SEDIMENTARY
ROCKS

HARPER'S GEOSCIENCE SERIES

Carey Croneis, Editor

SEDIMENTARY ROCKS

by

F. J. PETTIJOHN

PROFESSOR OF GEOLOGY
THE JOHNS HOPKINS UNIVERSITY

SECOND EDITION

HARPER & BROTHERS NEW YORK

Library of Congress catalog card number: 56–11820

Contents

Editor's Introduction
to the First Edition

PETTIJOHN's *Sedimentary Rocks* is the seventh in Harper's Geoscience Series. Our editorial suspicion is that it will become one of the more useful of the many textbooks on various of the fundamental aspects of geology. Of all these aspects, none is more central than the general process of sedimentation, and none is more important than the product of that process—the sedimentary rocks.

Dr. Pettijohn himself regards this volume as an "elementary treatment" of the subject. Students and colleagues are likely to agree that this is something of an understatement. For although *Sedimentary Rocks* presents none of the exhaustive topical treatments characteristic of the average monograph, it does nonetheless include essentially all major subjects in its field. In a certain real sense, however, the volume is elementary, for the author has taken pains to make the presentation of even the most complex concept simple, direct and clear.

Although the author has made no attempt to prepare a complete bibliography, approximately seven hundred carefully selected papers are cited. Well over one hundred useful tables are also included in the text, with which are incorporated general photographs, line drawings and photomicrographs. For the average reader the latter, numbering 104, are likely to prove especially helpful. Not only have the sections been chosen with care, but the photomicrography displays a high order of perfection. In this text the sedimentary rocks portrayed are not merely illustrated—they are illuminated.

But if the illustrative material commends itself to students, the text may be equally appreciated, for it is as sharply focused as are the photographs. The fifteen chapters which cover almost the entire gamut of sedimentary rock topics thus require less than 200,000 words—very few of them superfluous.

Dr. Pettijohn, for nearly twenty years a member of the Department of Geology at the University of Chicago, has recently become the third editor of the *Journal of Geology*. Like its first and second editors—Thomas Chrowder Chamberlin, and his son, Rollin T. Chamberlin—Dr. Pettijohn has devoted much of his research activity to the study of the pre-Cambrian sediments. But he has also found time to train many of the country's active students of modern as well as ancient sedimentation. All of these, among them Dr. William C. Krumbein, have contributed indirectly to this present volume; and yet it is these very researchers who may especially welcome its publication. This is true because *Sedimentary Rocks* was written to fill a long-felt need for a single-volume guide "to the observation, classification and interpretation of these deposits both in outcrop and as hand specimens."

Although Dr. Pettijohn's book may serve as a useful compendium for many professional geologists, both in and out of the field of sedimentology, the volume was designed chiefly as an aid in teaching. In this important area *Sedimentary Rocks* may well have wide use because of the philosophy of material presentation. As will be noted, the author has limited himself in the treatment of the processes of sedimentation and has devoted considerable space to analysis of the properties of rocks. Students particularly should appreciate this direct approach—and especially will they later appreciate the fact that he has been preoccupied with common rocks and structures, which they will actually see in the field, rather than with rare specimens and rare sedimentary phenomena commonly observed only in textbooks.

The style of Dr. Pettijohn's *Sedimentary Rocks* will be found refreshing in its vigor. He is not given to ambiguous or tentative explanations. He has not followed the all too common procedures of merely cataloguing unrelated observations, or listing conflicting interpretations without expressing judgment. In fact, in a recent letter, Dr. Pettijohn has written, "I have advanced some generalizations as though they were better established than they really are since I thought such treatment . . . stimulating and interesting. . . ." It seems probable that this type of text "treatment" characteristic of *Sedimentary Rocks*, will indeed prove stimulating and interesting, not alone to students but to their teachers.

CAREY CRONEIS

Beloit, Wisconsin

Editor's Introduction
to the Second Edition

THE second edition of Dr. Pettijohn's *Sedimentary Rocks* requires little editorial comment. The author's Preface suggests the important changes and improvements which characterize the largly rewritten present volume. Moreover, the editorial prediction concerning the widespread use and influence of the first edition—a prediction which, typically, Dr. Pettijohn deprecated— has been so completely confirmed that additional comment regarding the modernized version of *Sedimentary Rocks* would be superfluous. It is appropriate to point out, however, that since the first edition was published, Dr. Pettijohn has become Professor of Geology at The Johns Hopkins University; and that, not surprisingly, recognition of his contributions to the study of rocks has been demonstrated in many ways—among them his election to the Presidency of the Society of Economic Paleontologists and Mineralogists.

CAREY CRONEIS

The Rice Institute
April 14, 1956

Preface to the First Edition

THE chief interest of the geologist is the lithosphere—primarily the rocks of the lithosphere. His chief goal is to elucidate the natural history of these rocks, which constitute the sole record of the history of the earth itself. This history is reconstructed primarily from the study of the *sedimentary rocks*. This volume is intended, therefore, to be a guide to the observation, classification, and interpretation of these deposits both in outcrop and as hand specimens. It should serve also as a textbook in courses which have such an objective.

The author's aim is to write a book which will tell the user something about sedimentary *rocks* rather than *sedimentation*. A book which treats largely of the so-called processes of sedimentation, cannot of itself be of direct use to the geologist who must deal, not with process, but with the product—namely, rocks. Moreover, an adequate treatment of the processes of sedimentation—such as the fluid transport of sediments—would require another volume. Hence, in order to make this book practical and keep its contents within reasonable bounds, much of what is ordinarily considered "sedimentation" is omitted. Many of the transient phenomena, especially those of sediment transport, interesting and important as they are, leave no record and can best be left out. Even those which leave an imprint can be but briefly reviewed.

Likewise, the mechanics of sediment analysis—the measurement of particle size, microscopic determination of the mineral composition, and the like— are not included. Analytical methods have been treated in detail elsewhere and some knowledge of these procedures is assumed. Though methods as such are excluded, the properties of sedimentary deposits need some discussion, because upon these is based any interpretation of origin and any system of classification and nomenclature. Hence the first part of this volume is given over to the properties of the sedimentary rocks. Many analytical methods, moreover, are appropriate only for unconsolidated materials. Few sedimentary rocks so qualify—thus recourse to thin-section studies must be the main basis for investigation rather than the exception. The student, therefore, should have a working knowledge of the methods of micropetrology.

In this volume, the author has included much new data acquired by quantitative methods of analysis. These methods, which largely are a product of the last two decades of research, have yielded significant information which needs to be digested and organized in usable form. The writer has attempted to do this and to describe and interpret sedimentary rocks in the light of these newer researches. Rapid as the advances have been, more remains to be done than has so far been accomplished. This became evident as compilation of this work proceeded. Gaps, of larger or smaller size, in our knowledge appear everywhere. The author has pointed out many of these gaps in the hope that someone will undertake to fill them upon seeing the need.

There is notable overemphasis in the literature both of rare rocks and rare structures to the neglect of the common rocks and structures. The author has tried to strike a better balance in this volume.

The student of rocks, especially the beginner, can turn to no better source of instruction than the rocks themselves. Certainly the subject of sedimentary petrology should be pursued only if a well-collected representative set of specimens and thin sections is at hand. No course in this subject can be considered adequate unless accompanied by a well-organized program of laboratory work on such materials.

References to the literature are freely given. No attempt has been made, however, to make the bibliography complete. An attempt was made to provide a "working bibliography." For the most part the citations are to the large, more comprehensive works and to those with modern outlook. As is likely with any compilation covering a diverse field, some important references may have been inadvertently omitted.

A general work, such as this, is necessarily a compilation from many sources. A conscientious effort has been made to credit such sources. The contributions of the author, if any, lie in the direction of organization and classification, proper emphasis and balance between the various topics, and the choice of bibliographic items. It is inevitable, however, that some materials are not duly credited for one can never truly say how much is original and how much is unknowingly borrowed from fellow workers. The author is in heavy debt especially to Paul D. Krynine with whom he has had many stimulating discussions. He is likewise indebted to his colleagues at the University of Chicago—especially his former student and co-worker, W. C. Krumbein.

The preparation of this book has been made possible by the willing assistance and coöperation of many individuals and organizations. The author gratefully acknowledges the assistance of William Schmidt who took most of the photomicrographs and of Alfred Harris, D. J. Lehmer and Robert Nanz for preparation of most of the drawings. He is indebted also to those individuals and organizations that have permitted reproduction of published drawings or photographs or have supplied some of the needed illustrations. Specific acknowledgment of such has been made at appropriate places in the text. So also is the author indebted to those former students and others who, over a period of years, have send him many rock specimens the photomicrographs of which form the bulk of the illustrative matter of this text. Special thanks are due M. Macgregor, Assistant Director of the Geological Survey of Great Britain for a collection of Scottish graywackes; N. A. Riley of the University of Chicago for an excellent suite of Arbuckle rocks; Ada Swineford of the Kansas Geological Survey for numerous specimens from Kansas; and P. D. Krynine of Pennsylvania State College for much Pennsylvania material. F. F. Grout, J. H. C. Martens, and Ada Swineford were kind enough to loan the author certain thin sections for photographic purposes.

The writer is indebted to N. A. Riley who read parts of the manuscript and made many suggestions. Finally the author wishes to express his appreciation of the many helpful criticisms of Carey Croneis who as editor had the task of reading the whole volume. Dr. Croneis made many constructive suggestions and in general greatly facilitated the preparation of the manuscript for publication.

F. J. PETTIJOHN

Chicago, Illinois
August, 1948

Preface to the Second Edition

NEARLY ten years have elapsed since the manuscript for the first edition was completed. This decade has seen a flood of papers dealing with sediments and sedimentary rocks. Some, like those dealing with turbidity currents, have revolutionized our concepts of marine sedimentation and have made necessary a new interpretation of many sedimentary textures and structures. Others, such as those describing the plotting of vector properties and the making of paleocurrent maps and the quantitative measurement and mapping of sedimentary facies, provide new methods for the solution of the problems of paleogeography. The experimental work on the chemical precipitates and the complementary field studies of these deposits, and of the iron-bearing sediments in particular, have added much to our understanding of the origin of the chemical sediments. These new concepts and observations, as well as many others have made necessary the rewriting—not revision—of the first edition.

The author is convinced of the soundness of the geological science and believes that the study of rocks is most fruitfully advanced by a study of the rocks themselves. ". . . knowledge of theoretical interpretations is of no scientific value unless it is allied with (a) knowledge of the phenomena to be interpreted, and (b) knowledge of the evidence upon which the interpretations are based" (Doris L. Reynolds). The emphasis remains, therefore, on the geology of the sedimentary rocks.

The reader familiar with the first edition will note minor rearrangement of parts, a considerable increase in the number of references, collection of these into classified bibliographies at the ends of chapters or at other appropriate places. Rearrangement of the plate materials has made possible a net increase in the number of photographs. Many new line-drawings have been added; at least half of all those used are new.

The task of rewriting *Sedimentary Rocks* was a formidable one. It would not have been possible without the assistance of many persons. The author is especially indebted to John Spurbeck of The Johns Hopkins University and to William F. Schmidt of the University of Chicago for many of the new photographs, and to Philip W. Choquette for most of the new drawings. Others who have contributed photographs include H. L. James of the

PREFACE

U.S. Geological Survey, F. B. Van Houten of Princeton University, and W. L. Stokes of the University of Utah. The author is grateful to Gertrude Steffe and Mae Ann Stevens for typing the manuscript. The author also acknowledges with thanks the aid of Carey Croneis of Rice Institute and Editor of Harper's Geoscience Series for his assistance and encouragement in the preparation of both the old and the new editions.

F. J. Pettijohn

July, 1956

SEDIMENTARY
ROCKS

1

Introduction

GEOLOGY is primarily history—a history of the earth. Petrology has to do with the history of rocks and sedimentary petrology [1] is concerned with the history of the sedimentary rocks. Stratigraphy also has to do with geologic history. The primary task of stratigraphy is to ascertain the order of superposition of the strata at any given place and then to integrate the local geologic column thus constructed with the geologic columns of other places—places isolated or removed from one another. In short, the task of stratigraphy is to determine the temporal sequence of the strata the world over. This may be a difficult job; even the order of superposition is not easily determined in areas of complex structure, especially in the absence of fossils.[2]

At the present time, however, the composite geologic column is pretty well worked out—except, of course, for the Precambrian for which there is at present no world-wide rock or time scale. Students of sedimentary rocks are now turning to another and more difficult task, namely, reading the geologic history of a bed, the geologic age of which has been worked out by the stratigrapher. Although this is not a new task, it is one which is receiving renewed attention and is being attacked with new tools.

The history of any given bed involves determination of the source rocks and the source area from which the sediment came, or, in a word, its *provenance*. It involves also an understanding of the mechanism of *dispersal* of the residues formed in the source regions and the direction and distance of

[1] Miscalled "sedimentation"; also designated "sedimentology" (Wadell, 1932, 1933; Twenhofel, 1932; Goldman, 1950; Hough, 1950; Lohse, 1951; Doeglas, 1951).

[2] Shrock's book, *Sequence in layered rocks*, well illustrates the effort and ingenuity that may be required to establish the correct stratigraphic order.

transport and the area or petrologic province over which these materials were spread. Germane to the history of a sediment is a reconstruction of the *environment* of deposition—the physical and chemical milieu in which the materials accumulated. And finally the history involves those changes or modifications which the sediment underwent after deposition including internal physical and chemical rearrangements and the resultant *lithification.*

Not only is it of interest to determine what happened to a particular bed or layer, but the geologist is interested also in the long-time trends which may be a clue to the chemical and physical evolution of the earth's crust. About these secular trends little is known—it is not even known certainly whether or not there are any such trends.

THE ORIGIN OF SEDIMENTS

The origin and accumulation of sedimentary rocks might, at first thought, seem relatively simple. Sands and muds are seen to form and be carried by the rivers from the continents into the sea. The origin of sedimentary rocks, unlike that of many igneous and all metamorphic rocks, is apparently open to inspection and study. Unfortunately the matter is not so simple. Not all of the formative processes can be seen. The diagenetic changes, in particular, which include intrastratal solution, cementation, formation of concretions, and so forth, cannot be readily observed. Neither can the turbidity currents responsible for the transport, deposition, and structures of many marine sediments. The formation of many chemical sediments has never been seen. And so, as in the case of most other rocks, the history must be reconstructed from the geologic record—the effects produced by processes no longer operative. The "effects" are primarily the textures, the structures, and the minerals of the deposit in question. This, then, is the proper task of sedimentary petrology: to go to the rocks and read the record and thereby unravel the natural history of the rock.

The task of interpreting the history of a sedimentary rock is much more complex than that of an igneous or metamorphic rock. This follows from the more complex character of sedimentary rocks. Failure to understand this complexity comes about in part by the conventional separation of rocks into the traditional three categories—igneous, sedimentary, and metamorphic. The sediments, in fact, belong to *all three groups.* This vital and fundamental concept was well understood by Grabau (1904) but seems largely to be forgotten by his successors, who lump together rocks of fundamentally different origins merely because they were formed at or near the earth's surface at "relatively low temperatures and pressures."

As noted by Grabau, there are two fundamentally different groups of rocks, which he chose to call *exogenetic* and *endogenetic* (Fig. 1).[3] The exogenetic rocks are the fragmental or clastic rocks. The great bulk of the sediments (by volume) belong in this category. To this group also belong the pyroclastic igneous rocks, which are similar to the clastic sediments in all essential details of texture and structure, and therefore in their dynamics of accumulation.

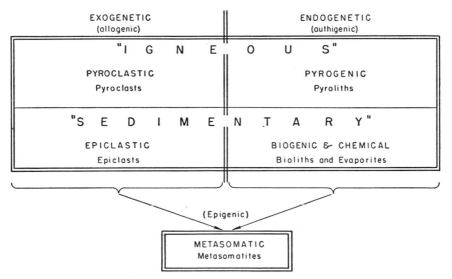

FIG. 1. Genetic classification of rocks.

In marked contrast to the exogenetic rocks are those termed endogenetic, which are both the amorphous and the crystalline precipitates from solution. Many sediments, including the saline deposits—rock salt, anhydrite, and the like—belong here, as do the bulk of the igneous rocks. These igneous rocks, like the chemical sediments, are precipitates from solution. Phase-rule chemistry governs the formation of each. In manner of origin, therefore, a rock-salt deposit is more akin to a granite than it is to a shale or a sandstone with which it is associated. On the other hand, the sandstone is closely related to a tuff of medium grain. Aerodynamic or hydrodynamic principles govern the accumulation of each. Similar textures and structures are found in each.

And finally sediments (and other materials) are subject to physical and chemical reorganization after they have formed. These changes modify greatly the original textures and structures and the mineralogical composition. In most cases there is little or no change in the bulk composition—in

[3] Exogenetic rocks owe their origin to external forces acting on the materials of which they are composed; endogenetic rocks are produced by forces resident within the material (chemical affinity).

others the change in composition is profound. If these changes take place at near-surface pressures and temperatures, they are termed diagenetic; if they take place at somewhat elevated temperature and pressure, they are termed metamorphic. The distinction is an arbitrary one. In either case the reorganization is accomplished primarily in the solid state. In sediments deformation is less marked than in the metamorphic rocks (in the restricted sense) although in some sedimentary facies, small scale mobilization, hydroplastic flow, and autoinjection are by no means rare (see p. 191). Chemical reorganization and the formation of new minerals, however, are widespread in sediments. These changes result in new textures superimposed on the primary textures. The latter may be partially to completely destroyed. Illustrative of the changes and the production of "metamorphic" or crystalloblastic textures is the conversion of limestone to dolomite with partial destruction of fossils and other original characters.

For the reasons previously outlined, it is desirable to discuss the textures of the exogenetic (clastic) rocks, the endogenetic (chemical) rocks, and the epigenetic (diagenetic) rocks separately.[4] It is essential to the interpretation of rock textures that the several fundamentally unlike processes of petrogenesis be clearly understood.[5]

Sediments are, however, complex rocks and may have a composite origin. As noted above, a rock may have diagenetic textures, structures, and minerals superimposed on textures, structures, and minerals produced by clastic (exogene) or chemical (endogene) processes. A given "primary" sediment may itself be a mixture and contain both exogene and endogene components. Such a mixture can be considered as a binary "system" if it contains two components, one exogene and one endogene. The two "end members" may vary in quantity between certain fixed limits [6] or they may vary in all possible proportions. In some sediments there may be three or, in rarer cases, even four end members.

The composition of a sediment, expressed in terms of these end members, may be shown graphically. A binary system can be represented by a two-coördinate diagram. Let M and N be detrital components; and X and Y be chemical components. Let M be the primary minerals (chiefly quartz and

---

[4] The diagenetic rocks are in the strict sense endogenetic as that term is used by Grabau, but as diagenesis leads to important modifications of the original textures and mineralogy it seems desirable to recognize these changes and to term the rocks so modified epigenetic rocks.

[5] The classification of "sediments" into the above three categories is not just a question of "training, personal experience, and psychology" as claimed (Twenhofel, 1950, p. 282). All we know about rocks is what can be deduced from their observable properties. The recognition that these three unlike geneses produce unlike textures, structures, and mineral composition is fundamental and basic—not a whim.

[6] For example, the cement of a sand, the endogene component, can vary only between zero and a limit set by the porosity, about 30 to 40 per cent.

feldspar) released from the source rock; and N, the secondary minerals (chiefly clay minerals) produced by weathering. The two chief chemical end members, X and Y, are the carbonates (calcite, dolomite) and silica (chalcedony and quartz). Let Z represent an additional nonclastic component such as the organic residues. The composition of a binary system may be represented as shown in Fig. 2. Any vertical line in this diagram represents

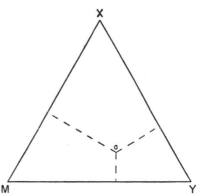

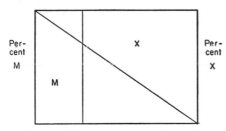

FIG. 2. Two-component sediment represented by a binary diagram.

FIG. 3. Three-component sediment represented by ternary diagram.

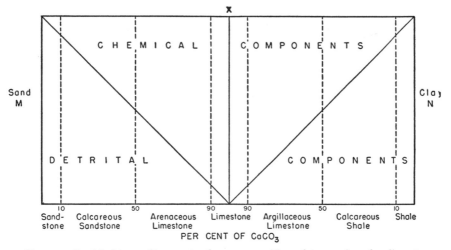

FIG. 4. Double binary diagram to show composition of two series of sediments.

a possible mixture of the two components. The possible mixtures of the various end members are many, but those involving significant amounts (several per cent or more) of each are few. Some common binary mixtures are given in Table 1.

A three-component mixture is graphically shown by a triangle diagram. Such a diagram depends on the proposition that the sum of the lengths of

Table 1. Representative Binary Mixtures

Clastic Component	Chemical Component	Remarks
Quartz	$CaCO_3$ (calcite or dolomite)	Common
Quartz	SiO_2 (quartz or chert)	Common
Clay	$CaCO_3$ (calcite)	Common
Clay	SiO_2 (chert)	Rare
Clay	C (bitumen or organic matter)	Common

the perpendiculars drawn from the sides of an equilateral triangle to any point within it are always the same. The length of each perpendicular may be taken as the proportional part of each component. Hence in Fig. 3, $X + Y + M = 100$. Each side of the triangle, in fact, is a two-component mixture. A ternary mixture therefore consists of three binary mixtures. Two of these three binary mixtures may be shown as a double binary mixture (Fig. 4).

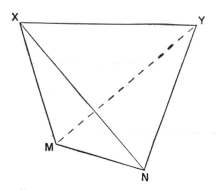

The rare four-component or quaternary mixture can be shown best by a solid, namely, the tetrahedron.[7] Here the sum of the perpendiculars to the four faces meeting in a common point within the solid body totals 100. A quaternary mixture consists of four ter-

Fig. 5. Four-component sediment represented by tetrahedron.

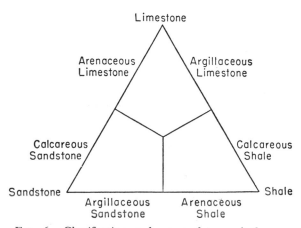

Fig. 6. Classification and nomenclature of the common sediments. (Modified after Pirsson and Schuchert.)

[7] If plotted on the triangular diagram, the fourth component will be represented by a smaller triangle within the diagram. See, for example, Fig. 78.

nary and six binary mixtures. Figure 5 summarizes the most common combinations shown by sediments. Probably less than 5 per cent of the sediments require some other type of diagram. Thus Z, representing organic carbon or some fifth component, can replace any corner of the tetrahedron, and all other possibilities are thereby accounted for. The common sediments are classified as shown in Figure 6.

THE STUDY OF SEDIMENTS

Sediments are the product of both *heritage* and *environment*. To trace their lines of descent and to reconstruct the environment which gave rise to the sedimentary rock are difficult tasks. A knowledge of the sedimentary processes, especially of those environmental factors that have had a major influence on the production, transportation, deposition, and subsequent modification of the sediment is important. But in the last analysis all the evidence for working out the history of a sedimentary rock must come from within the rock itself. The origin of the deposit is determined by this internal evidence alone.

The properties of a sedimentary rock which constitute such evidence need to be described properly and to be understood. Such properties are the *textures* and *structures* (including fossils), and the chemical and mineralogical *composition* of the rock. The first part of this volume deals with these properties.

The treatment of properties is followed by a synoptic review of the various classes of sedimentary rocks, or *products* of the sedimentary cycle. Sandstones, shales, and limestones are the most common; they form the bulk of any geologic section, and since the field geologist must deal mainly with these rocks they are treated at length.

Basic to any classification of sedimentary rocks, and hence to a rational plan of observation and description of these materials, is an understanding of the *processes of sedimentation*. These processes are not all of equal importance. Diastrophism plays the dominant role in controlling the production and deposition of a sediment—and to some extent its postdepositional history also. The last part of this book is an elaboration of this thesis, and is therefore an outline of the influence of tectonism on the origin, evolution, and lithification of the sedimentary materials.

TOTAL VOLUME OF SEDIMENT

By volume the sedimentary (and metasedimentary) rocks form only 5 per cent of the known lithosphere (outer shell ten miles thick), whereas the igneous (and meta-igneous) rocks form 95 per cent (Clarke, p. 34).[8] On the

---

[8] Assuming granite to be igneous and not metasedimentary.

other hand, the area of exposure of the sediments is 75 per cent of the total land area, whereas the igneous rocks crop out over only 25 per cent of the total (Fig. 7). It is evident, therefore, that the sediments must form only a thin surficial layer. Although their thickness ranges from 0 up to about 8 miles, they would average, according to Leith and Mead (1915) only 1.4 miles in thickness over the continental areas.

If we assume that all the sodium in the ocean is derived by leaching of primitive igneous rocks, it can be shown that the complete decomposition of an earth shell of such rock that is one-third of a mile thick would yield all the sodium of the sea (Clarke, 1924, p. 31). Because some of the sodium is retained in the sediment produced and thus is not all stored in the ocean,

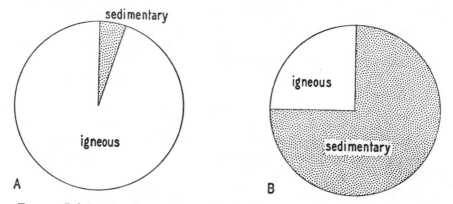

FIG. 7. Relative abundance of igneous and sedimentary rocks in the "crust" of the earth (data from Clarke, 1924, p. 34). A: By volume. B: By area.

the figure needs to be corrected. The revised figure is a scant half mile. This shell of igneous material, upon changing to a sediment, is increased in volume owing to oxidation, carbonation, and hydration. Assuming as Clarke does, that this increase is roughly 10 per cent, then the total volume of sediment corresponding to the igneous source rock would be about 9.3×10^7 cubic miles, or 3.7×10^8 cubic kilometers. This would be enough to form a rock shell about 2447 feet thick enveloping the whole earth. If this material were confined to the continental platform (roughly one-third of the area of the globe), its thickness would be about 7300 feet.

Leith and Mead (1915, p. 73) using a slightly different basis for their calculations, conclude that the thickness would be 1.39 miles or about 7400 feet, of which 600 feet are shale, 900 feet sandstone, and 500 feet limestone.

Other estimates have also been made of the total volume of sediment. Wickman (1954), for example, applied Mead's method to better data and has calculated the total mass of the sediments to be $(4.1 \pm 0.6) \times 10^8$ cubic kilometers, a value similar to that obtained by Clarke. Rankama (1954), basing his calculations on the assumption that all the ^{40}A now found in the atmosphere and the hydrosphere is a decay product of ^{40}K in the earth's crust and that all the ^{40}A formed has been released by weathering, concluded that a shell of "average" igneous rock 22 kilometers thick would have to be weathered to account for the ^{40}A now in the atmosphere. This is a figure about forty times larger than that estimated by Clarke, Goldschmidt (1933), and others. Obviously the total volume of sediment implied by Rankama's calculations is materially greater than others have supposed.

Kuenen (1941) gives the observed thickness of the Cambrian and post-Cambrian sediments in the United States as 1200 meters, or about 3940 feet. An average of 800 meters or 2620 feet proposed by Kuenen for the whole continent is about one-third the total volume of sediment implied by the calculations of Clarke and Leith and Mead referred to above. A large part of this sediment, moreover, is reworked. According to Krynine (1942), 30 per cent of the average sediment is derived by reworking of older deposits. Thus the total of new materials would be only 1500 feet thick. Because the Cambrian is a relatively late period in geologic history, the total amount of sediment produced would be materially greater than implied by Kuenen's figures.

Kuenen (1937, 1941) has taken exception to Clarke's estimate of the total volume of sediment and has shown from several lines of evidence that the bulk of the deep-sea deposits is several times that of the sediment on the continent. The latter sediments are estimated at about 2×10^8 cubic kilometers. Hence the total volume of all sediments derived from weathering is estimated at 8×10^8 cubic kilometers. To this Kuenen adds 5×10^8 cubic kilometers of disintegrated but not weathered material, making a total of 13×10^8 cubic kilometers (or solid on a pore-free basis of 11×10^8 cubic kilometers). These sediments are believed by Kuenen to have an average thickness (including pore space) of 3 kilometers over the floor of the oceans, 5 kilometers on the continental slope and 1.5 kilometers on the continent.

RELATIVE ABUNDANCE OF THE COMMON SEDIMENTS

Of the many kinds of sediment known, only a few are common. Three principal types constitute more than 99 per cent of all the sediments. But these three types, namely, shale, sandstone, and limestone, are not all equally abundant. Various workers have attempted to estimate their relative abundance.

Several methods of estimation of the relative proportions of the common sediments are employed. In the main they consist of either actual measurements of many stratigraphic sections (Table 2) or calculations of the proportions of the average shale, sandstone, and limestone (plus sea water) required to make the average igneous rock (Table 3; see also Fig. 8).

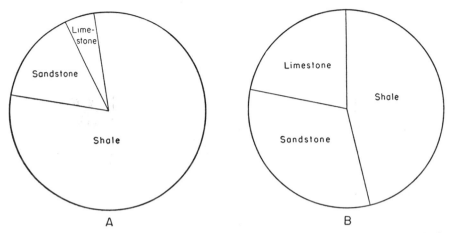

Fig. 8. Relative abundance of the common sediments (data from Tables 2 and 3). **A:** Determined by geochemical calculations. **B:** As averaged from stratigraphic measurements.

Inspection of Tables 2 and 3 shows that whereas the common types of sediment stand in the same order on both tables, there is a marked difference in the proportions assigned to each type. Several reasons have been advanced to explain these discrepancies. A part of the difficulty lies with the measurements of the sediments. These measurements take no account of the very

TABLE 2.   Percentage of Sedimentary Rocks as Measured

	Leith and Mead (1915)	Schuchert (1931)	Kuenen (1941)	Krynine (1948)
Shale	46	44	56	42
Sandstone	32	37	14	40
Limestone	22	19	29	18

TABLE 3.   Computed Proportions of the Sedimentary Rocks

	Mead (1907)	Clarke (1924)	Holmes (1937)	Wickman [a] (1954)
Shale	82	80	70	83
Sandstone	12	15	16	8
Limestone	6	5	14	9 [b]

[a] Percentage values calculated from Wickman's data.
[b] "Carbonate rock."

fine sediment carried out beyond the continents into the deep sea. The measurements are limited, moreover, to areas studied by geologists and may not be representative of the world as a whole. Some difficulties arise in averaging the measured sections and in deciding how to classify mixed formations.

As noted by Krynine and others, graywackes contain much clay (or authigenic derivatives thereof) and these and related sandstones contain sand-sized fragments of rocks, chiefly slates, phyllites, and similar materials. The older shales, as a result of metamorphism, have been rebuilt into coarser-grained materials, and are added to the sandstones, thereby increasing the proportion of sandstones at the expense of the shales. If we take Krynine's estimate for the relative proportions of graywacke, orthoquartzites, and arkose as 45, 23, and 32, respectively, and assume that graywacke is equivalent to two parts shale and one part arkose (see page 307), then two-thirds of the 45 per cent, or 30 per cent, of the graywacke is shale equivalent. Because sandstones are observed to form 32 per cent of the total section, 30 per cent of this 32 per cent, or 10 per cent, should be deducted from the sandstone portion and assigned to the shales; the proportions 46, 32, and 22 (Leith and Mead) then become 56, 22, and 22.

Likewise limestone tends to be overrated inasmuch as a little clay in a limestone changes its appearance very little and the rock is measured and reported as limestone. Assume 10 per cent of clay in the strata reported as limestone. Then 10 per cent of 22 per cent, or 2 per cent, should be deducted from the limestone and added to the shale. As thus amended the proportions of shale, sandstone, and limestone become 58, 22, and 20, respectively.

The large residual differences between the calculated and the observed proportions, as amended, must be due mainly to the loss of the clays to the deep sea.[9]

REFERENCES CITED AND BIBLIOGRAPHY

Clarke, F. W. (1924), Data of geochemistry, *U.S. Geol. Surv.*, Bull. 770.

Doeglas, D. J. (1951), From sedimentary petrology to sedimentology. *Proc. 3rd Int. Congr. Sedimentology*, pp. 15–22.

Goldman, M. I. (1950), What is "Sedimentology"? *J. Sediment. Petrol.*, vol. 20, p. 118.

Goldschmidt, V. M. (1933), Grundlagen der quantitativen Geochemie, *Fortschr. Mineral. Krist. Petrog.*, vol. 17, pp. 112–156.

Grabau, A. W. (1904), On the classification of sedimentary rocks, *Am. Geol.*, vol. 33, pp. 228–247.

[9] Lime is also lost to the deep sea owing to the lime-secreting habit of pelagic foraminifera. The ability of these forms to use lime, however, was acquired only in the Cretaceous; hence prior to that time the lime deposition was confined to the shallow seas.

Holmes, A. (1937), *The age of the earth*, London, Thomas Nelson and Sons, p. 75.

Hough, J. L. (1950), Editorial note, *J. Sediment. Petrol.*, vol. 20, pp. 118–119.

Krynine, P. D. (1942), *Report of a conference on sedimentation*, Am. Assoc. Petroleum Geol., p. 21.

Krynine, P. D. (1948), The megascopic study and field classification of sedimentary rocks, *J. Geol.*, vol. 56, p. 156, Table 4.

Kuenen, Ph. H. (1941), Geochemical calculations concerning the total mass of sediments in the earth, *Am. J. Sci.*, vol. 239, pp. 161–190.

Kuenen, Ph. H. (1947), On the total amount of sedimentation in the deep sea, *Am. J. Sci.*, ser. 5, vol. 34, pp. 457–468.

Leith, C. K. and Mead, W. J. (1915), *Metamorphic geology*, New York, Holt.

Lohse, E. A. (1951), Further discussion of "What is sedimentology?" *J. Sediment. Petrol.*, vol. 21, p. 121.

Mead, W. J. (1907), Redistribution of elements in the formation of sedimentary rocks, *J. Geol.*, vol. 15, p. 250.

Rankama, K. (1954), A calculation of the amount of weathered igneous rock, *Geoch. et Cosmoch. Acta*, vol. 5, pp. 81–84.

Schuchert, Chas. (1931), in The age of the earth, *Bull. Nat. Research Council*, no. 80, pp. 10–64, esp. p. 39.

Shrock, R. R. (1948), *Sequence in layered rocks*, New York, McGraw-Hill.

Twenhofel, W. H. (1932), Report of the Committee on Sedimentation, 1930–1932, *Bull. Nat. Research Council* 89, p. 18.

Twenhofel, W. H. (1950), *Principles of sedimentation*, New York, McGraw-Hill.

Wadell, H. (1932), Sedimentation and sedimentology, *Science*, n.s., vol. 75, p. 20.

Wadell, H. (1933), Sedimentation and sedimentology, *Science*, n.s., vol. 77, pp. 536–537.

Wickman, F. E. (1954), The "total" amount of sediment and the composition of the "average igneous rock," *Geoch. et Cosmoch. Acta*, vol. 5, pp. 97–110.

2

Textures

TEXTURE is the size, shape, and arrangement (packing and fabric) of the component elements of a sedimentary rock. These properties are geometrical. Expressions such as *coarse-grained, angular,* or *rounded,* and *openwork* are descriptive of texture. The geologist may require a more precise description. He may wish to know how coarse, how angular, or how well sorted a sand is. It is necessary, therefore, to formulate a clear definition of the property, then devise a method of measurement, and finally to make a statistical summarization for the sediment as a whole.

Some textures, porosity for example, are not simple properties but are complex and are dependent on the more fundamental grain characteristics—packing, shape, sorting, etc.

Unlike texture, *structure* deals with the larger features of the rock and is best seen in the field. Whereas texture has to do with the grain-to-grain relations, structure takes account of such features as bedding, ripple marking, and the like. Texture is commonly studied in thin section, in the hand specimen, or by analysis of a small sample. Structure, on the other hand, is usually studied in the outcrop, less commonly in the hand specimen or thin section.

Although the geometrical properties of a sediment are commonly described as textural or structural, they may also be classified as *scalar* or *vectorial* (Fig. 9). A scalar property is one which has magnitude but not direction, whereas a vector property has both magnitude and direction. The long diameter of a pebble in a gravel, for example, is a scalar property; its orientation is a vector property. Vector properties are in general properties

13

acquired at the time of deposition as a result of the earth's gravitational or magnetic fields (geopetal and geomagnetic fabrics) or as a response to current flow (current fabrics). Cross-bedding is another example of a vector property. A vector property is one which is lost upon collection of the sample by removal of a constituent element (pebble, sand grain, fossil) from its matrix or by breakdown of the structure of the deposit.

SEDIMENT PROPERTIES

SCALAR PROPERTIES

Size and sorting

Shape and roundness

Composition
    Gross= per cent sand, shale, lime
    Constituents= mineral frequencies, pebble
      counts, pollen count, etc.

Thickness
    Total
    Average of individual beds

VECTOR PROPERTIES

PLANAR =
    Cross-bedding

LINEAR =
    Primary sand lineation, striations, fluting
    Ripple marks
    Oriented fossils
    Fabric (long axis orientation)

FIG. 9. Properties of sediments, scalar and vector.

Although the classification of properties as scalar or vectorial is a useful one, and one given consideration in studying sediment dispersal, it is convenient to discuss the properties in the more conventional manner and consider them as textures or as structures. This chapter is devoted, therefore, to textures, and a subsequent chapter deals with structures. It is necessary, however, to deal separately with the textures of the clastic and the nonclastic rocks.

PARTICLE SIZE OF CLASTIC ROCKS

The grain size of a clastic sediment is of considerable importance. The size of the fragments of which the rock is composed is in part the basis of sub-division into conglomerates, sandstones, and shales. The size and uniformity of size or sorting is a measure of the competence and efficiency of the transporting agent. In the normal water-deposited materials, the size is in some way an index to the proximity of the source rock. Deposits of great coarseness usually have not moved far. The several agents and modes of transport lead to deposits which differ materially in their sorting and transporting ability. Turbidity flows are capable of transporting coarse materials appreciable distances without much sorting, whereas normal air or water currents deposit some of the best-sorted materials known, i.e., beach and dune sands.

A fuller understanding of the geologic significance of size can come only from a clearer concept of what is meant by "grain size" and by means of size analyses of sediments.

Concept of Size

If the particles composing a clastic sediment were all spheres, no special difficulty would arise in defining or in determining their sizes. A statement of their diameters would suffice. But the pebbles of a conglomerate, for example, are nonspherical and are commonly highly irregular and defy ordinary shape classification. Yet a conglomerate is said to be composed of pebbles of a certain "diameter." What is the "diameter" of an irregular solid?

Direct measurements of the particle diameter are commonly made though the irregular shape of the fragment creates difficulties. Some investigators report the *length, breadth*, and *thickness* of a fragment without clearly defining these terms. The long, intermediate, and short diameters of a triaxial ellipsoid are easily recognized but even casual inspection of a collection of pebbles will demonstrate the difficulty of defining such terms for irregular solids. Must the "diameters" or intercepts be at right angles? Must they pass through a common point? How should they be combined to give an "average" diameter? Or will the intermediate diameter alone suffice as a measure of size? Krumbein (1939) has reviewed these questions and framed objective operational definitions of these terms.

In practice the term *diameter* varies widely in meaning in accordance with the way in which it was measured. All methods of measurement are based on the premise that the constituent particles are spheres or that the measurements made can be expressed as diameters of equivalent spheres. In so far as these conditions are not fulfilled the reported sizes are incorrect or inaccurate.

One could, for example, measure the volume of a pebble and then *calculate* the diameter of a sphere having the same volume. Such a calculated diameter is the *nominal diameter* and it is indeed a true measure of size independent of either the shape or the density of the pebble. On the other hand, the settling velocity, commonly taken as a measure of size, is valid only if both the density and the shape are constant. Settling velocity measurements are usually reduced to a diameter (or radius) basis on the assumption of spherical form and density of 2.65 (quartz). Such is Oden's *equivalent radius* or Wadell's *sedimentation diameter* (Krumbein and Pettijohn, p. 94). Even sieves, commonly used to separate and measure particles of loose or friable materials, do not measure size alone. Long pencil-shaped particles may pass a sieve and be weighed with others of a lesser volume (and hence of smaller size). Sieves therefore classify particles on the basis of their least cross-sectional area.

It is not our purpose to discuss the methods or procedures to be followed in making analysis of the size of particles in a clastic sediment; that problem has been treated at length elsewhere (Krumbein and Pettijohn, 1938; Gessner, 1931; Dalla Valle, 1943). But a clear concept of size should be kept in mind in interpreting the results of size analyses, which, owing to the limitations of the analytical method, yield approximate results only.

Size Terms

Various size terms in common use have been adopted by the geologist. A lake sediment may be described as *clay* or an outwash deposit recorded as *gravel* or a beach reported as *sand*. Some writers have replaced such common language terms as sand and gravel with others less familiar. Several sets of such size terms (and their adjective modifications) are given in Table 4.

The terms *psephite, psammite,* and *pelite* and the equivalent terms *rudite, arenite,* and *lutite* [1] were proposed to supplant the common terms *gravel, sand,* and *clay.* The latter carry some implications of composition or other characters, and are therefore not strictly size terms. If a mineralogical restriction is to be placed on such a term as *clay,* then no size terms exist for material of fine grain. Even if the term *clay* were to be used with a double meaning, i.e., both as a size term and a particular sediment type, it is doubtful if geologists would be satisfied to call a pure lime mud a clay and the consolidated rock (lithographic limestone) a claystone. The term *lutite,* however, is readily acceptable for such materials, and the finely precipitated limestones

---

[1] Tyrrell does not regard the Greek-derived and corresponding Latin-derived terms as wholly equivalent and proposed that the Latin terms be applied to sedimentary rocks and the Greek terms be used for the metamorphic derivatives of such rocks, pelitic schist for example (Tyrrell, 1921, pp. 501–502.)

could be called *calcilutite*. Likewise a pure carbonate sand if lithified would more probably be called a limestone than sandstone. The terms *sand* and *sandstone* seem to have some mineralogical restrictions that render them inadequate as size terms.

TABLE 4. Descriptive Size Terms

| Texture | Common Terms | Greek-Derived Terms | Latin-Derived Terms[a] | |
			Clastics	Nonclastic Constructional[b]
Coarse	Gravel (gravelly)	Psephite (psephitic)	Rudite (rudaceous)	Spherite
Medium	Sand (sandy)	Psammite (psammitic)	Arenite (arenaceous)	Granulite
Fine	Clay (clayey)	Pelite (pelitic)	Lutite (lutaceous)	Pulverite

[a] A. W. Grabau, *Principles of stratigraphy*, New York, Seiler, 1913, pp. 269–298. The terms were spelled rudyte, arenyte, etc., by Grabau.
[b] Now generally obsolete.

Regardless of the choice the terms used are likely to mean different things to different people. The meaning attached to the word *sand*, i.e., the size limits to be placed on the sand grade or class, will vary greatly. This is well illustrated by Fig. 10, where one can see that there is wide diversity in usage. It is desirable, therefore, that usage be standardized or codified. Several such attempts have been made and within limits some agreement has been reached. Unfortunately there are several standards. The engineers, the soil scientists, and the geologist all use different standards.[2] Even among the geologists there is no universal agreement; European usage is different from that prevalent in North America.

The present generally accepted standard used by the students of sediments in North America stems from the work of J. A. Udden (1898, 1914). Udden devised a geometrical scale of size classes and redefined the common terms *boulder, gravel, sand, silt,* and *clay*. In 1922, Wentworth modified the definitions of Udden to conform to the prevailing opinion among research workers as indicated by returned questionnaires. The Udden grade scale and the Wentworth modification of the size limits for the common terms are generally used by sedimentologists in North America at the present time. It was used by the Committee on Sedimentation, Division of Geology and Geography of the National Research Council. This Committee prior to its discharge issued a series of reports in which the problems of nomenclature were reviewed and recommendations made (Wentworth and Williams, 1932;

[2] There has been some progress toward agreement. (See Lane *et al.*, 1947.)

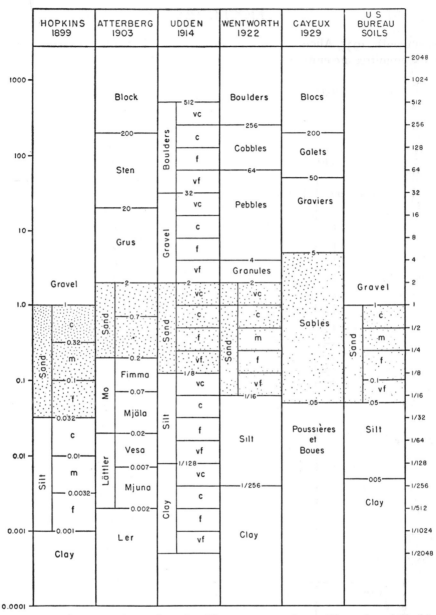

FIG. 10. Representative grade scales. Three types are shown. The scales of Hopkins and Atterberg are geometric, decimal, and cyclic. The starting points are 1.0 and 2.0 mm, respectively. The scales are, therefore, 0.001, 0.01, 0.1, 1.0, 10, etc.; and 0.002, 0.02, 0.2, 2.0, 20, etc. Subdivisions are obtained by finding the geometric mid-point between 0.1 and 1.0, and 0.7 is the corresponding mid-point between 0.2 and 2.0.

Udden's scale, later adopted by Wentworth and since accepted by the Lane committee, is geometric, but noncyclic and nondecimal. The Bureau of Soils scale and that of Cayeux are nonregular.

The diagram illustrates also the diverse meanings of the size terms and the need for standardization. Note the variations in the limits for sand (stippled).

Wentworth, 1935; Allen, 1936; Twenhofel, 1937). The recommendations of the Committee are embodied in Table 5.

TABLE 5.   Table of Size Limits of Common Grade and Rock Terms

Size	Sedimentary (epiclastic)				Volcanic (pyroclastic)	
	Rounded, Subrounded, Subangular		Angular		Fragment	Aggregate
	Fragment	Aggregate	Fragment	Aggregate		
	Boulder	Boulder gravel / Boulder conglomerate	Block		Block[a]	Volcanic breccia
256 mm	Cobble	Cobble gravel / Cobble conglomerate	. . . .	Rubble	Bomb[b]	Agglomerate
64 mm	Pebble	Pebble gravel / Pebble conglomerate	. . . .	Breccia	__32 mm__ Lapilli __4 mm__	Lapilli tuff
4 mm	Granule	Granule gravel	. . . .			
2 mm	Sand	Sand / Sandstone	. . . .	__1 mm__ Grit __½ mm__	Coarse ash	Coarse tuff
¹⁄₁₆ mm	Silt	Silt / Siltstone	. . . .	. . . .	__¼ mm__ Fine ash	Fine tuff
¹⁄₂₅₆ mm	Clay	Clay / Shale	. . . .			

("Roundstone" spans Boulder, Cobble, Pebble aggregate column)

a Broken from previously consolidated igneous rock.
b Solidified from plastic material while in flight.

More recently a committee of geologists and hydrologists recommended adoption of the Wentworth-Udden grade scale and size terms, omitting only the granule class (Lane et al., 1947).

Boulder was defined as "a detached rock mass, somewhat rounded or otherwise modified by abrasion in transport, and larger than a cobble" with a minimum size of 256 mm (about 10 in.). For those objects produced by weathering *in situ* such terms as *boulders of distintegration* or *boulders of exfoliation* are recommended. The term *block* was reserved for "a large, angular fragment showing little or no modification by transporting agencies" and similar in size to a boulder.

A *cobble* is defined in the same manner as a boulder except that it is restricted in size from 64 to 256 mm.[3] In like manner there may be *cobbles of exfoliation.*

A *pebble* is a "rock fragment larger than a coarse sand grain or granule and smaller than a cobble, which has been rounded or otherwise abraded by the action of water, wind, or glacial ice." It is therefore between 4 and 64 mm in diameter.

The unconsolidated accumulation of pebbles, cobbles, or boulders is *gravel,* which accordingly may be designated pebble-gravel, cobble-gravel, etc. The consolidated equivalent is *conglomerate,* likewise designated pebble-conglomerate, etc. *Rubble* is an unconsolidated accumulation of angular rock fragments coarser than sand. Its consolidated equivalent is *breccia.*

The term *sand* is used to denote an aggregate of mineral or rock grains greater than $\frac{1}{16}$ mm and less than 2 mm in diameter. Wentworth (1922) proposed the term *granule* [4] to cover material 4 to 2 mm in size; *silt* defined as from $\frac{1}{16}$ to $\frac{1}{256}$ mm in size, and *clay* [5] less than $\frac{1}{256}$ mm in diameter, complete the list of common size terms. Closer description requires modification of these terms, as very coarse sand, coarse sand, medium sand, fine sand, and so forth. Indurated equivalents are *sandstone, siltstone.*

The definitions as given above are defective in several respects. Several concepts other than size have been inadvertently introduced into definitions of what are supposed to be size or grade terms. The injection of roundness, the particular process of shape modification (abrasion), and the agents responsible (wind, water, or ice) is undesirable. Even granting the desirability of applying one term to the rounded fragments and another to the angular pieces, the Committee did not provide terms analogous to *block* for fragments of less than boulder size. Moreover, there is an unfortunate duplication of the term *block* under pyroclastics with a restricted and special

---

[3] Sayles (1914) has used the term *boulderet* for the 6- to 12-inch range.

[4] The Committee on Sedimentation failed to use this term and omitted any consideration of it in their reports. The term now seems abandoned as a size term. As it has been applied to precipitated bodies, notably certain iron silicates, e.g., glauconite, it does not seem wise to use it as a size term also. The Lane Committee assigned the 4 to 2 mm materials to the gravel class.

[5] Clay, of course, is also defined as a rock as well as a size term. See page 340 for such a definition.

meaning. The latter usage is a further example of giving a size term a genetic significance.[6]

Both prior to and following the publication of the Committee reports, there have been other attempts to modify the nomenclature applied to size terms. Fernald (1929), for example, proposed the term *roundstone* to designate collectively the largest sizes—boulder, cobbles, and pebbles. Shrock (1948) suggested the term *sharpstone* to designate the corresponding clastic elements of rubble, and would substitute the term *sharpstone conglomerate* for breccia. The term *roundstone conglomerate* would designate an ordinary conglomerate. Woodford (1925) had earlier proposed a series of terms to be applied to the sharp-edged unworn fragments of block size and smaller. Unlike Wentworth (1935), Woodford would extend the term *block* to designate any more or less equidimensional angular fragment over 4 mm in size. The term *slab* is reserved for flat fragments with maximum dimension over 64 mm and the terms *chip* and *flake* were likewise used for angular flat fragments the maximum dimensions of which were 64 and 4 mm, respectively.

The limits placed on the size terms *gravel*, *sand*, *silt*, and *clay* are in the main arbitrary and are to be considered "correct" only in so far as they are generally agreed upon and adhered to by students of sediments. Wentworth's original paper (1922) on the subject represented, in fact, prevailing usage as reflected by questionnaires. More recently (1933), Wentworth has stated his belief that there also is a "natural" basis for the grade limits chosen. This belief is founded on the notion that the several major classes of materials correlate closely with the several fundamental modes of transport by running water and with the several modes of derivation of sediment from parent rock. This concept is discussed elsewhere (p. 49).

It is obvious that other "natural" boundaries between the several size grades might be chosen if one's interest were in other properties or behavior of the granular materials.

Classification of Sedimentary Aggregates

Though some agreement has been reached respecting the terms to be applied to individual clastic grains or fragments, no such agreement has been attained concerning the names to be applied to an aggregate of such fragments. Because natural deposits or aggregates are rarely composed of frag-

---

[6] The above criticisms of the Committee reports should not be taken as meaning that they have no value. These reports are the most complete and most useful compendium on the subject to date. The criticisms offered here illustrate the difficulties encountered when terms are carried over from common speech and are redefined and quantified for scientific use. The Committee members were well aware of these difficulties.

A more recent compendium including both size and aggregate terms is that of Bonorino and Teruggi (1952).

ments of the same size, the problem is actually one of the nomenclature of mixed sizes. A *pebble*, for example, has been closely defined, but the term *gravel* or *conglomerate* has not been so circumscribed.

Various suggestions have been made. Perhaps to warrant the names gravel, sand, silt and so forth, an aggregate must have its chief ingredient (modal class or mode) within the limits set for these materials; or perhaps the mean size must fall within the prescribed range. Others have maintained that 50 per cent (or some other specified amount) of the whole distribution must fall within the specified size range. Thus a sand would have to have 50 per cent or more material within the sand size range.

The several methods suggested for naming an aggregate are not all equivalent or wholly satisfactory. A poorly sorted sediment, for example, which is a mixture of coarse gravel and sand, might be classed as a coarse sand if the mean size fell within this size grade, whereas in fact but 10 per cent of the material might be in the coarse sand class. Also, for example, the size classes of a poorly sorted sediment might be distributed equally between the sand, silt, and clay grades. Less than 50 per cent of the whole sample falls within the range of any one of these three materials. What name should be applied to this sediment?

There are numerous attempts at solution of the problem of classification and naming sedimentary aggregates. There have been two ways of solving this problem. One is to attempt to standardize prevalent usage. In this case existing practice is ascertained and the aggregate limits and terms are redefined to correspond. The other approach is to set more or less arbitrary limits to the various mixtures and to define and name them according to some systematic plan. The problem then is to change usage to conform to the proposed scheme. The first approach leads to irregular and seemingly illogical boundaries and definitions; the second leads to trouble with one's co-workers.

These two approaches are readily illustrated by the problem of the naming of mixtures of sand and gravel. This mixture constitutes a simple "binary system" which conceivably could be subdivided and named as shown in Fig. 11, A. Although this is a simple and logical scheme, it does not correspond to usage. Willman (1942) has noted that a large number of deposits which are called gravel and are commercially worked as such contain about 50 per cent sand and that many contain between 50 and 75 per cent sand. Analyses also show that many deposits which have been called gravel by the field geologist contain over 50 per cent sand. Willman therefore proposed the classification shown in Fig. 11, B. *Sand* accordingly would contain 75 to 100 per cent material of sand grade; *pebbly sand* would contain a conspicuous number of pebbles, but less than 25 per cent; *sandy gravel* contains 50 to 75 per cent sand and 25 to 50 per cent pebbles; and *gravel* contains 50 to 100 per cent material of pebble size. According to this classification a deposit with as little as 25 per cent of material of gravel size would be called *gravel*. Almost certainly the field geologist would call such a deposit, if consolidated, a conglomerate.

Three-component aggregates are readily represented by an equilateral triangular diagram. A single point within such a diagram is a graphic representation of a mixture of the three components.[7] It is therefore a very useful device for representing mixtures of sand, silt, and clay and for showing the limits of various mixtures for which specific names seem desirable.

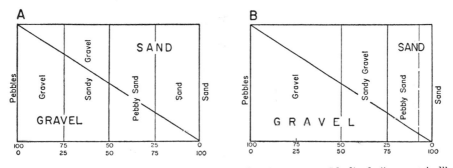

Fig. 11. Nomenclature of sand and gravel mixtures. **A**: Idealized "symmetrical" classification. **B**: Classification based on field usage (after Willman, 1942).

Some attempted solutions of the naming of sand-silt-clay mixtures are shown in Fig. 12. As can be seen by inspection of this figure there is no general agreement among geologists, oceanographers, pedologists, and engineers. The term *clay* as applied to aggregates, for example, is variously defined. As shown, it may contain as little as 50 per cent clay-sized material (A) or it may be defined as containing no less than 80 per cent of such materials (D).

As is apparent from inspection of Fig. 12, some workers have used special terms such as *mud*, *sansicl*, or *loam* for certain mixtures of sand, silt, and clay, generally those in which no component formed 50 per cent or more of the whole aggregate. *Wacke* has also been extended to designate such mixtures but except for the *graywackes* this term is rarely so used.

In general it can be seen that at present there is no accepted nor wholly satisfactory plan for designating sedimentary aggregates. Probably most of

---

[7] This results from the proposition that the sum of the perpendiculars from any such point to the respective sides is a constant. The length of each perpendicular, therefore, is proportional to each component (Fig. 3).

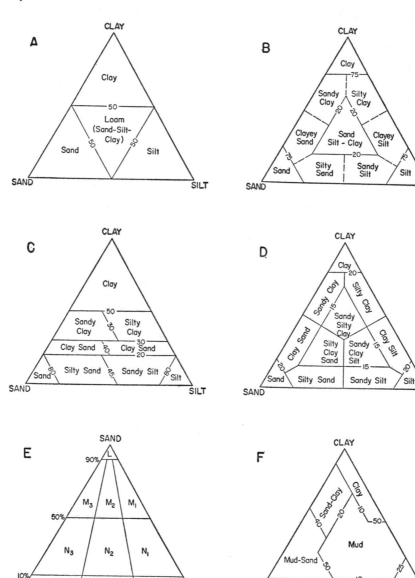

FIG. 12. Nomenclature of sand, silt, and clay mixtures. A: After Robinson (1949). B: After Shepard (1954). C: After Army Engineers. D: After Trefethen (1950). E: After Folk (1954). F: After A.P.I. Project 51 (Shepard, 1954).

the proposed systems of nomenclature could not be applied without a complete size analysis. Possible exception is that proposed by Folk (1954) which requires that the user decide whether silt or clay is the dominant fine component or whether these are present in subequal amounts. One must also be able to decide whether sand constitutes less than 10 per cent, more than 10 but less than 50 per cent, more than half but less than 90 per cent, or over 90 per cent of the sample. Such decisions would not seem to be difficult in most cases.

Instead of a ternary "system," i.e., one based on the proportions of three components, Baker (1920) and Niggli (1938) devised schemes for classifying the clastic sediments based on two parameters. Baker's system is based on the equivalent grade (mean size) and the grading factor (a sorting coefficient). His scheme is shown graphically in Fig. 13. Niggli's classification, like Baker's, is dependent upon knowledge of the whole size distribution. It is based on the ratio of two critical values on the distribution curves.

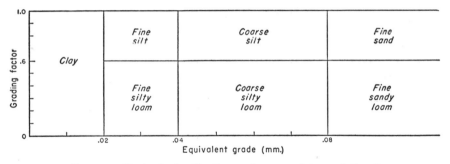

FIG. 13. Textural classification and nomenclature of the fine-grained clastic sediments (after Baker, 1920). Equivalent grade is arithmetic mean size; grading factor is a sorting coefficient. Perfect sorting has a grading factor of 1.0.

A modification of Niggli's scheme based on the Udden grade scale, and the first and third quartiles are shown in Fig. 14. If both quartiles fall within the limits set for any given size term, the unmodified term can be used for the aggregate. If one quartile falls in one size class and the other falls in another class, a suitable compound name is applied as indicated in the figure.

Although theoretically a clastic sediment could be a mixture of three (or even four) components, in *practice* such is rarely the case. Most deposits are gravels, sands, silts, or clays and are modified only by the introduction of materials from the preceding or following size grades. For that reason the complex ternary or quaternary classification schemes are largely unnecessary.

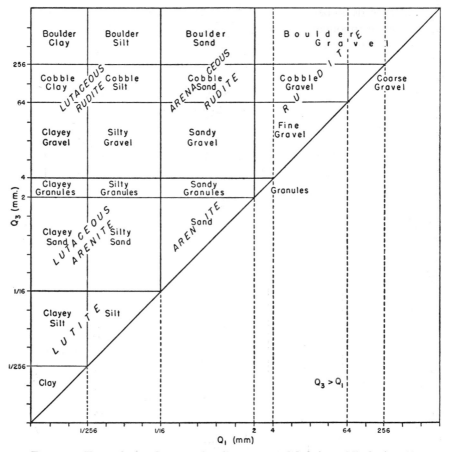

FIG. 14. Textural classification of sediments. Modified from Niggli (1938).

It is perhaps sufficient to follow the classification proposed by Wentworth in 1922 and shown in Table 6. As noted by Wentworth, this scheme does not take account of all possible mixtures but as noted above such mixtures, although theoretically possible, are exceedingly rare. Of 50 analyses chosen at random from Udden's compilation, Wentworth found that only till was not amenable to classification according to the plan shown in Table 6.

Essentially the same principle was utilized by Krynine (1948). He suggested that the terms *conglomerate, sandstone,* and *siltstone* be used and a modifying term be added if an appreciable content of a foreign size be present. A sandstone, for example, would be *conglomeratic* if it contained over 20 per cent pebbles, *pebbly* if over 10 but under 20 per cent pebbles, *silty* if more than 20 per cent of silt were present, and *clayey* if the clay content exceeds 20 per cent. In like manner a conglomerate would be *sandy* if the sand component exceeded 20 per cent and so forth. Presumably the foreign elements in each case must not exceed 50 per cent.

TABLE 6. Class Terms for Sediments (after Wentworth, 1922)

Percentage by Grade							Class Term
Gravel	>	80					Gravel
Gravel	>	sand	>	10,	others	< 10	Sandy gravel
Sand	>	gravel	>	10,	others	< 10	Gravelly sand
Sand	>	80					Sand
Sand	>	silt	>	10,	others	< 10	Silty sand
Silt	>	sand	>	10,	others	< 10	Sandy silt
Silt	>	80					Silt
Silt	>	clay	>	10,	others	< 10	Clayey silt
Clay	>	silt	>	10,	others	< 10	Silty clay
Clay	>	80					Clay

Classification of the breccias or aggregates with angular fragments is based on similar principles (Woodford, 1925). Using the term *rubble* for an aggregate of angular fragments of diameter over 2 mm, the following descriptive terms for the rocks may be used: *breccia,* over 80 per cent rubble; *sandy breccia,* over 10 per cent sand; *silty breccia,* over 10 per cent silt; and *clayey breccia,* over 10 per cent clay. In each case no second foreign component may exceed 10 per cent. If such be the case the term *earthy breccia* is used.

Alling (1934) and Shrock (1948) have also discussed the classification and naming of consolidated sedimentary aggregates.

Grade Scales

The class limits chosen by Wentworth and now generally followed by most American investigators, are based on the Udden *grade scale.* It is necessary, therefore, to examine this grade scale, to understand the basis of its construction, and to compare it with other proposed grade scales.

Although the particles of a sediment, such as a sand, differ in size from one another by infinitesimals from the largest to the smallest, it has been found convenient and necessary to divide the particle size range into a series of classes. Such a subdivision of an essentially continuous scale of sizes, a *grade scale,* is made for two reasons. One is the standardization of terms, which systematizes the description of sedimentary materials and thus avoids confusion of meaning. The other is the subdivision of the size distribution into a sufficient number of classes for statistical analysis. This latter requirement necessitates the use of a regular scale in which the subdivisions bear some simple relation to each other.

The range of sizes to be subdivided is very great. Consider boulder clay or till. The disparity between the extreme sizes is enormous. A boulder, a meter in diameter, is a million times as large as a clay particle one micron in size. For such a range the ordinary linear scale would be unsuitable because if such a scale had been used and one millimeter taken as the class unit, almost all the material known as sand, silt, and clay would be placed in one class and only the coarsest sand and gravel would be subdivided.

A graduated or geometric scale is clearly required for subdividing such a range of values. In this scale larger units are used for the larger sizes and smaller units for the smaller sizes. As Bagnold (1941) puts it, linear scales are seldom acceptable to Nature. Nature, if she has any preference, probably takes more interest in the ratios between quantities; she is rarely concerned with size for the sake of size. A millimeter difference between the diameters of two boulders is insignificant, but a millimeter difference between one sand grain and another is a large and important inequality.

The natural scale for size classification, therefore, is logarithmic. Udden, in the United States, recognized this as early as 1898. He chose one millimeter as the starting point and used the ratio ½ (or 2 depending on the sense of direction) and obtained thus the diameter limits to his size classes of 1, ½, ¼, and so forth, or 1, 2, 4, 8, and so forth in the other direction (Fig. 10). Udden's scale has remained in use to the present day and was adapted by Wentworth in 1922 and by the National Research Council in 1947 (Lane et al., 1947).

The Udden scale has some disadvantages. It is not suited to the analysis of well-graded sediments, because the number of classes into which such a sediment (dune sand, for example) will be divided is too small for statistical analysis. The scale therefore must be modified by dividing each class into two subclasses (or in some cases four subclasses). Such a scale is the $\sqrt{2}$ scale (Table 7). This subdivision, however, gives rise to a series of irrational numbers difficult to recall. Moreover, the mid-points (geometric means) of the various classes of this and the unmodified Udden scale required for statistical computation, also have irrational values. It might be desirable, therefore, to use a scale such as the "Tyler Standard," [8] in which the mid-point values of each size class are simple whole numbers or common fractions (Table 7).

To avoid both irrational class limits and irrational mid-points and also to simplify statistical computations, Krumbein (1934) proposed his phi scale. This scale is based on the observation that the class limits of the Udden scale can be expressed as powers of 2. Four millimeters is 2^2, 8 is 2^3, 1 is 2^0, ½ is 2^{-1}, and so forth. He therefore proposed to use the logarithm (to the base 2) of the diameter instead of the diameter. To avoid negative numbers for

[8] Catalog 53, 1952 edition, W. S. Tyler Company, Cleveland, Ohio.

the various sand grades and finer materials, the log was multiplied by -1, or in other words, phi $= -\log_2$ diam (mm).

Many other grade scales have been proposed or used (Truesdell and Varnes, 1950). As inspection of Fig. 10 will show, these fall into several categories. Some, like that of Udden, are regular geometric progressions.

TABLE 7. Standard Grade Scales

Udden $\sqrt{2}$		Tyler Standard			
		Class Limits		Mid-Point (mm)[a]	
Class Limits (mm)	Mid-point[a] (mm)	Mesh (in.)	(mm)	Exact	Approximate
32.00 to 22.61	26.82		26.67 to 18.85	22.67	
22.61 to 16.00	19.00		18.85 to 13.33	15.85	16.0
16.00 to 11.31	13.43		13.33 to 9.423	11.20	
11.31 to 8.00	9.50		9.423 to 6.680	7.925	8.0
8.00 to 5.75	6.78	3 to 4	6.680 to 4.699	5.613	
5.75 to 4.00	4.80	4 to 6	4.699 to 3.327	3.962	4.0
4.00 to 2.83	3.37	6 to 8	3.327 to 2.362	2.794	
2.83 to 2.00	2.38	8 to 10	2.362 to 1.651	1.981	2.0
2.00 to 1.414	1.68	10 to 14	1.651 to 1.168	1.397	
1.414 to 1.000	1.19	14 to 20	1.168 to 0.833	0.991	1.0
1.000 to 0.707	0.841	20 to 28	0.833 to 0.589	0.701	
0.707 to 0.500	0.595	28 to 35	0.589 to 0.417	0.495	0.5
0.500 to 0.354	0.420	35 to 48	0.417 to 0.295	0.351	
0.354 to 0.250	0.297	48 to 65	0.295 to 0.208	0.246	0.25
0.250 to 0.177	0.210	65 to 100	0.208 to 0.147	0.175	
0.177 to 0.125	0.149	100 to 150	0.147 to 0.104	0.124	0.125
0.125 to 0.088	0.105	150 to 200	0.104 to 0.074	0.088	
0.088 to 0.062	0.074				

[a] The mid-points on the Udden scale are very nearly the class limits of the Tyler Standard Scale, and conversely. These relations facilitate some transformations of data. Mid-points are square root of product of the class limits.

Some, like that of Atterberg (1905), are also geometrical but differ from Udden's in that they are also decimal and cyclical. In a decimal scale, the size limits are cyclical and are regularly repeated with only a change in the decimal point.

The Atterberg scale, for example, starts with 2 mm and the major subdivisions are 2, 20, 200, etc., in the upward direction and 0.2, 0.02, 0.002, etc., in the downward direction. This scale, however, does not provide a sufficient number of classes for analytical purposes so that subdivision is necessary. If the subdivision is to follow the logarithmic rule, the divisions will be the square root of the product (geometric mean) of the larger size grades. These values are also irrational and difficult to remember unless they be rounded off. Atterberg's scale has become the accepted standard of the International Soil Science Society and is widely used in Europe.

Some scales are neither wholly geometric nor linear. Such a nonregular scale is that long used by the U.S. Bureau of Soils (see Fig. 10) and commonly taken as a standard by the students of soils in the United States. The scale is a satisfactory one for descriptive purposes only for the materials of medium and fine grain, but it is not adequate for statistical analysis nor suitable for coarse materials.

Although many grade scales have been constructed and their adoption urged (Alling, 1943; Lane et al., 1947; Legget and Peckover, 1949) there has been no universally accepted scale which meets the needs of pedologists, civil engineers, oceanographers, geologists, etc. For geologists a standard scale should be a geometrical one to provide a sufficient number of classes for size analysis and statistical summarization. Though neither decimal nor cyclic, the Udden scale meets this need. It has been widely used and is the basis for the limits placed on various grade terms used in this book. It is also the basis of the grade terms or definitions recommended by the National Research Council Subcommittee on Sediment Terminology (Lane et al., 1947).

Size Frequency Distributions

If arranged according to size, the detrital elements in a clastic sediment (sand grains, pebbles, etc.) would be found to differ in size from one another by infinitesimals. The *size frequency distribution* is said to be continuous. To study a given size distribution and to summarize it statistically for comparison with other like distributions, it is necessary that the size values be grouped into classes or size grades. This subdivision is accomplished by use of a suitable grade scale.

Graphical Representation

Although a size frequency distribution of a sediment—its "mechanical analysis"—may be summarized in a table (see Table 8), it may also be presented graphically. Such graphical presentation is easier to grasp than columns of figures in a table. It facilitates comparison of several different analyses. Simplest of such graphical presentations is the *histogram* or frequency distribution pyramid. In this species of bar diagram the area of the bars is proportional to the quantity of material in each class. The width of the bars is determined by the class limits. If the limits are equal (or have an equal ratio, so that their limits may be plotted at equal intervals), the length of the bar will be directly proportional to the quantity in each size class. If, for example, one wishes to show the analysis given in Table 8, the class limits 16, 8, 4, 2, and so forth are appropriately marked off at equal intervals [9] on the x-axis and the lengths of the several bars are drawn proportional to the frequencies given.

The quantity in any given class may be measured by *weight* or *number*. If sieves were used to make a size analysis of a sand, the amount of material retained on each sieve would be weighed and the percentage or proportional part of the whole sample determined, whereas if the material were measured by a micrometer ocular under the microscope, the percentage present in a size class would be determined by count or number. The results in the two cases, though related, are quite different.

TABLE 8. Representative Mechanical Analyses

Size Grade (mm)	No. 6 %	No. 6 Cum. % [a]	No. 10 %	No. 10 Cum. % [a]	No. 3 %	No. 3 Cum. % [a]
16–8	6.3	6.3	....	....	....	....
8–4	11.3	17.6	....	....	....	....
4–2	20.1	37.7	1.4	1.4	....	....
2–1	24.5	62.2	10.0	11.4	0.1	0.1
1–½	22.2	84.4	30.4	41.8	0.3	0.4
½–¼	12.2	96.6	21.7	63.5	37.1	37.5
¼–⅛	2.6	99.2	20.9	84.4	56.5	94.0
⅛–1/16	0.6	99.8	11.6	96.0	5.7	99.7
Under 1/16	0.2	100.0	4.1	100.1	0.4	100.1
	100.0		100.1		100.1	

Samples are glacial outwash (Pleistocene, Wisconsin) from Dundee, Illinois. M. A. Rosenfeld, analyst.
  [a] Cumulative per cent.

The histogram has been criticized (Galliher, 1933; Dryden, 1934) as a means of representing the size composition of a sediment because the use of another grade scale (i.e., a different set of sieves in the case of sands) would markedly change the form of the graph and also because the analysis is represented by a series of steplike bars instead of a continuous curve. These objections are serious only if too few classes are present. If the size of the sample is increased and smaller class units used, both objections largely disappear (Fig. 15).

If the class interval be made smaller and the scale on the y-axis be changed so that the total area of the histogram remains the same, the "steps" between the several bars will grow smaller. If this process be continued, the limit which is approached is a smooth curve, known as a *frequency curve* (Fig. 16). Such a frequency curve is a better picture of the particle size distribution than the histogram, inasmuch as the difference between one grain and the next larger or smaller is an infinitesimal amount in comparison with the whole range of sizes involved. The curve cannot be plotted directly from the analytical data.

[9] Equivalent to plotting the logarithms of the size.

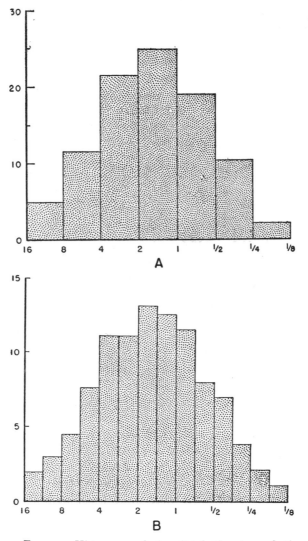

FIG. 15. Histograms of size distribution in a clastic sediment. **A**: Based on Udden size grades (analysis given in Table 8). **B**: Based on half Udden size grades.

The size distribution may be shown by means of a *cumulative curve* which can be constructed from the analytical data. The percentage larger than (or smaller than) each of the several size-grades used in making the analysis is computed. The quantities thus obtained are plotted as ordinates and the corresponding sizes as abscissas. The points located are joined by a smooth curve. The curves for several types of sediment are shown in Fig. 17.

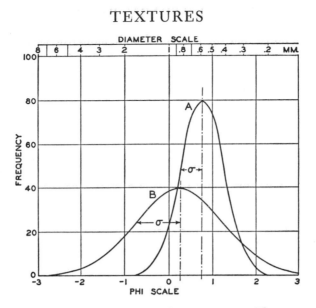

FIG. 16. Examples of size frequency curves. These are log normal frequency distributions (from Krumbein and Monk, *Am. Inst. Min. Eng.*, T. P. 1492, Fig. 1, 1942).

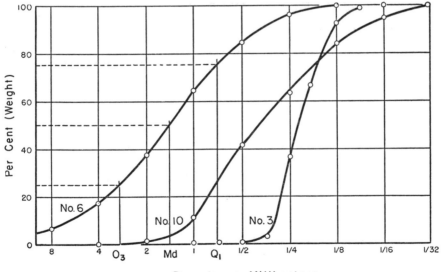

Diameter in Millimeters

FIG. 17. Size composition of clastic sediments represented by cumulative curves. The curve represents sediments, the analysis of which is given in Table 8, Sediments No. 6 and No. 10 have about the same sorting but differ markedly in average size, whereas sediments No. 10 and No. 3 have about the same average size but differ notably in sorting. The significant points for determination of median and coefficient of sorting are shown for curve No. 6. Here Md is median, Q_1 is first quartile, Q_3 is third quartile.

It should be noted that the horizontal scale along the x-axis of the cumulative curve—like that of the frequency curve and histogram—is logarithmic,
not linear. The distances scaled off on this axis are proportional to the
logarithms of the diameter, not to the diameter itself. This method of plotting has been generally adopted for particulate materials because it usually
symmetrizes the graph. The significance of this observation is discussed
elsewhere.

Another peculiarity of these plots is the reversed sense of direction on the
x-axis. The values decrease to the right instead of being the more conventional increase. This apparently is largely a matter of convenience and has
been widely though not universally practiced by students of the granular
materials.

A *sedimentation* curve also graphically portrays the sediment composition.
It is experimentally derived by weighing or otherwise measuring the quantity
of sediment deposited (or removed) in successively cumulated units of time
from an originally uniform suspension. The quantity of material in a given
size class or larger than a given size cannot be read directly from the graph.
Such information, however, may be determined by calculation or by graphic
means (Krumbein and Pettijohn, 1938, pp. 112–115).

Characteristics of Size Frequency Distributions

Comparison of histograms of several unlike sediments will disclose certain
similarities or differences. Udden (1914) noted the tendency of one size
grade or class to contain more than any other size grade or class. Udden

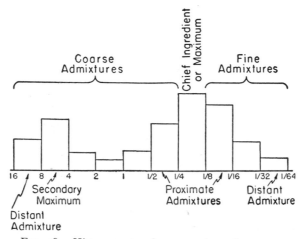

Fig. 18. Histogram to show meaning of terms employed by Udden to describe the size characteristics of a
clastic sediment. See Table 9.

referred to this dominant class as the "chief ingredient" or "maximum"
(Fig. 18). It is the *modal class*. The lesser or subordinate classes are the
"admixtures" and may be designated "coarse or fine admixtures" depending
on whether they consist of grades finer or coarser than the modal group.
The two classes adjacent to the modal class are the "proximate" grades or
classes, whereas those most different in size from the maximum are the
"distant admixtures."

Grades with less material than the maximum but dominant over their
neighbors, were described as *secondary maxima*. Size distributions with but
a single maximum are more appropriately called *unimodal* distributions;
those with several maxima or modes are *bimodal* if there bc but two and
polymodal if there are more. Bimodal distributions are rather common,
though the lesser mode is usually small (Fig. 19, F).

Inspection of many analyses reveals other characteristics. The analyses
plotted as histograms, for example, may contain many or few classes, i.e.,
have a wide or narrow *range*. The histogram may be symmetrical or otherwise, and if asymmetrical it may be marked by a dominance of coarse or of
fine admixtures (see Fig. 19). These differences are in part a reflection of
the conditions of deposition and may enable the geologist to read something
of the geologic history of the sediment from the analysis. The characteristics

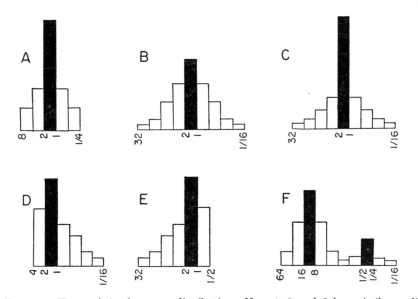

FIG. 19.   Types of size frequency distributions. Here A, B, and C have similar median
size; A and B differ in the sorting; C, though similar in median and sorting to B, differs
in its kurtosis; D and E are markedly skewed and differ in the direction of skewing; F is a
bimodal distribution; all others are unimodal.

described are features of any frequency distribution and there are methods for measuring these properties by means of a single number for each. The fundamental measures are those of the "average," the spread or "sorting" (or range) of the distribution, its symmetry or "skewness" (and its sign, i.e., whether positive or negative), and the "peakedness," or kurtosis of the frequency curve or histogram (Table 9).

TABLE 9. Attributes of Frequency Distributions

Attribute	Technical Name	Udden's Terminology	Statistical Measure[a]
"Average"	Measure of central tendency	Chief ingredient or maximum	Median or 50 percentile
"Sorting"	Dispersion	Number of size grades; index of sorting	Coefficient of sorting: $\sqrt{Q_3/Q_1}$
Symmetry	Skewness	Predominance of coarse or fine admixtures	Coefficient of skewness: $Q_1Q_3/(Md^2)$
Peakedness	Kurtosis	Quantity in the maximum plus range	Coefficient of kurtosis: $(Q_3 - Q_1)/2(P_{90} - P_{10})$

[a] There are various types of statistical measures. Those listed here are the "quartile measures," or measures based on the magnitude of the median (Md) and quartiles (Q_1 and Q_3) (and the 10 and 90 percentiles, P_{10} and P_{90}, respectively). Other types of measures, such as the moment measures and the several species of quartile measures, cannot be discussed here.

The advantages of single-number representation of these properties of the size-frequency distribution are obvious. Such summaries enable the geologist, not only to say a sediment is well sorted or better sorted than some other deposit, but also to say how well sorted or how much better sorted such sediment may be. Such values also enable the investigator to plot average size (or other characteristic) against distance, and to state in equation form the laws of size change with distance of travel and the like, or to plot the values of the median or other size parameter on a map, each value at the corresponding sampling point, and then to contour such a map and thereby deduce the direction of current flow and other data.

The parameters of the frequency distribution may be read or calculated from certain critical points on the cumulative curve. An easily determined measure of the "average" size is the *median*, which is that size such that 50 per cent of the material is larger and 50 per cent smaller.[10] The location of the median is determined by the point of crossing of the cumulative curve and the 50 per cent line (Fig. 17). The *sorting* or spread of the curve

[10] By weight in the case of sediments, the several grades of which are weighed.

is measured by the *coefficient of sorting*,[11] So, which is the square root of the ratio of the quartiles, Q_3/Q_1, where $Q_3 > Q_1$. The quartiles are the size values associated with the intersection of the 25 and 75 per cent values with the cumulative curve. A perfectly sorted sediment has a coefficient of 1.0. According to Trask (1932) a So value of less than 2.5 indicates a well-sorted sediment, whereas a value of about 3.0 is normal, and a value greater than 4.5 indicates a poorly sorted sediment. These values, which are based on a study of about 170 samples of Recent marine sediments, appear to be too high. Krumbein and Tisdel (1940) found that crystalline rocks which have disintegrated in place have a coefficient of sorting that places them within the range of Trask's well-sorted sediments. Hough (1940) and also Stetson (quoted by Hough) point out that most near-shore marine sediments of the sand grade have sorting coefficients between 1.0 and 2.0. Stetson gives 1.45 as the average.

The skewness or symmetry, Sk, may be measured by $Q_1Q_3/(Md)^2$, or the product of the quartiles divided by the square of the median. If $\log_{10}$ Sk instead of Sk itself be used, perfect symmetry has a value of 0 (zero), and all other values are either positive or negative depending on the direction in which the curve is skewed. With positive skewness, coarser admixtures exceed the fine; with negative skewness, the converse is true. Kurtosis may be expressed as $(Q_3 - Q_1)/2(P_{90} - P_{10})$, where Q_3 and Q_1 are the quartiles as before, and P_{90} and P_{10} are the percentiles, or the size associated with the percentage values, respectively.[12]

Representative size analyses are shown in Table 8; the five critical points on the cumulative curves and the four parameters computed from them for two of these analyses are summarized in Tables 10 and 11.

TABLE 10. Critical Size Values (mm)

Sample	Md	Q_3	Q_1	P_{90}	P_{10}
No. 6	1.45	3.0	0.72	6.00	0.39
No. 3	0.22	0.28	0.17	0.32	0.14

The simple indices given above are based on only a few specified points on the cumulative curve. More exact indices of average size, sorting, etc., based on the entire curve, are the so-called moment measures. Such measures

---

[11] *Sorting* is here used in a statistical sense. Actual materials that never were moved at all by air or water, such as the quartz grains in a residual soil derived from a granite, have a restricted size range, and hence show a statistical sorting.

[12] To conform with standard statistical usage, P_{90} is the size such that 90 per cent is larger and 10 per cent smaller; similarly with the P_{10}. So also Q_3 is the 75 percentile, i.e., 75 per cent is smaller and 25 per cent larger. See Fig. 17 and Table 10 (with actual values).

(mean, standard deviation, and the like) are described in any standard work on statistics, but because the methods usually given for their calculation generally require classes of equal size and because the grain size of sediments is usually summarized by classes of unequal magnitude (but usually of equal ratio), it is necessary to employ somewhat different methods of computation (Krumbein and Pettijohn, 1938).

TABLE 11.   Summary of Quartile Measures

Parameter	Values for Samples	
	No. 6	No. 3
Median (Md)	1.45 mm	0.22 mm
Coefficient of sorting (So)	2.04	1.27
Coefficient of skewness (Sk)	1.03	0.98
Kurtosis (K)	0.19	0.26

Interpretation of the Mechanical Composition of Clastic Sediments

J. A. Udden (1914) believed that the size composition of a sediment was controlled by the conditions prevailing during deposition of the sediment. It follows, therefore, that if ancient sediments were deposited under conditions similar to those now forming, study of modern sediments would reveal the grading characteristics of each type, which could then be used, in turn, to decipher the origin of the ancient deposits. Udden accordingly made many mechanical analyses of sediments, especially aeolian deposits, and published, in 1914, over 350 such analyses together with a summary of certain "laws" thought by him to govern the mechanical composition of clastic sediments.

Wentworth, in 1931, published more than 800 size analyses in graphic form. Inspection of the histograms shows that patterns of different sediments are different. Certain types, till and beach sand, for example, are strikingly unlike. On the other hand, some unlike types are strikingly similar in their mechanical composition as, for example, beach and dune sands. The similarities or differences between the grading curves of sediments from different environments are probably the result of similarities or differences in the hydro- or aerodynamic conditions in these several environments as Udden believed. Current velocity, turbulence, density, and viscosity of the transporting medium, and the stability of the flow conditions are no doubt largely responsible for the different types of size frequency distributions. The precise relations between these environmental characteristics and the resulting grading curves are as yet, however, largely unknown and can be stated only in the most general terms. It does not appear possible, at this time, therefore, to discriminate between closely related environments or agents by means of the grading curves of the sediments alone.

Whether size analyses will prove a reliable guide to the origin of a sediment is as yet uncertain. The success achieved to date is limited, in part because of inadequate data on modern sediments; inadequate analyses, i.e., analyses made with too large a class interval; improper sampling procedures which produce spurious bimodal curves; too great a reliance on a single size analysis; and failure to measure or interpret correctly the intersample variability caused by short time changes in the flow regimen within the environment of deposition.

The Nature of the Frequency Curve

Udden observed, as have others since, that the size distribution curve appears to be more or less symmetrical on a log basis, i.e., if the frequency be plotted against log size and not size itself. This is just another way of saying that a geometrical grade scale tends to symmetrize the frequency polygon or histogram. Udden (1914, p. 732) expressed this in his first two "laws" when he wrote:

In most sediments there is a mean size of clastic elements that is present in greater quantity than any other. . . . If we separate the mechanical elements in a sediment into a series of groups (grades) containing clastic elements, having diameters bearing a constant ratio to the diameters in their next group, we find that the mass in each group tends to have a fixed ratio to the mass of the other groups. Excepting some special condition, this ratio is such that the mass of any group is smaller the more its clastic elements differ in size from those of the mean size.

Bagnold (1941, p. 114) restated this observation of Udden's when he said:

It is now for the first time apparent that outside a definite central zone the grades to the right and to the left of the peak fall off each at its own constant rate; this means that we are again confronted with the same logarithmic law of distribution which runs through the whole subject.

The symmetrizing effect of the geometric scale led Krumbein (1938) to the conclusion that the grading curves of many clastic sediments were log normal and to express the size-frequency distributions as a Gaussian function in which log size is substituted for actual size.[13] Krumbein applied the test for normality and found that the requirements were reasonably well satisfied by many sediments.

Whether a size frequency distribution of a particular sediment is log normal or not is readily determined graphically by means of log probability

[13] The Gaussian distribution may be expressed as $Y = \dfrac{1}{b\sqrt{2\pi}} e^{-[(x-a)^2/2b^2]}$ where Y is the frequency, X is the magnitude of the independent variable, and a and b are constants or parameters that determine the position and shape of the curve; a is the arithmetic mean and b is the measure of spread of the data about the mean (standard deviation).

paper. A modified form of this paper and its use has been described by Otto (1939).[14] The size frequency, based on a weight percentage, is cumulated in the usual manner and plotted on this paper. As with the ordinary cumulative curve, size is plotted on one axis (in this case x) and the percentage frequency on the other (in this case y) (Fig. 20). Many sediments deviate

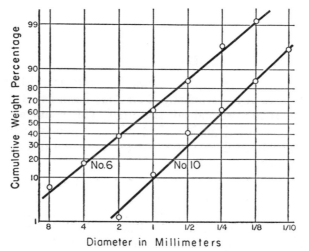

FIG. 20. Size composition of clastic sediment shown by cumulative weight percentage plotted on logarithmic probability paper. Sediment No. 6 is same as that shown in Figs. 15, 17, and Table 8.

but little from a straight line and some depart not at all. It is possible, by reading appropriate intercepts, to determine readily a series of statistical constants which are the essential parameters of the frequency distribution. The slope of the line is a measure of sorting. The parameters obtained are the "moment measures" and not the "quartile measures" given elsewhere (Krumbein and Pettijohn, 1938, p. 239).

Many sediments are not log normal, and even those which are approximately so show some departure from a strict log normal distribution. Even blown sands, which, as Bagnold (1941, p. 116) noted, approach a log normal type, show a small but definite departure from a log normal distribution. The deviation was great enough so that Bagnold concluded that "from the results of many analyses of sand samples, it seems clear that if sand grading is a random phenomenon, from which conclusion it is difficult to escape, then some special probability function must be looked for."

[14] Many sediment distribution curves satisfy all the geometrical requirements of the log normal curve, except the kurtosis. Krumbein noted that curves with zero kurtosis are rare among sediments. The significance of this anomaly is not known.

As the clays and silts depart widely from a log normal form, Doeglas (1936, 1947) and Doeglas and Smithuyzen (1941) were led to the conclusion that the size frequency distribution of sediments was an arithmetically normal Gaussian curve. Horner (1947, pp. 137–142) takes exception to this conclusion and notes, as Bagnold did, that the grading curves of most sediments, excepting for the "tails," better fit a log normal distribution.

Roller (1941, 1937) has also called attention to the theoretical and actual failure of the Gaussian probability law for both coarsest and finest grades of many sediments. The Gaussian function requires that the upper limits of size be infinite. The actual fact, however, is that there is a finite upper limit with an associated finite (not zero) frequency. Though the log probability function fits the coarser range rather well it fails systematically in the finer grades. Roller proposed and tested a different function [15] which was believed by him to describe most particulate materials.

There have been other attempts to relate size distribution curves to other laws than log probability. Krumbein and Tisdel (1940) believe that some materials, notably the products of weathering and certain peculiar sediments, such as boulder clay or till and some coarse pyroclastic deposits, appeared to follow Rosin's law. Rosin's law was devised to describe the distributions produced by artificial crushing of such materials as coal.[16] This may mean, therefore, that natural agencies of weathering, comminution by ice, and fragmentation by volcanic explosions yield a product similar to that formed by crushing but that the gradational agents yield a distribution of a different type, one that is essentially log normal. That this is the case is by no means certain. Dapples, Krumbein, and Sloss (1953) have shown that the grading of certain normal sediments, both arkoses and a normal quartz sandstone,

---

[15] According to Roller, $Y = aX^{1/2}e^{-b/x}$, where Y is the cumulative weight percentage of all sizes less than X, and a and b are the parameters of the distribution. The meaning and methods of graphical determination of the parameters are given by Roller. For a unimodal distribution, a plot of log $Y/X^{1/2}$ against $1/X$ yields a straight line which serves to determine the parameters a and b. The slope of the line is $-b/2.303$ and the intercept of the Y-axis and the line gives the log a. Bimodality is expressed by two straight-line segments of different slope. Extension of each line to meet the Y axis yields log a' and a'', and the two slope values provide the information to calculate b' and b''; a' and b' and a'' and b'' are the respective parameters of the two component size distributions.

The statistical constants S, surface area per gram; U, the coefficient of uniformity; R, the coefficient of regression (as a result of failure of the coarser sizes); and N, the number of particles per gram, are also defined and graphically determined, as is the mean size.

[16] Rosin's law may be expressed as $Y = 100(1 - e^{bx^n})$, where Y is the weight percentage passed by a sieve of mesh X; b is the reciprocal of the "average" size; and n is a reciprocal of the spread of the curve, a concept similar to the sorting coefficient of sediments, except that it decreases as the spread increases. If any size distribution plotted in cumulative fashion forms a straight line on the special graph paper devised by Geer and Yancy (Krumbein and Tisdel, 1940), that distribution conforms to Rosin's law (Fig. 21). As with probability paper, the slope is a measure of sorting or uniformity of the material (n), and a particular "average" size (b) can be read from an intercept.

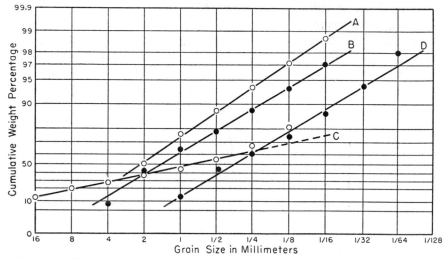

FIG. 21. Cumulative weight-percentage curves plotted on Rosin law paper. **A:** Artificially crushed quartz (after Krumbein and Tisdel, 1940). **B:** Disintegrated igneous rock (boulder in glacial outwash; after Krumbein and Tisdel, 1940). **C:** Tuff (after Moore, 1934). **D:** Detritus from weathered gneiss, District of Columbia (after Wentworth, 1931).

seem to follow the Rosin function. Roller, however, has pointed out that Rosin's law has both theoretical and practical drawbacks. Like the Gaussian function, it fails to satisfy the boundary conditions, since x (size) is infinite when y (cumulative frequency) is 100.

The Size Parameters

The three chief parameters of the frequency curve, namely, mean size, coefficient of sorting, and skewness are theoretically wholly independent of one another. Actually this is not the case. Hough (1942), for example, noted that the medium-grained beach and near-shore sands of Cape Cod Bay had a symmetrical size-distribution curve, i.e., one with no skewness. But the very fine offshore silts and clays (median under 0.1 mm) are both markedly skewed and materially less well sorted. The sediments with median near 0.2 are best sorted and those both coarser and finer showed less perfect sorting. Similar observations were reported by Krumbein and Aberdeen (1937) in the sediments of Barataria Bay. As noted by Hough, there is a remarkable similarity in the sorting and skewness between sediments within Cape Cod Bay and on the Continental Shelf, when samples of the same median diameter are compared. This suggests that similar marine processes, when they are of the same rigor (as indicated by the same median diameter), produce similar size distributions of the sediment.

The tendency of sediments of mean size of about 0.2 mm to be better sorted than those coarser or finer has been noted by Inman (1949) who concluded that "the general relationship of sorting coefficient to median diameter appears to be similar for all water environments, the difference being mainly in the degree of sorting. Sediments with median diameters near the grade of fine sand are the best sorted, sediments coarser and finer are more poorly sorted." The relations observed were attributed to the properties of fine sand which "would be most easily moved; the coarser and finer grades moved by surface creep would tend to lag behind."

The observations of Inman and earlier workers were further confirmed by analyses made by Griffiths (1951) who studied the size-sorting relationships in over 1200 Tertiary sediments from the Caribbean area. Griffiths attempted to express the relationships between these attributes in mathematical terms. Although a correlation between size and sorting is apparent, there is considerable scatter of the data. Individual sediments which departed widely from the expected norm were explained by Griffiths as related to abnormal events in the history of the deposit as, for example, flocculation of the finer clays. Griffiths furthermore concluded that the degree of scatter or deviation of the size-sorting parameter from the empirically established trend lines was a function of

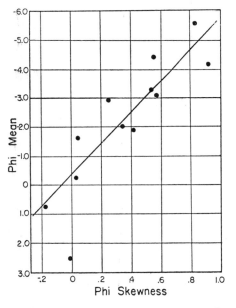

FIG. 22. Relation between mean size and skewness of samples of glacial outwash gravels (after Kurk, Plumley, 1948).

the "amount of sorting" the deposit had undergone. It was, in other words, an index of textural maturity of the sediment, and Griffiths believed it to be a very useful tool in ascertaining the environment of deposition, though Griffiths did not show how to use such relations as a working tool.

Unlike the Guiana gravels studied by Griffiths, the Black Hills gravels investigated by Plumley (1948) showed no correlation between mean size and the sorting. The gravels showed a marked downcurrent decrease in average size without any corresponding change in their sorting. They did show, however, a clear downcurrent decrease in skewness. The correlation between mean size and skewness is also shown by Kurk's (1941) data on glacial outwash gravels (Fig. 22). As Plumley points out the source materials (talus and the like) probably had a highly skewed size distribution, and stream abrasion and selective transport tend to symmetrize the distribution.

Fine-grained sediments show a somewhat different relation between mean size and skewness. As noted by Hough, the finer the sediment, the more skewed it is. The very fine offshore silts and clays of Cape Cod Bay (median under 0.1 mm) have a pronounced skewness. Fourteen bottom sediments all showed marked negative skewness, average −0.16, in contrast to 21 beach sands (average median of 0.57 mm) which had a skewness of 0.02 (see Table 65, p. 351). Inman has discussed the relations between size and skewness and has shown that the finest sediments should normally be highly skewed toward the fine fraction. As noted by him, however, Gripenberg (1934) has observed that many of the bottom sediments of the North Baltic sea are skewed toward the coarser grades.[17]

Bimodal Distributions

Published size analyses of many sediments show what Udden called secondary maxima. In modern statistical language these distributions are

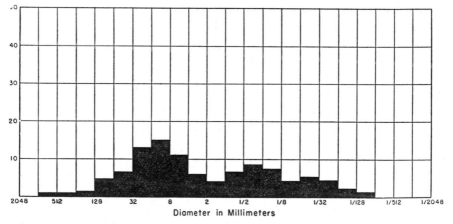

FIG. 23. Polymodal sediment. Average of twelve terrace sands and gravels, Piedmont region (after Wentworth Nos. 509–520, 1931).

termed polymodal (Fig. 23). As a rule but one secondary mode is present— the sediment is therefore bimodal.

[17] It is not certain what the actual size-skewness or size-sorting relations are in fine sediments, inasmuch as the deposits of finest grain size were deposited in a flocculated state, the size distribution found by analyses of deflocculated materials may bear little resemblance to the original size distribution.

In general it is the coarse gravels that are bimodal. Sands, on the other hand, tend to have a single mode. Of several hundred published analyses of California alluvial gravels, for example, 92 per cent had more than one mode (Conkling, Eckis, and Gross, 1934). Only 42 per cent of the associated sands were so characterized. In general the bimodal gravel has its chief mode in some gravel class and its secondary or lesser mode in the sand grades. The maxima are 4 to 5 grades apart on the average. The chief ingredient, therefore, has a diameter 16 to 32 times that of the material in the secondary mode. The quantity of material in the modal class is small in these gravels; this class has but 15 to 25 per cent, whereas in the associated unimodal sands, the modal class has nearly twice as much, or 30 to 50 per cent. In like manner other alluvial gravels are characteristically bimodal. Krumbein found 85 per cent of the flood gravels of the San Gabriel and Arroyo Seco to be bimodal (Krumbein, 1940, 1942). Ten of 25 samples of *single layers* in glacial outwash gravel were bimodal (Kurk, 1941) and 20 of 23 samples of Black Hills terrace gravels were bimodal (Plumley, 1948).

Various explanations have been suggested for the bimodal character of coarse alluvial sediments. According to Udden (1914)

When a transporting medium is supplied with sufficiently heterogeneous materials it will tend to carry and to deposit more of two certain sizes of material than of any other sizes. The principal deposit it makes will have an excess of another considerably coarser ingredient which it can roll, smaller in quantity. This makes what we call a secondary maximum. For water deposits, the secondary maximum will consist of elements having a diameter about sixteen times the diameter of the chief ingredient.

On the other hand, Fraser (1935) thought simultaneous deposition of cobbles and fine sand improbable, inasmuch as the velocity of a sand carrying cobbles 10 inches in diameter would have to be decreased 60 per cent before the 1 millimeter size could be deposited. He considers it unlikely that such violent changes in current velocity always occur when coarse materials are deposited. He concluded, therefore, that at any given instant a river usually deposits only a very limited size range of material and that the finer sizes in gravels are the result of later infiltration. Plumley (1948) is inclined to agree with Fraser and interpreted the fines—the secondary mode in most cases—as entrapped materials filling the voids between the primary matrix—the principal mode. To support this view Plumley noted that if one assume two sizes of spheres—the smallest small enough to be contained in the spaces between the larger—that the weight per cent of the smaller fraction would range from 22 to 32 per cent of the sample depending on the tightness of the packing. The natural gravels contained, on the average, 20 per cent of materials in the secondary mode and closely related grades. In view of the departure of the pebbles from spherical form, the nonuniform size of the two size fractions involved, and the chaotic nature of the packing, the agreement between theory and observation is surprisingly good.

It has been suggested that there is a dearth of materials in the grades between sand and gravel, i.e., in the 2 to 4 millimeter range (Hough 1942, p. 26, footnote). This scarcity of material has been explained by the mechanical instability of particles of the coarse-grained crystalline rocks. Moreover, some rocks undergo granular disintegration—and produce sand—whereas others break up into blocks, and thus produce gravel. A deficiency of material of intermediate nature seems probable. Would such a situation lead to a sag in the frequency distribution of some sediments so that their size distribution curve is bimodal?

Incomplete mixing of two sizes of materials by natural agencies might also produce bimodal curves. Ice deposits, notably till, are most likely to show this character. Study of many analyses shows that the small secondary modes are not just accidental. They probably express "loading" of the ice with some particular material which had a previous history of sorting and deposition. Ice moving over sandy outwash might pick up much of this material, so that analysis of the till deposited might show a small maximum in some sand grade, namely, the average grade of the contaminating sand. Whether analogous loading occurs in waterlain materials is uncertain. There is some evidence that it does and if the material added differs materially from the prevailing load, a secondary mode may be produced (Swensen, 1941; Rittenhouse, 1943).

A bimodal distribution could conceivably be the result of faulty sampling procedure. If in sampling a deposit, two distinct phases represented by two distinctly different layers, are sampled, the resulting curves express the mixing of two distinct distributions (Bagnold, 1941, pp. 118–124). If these distributions are slightly different, the resulting composite is notably skewed; if they are very unlike, two modes may result. A larger sample—such as a channel sample cutting many layers—would probably show a unimodal size distribution. That many bimodal distributions are not an artifact introduced by the sampling technique, however, is shown by the bimodal curves obtained from single layers.

In conclusion, it can be said that the possible causes of polymodal distributions are several and that present data are insufficient to show which are important and which are not. The prevalence of polymodal distributions in published analyses of stream gravels seems to be significant, whatever the explanation of such distributions.[18]

[18] Bimodal distributions are also known from some very fine-grained marine bottom deposits. These may be in part due to debris of organic origin mixed with normal bottom sediments (Revelle, 1944).

Relative Frequency of the Various Size Grades

In the discussion of polymodal distributions, attention was called to the most common types of bimodal curves in which one mode was in the sand range and the other was in the gravel sizes. It was suggested that the materials of the intermediate grades 2 to 4 millimeters in particular were less common in nature than materials either coarser or finer and that in this fact lies a possible explanation for the peculiar grading curves of the coarse fluviatile and related sediments.

That materials of this range are apparently not so abundant as other sizes has been suggested by several writers. Einstein, Anderson, and Johnson (1940) cite Nesper's work on the Rhine in Switzerland, in which the bed material ranges in size from 5 millimeters in diameter to "boulders" 100 millimeters in diameter and larger. Between the boulders and in protected pools, however, sand 1 millimeter in diameter and finer is found, whereas particles ranging in size from 1 to 5 millimeters are not present. These authors conclude that such particles "occur rarely for certain geologic or hydraulic reasons." In the Rhine of this area the coarse material was a part of the bed load of the stream, whereas the sand was a part of the suspended load.

Pettijohn (1940) concluded, after a statistical summary of about 1000 published mechanical analyses, that there was a deficiency in the 2 to 4 millimeter (granule) and the 2 to 1 millimeter (very coarse sand) range, and probably also in the $\frac{1}{8}$ to $\frac{1}{16}$ millimeter class. The evidence for the conclusion was based largely upon the observation that the modal class rarely fell in the grades cited. It seems probable that the modal group should fall in this range no less frequently than it does in the coarser or finer grades, unless there were a real shortage of such sizes. Published analyses of 241 fluvial (alluvial) gravels and sands of southern California (Conkling, Eckis, and Gross, 1934) showed that the chief mode fell in the 2 to 4 millimeter class but 3 times in contrast to 63 times in the $\frac{1}{2}$ to $\frac{1}{4}$ millimeter grades and 41 times in the 64 to 32 millimeter class. In this group of sediments 92 per cent of the gravels have more than one mode, whereas but 42 per cent of the sands were so characterized. Krumbein (1942, p. 9) made a statistical analysis of 100 bimodal gravels. The results of his study are shown in Table 12. Similar results appear in tabulations based on other analyses of fluvial sediments.

That fluvial sediments are not unique in this peculiarity is shown by data secured by Hough (1942, pp. 25–26) from shore and bottom sediments of Buzzard's and Cape Cod bays. Hough noted that the *medians* of several hundred samples rarely fell in the 2 to 4 millimeter class or in the $\frac{1}{16}$ to $\frac{1}{32}$ millimeter grade. Similarly a composite (average of 64 samples from Massa-

TABLE 12.   Distribution of Averages in Alluvial Gravel (after Krumbein, 1942)

Class (mm)	Geometric Means	Medians	1st Modes	2nd Modes	3rd Modes
256 to 128	....	....	2	6	1
128 to 64	....	....	7	2	....
64 to 32	....	7	34	13	....
32 to 16	3	20	21	7	1
16 to 8	31	16	11	4	1
8 to 4	34	30	....	2	2
4 to 2	32	21	2	1	2
2 to 1	....	6	8	21	2
1 to ½	....	....	10	31	5
½ to ¼	....	....	5	13	10
	100	100	100	100	24

chusetts Bay, published by Trowbridge and Shepard; 1932, p. 29) disclosed a low frequency in the 1 to 2 millimeter grade. This low frequency was explained as the gap between two sediment loads, one moved by storm waves and the other moved by the more usual gentle waves. It should be noted that in general the sediments, both offshore and beaches, are not themselves so characteristically bimodal as are the fluvial sediments, and the deficiency in certain grades is apparent only when all the available analyses are taken together.

Windblown sediments seem to show a deficiency in the ⅛ to 1/16 millimeter grade. This peculiarity was noted by Udden (1914, p. 741). Like the fine-grained stream deposits, aeolian sediments are rarely bimodal but only rarely does the chief ingredient fall into the ⅛ to 1/16 millimeter grade. Udden did not account for this peculiarity but suggests that it might not be general and other wind deposits might be found in which the maximum would fall in the apparently deficient grade.

Is the peculiar distribution of the modal class the result of geologic or hydraulic reasons? Why is it that sediments with a mode in the 2 to 4 millimeter size class are so very rare? Does the failure of the modal class to fall within these limits represent a real lack of such materials or is it merely a peculiarity of the depositing current that such sizes, though abundant, are unable to collect in significant quantities but appear only as a lesser constituent of both coarser and finer sediments? These questions must remain unanswered until further data are secured, and any conclusions made at this time are very tentative.

There are several possible explanations for the apparent scarcity of certain size grades or at least for the scarcity of sediments with their chief ingredient in these classes. One may assume that materials in the grades under consideration were produced by weathering and rock disintegration but that these materials were either never deposited as a modal class for certain hydraulic reasons or because of mechanical instability they disappear during the transport process, or we may suppose that there is a primary deficiency of certain size classes. It may be that all sizes of materials are not produced in equal quantity by breakdown of the source rocks.

As noted elsewhere, the bimodal character of coarse fluvial sediments has been explained by the dual nature of the load carried by the streams, i.e., bed load and suspension load. In torrential streams, the bed load is in the coarse gravel range, and the suspension materials are largely sand. The bimodal nature and consequent deficiency in the intermediate grades, 2 to 4 and 4 to 8 millimeters, is thereby explained. Where the stream is more sluggish, its traction or bed load is primarily sand and the suspension load is silt and clay. As noted by Lane (1938) such streams have a sand bed free from silt and clay. These sands, in the absence of coarser materials, are unimodal and record the bed load only.

The absence of the suspension load in the channel sands is ascribed by Lane to the abrupt change in the law governing the rate of settling of particles above 0.1 millimeter and those below that size. The energy required to keep particles below sand size in suspension decreases so rapidly with decrease in particle size, that most streams are able to carry in suspension all the materials which are brought into them having a diameter below 0.1 millimeter and hence very little of this material is present in the bed. Hence, perhaps, the "openwork" nature of sands in general in contrast to the chink-filled gravels. Wentworth (1933) had earlier expressed a similar idea which he extended to the other natural aggregates. He suggested that each of the chief aggregates—sand, gravel, silt, and clay—was closely correlated with the principal mode of transport (Table 13). Though the different modes of transport have overlapping ranges, there is an optimum for each, and therefore the detrital materials found in natural deposits occur more abundantly

TABLE 13.   Modes of Transport and Chief Natural Aggregates (after Wentworth)

Mode of Transport	Usual Source	Name of Aggregate
Traction	All available hard rocks	Gravel
Inertia suspension[a]	Monomineral grains of phanerites (chiefly)	Sand
Viscous suspension[b]	Monomineral grains of any rocks (chiefly)	Silt
Colloidal suspension	Molecularly decomposable materials	Clay

[a] Traction and inertia suspension take place approximately in accordance with the so-called sixth power law, which postulates a complete transfer of kinetic energy from the water to a particle and which makes no allowance for the subsidiary effect of viscous drag.
[b] Viscous suspension accounts for the transport of finer particles in which the surface effect is greater relative to the mass. The size-velocity relationship in this range is defined by the well-known Stokes law. Still smaller particles are kept in suspension, chiefly by the kinetic effects found in dispersed systems, i.e., colloid.

well within the individual coarseness ranges of each type of aggregate rather than in the ranges that are transitional between these groups.

It is difficult to see, under any of the hypotheses accounting for the apparent deficiencies of certain sizes, if these sizes were produced by weathering or abrasion, what has become of them. Hydraulic considerations might prevent their deposition in some particular place or with certain other sizes but can hardly prevent their deposition everywhere. Either they have been produced by rock disintegration but are mechanically unstable or they never were formed in appreciable volume. The first hypothesis has been invoked to explain the apparent deficiency of the particles in the 2 to 8 millimeter range. The mineral grains which compose particles of this size are likely to be relatively large compared to the whole fragment. Such granules, therefore, would be structurally weak and hence unable to survive rigorous stream action.

TABLE 14.   Percentage of Monomineralic Grains in Size Grades

Diam. (mm)	A	B
8 to 4	0	0
4 to 2	17	0
2 to 1	36	10
1 to ½	64	42
½ to ¼	80	78
¼ to ⅛	94	90

A. Sand from dry wash near El Centro, Calif. Essentially a disintegrated granite.
B. Disintegrated gneissic quartz diorite boulder from glacial outwash, Cary, Ill.

On the other hand, it may be that the processes of rock disintegration which yield products of varying grain size produce more of certain sizes and less of others. In other words, there is an initial or primary deficiency of certain sizes. Some rocks characteristically yield *blocks* upon breakdown, whereas others undergo granular disintegration and yield *grains* of sand size. The first type is illustrated by quartzite; the latter by many coarse-grained acid igneous rocks and gneisses. Products of disintegration of intermediate sizes may be relatively rare. Present data, however, are inconclusive as five samples of disintegrated (but not decayed) rocks of granitic composition analyzed by Tisdel (Tisdel and Krumbein, 1940) showed the largest quantity of material in the 2 to 4 millimeter class. Nevertheless as pointed out by Dake (1921, p. 162) the size distribution of the quartz grains must be closely restricted by the size distribution of the quartz in the phaneritic crystalline rocks. Grains larger than 1 millimeter are rare (under 10 per cent) so that the larger grains found by Tisdel are mainly aggregates (Table 14). The apparent deficiency of silt (or very fine sand, ⅛ to ¹⁄₁₆ millimeter) may result from the greater quantity of sand (disintegration product) and clay (decomposition product) than the intermediate sizes. It may be that neither disintegration nor decomposition yields silt in appreciable amounts.

REFERENCES CITED AND BIBLIOGRAPHY

Allen, V. T. (1936), Terminology of medium-grained sediments, *Rept. Comm. Sedimentation 1935-1936* (mimeographed), Nat. Research Council, pp. 18–47.

Alling, H. L. (1943), A metric grade scale for sedimentary rocks, *J. Geol.*, vol. 51, pp. 259–269.

Atterberg, A. (1905), Die rationelle Klassifikation der Sande und Kiese, *Chem. Z.*, vol. 29, pp. 195–198.

Bagnold, R. A. (1941), *The physics of blown sand and desert dunes*, London, Methuen, p. 2.

Baker, H. A. (1920), On the investigation of the mechanical constitution of loose arenaceous sediments, etc., *Geol. Mag.*, vol. 57, p. 415.

Bonorino, F. G., and Teruggi, M. E. (1952), *Lexico Sedimentologico*, Inst. Nacional de Invest. de las Ciencias Nat., etc., Public. No. 6, pp. 164.

Cailleux, Andre (1954), Limites dimensionnelles et noms des fractions granulometriques, *Bull. Soc. géol. France*, ser. 6, vol. 4, pp. 643–646.

Conkling, H., Eckis, R., and Gross, P. L. K. (1934), Ground water storage capacity of valley fill, *Calif. Div. Water Resources, Bull.* 45.

DallaValle, J. M. (1943), *Micromeritics*, 2d ed., New York, Pitman, pp. 31–79.

Dake, C. L. (1921), The problem of the St. Peter sandstone, *Univ. Missouri School of Mines and Metall., Bull.*, tech. series, vol. 6, pp. 158f.

Dapples, E. C., Krumbein, W. C., and Sloss, L. L. (1953), Petrographic and lithologic attributes of sandstones, *J. Geol.*, vol. 61, pp. 291–317.

Doeglas, D. J. (1946), Interpretation of results of mechanical analyses, *J. Sediment. Petrol.*, vol. 16, pp. 19–40.

Doeglas, D. J. (1947), Recherches granulometrique aux Pays-Bas, *La Geologie des Terrains Recents*, Sess. Extraordinaire 1946, Soc. Belges de Géol., pp. 125–137.

Doeglas, D. J., and Smithuyzen, N. C. B. (1941), De interpretatie van de resultaten von Korrelgroote-analysen, *Geol. en Mijnbouw*, Jaargan 8, pp. 273–296.

Dryden, A. L. (1934), Cumulative curves and histograms, *Am. J. Sci.*, 5th ser., vol. 27, pp. 146–147.

Einstein, H. A., Anderson, A. G., and Johnson, J. W. (1940), A distinction between bed load and suspended load in natural streams, *Trans. Am. Geophys. Union*, 21st Ann. Meeting, part II, p. 628.

Fernald, F. A. (1929), Roundstone, a new geologic term, *Science*, vol. 70, p. 240.

Folk, R. (1954), The distinction between grain size and mineral composition in sedimentary rock nomenclature, *J. Geol.*, vol. 62, pp. 344–359.

Fraser, H. J. (1935), Experimental study of the porosity and permeability of clastic sediments, *J. Geol.*, vol. 43, pp. 910–1010.

Galliher, E. Wayne (1933), Cumulative curves and histograms, *Am. J. Sci.*, 5th ser., vol. 26, pp. 475–478.

Gessner, H. (1931), *Die Schlammanalyse*, Leipzig, Akademische Verlagsgesellschaft.

Griffiths, J. C. (1951), Size versus sorting in some Caribbean sediments, *J. Geol.*, vol. 59, pp. 211–243.

Gripenberg, Stina (1934), A study of the sediments of the North Baltic and adjoining seas, *Fennia* 60, no. 3.

Horner, Nils (1947), (Discussion) *La Geologie des Terrains Recents*, Sess. extraordinaire 1946, Soc. Belges de Géol., pp. 137–142.

Hough, J. L. (1942), Sediments of Cape Cod Bay, Massachusetts, *J. Sediment. Petrol.*, vol. 12, pp. 10–30.

Inman, D. L. (1949), Sorting of sediments in the light of fluid mechanics, *J. Sediment. Petrol.*, vol. 19, pp. 51–70.

Krumbein, W. C. (1934), Size frequency distributions of sediments, *J. Sediment. Petrol.*, vol. 4, pp. 65–77.

Krumbein, W. C. (1938), Size frequency distributions of sediments and the normal phi curve, *J. Sediment. Petrol.*, vol. 18, pp. 84–90.

Krumbein, W. C. (1939), Application of the photo-electric cell to the study of pebble size and shape, *Proc. 6th Pacific Science Congress*, pp. 769–777.

Krumbein, W. C. (1940), Flood gravel of San Gabriel Canyon, California, *Bull. Geol. Soc. Amer.*, vol. 51, pp. 639–676.

Krumbein, W. C. (1941), Measurement and geological significance of shape and roundness of sedimentary particles, *J. Sediment. Petrol.*, vol. 11, pp. 64–72.

Krumbein, W. C. (1942), Flood deposits of Arroyo Seco, Los Angeles County, California, *Bull. Geol. Soc. Amer.*, vol. 53, pp. 1355–1402.

Krumbein, W. C. (1942), Statistical summary of some alluvial gravels, *Rept. Comm. Sed. 1940–1941* (mimeographed), Nat. Research Council, p. 9.

Krumbein, W. C., and Aberdeen, Esther (1937), Sediments of Barataria Bay, *J. Sediment. Petrol.*, vol. 17, pp. 3–17.

Krumbein, W. C., and Pettijohn, F. J. (1938), *Manual of sedimentary petrography*, New York, Appleton-Century, pp. 91–181.

Krumbein, W. C. and Tisdel, F. W. (1940), Size distributions of source rocks of sediments, *Am. J. Sci.*, vol. 238, pp. 296–305.

Krynine, P. D. (1948), The megascopic study and field classification of sedimentary rocks, *J. Geol.*, vol. 56, pp. 130–165.

Kurk, E. H. (1941), *The problem of sampling heterogeneous sediments*, Thesis (unpublished), Univ. Chicago.

Lane, E. W. (1938), Notes on the formation of sand, *Trans. Am. Geophys. Union*, 19th An. Meeting, pp. 505–508.

Lane, E. W. and others (1947), Report of the sub-committee on sediment terminology, *Trans. Am. Geophys. Union*, vol. 28, pp. 936–938.

Legget, R. F., and Peckover, F. L. (1949), Discussion of "Report of the sub-committee on sediment terminology," *Trans. Am. Geophys. Union*, vol. 30, pp. 134–137.

Niggli, J. (1938), Zusammensetzung und der Klassification der Lockergesteine, Schweiz. Archiv f. angewandte Wissensch. u. Tech., vol. 4.

Otto, G. H. (1939), A modified logarithmic probability graph for the interpretation of mechanical analyses of sediments, J. Sediment. Petrol., vol. 9, pp. 62–76.

Pettijohn, F. J. (1940), Relative abundance of size grades of clastic sediments, (abstract) S.E.P.M. program.

Plumley, W. J. (1948), Black Hills terrace gravels: a study in sediment transport, J. Geol., vol. 55, pp. 526–577.

Revelle, Roger (1944), Marine bottom samples collected in the Pacific Ocean by the Carnegie on its seventh cruise, Carnegie Inst. of Washington, Pub. 556.

Rittenhouse, Gordon (1943), Sedimentation near junction of Maquoketa and Mississippi rivers.—A discussion, J. Sediment. Petrol., vol. 13, pp. 40–42.

Roller, P. S. (1937), Law of size distribution and statistical description of particulate materials, J. Franklin Inst., vol. 223, pp. 609–633.

Roller, P. S. (1941), Statistical analysis of size distribution of particulate materials with special reference to bimodal frequency distributions, J. Phys. Chem., vol. 45, pp. 241–281.

Sayles, R. W. (1914), The Squantum tillite, Bull. Harv. Mus. Comp. Zool., vol. 66, p. 145.

Shrock, R. R. (1948), A classification of sedimentary rocks, J. Geol., vol. 56, pp. 118–129.

Swensen, F. A. (1942), Sedimentation near junction of Maquoketa and Mississippi rivers, J. Sediment. Petrol., vol. 12, pp. 3–9.

Trask, P. D. (1932), Origin and environment of source sediments of petroleum, Houston, Gulf Publ. Co., pp. 67ff.

Trefethen, J. M. (1950), Classification of sediments, Am. J. Sci., vol. 248, p. 55–62.

Trowbridge, A. C. and Shepard, F. J. (1932), Sedimentation in Massachusetts Bay, J. Sediment. Petrol., vol. 2, p. 29.

Truesdell, P. E. and Varnes, D. J. (1950), Chart correlating various grain-size definitions of sedimentary materials, U. S. Geol. Survey.

Twenhofel, W. H. (1937), Terminology of the fine-grained mechanical sediments, Rept. Comm. Sedimentation 1936–1937 (mimeographed), Nat. Research Council, pp. 81–104.

Tyrrell, G. W. (1921), Some points in petrographic nomenclature, Geol. Mag., vol. 58, pp. 501–502.

Udden, J. A. (1898), Mechanical composition of wind deposits, Augustana Library Publications, no. 1.

Udden, J. A. (1914), Mechanical composition of clastic sediments, Bull. Geol. Soc. Amer., vol. 25, pp. 655–744.

Wentworth, C. K. (1922), A scale of grade and class terms for clastic sediments, J. Geol., vol. 30, pp. 377–392.

Wentworth, C. K. (1931), The mechanical composition of sediments in graphic form, Univ. Iowa Studies in Nat. Hist., vol. 14, no. 3.

Wentworth, C. K. (1933), Fundamental limits to the sizes of clastic grains, Science, vol. 77, pp. 633–634.

Wentworth, C. K. (1935), The terminology of coarse sediments, *Bull. Nat. Research Council*, 98, pp. 225–246.

Wentworth, C. K. and Williams, Howel (1932), The classification and terminology of the pyroclastic rocks, *Bull. Nat. Research Council*, 89, pp. 19–53.

Willman, H. B. (1942), Geology and mineral resources of the Marseilles, Ottawa, and Streater quadrangles, *Bull. Ill. State Geol. Survey*, 66, pp. 343–344.

Woodford, A. O. (1925), The San Onofre breccia, *Bull. Univ. Calif., Dept. Geol.*, vol. 15, p. 183.

SHAPE AND ROUNDNESS

The shape and roundness of pebbles and sand grains have long been used to decipher the history of a deposit of which they are a part. The distinctive shapes of ice-faceted pebbles and wind-whetted ventifacts are known even to beginners. The effect of other agents is less clear and is the subject of much controversy. Are beach pebbles flatter than river pebbles? Does wind round sand grains more effectively than water? What is the lower size limit, if any, of water rounding? Such questions have not yet been answered in a conclusive manner. It is obvious that a conclusive answer would materially aid us in the interpretation of the geologic history of a sediment.

Shape

The shapes of objects may be classified in a number of ways. The geometrician has defined a series of regular shapes such as a cube, prism, sphere, cylinder, cone, etc. The crystallographer has likewise a classification of solids bounded by plane surfaces. Neither system is adequate for the natural sediments. At best, pebble shapes only approximate the regular solids of the geometrician. Terms to indicate similarity, such as prismoidal, bipyramidal, pyramidal, wedge-shaped, parallel-tabular, may be used (Wentworth, 1936a). Such a classification, however, is at best a qualitative description and does not, as a rule, bear any relation to the dynamical behavior of these objects during transportation. Instead, a single-number index of shape is required which is amenable to mathematical or graphic analysis and by means of which a shape distribution or frequency curve can be constructed.

There are, however, certain distinctive shapes not described in a simple numerical manner. Such are the crystal euhedra and the diagnostic curving forms assumed by glass fragments—the *shards* of tuffs and tuffaceous sediments. Crystal euhedra arise in several ways. They may be but slightly worn detrital grains, as are some zircons (Pl. 1, D), or crystals reconstructed by secondary overgrowth (Pl. 1, C and Fig. 168), or euhedra which have grown *de novo* in the rock in which they are found, as are certain quartz crystals in limestone. The forms of such crystals can be described crystallographically, though some workers, such as Smithson (1939) have found it advantageous to adopt shape ratios, such as l/b, where l is length and b is breadth. The distinctive shapes of wind-faceted stones—the familiar einkanter and drei-kanter—as well as the flatiron form of the glacial cobble likewise cannot be reduced to numerical terms.

A quantitative or numerical index of shape requires some standard of reference. The sphere may be taken as such a standard. Not only is the limiting shape assumed by many rock and mineral fragments upon prolonged abrasion that of a sphere, or approximately so, but the sphere has certain unique properties which make it an acceptable standard of reference. Of all possible shapes, the sphere has the least surface area for a given volume. As a consequence of this property, the sphere has the greatest settling velocity in a fluid of any possible shape (volume and density being fixed) (Krum-bein, 1942).[19] Hence under conditions of suspension transport, the more spherical particles tend to become separated from others of the same size and density but of less spherical form. The more spherical particles tend to be deposited, whereas those less spherical tend to be carried away. The reverse situation should prevail under conditions of traction transport. In this case, of two particles of the same volume and density, the less spherical should remain behind and the more spherical should roll away. Field studies have shown that the first of these concepts is valid but evidence on the second is lacking (page 552).

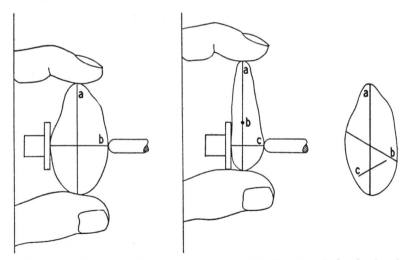

Fig. 24. Concept and measurement of pebble diameters. Left, the b axis in position; center, the c axis in position; right, the pebble in perspective (from Krumbein, 1941).

[19] Excepting at high velocities, at which the pear- or tear-drop forms move with less resistance through a fluid. Such streamlining effects are not likely to be of importance under the lower velocities of nature.

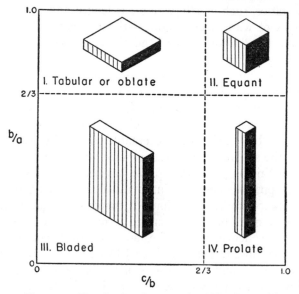

FIG. 25. Zingg's classification of pebble shapes. Note that although the representative solids shown (rectangular parallelopipeds) have the same roundness (o), they have different shapes.

Ideally, the property of *sphericity* might be defined as s/S (Wadell, 1932), where s is the surface area of a sphere of the same volume as the fragment in question and S is the actual surface area of the object. For a sphere the ratio has the value of 1.0. For all other solids the value would be less than 1.0. Because of the difficulties of measuring the surface area of irregular solids, the sphericity may also be expressed as d_n/D_s, where d_n is the nominal diameter (diameter of a sphere of the same volume as the object; Wadell, 1935) and D_s is the diameter of a circumscribing sphere (generally the long diameter). As before, a sphere has a sphericity of 1.0 and all other objects have values less than 1.0.

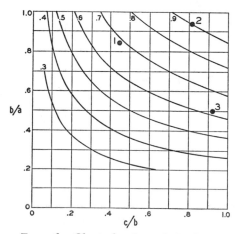

FIG. 26. Chart showing relationship between sphericity and Zingg shape indices. The curves represent lines of equal sphericity (from Krumbein, 1941).

In a sample of sand or gravel, each fragment or particle will have its own sphericity value. Some, however, will be disk-shaped or notably flat and elongated in two directions, shortened in the third. Others will be elongated in one direction only and will be roller-shaped. Both such shapes yield a low sphericity value. In some cases it is important to distinguish between the two. The sphericity index as defined above fails to do so.

Distinction between the prolate and oblate forms, however, is made possible by means of diameter ratios (Zingg, 1935). The ratios b/a and c/b (where a, b, and c are length, breadth, and thickness, respectively) can be made to define four shape classes (Fig. 25 and Table 15). These classes, oblate, prolate, equiaxial, and triaxial, and their relation to the Wadell sphericity index are shown in Fig. 26.

TABLE 15. Zingg Shape Classes[a]

Class No.	b/a	c/b	Shape
I	$> \frac{2}{3}$	$< \frac{2}{3}$	Oblate (discoidal)
II	$> \frac{2}{3}$	$> \frac{2}{3}$	Equiaxial (spherical)
III	$< \frac{2}{3}$	$< \frac{2}{3}$	Triaxial (bladed)
IV	$< \frac{2}{3}$	$> \frac{2}{3}$	Prolate (rod-shaped)

[a] a, length; b, breadth; c, thickness.

Roundness

Roundness has to do with the sharpness of the edges and corners of a clastic fragment. It is independent of shape. The several right-angled geometrical forms, cube, plate, prism, and the like (Fig. 25) all have equally sharp edges—in that their radii of curvature are zero—yet differ from one another in shape (and therefore in sphericity). The term *roundness*, however, has been used or misused in the literature and in many cases has been used interchangeably with shape (Russell and Taylor, 1937a). The distinction between the two is fundamental and should be kept clearly in mind. Roundness may be expressed as the ratio of the average radius of curvature of the several corners or edges to the radius of curvature of the maximum inscribed sphere or to the nominal radius of the fragment. Actually it is more convenient, and in many cases necessary, to work with a two-dimensional figure—a section or a projection of the fragment in question—rather than the three-dimensional object itself. In this case roundness is defined as the average radius of curvature of the corners of the grain image divided by the radius of the maximum inscribed circle. This is expressed as P (rho) $= \Sigma (r_i/R)/N$, where r_i are the individual radii of the corners, N is the number of corners, and R is the radius of the maximum inscribed circle (Fig. 27). By such a definition a sphere has a roundness of 1.0 as well as a sphericity of 1.0. Other objects, however, which are nonspherical, may also have a roundness of 1.0—such as a capsule-shaped body which is essentially a cylinder capped by two hemispheres.

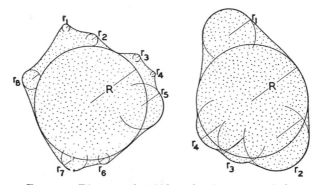

Fig. 27. Diagram of pebbles, showing geometrical nature of roundness (from Krumbein, 1940).

As pointed out, the term *roundness* has been used carelessly. Loosely used also are such terms as *rounded, subrounded, subangular,* and *angular.* In order that these terms have a more precise meaning, they have been redefined in quantitative terms in a manner analogous to the more exact redefinitions of the common size terms.[20] Russell and Taylor (1937b) set up five roundness grades. As can be seen from Table 16, Russell and Taylor's five classes are not of equal size. This inequality arises from the observation that it is difficult to distinguish slight differences in roundness if the roundness values are high but similar slight differences can be readily ascertained at the lower end of the scale. The author therefore redefined the class limits in such a way that the mid-points of the classes form a geometric progression[21] (Table 16). More recently Powers (1953) named and defined six roundness grades in such a way that the ratio of the upper limit to the lower limit of each class is o.7. Powers's scale is useful where closer discrimination is required and where a more rigorous statistical analysis is to be made of the results.

The author's roundness grades (as defined in Table 16 and Fig. 28) are as follows:

Angular (o–0.15): showing very little or no evidence of wear; edges and corners sharp. Secondary corners[22] numerous (15–30) and sharp.

[20] For actual procedures in measuring or estimating roundness and sphericities, the reader is referred to a paper by Krumbein (1941).
[21] Approximately. Class limits slightly changed to facilitate memory. The angular class has been extended to zero in violation of the requirements of the progression. Actually most particles, even freshly broken, have a finite roundness and few fragments will be appreciably below 0.10 in roundness. The "mid-point" value chosen for this class will probably fall near the mid-point of the actual values which lie within the class.
[22] Secondary corners are the minor convexities seen in the grain profile. Primary corners are the principal interfacial edges and are few in number (3–5). The secondary corners quickly disappear during abrasion, whereas the primary corners remain and are discernible, though rounded, in much abraded grains. See Fig. 28.

TABLE 16.   Roundness Grades

| Grade Terms | Russell and Taylor | | | This Book | |
	Class Limits	Mid-Point[a]	Class Limits	Mid-Point[b]
Angular	0 to 0.15	0.075	0 to 0.15	0.125
Subangular	0.15 to 0.30	0.225	0.15 to 0.25	0.200
Subrounded	0.30 to 0.50	0.400	0.25 to 0.40	0.315
Rounded	0.50 to 0.70	0.600	0.40 to 0.60	0.500
Well rounded	0.70 to 1.00	0.850	0.60 to 1.00	0.800

[a] Arithmetic mid-points.
[b] Geometric (approximately) except for angular class. Most particles, even freshly broken, have a finite roundness, rarely less than 0.10. Hence lower limit of the angular class is not, in practice, zero. The mid-point of the fragments in the group therefore is probably near 0.125.

Subangular (0.15–0.25): showing definite effects of wear. The fragments still have their original form, and the faces are virtually untouched; but the edges and corners have been rounded off to some extent. Secondary corners numerous (10–20), though less so than in angular class.

Subrounded (0.25–0.40): showing considerable wear. The edges and corners are rounded off to smooth curves, and the area of the original faces is considerably reduced, but the original shape of the grain is still distinct. Secondary corners much rounded and reduced in numbers (5–10).

FIG. 28.   Roundness classes. A: Angular. B: Subangular. C: Subrounded. D: Rounded. E: Well Rounded.

Rounded (0.40–0.60): original faces almost completely destroyed, but some comparatively flat surfaces may be present. There may be broad re-entrant angles between remnant faces. All original edges and corners have been smoothed off to rather broad curves. Secondary corners greatly subdued and few (0–5). At roundness 0.60 all secondary corners disappear. Original shape still readily apparent.

Well-rounded (0.60–1.00): no original faces, edges, or corners left. The entire surface consists of broad curves; flat areas absent. No secondary corners. The original shape is suggested by the present form of the grain.

Relations of Shape, Roundness, and Size

Theoretically sphericity and roundness are geometrically distinct and independent properties. Theoretically both are independent and unrelated to size—another geometrical property of clastic particles. Actually in natural sediments not only are sphericity and roundness closely correlated with each other but each in turn is a function of size.

In river sands, Russell and Taylor (1937b) found the better-rounded quartz grains to be the more spherical. A similar relationship was observed

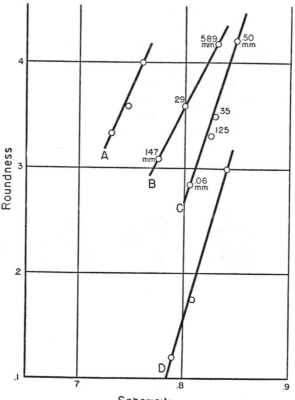

Fig. 29.   Relation of sphericity and roundness. **A:** Lake Erie beach sand, three samples (0.351-to-0.246 mm class only), intercept sphericity (Pettijohn and Lundahl, 1943). **B:** Lake Erie beach sand, three grade sizes, average of seven samples, projection sphericity (Pettijohn and Lundahl, 1943). **C:** St. Peter sandstone, four size grades, projection sphericity (Wadell, 1935). **D:** Mississippi River sand, weighted mean of three samples, projection sphericity (Russell and Taylor, 1937).

in the beach sands of Lake Erie by Lundahl and Pettijohn (1943) who believed that roundness bore a linear relation to sphericity. The relation could be expressed as $y = mx - b$, where y is the roundness, x is the sphericity, and m and b are constants. The Lake Erie sands yield the expression $y = 2.01x - 1.25$ (curve B, Fig. 29). For a zero value of roundness, the sphericity value should be 0.65. Thiel (1940) found crushed quartz to have sphericities of 0.70 and 0.72 for the 2 to 1 and 1.0 to 0.5 millimeter size grades, respectively. But as these values were based on a projected image, they are about 0.1 too high and should be, therefore, about 0.60 to 0.62. These corrected values, for

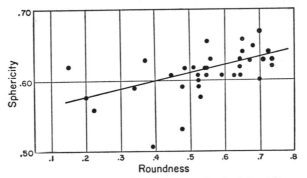

FIG. 30.   Relation of roundness and sphericity. Minnekahta limestone pebbles (16–32 mm). Arithmetic mean values of 35 samples of 50 pebbles each (from Plumley, 1948).

slightly coarser materials than the Lake Erie sands show good agreement with the values calculated from the equations. Of primary importance is the observation that a small change in sphericity is correlated with a rather large change in roundness. A sphericity change from 0.7 to 0.8, a 14 per cent increase, results in an increase of roundness from 0.16 to 0.36, a 125 per cent increase.

Plumley (1948) showed a close correlation between roundness and sphericity of limestone pebbles (16 to 32 mm grade) in Black Hills stream gravels (Fig. 30) and in quartz (1.0 to 1.414 mm grade) from the same deposits. For an increase of 4.6 per cent in sphericity, an increase of 119 per cent is noted for the roundness of the quartz grains. In the case of the limestone pebbles, a 12.3 per cent increase in sphericity is associated with a 380 per cent increase in roundness.

Wentworth (1922a) studied the relation between shape and roundness of beach pebbles. He found that flatness (a shape modulus) and roundness bore an inverse relation to each other, i.e., the flatter the pebble the less round it was, and conversely (Fig. 31). Wentworth explained the relation-

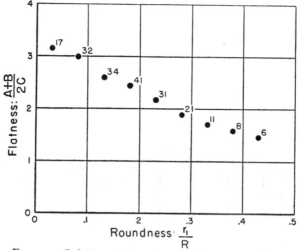

FIG. 31. Relation of roundness to flatness of 201 pebbles, Nantasket Beach, Massachusetts. For sake of simplicity, the pebbles were arranged in subgroups and each large dot shows the mean position of the number of pebbles that is indicated by the associated figure. It is apparent that as the roundness increases the flatness decreases (after Wentworth, 1922).

ship by assuming the rounder the pebble, the longer its abrasion history and that the flat pebbles were therefore least modified pieces. Inasmuch as the rounder they became, i.e., the more they were abraded, the less flat they are, beach action tends to destroy rather than produce flat pebbles (see also Fig. 32).

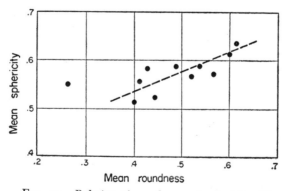

FIG. 32. Relation of roundness and sphericity. Rhyolite pebbles (25–75 mm) from Lake Superior beach. As the better rounded pebbles are also the more spherical, it follows that prolonged abrasion on a beach tends to make pebbles more spherical and hence less flat (after Grogan, 1945).

There is a marked correlation between roundness and size. The larger sizes of any given natural sand or gravel are much better rounded than the smaller grades.[23] This relationship has been explored by Pettijohn and Lundahl (1943) for beach sand. In nearly every sample examined by them, the coarsest fraction was the best rounded. The same proved to be true of the sands of the Mississippi River (Russell and Taylor, 1937b) and the St. Peter sandstone (Wadell, 1935). Incomplete data suggest a similar relation for fluvial gravels.[24]

The functional relationship between size and roundness can be established readily by plotting size against roundness (Fig. 33). From available data the

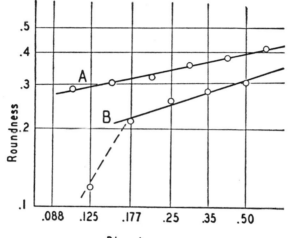

FIG. 33. Relation between mean roundness and mean diameter of size classes. A: Average of seven samples Lake Erie beach sand. B: Average of three samples, Mississippi River sand (from Pettijohn and Lundahl, 1943).

[23] Wentworth (in Twenhofel et al., 1932, p. 222) says "that in most sands the roundest grains are neither the largest nor the smallest, but belong to grades just short of the coarsest which are abundant in the deposit." MacCarthy's data (1933) seem to bear out this view, although, as noted elsewhere (Russell and Taylor, 1937a), MacCarthy's "roundness" is in fact a measure of shape. Furthermore, other data published by MacCarthy (1955) show the relationship not to be true of aeolian sands nor even of all beach materials. Possibly the coarsest material, a little less spherical and also a little less rounded, is not quartz like the remainder of the sand, but is shell or other materials sorted out and deposited with the sand. Unless similar materials are compared, the results are open to question.

[24] Plumley's (1948) analysis of limestone pebbles from Rapid Creek gravels in the Black Hills shows that the roundness of the 32 to 64 mm grade was at all stations sampled the same as or larger than most of the 16 to 32 mm material from the corresponding localities. A sample of gravelly sand from the Brandywine formation of Maryland, probably fluvial, showed roundness to increase with size throughout the size ranges studied (Calderon, 1953). These results are essentially like those earlier reported in Pleistocene fluvioglacial gravels (Krumbein, 1941).

relation seems to be of the type $y = mx^b$, where y is the roundness, x is the size, b is a coefficient, and m is a constant. For the Lake Erie beach sands the expression is $y = 0.46x^{0.21}$. When x is zero, then y is zero, but for any finite size, y will have a certain finite value. Hence this would mean that there is no lower limit of rounding. Russell and Taylor's curve (1937b) "breaks" between 0.177 and 0.888 millimeter, which suggests that the law expressed by the above equations breaks down near 0.1 millimeter, which might be therefore the lower limit of rounding in water. The size-roundness relations given in the equation, derived from study of the Lake Erie beaches, cannot be extrapolated too far in the direction of the larger sizes because roundness values greater than 1.0 which have no meaning, are obtained for the larger sizes.

It might be presumed that freshly broken materials, no matter what the size, would all be sharp-edged and equally angular. As sands which have undergone considerable abrasion show, on the other hand, a close correlation between roundness and size, the larger being the better rounded, it follows that the size-roundness relations must change as the sand or gravel is abraded. Accordingly the relation expressed by the equation for the Lake Erie sands cannot be applied to other sands with a shorter or with a longer abrasion history. In general a mature sand should show a well-marked relation between size and roundness, whereas in an immature sediment, such a relationship is less pronounced. A reversal of the normal relations is virtual proof of a dual source of a sediment. Local material of coarser grain may not be so well rounded as finer far-traveled materials.

Some abrasion mill studies (Sarmiento, 1945) have shown that the larger fragments tend to round much more rapidly than the smaller sizes (Table 102).

Inasmuch as roundness and sphericity are positively correlated and as roundness increases with size, it should follow that sphericity also should increase with size. Such proves to be the case although the relation between sphericity and size is less pronounced. Again, as in the case of roundness, the correlation of sphericity and size is absent in freshly crushed materials and appears only in sediments which have undergone appreciable wear or abrasion. Pettijohn and Lundahl (1943), for example, found that in every sample of Lake Erie beach sand studied by them, the larger the size the more spherical were the grains (Fig. 34). Similar relations were found in the Mississippi River sands by Russell and Taylor (1937b). The 35-mesh fraction (average of 3 samples) had a sphericity of 0.84; the sand retained on the 150 mesh screen had a sphericity of 0.79. These values are approximately the same as those of the Lake Erie beaches for the comparable sieve fraction. In the Lake Erie sands the average sphericity of the coarser fraction (0.70 to 0.495 mm) was 0.83, whereas that of the finer fraction (0.175 to 0.125 mm) is 0.774.

Wadell's (1935) work on the St. Peter sandstones as well as that by Lamar (1927) demonstrates the same law. MacCarthy's (1935) work on aeolian sands further substantiates it.[25] No satisfactory data exist for coarse materials though it is probably true that the coarser sizes are also the more spherical.[26]

Thiel's (1940) experimental work on sand showed a clear correlation between size and the sphericity of the grains. In the case of the apatite grains, three sizes, 2 to 1, 1 to 0.5, and 0.5 to 0.25 millimeters were studied. The sphericities after prolonged abrasion of these three grades were 0.91, 0.87, and 0.81, respectively. Initially the sphericity of all three sizes was essentially the same, namely, 0.74 to 0.76.

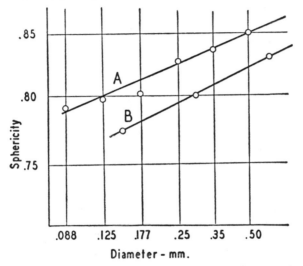

FIG. 34. Relation of mean sphericity and geometric mean diameter of size classes. A: Average of seven beach samples. B: Average of three Mississippi River samples (from Pettijohn and Lundahl, 1943).

The nature of the function represented by the curves of Fig. 34 is not known because of incompleteness of the data. A study of the size-roundness equation and the sphericity-roundness relations given above suggest that it must be of the type $y = a + mx^n$.

It follows from Thiel's observations, therefore, that in immature or primitive sands sphericity is probably the same, or nearly the same, for all sizes. A marked differentiation of sphericity values and distinct correlation with size is indicative of a long abrasion history.

[25] Both Lamar and MacCarthy term the shape factor "roundness" whereas they actually measure sphericity or a closely related property (Russell and Taylor, 1937a).

[26] Plumley's (1948) data on limestone pebbles in the gravels of Rapid Creek, South Dakota, show the sphericity of the 32 to 64 mm class to be the same as or larger than that of the 16 to 32 mm class in 7 of the 8 samples studied.

Geologic Significance of Shape and Roundness

Owing to incompleteness of data at the present time, it is difficult to evaluate the properties of shape and roundness and to state their geologic significance. Apparently rounding is a good index to the maturity of a sediment. Only well-washed, many times reworked sands are well rounded or even moderately rounded. A well-rounded gravel, although more mature than an angular gravel, does not signify the same degree of maturity as a well-rounded sand. Both experimental and field studies show that gravel sizes are readily rounded, even by comparatively short transport, whereas prolonged abrasion is required for the rounding of sand.

A further difference between immature sands and gravels and those of greater maturity appears in the relation between size and roundness. Where the sediment is *not* derived from pre-existing sediments and where it has been little transported (and hence little worn) all sizes have the same, or nearly the same, roundness. The products of prolonged abrasion, on the other hand, show marked differences between the rounding of the several size grades. The larger sizes are the better rounded.

In a word, then, the roundness of a clastic particle sums up its abrasion history.

Sphericity, on the other hand, more largely reflects the conditions of deposition at the moment of accumulation, though to a more limited extent sphericity is modified by the abrasion processes. Unless marked inequalities due to structure exist, the more rounded fragments are also the more spherical in mature deposits. Except for the slight shape modifications produced by abrasion, the end shape of a sand grain or pebble appears to be determined by its original shape (see page 119).

Some few shapes, however, are distinctive of certain processes. The glacial cobble of flatiron shape (Wentworth, 1936) and the wind-faceted ventifacts (Bryan, 1931) are indices of glacial and wind action, respectively. Other shapes thought to be diagnostic of particular agents or environments include chink-faceted pebbles (Wentworth, 1925) or pebbles with small facets produced by localized grinding. Such pebbles are lodged in chinks of various sizes or shapes on rock beaches and are so lodged that they can move to and fro to a slight extent but cannot escape. Kuenen (1947) has shown that water can also produce facets and edges on cobbles and boulders similar to those produced by wind. The *aquafacts*, produced by such "wet blasting" in streams and on some beaches, unlike ventifacts, are not polished, are restricted to the larger sized pieces, and although not rare, are generally less common and of less perfect form.

Also worthy of mention are broken rounds (Bretz, 1929) which, as the name implies, are roundstones which have undergone breakage. Such broken rounds and pebbles or cobbles with spalled corners are thought to be indicative of exceptionally high-velocity currents.

In all these cobbles of rather special form, the shape alone is not the only or the decisive character in determining origin. Special markings (striations, percussion scars, and the like) and surface textures are equally important.

If shape be less indicative of the abrasion history than rounding, it is more important in the sorting history of the deposit. Sedimentary mica illustrates the principle. Such material is deposited with the fine sand and silt sizes rather than with the coarse sands with which it was originally associated. Less striking, but perhaps equally important is the shape sorting that is going on in the sands of both streams and beaches (see page 552).

REFERENCES CITED AND BIBLIOGRAPHY

Bretz, J Harlen (1929), Valley deposits immediately east of the channeled scabland of Washington, *J. Geol.*, vol. 37, p. 507.

Bryan, Kirk (1931), Wind-worn stones or ventifacts—a discussion and bibliography, *Rept. Comm. Sedimentation, 1929–1930*, Nat. Research Council, reprint and circular series, no. 98, pp. 29–50.

Calderon, Alejandro (1953), *Unpublished manuscript*.

Krumbein, W. C. (1941), Measurement and geologic significance of shape and roundness of sedimentary particles, *J. Sediment. Petrol.*, vol. 11, pp. 64–72.

Krumbein, W. C. (1942), Settling velocity and flume-behaviour of non-spherical particles, *Trans. Am. Geophys. Union, 1942*, pp. 621–633.

Kuenen, Ph. H. (1947), Water-faceted boulders, *Am. J. Sci.*, vol. 245, pp. 779–783.

Lamar, J. E. (1927), Geology and economic resources of the St. Peter sandstone of Illinois, *Bull. Ill. State Geol. Survey*, 53, pp. 148–151.

MacCarthy, G. R. (1933), The rounding of beach sands, *Am. J. Sci.*, ser. 5, vol. 25, pp. 205–224.

MacCarthy, G. R. (1935), Eolian sands: A comparison, *Am. J. Sci.*, ser. 5, vol. 30, pp. 81–95.

Pettijohn, F. J. and Lundahl, A. C. (1943), Shape and roundness of Lake Erie beach sands, *J. Sediment. Petrol.*, vol. 13, pp. 69–78.

Plumley, W. J. (1948), Black Hills terrace gravels: A study in sediment transport, *J. Geol.*, vol. 56, pp. 526–577.

Powers, M. C. (1953), A new roundness scale for sedimentary particles, *J. Sediment. Petrol.*, vol. 23, pp. 117–119.

Russell, R. D., and Taylor, R. E. (1937a), Bibliography on roundness and shape of sedimentary rock particles, *Rept. Comm. Sedimentation 1936–1937*, Nat. Research Council, pp. 65–80.

Russell, R. D. and Taylor, R. E., (1937b), Roundness and shape of Mississippi River sands, *J. Geol.*, vol. 45, pp. 225–267.

Sarmiento, A. (1945), *Experimental study of pebble abrasion*, Univ. of Chicago, M.S. thesis (manuscript).

Smithson, F. (1939), Statistical methods in sedimentary petrology, *Geol. Mag.*, vol. 76, p. 351.

Thiel, G. A. (1940), The relative resistance to abrasion of mineral grains of sand size, *J. Sediment Petrol.*, vol. 10, pp. 103–124.

Twenhofel, W. H. and others (1932), *Treatise on sedimentation*, 2d ed., Baltimore, Williams and Wilkins, p. 222.

Wadell, Hakon (1932), Volume, shape, and roundness of rock particles, *J. Geol.*, vol. 40, pp. 443–451.

Wadell, Hakon (1935), Volume, shape and roundness of quartz particles, *J. Geol.*, vol. 43, pp. 250–280.

Wentworth, C. K. (1922b), A field study of the shapes of river pebbles, *Bull. U.S. Geol. Survey*, 730–C, p. 114.

Wentworth, C. K. (1922a), The shapes of beach pebbles, *Prof. Paper, U.S. Geol. Survey*, 131–C, pp. 75–83.

Wentworth, C. K. (1925), Chink-faceting: A new process of pebble-shaping, *J. Geol.*, vol. 33, pp. 260–267.

Wentworth, C. K. (1936a), An analysis of the shapes of glacial cobbles, *J. Sediment. Petrol.*, vol. 6, p. 89.

Wentworth, C. K. (1936b), The shapes of glacial and ice jam cobbles, *J. Sediment. Petrol.*, vol. 6, pp. 97–108.

Zingg, Th. (1935), Beitrag zur Schotteranalyse, *Schweiz. mineralog. petrog. Mitt.*, Bd. 15, pp. 39–140.

SURFACE TEXTURES

The minor features of the grain surface, independent of size, shape, or roundness, are termed *surface textures* of the grain. Polish, frosting, striations, and the like belong in this category. That such features are of genetic significance is readily apparent. The striations on glacial cobbles illustrate the point. The frosting on sand grains has been commonly attributed to aeolian action.

But just as a sand grain or pebble may inherit its shape and roundness from an earlier deposit of different origin, so too a particle or fragment may inherit the surface markings which it bears. However, less abrasion, and hence less transport, is required to modify these details than to change roundness, shape, or size. The surface markings are easily erased or imparted to a grain or fragment. Wentworth (1922), for example, determined experimentally that about 0.35 mile of travel would remove striae from glaciated limestone pebbles. These pebbles, however, were still recognizable as glacial in origin by their facets, though not so conclusively as before. The surface textures therefore are more likely to record the last cycle of transportation. But as with other characteristics, a sand of mixed parentage will contain grains with a diversity of surface textures. These features therefore tell us only that such is the case and that the last epoch of transportation and deposition was inadequate to erase the surface markings of previous cycles. On the other hand, in a sand in which all the grains exhibit but one type of surface texture, such as frosting, the surface shown may be useful in deciphering the natural history of the deposit.

Surface textures are diverse, but they may be grouped into two categories. One class has to do with the dullness or the polish of the surface of the fragment. The other has to do with the markings on the surface, such as striations, percussion scars, and the like.

Polish or gloss has to do with the surface luster. This property is a quality related to the regularity of reflection. Scattering or diffusion of light produces a *dull* surface. Polish is indicated by the presence of highlights. The cause of polish or lack of it, its nature, and its geologic significance is not fully understood.[27] Very probably the causes are several in number. Polish may be mechanically produced by gentle attrition or wear, particularly if the abrasive agent is of fine grain. Such is thought to be the cause of the wind polish on some quartzite outcrops and fragments (*ventifacts*). It may also be produced by the deposition of a vitreous film or glaze, such as that known as *desert varnish*. Though the origin of this feature is not certain, prevailing opinion (Laudermilk, 1931) is that desert varnish seems to have been produced by water, which is present in the rocks and is drawn to the surface and evaporated by the heat of the sun, depositing the substances dissolved in a relatively insoluble form, as thin hard coatings consisting of silica, iron oxide, and some manganese oxide. Some geologists have attributed the high polish to subsequent sandblasting. Laudermilk thought that certain lichens played an important role as accumulators of iron and manganese compounds. The lichen growth was terminated by the accumulation of these products, which were then spread over the pebble surface by the acids generated upon death of the lichens, onto adjacent rocks that had no manganese content themselves. Dehydration and oxidation under action of the desert sun leaves the varnish-like residue.

A most enigmatic polish is that which appears on some pebbles embedded in clay such as the *gastroliths* or "stomach stones" of ancient reptiles of the plesiosaurian type. Most famous of these are pebbles found in marine shales of Cretaceous age. Though much has been written about these objects, no agreement has been reached concerning the origin of their polish, which has been attributed to wind action, to abrasion in the stomach of the animal, and to compaction movements of the shale matrix.

Polish, or certainly a high polish or gloss, is the exception. Most pebbles have dull surfaces. The same is true of quartz sand grains. Rarely do the quartz grains show a high polish. Some sand grains, on the other hand, have a

[27] For a resume of this subject and bibliography dealing with the same, see Williams (1937).

striking surface character variously described as "mat," "frosted," or "ground-glass." This surface character is most commonly seen on the grains of highly quartzose and well-rounded sands of which the St. Peter (Ordovician) is the best example in the United States. Frosting has been commonly attributed to aeolian action and has even been mapped in the European Pleistocene deposits by Callieux (1942), who considered the feature a criterion of peri-glacial wind action. The similarity of the surface to that produced on glass by sandblast gives credence to this theory, though there is little or no field evidence to support the concept. Glass subject to the action of hydrofluoric acid, however, also acquires a frosted surface, and perhaps therefore this type of surface is a product of prolonged action by natural solvents. The quartz of many sandstones with a carbonate cement and the scattered quartz grains found in some limestones commonly shows an encroachment of the quartz by the surrounding carbonate (Pl. 17, B). Extended encroachment would produce rough pitted grains. Incipient action of this type might produce a frosted grain. Roth (1932), on the other hand, thought that frosting must be the result of incipient secondary enlargement rather than incipient solution.

Surface markings on detrital fragments include striations and scratches, percussion marks, and indentations or pits. *Striations* are confined to the larger pieces, namely, pebbles, cobbles, and boulders. Most commonly these scratches are the product of ice action, generally glacial ice. Wentworth (1932, 1936b) has called attention to the work of subarctic streams in pro-ducing striated cobbles. The percentage of cobbles striated in some streams is high, and in many places a majority of all these above certain sizes are so marked. The percentage may equal or exceed that shown in the most favor-able deposits of glacial boulders. The cobbles striated by action of river ice lack the characteristic glacial facets. Even in bona fide glacial deposits the striated stones are not very abundant. Wentworth (1936a) studied several Wisconsin morainal deposits that are noted for the excellence of their stri-ated stones. Of over 600 pebbles or cobbles examined, of which a little over half were limestone, 40 per cent had no striations at all, 50 per cent had faint striations or clear striations only on one side; and as few as 10 per cent were conspicuously marked. On limestone the striations were most prevalent and most conspicuous (Pl. 14). The siliceous cobbles and the coarse-grained igneous rocks were virtually unmarked. It is not surprising, therefore, that ancient well-indurated tillites, from which extraction of entire pebbles or cobbles is well-nigh impossible, show few striated stones or none.

Striations are ideally narrow, straight, or nearly straight scratches clearly cut below the surface on which they appear, and are not in any way de-pendent on alteration of the surface adjacent to them (Pl. 14). In other words, excluded are those markings produced by differential weathering of a primary rock structure. Related to striations are *bruises*, which are cruder, shorter, and broader than striations, and are commonly found in *en echelon* patterns. *Nailhead* scratches are striations which have a definite head or point of origin. Such scratches tend to narrow or taper slightly from this point and come to an indefinite end. If the marked cobbles are embedded in the matrix, their striations tend to be aligned with the direction of ice flow. They are therefore, in general, parallel to the long axes of the cobbles (see page 80 on fabric).

Four chief striation patterns can be defined, namely, parallel, subparallel, scatter or random, and grid. The last-named is marked by the crossing of two or more parallel systems. Subparallel and random patterns appear to dominate in glacial cobbles. Parallel and subparallel striation patterns tend to run lengthwise of the cobble. Wentworth (1936b) states that grid patterns, especially those with widely spaced striations, are much more abundant, relatively, on ice-jam cobbles than on glacial cobbles, as are also curved striations.

Pebbles or cobbles embedded in a rather fine-grained matrix may be striated or slickensided as a result of internal movements during deformation of the rock under pressure. Such pebbles are likely to be minutely faulted and otherwise different from those striated prior to consolidation of the rock.

Crescentic impact scars or *percussion marks* are notable on some pebbles, especially the cherts and some quartzites. These small crescentic marks are caused by blows upon the pebble or cobble surface and are the traces of cones of shear, commonly incomplete, on the pebble surface. They are indicative, perhaps, of high-velocity flow.

Many clastic particles, both sand grains and pebbles, have surface indentations and pits. These are produced in part by etching and differential solution of inhomogeneities of the rock. The coarse-grained igneous rocks are characteristically pitted and rough, whereas the fine-grained rocks are smooth. In the latter category are the cherts, quartzites, many limestones, and the fine-grained lavas, though under some conditions of abrasion even the coarse-grained rocks may be very smooth. More generally, however, the term *pitted pebble* is applied to those pebbles or cobbles which have marked concavities not related to the texture of the rock or differential weathering. Such depressions are common at the contacts between adjacent pebbles. They vary in size from minute pits caused by sand grains to cups a few centimeters across and a centimeter deep. Normally the pits are also smooth and sharply cut as if scooped out with a small spoon. The literature on such pitted pebbles and the problem of their formation has been reviewed by Kuenen (1942). They have been explained as mutual indenture by pressure, a hypothesis readily shown to be untenable, and by solution induced by pressure at points of contact (Sorby, 1863).

Pitted pebbles are rather common in some conglomerates. A noted example is the "Potomac marble," a Triassic conglomerate from Maryland, in which many limestone pebbles show such pitting or even mutual stylolitic penetration (Bastin, 1940).

Pitted pebbles should not be confused with "cupped pebbles." The latter are pebbles which have been subject to solution on their upper side and have been so corroded that some are mere shells (Scott, 1947).

REFERENCES CITED AND BIBLIOGRAPHY

Bastin, E. S. (1940), Discussion. A note on pressure stylolites, *J. Geol.*, vol. 48, pp. 214–216.

Cailleux, André (1942), Les actions éoliennes périglaciaires en Europe, *Bull. soc. géol. France*, Ser. 5, vol. 6, pp. 495–505.

Kuenen, Ph. H. (1942), Pitted pebbles, *Leidsche Geol. Mededeel.*, vol. 13, pp. 189–201.

Laudermilk, J. D. (1931), On the origin of desert varnish, *Am. J. Sci.*, ser. 5, vol. 21, pp. 51–66.

Roth, R. (1932), Evidence indicating the limits of Triassic in Kansas, Oklahoma, and Texas, *J. Geol.*, vol. 40, pp. 718–719.

Scott, H. W. (1947), Solution sculpturing in limestone pebbles, *Bull. Geol. Soc. Amer.*, vol. 58, pp. 141–152.

Sorby, H. C. (1863), Ueber Kalkstein-Geschiebe mit Eindrucke, *Neues Jahrb. Mineral.*, pp. 801–807.

Wentworth, C. K. (1922), A field study of the shapes of river pebbles, *Bull. U.S. Geol. Survey*, 730–C, p. 114.

Wentworth, C. K. (1932), The geologic work of ice jams in subarctic rivers, *Wash. Univ. Studies, Sci. and Tech.*, no. 7, p. 72.

Wentworth, C. K. (1936a), An analysis of the shapes of glacial cobbles, *J. Sediment. Petrol.*, vol. 6, pp. 85–96.

Wentworth, C. K. (1936b), The shapes of glacial and ice jam cobbles, *J. Sediment. Petrol.*, vol. 6, pp. 97–108.

Williams, L. (1937), Classification and selected bibliography of the surface textures of sedimentary fragments, *Rept. Comm. Sedimentation 1936–1937*, Nat. Research Council, pp. 114–128.

FABRIC AND PACKING

Definitions

Fabric is the orientation, or lack of it, of the elements of which a rock is composed. Any nonspherical object (such as a pebble) has an orientation. When, out of all possible orientations, a significant number of like elements has assumed a certain orientation or orientations in preference to all others, these objects (or the gravel containing such oriented pebbles, for example) are said to show a preferred orientation, or to have an anisotropic fabric pattern. Such a pattern may be expressed by the alignment of the long axes of pebbles, the subparallelism of graptolites in a shale, the uniform convex-upward arrangements of the valves of mollusks, and the like. Such fabric is dimensional because the actual dimensions of the elements govern the alignment observed. If the fabric is shown by the alignment of the crystallographic directions, c-axes of the quartz grains for example, it is termed crystallographic. The dimensional and crystallographic fabrics may or may not be closely related, and in the case of rock fragments, of course, no crystallographic fabric is possible.

Packing is the spacing of the elements or "density" of the pattern. Even in a rock composed wholly of uniformly sized spherical elements, there are several ways in which these spheres can be arranged or packed. When the size and shapes are more varied, the manner of packing becomes more complex. Though packing and fabric are closely related, they are not the same thing.

Fabric

Types and Geologic Significance of Fabric

Genetically, there are two kinds of fabric, namely, deformation and apposition. A *deformation fabric* is produced by external stress on the rock and results from a rotation or movement of the constituent elements under that stress or the growth of new elements in common orientation in the stress field. This type of fabric is essentially that exhibited by metamorphic rocks. An *apposition fabric* is one formed at the time of deposition of the material and is a "primary" fabric. For the most part, the fabrics of sedimentary rocks are apposition or primary fabrics, though compaction of shales or clays, accompanied by decrease in porosity, is in part a deformation phenomenon which might appreciably modify the primary fabric.

An apposition or primary fabric records a response of the linear elements (long axes of pebbles, etc.) to a force field. Normally this is the flow field of the fluid from which the sediment is deposited. The elements tend to come to rest in some stable position with reference to the direction of flow. Conceivably some fabrics may arise in response to the gravitational and magnetic fields. The chief interest in sedimentary fabrics arises from their usefulness in determining direction of current flow, their correlation with vectorial permeability, the determination of the direction of elongation of sand bodies (especially "shoestring" sands) from single samples, and the like.

Where the orientation of the fabric elements is random, the fabric is *isotropic*; where preferred orientation is present, the fabric is *anisotropic*.

Fabric Elements and Fabric Analysis

A fabric element is a rock component having dimensional inequalities. A sphere, lacking such inequalities, cannot be such an element. A triaxial ellipsoid, on the other hand, is oriented in space and its space position can be determined. The orientation of the long axis, if the object is prolate, or of the short axis, if the object is oblate, is commonly determined.

Almost any detrital component is a potential fabric element, though those with greatest dimensional inequalities are most useful. Pebbles and sand grains are most commonly studied for the space position of their most atypical axes. Mica flakes, even the clay micas, and much organic debris are usable fabric elements. Among the latter are the orthocerids, chitonous stalks of graptolites, *Tentaculites*, the bivalve shells, and the high-spired gastropods.

The orientation of a fabric element, a pebble for example, may be described in terms of two angles. One is the direction ("strike") or azimuth angle between some axis of the pebble and the north; the other is the inclination ("plunge" or "dip") of this axis—the angle between the axis in question and the horizontal plane. The long axes [28] may show a preferred orientation, but for some pebbles, such as those approaching a disk, a preferred orientation of the long axes may be lacking, or at best be very feeble. In this case the orientation may be controlled by the large flat faces of the object. The position of these faces is closely approximated by giving the azimuth and angle of dip of the normal or "face pole" of the maximum projection area. This direction is essentially that of the c-axis or shortest diameter of the pebble.[29]

The position of a triaxial pebble is not fully stated by locating either the long axis alone or the c-axis alone. Such a pebble that has a horizontal long axis, for example, either may lie "flat," i.e., have the pole of the maximum projection area vertical; or it may "stand on edge," i.e., have the normal to the maximum projection area lie in the horizontal plane.

If a pebble be suitably marked in the outcrop so that it can be reoriented in the same position with reference to the meridian and zenith in the laboratory as it had in the field, it is possible, by use of a goniometer, to measure the azimuth and angle of dip of both the long axis and the normal to the maximum projection area (Karlstrom, 1952).

The observations thus made on a sample of 100 or more pebbles can be graphically summarized in several ways. One can study either the azimuth directions or the inclinations. It may be necessary, for example, to find the

[28] The length or long axis, designated the a-axis, is the distance between the two points most removed from each other on the pebble (Krumbein, 1939, p. 122). In exceptional cases the long axis may even pass outside of the pebble at some place.
[29] The thickness or c-axis is the maximum intercept normal to the a-axis, measured in the plane perpendicular to that of maximum projection (Krumbein, 1941).

direction of ice flow from the many observed azimuths of the long axes of the till stones. The azimuth readings may be collected into classes, using an appropriate interval, such as 20 degrees, and the modal class may be observed. The arithmetic mean azimuth or the mode itself may then be computed. The scattering of the azimuths about such a mean or standard deviation may also be determined.[30] A similar analysis of the dip angles can be made. If such frequency distributions appear as straight lines when plotted on probability paper, the deviation from the mean is random. The median azimuth (50 per cent value) can be read from the probability graph. Either the median or mean azimuth can be plotted graphically on a map, and the ice-flow or other current lines reconstructed.

Studies of the frequency distribution of inclinations may show the mean inclination to bear some relation to the direction of current flow. The long axes of pebbles, for example, dip upstream, and a study of the frequency distribution of the long axes may not only give the upstream direction but may yield other data that make possible determination of initial dip of the bed (White, 1953).

A diagram that shows *both* the azimuth and the inclination of the long axis of a fabric element is the "petrofabric diagram" (Knopf and Ingerson, pp. 226–262). The position of each long axis measured is represented by a point or dot on polar coördinate paper or by a point on a Lambert equiareal polar net, or on the so-called Schmidt net (Fig. 35). The clustering of points, or lack of it, shows whether any preferred orientation is present or not. Such diagrams are readily visualized if one imagines that each pebble in turn is placed at the center of a hollow sphere in precisely the position that this pebble had in the undisturbed outcrop. The long axis (or any other axis) of the pebble is extended until such axis intersects the surface of the sphere. The piercing point in the southern hemisphere is then plotted on the "polar" map of that hemisphere.

The orientation of a line in space (pebble axis, and so forth) is thus represented on the diagram by a point. A plane may also be represented by a point which is the piercing point of the normal or perpendicular to the plane. One might wish, for example, to show the orientation of a cross-bedding lamination in this way. By so doing the orientation of a good many such laminations in a cross-bedded deposit might be shown on a single diagram.

If the linear elements are randomly oriented, the points representing these lines are scattered in haphazard manner over the diagram. If they are prefer-

[30] Arbitrary grouping into classes as indicated would give in many cases a bimodal distribution because classes 180 degrees apart are equivalent and they must be combined. In general the histogram is constructed or built around the modal class. The statistical parameters of the azimuth distribution can be computed in the usual manner (Krumbein, 1939a, p. 673).

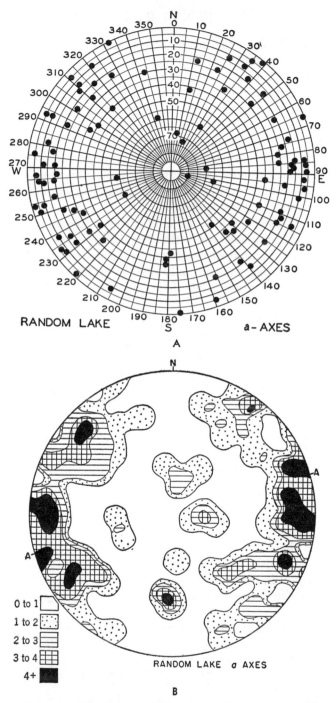

FIG. 35. Till fabric. A: Distribution of long (a) axes of late Wisconsin till plotted on equiareal polar coördinate paper. B: Same contoured as "petrofabric" diagram. Black: 4 per cent maxima (from Krumbein, 1939).

entially oriented in one direction, there will be a cluster of points on the diagram. In order to show the clustering or density of points, appropriate contours are drawn. Just as on a population density map contours may be drawn to show the number of people per square mile, so on the petrofabric diagram contours are drawn to show the density of points per unit area. Relative number (per cent) rather than actual numbers are usually shown. The unit area is commonly 1 per cent of the area of the diagram.

The points representing axes of the fabric elements or the normals to specified planes (cross-bedding laminations for example) may show centers of concentration, termed *poles*, or zones or belts, termed *girdles*.

Fabric Patterns of Gravels and Sands

Although there are many conceivable fabric patterns, sedimentary deposits show a relatively few simple arrangements. As the orientation of a fabric element—pebble for example—is dependent on the shape of the element, it is profitable to review briefly the common patterns shown by the principal shape classes.

Spheres, of course, cannot display a fabric pattern. None is possible. The orientation of prolate forms is described in terms of the fabric pattern of

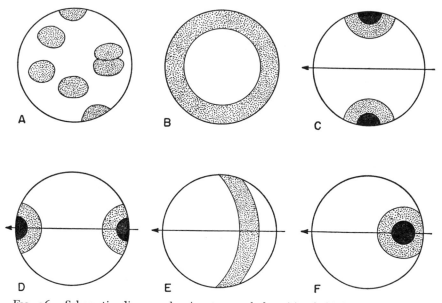

Fig. 36. Schematic diagram showing types of depositional fabric. **A:** Isotropic or random. **B:** Girdle in plane of bedding. **C:** Transverse pole in plane of bedding normal to current (arrow). **D:** Longitudinal pole in plane of bedding. **E:** Girdle dipping up-current. **F:** Pole dipping up-current. Various combinations of these types are also possible (see Fig. 71).

their long axes. These may be random (isotropic fabric), Fig. 36, A; bedding-plane girdle, Fig. 36, B; one or two poles in plane of bed (parallel with and transverse to prevailing current), Fig. 36, C; or a single pole with upcurrent dip ("monoclinic" fabric), Fig. 36, F. The orientation of oblate or disk-shaped elements may be described in terms of the fabric pattern of the short axes—essentially the normals to the disk. The disks may lie in the bedding plane with a short-axis pole perpendicular to the bed, or they may be imbricated with upstream dip, in which case the short-axis pole is "off-center." Triaxial forms may have the long axes concentrated in a bedding-plane girdle or in a girdle slightly inclined to the bed. In the latter case the girdle appears in only one-half of the diagram and follows a great circle, Fig. 36, E. The short axis in this case is an "off-center" pole as in the case of disks.

The preferred orientation of pebbles in some gravel accumulations has long been noted. The overlapping, shingling effect of flat pebbles in certain gravels and conglomerates has been commonly described as an "imbricate structure" (Fig. 37). Its manner of formation and relation to current flow has been discussed by Becker (1893, pp. 53–54).

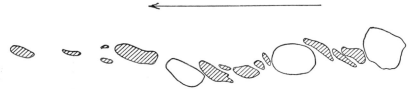

Fig. 37. Sketch showing the imbricate arrangement of pebbles. Archean conglomerate, Little Vermilion Lake, Ont., Can. (from Pettijohn, 1930).

Wadell (1936) and others (Cailleux, 1938; Krumbein, 1940, 1942; White, 1953) also studied the fabric of gravels. Wadell studied openwork esker and glacial delta gravels. He found the long axes of the pebbles of each to have a preferred orientation. In the esker gravel the majority of the fragments dip essentially in the same direction as the bed itself. Such a condition has also been noted on subaerial talus slopes. In the delta gravel, on the other hand, the pebble axes generally are inclined upstream in a direction opposite to the initial dip of the bed itself. This upcurrent imbrication was also found by Krumbein (1940, 1942) in the gravel deposits of the San Gabriel and Arroyo Seco canyons. The Arroyo Seco diagrams (Fig. 38) show the fabric to have a monoclinic symmetry, with the long axes of the pebbles dipping upstream.

The observations of Wadell and Krumbein are in accord with the statement of Johnston (1922, pp. 387–390) that "the longer axes of the stones usually lie in the direction of the current." This statement has been challenged by Fraser (1935, p. 985) who quotes Twenhofel and others to the

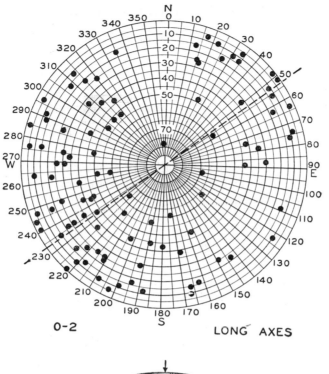

0-2

LONG AXES

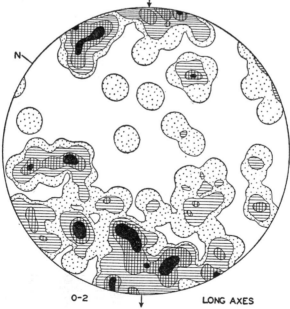

0-2

LONG AXES

FIG. 38. River gravel fabric (from Krumbein, *Bull. Geol. Soc. Amer.*, 51, 1940, Fig. 7, p. 662).

effect that the longest axes lie perpendicular to the current and it is the median axis that dips upstream. The correctness of Johnston's statement, however, is further confirmed by the work of Murray and Schlee (1953), who found a clear alignment of the long axes of rod-shaped pebbles of Patapsco River gravels parallel to current flow. Considering the numerous swirls, eddies, and reverse currents present in swift, turbulent streams, the general agreement of the preferred orientation to valley trend is significant.

Cailleux (1945) studied the inclination of about 4000 pebbles in formations ranging from Paleozoic to Recent in age. Imbrication was very common, and in marine formations was somewhat variable in direction, whereas in river deposits the inclination was notably uniform. The mean upstream inclination in fluvial deposits was 15 to 30 degrees, whereas marine deposits showed inclinations of only 2 to 12 degrees. Cailleux studied the effect of shape, size, and contiguity on the inclination. In general, flat pebbles had a lower inclination than less flat ones, the larger sizes were better oriented than the smaller, and pebbles in contact were better oriented than those wholly isolated.

The apparent inclination of pebbles in the plane parallel to the direction of current flow was studied statistically by White (1953). White found the inclination of pebbles in a Keweenawan conglomerate to be essentially "normally" dispersed about their mean inclination. There was, however, an excess number with inclinations of near 40 degrees to the bedding. These irregularities in an otherwise apparently normal distribution of pebble in-clinations were interpreted by White as due to concentrations of pebbles on the flanks of scour pits and representing the angle of repose of materials on the sides of such pits. If this be true, then, as White points out, the obtuse bisectrix of angle between crater walls should have a fixed relationship to a horizontal line at the time of deposition. The difference in inclination between the obtuse bisectrix and the normal to the bedding plane is therefore the initial dip of the bed.

The preferred orientation of till stones has been used as a criterion of the direction of ice flow (Richter, 1932, 1936; Krumbein, 1939a; Holmes, 1941; Karlstrom, 1952). In general the long axes are parallel to the direction of ice flow as determined independently by bedrock striae or other means. As Holmes notes, however, there tends to be a lesser concentration of long axes transverse to the ice movement (see Fig. 70).

The fabric of sands and sandstones is less well known than that of gravels owing primarily to the difficulties of study of the finer-grained materials. Attempts have been made to measure the position of the actual long axes of the grains (Schwarzacher, 1951), the apparent long axes (Griffiths, 1949; Griffiths and Rosenfeld, 1950, 1953) and to measure the orientation of the crystallographic c-axis (Rowland, 1946) on the premise that the dimensional long axis and the c-crystallographic axis are closely correlated.

Wayland (1939) showed that the long axes of clastic quartz grains and the c-crystallographic axis tend to be the same. Ingerson and Ramisch (1942) have confirmed Wayland's observation. Accordingly it might be expected that if nonspherical quartz grains tend to be preferentially oriented by bottom currents at the time of deposition, sandstones would therefore display a crystallographic fabric. A petrofabric analysis of the St. Peter sandstone by Wayland showed that the optic axes of quartz did indeed show such an orientation. Rowland (1946) attempted to explore further the relations between dimensional and crystallographic directions in clastic quartz and on the basis of this knowledge to convert quartz optic axis diagrams into diagrams showing the poles to the maximum projection area of the quartz grains or the long axes of such grains. The results are rather inconclusive. In Ingerson's (1940) earlier work the c-axis of quartz in sandstones had little or no preferred orientation.

Dapples and Rominger (1945) showed experimentally that the azimuths of the long axes of sand grains tended to be oriented parallel to the direction of current flow (both wind and water) and also that the larger end of the asymmetric grains was generally (62 per cent in the water-deposited grains) upstream. Schwarzacher (1951) studied the dimensional fabrics both experimentally and in consolidated sandstones. He observed also that the long axes of the sand grains were concentrated mainly in the direction of current flow and tend to dip upstream as do the pebbles of fluvial gravels. A lesser concentration of long axes was observed to lie transverse to the prevailing current. Some of the sandstones studied by Schwarzacher showed a tendency to a "double maximum" the bisectrix of which was parallel to the current direction. The bimodal concentration of long axes was explained as a consequence of a packing pattern of triaxial grains.

Griffiths (1949) and Griffiths and Rosenfeld (1950, 1953) studied the orientation of the *apparent* long axes of quartz grains in thin section cut parallel and perpendicular to the bedding of the Bradford Sand of Pennsylvania. As this sandstone shows marked vectorial permeability, sections parallel to maximum and minimum permeability were also examined. Sections normal to the bedding disclosed preferential arrangement of the apparent long axes. No such orientation was observed in the section parallel with the bedding. Griffiths and Rosenfeld (1953) thought the most perfect alignment of long axes occurred in the direction of maximum permeability though the published data are somewhat ambiguous.[31] Work of Nanz (1955)

---

[31] The standard deviation of the measured inclinations of the apparent long axes of the quartz grains did not vary significantly between sections cut parallel to and perpendicular to the direction of maximum permeability.

on modern beach and river sands showed that the apparent long axes of the grains in the plane of the bedding have a distinct preferential arrangement. Work by Rusnak (1952) showed that such arrangements were regionally persistent in some Pennsylvanian sandstones of Illinois.

Fabric of Clays and Shales

It has been shown that the particles of clays, especially the clay minerals, are micaceous in habit and that the clastic fragments are platelike (Marshall, 1941). Even though these may be randomly deposited (probably not wholly so), gravitational pressure and resultant compaction rotate them into the same plane, so that they have a parallel or subparallel orientation. Such reorientation reduces the porosity and gives the shale or clay an anisotropic fabric and a fissility.

Keller (1946), however, has shown that some fire clays have the clay mineral plates randomly oriented and believed this to be the result of growth of these plates in a clay gel after deposition. Laminated shales appear to have the clay mica plates parallel to bedding and to impart a fissility to the rock. The claystones without such fabric have a conchoidal to irregular fracture.

Fabric of Limestones and Dolomites

The primary depositional fabrics of limestones and dolomites have been investigated by Sander (Knopf, 1951), Hohlt (1948), and F. W. Johnson (1951). Although well-defined crystallographic fabrics were reported by Hohlt; Johnson, who examined a number of similar rocks, found no such fabric patterns. The patterns described by Sander are largely growth fabrics in pores and other openings produced by druselike implantations of crystals on the walls of such cavities. It seems unlikely that pronounced crystallographic fabrics will be found in unstressed limestones or dolomites.

Oriented Fossils

Organic structures also respond to current flow. The detached valves of concavo-convex form may lie either with the concave or convex side upward, but if moved by current action the orientation becomes uniform, in this case with the convex side upward. The preferred orientation of such shells therefore is an index to both current *velocity* and to the upper and lower surface of steeply tilted or overturned strata (Shrock, 1948, p. 314).

Oriented fossils may also be indices of current *direction*. As noted long ago, *Tentaculites*, graptolite colonies, and the like, tend to show preferred orientation in the plane of the bedding. Chenowith (1952, pp. 556–559) showed that orthoceracone cephalopods and high-spired gastropods were well oriented in the Trenton of New York State. They tended to have their longest dimension either parallel to or perpendicular to the pararipples of the same beds. Chenowith believed those normal to the ripples and parallel to current flow became so oriented because of their displaced centers of gravity. This view was supported by plotting the position not only of the long axes but also noting the direction of the apical end of the gastropods studied.

Packing

Packing has to do with the manner of arrangement of the solid units in which each constituent is supported and held in place in the earth's gravitational field by tangent contact with its neighbors (Graton and Fraser, 1935, p. 790). Although the manner of arrangement of these units is in a sense a fabric, it is a scalar fabric rather than a vectorial fabric. The latter is that referred to when the term *fabric* is used alone.

The solid units of the coarser clastic sediments—the gravels and sands— are the pebbles and sand grains of which these deposits are composed. These clastic elements are nonspherical and nonuniform in size. An understanding of the phenomenon of packing, however, and of the effects of packing on porosity and permeability is furthered by assuming the solid units to be spheres (in most cases the constituents of the coarser sediments are nearly spherical, with average sphericity of 0.80 and higher). Consideration must first be given to an aggregate of uniformly sized spheres and then to nonuniform mixtures.

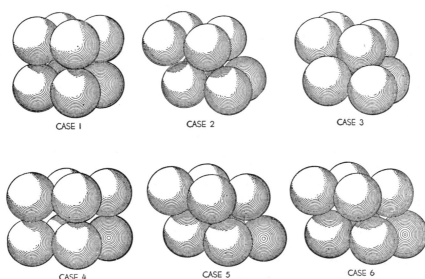

FIG. 39.   Packing of spheres (from Graton and Fraser, 1935, p. 796). Shows the six possible packing arrangements. Case 1 is most "open" or cubic packing: Case 6 is the "closest" or rhombohedral packing.

The packing of spheres of uniform size may be disorderly or may be constantly repetitive and geometrically systematic. Consideration of the problem shows that although there are six fundamentally different methods of systematic packing, one case, that of rhombohedral packing (Slichter, 1899, p. 305) is the "tightest," i.e., has minimum porosity and is the most compact possible arrangement of solid spheres. Because this is also the most stable, most natural, closely sized aggregates approach the rhombohedral arrangement. A considerable degree of disorder occurs in most deposits, though within any given deposit may be "colonies" or regions in which the tightest packing prevails. Rhombohedral packing is characterized by a unit cell of six planes passed through eight sphere centers situated at the corners of a regular rhombohedron, each edge of which measures $2R$ (Fig. 39). Rhombohedral packing stands in marked contrast with cubic packing—the "loosest" possible systematic packing, in which the unit cell is a cube, the eight corners of which are centers of the spheres involved (Fig. 39). In rhombohedral packing the porosity is 25.95 per cent, whereas for cubic packing it is 47.64 per cent.

Any plane passed at random through systematically packed spheres reveals alternating areas of solid materials and voids. The area of voids, however, is not a true measure of the total area available for transfer of fluid, because part of the voids is closed above or below by other grains which block the passageway. If, however, a plane is passed through the centers of the sphere in one of the rhombohedral layers of tightest packing, i.e. a "throat plane," the void area in this plane is a true measure of the minimum cross-sectional area of the channelways or of what might be called the "useful porosity." In the tightest rhombohedral packing, with total porosity of 25.95 per cent, the effective porosity is 9.30 per cent.

If a large number of spheres of equal diameter is arranged in any strictly systematic packing, there is a certain diameter ratio for a smaller sphere which can just pass through the throats between the larger spheres into the interstices. For the tightest packing the critical diameter is $0.154D$ (where D is diameter of the larger spheres). Similarly, there is a critical ratio for the diameter of a sphere which, although too large to pass into the void from without, can exist in such void and therefore must have entered such position at the time of deposition. The critical ratios of occupation are $0.414D$ and $0.225D$ for the rhombohedral arrangement.[32] These theoretical concepts cannot be applied too literally to natural deposits because the latter neither are composed of spheres nor are they packed in a wholly systematic manner. Nevertheless, if the materials filling the interstices of a gravel are mostly larger than 0.154 times the diameter of the larger pebbles, then the "fines" have not been washed in but have been laid down contemporaneously.

[32] Two types and sizes of voids are present in this packing system.

POROSITY AND PERMEABILITY

Introduction

Unlike the crystalline rocks in which the porosity is nil, the clastic sediments are moderately to highly porous. This porosity is due to the fact that the clastic components could not be, at the time of deposition, in continuous contact with one another. The porous nature of these sediments is a major cause and condition for diagenetic reorganization. The porosity, for example, leads to inhomogeneities in the distribution of the pressure due to the weight of the superincumbent beds, the weight being carried on the relatively small area of contact between grains. This leads to solution at points of contact and precipitation in the voids. Moreover, the fluid which occupies the pores constitutes a medium in which chemical reactions occur or which itself reacts with the solid framework of the sediment. The pore system is also the channelway for movement of fluid as well as for the storage of fluids. Hence the volume of such spaces and resulting storage capacity of the rock and its transmissibility are of great importance in the study of oil and gas, brines, and ordinary ground waters.

As a result of solution and precipitation, infilling, and other diagenetic changes, the porosity of a sediment is diminished with time. The higher the grade of diagenesis, the closer the similarity of the rock to those of metamorphic or igneous origin.

A consideration of the nonsolid portion of a sedimentary rock involves the composition of the contained fluids and the geometry of the void or pore system. The latter will be considered here. This problem is resolved into two, namely, the total (or relative) volume of voids and the framework elements and the pore pattern. The first is expressed by the term *porosity*.

Porosity

The porosity of a rock is defined as the percentage of pore space in the total volume of the rock, i.e., the space not occupied by the solid mineral matter. The porosity thus expressed is the *total* pore space as contrasted with the *effective* or available pore space. The total pore space includes all interstices or voids, whether connecting or not, and hence is larger than the effective pore space.

Porosity may be considered as either original or secondary (Fraser, 1935). Original porosity is an inherent characteristic and was determined at the time the rock was formed. Secondary porosity results from later changes which may increase or decrease the original porosity. Such changes include cementation, fracturing, and solution.

The original porosity of a sediment is affected by (1) uniformity of grain size, (2) shape of the grains, (3) method of deposition and packing of the sediment, and (4) compaction during and after deposition.

Theoretically, the actual size of grain has no influence on porosity. In fact, however, the finer-grained sediments have a higher porosity than the coarse-grained sediments (Table 17). This observation, however, does not establish a cause-and-effect relation inasmuch as size may be closely correlated with other properties, such as shape (p. 65), which may be the primary cause of the porosity differences noted.

TABLE 17. Relation Between Porosity and Grain Size (after Lee, 1919, p. 121)

Size of Material	Porosity (per cent)
Coarse sand	39 to 41
Medium sand	41 to 48
Fine sand	44 to 49
Fine sandy loam	50 to 54

Whether the size is uniform or nonuniform is of fundamental importance. The highest porosity is commonly obtained when the grains are all of the same size. To such an assemblage the addition of grains, either larger or smaller, tends to lower the porosity; and this lowering, within certain limits, is directly proportional to the amount added. No simple relation, however, has been found between the size distribution and porosity. Fraser and others have shown that quite different mixtures can have the same porosity.

The effect of shape of the grains on porosity is little understood. In general grains of high sphericity tend to pack with minimum pore space. Fraser found, for example, that uniformly sized beach and dune sands that had been experimentally compacted, had porosities of about 38 and 39 per cent, respectively, whereas crushed quartz had a porosity of about 44 per cent. As the sphericity of crushed quartz is about 0.60 to 0.65 (p. 61) and that of beach sand is probably near 0.82 to 0.84 (p. 60), it is clear that grain shape has a small but noticeable effect on porosity. Fraser found that the effect is most marked in the case of very flat particles. Freshly deposited clays have very high porosities—even up to 85 per cent. Unlike sands, the clay shows a large and regular decrease in porosity upon compaction.

The method of deposition and packing should have a marked influence on the porosity. For uniform spheres calculations show porosities ranging from 26 to 48 per cent for the closest packed to the most open arrangement, respectively. A given sand, experimentally packed, has been found to vary from 28 to 36 per cent. In nature, however, the tightest packing with minimum voids tends to prevail, so that in general the importance of packing is minimized.

The effect of compaction on the porosity has been reviewed elsewhere (p. 354). The effect on clay and shale is very great; the porosity seems to be a function of depth of burial according to the expression $P = p(e^{-bx})$, where P is the porosity, p is the average porosity of surface clays, b is a constant, and x is the depth of burial. The compaction of sands, however, is negligible. The initial porosity of sands (35 to 40 per cent) may be reduced to a very small figure by solution and reprecipitation or by infilling with introduced cement. The average sandstone has a porosity of 15 to 20 per cent. The high porosity of some sandstones, such as the Oriskany, has been attributed to the leaching of preëxisting carbonate cement (Krynine, 1941).

Permeability

Permeability is the property of a rock which allows the passage of fluids without impairment of its structure or displacement of its parts. A rock is said to be permeable if it permits an appreciable quantity of fluid to pass through in a given time, and impermeable if the rate of passage is negligible. Obviously, the rate of discharge through a given cross section depends not only upon the rock, but also upon the nature of the fluid and the hydraulic head or pressure.

Permeability may be expressed by the velocity of flow, Q (cm³ of fluid per sec) which passes through a cylindrical rock specimen of cross section F (cm²) and length L (cm). As the velocity of flow depends also on the pressure difference P (in atmospheres) and the viscosity of the fluid M (in centipoises), the relations observed may be expressed as

$$Q = K \frac{FP}{ML}$$

The proportionality factor K is the permeability, a factor characteristic of the rock under consideration. This permeability coefficient has been called a darcy. A sand is said to have a permeability of one darcy when it yields one cubic centimeter of fluid, viscosity one centipoise, per second through a cross section of one square centimeter under a pressure gradient of one atmosphere per centimeter of length. The permeability of oil sands ranges from one to over three thousand millidarcys.

The coefficient of permeability, K, of an unconsolidated rock is affected by the grain size and sorting of the rock, the grain shape, and the packing. The effects of size and uniformity of size have been studied experimentally by various workers. Krumbein and Monk (1942), for example, used glacial outwash sand which was sieved and recombined into sand mixtures of desired composition. Since many natural sands have log normal size distributions, the prepared mixtures were made log normal. They were made into sets with either (a) a common mean size but variable standard deviation, or (b) a common standard deviation but variable mean size. Thus the effects of mean size and sorting could be studied separately. Krumbein and Monk found the coefficient of permeability to vary as the square of the diameter

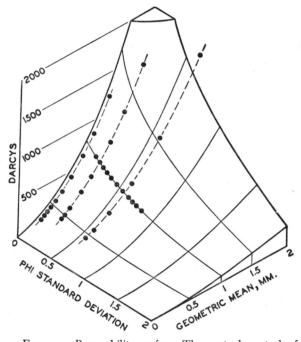

FIG. 40. Permeability surface. The mutual control of permeability by the mean size and the standard deviation is shown. The vertical axis represents the permeability in darcys, and the horizontal axes are the geometric mean diameter in millimeters and the phi standard deviation. The nature of the surface is shown by the grid lines, which are parabolas parallel to the darcy-size plane, and negative exponentials parallel to the darcy-standard deviation plane (Krumbein and Monk, A.I.M.E., T. P. 1492, Fig. 5, 1942).

and inversely as the log of the standard deviation. These relations may be expressed as $k = bd^2e^{-a\sigma}$, where K is the permeability in darcys, d is the geometric mean diameter in millimeters, σ is the geometric standard deviation, a and b are constants. In other words, permeability is increased by increase in size of grain and increased by an improvement in sorting (Fig. 40).

The shapes of the constituent grains, expressed by their sphericity, in some way affect the permeability. Inasmuch as sands with lower sphericities have higher porosities, presumably they would also have a higher permeability.

Because the permeability is dependent on the size and shape of the pores, it is dependent not only on the size of the grains but also on their packing arrangement. For a given size of grain the permeability is dependent solely on the packing. Under these conditions any change in packing which increases the porosity will increase the permeability. This is well shown by experimental work of Engelhardt and Pitter (1951), who varied the packing of a given sand and found the permeability to be positively correlated with the varying porosity. Looser packing, expressed by higher porosities, was accompanied by higher permeabilities.

In actual stratified sediments, the permeability has been found to be greater parallel to the bedding than perpendicular to it. In some such sediments it has been found to vary in a direction parallel to the bedding. Presumably this latter variation is related to some kind of anisotropic fabric.

Although porosity and permeability are geometrically distinct they are correlated in some ways. Obviously a nonporous rock is also impermeable. On the other hand, a highly porous rock is not necessarily permeable. Fine-grained rocks, although porous, are only slightly permeable. The relations between porosity, permeability and grain-size distributions have been studied by Engelhardt and Pitter (1951). Theoretically

$$K = 2 \times 10^7 \times \frac{\Theta^3}{(1 - \Theta)^2} \times \frac{1}{S^2}$$

where K is the permeability in darcys, Θ is the porosity, and S is the specific surface (square centimeters per cubic centimeter) of the sand. The specific surface is a function of grain shape and size; it can be calculated from the size analysis if the grains are assumed to be spheres. The theoretical relations were substantiated by experimental study of loose sands.

If S is calculated for a consolidated sediment from the grain size distribution and calculated from actual measurement of porosity and permeability, the results will not agree. The difference found is a measure of the degree of cementation. Obviously the deposition of mineral matter in the interstices reduces both porosity and permeability.

Not usually considered in permeability studies is the effect of the reaction between the minerals of the sediment and the contained fluids. If interstitial clays of the expanding lattice type are present, the introduction of water (as in "secondary recovery" operations) will result in swelling and blocking off the circulation. The action of such interstitial clay linings has been termed the "wall-paper" effect (Krynine, 1938).

REFERENCES CITED AND BIBLIOGRAPHY

Becker, G. F. (1893), Finite homogeneous strain, flow, and rupture of rock, *Bull. Geol. Soc. Amer.*, vol. 4, pp. 13–90.

Cailleux, A. (1938), La disposition individuelle des galets dans les formations détritiques, *Rev. géogr. phys. Géol. Dynam.*, vol. 11, pp. 171–196.

Cailleux, A. (1945), Distinction des galets marins et fluviatiles, *Bull. Soc. géol. France*, ser. 5, vol. 15, pp. 375–404.

Chenowith, Philip A. (1952), Statistical methods applied to Trentonian stratigraphy in New York, *Bull. Geol. Soc. Amer.*, vol. 63, pp. 521–560.

Dapples, E. C., and Rominger, J. F. (1945), Orientation analysis of fine-grained clastic sediments, *J. Geol.*, vol. 53, pp. 246–261.

Engelhardt, W. v. and Pitter, H. (1951), Über die Zusammenhänge zwischen Porosität, Permeabilität und Korngrösse bei Sanden und Sandsteinen, *Heidelberger Beitr. Min. Petrog.*, vol. 2, pp. 477–491.

Fraser, H. J. (1935), Experimental study of the porosity and permeability of clastic sediments, *J. Geol.*, vol. 43, pp. 910–1010.

Graton, L. C., and Fraser, H. J. (1935), Systematic packing of spheres with particular relation to porosity and permeability, *J. Geol.*, vol. 43, pp. 785–909.

Griffiths, J. C. (1949), Directional permeability and dimensional orientation in Bradford sand, *Penn. State Coll. Mineral Ind. Expt. Sta. Bull.* 54, pp. 138–163.

Griffiths, J. C. and Rosenfeld, M. A. (1950), Progress in measurement of grain orientation in Bradford sand, *Penn. State Coll. Mineral Ind. Expt. Sta. Bull.* 56, pp. 202–236.

Griffiths, J. C. (1953), A further test of dimensional orientation of quartz grains in Bradford sand, *Am. J. Sci.*, vol. 251, pp. 192–214.

Helmbold, R. (1952), Beitrag zur Petrographie der Tanner Grauwacken, *Heidelberger Beitr. Min. Petrog.*, vol. 3, pp. 253–288.

Hohlt, R. B. (1948), The nature and origin of limestone porosity, *Colo. School Mines Quart.*, vol. 43, no. 4.

Holmes, C. D. (1941), Till fabric, *Bull. Geol. Soc. Amer.*, vol. 51, pp. 1299–1354.

Ingerson, Earl (1940), Fabric criteria for distinguishing pseudo-ripple marks from ripple marks, *Bull. Geol. Soc. Amer.*, vol. 51, pp. 557–570

Ingerson, Earl and Ramisch, J. L. (1942), Origin of shapes of quartz sand grains, *Am. Mineralogist*, vol. 27, pp. 595–606.

Ingerson, Earl (1954), Studies of unconsolidated sediments I: Quartz fabric of current and wind ripple marks, *Tschermak's min. petrog. Mitt.*, ser. 3, vol. 4, pp. 117–124.

Johnson, F. W. (1951), Unpublished Ph. D. thesis, Univ. Chicago.

Johnston, W. A. (1922), Imbricated structure in river gravels, *Am. J. Sci.*, ser. 5, vol. 4, pp. 387–390.

Karlstrom, T. N. V. (1952), Improved equipment and techniques for orientation studies of large particles in sediments, *J. Geol.*, vol. 60, pp. 489–493.

Keller, W. D. (1946), Evidence of texture on the origin of the Cheltenham fireclay of Missouri and associated shales, *J. Sediment. Petrol.*, vol. 16, pp. 63–71.

Knopf, E. B., and Ingerson, Earl (1938), Structural petrology, *Geol. Soc. Amer. Mem.,* 6.

Kopstein, F. P. H. W. (1954), *Graded bedding of the Harlech Dome,* Rijksuniversetiet Groningen, pp. 57–64.

Krumbein, W. C. (1939a), Preferred orientation of pebbles in sedimentary deposits, *J. Geol.,* vol. 47, pp. 673–706.

Krumbein, W. C. (1939b), Application of photoelectric cell to the measurement of pebble axes for orientation analysis, *J. Sediment. Petrol.,* vol. 9, p. 112.

Krumbein, W. C. (1940), Flood gravel of San Gabriel canyon, *Bull. Geol. Soc. Amer.,* vol. 51, pp. 636–676.

Krumbein, W. C. (1941), Measurement and geologic significance of shape and roundness of sedimentary particles, *J. Sediment. Petrol.,* vol. 11, pp. 64–72.

Krumbein, W. C. (1942), Flood deposits of Arroyo Seco, Los Angeles County, California, *Bull. Geol. Soc. Amer.,* vol. 53, pp. 1355–1402.

Krumbein, W. C. and Monk, G. D. (1942), Permeability as a function of the size parameters of unconsolidated sands, *Am. Inst. Mining Met. Engrs., Tech. Publs.,* 1492.

Krumbein, W. C. and Griffith, J. S. (1938), Beach environment in Little Sister Bay, Wisconsin, *Bull. Geol. Soc. Amer.,* vol. 49, pp. 629–652.

Krynine, P. D. (1938), Mineralogy of water flooding, *Producers Monthly,* vol. 3, Dec.

Lane, E. W., and Carlson, E. J. (1954), Some observations on the effect of particle shape on the movement of coarse sediments, *Trans. Am. Geophys. Union,* vol. 35, pp. 453–462.

Lee, C. H. (1919), Geology and ground waters of the western part of San Diego County, California, *U.S. Geol. Surv., Water Supply Paper 446,* pp. 121.

Marshall, C. E. (1941), Studies in the degree of dispersion of clays. IV. The shapes of clay particles, *J. Phys. Chem.,* vol. 41, pp. 81–93.

Nanz, R. H. (1955), Grain orientation in beach sands: A possible means for predicting reservoir trend, *J. Sediment. Petrol.,* vol. 25, p. 130. (abstract)

Richter, K. (1932), Die Bewegungsrichtung des Inlandeises, rekonstruiert aus den Kritzen und Langsachsen der Geschiebe, *Z. Geschiebeforschung,* vol. 8, pp. 62–66.

Richter, K. (1936), Ergebnisse und Aussichten der Gefügesforschung im pommerschen Diluvium, *Geol. Rundschau,* vol. 27, pp. 197–206.

Rowland, R. A. (1946), Grain-shape fabrics of clastic quartz, *Bull. Geol. Soc. Amer.,* vol. 57, pp. 547–564.

Rusnak, G. A. (1952), Personal communication.

Sander, B. (1936) (trans. by E. B. Knopf, 1951), *Contributions to the study of depositional fabrics,* Tulsa, American Association of Petroleum Geologists.

Schlee, J., and Murray, Harrison (1953), Personal communication.

Schwarzacher, W. (1951), Grain orientation in sands and sandstones, *J. Sediment. Petrol.,* vol. 21, pp. 162–172.

Shrock, R. R. (1948), *Sequence in layered rocks,* New York, McGraw-Hill.

Slichter, C. S. (1899), Theoretical investigation of the motion of ground water, *U.S. Geol. Survey, 19th Ann. Rept.,* Part II, p. 305.

Wadell, Hakon (1936), Shape and shape position of rock fragments, *Geografiska Annaler*, pp. 74–92.
Wayland, Russell G. (1939), Optical orientation in elongate clastic quartz, *Am. J. Sci.*, vol. 237, pp. 99–109.
White, Walter S. (1952), Imbrication and initial dip in a Keweenawan conglomerate bed, *J. Sediment. Petrol.*, vol. 22, pp. 189–199.

TEXTURES OF NONCLASTIC (CHEMICAL) SEDIMENTS

The textures of the nonclastic or chemical sediments are distinctive and notably different from those of the clastic sediments. The textures seen are primarily the result of recrystallization from solution or the gel state or of recrystallization of microcrystalline or near-amorphous materials. The textures therefore are analogous to, if not identical with, the textures seen in many igneous and metamorphic rocks.

Crystalline Texture

In a strict sense virtually all rocks are crystalline—even the clays—but the term "crystalline" is usually reserved for those rocks which show an *interlocking* aggregate of crystals such as shown by rock salt. Such rocks are also called crystalline granular, or saccharoidal. They may be coarse (macrocrystalline), medium-grained (mesocrystalline), or fine-grained (microcrystalline or cryptocrystalline) (Table 18).[33] The individual crystals may be euhedral, subhedral, or anhedral, according to whether they exhibit good crystal boundaries (faces), a few such boundaries, or are devoid of crystal outlines.

Some crystalline sediments are equigranular or about uniform in size. Others are uneven-grained in that large crystals ("porphyroblasts") are scattered through a crystalline matrix of fine-grained materials. Some anhydrite beds, for example, have large conspicuous euhedra of gypsum in a finer-grained, microcrystalline matrix of anhydrite. Such a texture might be called porphyroblastic.

Other terms, borrowed from the students of metamorphic rocks, may be appropriate to describe special crystal habits. The crystals may be equigranular (equidimensional), nematoblastic (threadlike) or fibroblastic, lepidoblastic (leaf-shaped or scaly), and the like.

In the crystalline rock special attention is given to the nature of the grain boundaries. If the contacts are more or less regular, the texture is a simple mosaic; if the contacts are markedly sutured the texture is a sutured mosaic. In some cases the crystalline grains are separated by a microcrystalline mosaic —the mortar texture.

[33] For other attempts to designate size terms for the nonclastic rocks, the carbonate rocks in particular, see DeFord (1946) and Rodgers (1955).

TABLE 18. Crystalline Textures (after Hirschwald, 1912, and Howell, 1922)

I. Macrocrystalline (granoblastic: over 0.75 mm).
   A. Subequal grains.
      1. Sutured.
      2. Mosaic.
   B. Unequal grains.
      1. Sutured.
      2. Mortar.

II. Mesocrystalline (porphyroblastic: 0.20 to 0.75 mm).
   A. Porphyroblasts dominant (in contact, forming a loose net).
      1. Groundmass microcrystalline.
      2. Groundmass cryptocrystalline.
   B. Porphyroblasts subordinate (scattered or isolated).
      1. Groundmass microcrystalline.
      2. Groundmass cryptocrystalline.
      3. Groundmass pelitomorphic.

III. Microcrystalline (crystalline nature recognizable only under the microscope: 0.01 to 0.20 mm).
   A. Even-grained.
   B. Uneven-grained.
      1. Cryptocrystalline material subordinate.
      2. Cryptocrystalline material dominant.

IV. Cryptocrystalline (less than 0.01 mm).

The crystalline texture of sedimentary rocks is formed in several ways. The texture of some rocks, such as rock salt and rock gypsum, is produced by precipitation from a saturated solution. Crystals growing from many centers in a supersaturated brine settle to the bottom, where growth continues until an interlocking mosaic is formed. A crystalline mosaic may also be the result of "secondary enlargements" of the detrital grains of a highly quartzose sandstone. The worn detrital grains constitute seed "crystals" which grow until they interlock with their neighbors and produce a crystalline mosaic (an orthoquartzite). Likewise echinoderm debris sorted and assembled into a calcareous sand may be secondarily enlarged to form a "marble" or crystalline limestone.

The crystalline texture of many rocks, however, seems to be wholly a secondary attribute. The conversion of a limestone to a dolomite results in a coarse crystalline mosaic of dolomite crystals. The microcrystalline texture of chert is presumed to be the result of the neocrystallization of a silica gel. Crystallization or recrystallization in the solid state produces textures essentially "metamorphic" or crystalloblastic in character. The conversion of anhydrite to gypsum is also a good example of this type of transformation. Crystals that have grown in this way in an essentially solid medium are likely to be filled with inclusions. In a dolomite, for example, formed from a silty limestone or calcareous siltstone, many of the porphyroblastic dolomite rhombs may engulf or include some of the particles of quartz or foreign matter. Such inclusions may be scattered at random through the crystal or they may be collected near the center or be zonally distributed. A most interesting example of the engulfment of foreign materials in crystals is afforded by the "crystalline" or "luster-mottled" sandstones—quartz sand cemented by coarsely crystalline calcite (see p. 653). Sand crystals, or inclusion-loaded euhedra of calcite (Pl. 8) are the sedimentary analogue of the "poikiloblastic" crystals of the metamorphic rocks.

As might be expected, the rocks which owe their crystallization to diagenetic changes would carry, like their metamorphic counterparts, relict textures and structures. These are traces of the original textures and structures of the rock which have not been wholly destroyed by the postdepositional reorganization. Bedding laminations, oolites, fossils, and even clastic textures may persist and be recognizable.

Colloform and Related Textures

Many minerals and rocks are now thought to be of colloid origin (Rogers, 1917). Colloids enter into many geological processes, especially those connected with the deposition of the sedimentary rocks.

Liquid colloids are termed sols, and when the particles of a sol coagulate into a gelatinous mass, the product is known as a gel. In time gels lose a portion of their water and harden and produce various types of amorphous minerals. Inasmuch as colloid systems are unstable, further changes lead to crystallization, which may be fibrous at first, but may finally be coarse and granular. Even following such recrystallization, the original form of the gel may remain. Many concretionary, botryoidal, reniform, nodular, oolitic, and pisolitic textures and structures are believed characteristic of minerals of colloidal origin. In addition to the concentric colloform features, other evidences of a former gel state are "syneresis" or shrinkage cracks, including the septarian structure, lenticular cracks, and other contraction phenomena (Taliaferro, 1934). The criteria for the recognition of an original gel state have been best formulated by the students of ore deposits (Boydell, 1924; Lindgren, 1925; Rust, 1935).

Pellets and Granules

Small bodies of ovoid form, generally under one millimeter in size, are common in some rocks. These bodies are roundish, ellipsoidal to subspherical, polylobate (in section) to somewhat irregular. Some closely resemble oolites and some have been termed "false oolites." Unlike oolites they have no radial or concentric structure; they are amorphous or microcrystalline. Syneresis cracks may be present. Glauconite, greenalite, and other iron silicates, collophane, and even lime carbonate commonly assume this form.

Some of these bodies, especially those of calcareous and phosphatic composition, have been interpreted as faecal pellets (see p. 220). Other pelletizing processes have been suggested for the carbonate granules (p. 403). The iron silicate granules have been thought to form by ". . . slight current or wave action on a fine-grained precipitate" (James, 1954, p. 268).

Oolites and Pisolites

A rock may be said to possess an *oolitic* texture if it consists largely of *oolites*. Oolites are small spherical or subspherical, accretionary bodies, 0.25 to 2.00 millimeters in diameter; most commonly they are 0.5 to 1.0 millimeter in size. If they are over 2.0 millimeters in diameter they are termed *pisolites*. Although the spherical form is the rule, some oolites are oblate ellipsoidal. Within any given rock, however, they are highly uniform in both size and shape. Oolites are found in deposits of all ages.

The term *oolite* has been applied both to the minute accretionary bodies described above and to the rock composed of such objects. To avoid confusion some writers apply the term oolite only to the rock and use the term *oolith* for the spherites of which the rock is made (DeFord and Waldschmidt, 1946). The suffix *-lith*, however, has been used by some petrographers to denote a rock and hence the term oolith is also ambiguous. The terms *ooid* (also *ooide*) and *ovulite* also have been used (Deverin, 1945). Twenhofel (1950) would avoid ambiguities by restricting the term *oolite* to the microconcretionary bodies and would use the adjective *oolitic* for the rocks. The terms *oolitic phosphate, oolitic limestone* are certainly clear enough.

In section oolites appear radial, or concentric or both. Some oolites, owing to replacement, have lost their original structure and show only a crystal mosaic. These are not to be confused with false oolites. Oolites appear to have grown outward from a center. In some oolites the growth has taken place around a nucleus—such as a quartz sand grain or a small fragment of shell. In others no nucleus can be seen, either because the section did not pass through the nucleus or because there was none.

Oolites formed at the present time are calcareous—aragonite or calcite. "Fossil" oolites, however, may be siliceous, dolomitic, hematitic, pyritic, and so forth. Some of these may be replacements of a calcareous oolite; others may be original precipitates. In the calcareous oolites, aragonite or calcite fibers radiate from a center. Under crossed nicols this structure is expressed by a black cross, and in theory at least, by concentric interference rings—a pseudo-interference figure of the uniaxial type. Instability of aragonite leads to conversion to calcite with loss of the radial structure and its replacement by a mosaic of carbonate crystals, within which traces of the original radial or concentric structure can still be seen.

The calcite, in turn, may be replaced by dolomite, which first appears as rhombic euhedra—veritable metacrysts—in the oolite. Such rhombs lie athwart the concentric structure and may even lie across the boundary of the oolite itself.

Silica may also replace a calcareous oolite—in some cases before dolomitization and in some cases, afterward. Evidence of the secondary nature of the siliceous oolite includes (1) chert pseudomorphs of the dolomite rhombs (Pl. 32, F), (2) the secondary enlargement of the detrital quartz nuclei of some oolites with a thin carbonate ring at the interface between the detrital grain and the quartz overlay (indicating entrapment of the calcareous matrix at the time of overgrowth) (Pl. 39, F), (3) the clear encroachment of the reconstructed quartz crystals on the oolitic structure (Pls. 39, C), and (4) the "hybrid" oolites, which are in part carbonate and in part chert with the original concentric structure crossing the chert-carbonate boundary (Pl. 40, A).

Not all noncalcareous oolites are replacements. Although their formation has not been observed, petrologic data indicate a primary origin for both the oolitic phosphates and the oolitic ironstones.

Many theories have been advanced to explain the formation of oolites. Some theories demand direct or indirect intervention of organisms; others require formation in a gel medium; some theories presume the oolites to form by replacement of calcareous nonoolitic detritus. The interested reader is referred to the original papers for details (Bradley, 1929a, 1929b; Brown, 1914; Bucher, 1918; Eardley, 1938; Mathews, 1930; Krynine, Honess and Myers, 1941; Choquette, 1955). Some oolitic bodies are certainly algal ("algal pisolites," see Pl. 30, D); some are products of replacement of calcareous oolites (Pl. 40, B); some, such as those found in pisolitic bauxite, may be products of replacement on nonoolitic materials. Most calcareous oolites, however, and many noncalcareous oolites, seem to be the product of direct precipitation of dissolved materials on nuclei in a "free-rolling" environment. The close association of oolites and detrital quartz grains (Fig. 95); the cross-bedded character of the deposit, and the sorting indicate accumulation in a turbulent medium. Illing (1954), who has given a good review of the oolite problem, concluded that the oolitic sands of the Bahamas are forming today only where the sediment is subjected to strong tidal current action and that the oolites form where the oceanic waters moving onto shallow banks are sufficiently warmed to become appreciably supersaturated with calcium carbonate. Neither algae nor other organisms play any part in their formation.

Spherulites

The term "spherulite" has been applied to any spherical body with a radial structure. Certain concretionary bodies are spherulitic. Many oolites are also spherulitic. As here used, however, the term is reserved for those minute subspherical bodies with a radial structure which has formed *in situ*. They are somewhat similar to the spherulitic bodies which form by the devitrification of a glass. Spherulites of chalcedony, for example, form in some limestones (Pl. 40, C). Spherulites of this type, unlike oolites, have a somewhat irregular surface. Moreover, if the centers of growth are too closely spaced, mutual interference of these bodies may take place. If mutual interference is common, the growing spherulites become closely packed polyhedra. Oolites may become broken and the broken parts become the nucleus for new oolites; this feature is obviously impossible in spherulitic formation.

Spastoliths

Spastoliths are deformed oolites. Some oolites, especially those composed of chamosite, are closely appressed, twisted, or misshapen. The distortion has been attributed to the soft condition of the oolite at the time of its burial. Spastoliths of chamosite therefore are said to establish the primary nature of this mineral. Oolites, of course, may be subject to flattening and elongation by the tectonic forces which deform the rock and all structures which it exhibits (Cloos, 1947).

Summary

The nonclastic or chemical rocks show either a crystalline texture, in which the grains are in contact with one another over the whole of their surface, or an oolitic (or granuloid) texture in which the constituent crystal aggregates, like the elements of a clastic rock, show only tangential contacts with one another. The latter rocks are subject to the same type of infilling and condensation as are the clastic rocks.

In addition the nonclastic rocks may show textures resulting from organic growth—spicules and so forth. Such organoform or bioform features have been described in the section on organic structures (p. 218).

REFERENCES CITED AND BIBLIOGRAPHY

Barbour, E. H., and Torrey, J., Jr. (1890), Notes on the microscopic structure of oolites, with analyses, *Am. J. Sci.*, ser. 3, vol. 40, pp. 246–249.

Boydell, H. C. (1924), The role of colloidal solutions in the formation of mineral deposits, *Bull. Inst. Mining Metall.*, 234.

Bradley, W. H. (1929), Algal reefs and oolites of the Green River formation, *U.S. Geol. Survey, Prof. Paper* 154-G, pp. 203–224.

Bradley, W. H. (1929b), Cultures of algal oolites, *Am. J. Sci.*, ser. 5, vol. 18, pp. 145–148.

Brown, T. C. (1914), Origin of oolites and the oolitic texture in rocks, *Bull. Geol. Soc. Amer.*, vol. 25, pp. 745–780.

Bucher, W. H. (1918), On oolites and spherulites, *J. Geol.*, vol. 26, pp. 593–609.

Choquette, P. W. (1955), A petrographic study of the "State College" siliceous oolite, *J. Geol.*, vol. 63, pp. 337–347.

Cloos, E. (1947), Oolite deformation in the South Mountain fold, Maryland, *Bull. Geol. Soc. Amer.*, vol. 58, pp. 843–918.

DeFord, R. K. (1946), Grain size in carbonate rocks, *Bull. Am. Assoc. Petroleum Geol.*, vol. 30, pp. 1921–1927.

DeFord, R. K. and Waldschmidt, W. A. (1946), Oolite and oolith, *Bull. Am. Assoc. Petroleum Geol.*, vol. 30, pp. 1587–1588.

Eardley, A. J. (1938), Sediments of Great Salt Lake, Utah, *Bull. Am. Assoc. Petroleum Geol.*, vol. 22, pp. 1359–1387.

Henbest, L. G. (1945), Unusual nuclei in oolites from the Morrow group near Fayetteville, Arkansas, *J. Sediment. Petrol.*, vol. 15, pp. 20–24.

Hirschwald, J. (1912), *Handbuch der bautechnischen Gesteinsprüfung*, Berlin, Gebrüder Borntraeger, p. 511–516.

Hovey, E. C. (1894), Microscopic structure of siliceous oolites, *Bull. Geol. Soc. Amer.*, vol. 5, pp. 627–629.

Howell, J. V. (1922), Notes on the pre-Permian Paleozoics of the Wichita Mountain area, *Bull. Am. Assoc. Petroleum Geol.*, vol. 6, pp. 413–425.

Illing, L. V. (1954), Bahaman calcareous sands, *Bull. Am. Assoc. Petroleum Geol.*, vol. 38, pp. 1–95.

James, H. L. (1954), Sedimentary facies of iron-formation, *Econ. Geol.*, vol. 49, pp. 235–293.

Krynine, P. D., Honess, A. P., and Myers, W. M. (1941), Siliceous oolites and chemical sedimentation, *Bull. Geol. Soc. Amer.*, vol. 52 (abstract), pp. 1916–1917.

Lindgren, W. (1925), Gel replacement, a new aspect of metasomatism, *Proc. Nat. Acad. Sci. U.S.*, vol. 11, pp. 5–11.

Mathews, A. A. L. (1930), Origin and growth of Great Salt Lake oolites, *J. Geol.*, vol. 38, pp. 633–642.

Rogers, A. F. (1917), A review of the amorphous minerals, *J. Geol.*, vol. 25, pp. 515–541.

Rust, G. W. (1935), Colloidal primary copper ores at Cornwall Mines, southeastern Missouri, *J. Geol.*, vol. 43, pp. 398–426.

Taliaferro, N. L. (1934), Contraction phenomena in cherts, *Bull. Geol. Soc. Amer.*, vol. 45, pp. 189–232.

Twenhofel, W. H. (1950), *Principles of sedimentation* (2d ed.), New York, McGraw-Hill, pp. 625–626.

3

Composition of
Sedimentary Rocks

CHEMICAL COMPOSITION AND CLASSIFICATION OF SEDIMENTARY ROCKS

Introduction

THE composition of a sediment may be expressed in terms of the chemical elements of which it is composed. The composition thus expressed is determined by a chemical analysis and is referred to as the chemical composition of the rock.

1 0 4 2 1 6

Chemical data of this sort are very useful in the study of sedimentary rocks. The sediments are, in a sense, the products of large-scale chemical and mechanical fractionation processes—they are in fact concentrates, sharply contrasted chemically as well as physically. In this respect they show much greater diversity in composition than do the igneous rocks. To understand fully the geochemical processes and the evolution of the various types of sediments or differentiates, chemical analyses are needed. Moreover, in some sediments the grain size is so fine as to make ordinary petrographical studies difficult or impossible, so that much of our knowledge of the composition of these sediments is obtained by chemical studies.

The interpretation of a chemical analysis calls for considerable skill and judgment when the mineral composition is partially or wholly unknown. An indispensable aid to such interpretation is a well-chosen set of analyses of typical sedimentary rocks. The author has endeavored to compile such analyses in connection with the discussion of each group of sediments. It is also desirable to have some notion of what the chemical composition of the average sedimentary rock is like and to know, also, what the average shale, sandstone, and limestone contain. Such averages, based on data by Clarke, are given in the various chapters dealing with these materials and in Table 20.

The chemical composition of a rock is ordinarily reported by the chemist in terms of "oxides." Clearly the oxides as such are not necessarily present. They are instead usually bound up with other oxides to form the various minerals—such as calcite, kaolinite, chlorite, and so forth. In some rocks, however, there is much more of one oxide than can be accounted for by such combinations, so that it must occur in a "free" or uncombined state. An excess of silica in the clastic rocks, for example, means that "free" silica— usually quartz—is present. As the oxygen content of a rock is not actually determined, the practice of reporting the constituents as oxides is based on the assumption that the elements determined are combined with oxygen in stoichiometric proportions. This assumption is not always valid. If sulfides are present, for example, it is obviously incorrect to report the iron as FeO and the sulfur as SO_3. In most sediments, fortunately, sulfides are rather minor, and this exception and others like it are unimportant.

Chemical analyses vary a great deal in reliability and completeness. To evaluate and use analyses requires considerable judgment and some knowledge of how analyses are made (Washington, 1930; Hillebrand, 1919; Groves, 1937; Fairbairn et al., 1951). Many analyses are woefully incomplete. Even major constituents may not be separately determined. Some analysts report "loss on ignition." The loss may include free and combined water, carbon dioxide, sulfide sulfur, and carbon or organic matter. Titania (TiO_2), an important constituent of some shales and clays, may not be determined. If it is unreported, it appears in the figure given for alumina (Al_2O_3), which is therefore too high. In many sedimentary rocks the alkalies Na_2O and K_2O are not separately determined. The lesser constituents, MnO, P_2O_5, BaO, SO_3, S, and even CO_2 are commonly omitted. Such incomplete analyses are a decided handicap in the study of sediments. Washington (1930) has given an excellent discussion of the completeness of chemical analyses as well as the methods of evaluating analyses.

Factors Affecting the Chemical Composition of Clastic Sediments

The chemical composition of clastic sediments varies widely. In order to understand the significance of chemical composition, it is necessary to understand the nature of these variations and their causes.

The chemical composition of a clastic sediment is very closely related to its *grain size*. The relations between the composition and grain size is well shown by Grout's chemical analyses of the several size fractions of the same

TABLE 19. Relation of Chemical Composition to Size of Grain (after Grout)[a]

Constituent	Fine Sand	Silt	Coarse Clay	Fine Clay
SiO_2	71.15	61.29	48.07	40.61
TiO_2	0.50	0.85	0.89	0.79
Al_2O_3	10.16	13.30	18.83	18.97
Iron Oxides	3.72	3.94	6.91	7.42
MgO	1.66	3.31	3.56	3.19
CaO	3.65	5.11	4.96	6.24
Na_2O	0.86	1.32	1.17	1.19
K_2O	2.20	2.33	2.57	2.62
Ignition	5.08	7.05	10.91	12.51

[a] Based on average of 12 clays: 1 residual clay, 1 Ordovician shale, 2 Cretaceous clays, and the remainder (8) of glacial or recent origin. "Fine clay" is under 1 micron, "coarse clay" is 1 to 5 microns, and "silt" is 5 to 50 microns. See Table 21 for recalculated mineral composition of the same materials.

materials (Grout, 1925). It is obvious that the coarser fractions are richer in silica and poorer in alumina, the oxides of iron and potash than are the finer-grained portions.[1] This is, perhaps, to be expected as the excess silica is largely detrital quartz which characterizes the sand portion, whereas alumina and potash are contained in the finer-grained clay fractions as is the iron. It is obvious, therefore, that comparison of chemical analyses of clastic sediments must be made on materials of like grain size.

That these relations are rather common is shown also by analyses of naturally fractionated materials. The differences in chemical composition between the winter and summer fractions of the same varve are of the same kind and magnitude as those shown by Grout (see Table 62).

The low silica content of many residual clays and the low silica content in the clay fractions analyzed by Grout lead to the conclusion that the somewhat higher silica content of the "average shale" (Clarke, 1924) (Table 20) must be due to a mixture of clay and silt or fine sand. Inspection of Grout's figures shows that about two parts of silt and one part of clay would yield a product with about the same silica and same alumina content as the average shale.

A second major influence on the chemical character of clastic sediments is *maturity*. Maturity has to do with the degree to which a sediment has been differentiated or evolved from the parent materials from which it came. Sand, one of the products of disintegration and decomposition of the coarse-grained crystalline rocks, tends to become a high-purity quartz concentrate. Immature sands, however, may contain undecomposed feldspars and other minerals. It is self-evident, therefore, that sands and sandstones will show a wide range of chemical composition depending on their maturity. The silica content, for example, varies from 65 to 70 per cent in the arkoses to over 99 per

[1] Grout's work showed the very coarsest fractions to contain less silica than the next smallest grain. The coarser fraction contained rock particles in addition to free quartz.

cent in the orthoquartzites. On the other hand, the chemical composition of shales of about the same grain size varies within comparatively narrow limits. The finer-grained clastics are clearly much less differentiated (see Fig. 41).

By comparison of weathered materials and the rocks from which they were derived, it is possible to ascertain what has been lost by weathering and in what constituents the original material has been thereby enriched. Such studies show that some oxides are more inert than others and tend to remain in the weathered residue, whereas others are more mobile and tend to be removed. The average order of loss of the oxides can be determined by the

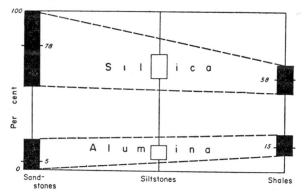

Fig. 41. Diagram showing mean and range in silica and alumina content of sandstones, siltstones, and shales. Data for siltstones are incomplete. Note greater variability of coarser sediments which shows that these are more highly differentiated chemically than are the finer sediments.

study of large numbers of rocks and their weathered residues. The order in which the constituents are lost, as interpreted by several investigators, is given in Table 93. The variation in the order of loss of the oxides found by the several workers probably results from sample inadequacies. Perhaps also some differences might be expected in different rocks; more marked differences may be related to differences in climate in the cases studied.

In nearly all cases, however, the residues tend to be enriched in silica, iron, and alumina and impoverished in lime, magnesia, soda, and potash. The sediments, however, are washed residues and differ from the residual products in two important ways. First, the washing process tends to produce a mechanical separation of the sand from the clay and therefore a separation of the silica from the alumina and iron. Sands are washed products enriched in silica, whereas the shales are products enriched in alumina and iron. In the second place, some of the oxides lost on weathering may reappear in the sediments—especially the fine-grained sediments—by reason of chemical or biochemical addition of these constituents during the sedimentation process.

Thus precipitated carbonates may add CaO or FeO to the shales; likewise the addition of silica is probable in the case of the siliceous shales. Of special interest in this connection is K_2O which, though not directly precipitated, is also restored to the shales.

Apparently alumina and in most cases soda are the two constituents not likely to be either added or subtracted from the sediments during or after the processes of deposition. As alumina is perhaps the most inert oxide whereas soda is the most mobile, the Al_2O_3/Na_2O ratio is therefore the most appropriate index of maturity for the fine-grained sediments.

The differential mobility of the oxides has led several investigators, notably Reiche (1943) to devise indices of "weatherability." Such an index—Reiche's weathering potential index, for example—is in effect the reciprocal of the maturity of the weathered residue. The weathering potential falls as the material approaches a stable end state. Reiche's index is, in effect, the mol percentage of the mobile oxides (MgO, CaO, Na_2O, K_2O) in the residue. (Reiche actually uses the difference between the sum of these oxides and combined water content.) Such an index, however, is not an appropriate index of maturity for the sediments inasmuch as the index will be vitiated by the biochemical or chemical additions to the sediment as well as by the silica content, which is a function also of the grain size.

An essentially similar concept was earlier expressed by Vogt (1927) and restated by Kennedy (1951). These authors refer to the "degree of residual character" exhibited by shales and like materials. As pointed out by Vogt, the enrichment in alumina is the best index of such a property. The enrichment, however, may be obscured by a change in the amount of the quartz present—the result of fortuitous sorting action—and in order to neutralize this blurring effect of silica, Vogt recalculated the proportion of the oxides to the sum of 100 excluding SiO_2 (and TiO_2). When this is done the alumina gives a truer picture of the residual character of the rock and can be used as the reference oxide against which the molecular percentages of the other oxides can be plotted (Kennedy, p. 260).

In the coarser clastics the silica is a measure of the maturity of a sediment. The highly mature orthoquartzites have over 99 per cent silica. The silica percentage alone can be misleading because it may be reduced, relatively, owing to presence of introduced cements—generally carbonate—in these rocks. Inspection of the analysis will usually show whether such is the case.

Postdepositional Changes in Chemical Composition

The primary chemical nature of a sediment is determined by the completeness of the weathering processes which gave rise to the sediment and to the thoroughness of the mechanical fractionation processes (washing) attendant on transportation and deposition. The original composition may be modified, however, in various ways after deposition by the processes of diagenesis, lithification, and metamorphism.

The chemical changes that are caused by diagenesis and lithification may be minor though in some cases they are profound. Shales appear to be little modified in their gross composition even by moderate metamorphism. The sands, on the other hand, may be materially changed chemically by introduction of cementing minerals. The high calcium content of some sands is obviously in the cement if the carbon dioxide content is also high. Carbonate rocks, including the carbonate-cemented sands may be dolomitized or silicified with pronounced corresponding changes in their gross chemical composition.

Metamorphism may also alter the chemical composition of the sedimentary rock, though such changes may be smaller than is commonly claimed. The chief difference between shales and slates seems to be in the reduction of the iron to the ferrous state and the loss of hygroscopic water (Table 61). Many of the purported wholesale changes in composition are suspect, inasmuch as erroneous assumptions were made as to the original character of the metamorphic rock. The supposed unique chemical properties of sediments, cited by Bastin (1909) are statistically correct but individual sediments range widely from the norm. Even the same sedimentary sequence can show lateral variations in its primary chemical nature and lead to erroneous conclusions about the effects of regional metamorphism (Kennedy, 1951). The question of differences in chemical composition between sedimentary and metamorphic rocks has recently been reviewed by Albee (1952) who studied the range of variation in original composition of the argillaceous and arenaceous rocks.

Chemical Composition and Geologic Age

The chemical composition of the shales, and perhaps the coarser clastics and some of the nonclastics as well, may be in a minor way related to their age. See Table 61. Paleozoic and older shales seem to be poorer in lime perhaps because the lime-secreting habit of pelagic foraminifera did not become important until the Cretaceous. Deep-water shales, therefore, of the later times are enriched in the calcareous materials. There are other apparent differences between the earlier lutites and those of a later age, but at present such differences have not been adequately explained (Nanz, 1953). There is some evidence that the cement of the older sandstones tends to be more siliceous or more dolomitic (Tallman, 1949) and the older carbonate rocks seem to be richer in magnesium (Daly, 1909).

Chemical Character and Classification of Sedimentary Rocks

Sediments may be considered the end products of a large-scale chemical fractionation process and as such they may be classified as chemical entities.

Such a classification was proposed by Goldschmidt (1937) and restated and revised by Rankama and Sahama (1950). Goldschmidt's classification is given below:

I	II	III	IV	V
Si	Al, Si, (K)	Fe	Ca, (Mg)	(Ca), Na, (K), (Mg)
Resistates	Hydrolysates	Oxidates	Carbonate precipitates	Evaporates
SiO_2	Clay minerals (hydrolyzed bases)	$Fe(OH)_3$	$CaCO_3$ $CaMg(CO_3)_2$	NaCl KCl $MgCl_2$, $MgSO_4$, etc.

To these Rankama and Sahama would add a sixth (VI) group, namely, the *reduzates* or those abnormally reduced sediments containing C, Fe^{2+}, Mn^{2+}, and S, principally the coals, siderite, and sedimentary sulfide. Chemically the fully differentiated sandstones belong to group I; the shales, on the other hand, are a mixed deposit and include groups I, II, and III. The limestones and dolomites belong to group IV and the saline sediments belong in group V.

It will be noted that the order in which the principal elements are presented and grouped is essentially the order in which they are stated in a chemical analysis and essentially the order in which they were determined by the analyst (Barth, 1952; Mason, 1952). The separations of the various elements in most cases are not sharp. The shales, for example, are not markedly differentiated chemically. On the other hand, some sandstones, limestones, and saline residues are abnormally pure and constitute segregations of certain elements far greater than that found in any igneous body (Fig. 42).

The significant features of the chemical composition of sediments, according to Bastin (1909) are the dominance of magnesia over lime,[2] potash over soda, excess of alumina,[3] high silica, and in the carbonate formations excessively high lime and magnesia. To these, perhaps, should be added the dominance of ferric iron over ferrous iron. There are, however, many exceptions to these generalizations. The comparison of those sediments produced by mechanical disintegration only, and unsorted, is much like that of the rock from which it was derived (see arkose, p. 324).

[2] The average shale (Table 20,) does not seem to have an excess of magnesia over lime. This is probably due to inclusion in the Clarke average some 27 Mesozoic and Cenozoic shales with a magnesia to lime ratio of 2.67 to 5.96. Paleozoic shales are said to have a magnesia to lime ratio of 2.32 to 1.41 (Clarke, 1927). Roughly 77 to 84 per cent of the metasedimentary slates and schists tallied by Bastin had an excess of magnesia over lime against but 8 per cent of the acid igneous rocks and 35 per cent of the basic igneous rocks.

[3] Excess over that necessary to satisfy the 1 to 1 ratio in which it is combined with lime and the alkalies in the common rock-forming silicates.

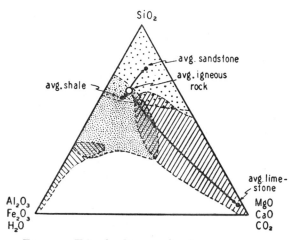

FIG. 42. Triangle diagram showing range in composition of the common sediments (after Brian Mason (1952), *Principles of geochemistry*, New York, Wiley; and Clarke, 1924). Coarse stipple, sandstone; fine stipple, shale; large diagonal ruled area, limestones; small diagonal ruled area, laterites and other residual accumulations.

Comparison of the chemical composition of the average sediment with that of the average igneous rock (Table 20) shows differences due to (1) additions from the atmosphere, and (2) losses to the ocean. To each 100 grams of igneous rock have been added, during weathering, 5.30 grams of CO_2, 1.99 grams of H_2O, 0.30 grams of SO_3, 0.72 grams of C, and 1.0 grams of O_2.

TABLE 20. Chemical Composition of Average Rocks (after Clarke)

Constituent	Igneous Rock	Shale	Sandstone	Limestone	Sediment[a]
SiO_2	59.14	58.10	78.33	5.19	57.95
TiO_2	1.05	0.65	0.25	0.06	0.57
Al_2O_3	15.34	15.40	4.77	0.81	13.39
Fe_2O_3	3.08	4.02	1.07	0.54	3.47
FeO	3.80	2.45	0.30	....	2.08
MgO	3.49	2.44	1.16	7.89	2.65
CaO	5.08	3.11	5.50	42.57	5.89
Na_2O	3.84	1.30	0.45	0.05	1.13
K_2O	3.13	3.24	1.31	0.33	2.86
H_2O	1.15	5.00	1.63	0.77	3.23
P_2O_5	0.30	0.17	0.08	0.04	0.13
CO_2	0.10	2.63	5.03	41.54	5.38
SO_3	....	0.64	0.07	0.05	0.54
BaO	0.06	0.05	0.05	....	....
C	....	0.80	....	....	0.66
	99.56	100.00	100.00	99.84	99.93

[a] Shale 82 per cent, sandstone 12 per cent, limestone 6 per cent (after Leith and Mead, 1915).

REFERENCES CITED AND BIBLIOGRAPHY

Albee, A. L. (1952), Comparison of the chemical analyses of sedimentary and metamorphic rocks, *Bull. Geol. Soc. Amer.*, vol. 63, p. 1220 (abstract).

Barth, T. F. W. (1952), *Theoretical petrology*, New York, Wiley, especially pp. 37–60.

Bastin, E. S. (1909), Chemical composition as a criterion in identifying metamorphosed sediments, *J. Geol.*, vol. 17, pp. 445–472.

Clarke, F. W. (1924), Data of geochemistry, *U.S. Geol. Survey, Bull.* 770, especially pp. 543–593.

Daly, R. A. (1909), First calcareous fossils and the evolution of the limestones, *Bull. Geol. Soc. Amer.*, vol. 20, p. 165.

Fairbairn, H. W. and others (1951), A cooperative investigation of precision and accuracy in chemical, spectrochemical and modal analyses of silicate rocks, *U.S. Geol. Survey, Bull.* 980.

Goldschmidt, V. M. (1937), The principles of the distribution of the chemical elements in minerals and rocks, *J. Chem. Soc. London.*, pp. 655–673.

Grout, F. F. (1925), Relation of texture and composition of clays, *Bull. Geol. Soc. Amer.*, vol. 36, pp. 393–416.

Groves, A. W. (1937), *Silicate analysis*, London, Murby.

Hillebrand, W. F. (1919), The analysis of silicate and carbonate rocks, *U.S. Geol. Survey, Bull.* 700.

Kennedy, W. Q. (1951), Sedimentary differentiation as a factor in the Moine-Torridonian correlation, *Geol. Mag.*, vol. 88, pp. 257–266.

Mason, Brian (1952), *Principles of geochemistry*, New York, Wiley.

Mead, W. J. (1907), Redistribution of elements in the formation of sedimentary rocks, *J. Geol.*, vol. 15, pp. 238–256.

Nanz, R. H. (1953), Chemical composition of pre-Cambrian slates with notes on the geochemical evolution of lutites, *J. Geol.*, vol. 61, pp. 51–64.

Rankama, K., and Sahama, T. (1950), *Geochemistry*, Chicago, Univ. Chicago Press, especially pp. 189–242.

Reiche, Parry (1943), Graphic representation of chemical weathering, *J. Sediment. Petrol.*, vol. 13, pp. 58–68.

Tallman, S. L. (1949), Sandstone types: their abundance and cementing agents, *J. Geol.*, vol. 57, pp. 582–591.

Vogt, T. (1927), Geology and petrology and the Sulitelma district, *Norges Geol. Undersökelse*, Nr. 121.

Washington, H. S. (1930), *The chemical analysis of rocks*, 4th ed., New York, Wiley.

MINERAL COMPOSITION OF THE SEDIMENTARY ROCKS

Introduction

The mineral composition of a sedimentary rock is one of its most important attributes. The presence or absence of a given mineral may be an important clue to the history of the rock.

Minerals in sedimentary rocks belong to one or another of two main groups, namely, detrital or chemical. The first group are released or formed by weathering of the source rock and are mechanically transported and deposited; the second group are precipitated from solution. In general the detrital minerals are documents of provenance and dispersal; the chemical minerals are documents of milieu.[4]

The kinds of detrital minerals present are related to the character of the source rocks (provenance) from which the sediment was derived. Those which survive weathering constitute important evidence on the duration and intensity of the weathering processes and may be indicative of the nature of the climate and relief of the source area. Detrital minerals also carry a record of the transport history—its duration and rigor. In the basin of deposition the detrital suite defines the area over which the debris from a given source is spread—the sedimentary petrographic province. The geographic limits of this province, the recognition of interfingering or mingling of materials from several sources, and the changing character of the suite from a given source because of progressive denudation may be determined from careful study of the detrital minerals—especially those of sandstones. The changing character of the suite is, of course, the basis of the so-called "heavy mineral correlation."

The precipitated minerals are guides to the chemical milieu of deposition. Certain minerals are restricted to a limited range in pH and Eh, and others are formed only from solutions of higher than normal salinity or temperature. Their isotopic composition may carry a record of their age or a record of the temperature of their formation (paleotemperature).

The clay minerals are in a class apart from the normal detrital minerals in that they are not, in general, "inherited" from the source rock. They afford little clue, therefore, as to the nature of that source rock. Moreover, they are especially susceptible to change, since they are reactive and may be modified by exchange of ions with the surrounding medium. Thus the clay minerals, though detrital, are environment sensitive and in some degree are indicative of the chemical milieu of that environment.

The principles utilized in interpretation of the mineral composition are outlined in later chapters. Such interpretation, however, is contingent upon a proper genetic classification of the minerals of a sedimentary rock and

---

[4] The terms "allogenic" and "authigenic" have been used to describe, in a general way, the two main classes of minerals. *Allogenic* minerals originate outside of the sediment and are transported to the place of deposition. *Authigenic* minerals, on the other hand, originate in the place where they are now found: they are generated on the spot. The clay minerals are usually called authigenic, yet it is difficult to so classify them, since they may be transported like any other detrital mineral. Only if the clay minerals grow in place in the sediment after deposition, as does some illite and chlorite, should they be considered authigenic.

upon a proper interpretation of the time sequence of their formation.

Classification of Sedimentary Minerals and Criteria for Their Recognition

In light of the foregoing, therefore, the minerals of the sedimentary rocks belong to three main groups, namely, the residual detrital minerals, the secondary detrital minerals, and the chemical precipitates (Fig. 43). The first group, the residual detritals, are those minerals of the source rocks which survive the processes of weathering and are mechanically transported

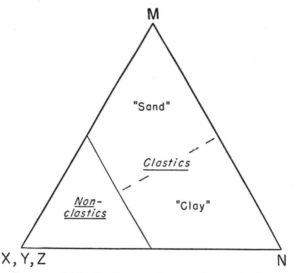

Fig. 43. Triangle diagram showing the usual relations between the three classes of minerals in sedimentary rocks. A sediment may be a mixture of any two or of all three. M is detrital sand, N is detrital clay and iron hydroxide, X, Y, and Z are carbonate, silica, and carbonaceous (organic) materials, respectively.

and redeposited. They include both stable species, like quartz, and the relatively unstable species such as feldspar. The secondary detrital minerals are those generated by the weathering processes, such as the clay minerals, which are likewise mechanically transported and deposited. The chemical precipitates are the minerals deposited from true solution by chemical and biochemical processes. Some are directly precipitated and constitute the bulk of the rock; others are added to the rock after deposition by precipitation from permeating solutions.

A given sedimentary rock, therefore, may have a complex mineralogy (Figs. 43 and 44). It may consist of few or many mineral species, some of which are detrital and some of which are chemical in origin. And moreover,

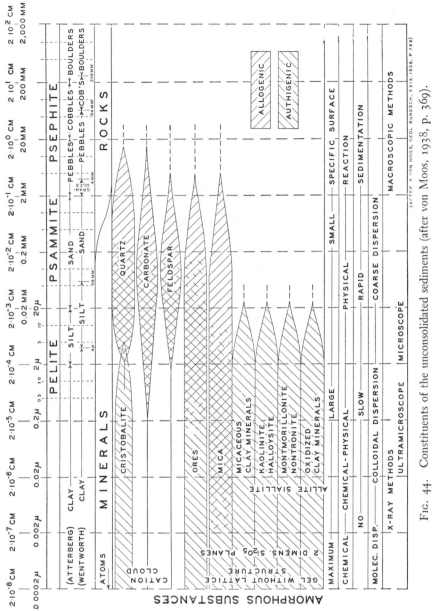

FIG. 44. Constituents of the unconsolidated sediments (after von Moos, 1938, p. 369).

a given mineral species may be in part detrital and in part chemical. The minerals which are chemically precipitated may be formed at the time of accumulation of the sediment; or they may be formed later, perhaps precipitated in the interstices of the sediment, or perhaps in part replacing pre-existing minerals, either detrital or chemical. It is evident, therefore, that to understand the history of a sedimentary rock, it is necessary: first, to discriminate between the detrital minerals and those chemically precipitated; second, to determine the relative age of the several precipitated minerals; and finally, to ascertain the manner of emplacement of the precipitated materials whether formed in openings or formed by replacement. To make these discriminations, the student will need criteria and will need to evaluate these criteria in reading the history of the rock (Grout, 1932, pp. 1–3).

In the coarser clastic deposits, the distinction between minerals of detrital origin and those which are chemical precipitates is usually self-evident. The detrital elements, whether rock particles or single mineral grains, are usually somewhat rounded by abrasion, are somewhat sorted as to size and are usually the dominant component (of the sands or gravels), thus forming the framework of such deposits in which the subordinate chemically precipitated materials fill the voids or interstices. The distinction between minerals of detrital and chemical origin in the shales, in which the clay minerals may be in part detrital and in part diagenetic, is much less easy. So also in those sandstones which contain interstitial clay, it is difficult to be sure whether the clay is an original detrital component, a mechanically infiltrated product, or a chemical precipitate. Troublesome also is the chlorite of both siltstones and shales and the interstitial chlorite of some sandstones (graywackes). Is the chlorite detrital material or a product of authigenesis?

Minerals such as quartz and feldspar, which may be both detrital and chemical, even in the same grain, are rarely hard to classify. The detrital character of the quartz and feldspar is generally clear; the authigenic quartz and feldspar occur either as overgrowths on detrital cores or as euhedra (generally in a carbonate rock). Not uncommonly, however, the boundary between the detrital nucleus and the overgrowth is obscure, so that it may be difficult to be sure which portion of a given grain is detrital and which portion is chemical.

For full understanding of the history of the rock, it is imperative that the relative ages or paragenesis of the several minerals present be determined. The problem of mineral paragenesis and the related problem of replacement of one mineral by another have occupied the attention of petrographers and students of the ore deposits for many years. The students of ores, in particular, have been astute observers of the textures of both ores and rocks and have formulated many criteria for attacking the problem of relative age and replacement (Bastin and others, 1931; Bastin, 1950; Edwards, 1947). The student of sedimentary rocks, including both those predominantly detrital and those predominantly chemical, should study those papers dealing with mineral paragenesis in order that the needed criteria may be fully understood and be properly evaluated. It does not seem feasible to outline or discuss in detail these criteria in such a book as this. The interested reader is referred to the works of Grout, Bastin, and others in which such criteria are collected, summarized, and evaluated. The criteria are best understood with reference to specific cases. Many such cases are cited elsewhere in this volume and are illustrated by appropriate photomicrographs or sketches.

Most of the microtextures and mineral contact relations found in other rocks and in ores are also present in sediments. The relative age of two minerals in contact with each other is in part determined by the fabric of the rock. The minerals of the detrital framework are obviously earlier than those which fill the voids within the framework. Some have contended, however, that the cementing minerals are penecontemporaneous with the detrital materials which they bind together (Krynine, 1941, for example). Minerals filling vugs or fractures as well as voids are obviously later than the host rock. Where several minerals fill the same cavity, their relative ages are determined by the mutual contact relations. In general, the younger mineral is moulded about the older. Because the early formed minerals grew into empty or fluid-filled cavities, they will be euhedral; the later minerals will therefore conform to the remaining space between such early euhedra, and are themselves anhedral. Unfortunately euhedralism is not an infallible criterion of early formation. If the euhedral crystal was formed by *replacement*, it may be later than the material which surrounds it. The quartz euhedra found in some limestones are excellent illustrations of this principle (Pl. 39, C). It is necessary therefore to discriminate between euhedra formed by growth in a fluid medium and euhedra formed by replacement within a solid matrix.

The criteria of replacement are many and include automorphic crystals which transect earlier structures such as bedding, fossils, and oolites (Pl. 39, C). Minerals formed by replacement contain inclusions of the material replaced. These unreplaced residuals may have a common crystallographic orientation, or may be distributed in a relict or ghost pattern inherited from the structure replaced (Pl. 39, E). Embayed contacts, as well as the residuals isolated by extreme embayment, are indicative of replacement relations (Pl. 17, B). The best-known criterion of replacement, perhaps, is pseudomorphism. Pseudomorphic replacement of organic structures (fossil wood, shells, etc.) and crystal pseudomorphs (silica after dolomite, for example) are common and conclusive evidences of replacement (Pl. 32, F). The alert observer will discover and use other criteria of relative age and replacement. It is essential that these relations be carefully worked out.

Mineralogy and Grain Size

As might be expected from a study of the relation between the grain size of clastic sediments and their chemical composition, there is a close correlation also between the mineral composition and grain size. In general, the stable primary detritals are of sand size, since they were the predominant constituents of the phaneritic crystalline source rocks. The stable secondary products, produced by the decomposition of the unstable primary constituents of the source rock, are of clay size. Though mostly crystalline, they are very fine-grained. The original residues, consisting of both sand-sized primary residuals and clay-sized secondary residuals, are washed and mechanically separated into sands, silts, and clays. As the fractionation is commonly imperfect, there is a gradation in grain size and corresponding gradation in both chemical and mineralogical composition.

TABLE 21.   Calculated Mineral Composition of Size Fractions of Clay
(after Grout, 1925)

Constituent	Size Fraction of "Clay"[a]		
	Silt[b]	Coarse Clay[b]	Fine Clay[b]
Kaolinite and Clay Minerals	7.5	17.0	23.2
Sericite and Paragonite	16.6	21.2	22.1
Quartz	36.7	19.3	13.1
Chlorite and Serpentine	8.2	10.3	7.3
Limonite, Hematite, and Pyrite	3.0	5.5	8.0
Calcite and Dolomite	10.5	7.5	5.7
Feldspars	12.6	7.2	7.3
Zeolites	3.0	7.5	6.9
Titanite and Rutile	1.7	2.0	1.7
Carbonaceous Matter	0.2	0.9	0.6
Moisture	0.9	1.3	4.1
	100.9	99.7	100.0

[a] Includes 1 residual clay, 1 Ordovician shale, 2 Cretaceous clays, and the remainder (8) of glacial or recent origin.
[b] "Fine clay" is under 1 micron; "coarse clay" is 1 to 5 microns; and silt is 5 to 50 microns.

The relation between grain size and composition is illustrated by the silts and clays artifically fractionated by Grout (1925). The chemical composition of each size fraction was determined by laboratory analysis (Table 19). If the finer fractions consist of the same minerals observed in the coarser fractions (though in different proportions), it is possible to calculate the probable mineral composition of each fraction. The results of such calculations are given in Table 21. As can be seen from this table the finer fractions are poorer in quartz and richer in the clay minerals (kaolinite, sericite, and paragonite and the iron oxide minerals). These mineralogical differences are closely correlated, of course, with the differences in chemical composition (p. 101).

The mineralogical composition of the average sandstone and average shale, calculated from the chemical analyses of average or composite sandstone and shale samples, shows differences related to grain size of the same kind found by Grout (Table 22). The average sandstone, as would be expected, is richer in quartz and poorer in the clay materials than the shales. As noted before,

TABLE 22. Mineral Composition of Average Sedimentary Rocks

Mineral	Shale		Sandstone		Limestone	Average Sediment[a]
	Leith and Mead (1915)	Clarke (1924)	Leith and Mead (1915)	Clarke (1924)	Leith and Mead (1915)	Leith and Mead (1915)
Quartz	31.91	22.3	69.76	66.8	3.71	34.80
Orthoclase	12.05⎫		8.41⎫		2.20⎫	11.02
Albite	5.55⎭	30.0	....⎭	11.5	....⎭	4.55
Sericite	18.40⎫		....⎫		....⎫	15.11
Kaolin	10.00⎭	25.0	7.98⎭	6.6	1.03⎭	9.22
Calcite	....⎫		7.21⎫		56.56⎫	4.25
Dolomite	7.90⎭	5.7	3.44⎭	11.1	36.25⎭	9.07
Limonite	4.75	5.6	0.80	1.8	....	4.00
Gypsum	1.17		0.12		0.10	0.97
Chlorite	6.40		1.15		....	5.29
Carbon	0.81		....		....	0.73
Miscellaneous	1.06	11.4	1.13	2.2	0.15	0.99
	100.00	100.00	100.00	100.00	100.00	100.00

[a] Weighted: shales 82%, sandstones 11%, and limestones 7%.

the average shale must be, in fact, a mixture of silt and clay, since it is richer in quartz and poorer in clay materials than the more closely fractionated clays. Grout's "fine clay," for example, contains but 13 per cent quartz and about 59 per cent of "clay minerals" (kaolinite, clay micas, chlorites, and "zeolites"). The average "shale," in contrast, has 32 per cent quartz and but 34 per cent of clay minerals, according to Leith and Mead.

The Minerals of Sediments

A comparison of the mineralogical composition of the average igneous rock with that of the average sediment shows significant differences. The sediments are enriched in quartz and impoverished in feldspar. The sedimentary feldspar, moreover, is not wholly a survival product: some of it is secondary or authigenic. The gain in quartz and decline in feldspar both result from the desilication of the feldspars on weathering. It follows therefore that the amount of free silica (quartz) is greatly increased during repeated cycles of weathering and erosion. The ferromagnesian constituents of the igneous rocks are almost wholly destroyed (except perhaps the mica which finds its way into some micaceous sand- and siltstones). The constituents of the ferromagnesian minerals are reorganized and appear as new minerals in the sediments, notably as magnesian and iron-bearing carbonates, chlorite, and the iron hydroxides. Together with kaolinite, or other clay minerals, these materials form a large part of the average sediment, especially the shales.[5]

TABLE 23. Comparison of the Calculated Mineral Composition of the Average Igneous Rock and the Average Sediment

Mineral	Average Igneous Rock[a]		Average Sediment
	Clarke (1924)	Leith and Mead (1915)	Leith and Mead (1915)
Quartz	12.0	20.4	35
Feldspars	59.5	50.2	16[b]
Ferromagnesian Minerals	16.8⎰	24.8	⎰ ....
Mica	3.8⎱		⎱ 15[b]
Miscellaneous	7.9	4.6	34[c]

[a] Leith and Mead's average igneous rock is based on 65 parts average granite plus 35 parts average basalt. Clarke's average is based on a statistical summary of 700 rocks described petrographically.
[b] Authigenic in part.
[c] Carbonates 13, kaolin 9, limonite 4, chlorite 5, etc.

The minerals of sedimentary rocks are, in general, of rather simple composition—simple oxides, hydroxides, carbonates, etc., for the most part—that are rich in H_2O, CO_2, and O_2 (the chemically active components of the atmosphere) and by a rather low density. These minerals are necessarily fairly stable under the low-temperature, low-pressure, hydrous environment found at the surface of the earth. The stable primary minerals of the plutonic rock crystallized last from the magma or under near-magmatic conditions, and therefore were formed at lower temperatures and in the presence of more water than were the products of early crystallization. For these reasons, probably, they appear to be the most stable under surface conditions and survive weathering and become part of these sediments. The question of mineral stability is discussed elsewhere (p. 502).

[5] The data contained in Tables 21, 22, and 23, are based on calculations from chemical analyses. The compositions thus computed, according to certain rules, are called *normative* or just *norms*. Data are not yet adequate to summarize the mineral composition of the sediments as actually measured (the *mode*). This can be done partially for the sandstones, and in the section on sandstones, a few such partial summaries are given. Owing to the fineness of grain of the shales, they are not very amenable to modal analyses. Hence no such summaries can be given for the peletic rocks.

REFERENCES CITED AND BIBLIOGRAPHY

Bastin, L. S. (1950), Interpretation of ore textures, Geol. Soc. Amer., Memoir 45.

Bastin, E. 3., and others (1931), Criteria of age relations of minerals, etc., Econ. Geol., vol. 26, pp. 562–610.

Clarke, F. W. (1924), Data of geochemistry, U.S. Geol. Survey, Bull. 770.

Edwards, A. B. (1947), Textures of the ore minerals and their significance, Melbourne, Australian Inst. Min. Metall.

Grout, F. F. (1925), Relation of texture and composition of clays, Bull. Geol. Soc. Amer., vol. 36, pp. 393–416.

Grout, F. F. (1932), Petrography and petrology, New York, McGraw-Hill.

Krynine, P. D. (1941), Petrographic studies of variations in cementing material in the Oriskany sand, Penn. State Coll., Bull., No. 33, pp. 108–116.

Leith, C. K. and Mead, W. J. (1915), Metamorphic geology, New York, Holt.

THE DETRITAL MINERALS

The list of primary detrital minerals which have been found in sediments is long (Table 24). If the source rock was subjected to incomplete weathering and the transportation was short, almost any known mineral can occur in sands that is of sand size in the parent rock. For a detailed description of the common detrital minerals the reader is referred to standard works by Milner (1940), Krumbein and Pettijohn (1938), and Tickell (1939).

Although the list of possible detrital minerals is long, in practice relatively few species are encountered and in most thin sections the number of minerals is even more restricted. Quartz is dominant in most sandstones and in many samples it forms more than 90 per cent of the detrital portion. The feldspars, though common, play a subordinate role in contrast to their importance in the igneous rocks (Table 23). In addition to quartz and feldspar, mica is the only other constituent of the parent rock likely to form an appreciable part of the detritus in the normal sandstone. Rock particles occur in some sandstones and are abundant in a few.

Quartz

Occurrence and Abundance

Quartz, the most ubiquitous mineral of sediments, is the chief constituent of most sandstones and in some it forms 99 or more per cent of the whole rock. It is an important constituent of siltstones and shales and may even occur in some limestones and dolomites. The average sandstone (Table 22) is composed of about two-thirds quartz although Krynine (1948) has estimated a lower figure, namely, 51 per cent.[6] The quartz content of the average shale is calculated by Leith and Mead (1915) to be about 32 per cent (Table 22); Clarke, however, gives 22 per cent. Although quartz occurs in abundance in some carbonate rocks, it is rare in most.

TABLE 24.   Detrital Minerals of the Arenaceous Sediments

The table lists the fifty most common detrital minerals of sands. The twenty-five most common minerals in recent sands are capitalized. "Light" minerals (sp gr less than 2.85) are italicized; all others are the "heavy" minerals (sp gr over 2.85). The latter total less than 1 per cent in most sands.

1. Actinolite-tremolite	26. Hematite
2. Anatase	27. HORNBLENDE
3. ANDALUSITE	28. HYPERSTHENE-ENSTATITE
4. APATITE	29. ILMENITE
5. AUGITE	30. KYANITE
6. Barite	31. LEUCOXENE
7. BIOTITE	32. Limonite
8. Brookite	33. MAGNETITE
9. *CALCITE*	34. Monazite
10. Cassiterite	35. *MUSCOVITE*
11. *Chalcedony*	36. Olivine
12. CHLORITE	37. Pyrite
13. Chloritoid	38. *QUARTZ*
14. Clinozoisite	39. RUTILE
15. Collophane	40. Serpentine
16. Cordierite	41. Siderite
17. Corundum	42. Sillimanite
18. DIOPSIDE	43. Spinel
19. *DOLOMITE*	44. SPHENE
20. Dumortierite	45. STAUROLITE
21. EPIDOTE	46. Topaz
22. *FELDSPAR*	47. TOURMALINE
23. Fluorite	48. Xenotime
24. GARNET	49. ZIRCON
25. Glauconite	50. ZOISITE

Quartz is primarily a detrital mineral, although it may also be authigenic in origin. In sandstones authigenic quartz occurs as overgrowths on the detrital grains and as such it may be an important constituent of the rock (upwards of 25 to 30 per cent in some cases). It also occurs as authigenic crystals in some limestones, either as overgrowths on detrital quartz (Pl. 39) or as crystals grown de novo in the carbonate.

[6] The values given by Leith and Mead (1915) and by Clarke (1924) are computed from the chemical composition of the "average sandstone." Krynine's figure is presumed to be an estimate based on modal analyses.

Observations

The detrital quartz grains of most sandstones are under 1.0 millimeter in diameter and most are less than 0.6 millimeter (Dake, 1921). Grains larger than 1.0 millimeter are generally composite grains of quartzite or like material. The size of the quartz grains is probably determined largely by the size of the quartz grains in the source rock. The quartz-bearing plutonic rocks, principally the granites, are the ultimate source of nearly all detrital quartz. Dake (1921) was able to show that such rocks would rarely yield grains larger than 1.0 millimeter in diameter. Examination of 14 granites shows about one-fourth the quartz grains were 1.0 millimeter or more in diameter. But of these, most were fractured or badly broken and would not yield large grains. Dake estimated, therefore, that only 9 per cent of the quartz would exceed 1.0 millimeter and but 20 per cent of the quartz would exceed 0.6 millimeter in diameter.

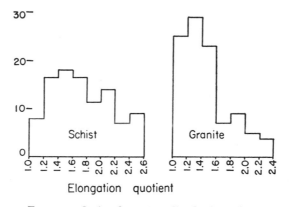

Fig. 45. Grain elongation distribution of quartz in source rocks (after Bokman, 1952, p. 23).

The quartz grains of sediments are variable in shape. In the main they tend to be subspherical. Even in the most mature sands, however, they tend to show a slight elongation. The elongation of detrital quartz may be expressed by an elongation quotient (long axis/short axis ratio) (Bokman, 1952). This varies, for example, from near 1.0 to 2.5 in the sandstones of the Stanley and Jackfork formations of Oklahoma and Arkansas. The means for these formations were about 1.5 and 1.75, respectively. As shown by Bokman these differences result in part from differences in provenance of the quartz. Quartz from granite is more nearly equiaxial than that from schists (Fig. 45). The mean elongation of the former was 1.43 and the latter, 1.75 for materials studied by Bokman.

Wayland (1939) noted the tendency for the elongation of detrital quartz grains to be greatest in the direction of the c-crystallographic axis. Wayland supposed that this elongation was produced by vectorial abrasion resulting from slight differences in hardness between the c-direction and the a-direction of quartz. Ingerson and Ramisch (1942), however, observed that the quartz grains of igneous and metamorphic source rocks, even those of granites, tended to be elongated and such elongation was very commonly parallel to the c-crystallographic axis. The final or end shape of sedimentary quartz is determined, therefore, in large part by the initial shape.

The surface of detrital quartz grains varies from highly polished to frosted. Most quartz is neither polished nor frosted. The quartz grains embedded in carbonate matrix tend to be slightly to strongly corroded by the cement. Incipient corrosion by the carbonate may be, in fact, the cause of the frosting.

Most quartz grains contain inclusions. These, usually small, are commonly scattered at random within the grain, although there is a tendency for some to be arranged in planes. Close attention has been given to the character of the inclusions, as their nature may be indicative of the provenance of the quartz. Mackie (1896) classified quartz inclusions into four groups, namely, regular, acicular, irregular, and inclusionless. Regular inclusions are mineral inclusions of automorphic habit; acicular inclusions are fine to needle-like, probably rutile; irregular inclusions are fluid lacunae with or without gas bubbles. Mackie examined a number of granites, gneisses, and other rocks and observed that the acicular and irregular inclusions were characteristic of the quartz of the granitic rocks, whereas the quartz of schists and gneisses contained regular inclusions. Mackie's observations were supported by those of Gilligan (1920) and Tyler (1936). Keller and Littlefield (1950) made a study of the inclusions of quartz in some 35 igneous and 16 metamorphic rocks. They concluded that Mackie's findings were in general correct. Although no one type of inclusion was diagnostic either of igneous or metamorphic quartz, a predominance of acicular and irregular inclusions was found to characterize the igneous rocks, whereas regular inclusions are more indicative of quartz-bearing schists. Liquid and gas inclusions, however, were common both in granites and in gneisses.

The extinction of quartz varies from sharp to wavy. Quartz which has been subjected to considerable pressure shows "strain shadows" or "undulatory extinction" observable under crossed nicols. The stronger the pressure, the more pronounced the strain shadows. In general, therefore, the quartz of metamorphic rocks is characterized by marked wavy extinction.

The detrital quartz of many sediments is seen to have been "secondarily enlarged" by the addition of a quartz overgrowth in crystallographic and optical continuity with the detrital nucleus (Sorby, 1880). Such overgrowths are very common and have been described and figured many times (Irving and Van Hise, 1884) (Pl. 39; Fig. 168). If the quartz is free to do so, it may become completely reconstructed and become a doubly terminated crystal. The quartz of many limestones tends to assume such a euhedral form in which case the overgrowth is commonly filled with many minute carbonate inclusions. Overgrowths in sandstones rarely assume a complete crystal form. Mutual interference of the growing nuclei leads to irregular boundaries or contacts with adjacent grains. Many partial facets are formed, however, which are made evident, even to the naked eye, because of the manner in which they reflect light.

Stability

Quartz is an exceedingly stable detrital mineral. The average igneous rock contains 12.0 (Clarke, 1924) to 20.4 (Leith and Mead, 1915) per cent quartz, whereas the average sandstone derived from the igneous rocks contains 67 to 70 per cent quartz (Table 22). Such enrichment in quartz implies a high degree of both mechanical and chemical stability. Quartz is not wholly insoluble, however, as the etching and pitting of some grains demonstrate. In general it is stable within the stratum and even tends to grow as the secondary outgrowths show. It is notably more stable than chert, which is commonly subject to intrastratal solution (Sloss and Feray, 1948).

Not only is quartz chemically inert but it is also mechanically durable. Daubrée (1879) showed experimentally that quartz grains lost only 1 part in 10,000 per kilometer of travel. Abrasion mill studies by Thiel (1940) confirm Daubrée's findings. Quartz grains 1 to ½ millimeter in diameter lost 22.4 per cent of their weight in 100 days of abrasion (about equivalent to 5000 miles of travel). Such a weight loss implies only an insignificant reduction in diameter (about 5 per cent). Quartz, therefore, even after several cycles of abrasion, undergoes only minor size reduction, just enough to round the corners but not enough to alter materially its original size or shape (p. 536). Anderson's (1926) earlier work likewise showed the slowness with which quartz was abraded.

Provenance

Quartz is ultimately derived from the quartz-bearing plutonic rocks, both igneous and metamorphic. It is also, of course, derived from preëxisting quartzose sediments, mainly sandstones, and from related metamorphic rocks, especially quartzite. Krynine (1942) has estimated that of the detrital quartz of the average sandstone, 25 per cent is derived from igneous and other crystalline rocks, 45 per cent comes from metamorphic rocks (mostly low rank), and 30 per cent is traceable to preëxisting sediments. As noted above, various criteria have been used to determine the provenance of the quartz. The attributes most used are (1) inclusions, (2) extinction, and (3) shape of the grains. On the basis of these properties, Krynine (1940) classified the quartz of the Bradford sand into eight types, four of which are of igneous derivation, three of metamorphic origin, and one of sedimentary origin. Krynine (1946) later modified his classification of quartz so that there were three types of igneous quartz, namely, plutonic, volcanic, and hydrothermal (including pegmatitic quartz), two types of metamorphic quartz, namely, pressure quartz and injection quartz, and finally several types of sedimentary quartz, authigenic overgrowths and new crystals and vein fillings. The criteria for the recognition of all major and minor types of quartz are given in detail by Krynine.

REFERENCES CITED AND BIBLIOGRAPHY

Anderson, G. E. (1926), Experiments on the rate of wear of sand grains, *J. Geol.*, vol. 34, pp. 144–158.

Bokman, John (1952), Clastic quartz particles as indices of provenance, *J. Sediment. Petrol.*, vol. 22, pp. 17–24.

Cayeux, L. (1929), *Les roches sedimentaires de France, Roches siliceuses*, Paris, Mason, pp. 30–31.

Clarke, F. W. (1924), Data of geochemistry, *U.S. Geol. Survey, Bull.* 770.

Dake, C. L. (1921), The problem of the St. Peter sandstone, *Missouri Univ. School Mines and Met. Bull.*, vol. 6, no. 1, pp. 158–163.

Daubrée, A. (1879), *Etudes synthetiques de geologie experimentale*, 2 vols., Paris, Dunod.

Gilligan, A. (1920), The petrography of the Millstone Grit in Yorkshire, *Quart. J. Geol. Soc. London*, vol. 75, pp. 251–294.

Ingerson, E., and Ramisch, J. L. (1942), Origin of shapes of quartz grains, *Am. Mineralogist*, vol. 27, pp. 595–606.

Irving, R. D., and Van Hise, C. R. (1884), On secondary enlargements of mineral fragments in certain rocks, *U.S. Geol. Survey, Bull.* 8, pp. 8–43.

Keller, W. D., and Littlefield, R. F. (1950), Inclusions in the quartz of igneous and metamorphic rocks, *J. Sediment. Petrol.*, vol. 20, pp. 74–84.

Krumbein, W. C., and Pettijohn, F. J. (1938), *Manual of sedimentary petrography*, New York, Appleton-Century.

Krynine, P. D. (1940), Petrology and genesis of the Third Bradford Sand, *Penn. State Coll. Mineral Ind. Expt. Sta., Bull.* 29, pp. 13–20.

Krynine, P. D. (1942), in *Report of a conference on sedimentation*, Tulsa, Research Comm., Am. Assoc. Petroleum Geol., pp. 66–67.

Krynine, P. D. (1946), Microscopic morphology of quartz types, *Anales Segundo Congr. Panamericano de Ing. de Minas y Geol.*, vol. 3, pp. 35–49.

Krynine, P. D. (1948), Megascopic and field classification of the sedimentary rocks, *J. Geol.*, vol. 56, pp. 130–165.

Leith, C. K., and Mead, W. J. (1915), *Metamorphic geology*, New York, Holt.

Milner, H. B. (1940), Sedimentary petrography, 3d ed., London, Murby.

Mackie, W. (1896), The sands and sandstones of Eastern Moray, Trans. Edinburgh Geol. Soc., vol. 7, pp. 148–172.

Sloss, L. L., and Feray, D. E. (1948), Microstylolites in sandstone, J. Sediment. Petrol., vol. 18, pp. 3–13.

Sorby, H. C. (1858), On the microscopical structure of crystals, indicating the origin of minerals and rocks, Quart. J. Geol. Soc. London, vol. 14, p. 474.

Sorby, H. C. (1880), On the structure and origin of non-calcareous stratified rocks, Proc. Geol. Soc. London, vol. 36, pp. 62–64.

Thiel, G. A. (1940), The relative resistance to abrasion of mineral grains of sand size, J. Sediment Petrol., vol. 10, pp. 103–124.

Tickell, F. G. (1939), The examination of fragmental rocks, 2d ed., Stanford University, Stanford Univ. Press.

Tyler, S. A. (1936), Heavy minerals of the St. Peter sandstone in Wisconsin, J. Sediment. Petrol., vol. 6, pp. 72–77.

Wayland, R. G. (1939), Optical orientation in elongate clastic quartz, Am. J. Sci., vol. 237, pp. 99–109.

Feldspar

Occurrence and Abundance

Feldspar, although the most abundant mineral of igneous rocks, plays a role subordinate to that of quartz in the sediments. It is a common detrital mineral in sandstones (in great quantity in some); it occurs also in the finer siltstones and shales in which it is probably authigenic; and it is a minor constituent in some limestones.

The average sandstone is calculated to contain, according to Clarke (1924), 11.5 per cent feldspar; Leith and Mead estimate 8.4 per cent. The observed average of 74 pre-Pleistocene sandstones is 12 per cent (Table 26). According to Krynine (1948) the average sandstone has about 11–12 per cent feldspar. In general, the agreement between the values calculated from the chemical composition and the observed content are rather good.

As can be seen from Table 25, modern sands from Europe and North America seem to be richer in feldspar than those of the past. The feldspar content of 214 samples ranges from 1 to 77 per cent and averages 19.3 per cent. No doubt many of these sands are enriched in feldspar by erosion of Pleistocene glacial materials although recent sands from unglaciated areas are also high in feldspar. There seems to be no difference in feldspar content of dune, beach, or stream deposits.

The feldspar content of the ancient sands shows much more striking variation than does that of the younger sands. The nearly feldspar-free sandstones, such as the St. Peter (Ordovician) of the mid-continent region, stand in marked contrast with the sediments of orogenic regions, which may contain feldspar in excess of the quartz and are properly designated arkoses

TABLE 25.   Feldspar Content of Recent and Pleistocene Sands

Type	Locality	No. of Samples	Range	Average	Reference
Beach, Lake	Lake Erie	7	22 to 28	25	Pettijohn and Lundahl (1943)
Beach, Lake	Lake Michigan	4	....	14	Willman (1942)
Beach, Sea	Quebec, Labrador, Greenland	9	27 to 77	49	Martens (1929)
Beach, Sea	Massachusetts	17	1 to 26	8	Trowbridge and Shepard (1932)
Beach, Sea	Scotland	5	7 to 15	10	Mackie (1896)
Dune	Illinois	47	8 to 29	18	Willman (1942)
Dune	Scotland	2	8 to 13	13	Mackie (1896)
River	Illinois river	3	9 to 12	10	Willman (1942)
River	Ohio river	4	6 to 21	15	Willman (1942)
River	Wabash river	2	17 to 19	18	Willman (1942)
River	Mississippi (Illinois)	13	16 to 34	25	Willman (1942)
River	Mississippi (Illinois to Gulf)	62	15 to 26	21	Russell (1937)
River	Scotland	10	12 to 42	21	Mackie (1896)
Glacial, Outwash	Illinois	24	....	14	Willman (1942)
Glacial, Till (sand portion)	Illinois	5	15 to 20	17	Willman (1942)
Glacial, Till (sand portion)	Scotland	..	....	13½	Mackie (1896)
Summary		214	1 to 77	19.3	

TABLE 26.   Feldspar Content of Pre-Pleistocene Sandstones

Age	Number of Formations	Per cent Feldspar
Precambrian	10	9
Early Paleozoic	16	2
Late Paleozoic	24	4
Mesozoic	12	19
Cenozoic	12	27
Total	74 Average	12

or feldspathic graywackes. There seems to be a general increase in feldspar content from the early Paleozoic to the present (Table 26). The pre-Pennsylvanian sandstones average 2.2 per cent, whereas the Tertiary average is 27.3 per cent.

Feldspar occurs in shale also. The normative feldspar content, calculated from the chemical composition of the "average" shale, is given as 17.6 per cent by Leith and Mead (1915) and as 30.0 per cent by Clarke (1924). Owing to uncertainties underlying the calculations, the actual feldspar content is in doubt. Some shales, however, have been shown by x-ray analysis to have a high feldspar content (Gruner and Thiel, 1937). The feldspar is presumed to be largely or wholly authigenic.

A little feldspar, both detrital and authigenic, is reported from some limestones and dolomite. In rare cases it is abundant, as in the Altyn limestone of the Belt series (Precambrian), in which authigenic feldspar makes up as much as 40 per cent of some specimens (Daly, 1917).

Identification

In sediments the particular species of feldspar does not carry the same significance that it does in the igneous rocks, i.e., the classification of the rock does not depend on the kind of feldspar present. Moreover, the "statistical method" of Michel-Lévy, which assumes one and only one plagioclase to be present, is not a workable method of identification of the feldspars of sandstones, which may have as many kinds or varieties of feldspar as there are different feldspar-bearing source rocks in the region from which the sediment was derived.

The principal problem in identification is to distinguish the feldspars from quartz (Russell, 1935; Doeglas, 1940). This may be done by:

1. *Refractive index.* The potash and soda-rich feldspars have an index less than quartz (and less than Canada balsam). The calcium-rich members are of higher index than quartz. Oligoclase and andesine, however, are too near quartz to be readily distinguished on basis of index.

2. *Cleavage.* The feldspars exhibit two good cleavages at or nearly at right angles to each other, (001) perfect and (010) somewhat less so; also (110) imperfect. Quartz may show at times a rude cleavage (rhombohedral) or parting.

3. *Twinning.* The multiple twinning of the plagioclase is well known. Unfortunately many feldspars lie on the (010) plane and therefore do not show the twinning lamellae, but only an imperfect extinction. Quartz commonly shows optical anomalies which give rise to imperfect extinction also.

4. *Staining.* This method is regarded by most workers as the most rapid and reliable where quantitative data are required. It is accomplished by treatment of the polished surface, thin section, or suitably mounted grains with a solution of hydrofluoric acid. The material so treated is then washed and stained with a water-soluble organic dye, such as malachite green. The feldspars absorb the stain whereas the quartz does not.

Stability

Study of the granitic source rocks and the derived sands show a marked difference in the relative proportions of feldspar and quartz. The average igneous rock contains about one-half feldspar; the average sand has about one-fifth as much. It is clear, therefore, that the feldspar is much less stable than quartz, so that the residues derived from the plutonic rocks are impoverished in feldspar and enriched in quartz. The impoverishment may be the result of decomposition of the feldspars in the weathering profile or it may result from destruction of this mineral during transport by abrasive processes.

That feldspar is unstable in the soil profile and that the several varieties are not equally unstable is well shown by data published by Goldich (1938). Goldich showed that the lime-rich varieties are less stable than the pure alkali feldspars. This observation explains why the alkali feldspars, especially microcline, are so much more common in most sandstones than the lime-bearing plagioclases.

The stability of the feldspars *within* a sandstone is not the same, however, as that in the soil. Within many sediments the feldspar is not only stable but is prone to acquire secondary outgrowths. As the latter are nearly pure soda or pure potash feldspar it seems likely that these species are stable and that the lime-rich varieties are not so stable at the lower temperatures and pressures. In those sandstones, however, which have a carbonate cement, the detrital feldspar is commonly corroded by the cement. On the other hand, authigenic feldspar has grown in many limestones or dolomites. Quartz, as pointed out above, also shows this somewhat contradictory behavior.

Feldspar is supposed to be more susceptible to mechanical wear than quartz. Hence sands during transport would be enriched in quartz and impoverished in feldspar. Data on this subject are somewhat contradictory. Mackie (1896), for example, observed that the feldspar content of the Findhorn River of Scotland showed a decrease from 42 per cent feldspar to 21 per cent in 30 to 40 miles downstream. In the Mississippi River, however, Russell (1937) found the feldspar content of the stream sand to decrease from about 25 per cent near Cairo, Illinois, to about 20 per cent at the Gulf of Mexico some 1100 miles distant. Plumley (1948) found a decrease in feldspar content in the sands of Battle Creek, in the Black Hills of South Dakota, of about 50 per cent (35 per cent to 17 per cent) in 40–45 miles of downstream travel. This decrease is of the same order of magnitude as that observed by Mackie. In the Cheyenne River of the same region Plumley found the decline in feldspar content to be slight, from about 29 per cent to 24 per cent in 150 miles. One may conclude, perhaps, that feldspar is reduced rather rapidly in turbulent, high-gradient streams but is lost very slowly in larger streams. Much feldspar, therefore, would normally survive transport over long distances. It is probable, too, that vigorous beach action would tend to reduce materially the feldspar content of a sand. Some experimental work (Thiel, 1940; Friese, 1931) tends to confirm the field observations and show quartz to be mechanically more durable than orthoclase or microcline.

Provenance

The feldspar of sand grade is derived principally from the coarse-grained plutonic rocks, both the feldspar-bearing igneous rocks such as granite, and from the corresponding gneisses. To a lesser extent, it is derived from volcanic sources, both the effusive rocks and their pyroclastic equivalents.

The igneous feldspars include both the potash-bearing species and the soda-lime feldspars. The potash varieties are indicative of the more acid igneous rocks, notably the granites, whereas the lime-rich varieties, although present in many granites, are most characteristic of the igneous rocks of intermediate composition. Volcanic feldspar is characterized by its finely zoned structure, and in the more recent sediments, by its association with volcanic glass which in many cases appears as inclusions and as a thin pellicle around the feldspar grain. Metamorphic feldspar, is, on the whole, more prone to show numerous mineral inclusions, especially epidote. It is commonly saussuritized and otherwise altered.

Significance

The significance of detrital feldspar has been the subject of considerable controversy. The presence of a large quantity of feldspar in some sandstones (the arkoses) has led to the prevalent theory that certain special climatic conditions, which inhibited the decomposition of feldspar, were required to insure its survival and accumulation in the sediment (Mackie, 1899). Accordingly, very arid climate (implying absence of water and hence arrested chemical decay) or very cold climate (and hence much retarded chemical action) were postulated. Sufficient evidence has now accumulated to make necessary a modification of the rigorous climate theory. Barton (1916) has shown that arkosic sediments could and did form under moist, temperate conditions. Krynine (1935) *observed* arkose accumulation under humid tropical conditions, with average temperatures of 80 degrees and annual rainfall of 120 inches. Not only is feldspar seen to accumulate in sediments under such conditions, but critical study of the ancient arkose deposits yield abundant evidence that many of these were not the products of rigorous climate. Reed (1928), for example, has noted that the Eocene sandstones of California, which contain nearly 50 per cent of feldspar, yield a flora which could only have lived under warm humid conditions. The Catahoula sandstone of Texas, also of Eocene (?) age, contains a tropical coastal flora, although it also contains nearly 50 per cent feldspar (Goldman, 1915). As noted by Barton, the arkosic sandstones produced under humid conditions contain a high proportion of weathered or partially weathered feldspars. The mixture of brilliantly fresh with somewhat clouded and altered feldspar in the same sediments may be explained as the product of torrential erosion of a deeply dissected highland area underlain by feldspar-bearing rocks under warm climate conditions. A rigorous climate arkose should contain little or no altered feldspar.

If the feldspar content is independent of climate, what then is its significance? The weathering of feldspar requires not only a suitable climate but also a proper length of time. The *intensity* of the decay process is climate-controlled but the duration of *time* through which the processes of decomposition act is determined by relief. Regions of high relief undergo rapid erosion, so that feldspar escapes destruction and is contributed to the basin of deposition. If the relief is low, the rate of erosion is slow and if the climate is favorable, the feldspar will be wholly decomposed. The presence or absence of feldspar is therefore the result of the balance struck between the rate of decomposition and the rate of erosion. Detrital feldspar is therefore an index of both climatic rigor and tectonic activity. Whether, therefore, it is indicative of one rather than the other will have to be decided by other criteria than just the presence or absence of feldspar.

In general, it seems probable that high relief is more important than rigorous climate in the production of most highly feldspathic sediments. Sandstones of present-day and ancient orogenic belts seem to be richer in feldspar than those deposited in tectonically stable environments. In particular those sandstones deposited just prior to or contemporaneous with the principal orogenies are the most feldspathic.

Authigenic Feldspar

Authigenic and secondary feldspar occurs in rocks of all ages. It occurs in sandstones, shales, and limestone although its occurrence in shale is demonstrated or reported only rarely. In sandstone it appears most commonly as secondary rims or overgrowths on detrital feldspars. In limestones the feldspar forms minute euhedra (see p. 388).

REFERENCES CITED AND BIBLIOGRAPHY

Barton, D. C. (1916), Geological significance and genetic classification of arkose deposits, *J. Geol.*, vol. 24, pp. 417–449.

Boswell, P. G. H. (1933), *On the mineralogy of the sedimentary rocks*, London, Murby, pp. 87–96.

Clarke, F. W. (1924), Data of geochemistry, *U.S. Geol. Survey, Bull.* 770, p. 33.

Doeglas, D. J. (1940), Reliable and rapid method for distinguishing quartz and untwinned feldspar, *Am. Mineralogist*, vol. 25, pp. 286–296.

Friese, F. W. (1931), Untersuchung von Mineralen auf Abnutzbarkeit bei Verfrachtung im Wasser, *Mineralog. petrog. Mitt.*, vol. 41, new ser., pp. 1–7.

Goldich, S. S. (1938), A study in rock-weathering, *J. Geol.*, vol. 46, pp. 17–58.

Goldman, M. I. (1915), Petrographic evidence on the origin of the Catahoula sandstone, *Am. J. Sci.*, ser. 4, vol. 39, pp. 261–287.

Krynine, P. D. (1935), Arkose deposits in the humid tropics. A study in sedimentation in southern Mexico, *Am. J. Sci.*, ser. 5, vol. 29, pp. 353–363.

Krynine, P. D. (1948), The megascopic study and field classification of sedimentary rocks, *J. Geol.*, vol. 56, fig. 11.

Leith, C. K. and Mead, W. J. (1915), *Metamorphic geology*, New York, Holt, p. 76.

Mackie, Wm. (1896), The sands and sandstones of Eastern Moray, *Trans. Edinburgh Geol. Soc.*, vol. 7, pp. 148–172.

Mackie, Wm. (1899), The felspars present in sedimentary rocks as indicators of contemporaneous climates, *Trans. Edinburgh Geol. Soc.*, vol. 7, pp. 443–468.

Martens, J. H. C. (1929), The mineral composition of some sands from Quebec, Labrador, and Greenland, *Field Museum Nat. History, Pub.* 260.

Pettijohn, F. J. and Lundahl, A. C. (1943), Shape and roundness of Lake Erie beach sands, *J. Sediment Petrol.*, vol. 13, pp. 69–78.

Plumley, W. J. (1948), Black Hills terrace gravels: A study in sediment transport, *J. Geol.*, vol. 56, pp. 526–577.

Reed, R. D. (1928), The occurrence of feldspar in California sandstones, *Bull. Am. Assoc. Petroleum Geol.*, vol. 12, pp. 1023–1024.

Russell, R. D. (1935), Frequency percentage determinations of detrital quartz and feldspar, *J. Sediment. Petrol.*, vol. 5, pp. 109–114.

Russell, R. D. (1937), Mineral composition of Mississippi River sands, *Bull. Geol. Soc. Amer.*, vol. 48, pp. 1307–1348.

Thiel, G. A. (1940), The relative resistance to abrasion of mineral grains of sand size, *J. Sediment. Petrol.*, vol. 10, pp. 103–124.

Trowbridge, A. C. and Shepard, F. J. (1932), Sedimentation in Massachusetts Bay, *J. Sediment. Petrol.*, vol. 2, p. 29, etc.

Willman, H. B. (1942), Feldspar in Illinois sands, *Illinois State Geol. Survey, Rept. Invest. No. 79.*

Micas

The micas are found in sediments as both clastic and authigenic constituents. Clastic mica is most characteristic of the "microbreccias," both the graywacke type of sandstone and the arkoses, and of some tuffs. The micas are more common in the finer silty sandstones. Because of their flakiness they are not ordinarily deposited with the clean-washed sands. Biotite, being less stable than muscovite, is less abundant than the latter. It is commonly altered to chlorite, or more rarely to glauconite (Galliher, 1935).

The habit of the clastic micas varies from well-defined plates, some of which show good rounding, to very finely comminuted flakes and shreds. The excellent hexagonal plates of biotite in some sediments have been interpreted as volcanic, i.e., part of an infall from showers of ash (Krynine, 1940, p. 22). The well-rounded micas are said by Krynine (1940, p. 82) to indicate "a specialized set of sluggishly moving currents with gentle to-and-fro motion." Mica has been cited by some as a criterion of continental and littoral sedimentation (Lahee, 1941, p. 36).

The orientation of mica flakes, parallel to the bedding, imparts a sheen or luster to such bedding surfaces and probably enhances the original bedding-plane fissility.

Authigenic or secondary mica, sericite, and the clay-mica (illite), occur in a finely divided state in the shales and in the graywackes as a replacement of the clay minerals and even as a replacement of the detrital quartz. Chlorite has been noted in the same role.

"Heavy Minerals"

Among the minerals of the parent rock surviving destruction by weathering, abrasion, or interstratal solution are the so-called "heavy" minerals (specific gravity greater than bromoform, 2.85). These are the minor accessory minerals of the sandstones that are marked by a higher than average specific gravity. These minor constituents—rarely exceeding 1 per cent and more commonly forming less than 0.1 per cent of the rock—are derived from the very stable minor accessory minerals of the parent rock, or more exceptionally, they are the surviving remnant of the rather abundant but unstable mafic components of the source rocks. Zircon is an example of the stable minor accessories, and hornblende is representative of the more abundant but unstable mafic components of the source rock. The number and kinds of heavy minerals vary between wide limits. Although almost any mineral present in the source rock may appear in the sediment, only a relatively few species are common in the sands (Table 24).

If the heavy minerals are newly derived from the crystalline rock, they are comparatively little worn. Cleavage fragments and more or less euhedral crystals characterized the assemblage (Pl. 1, D). If, however, the "heavies" are derived from earlier sediments, the less stable species tend to be absent. The more stable varieties which survive show notable rounding (Pl. 1, E).

So rare are the heavy minerals that, except for an occasional grain or two, they are seldom seen in thin section. In order to investigate them, it is necessary that they be concentrated and isolated from the bulk of the light minerals with which they are associated. Methods for achieving this separation are discussed in the standard works on sedimentary petrography.

Study of the heavy-mineral residue has proved useful in some cases of stratigraphic correlation because, theoretically, each stratigraphic unit differs in some degree from every other in the character and abundance of its suite of minor accessory minerals.[7]

[7] A general summary of our knowledge of the individuality of sediments and of the usefulness of this characteristic for purposes of correlation is given by Boswell (1933, pp. 29–36, 60–72).

That the heavy mineral assemblage recovered from certain strata is distinct and unlike that of overlying or underlying strata has been confirmed many times. This observation is the basis for "petrographic correlation." Such correlation depends for its success not only on the recognition of a distinctive association of minerals, but also on peculiar varieties and on changing proportions of the constituent minerals with time. Such differences are secured by progressive denudation of a varied terrane. Each new rock mass unroofed contributes new species or varieties to the accumulating sediment or changes the proportions of the species already being deposited. Correlation is complicated, however, by reworking of earlier-formed sediments and incorporation of such materials in younger strata. A sediment produced by such reworking necessarily has many species in common with the deposit from which it was derived.

The heavy-mineral assemblage has also proved to be a useful guide to the kind of source rock from which the sediment came (Boswell, 1933, pp. 47–59). Some minerals are diagnostic of certain source rocks. Others, like quartz, are more nearly ubiquitous and occur in nearly all possible parent materials. In this case the varietal features, such as inclusions, serve as a guide to the rock type. Krynine's work on tourmaline in which he was able to recognize thirteen varieties or subtypes, illustrates the use of varietal features (Krynine, 1946).[8]

The more common mineral suites indicative of source rock types are given in Table 98 (p. 513).

The problem of interpreting heavy-mineral suites is complicated by the selective dissolution which the assemblage undergoes after deposition. The actual assemblage, therefore, is a function of both source rock composition and mineral stability (and hence capacity for survival both in the weathering profile and in the sediment itself) (Boswell, 1933, pp. 37–46). The question of stability has been treated at length elsewhere (p. 502) as has the problem of durability and resistance to abrasion (p. 558).

Rock Fragments

The coarser-grained rocks, both igneous and metamorphic, cannot by the nature of things appear as detrital grains in the medium-grained clastics. The latter are derived primarily by the disintegration of the former.

On the other hand, fragments of rocks of fine grain may appear in the arenites, and in some sands they form the dominant clastic constituent,

[8] Krynine described five main types of large-scale provenance. These are (1) granitic tourmaline, (2) pegmatitic tourmaline, (3) tourmaline from pegmatized, injected metamorphic terranes, (4) sedimentary authigenic tourmaline, and (5) tourmaline reworked from older sediment. Each tourmaline variety has distinctive optical and morphologic properties which enable one to recognize and correctly interpret the provenance of the sediment.

exceeding even quartz. Almost any fine-grained rock can appear as a detrital grain. Most common, however, are those most resistant to chemical or mechanical breakdown. Of special interest, therefore, is *chert*. This rock appears as a detrital constituent in the sandstones, both the orthoquartzites and the graywackes and subgraywackes. Its presence is one of the best indications that the containing rock has been derived from pre-existing sediments. In most cases the presence of chert is the record of the condensation of a great body of limestone in which it was once a minor constituent. Similar to chert and difficult to distinguish from metamorphic chert, are fine-grained *quartzite* particles. Those of coarser grain, consisting of but a few quartz grains, are more readily recognized. As is typical of quartzites, the constituent grains exhibit sutured contacts with one another.

Less common in most arenites but very abundant in the graywackes and subgraywackes, are fragments of *slate, phyllite,* and *schist*. These rock particles are recognized by the parallel arrangement of their constituent grains (micas and related minerals) and by the resulting rock cleavage and flakelike form of the fragment. Some of the shale or slate fragments have ill-defined boundaries, which suggest partial disintegration of the particle following burial. These may be in part intraformational debris.

Clastic *limestone* particles are rare in most arenites, but the calcarenites are composed of little else. Such particles, however, were probably of subaqueous fragmentation and are not the product of normal rock weathering.

The aphanitic igneous rocks, such as *rhyolite* and *trachyte*, may appear in some arenites and be abundant in those which contain a generous amount of volcanic glass and other tuffaceous debris. The microstructures and textures of these particles and their associations serve to identify them.

Clay Minerals

When the silicates of the primary crystalline rocks are decomposed by weathering, they yield, among other things, a group of minerals known as the "clay minerals." [9] These minerals are hydrated silicates of aluminum, commonly with some replacements by iron and magnesium. They are of fine grain, generally less than 5 microns (0.005 mm) in size, commonly even smaller, in some cases as small as a millimicron (0.000001 mm). These minerals not only occur in the residual clays formed by decomposition of the parent materials, but they are transported and deposited as sediments. They form a most important part of clays and shales and give these rocks their distinctive properties. They also occur mixed with precipitated carbonates in the argillaceous limestones, and mixed with sand-sized materials in the

---

[9] The study of the clay minerals has become a highly specialized branch of mineralogy. The interested reader is referred to the literature for a more complete treatment of this subject (Grim, 1939, 1942, 1953; Marshall, 1936).

graywackes and related rocks. They are therefore an important group of minerals in the sediments.

Mineralogy

Owing to their very fine size, the clay minerals are difficult to identify with certainty. Positive identification can rarely be made from the thin section alone. Special techniques for the isolation of the clay minerals and study by chemical, optical, x-ray, and other means are required for certain identification. The specialized techniques and laboratory equipment needed for the

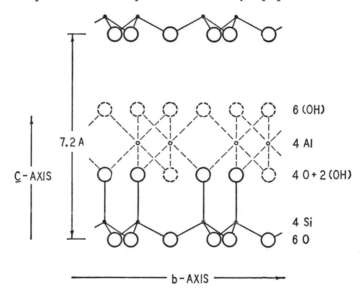

KAOLINITE $(OH)_8 Al_4 Si_4 O_{10}$

FIG. 46. Schematic presentation of the crystal structure of kaolinite. An example of a two-layer (1:1) clay mineral (after Gruner, from Grim, 1942, p. 246).

study of the clay minerals are not available to most geologists, and hence clay mineral analyses, like chemical analyses, are best made by the specialist. One should know, however, what the clay minerals are and what the salient facts concerning their origin are in order to understand fully the origin of the shales and other sediments in which these minerals occur.

The clay minerals are phyllosilicates, that is, they have a sheet structure somewhat like that of the micas. They consist essentially of two types of layers. One is a silica tetrahedral layer consisting of SiO_4 groups linked together to form an hexagonal network of the composition Si_4O_{10} repeated indefinitely. The other type of layer is the alumina or aluminum hydroxide unit, which consists of two sheets of close-packed oxygens or hydroxyls between which octahedrally coördinated aluminum atoms are embedded in such a position that they are equidistant from six oxygens or hydroxyls. Actually only two-thirds of the possible aluminum positions are occupied in this layer, which is the gibbsite structure. The mineral brucite has such a structure except that all possible aluminum positions are occupied.

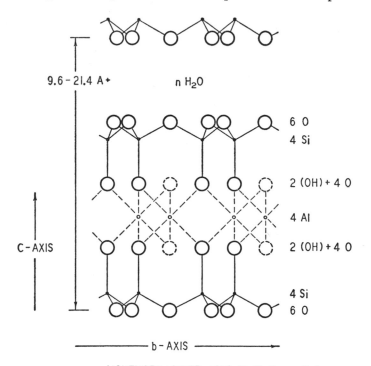

MONTMORILLONITE $(OH)_4 Al_4 Si_8 O_{20} \cdot n H_2O$

FIG. 47.   Schematic presentation of the crystal structure of montmorillonite. An example of a three-layer (2:1) clay mineral (after Hofmann, Endell, and Wilm, from Grim, 1942, p. 239).

The clay minerals belong to two contrasting groups. In one, the *kaolinite* group, the mineral is characterized by a two-layer (1:1 layer) lattice consisting of a gibbsite sheet and a silica tetrahedral sheet (Fig. 46). This lattice does not expand with varying water content, and no replacements by iron or magnesium in the gibbsite layer are known. The other group of clay minerals is characterized by a three-layer (2:1) lattice (Fig. 47). In this type of lattice there are two layers of tetrahedrally coördinated Si ions between which is sandwiched a gibbsite layer of octahedrally coördinated Al ions (or ions proxying for Al). Several important clay minerals belong to the three-layer group. In *montmorillonite* these three-layer units are loosely held together in the c-direction with water between them. The amount of water varies so that the c-dimension ranges from 9.6 to 21.4 angstrom units. The mineral is said to have an expanding lattice. The three-layer unit may also be held together by potassium which, owing to favorable ionic diameter and

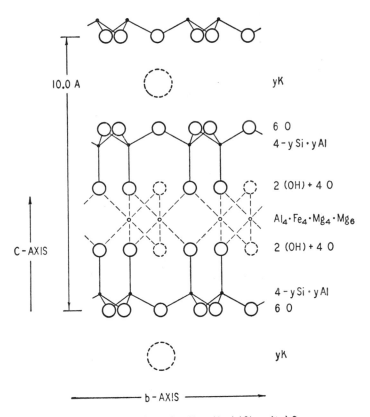

ILLITE $(OH)_4 K_y (Al_4 \cdot Fe_4 \cdot Mg_4 \cdot Mg_6) (Si_{8-y} \cdot Al_y) O_{20}$

FIG. 48. Schematic presentation of the crystal structure of the clay mica, illite (after Grim, Bray, and Bradley, from Grim, 1942, p. 244).

coördination capacity, binds the structure together so tightly that expansion is impossible (Fig. 48). The clay mineral thus formed is *illite* (the "clay mica"). The sedimentary *chlorites* can be thought of, perhaps, as being derived from montmorillonite by insertion of $Mg(OH)_2$ sheets between the three-layer units.

The principal clay mineral groups are therefore the kaolinite group, the montmorillonite group, the clay mica (illite), and the sedimentary chlorites.

The chief member of the kaolinite group (Ross and Kerr, 1931) is kaolin or *kaolinite*, which has the composition $(OH)_8Al_4Si_4O_{10}$. *Anauxite*, similar to kaolin except for a $SiO_2:Al_2O_3$ molecular ratio of about three instead of two, is much less common. *Dickite* and *nacrite*, similar to kaolinite in composition but with slightly different crystal form, are also members of this group. They rarely occur, however, in sediments.

The montmorillonite group (Ross and Hendricks, 1945), named for the chief member of the group, *montmorillonite*, has the composition $(OH)_4Al_4Si_8O_{10}\cdot xH_2O$. Magnesium generally replaces some of the aluminum in the lattice. *Beidellite*, which has a $SiO_2:Al_2O_3$ molecular ratio of three, and *nontronite*, in which ferric iron replaces the aluminum, are placed in the montmorillonite group.

The illite group (Grim, Bray, and Bradley, 1937) is a less well-known group. It is related to the white micas but differs in that it contains less potash and more water than do the micas proper. *Illite* has the general formula $(OH)_4K_y(Al_4\cdot Fe_4\cdot Mg_4\cdot Mg_6)Si_{8-y}\cdot Al_yO_{20}$, with y varying from 1 to 1.5.

The *chlorites* have only recently been recognized as constituents of certain clays and modern sediments (MacEwan, 1948). They are magnesium-rich minerals.

In addition to the principal groups listed above, there are some clay minerals of less common occurrence and of somewhat different crystal structure. These include *halloysite*, $(OH)_{16}Al_4Si_4O_6$, together with the less hydrated *metahalloysite*, $(OH)_8Al_4Si_4O_{10}$, and *allophane*, a noncrystalline mutual solution of silica, alumina, and water in varying proportions. Also found in some clays are the *vermiculite* and *palygorskites* (sepiolite and attapulgite). None of these minor clay minerals appears to be found in the shales or related rocks.

The clay minerals (excepting the rare palygorskites) are probably all monoclinic. All have a pronounced basal cleavage. A compilation of their optical properties is given by Grim and is reproduced here (Table 27).

"Base exchange" [10] is the exchange of ions in solution for those of a solid. It follows, therefore, that upon contact with a solid, the solution will undergo a change reciprocal to that of the solid. The clay minerals exhibit this property in varying, though marked, degrees. In general, montmorillonite shows a large exchange capacity, whereas kaolinite has only slight exchange ability. Illite is intermediate in behavior.

The exchangeable ion can be displaced only by other ions. It does not of itself move freely out into the liquid. The manner in which the exchangeable ions are held and the exact mechanism by means of which base exchange takes place is not fully understood. A discussion of rival concepts is not in

[10] For a good summary of this subject see Kelly (1939, 1942) or Grim (1953).

TABLE 27.   Optical Properties of Clay Minerals

		γ	β	a	γ-a	$2V$	Optic Sign	Orientation of Bisectrices
Kaolinite Group	Kaolinite-anauxite	1.570–1.560	1.569–1.559	1.563–1.553	0.006	24°–50°	(−)	$Bx_a = X \wedge base$ $normal = 1°$-$3\frac{1}{2}°$
	Nacrite	1.566–1.563	1.563–1.562	1.560–1.557	0.006	40°–90°	(+) or (−)	$Bx_a = X \wedge base$ $normal = 10°$-$12°$
	Dickite	1.566	1.563–1.561	1.560	0.006	52°–80°	(+)	$Bx_a = X \wedge base$ Normal $= 15°$-$20°$
Montmorillonite Group	Montmorillonite	1.530–1.500		1.505–1.470	0.035–0.025	7°–25°	(−)	$Bx_a = X$ about ⊥ to base
	Beidellite	1.560–1.530		1.530–1.500	0.035–0.025	small	(−)	do
	Nontronite	1.610–1.560		1.575–1.530	0.035–0.030	small	(−)	do
Illite Group		1.605–1.565		1.570–1.535	0.035–0.030	small	(−)	do
Halloysite Group	Metahalloysite	mean index 1.561–1.549			very slight			
	Halloysite	mean index 1.542–1.526			very slight			
Allophane		amorphous: 1.496–1.470						

NOTE: Table abbreviated from R. E. Grim. Properties of clay, in *Recent Marine Sediments,* Tulsa, Amer. Association Petroleum Geologist, 1939, p. 470.

order here. The replacing power of the several ions, however, is variable. There is also a definite order of replaceability, namely, Na < K < Mg < Ca < H which means that hydrogen will replace calcium, etc.

Geology

Although the mineralogy of clay is now becoming rather well understood, the geology of this material is as yet far from clear. The occurrence, origin, and transformation of the clay minerals are poorly known. As recently as 1942 Kelly concluded that "it is not possible at present to trace the clay minerals of soils to specific parent-rocks or to specific conditions of weathering," i.e., climate. Kaolin, montmorillonite, and illite all appear to arise from the weathering of many kinds of rocks under various climatic conditions. All, therefore, are found in residual soils. Certain general requirements for each of the major clay mineral groups have been specified (Keller, 1955). Kaolinite seems to require an acid environment from which Ca, Mg, and Fe are effectively removed; montmorillonite, on the other hand, requires an alkaline environment in which Mg, ferrous Fe, and Ca are present. Partial or incomplete leaching tends to yield a montmorillonite clay; thorough leaching is conducive to formation of a kaolinitic residue. Illite seems to be formed in the oceans and requires an alkaline environment and the presence of Ca, Mg, ferrous iron, and potassium. The conditions under which the chloritic clay minerals form are less clear. Since they contain considerable magnesium, their formation would proceed more rapidly in a marine environment rather than one subject to strong leaching.

Some clay minerals themselves can be weathered. Extraction of the potassium from illite, for example, is possible under certain climatic conditions. Kaolin may be altered to bauxite. The changes are reversible, however, and in the proper environment the degraded illite may take up potassium; the bauxite may even be converted to kaolinite (Gordon and Tracy, 1952).

Although the clay minerals occur in recent sediments, only the mineralogy of the modern marine sediments is reasonably well known. Some effort has been made to relate the type of clay mineral to the environment of deposition on the notion that the clay materials that enter the environment will be modified or transformed to those stable within the environmental complex. Kaolinite, for example, is presumed to characterize an acid, fresh-water environment; illite and the chloritic clay minerals are presumed to be products of transformation of montmorillonite or perhaps kaolinite in the marine environment. Most pronounced diagenetic change is the reconstitution of illite from "degraded" or depotassicated illite (Grim, Dietz, and Bradley, 1949). Too little is known of the distribution of clay minerals in present-day marine environments. Some observations suggest that the distribution of the clay minerals is due to factors at present unknown and perhaps not due to diagenetic reactions in the present environment (van Andel, 1954).

The occurrence and distribution of the clay minerals in the "fossil" sediments is least known. Illite appears to be the dominant mineral in most shales; chloritic material, however, is also common. Montmorillonite is likely to be rare in the Paleozoic or older lutites and abundant only in those of Mesozoic or younger age. Kaolinite is common in all shales but only in minor amounts. Millot (1949) has attempted to correlate the clay minerals of the shales and mudstones with the environment of deposition as established by paleontologic and stratigraphic evidence. Dominant in marine shales was illite; kaolinite was subordinate. Montmorillonite characterized the lagoonal sediment. Kaolinite is the characteristic mineral of an acid fresh-water environment whereas illite or montmorillonite signify an alkaline or soda lake. The presumed differences, however, seem not to be applicable to the fresh, brackish, and marine facies of the Molasse (Lemcke et al., 1953, p. 57). Some students of shales even deny any correlation between the clay mineralogy and the environment, and attribute differences between one shale and the next as a record of variations in character and of the source rocks and the climate which prevailed at the time of accumulation.

Montmorillonite and kaolinite tend to disappear in sediments with increasing age; illitic and chloritic materials take their place.

The salient facts relative to the occurrence of the clay minerals are summarized in Table 28.

TABLE 28. Occurrence of Clay Minerals

	Soils	Recent Marine Sediments	Ancient Sediments	Hydrothermal Materials
Kaolinite Group				
Kaolinite	common	common	common	present?
Anauxite	very rare	?	very rare	?
Nacrite	none	?	?	present
Dickite	none	?	?	present
Montmorillonite Group	very common	common	common in post-Paleozoic only	present?
Illite Group	present (unstable?)	very common	very common	?
Chlorite Group	present (unstable?)	present	common	present

Oxides of Iron and Alumina

The sesquioxides of iron and alumina are widely distributed among the products of weathering. The oxides of iron of importance are (1) limonite, (2) goethite, (3) hematite and magnetite.[11] The first of these is an ill-defined amorphous product of hardening of gel masses of hydrous basic ferric oxide, $FeO(OH) \cdot nH_2O$. Such material is isotropic, without internal structure, and externally colloform.

Goethite, $HFeO_2$, is a crystalline substance that is characterized by a radial fibrous habit. It is commonly found as reniform, botryoidal, or other colloform masses with an internal concentric or radial (or both) fibrous structure.

Hematite, Fe_2O_3, is of more varied character and may be of specular, compact columnar, or ocherous habit.

The relations between these minerals and their occurrence in sedimentary rocks is but partially known. In sediments, at least, the three may form a series representing progressive dehydration and hardening of a gel, analogous to that shown by silica (Crosby, 1891). Certain it is that the external forms of goethite suggest an original gel state; in some cases the hematite exhibits a similar structure. It is, perhaps, pseudomorphic after goethite.

Sedimentary magnetite, Fe_3O_4, is also known. It is most common as a "heavy mineral" of sand size, in which case it is a stable detrital left from the

[11] For full description, see Palache, Berman, and Frondel (1944, pp. 525–532, 680–696).

breakdown of magnetite-bearing crystalline rocks. Rarely it appears as a low-temperature precipitate in some iron formations.

The iron oxides play the role of both pigment and cement in the clastic sediments. The "red beds" are shales and sandstones which owe their red coloration to disseminated hematite. In the sandstones the hematite forms a thin film on the sand grains, although in a few cases it may constitute the cement. Less commonly the iron oxides occur as an alteration product of siderite or other ferrous iron compounds. Many shales and sandstones buff or brown in outcrops are gray in deep cuts and drill core. The iron oxides, in rare cases, form bedded deposits; best known are the oolitic hematites. These are regarded by most students as original precipitates.

The iron oxides tend to accumulate in residual soils, and such deposits if exceptionally rich in iron constitute the ferruginous laterites. In the normal course of events, however, the iron oxides form "hardpans" in some soils or are precipitated as a bog iron or more commonly are dispersed in a finely divided state and are mechanically transported and deposited with the finest clay fraction of many muds.

Aluminum hydrate (gibbsite) is rare and virtually unknown as a constituent of sedimentary rocks. Like the ferric hydroxides it may occur as an important constituent of some soils, notably the laterites. The latter are products of tropical weathering.

The properties of the oxides and hydroxides or iron and aluminum are summarized in Table 29.

TABLE 29. Sedimentary Oxides and Hydroxides of Iron and Alumina

Mineral	Composition	Structure	Microscopical Characteristics [a]				Remarks
			Color	Median Index	Bire-fringence	Other Optical Properties	
"Limonite"	$FeO(OH) \cdot nH_2O$	colloform; amorphous	trans-lucent; yellow	2.0–2.1	0 to weak		soluble in hot HCl
Goethite	$HFeO_2$	colloform; fibrous	yellow, orange	2.1–2.3	0.06–0.14	pleochroic; strong dispersion	soluble in hot HCl
Hematite	Fe_2O_3	scaly or specular; fibrous; earthy	blood red	3.2[b]	0.28	weakly pleochroic	soluble in HCl
Bauxite	$Al_2O_3 \cdot nH_2O$	pisolitic, concre-tionary; amorphous	colorless	1.56–1.61	0		attacked by alkalies
Gibbsite	$Al_2O_3 \cdot 3H_2O$	finely lamellar; concre-tionary	colorless	1.55–1.57	0.022	positive; 2V small	soluble in H_2SO_4 and hot NaOH

[a] Taken from Winchell, 1933.
[b] N_o.

REFERENCES CITED AND BIBLIOGRAPHY

Boswell, P. G. H. (1933), *On the mineralogy of sedimentary rocks*, London, Murby.

Galliher, E. W. (1935), Geology of glauconite, *Bull. Am. Assoc. Petroleum Geol.*, vol. 19, pp. 1569–1601.

Gordon, M., and Tracey, J. I. (1952), Origin of the Arkansas bauxite deposits, *Problems of clay and laterite genesis*, Am. Inst. Mining Engrs.

Grim, R. E. (1939), Properties of clay, in *Recent marine sediments*, Tulsa, Am. Assoc. Petroleum Geol., pp. 466–495.

Grim, R. E. (1942), Modern concepts of clay materials, *J. Geol.*, vol. 50, pp. 225–275.

Grim, R. E. (1953), *Clay mineralogy*, New York, McGraw-Hill.

Grim, R. E., Bray, R. M., and Bradley, W. F. (1937), The mica in argillaceous sediments, *Am. Mineralogist*, vol. 22, pp. 813–829.

Grim, R. E., Dietz, R. S., and Bradley, W. F. (1949), Clay mineral composition of some sediments from the Pacific Ocean off the California coast and the Gulf of California, *Bull. Geol. Soc. Amer.*, vol. 60, pp. 1785–1808.

Hendricks, S. B. (1942), Lattice structure of clay minerals and some properties of clays, *J. Geol.*, vol. 50, pp. 276–290.

Keller, W. D. (1955), *The principles of chemical weathering*, Columbia, Mo., Lucas.

Kelly, W. P. (1939), Base exchange in relation to sediments, in *Recent marine sediments*, Tulsa, Amer. Assoc. Petroleum Geol., pp. 454–465.

Kelly, W. P. (1942), Modern clay researches in relation to agriculture, *J. Geol.*, vol. 50, pp. 307–315.

Krynine, P. D. (1940), Petrology and genesis of the Third Bradford Sand, *Penn. State Coll. Bull.* 29.

Krynine, P. D. (1946), The tourmaline group in sediments, *J. Geol.*, vol. 54, pp. 65–87.

Lahee, F. H. (1941), *Field geology* (5th ed.), New York, McGraw-Hill, p. 39.

Lemcke, K., von Engelhardt, W., and Fuchtbauer, H. (1953), Geologische und sedimentpetrographische Untersuchungen im Westteil der ungefalteten Molasse des suddeutschen Alpenvorlandes, *Beihefte Geol. Jahrb.*, vol. 11.

MacEwan, D. M. C. (1948), Chlorites and vermiculites in soil clays, *Verre et silicates ind.*, vol. 13, pp. 41–46 (cited by Grim, 1953).

Marshall, C. E. (1936), The constitution of the clay minerals, *Science Progr.*, vol. 30, pp. 422–433.

Millot, G. (1949), Relations entre la constitution et la genese des roches argileuses, *Bull. Assoc. Ingen. Geol. de l'Univ. Nancy*, vol. 2.

Palache, G., Berman, H., and Frondel, C. (1944), *Dana's system of mineralogy*, New York, Wiley, vol. 1, pp. 680–696.

Riviere, A., and Visse, L. (1954), L'origine des mineraux des sediments marins, *Bull. Soc. Geol. France*, ser. 6, vol. 4, pp. 467–473.

Ross, C. S. (1943), Clays and soils in relation to geologic processes, *J. Wash. Acad. Sci.*, vol. 33, pp. 225–235.

Ross, C. S. and Kerr, P. F. (1931), The kaolin minerals, *U.S. Geol. Survey,*
Prof. Paper 165E, pp. 151–175.

Ross, C. S. (1931), The clay minerals and their identity, *J. Sediment Petrol.,*
vol. 1, pp. 55–65.

Ross, C. S. (1934), Halloysite and allophane, *U.S. Geol. Surv., Prof. Paper*
185G, pp. 135–148.

Ross, C. S. and Hendricks, S. B. (1945), Minerals of the montmorillonite group,
U.S. Geol. Survey, Prof. Paper 205B, pp. 23–77.

Van Andel, Tj. and Postma, H. (1954), Recent sediments of the Gulf of Paria,
Verhandel. Koninkl. Ned. Akad. Wetenschap., vol. 20, no. 5.

Winchell, A. N. (1933), *Elements of optical mineralogy* (3d ed.), Part 2, New
York, Wiley.

THE CHEMICAL PRECIPITATES

Carbonates

Most common of the materials precipitated directly, or in some cases
through the intervention of organisms, are the carbonates. Of these calcite
and dolomite are the most abundant; less so are aragonite, ankerite, and
siderite. All except aragonite are hexagonal, uniaxial, negative, and with excellent rhombohedral ($10\bar{1}1$) cleavage. Dolomite, siderite, and ankerite have
curved cleavage faces. Aragonite is orthorhombic. The principal properties
of these carbonates are summarized in Table 30.

TABLE 30.   Properties of Common Carbonate Minerals (mainly after Larsen, 1921)

Mineral	Composition	Specific Gravity	Indices	Index on Cleavage[b]	Birefringence	Solubility Cold Dil. HCL	Remarks
Calcite	$CaCO_3$	2.71	1.658 1.486	1.566	0.172	marked	colorless in section
Dolomite	$CaMg(CO_3)_2$	2.87	1.681 1.500	1.588	0.181	slow	rhombic habit; colorless
Siderite	$FeCO_3$	3.89	1.875 1.633	1.747	0.242	insol.	alters to limonite; yellow
Ankerite	$Ca(Mg \cdot Fe)(CO_3)_2$	2.9–3.1	1.698[a] 1.518[a]		0.180[a]	slow	
Aragonite	$CaCO_3$	2.94	1.686 1.682 1.531		0.155	marked	biaxial (−); 2V 18°; acicular; colorless

[a] 10.7 per cent $FeCO_3$.
[b] After Winchell (1933).

PLATE I

SAND GRAINS

A: Angular quartz sand, ordinary light, $\times 35$. Artificially crushed and screened.

B: Rounded quartz sand, ordinary light, $\times 35$. St. Peter sandstone (Ordovician), St. Paul, Minn.

C: Secondary enlargement of quartz, ordinary light, $\times 35$. St. Peter sandstone, Klondike, Missouri.

Pyramidal outgrowths of limpid quartz shown on several grains.

D: Heavy minerals from Jorgan sand, Cleveland County, North Carolina, ordinary light, $\times 60$.

Principally euhedral to slightly worn zircon.

E: Heavy minerals from St. Peter sandstone, ordinary light, $\times 60$.

Mainly well-rounded zircon (Z) and tourmaline (T) (Thiel, *Bull., Geol. Soc. Amer.*, vol. 46, 1935, pl. 48).

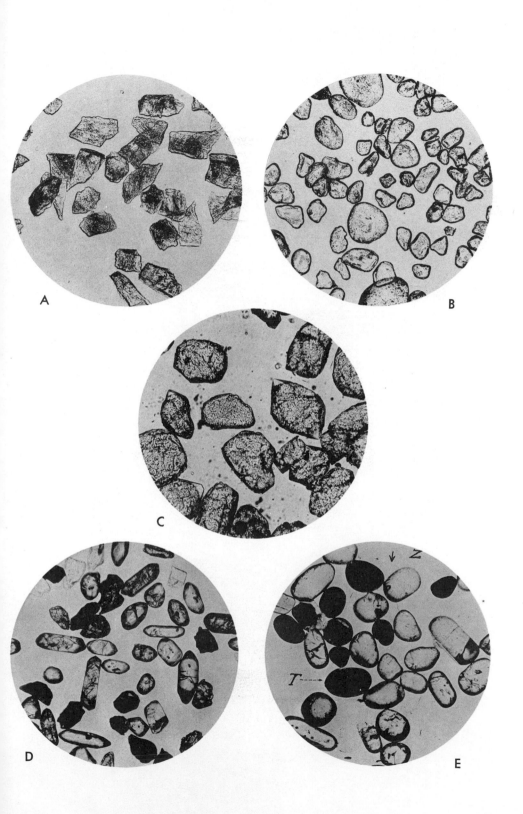

A

B

C

D   E

PLATE 2

CURRENT STRUCTURES I

Top: Cross-bedded Sturgeon quartzite, Precambrian, Dickinson County, Michigan.

Cross-bedded layer about seven inches thick; inclination of cross laminations is about twenty-five degrees.

Center: Ripple-marked Baraboo quartzite, Precambrian, Devils Lake, Wisconsin.

Bottom: Flow casts on base of siltstone bed, Upper Devonian, New Brunswick.

Length of specimen about nine inches.

Calcite

Calcite is most difficult to distinguish from dolomite; the definitive properties of calcite and dolomite are summarized in Table 30.

The normal crystal habit of calcite is scalenohedral; seldom does it assume the rhombic form characteristic of dolomite. Except for certain vein and geode fillings, and the rare "sand crystals," calcite rarely shows any euhedral outlines but forms instead an anhedral mosaic. In oolites it may show a radial structure.

Calcite occurs as a crystalline or microcrystalline aggregate forming the bulk of the limestones and an appreciable part of the calcareous sandstones and shales, as a constituent of many shells, nearly all calcareous fossils, and as a constituent of minor concretionary bodies in noncalcareous rocks, especially the clays and shales.

The calcite of some limestones (the calcarenites) is present as both the detrital and the cementing material. The detritus, however, is intrabasinal in origin and is largely shell debris; the calcite cement is water clear and readily distinguished from the calcitic fragmental debris. Some calcite is an authigenic modification of aragonite. Aragonite is unstable and in the older rocks is converted to calcite.

Aragonite

Aragonite is the form commonly assumed by calcium carbonate when it is precipitated inorganically. Many oolites seem to have formed originally of concentric layers of aragonite which were later converted either to an anhedral mosaic of calcite, or more commonly, to calcite with radial arrangement.

Aragonite is the chief constituent of pelecypod and gastropod shells and of some corals. The aragonite of such organic structures, like that of the oolites, is spontaneously changed to the more stable calcite. Shells which originally consisted of this mineral are found only as open molds or as coarsely crystalline calcite. The instability of aragonite precludes its occurrence in the older limestones.[12]

Dolomite

Dolomite is intimately associated with calcite in some limestones. It is commonly difficult to distinguish between these two minerals. The chief differences are summarized in Table 31. Both calcite and dolomite may show lamellar twinning. As pointed out elsewhere (p. 421), dolomite is not com-

---

[12] A good discussion of the properties and occurrence of both aragonite and calcite is given by Johnston, Merwin, and Williamson (1916). The factors governing the distribution and occurrence of calcite and aragonite in the shell materials have been described by Lowenstam (1954).

monly primary; it is in most cases a replacement of calcite or other mineral. No shell structures are originally dolomite; dolomitic shells therefore are a product of postdepositional replacement. Scattered dolomite rhombs or irregular aggregates or patches of dolomite may be products of diagenetic differentiation or the unmixing of a biochemically formed magnesian calcite.

TABLE 31.   Chief Differences Between Calcite and Dolomite

	Calcite	Dolomite
Crystal Habit (in rocks)	anhedral; rarely rhombohedral	rhombohedral; may be zoned
Refractive Indices	O 1.658	O 1.680
	E 1.486	E 1.501
On Cleavage Face	1.566	1.588
Birefringence	0.172	0.179
Specific Gravity	2.71	2.87
Solubility in Acid	readily soluble in cold dilute acid	very slowly soluble in cold dilute acid
Staining[a]	readily takes a silver chromate stain	not stained by silver chromate
Weathering	does not become buff or pink	weathers buff or pink owing to small amount $FeCO_3$ present

[a] See Rodgers (1940) for use of stains.

Ankerite

Ankerite or ferriferous dolomite is rarely identified in sediments although it is said to occur in some graywackes as small isolated patches replacing both the coarser detrital grains, especially feldspar, and the matrix.

Siderite

Siderite, like ankerite, is not often reported from the sediments. It is, however, a constituent of certain argillaceous nodular masses ("clay ironstone concretions") and the principal component of some rare sedimentary strata—the sideritic ironstones. The bedded siderites are associated with some iron silicates, commonly chamosite, and bedded cherts. Siderite is also present in some limestones, a few of which are more or less sideritized. The circumstances leading to the formation of these siderite-rich rocks are not well understood; the problem of siderite precipitation is reviewed elsewhere (p. 460).

Siderite is probably a more common constituent of many sandstones, as a minor cement, and some shales than is generally believed. Owing to its susceptibility to oxidation, it is readily destroyed in the outcrop. Many of the buff-colored sandstones and yellow shales are gray in drill cores or in very fresh deep cuts. No doubt the change in color is related to oxidation; in many cases the mineral oxidized is siderite.

Silica

Silica may be precipitated as quartz, chalcedony, or as opal.

The chemically precipitated *quartz* of the sedimentary rocks is the low-temperature form of that mineral. It appears as secondary outgrowths on detrital quartz (p. 663) or as microscopic, doubly terminated crystals in limestone and dolomite. It is present in some cherts but appears to be derived from chalcedony. The quartz of sediments has all the usual properties of that mineral.

Chalcedony is the dominant constituent of most cherts. It is a natural microscopic fibrous silica with atomic arrangement of quartz. Sosman (1927) did not regard chalcedony as a variety of quartz because of its distinctive properties. It is dominantly fibrous, shows negative elongation, indices of 1.533 and 1.540, a birefringence of 0.009 to 0.011, density of 2.55 to 2.63, an absence of inversion at 573° C, and a heat capacity unlike that of quartz. Although chalcedony consists dominantly of microfibrous silica, some investigators have explained the anomalous properties by supposing that various amounts of submicroscopic amorphous silica or opal were present. Washburn and Navais (1922) concluded that "flint and chalcedony consist of colloidal quartz. In the purer form of chalcedony, the colloid is of the gel type and the individual colloid particles are microscopic or submicroscopic in size." Sosman, however, emphasized shape, not size, of the particles and notes that the particles are threadlike or fibrous. If these are short and randomly oriented, the fracture is conchoidal, as in flint or chert. Electron micrographs of chalcedonic or fibrous silica show that the material has a spongy texture presumed to be due to minute spherical water-filled cavities. There is no evidence of fibrous structure or that opal is present (Folk and Weaver, 1952).

Tarr's study of thin sections (1926, 1938) convinced him that although chalcedony predominates in chert, quartz is also present, and in some deposits it is predominant. He thought that the microfibrous forms of chalcedony would in time pass over into quartz. The sequence of changes probably are (1) original hydrous gel (opal), (2) chalcedony, and (3) quartz. James (1954) has shown that the grain size (of quartz) in some Precambrian cherts is closely correlated with the degree of metamorphism; the higher the grade, the coarser the chert.

Opal, $SiO_2 \cdot nH_2O$, is primarily amorphous silica with some water which is perhaps merely absorbed. It is marked by its low density, about 2.1, and its solubility in KOH. It has a low index which varies from 1.38 to 1.46, depending on the water content (Taliaferro, 1935). Opal occurs in many cherts and is the dominant constituent of some. The dehydration of this material gives rise to certain shrinkage effects, notably concentrically banded spheroids (Taliaferro, 1934).

Chemically precipitated silica occurs intimately mixed with certain sediments, as discrete bodies in other sediments, and as relatively pure deposits devoid of foreign materials. The silica occurs as quartz or as the mineralogic complex known as chert. The silica may have been deposited penecontemporaneously with the associated materials or it may be a postdepositional replacement (Storz, 1928).

TABLE 32. Mineralogical Classification and Occurrence of Sedimentary Silica

I. Quartz
    1. Detrital grains (mainly sandstones and silts)
    2. Secondary (authigenic) quartz
        a. Overgrowths on detrital quartz
        b. Euhedra (in limestones and related rocks)
        c. Veins, geodes, etc.

II. Chalcedony
    1. Detrital chert (mainly sandstones)
    2. Precipitated chalcedony
        a. Chert nodules
        b. Bedded cherts
        c. Spherulites (in limestones); oolites
        d. Cement (in sandstones)

III. Opal
    1. Chert nodules and beds
    2. Cement of sandstones
    3. Siliceous earths (diatomite)

IV. Cristobalite
    1. Crystallites in opal
    2. Crystallites in bentonitic clays

Silicates

Few silicates are sedimentary precipitates; most silicates in sediments are either undecomposed residues from the source rock or the secondary products of weathering; both are transported and deposited mechanically. Silicates are also formed in the sediment after deposition—the authigenic feldspars, micas, and chlorites, for example. These are diagenetic rather than original precipitates. Complex silicates seem to be characteristic of magmatic or metamorphic rather than sedimentary environments.

The silicates, which in rare cases form a large or important part of the deposit in which they occur, are the iron-bearing silicates glauconite, chamosite, greenalite, minnesotaite, and stilpnomelane. Some or even all of these may be strictly diagenetic rather than original precipitates.

Of these glauconite is the most widespread. It occurs in many Paleozoic or younger marine sandstones or limestones. It is found and presumed to be forming on the present-day sea floor. Glauconite rarely occurs as the chief constituent of the rock; it is generally an accessory. Chamosite is a principal component of some of the Paleozoic or younger ironstones; greenalite is most characteristic of some of the Lake Superior iron formations; stilpnomelane is found in both Precambrian and later ironstones; minnesotaite is less well known and has thus far been reported only from the Precambrian. Some iron-rich chlorites (aphrosiderite and thuringite) are also present in some ironstones.

Chamosite

Chamosite is an important constituent of the marine clay ironstones, which are chemically precipitated muds more or less enriched with siderite. Chamosite is mixed with calcite, clay, and quartz in the shales and sandstones associated with some of the ironstones.

Chamosite is a chlorite. Analyses show that it has the composition $2SiO_2 \cdot Al_2O_3 \cdot 3FeO \cdot nH_2O$ with some Fe_2O_3 replacing the Al_2O_3 and some MgO replacing the FeO (Hallimond, 1925). Accordingly it has a micaceous habit, is marked by perfect cleavage; the pleochroism is pale green or colorless to dark olive-green parallel with cleavage; mean index near 1.62; optically biaxial negative with small 2V; birefringence lower than quartz; specific gravity is near 3.0 to 3.5. Chamosite is completely soluble in hot dilute (2N) HCl. It is bleached by cold dilute sulfuric acid.

Chamosite may occur in many minute scales that are oriented parallel to the bedding so as to give the mudstone a weak birefringence and composite extinction; or it may occur as concentric shelled oolites (Pl 34, E) in a chamosite matrix or be associated with sand grains, shell debris, etc.

According to Hallimond, chamosite apparently was an original precipitate, perhaps an amorphous gel which later assumed the form it now shows, or it may have originated by progressive replacement of clay in which oolites of the same material may or may not have formed. According to Deverin (1945) chamosite is not an original precipitate but is rather a replacement of carbonate detritus, chiefly echinoderm debris.

Glauconite

Glauconite is a complex silicate of iron, aluminum, magnesium, and unlike the other iron-bearing silicates, it contains potassium. Its composition is expressed as $KMg(Fe, Al)(SiO_3)_6 \cdot 3H_2O$. Glauconite is commonly granular, generally as small, sand-sized, rounded, ovoid, papilliform, spherical, or polylobate in form. Their surfaces are lustrous; in some cases cracked. The interior is a fine-grained or microcrystalline aggregate. In thin section the glauconite granules are olive- to grass-green. Indices vary from 1.597 to 1.630 (beta 1.618 to 1.630); birefringence is moderate (0.013 to 0.027). Oxidation results in change from a green to a yellow or yellow-brown color.

Glauconite grains occur in sandstones and in limestone—notably the clastic limestones. Probably the glauconite granules are detrital because they are of the same order of size as is the associated quartz and carbonate detritus, and they are cemented in the same manner as the other grains (Pl. 29, E). The glauconite grains may show syneresis cracks and shrinkage away from the matrix in which they are embedded. In dolomites they may show partial replacement by dolomite (Pl. 29, F).

Not all glauconite has a detrital habit. In one case at least it forms a jacket or envelope surrounding common heavy minerals (Grim, 1936); in still other cases it occupies openings in fossils (Takahashi, 1939) and in still others it is finely divided and disseminated (in shales).

Other Iron-bearing Silicates

Other iron-bearing silicates include stilpnomelane, greenalite, minnesotaite, and some iron-rich chlorites.

Stilpnomelane is a hydrous iron silicate of chlorite-like character containing both ferrous and ferric iron and small amounts of alumina and magnesium. It occurs as microscopic needles and plates of dark brown to medium olive-green color. Pleochroism is strong. Indices are highly variable; alpha varies from 1.54 to 1.625 and gamma ranges from 1.594 to 1.735. The higher values are associated with a greater content of ferric iron. Stilpnomelane occurs in the silicate ironstones as disseminated micaceous grains or in thin silicate-rich laminations in the sideritic ironstones.

Minnesotaite has the structure of a talc to which it is equivalent in composition if the magnesium be almost wholly replaced by ferrous iron. It occurs as colorless microscopic needles and plates. It is soft, light greenish-gray in hand specimen. It is marked by parallel extinction, small optic angle, fairly high birefringence (0.035). Alpha and gamma are 1.580 and 1.615, respectively. Elongation is positive. Minnesotaite occurs in some of the silicate iron formations of the Lake Superior district (Gruner, 1946; James, 1954).

Greenalite is a ferrous silicate of doubtful composition ($FeSiO_3 \cdot nH_2O$?) in which there is some ferric iron and a little magnesium. It is related to glauconite and chamosite. It is olive- to yellow-green in color, is isotropic, has a refractive index near 1.65 and a specific gravity of about 2.8. Greenalite is soluble in concentrated hydrochloric acid. It has a granular habit like that of glauconite (Pl. 34, F). Greenalite is a major constituent of the ferrugi nous cherts of the Mesabi Range prior to their oxidation and leaching. It is regarded by Leith (1903) as a primary colloidal precipitate formed by interaction of ferrous salts and colloidal silica in a standing body of water.

Chlorite

Iron-rich chlorite (aphrosiderite and possibly thuringite) has been shown to be a major constituent of the iron formation in the Iron River and Crystal Falls districts (James, 1951). It occurs as exceedingly fine-grained material associated with siderite and magnetite. As it is restricted to those rocks that contain recognizable clastic materials it is considered by James (1954) to be a product of reaction between iron-rich sea water and the finer fraction of the clastic load.

Other Silicates

Other silicates, the products of diagenesis, include feldspar and various clay minerals. These have been described elsewhere.

Phosphates

The only common phosphate mineral in sediments is collophane (Rogers, 1922). It is a tricalcium phosphate of somewhat variable composition, the formula being usually given as $3Ca_3(PO_4)_2 \cdot nCa(CO_3,F_2,O)(H_2O)_x$. Collophane is amorphous; refractive index varies from 1.57 to 1.62; color is light yellow to brown in thin section. In habit it is massive, oolitic, colloform granular, or a replacement of shell or bone with retention of original internal structure.

Collophane occurs as scattered grains or pellets in the phosphatic limestones, as isolated nodules, or as the chief constituent of bone beds and bedded phosphorites. It may replace other materials, especially in the phosphatized limestones.

Sulfides

Marcasite and pyrite occur as minor constituents of most sediments. They are especially abundant in rocks that are rich in organic matter, such as the black shales and coal beds. They are less common, though by no means rare, in many limestones and even sandstones. The sulfide of coal is said to be marcasite; that of other rocks, pyrite. Some muds deposited at the present time under anaerobic conditions owe their black color to *melnikovite*, the amorphous disulfide of iron.

Marcasite and pyrite occur as nodules, as scattered crystals or spherulites and as disseminated microcrystalline grains. Only rarely do they form the dominant constituent of the rock (p. 450). Even in this case the sulfide beds are thin and interstratified with other rocks, usually black shale (Pl. 33).

Marcasite is very unstable and undergoes oxidation, which is accompanied by swelling and efflorescence. Pyrite is more stable although in the finely divided state, it also oxidizes.

Sulfates

Three common sulfate minerals are known in sedimentary rocks, namely gypsum, anhydrite, and barite. Gypsum and anhydrite may occur in the relatively pure state as a chemical deposit of considerable thickness. Barite, on the other hand, occurs only as nodules (rosettes) or as a minor authigenic cement of some sandstones. Anhydrite is also common as a minor authigenic constituent of sandstones; gypsum forms authigenic crystals or crystal aggregates in some clays and shales.

The properties of the three common sulfates are summarized in Table 33. All are normally colorless.

TABLE 33.   Properties of the Common Sulfate Minerals (after Larsen, 1921)

Mineral	Composition	Crystal System	Cleavage	Specific Gravity	Hardness	Indices	Birefringence	2V
Gypsum	$CaSO_4 \cdot 2H_2O$	mono-clinic	010 mic	2.32	1.5–2	1.530 1.523 1.520	0.010	58°
Anhydrite	$CaSO_4$	ortho-rhombic	001 perf 010 perf 100 distinct	2.93	3	1.614 1.576 1.571	0.043	42°
Barite	$BaSO_4$	ortho-rhombic	001 perf 110 perf 010 imperf	4.5	3	1.648 1.637 1.636	0.012	37½°

Halides

Of the various halides only halite (NaCl) is common. Inasmuch as it is water-soluble it occurs neither in the outcrops of humid regions nor in the ordinary thin section. Rocks suspected of being halite-bearing must be sectioned by special processes. Halite is the chief constituent of bedded rock salt.

Other chlorides and sulfates occur in the potash-bearing salt beds. These minerals are so rare, however, that there is no need to review their properties in this book. The interested reader is referred to special papers dealing with this group of minerals (Clarke, 1924, pp. 222–229).

REFERENCES CITED AND BIBLIOGRAPHY

Clarke, F. W. (1924), Data of geochemistry, U.S. Geol. Survey Bull. 770.

Deverin, L. (1945), Etude petrographique des minerals de fer oolithique du Dogger des Alpes suisses, Beitrage Geol. Schweiz, Lieferung 13, vol. 2.

Folk, R. L. and Weaver, C. E. (1952), A study of the texture and composition of chert, Am. J. Sci., vol. 250, pp. 498–510.

Grim, R. E. (1936), The Eocene sediments of Mississippi, Mississippi State Geol. Survey, Bull. 30, pp. 201–203.

Gruner, J. W. (1946), Mineralogy and geology of the Mesabi Range, Iron Range Resources and Rehabilitation Com., St. Paul, pp. 7–14.

Hallimond, A. F. (1925), Iron ores: bedded ores of England and Wales, Special Repts. Mineral Resources Great Britain, vol. 29, pp. 26–27.

James, H. L. (1951), Iron formation and associated rocks in the Iron River district, Michigan, Bull. Geol. Soc. Amer., vol. 62, pp. 251–266.

James, H. L. (1954), Sedimentary facies of iron-formation, Econ. Geol., vol. 49, pp. 238–239.

Johnston, J., Merwin, H. E., and Williamson, E. D. (1916), The several forms of calcium carbonate, Am. J. Sci., ser. 4, vol. 41, pp. 473–512.

Larsen, E. S. (1921), The microscopic determination of the nonopaque minerals, U.S. Geol. Surv., Bull. 679.

Leith, C. K. (1903), The Mesabi iron-bearing district of Minnesota, U.S. Geol. Survey, Mono. 43, pp. 101–115.

Lowenstam, H. A. (1954), Factors affecting the aragonite:calcite ratios in carbonate-secreting marine organisms, J. Geol., vol. 62, pp. 284–322.

Rodgers, John (1940), Distinction between calcite and dolomite on polished surfaces, Am. J. Sci., vol. 238, pp. 788–798.

Rogers, A. F. (1922), Collophane, a much neglected mineral, Am. J. Sci., ser. 5, vol. 3, pp. 269–276.

Sosman, R. B. (1927), The properties of silica, New York, Chem. Catalogue Co., p. 794.

Storz, Max (1928), Die sekundare authigene Kieselsaure in ihrer petrogenetische-geologischen Bedeutung, Monograph Geol. Paleo, ser, 2, vol. 4.

Takahashi, Jun-Ichi (1939), Synopsis of glauconitization in Recent marine sediments, Tulsa, Amer. Assoc. Petroleum Geologists, pp. 503–512.

Taliaferro, N. L. (1934), Contraction phenomena in cherts, Bull. Geol. Soc. Amer., vol. 45, pp. 189–232.

Taliaferro, N. L. (1935), Some properties of opal, Am. J. Sci., ser. 5, vol. 30, pp. 450–474.

Tarr, W. A. (1926), The origin of chert and flint, Univ. Missouri Studies, vol. 1, pp. 8–12.

Tarr, W. A. (1938), Terminology of the chemical siliceous sediments, Rept. Nat. Research Council, Comm. Sedimentation 1937–1938, pp. 8–27 (mimeographed).

Washburn, E. W. and Navias, L. (1922), The relation of chalcedony to other forms of silica, Proc. Nat. Acad. Sci., vol. 8, p. 12.

Winchell, A. N. (1933), *Elements of optical mineralogy*, Part 2 (3d ed.), New York, Wiley.

MISCELLANEOUS CONSTITUENTS

Volcanic Debris

Many sediments are contaminated with volcanic debris; a few are composed largely of volcanic ejectamenta. The *pyroclastic rocks* are but a class of sediments in which such materials predominate. The total quantity of volcanic debris contributed to the sediments is probably larger than commonly believed. Kuenen (1937) has estimated that the sediments of the deep sea are notably augmented by such contributions.

Volcanic debris is of three sorts: (1) rock fragments, (2) crystals and crystal fragments of intratelluric origin, and (3) glass. Glass is the most important of the three.

The rock fragments include both cognate and noncognate, or accidental, blocks. Cognate blocks are parts of the solidified lava which had been broken by later eruptions; noncognate blocks are fragments of the wall rock through which the volcanic vents are blasted. Blocks of volcanic origin are rare in sediments, excepting the volcanic breccias which accumulate nearest the centers of eruption.

Crystal debris is more widespread. The crystals are those which commonly form phenocrysts in lava. They may be entire but generally they are broken euhedra. In many cases they are surrounded by a thin envelope or pellicle of glass. Biotite plates are especially likely to be widely distributed.

Generally, however, the crystals are associated with a larger quantity of volcanic glass, which may be very fine-grained, and if reworked or redeposited it may be mingled with normal sedimentary materials in all proportions. The fresh glass is characterized by its colorless appearance in thin section, by its low index (mostly 1.50 to 1.52), its isotropic character, and principally by its shape. The glass fragments exhibit curious curved spicule-like forms, termed "shards" (Pl. 21, A). The whole rock is said to have a "bogen structure." The glass in time undergoes alteration and becomes devitrified. The devitrification is marked by development of aggregate polarization (with low birefringence). Complete decomposition of an ash bed composed largely of volcanic glass results in conversion of the ash to a bentonitic clay seam or bed. Recognition of the original volcanic character of such materials may be difficult (see bentonites).

Organic Matter

Organic matter is present in nearly all sediments; it is the major constituent of some. The quantity of organic matter varies greatly among different deposits. According to Trask (1939) few typically marine sediments contain more than 10 per cent, and equally few contain less than 0.5 per cent. The average near-shore sediments have 2.5 per cent and the deposits of the open ocean average approximately 1 per cent organic matter. The organic content is also closely related to the texture of the sediment. The clayey sediments contain twice as much organic matter as the silty deposits which, in turn, contain twice as much as the sandy strata.

The amount of organic matter preserved is a "product of an equation between the rate of supply of organic matter and the rate of decomposition" (Goldman, 1924). It depends on the chemical composition and rate of growth of the organic materials, the rate of burial, and the rate of decay after burial.

Organic residues (in sediments) take various forms. In general such residues are difficult to detect and identify unless they form an appreciable part of the rock. Generally the quantity and character of the organic materials are best determined by extraction and analysis by chemical methods. In some sediments, however, organic residues may be seen under the microscope. Most easily recognized are the resinous bodies and spores. These materials, when viewed in transmitted light, are generally yellow, or amber-colored. They are polarizing and look much the same between crossed nicols as in ordinary light. They show little or no internal structure with the exception of the fact that the spore walls can be distinguished from the internal cavity. The spores are generally collapsed or greatly flattened. In the oil shales and related rocks the organic matter appears as a yellow to reddish-brown translucent material. In coal the translucent constituent ("vitrinite") is anisotropic in polarized light; is apparently uniaxial (a strain phenomenon) with optic axis perpendicular to the bedding; it has a refractive index varying from 1.76 to 1.87, and a low birefringence (Fisher, 1934). These materials become darker and have a higher refractive index upon metamorphism.

In some sediments the residues are more carbonaceous and are opaque or nearly so. If cell structure is present the organic origin is clear; if not, the nature of the opaque material is uncertain.

Recent work, based on extraction methods and organic analysis, has shown that organic compounds can be identified in many of the older sediments—even those of Precambrian age (Abelson, 1954).

Two facies of sedimentation seem to be the most favorable for the accumulation and preservation of organic matter. These are the "euxinic" or black shale facies and the "saline" facies. In both facies the high content of organic matter is due to inhibition of decay rather than accelerated production. For an analysis of these environments and the factors involved the reader is referred to Chapter 13.

Trace Elements

All sediments contain certain elements which are not present in separate or distinct minerals but which are found in small quantities in the lattice of the common minerals or are adsorbed on the surface of such minerals. These are the so-called "trace elements." Included among these are strontium, selenium, vanadium, uranium, and the like. Mainly owing to the work of Goldschmidt (1954) there has been a growing interest in the distribution of these elements in nature, including a study of their occurrence in sedimentary rocks. And because some of these elements are radioactive they have been intensively studied in recent years. The literature of these trace constituents, especially the radioactive elements, is very extensive. As the distribution of these elements and the problems connected with them have been ably summarized in comprehensive works and annotated bibliographies (Rankama and Sahama, 1950; Goldschmidt, 1954; Mason, 1952; Ingerson, 1953) no attempt will be made to review or digest this vast literature.

The student of sedimentary rocks, however, needs to understand the usefulness of these studies in the interpretation of the environment of deposition as the distribution of some rare elements seem to be environment-controlled. Boron, for example, is said to be indicative of marine sedimentation (Landergren, 1948). Moreover, the interpretation of some geophysical well surveys, such as gamma ray logs, requires an understanding of the nature and distribution of radioactive materials in the sedimentary rocks (Russell, 1941, 1944, 1945; Beers and Goodman, 1944; Beers, 1945). In some cases also the trace element is injurious to health, such as selenium, and its distribution can be understood only if the sedimentary history of the rock containing it is known. Despite the low concentration of some of the elements, the rocks containing them may be an ore of the element in question or it may be that the ores of the element were derived from such rocks by natural processes of leaching and concentration. The interested reader is referred to the larger and specialized works cited above dealing with the minor elements.

REFERENCES CITED AND BIBLIOGRAPHY

Abelson, P. H. (1954), Annual report of the Director of the Geophysical Laboratory, *Carnegie Inst. Wash. Yearbook* No. 53, pp. 97–101.

Beers, R. F. (1945), Radioactivity and organic content of some Paleozoic shales, *Bull. Am. Assoc. Petroleum Geol.*, vol. 29, pp. 1–22.

Beers, R. F. and Goodman, Clark (1944), Distribution of radioactivity in ancient sediments, *Bull. Geol. Soc. Amer.*, vol. 55, pp. 1229–1253.

Fisher, D. J. (1934), Coal composition, *Proc. Geol. Soc. Amer.*, 1933, pp. 444–445.

Goldman, M. I. (1924), "Black shale" formation in and about Chesapeake Bay, *Bull. Am. Assoc. Petroleum Geol.*, vol. 8, pp. 195–201.

Goldschmidt, V. M. (1954), *Geochemistry* (ed. Alex Muir), Oxford.

Ingerson, Earl (1953), Nonradiogenic isotopes in geology: A review, *Bull. Geol. Soc. Amer.*, vol. 64, pp. 301–374.

Kuenen, Ph. H. (1937), On the total amount of sedimentation in the deep sea, *Am. J. Sci.*, ser. 5, vol. 34, pp. 457–468.

Landergren, Sture (1948), On the geochemistry of Swedish iron ores and associated rocks. A study on iron-ore formation, *Sveriges Geol. Undersökn., Ser. C, Avhandl. och Uppsat.*, no. 496, Arsbok 42, no. 5.

Mason, Brian (1952), *Principles of geochemistry*, New York, Wiley.

Rankama, K. and Sahama, T. (1950), *Geochemistry*, Chicago, Univ. Chicago Press.

Russell, W. L. (1941), Well logging by radioactivity, *Bull. Am. Assoc. Petroleum Geol.*, vol. 25, pp. 1768–1788.

Russell, W. L. (1944), The total gamma ray activity of sedimentary rocks as indicated by Geiger counter determinations, *Geophysics*, vol. 9, pp. 180–216.

Russell, W. L. (1945), Relation of radioactivity, organic content, and sedimentation, *Bull. Am. Assoc. Petroleum Geol.*, vol. 29, pp. 1470–1494.

Trask, P. D. (1939), Organic content of recent marine sediments, in *Recent marine sediments*, Tulsa, Amer. Association Petroleum Geologist, pp. 428–453.

4

Structures

INTRODUCTION AND CLASSIFICATION

THE structures of sediments are those larger features that, in general, are seen or studied best in the outcrop rather than hand specimen or thin section. They are the larger features of the rock.

Structures are both inorganic and organic in origin (Table 34). The inorganic structures are classed either as "primary" or "secondary." The primary structures are mainly dependent on current velocity and rate of sedimentation. The rate of sedimentation, in turn, is governed by the rate of sediment supply and the relation of the surface of deposition to the profile of equilibrium or surface of balance between erosion and deposition. Here belong "bedding" in the broad sense, and all features included thereunder such as cross-bedding, graded-bedding, ripple mark, and other bedding-plane phenomena. The secondary structures are mainly the products of chemical action penecontemporaneous with sedimentation or shortly thereafter. Concretions, nodules, cone-in-cone, septaria, geodes, and the like, are included here. The organic structures are the direct or indirect consequences of organic action. They are the "fossils" in the broadest sense of the term and include not only the petrifactions, but also tracks, trails, borings, and so forth.

MECHANICAL ("PRIMARY") STRUCTURES: BEDDING

The most nearly universal primary structure of sedimentary rocks—their single common characteristic—is their bedding or stratification. In fact the expression "stratified rocks" is virtually synonomous with "sedimentary

TABLE 34. Classification of Structures of Sedimentary Rocks

Inorganic Structures		Organic Structures
Mechanical ("Primary")	Chemical ("Secondary")	

A. Planar bedding structures
  1. Laminations
  2. Cross-bedding
  3. Graded-bedding
	A. Solution structures
	  1. Stylolites
	  2. Corrosion zones
	  3. Vugs, oolicasts, etc.
		A. Petrifactions

B. Linear bedding structures
  1. Striations
  2. Sand lineation
  3. Spatulate casts
  4. Ripple marks
	B. Accretionary structures
	  1. Nodules
	  2. Concretions
	  3. Crystal aggregates
	    (Spherulites and
	    rosettes)
	  4. Veinlets
	  5. Color banding
		B. Bedding ("weedia"
		    and other stro-
		    matolites)

C. Bedding-plane irregularities
  and markings
  1. Wave and swash marks
  2. Pits and prints (rain, etc.)
  3. Cut-outs, scoops, etc.
	C. Composite structures
	  1. Geodes
	  2. Septaria
	  3. Cone-in-cone
		C. Miscellaneous
		  1. Borings
		  2. Tracks and trails
		  3. Casts and molds
		  4. Faecal pellets and
		    coprolites

D. Deformed and disrupted bedding
  1. Soft-sediment folding
  2. Soft-sediment boudinage
  3. Disrupted bedding (brecciation, pull-aparts, mud cracks, clay galls, etc.)
  4. Sedimentary sills and dikes		

rocks," although a few rare sediments, such as tillite, are without internal stratification, and some igneous rocks, the surface flows, are bedded.

The Sedimentation Unit

Bedding or stratification is expressed by rock units of general tabular or lenticular form that have some lithologic or structural unity, and are thus set off from other strata with which they are interleaved. These units are of various sizes. Largest is the "formation," a mappable unit of considerable thickness and extent. The formation is composed of lesser units, "members" and "sedimentation units," which, in turn, may show the smallest recognizable units or laminations.

Payne (1942) has used the term *stratum* for a layer "greater than 1 centimeter in thickness . . . visually separable from other layers above and below, the separation being determined by a discrete change in lithology, a sharp physical break in lithology, or by both." The term *lamination* is restricted to similar units under 1 centimeter in thickness. The difference, therefore, is wholly one of degree. Payne further redefined the common terms applied to strata, namely, *fissile, shaly, flaggy,* and *massive,* and assigned specific thickness limits to each. McKee and Weir (1953) have attempted to discriminate between terms applied to the *thickness* of the strata and the terms which describe the *splitting property.* Like Payne, McKee and Weir call all units less than 1 centimeter thick *laminations* and those thicker than 1 centimeter *beds.* Beds 1–5 centimeters thick are *very thin,* 5–60 centimeter layers are *thin,* those from 60–120 centimeters are *thick,* and if over 120 centimeters the term *thick-bedded* is applied. If the beds split into units of the same orders of thickness, they were termed *flaggy, slabby, blocky,* and *massive,* respectively. The thinner strata are *laminated,* or if less than 2 millimeters thick, *thinly laminated.*

Otto (1938) attempted to define two genetically significant units, namely, the *sedimentation unit* and the *lamination.* The sedimentation unit is defined as "that thickness of sediment which was deposited under essentially constant physical conditions." Current flow in nature is never absolutely uniform; hence no sediment, for example, is composed of particles of uniform size. Actually there is some prevailing current that deposits some prevailing size. This prevailing current has a mean velocity and deposits some mean size for a considerable period of time. The sedimentation unit is the deposit made during this time period. When the current is radically changed and a new set of conditions is established at another time, a new unit will be formed. There are momentary fluctuations in the current velocity, of course, which accounts for *laminations* or *phases* [1] differing slightly from each other. A cross-bedded layer of sand or sandstone, for example, is a sedimentation unit. It was deposited under essentially uniform conditions. The depositing current maintained more or less uniform direction and velocity of flow. The cross-laminations, however, record local and short-timed fluctuations in the velocity of the depositing current and are phases. A second cross-bedded unit above the first, either with the same or differently oriented cross-laminations is a separate and distinct sedimentation unit and records a new and different episode of deposition.

The distinction between sedimentation unit and lamination is not, according to Otto, a matter of thickness. The annual layers or varves of the Pleistocene proglacial lakes, though commonly over 1 centimeter in thickness may also be, in part, less than 1 centimeter thick. It does not seem reasonable to

[1] Apfel (1938) has defined a phase as the product of "deposition during a single fluctuation in the competency of the transporting agent." Such a subunit is probably a lamination—the smallest recognizable unit layer of particles of a sediment.

class some as beds or strata and others as laminations. All are, instead, very thin sedimentation units. As some of the thicker silty and sandy portions of the varves are commonly laminated, it does seem necessary and desirable to discriminate between such laminations and the varves proper, and therefore between beds and laminations on some other basis than a predetermined arbitrary thickness.

Under some conditions the velocity of the prevailing current declines in a gradual manner. A sedimentation unit formed under these conditions is marked by a gradual decrease in the size of grain from the base upwards.

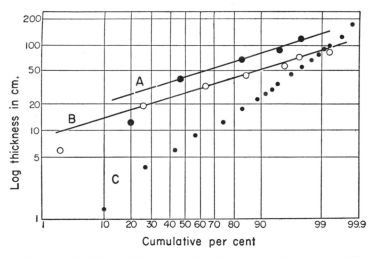

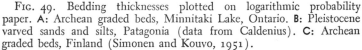

FIG. 49. Bedding thicknesses plotted on logarithmic probability paper. **A**: Archean graded beds, Minnitaki Lake, Ontario. **B**: Pleistocene varved sands and silts, Patagonia (data from Caldenius). **C**: Archean graded beds, Finland (Simonen and Kouvo, 1951).

Such a unit is a graded bed. A graded bed may also be deposited from a single and short-lived turbidity flow. In either case it is a sedimentation unit and records a single self-contained episode or event.

Sedimentation units vary in their thickness and persistence. The variations in thickness, in many cases, seem to have a logarithmic normal distribution. When the measured units are grouped into thickness classes and the frequencies cumulated, they are found to plot as a straight line on logarithmic probability paper (Fig. 49). Such was shown to be the case for 124 Pleistocene varved sands and silts of Patagonia and for 44 graded beds in the Archean of Ontario (Pettijohn, 1949). It has also been found to be true of over 3500 graded beds in the Archean of Finland (Simonen and Kouvo, 1951) and of 208 graywacke beds in the Stanley formation of Arkansas (Bokman, 1953). Schwarzacher (1953) noted that the thickness frequency of 100 randomly chosen cross-bedded sandstone layers, 5 to 250 centimeters in thickness, of the Lower Cretaceous of England, also tended to have a log normal distribution (Fig. 50). It is apparent, therefore, that many sedimentation units of unlike origins tend to show thickness fluctuations that are log normal.

In general, though by no means invariably, the coarseness of grain and the thickness of a unit are related. Kurk (1941), who studied 25 beds of sand and gravel in a glacial outwash deposit, showed that the mean grain size in-

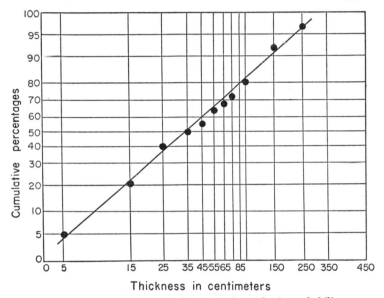

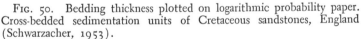
Thickness in centimeters

FIG. 50.   Bedding thickness plotted on logarithmic probability paper. Cross-bedded sedimentation units of Cretaceous sandstones, England (Schwarzacher, 1953).

creased in a linear manner with the thickness of the unit (Fig. 51). Though statistically true, there were many marked exceptions to this rule. Schwarzacher (1953) showed that in general the median grain size of cross-bedding units of the Lower Cretaceous of England was positively correlated with the thickness of these units. Twenty-five paired values had a correlation coefficient of 0.58 (Fig. 52). Fiege (1937) has also observed that the grain size increases with the thickness of the bedding unit.

Sedimentation units vary not only in thickness but also in lateral persistence. Some, like the varves of glaciolacustrine origin, have remarkable lateral continuity. Others, like the festoon cross-bedded sands, are of very limited extent. Such stratigraphic variability is not so easily measured as the thickness variability but it is an important characteristic of any group of beds and is perhaps diagnostic of some types of sedimentation.

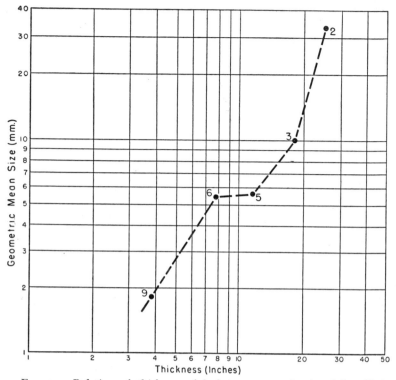

FIG. 51. Relation of thickness of bed to mean grain size (after Kurk, 1941). Figures denote number of measurements averaged.

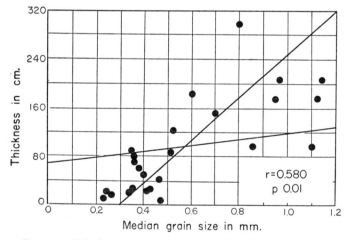

FIG. 52. Thickness and median grain size of cross-bedded sedimentation units of Cretaceous sandstones, England (Schwarzacher, 1953).

Laminations

Laminations are the smallest units of bedding. They are in some cases very thin sedimentation units (millimeter varves), but in other cases they are merely records of transitory "phases" or minor chance fluctuations in the velocity of the depositing current. It is not always possible to determine which type of lamination one has. The first type is best illustrated by the annual laminations in some shales; the second type is represented by the cross-laminations in many sandstone beds.

Laminations are most characteristic of the finer-grained sediments, notably siltstones and shales. They appear as more or less distinct alternations of material which differ one from the other in grain size or composition. Commonly they are 0.05 to 1.0 millimeter thick. They may be continuous and distinct or discontinuous and obscure. Examples of laminations are those formed by alternations of coarse and fine particles (silt and even fine sand and clay) (Pl. 24, A and B), dark- and light-colored silt layers caused by differences in organic matter (Pl. 24, C), and by alternations of calcium carbonate and silt.

The causes of such laminations are variations in the rate of supply or deposition of the different materials. These variations might result from changes in the quantity of silt, clay, or calcium carbonate, or organic matter in the sea water or to changes in the rate of accumulation of these materials. Such variations have been attributed to the fortuitous shift in the depositing current, to climatic causes (especially cyclical changes related to diurnal or annual rhythms), and also to aperiodic storms or floods. For a discussion of the conditions needed for the formation and preservation of annual layers and the criteria for their recognition, the reader is referred to the more extended discussion by Bradley (1929) and Rubey (1930).

Some shales are noted for the excellence of their laminations; others are conspicuous by reason of the absence of this structure. The most perfect examples of laminated shales are said to be lacustrine. Least perfect are the blocky mudstones found in some terrestrial sediments.

The distinctness and degree of preservation of the laminations is in part a rough measure of the quietness of the waters in which the sediments accumulated. Even slight bottom currents would destroy any previously formed laminations. Hence laminations record deposition below wave base. The distinctness of the laminations is also related to the salinity of the water as Sauramo (1923) has shown. Certain electrolytes, of which sodium chloride is the most common, induce flocculation or *symmixis*, which results in mixing of the silt and clay particles and results in a nearly homogeneous rather than laminated clay. It is probable also that the stratification of a sediment may be destroyed by organisms that feed on the organic matter contained in the bottom muds. Repeated ingestion of the muds results in a thorough working over of the sediment and partial or complete destruction of the laminations.

In general, the thinner the laminations the slower the rate of accumulation. This is obviously true of the paired laminations that were formed during equal time intervals such as the year.

INTERNAL STRUCTURE

Next to the grosser dimensions—thickness and lateral extent—the internal structure of a bed is its most important property (Fig. 53). There are two principal types of internal structure, namely, cross-bedded and graded.

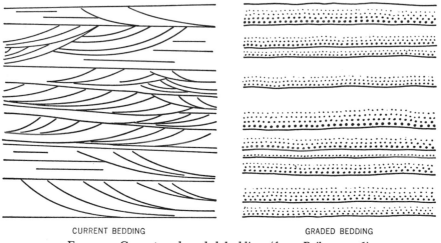

CURRENT BEDDING   GRADED BEDDING

FIG. 53.   Current and graded bedding (from Bailey, 1936).

Though these structures are most characteristic of sandstone beds, they may also be present in both coarser and finer clastic sediments and are found, in rare cases, in some limestones. Bailey (1930) has noted that these structures are more or less mutually exclusive and are in all probability the earmarks of two contrasting facies of deposition. This observation seems to be generally true, though Kuenen (1953a, p. 1051) and others have pointed out that cross-bedding, albeit on a small scale, is more common in graded sequences than once supposed.

Cross-Bedding

Cross-bedding is a common and well-known property of many granular sediments. Since it is a useful character to ascertain current direction, and since it is also a criterion of top and bottom of vertical or overturned beds, it should be carefully examined and its attitude or orientation recorded.

Though much remains to be learned about cross-bedding and the mechanism of its formation, it is now clear that the important attributes of this structure are (1) its scale, and (2) its variability, both in inclination and direction. By scale is meant the thickness of the cross-bedded unit. The scale or thickness frequency distribution can be established by measurements of a number of cross-bedded units and by a statistical summarization of such measurements.

The mean thickness and the standard deviation from the mean can be ascertained. Whether or not the distribution of thickness is log normal should also be determined.

The variability of cross-bedding is expressed by the variability of its strike and dip. Should the bed itself have been deformed, the observed strike and dip of the cross-laminations should be corrected for such deformation by appropriate rotation of the cross-bedded plane about the strike of the true bedding.[2] The attitude of the cross-bedded planes is expressed by two angles, namely, the angle of strike and the angle of dip. More commonly the strike is of less interest than the normal to it, more specifically, the dip direction. As both the direction and the angle of inclination are somewhat variable in the same outcrop and even within the same bed, it is necessary to make a number of measurements.[3] Reiche (1938) recorded the pole of each cross-lamination on a stereographic polar net (polar coördinate paper could be used in beds that are undisturbed, but if rotation to correct for dip of beds is required, the stereographic net is better) (Fig. 54).

The measurements may be summarized statistically (Fig. 55) and both the mean and standard deviation of the azimuthal directions (and of the inclination if so desired) computed. The results can be plotted on a map so that the regional pattern can be seen and paleogeographic interpretations made (Fig. 150). Reiche summarized his measurements at any one observation point by means of a special symbol consisting of (1) an arc indicating the range in directions represented by 90 per cent of the plotted directions, (2) an arrow having the direction determined by addition of vectors which themselves have the direction of the dip of the cross-lamination and the length proportional to the tangent of half the dip angle, and (3) the length

[2] The so-called "two-tilt" problem on which many papers have been written. It can be solved graphically (Fisher, 1938) or mechanically (Cloos, 1938).

[3] It is important that measurements of both inclination and direction of inclination be made on the actual cross-bedded planes. Much of the apparent variability of cross-bedding may be due to observations of the traces of cross-laminations on other planes. In that vertical plane which is normal to the mean direction of current flow the cross-bedding may appear quite random; in the vertical plane parallel to the mean direction of current flow the cross-laminations may appear remarkably uniform (Fig. 58).

of the arrow which is a measure of the "consistency ratio," or ratio secured by dividing the length of the vector resultant by the sum of the length of the individual vectors (the longer the arrow, the more consistent the observed dip directions). A more recent example of the statistical treatment of cross-bedding measurements is given by the work of Olson and Potter (1954).

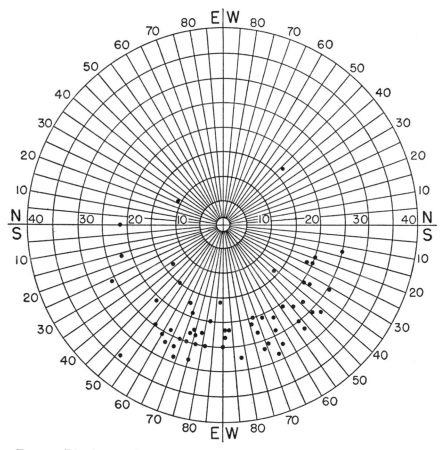

FIG. 54. Distribution of poles of cross-lamination in the Coconino sandstone (Permian) at Clear Creek, east of Winslow, Arizona (after Reiche, 1938).

Various attempts have been made to classify cross-bedding into types presumed to be indicative of the agent responsible for their formation, or into classes or types based on the character and arrangement of the cross-laminations.[4] It now seems doubtful whether genetic types of cross-bedding exist

[4] An example of a classification and nomenclature based on characteristic structural features rather than supposed genesis is that of McKee and Weir (1953).

and whether the classifications now used have any genetic significance. Only the scale, the mean direction, and the variability of the cross-bedding appear to be significant. The scale is a function of the current velocity, the orientation of the cross-bedding is a function of the direction of current flow, and the variability is a function of the stability of the current system. As these vary regionally and are of great paleogeographic importance, it is as necessary to record and map these characteristics as it is to note and map the distribution of rock types.

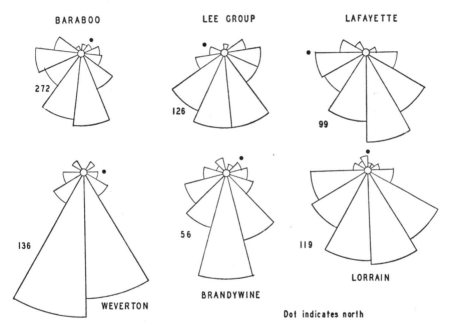

FIG. 55. Azimuthal distribution of cross-bedding in Precambrian (Baraboo and Lorrain); Cambrian (Weverton), Pennsylvanian (Lee Group) and Pliocene or Pleistocene (Lafayette and Brandywine).

In general the dip of the cross-bedding is in the local direction of current flow. If such directions of current flow show a regionally consistent pattern, that is, one with a strong preferred orientation instead of a random scatter, then the implied current movement was probably down the regional slope at the time of deposition of the bed in question. In general, therefore, the current flow is from source to site and hence from older rocks toward younger. The paleogeographic significance of cross-bedding and other vector properties is discussed in Chapter 12.

The *angle* of inclination of the cross-bedding is probably of much less importance than the *direction* of inclination. Statistical studies of inclination show that in undisturbed beds there is a preferred angle of inclination. Potter and Olson (1954), for example, obtained a mean of 16.5 degrees from 531 measurements of the Lower Pennsylvanian sandstones (Caseyville and Mansfield) of the Eastern Interior Basin. No cross-lamination exceeded 36 degrees.

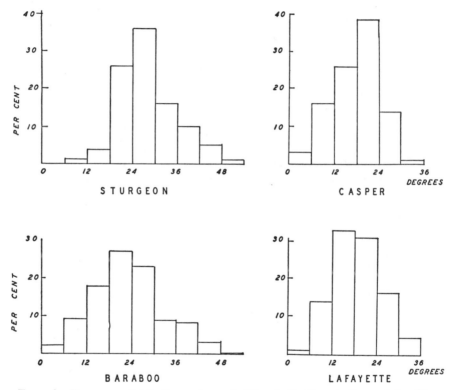

Fig. 56. Frequency distributions of cross-bedding inclinations in Precambrian (Baraboo and Sturgeon), Pennsylvanian (Casper) and Pliocene or Pleistocene (Lafayette).

Similar results were obtained by Potter (1955) in his study of the Lafayette formation of western Kentucky and environs (about 19 degrees) and by Knight (1929) in his study of the Casper formation (Carboniferous) of Wyoming (about 18 degrees). The maximum angle observed is near 34 degrees—the angle commonly cited as the angle of repose of sand (Bagnold, 1942). Angles of inclination, therefore, in excess of 36 degrees indicate post-depositional deformation.

A statistical analysis of 283 cross-bedding measurements in the Baraboo quartzite of Wisconsin (Brett, 1955) and of 80 similar measurements in the

Sturgeon quartzite of Michigan (Trow, 1948), both Precambrian in age, shows that the mean inclination and the maximum inclination observed were much greater than those of the younger still flat-lying sands (Fig. 56). The mean value of the Baraboo is near 24 degrees and the maximum is near 50 degrees; the Sturgeon averaged about 29 degrees and likewise it had a maximum of near 50. The higher angles for the deformed Precambrian beds must be the result of the internal shear during folding (Fig. 57). It might be supposed, however, that such internal deformation would *lower* the angle in as many cases as it would raise it so that the mean inclination would remain the same. Such does not appear to have been the case.

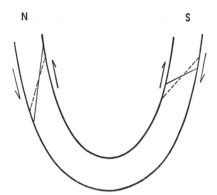

FIG. 57. Effect of deformation on cross-bedding inclination. Note that the inclination, or angle between cross laminations and bedding, is decreased on one fold limb and increased on the other.

In the foregoing section, the cross-bedding laminations have been assumed to be planes, the position in space of which could be described in terms of their strike and dip. As a first approximation this assumption is acceptable and the cross-laminations may be treated as planes. Close inspection, however, shows that many are in fact curved surfaces. In section, some laminations appear to become tangential to the base of the beds. Even the strike of a cross-lamination may be curvilinear. If examined in three dimensions some cross-beds appear to have been deposited in a plunging trough or scooplike structure and to be confluent with the walls of such a structure. These are the so-called "festoon" cross-beds. Rarely is a complete trough or scoop preserved; each one seems to have been cut into by a younger one (Fig. 58).

The scoops or troughs range widely in scale. Knight (1929) describes these structures which are from 50 to several thousand feet long, 10 to 1000 feet wide, and 1 to 100 feet deep in the Casper formation. Similar structures described by Stokes in the Salt Wash sandstone of Utah were on the order of 5 feet wide, 20 feet long, and 18 inches deep. Perhaps the so-called "flowcasts" or spatulate casts found at the base of some siltstone beds, and shown by Kuenen (1952) to be cross-bedded, are but scoops of a very small size.

The origin and mechanism of deposition of cross-beds is not clear. The factors which govern scale and which result in scoop formation and scoop-filling (in the case of festoon cross-bedding) are not known. Cross-bedding is certainly both marine and nonmarine. Whether there are any differences in scale, variance, or structure between marine and nonmarine cross-laminations is not known. Even the characteristics of aeolian cross-bedding have never been quantitatively determined (in terms of scale, variance of same, or of direction, or of inclination).

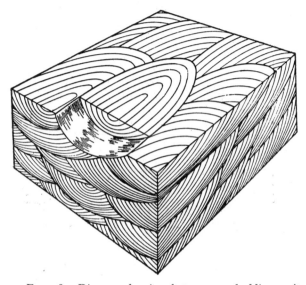

Fig. 58. Diagram showing festoon cross-bedding as it appears on horizontal, transverse, and longitudinal sections (after Knight, 1929).

Graded Bedding

Graded bedding, a common feature of certain kinds of sediments, has been called to our attention by the field geologists who have found it exceptionally useful in the determination of the order of superposition in isoclinally folded and overturned strata. The geological significance of graded bedding and the recognition of graded bedding and cross-bedding as the distinguishing attributes of two contrasting facies of sand deposition, have only more recently been made clear by the writings of Bailey (1930, 1936), Pettijohn (1943), and Kuenen and co-workers (Kuenen and Migliorini, 1950; Kuenen, 1951a, 1952, and 1953a, 1953b; Kuenen and Menard, 1952).

Graded beds are sedimentation units, marked by a gradation in grain size, from coarse to fine, upward from the base to the top of the unit. Theoretically two types of grading are possible. In one type, decrease in the grain size upward is the result of addition of successive increments of material each of which is finer than the preceding (Fig. 59, A); in the other, each successive increment is similar to the preceding excepting that it contains one less coarse grade (Fig. 59, B). In the first type there are no fines in the lowest part of the graded bed; in the second type, the fines are distributed through-out. The first type is, perhaps, the product of a normal waning current, the decline in competency taking place over an extended period of time. At any given moment but a single size is being deposited. The second type is the product of sedimentation from a suspension in which all sizes are carried and out of which they settle. The deposits in both cases are "graded" but in the first case the mean size would decrease upward but the sorting would remain

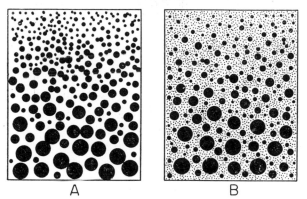

FIG. 59. Types of graded bedding. **A**: Grading produced by waning current. **B**: Grading produced by differential set-tling from turbidity flow.

constant, whereas in the second case mean size would diminish but the sort-ing would improve. Meager experimental and observational data available seem to bear out these concepts. An analysis of a graded glacial outwash sand about 15 inches thick shows the geometric mean diameter to decrease ex-ponentially from the base of the bed upward; the standard deviation, how-ever, shows a slight *increase* from the base upward. On the other hand,

TABLE 35.   Size Parameters of Graded Beds

	Ventura River[a] (Pliocene) 120 cm bed		Glacial Outwash[b] (Pleistocene) 38 cm bed	
Sample	Mean (mm)	ϕ_σ	Mean (mm)	ϕ_σ
1 (base)	0.66	1.89	0.25	0.44
2	0.35	1.49	0.24	0.43
3	0.31	1.52	0.21	0.52
4	0.24	1.47	0.16	0.60
5	0.13	0.87	0.14	0.66
6 (top)	0.12	1.04	....	....

[a] Calculated from diagrams published by Kuenen and Menard (1952, p. 86).
[b] M. A. Rosenfeld, analyst.

inspection of the analyses published by Kuenen and Migliorini (1950) of the graded beds deposited from experimentally produced turbidity flows and calculations based on the data published on the naturally graded graywackes of the Ventura Basin of California (Kuenen and Menard, 1952) show that the mean size decreases in regular fashion upwards from the base and that the sorting becomes progressively better (Table 35).

Most of the graded bedding observed in the field seems to belong to the second type. The graded beds of this type have an abrupt contact, never gradational, with the underlying stratum. Normally they are sands or coarse silts which grade upward into finer materials—in some cases into shale or slate. The sand bed proper therefore has a sharp lower contact but a gradational upper contact. The individual graded beds may be quite thin—4 or 5 to the inch—though more commonly they are several inches to several feet thick (Pls. 22 and 24, A, and Table 36). These units are characterized by their tendency to occur in long sequences. The thin graded beds have an appearance strongly suggesting the varve structure of the late Pleistocene lacustrine clays.[5] In fact, the structure exhibited by the varved clays and silts is one type of graded bedding.

TABLE 36.   Thicknesses of Graded Bedding

Locality	Age	No. of Beds Measured	Thickness (in.)			S. D.[b]	Coeff. of Variation
			Avg.[a]	Max.	Min.		
Minnataki Lake, Ont., Canada	Archean	44	20.2	50	5	10.8	54%
Minnataki Lake, Ont., Canada	Archean	34	9.9	25?	2	5.1	51%
Patagonia [c]	Pleisto-cene	140	15.2	66	4	7.0	46%

[a] Arithmetic mean.
[b] Standard deviation.
[c] Calculated from measurements of published diagram (Caldenius, 1932, p. 23); two catastrophic drainage varves omitted.

Normally the graded beds, especially the coarser sandy beds, have no internal structure or lamination of any kind other than grading. But, as noted by Kuenen (1953a) and others, there are some exceptions. Most exceptions appear in the graded siltstones or finer sandstones and consist of an internal lamination which is commonly much disturbed. The disturbed laminations are closely and intricately folded or crumpled—a structure obviously acquired

[5] Although the graded beds of some siltstone-slate sequences have been called varved (Eskola, 1932; Pettijohn, 1936; Simonen and Kouvo, 1951) it is unlikely, for reasons given on p. 177, that such layers are truly year layers.

while the sediment was still soft and before deposition of the overlying layer. In other cases the graded bed may show a very small-scale cross-bedding; in still other cases the base of the bed exhibits downward protuberances into the underlying shale or slate. Such spatulate depressions in the underlying bed appear as casts on the underside of the overlying silt or sandstone bed. As a rule, however, the graded bed is characterized by lack of internal structure or organization. In fact the toughness and lack of fissility of the graywackes—which so commonly are graded—is due to the randomness in the orientation of their component elements, i.e., their lack of bedding or fabric parallel to the surface of deposition.

Associated with graded beds are dikes and sills of the same composition and internal structures as the graded beds themselves. It is perhaps significant that the dikes consist of the graywacke sands, not the associated mudstones, and like the bedded graywackes are without conspicuous internal bedding or fabric. Both would seem to have a common mode of transport and emplacement.

Graded bedding is widespread both in time and place. It is a common structure in virtually all Temiskaming-like sequences of the early Precambrian of the Canadian shield (Pettijohn, 1943). Similar graded bedding in the early Precambrian (Bothnian) of Finland was early described by Sederholm (1931) who recognized the similarity of this structure to that shown by the glacial clays of the Pleistocene. Eskola (1932) and Simonen and Kouvo (1951) have described in some detail the structure and composition of these graded beds. They are also reported from the Archean of central Sweden (Sundius, 1923).

As Bailey (1930, 1936) has pointed out, graded bedding is not exclusively an Archean feature, since it is well displayed by rocks of later times. Bailey, for example, cited its occurrence in ". . . the younger Dalradian (probably late Precambrian), Cambrian, Ordovician, and Silurian of Scotland, Ireland, and Wales within the compass of the Caledonian geosyncline . . . it characterizes some of the Carboniferous of the Armorican geosyncline of the Devon peninsula and . . . the Tertiary Flysch of the Alpine geosyncline." Graded bedding has received much study from Kuenen and his associates. Kuenen (1953b) has described in some detail the graded beds of the Lower Paleozoic rocks of Great Britain. The Pliocene of the Ventura Basin of California has been studied by Natland and Kuenen (1951). Graded beds are reported in rocks varying from Cretaceous to Pliocene in age in various parts of California (Kuenen, 1953, p. 1063). It is also reported from the Tertiary of Peru (Dorreen, 1951). Graded bedding probably characterizes all thick geosynclinal accumulations of graywackes interbedded with shales or slates.

An occasional graded bed is seen in quartzites, sandstones, and recent sand deposits. In such cases, however, the graded bed is a solitary or sporadic

PLATE 3

CURRENT STRUCTURES II

Lower side of flagstone from Hatch formation, Naples Group ("Portage") Upper Devonian, Conesus Lake, New York. Marked by striation and groove casts and by less persistent flow casts. Current presumably flowed from upper to lower part of picture. Base of specimen about fifteen inches.

PLATE 4

CURRENT STRUCTURES III

Top: Specimen of Salt Wash sandstone (Jurassic) of Arizona showing lineation. Current flowed parallel to scale. (Stokes, U.S. Atomic Energy Commission, RME–3043, Pt. 1, Fig. 7.)

Bottom: Rib-and-furrow markings showing direction of current movement. Salt Wash sandstone, Carrizo Mountains, Arizona. (Stokes, U.S. Atomic Energy Commission, RME–3043, Pt. 1, Fig. 6.)

occurrence and is probably of the type in which the fines are not present in the lower part of the bed. Such beds may even show reversed grading.

The origin and significance of graded beds is just beginning to be understood. Bailey (1930) has said that "current bedding and graded bedding are distinguishing marks of two different sandstone facies. Current-bedded sandstones are obviously the products of bottom currents. Graded-bedded sandstones are the products of settling through comparatively still bottom water, which allows sand and mud to accumulate in one and the same locality, though with a lag on the part of the mud determined by its finer texture. . . . Thus current-bedded sandstones belong to relatively shallow water (or to the air), and graded-bedded sandstones belong to relatively deep water." In general the author's observations support Bailey's thesis that graded-bedding and current-bedding are the earmarks of two facies of sediments. These two types of bedding are mutually exclusive, except, as Bailey noted, "sometimes there is an admixture of type, even in one and the same bed," but where this is the case, the cross-bedding is on a small scale and is confined to a single layer.

Graded beds have been explained in several ways. Bailey ascribed them to earthquakes which served as "intermittent distributors of sand and mud." According to Bailey, the sand and mud, which formed unstable accumulations on the borders of the geosyncline, are periodically dislodged by submarine temblors and thrown into suspension to settle out in comparatively deep and quiet water with the graded structure. Slip-bedding, a product of subaqueous slumping, is produced by the same means, and therefore should be associated with the graded bedding, as it commonly is.

Kuenen and Migliorini (1950) first expressed the view that turbidity currents are the probable cause of most graded bedding. Kuenen (1953a) has presented a detailed review of the evidence for the turbidity flow origin of graded beds. In part, this evidence has been presented in the discussion of graywackes (p. 312) which are characteristically graded. The most compelling evidence lies in the structure of the bed itself, i.e., grading and distribution of the fines throughout the bed, features which can be experimentally reproduced by turbidity flows (Kuenen and Migliorini, 1950; Kuenen and Menard, 1952). Also significant is the uniformity of thickness, even of the coarsest graded units (normal swift currents would produce lenticular cross-bedded units), absence of cross-bedding, evidence of deepwater origin (deep-water microfauna of associated shale interbeds), deposition of coarse debris on underlying mud without disturbance of the mud surface (delicate worm trails preserved as casts on underside of overlying sand bed, Kuenen and Migliorini, 1950). Obviously each graded unit records a single short-lived episode and is a product of deep-water sedimentation beyond the reach of normal bottom currents and waves. The accumulated evidence now almost certainly indicates deposition from a dense turbidity flow, which may be the product of submarine slump, triggered perhaps by earthquakes.

Graded beds conceivably might originate in other ways. The close resemblance of the thinner graded beds to the varves of glacial lakes led to the view that a seasonal influx of sediment that was controlled by glacial melting was responsible for the graded structure. Coleman (1926) so interpreted the graded beds of the Sudbury series of Ontario, Canada. Eskola (1932), however, noted the greater thickness of the Archean "varved" sequences, the failure of the "varves" to show a diminution in thickness upwards from the base, as is common in the glacial varves owing to the withdrawal of the ice, and the absence of tillites in the Archean. Eskola, however, did conclude that "these Archean sediments exhibit such a close similarity to analogous Pleistocene sediments that similar conditions of origin, i.e., weathering and deposition in temperature or cold climates must be inferred." Kuenen himself (1951a, 1951b) suggested that the late-glacial varved silts and clays were produced by deposition from heavy melt-water underflows in the glacial lake which in fact are a species of turbidity flow. Sundius (1923) has rejected the idea that the graded graywackes and slates of central Sweden were seasonal. The beds, 2 to 50 decimeters thick, are not sufficiently uniform. Sundius attributed them to local conditions.

Were the graded beds seasonal, their thickness would imply an unreasonably high rate of deposition. Although Caldenius (1932) has measured Pleistocene lake sediments in Patagonia which were in excess of 100 feet thick and were deposited at an average rate of 15.2 inches per year, it is highly improbable that the older graded beds were similarly deposited. If instead, the time usually estimated for the whole series is divided by the number of graded beds, one must conclude that the graded beds recorded events widely spaced in time. Kuenen (1953) thus estimated that several hundred to several thousand years elapsed between the formation of one graded bed and the next.

The diadactic or graded structure of the varves of the Fennoscandian Pleistocene has been cited as evidence of their fresh-water origin (Sauramo, 1923). Salt water is supposed to flocculate the mud and produce a structureless deposit or a sedimentation unit with a symmict structure. The interstitial mud (or its authigenic derivatives) seen under the microscope, common in many grits and graywackes, has been attributed to the flocculating effect of salt water (Woodland, 1938). But as shown by Kuenen and Menard (1952), the interstitial material is a normal consequence of turbidity current transport. Grading or the absence of it is not necessarily dependent on the salinity of the surrounding water.

Although some isolated or sporadic graded beds can be produced by volcanic eruptions, heavy floods, or even periodic silting of delta distributaries and shifting of discharge points or river mouths, most marine graded beds are almost certainly the product of short-lived turbidity flows. Graded beds due to other causes apparently are relatively rare and different in structure or associated features so that confusion with grading due to turbidity flow is unlikely. Possible exceptions are the much thinner, evenly bedded, fine-grained siltstones. Discrimination between these deposits and truly seasonal sediments may be less easy.

REFERENCES CITED AND BIBLIOGRAPHY

Andersen, S. A. (1931), (Review of paper by Andersen, in *J. Geol.*, 1934, vol. 42, p. 551).

Andrée, K. (1915), Ursachen und Arten der Schichtung, *Geol. Rundschau*, vol. 6, pp. 351–397.

Apfel, E. T. (1938), Phase sampling of sediments, *J. Sediment. Petrol.*, vol. 8, pp. 67–68.

Bagnold, R. A. (1941), *The physics of blown sand and desert dunes*, London, Methuen.

Bailey, E. B. (1930), New light on sedimentation and tectonics, *Geol. Mag.*, vol. 67, pp. 77–92.

Bailey, E. B. (1936), Sedimentation in relation to tectonics, *Bull. Geol. Soc. Amer.*, vol. 47, pp. 1713–1726.

Bieber, C. L. (1952), Current directions indicated by cross-bedding in deposits of early Mansfield age in southwestern Indiana, *Proc. Indiana Acad. Sci.*, 1952, vol. 62, pp. 228–229.

Bokman, John (1953), Lithology and petrology of the Stanley and Jackfork formations, *J. Geol.*, vol. 61, pp. 152–170.

Bradley, W. H. (1929), The varves and climate of the Green River epoch, *U.S. Geol. Survey, Prof. Paper* 158E.

Bradley, W. H. (1931), Non-glacial marine varves, *Am. J. Sci.*, ser. 5, vol. 22, pp. 318–330.

Brett, G. W. (1955), Crossbedding in the Baraboo quartzite of Wisconsin, *J. Geol.*, vol. 63, pp. 143–148.

Brinkman, R. (1932), Über Kreuzschichtung in deutschen Bundsandsteins-becken, *Nachr. Ges. Wissen. Göttingen, Math-Phys. Kl. IV*, 32.

Caldenius, C. C. (1932), Las glaciaciones Cuaternarias en la Patagonia y Tierra del Fuego, *Geog. Annalen*, vols. 1 and 2.

Cloos, Hans (1938), Primäre Richtungen in Sedimenten der rheinischen Geo-synkline, *Geol. Rundschau*, vol. 29, pp. 357–367.

Coleman, A. P. (1926), *Ice ages, recent and ancient*, New York, Macmillan, pp. 77f.

Dorreen, J. M. (1951), Rubble bedding and graded bedding in Talara formation of northwestern Peru, *Bull. Am. Assoc. Petroleum Geol.*, vol. 35, pp. 1829–1849.

Eskola, P. (1932), Conditions during the earliest geological times, as indicated by the Archean rocks, *Ann. Acad. Sci. Fennicae*, ser. A, vol. 36, no. 4.

Fiege, K. (1937), Untersuchungen über zyklische Sedimentation geosynklinaler und epikontinentaler Räume, *Abhandl. preuss. geol. Landesanstalt*, n.f., h. 177.

Fisher, D. J. (1938), Problem of two tilts and the stereographic projection, *Bull. Am. Assoc. Petroleum Geol.*, vol. 22, pp. 1261–1271.

Illies, Henning (1949), Die Schrägschichtung in fluvialtilen und litoralen Sedimenten, etc., *Mitt. geol. Staatsinst. Hamburg*, H. 19, z. 89–109.

Jüngst, H. (1939), Paleogeographische Auswertung der Kreuzschichtung, *Geol. der Meere und Binnengewässer*, Bd. 2, pp. 229–277.

Knight, S. H. (1929), The Fountain and Casper formations of the Laramie Basin, *Univ. Wyoming Publ. Sci.*, Geology 1, no. 1, pp. 1–82.

Kuenen, Ph. H. (1951a), Mechanics of varve formation and the action of turbidity currents, *Geol. Fören. i. Stockholm Forh.*, vol. 73, pp. 69–84.

Kuenen, Ph. H. (1951b), Turbidity currents as the cause of glacial varves, *J. Geol.*, vol. 59, pp. 507–508.

Kuenen, Ph. H. (1952), Paleogeographic significance of graded bedding and associated features, *Proc. Koninkl. Ned. Akad. Wetenschap*, ser. B., vol. 55, nr. 1, pp. 28–36.

Kuenen, Ph. H. (1953a), Significant features of graded bedding, *Bull. Am. Assoc. Petroleum Geol.*, vol. 37, pp. 1044–1066.

Kuenen, Ph. H. (1953b), Graded bedding with observations on Lower Paleozoic rocks of Britain, *Verhandel. Koninkl. Ned. Akad. Wetenschap.*, Afdel. Natuurk., vol. 20, no. 3, pp. 1–47.

Kuenen, Ph. H., and Migliorini, C. I. (1950), Turbidity currents as a cause of graded bedding, *J. Geol.*, vol. 58, pp. 91–127.

Kuenen, Ph. H., and Menard, H. W. (1952), Turbidity currents, graded and non-graded deposits, *J. Sediment. Petrol.*, vol. 22, pp. 83–96.

Kurk, E. H. (1941), *The problem of sampling heterogeneous sediments*, Thesis (S.M.) University of Chicago.

McKee, E. D. (1939), Some types of bedding in the Colorado River delta, *J. Geol.*, vol. 47, pp. 64–81.

McKee, E. D., and Weir, G. W. (1953), Terminology for stratification and cross-stratification, *Bull. Geol. Soc. Amer.*, vol. 64, pp. 381–390.

Olson, Jerry, and Potter, P. E. (1954), Variance components of cross-bedding direction in some basal Pennsylvanian sandstones of the Eastern Interior Basin: Statistical methods, *J. Geol.*, vol. 62, pp. 50–73.

Otto, G. H. (1938), The sedimentation unit and its use in field sampling, *J. Geol.* vol. 46, pp. 569–582.

Payne, T. G. (1942), Stratigraphical analysis and environmental reconstruction, *Bull. Am. Assoc. Petroleum Geol.*, vol. 26, pp. 1697–1770.

Pettijohn, F. J. (1936), Early Precambrian varved slate in northwestern Ontario, *Bull. Geol. Soc. Amer.*, vol. 47, pp. 621–628.

Pettijohn, F. J. (1943), Archean sedimentation, *Bull. Geol. Soc. Amer.*, vol. 54, pp. 925–972.

Pettijohn, F. J. (1949), *Sedimentary rocks*, 1st ed., New York, Harper & Brothers, p. 135.

Potter, Paul (1955), The petrology and origin of the Lafayette gravel: Part 1. Mineralogy and petrology, *J. Geol.*, vol. 63, pp. 1–38.

Potter, P. E. and Olson, Jerry (1954), Variance components of cross-bedding direction in some basal Pennsylvanian sandstones of the Eastern Interior Basin: Geological applications, *J. Geol.*, vol. 62, pp. 26–49.

Reiche, Parry (1938), An analysis of cross-lamination: The Coconino sandstone, *J. Geol.*, vol. 46, pp. 905–932.

Rubey, W. W. (1930), Lithologic studies of fine-grained Upper Cretaceous rocks of the Black Hills region, *U.S. Geol. Survey, Prof. Paper* 165A.

Sauramo, Matti (1923), Studies on the Quaternary varved sediments in southern Finland, *Bull. comm. géol. Finlande*, 60.

Schwarzacher, W. (1953), Cross-bedding and grain size in the Lower Cretaceous sands of East Anglia, *Geol. Mag.*, vol. 90, pp. 322–330.

Sederholm, J. J. (1931), On the sub-Bothnian unconformity and on Archean rocks formed by secular weathering, *Bull. comm. géol. Finlande*, no. 95, p. 78.

Shotton, F. W. (1937), Lower Bunter sandstones of north Worcestershire and east Shropshire, *Geol. Mag.*, vol. 74, pp. 534–553 (cross-bedding).

Shrock, R. R. (1948), *Sequence in layered rocks*, New York, McGraw-Hill. (Various chapters on bedding, ripple marks, etc.).

Simonen, A. and Kouvo, O. (1951), Archean varved schists north of Tampere in Finland, *C. R. Soc. géol. de Finlande*, no. 24, pp. 93–114.

Sundius, N. (1923), Grythytte fältets geologi, *Sver. Geol. Undersökn.*, ser. C, no. 312.

Trow, J. W. (1948), *The Sturgeon quartzite of the Menominee district, Michigan*, Ph.D. dissertation, Univ. of Chicago.

BEDDING-PLANE IRREGULARITIES AND MARKINGS

Primary Current Lineation and Other Current Markings

The bedding planes of some sediments are characterized by linear structures. Such structures include ripple mark, striations and grooves, spatulate depressions, and so forth. Some, notably the striations, grooves, and spatulate depressions, occur in shales or mudstones just below siltstone or sandstone beds, and are therefore preserved only as *casts* on the underside of the overlying more durable stratum (Pl. 3).

The linear structures are largely the product of current action and may be parallel to current flow as in case of the striations, etc., or perpendicular to it as in the case of the ripple markings. Because of their value in establishing a regional flow pattern these structures should be mapped.

Striations, striation casts, and similar structures are of several kinds. Best known are the glacial striations produced by the movement of glacial ice over a rock surface. Such markings, though common beneath Pleistocene tills, are exceedingly rare in the older geologic record. They would occur only below a tillite bed.

A more common but less well-known linear structure is a faint but distinct structure found along the bedding planes of some thin-bedded sandstones. This feature, termed primary current lineation by Stokes (1947),[6] was described and figured by Hans Cloos (1938) who pointed out its significance and relation to current direction as disclosed by cross-bedding and other structures. Primary current lineation appears as a faint or weakly defined series of parallel ridges or grooves (Pl. 4, top). Stokes (1953) has more recently mapped this type of lineation and other primary current structures in the Saltwash sandstone member of the Morrison formation in Utah. This structure is abundant also in Devonian flagstones of Pennsylvania and no doubt is common elsewhere. According to Stokes (1953), primary current lineation of sands is indicative of "formation in a fluvial environment or at least under shallow sheets of flowing water."

A superficially similar but in fact somewhat different feature is the striations of certain mudstones which are now preserved only as casts on the underside of some siltstone and fine sandstone beds. These markings are a millimeter or two in depth and many centimeters in length. They are characteristic of many thin-bedded interlayered siltstone and mudstone sequences. Such striations or *striation casts* ("groove-casts" of Shrock, 1948) have been figured and described by Clarke (1918) in the Devonian sandstones of New York (Pl. 3). Associated with these markings are spatulate or lingual structures which also occur only at the interface of shale and overlying siltstone or sandstone bed. These structures are both larger and less continuous than the striations and are essentially downward protrusions of the sandstone bed into the underlying mudstone. The structure, or cast ("lobate rill marks" of Shrock, 1948, p. 131) resembles the bowl of an inverted spoon (Pl. 2, bottom). Such spatulate or linguloid forms are subparallel and appear to have their blunt ends oriented in the same direction. The blunt end is presumed to be the upcurrent end. In some flagstones a second set of lingual forms crosses the first set. Both the striation casts and the spatulate casts are closely associated, not only with each other, but with graded graywackes or subgraywackes which are presumed to have been deposited by turbidity flows. Kuenen (1953, p. 24) who observed these markings in the Llandoverian grits near Aberystwyth, Wales, noted that they were parallel over large areas and that they were parallel to the presumed direction of current flow as shown by both ripple marks and cross-bedding. They were

[6] Stokes's term is perhaps not altogether appropriate, since other and different lineations may also be primary and also due to currents. This term and some terms applied to other structures are also unsatisfactory in that the origin of the structure is implied. As long as the origin is in doubt, nongenetic terms should be used.

PLATE 5

PENECONTEMPORANEOUS DEFORMATION

Top: Intraformational folding of siltstone bed in Martinsburg slate (Ordovician), New Jersey. Length of specimen about five inches. Photograph by W. S. Starks. (van Houten, *Bull. Geol. Soc. Amer.*, vol. 65, pl. 2.)

Convolutions of laminated, very fine-grained sandstone.

Bottom: Sandstone dike cutting Espanola formation (Huronian) near Espanola, Ontario, Canada.

The dike, essentially a graywacke, cuts the Espanola formation, an impure, thin-bedded carbonate silt. The weathered surface is etched into relief and harshly corrugated.

See Pl. 18, **C** for photomicrograph of the dike rock.

PLATE 6

ARMORED MUD BALLS

These have rolled approximately three miles. Note remarkably heavy armor and the high degree of sphericity. Las Posas Barranca, California. Soil Conservation Service photograph. (Bell, *J. Geol.*, vol. 48, 1940, p. 18.)

attributed by Kuenen, and also by Rich (1950), to the action of "density currents rendered abrasive with respect to the underlying mud." Although these flow markings have been attributed to other agencies,[7] the consistent areal pattern, relation to other current structures, and relations to certain sedimentary facies, leaves little doubt of their current origin. The spatulate or lingual casts and associated striation or groove casts are common in the Devonian Portage beds of New York (Clarke, 1918), the Mississippian Horton-Windsor series of Nova Scotia, and the Carboniferous Stanley of Arkansas (Bokman, 1953, Pl. 1). Without doubt they occur in all similar graywacke and siltstone-shale sequences throughout the world.

Another primary bedding-plane feature produced by current action is the *rib-and-furrow* structure of Stokes (1953). Rib-and-furrow structures are small, transverse markings which occur in sets confined to relatively long, narrow grooves separated from one another by very narrow and not altogether continuous ridges (Pl. 4). The longitudinal grooves are essentially parallel to one another and to the current flow. They are an inch or two wide and several inches to several feet in length. The small transverse markings within the grooves are arcuate; the convex side is upcurrent, and the bisectrix is parallel to the current flow. These transverse markings are the eroded edges of an imbricate structure—upturned arcuate laminations.

The origin of the rib-and-furrow structure is somewhat in doubt though it appears to be a species of small-scale cross-bedding (hence imbrication). This is by no means clear although in any case the structure is a reliable guide to current direction. Rib-and-furrow structure is closely associated with ripple marking and with the primary current lineation of sands. It is described by Stokes in the Moenkopi formation (Triassic) and the Saltwash sandstone (Morrison, Jurassic) of Utah. The author has observed it in the Devonian flagstones of Pennsylvania.

Ripple Marks

When a current flowing over a bed of sands reaches a certain velocity, the sand particles begin to move, and a rippling appears on the surface of the sand. These current ripples consist of numerous, essentially parallel, long, more or less equidistant ridges, trending in straight or gently curved lines at right angles to the current (Pl. 2, center). The pattern of some current ripples is less regular and the ripples are crescent-like or linguloid. The ideal current ripple is asymmetrical in cross section and has a gentle stoss or up-current slope and a steep lee slope. Study of Fig. 60 will make clear most of the terms used in connection with ripple mark. The *length* is the distance

[7] Shrock ascribes his "lobate rill marks" to the "ebbing tidal currents or retreating storm waves" and to be indicative, therefore, of the intertidal or strand zone. This seems to have been the view of other authors (Rich, 1950, p. 727).

between two corresponding points on two consecutive ripples. *Amplitude* is the vertical distance between the crest and the trough. The *ripple index* is the ratio of length to amplitude.

Current ripples are a product of both air and water action. Theoretically, aeolian and aqueous current ripples can be distinguished by the ripple index and by the concentration of coarse grains on the crests of the aeolian type. Virtually all fossil current ripples are aqueous. It is doubtful if the aeolian type can be preserved.

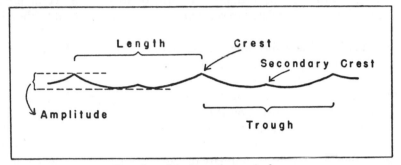

FIG. 60.   Ripple-mark terminology.

Shallow sandy bottoms of standing water bodies are commonly covered by oscillation ripple marks generated by the to-and-fro motion of the water agitated by waves. The ground plan of oscillation ripples is much like that of current ripples, but may be even more regular. In profile, however, the oscillation ripples are strictly symmetrical, which together with the sharp crests and the broadly rounded troughs within which a minor medial ridge is commonly present, distinguish these ripples from the current type. The contrast between the original and the cast make these structures a valuable criterion for distinguishing the top and the bottom of steeply upturned beds (Dake and Cox, 1916; Shrock, 1948).

Interference ripples ("tadpole nests") are the product of two superimposed ripple patterns.

In general ripple mark is a small-scale structure. The wave length is but a few inches and the amplitude but a small fraction of an inch. In certain environments, notably the fluvial, giant ripples are common. These megaripples are characterized by a wave length of several feet and by an amplitude of about a foot more or less. These large ripples are rare in the geologic record but the common torrential cross-bedding of many sandstones is attributed to the deposition and migration of these sand waves (Kindle, 1917, p. 56). They have been reported also from limestones (Tansey, 1953).

The orientation as well as the scale of ripple mark is a significant attribute—perhaps the most significant attribute. Recorded "strikes" of ripples may be summarized graphically and statistically. The orientation of ripples at numerous observation points may be plotted on a map and the regional pattern of orientation determined as was done by Hyde (1911) for the Berea (Mississippian) sandstone of Ohio. The pattern, if produced by currents, will be about perpendicular to the regional current pattern and therefore closely correlated with the cross-bedding orientation. The polarity of the pattern will be determined by ripple asymmetry which, of course, should be noted. The pattern of symmetrical or oscillation ripples will not necessarily be correlated with the cross-bedding azimuths or with other vector properties. It may, however, be related to prevailing wave directions and to shoreline trends.

Ripple mark and cross-bedding are commonly associated. Both are more characteristic of the orthoquartzitic sandstones. They are seldom found in the graded-bedded graywackes.

The mechanics of ripple formation is as yet only partially understood though much has been written on the subject. The effects of velocity, depth of water, viscosity, and sand and density of the grains have been investigated. For a good review of our present knowledge of these topics, the reader is referred to Bucher's excellent summary of the subject (Bucher, 1919) and to the summary of Kindle and Bucher (in Twenhofel, 1932).

The significance of ripple mark is incompletely understood. Asymmetric ripples are certainly the product of current action and their orientation is a means of deducing the direction of ancient current flow. To a degree they are indicative of current velocity as well as direction. Below a certain critical velocity ripples do not form and above a second critical velocity they are destroyed. The value of the limiting velocities are only roughly known. The symmetrical ripples are produced by an oscillating current presumably wave-generated. They are therefore indicative of a standing body of water. Presumably they form, or certainly are abundant, only in depths affected by wave motion. As wave-generated movement dies out rapidly with depth, oscillation ripples are indicative of shallow waters, generally waters but a few tens of feet deep.[8] Current ripples, on the other hand, though also more commonly found in shallow waters have been found in deep waters. The orientation pattern of oscillation ripples is less clearly understood than that of ripples related to polarized currents. It might be expected that the oscillation ripples would be related to the prevailing wave movements, in turn controlled by the prevailing wind pattern, and by the orientation of the shore line. Trow's study of the ripple orientation in the Sturgeon quartzite

[8] Recently oscillation ripples have been reported from very deep water (Menard, 1952). Symmetrical ripples occur in Globigerina ooze at about 4500 feet. It is doubtful, however, if profusely ripple-marked sands can form in such depths and such materials may confidently be ascribed to very shallow waters.

(Precambrian) showed two preferred directions of ripple orientation, namely, normal to the current flow pattern disclosed by cross-bedding, and about perpendicular to the same (Trow, 1948). The symmetrical ripples studied by van Bertsbergh in the Devonian of the Rhine areas were parallel, in general, to the asymmetrical forms and transverse to the region current system as shown by other criteria. (van Bertsbergh, 1940; Chenowith, 1952).

Miscellaneous Markings

Bedding planes may exhibit a host of markings other than those produced by currents. These markings or impressions include tracks and trails made by organisms, rain prints, hail and spray pits, and so forth. Unlike the current generated markings these features have no value in paleocurrent studies and in determination of either direction or angle of the depositional slope. They are, however, of some value in determining the environment of deposition—whether above or below the water surface, and so forth.

Tracks, trails, and related structures are produced by various organisms. Only if the organism responsible for the structure is known can it be determined whether the markings are subaqueous or subaerial. Rain, drip, and hail impressions are small, circular to elliptical pits formed in wet muds by the agents named. "Fossil" rainprints have been reported from many strata. Like mud cracks they indicate subaerial exposure and are most likely to be preserved in continental beds.

Swash and rill marks are current produced although they are very restricted in their distribution. Swash marks are the delicate, somewhat arcuate (convex landward), anastomosing patterns of fine lines or microridges left on a sandy surface by waves. Rill marks are small branching channels with dendritic or plantlike patterns. Swash and rill marks are rarely found in "fossil" form.

Though many other structures have been described from modern beaches and mud flats, their geological counterparts are unknown. The interested reader will find a good resume of many of these structures as well as those due to organisms in the *Treatise on Sedimentation* (Twenhofel, 1932) and in a paper by Bucher (1938).

REFERENCES CITED AND BIBLIOGRAPHY

Bokman, John (1953), Lithology and petrology of the Stanley and Jackfork formations, *J. Geol.*, vol. 61, pp. 152–170.

Bucher, W. H. (1919), On ripples and related sedimentary surface forms and their paleogeographic interpretation, *Am. J. Sci.*, ser. 4, vol. 47, pp. 149–210; 241–269.

Bucher, W. H. (1938), Key to papers published by an institute for the study of modern sediments in shallow seas, *J. Geol.*, vol. 46, pp. 726–755.

Chenowith, P. A. (1952), Statistical methods applied to Trentonian stratigraphy in New York, *Bull. Geol. Soc. Amer.*, vol. 63, pp. 521–560.

Clarke, J. M. (1918), Strand and undertow markings of Upper Devonian time, etc., *Bull. N.Y. State Mus.*, vol. 196, pp. 199–238.

Cloos, Hans (1938), Primäre Richtungen in Sedimenten der rheinischen Geosynkline, *Geol. Rundschau*, vol. 29, pp. 357–367.

Dake, C. L., and Cox, G. H. (1916), Geological criteria for determining the structural position of sedimentary beds, *Missouri Univ. School Mines, Bull.* 2, no. 4.

Hyde, J. E. (1911), The ripples of the Bedford and Berea formations of central Ohio; with notes on the paleogeography of that epoch, *J. Geol.*, vol. 19, pp. 257–269.

Kindle, E. M. (1917), Recent and fossil ripple mark, *Canadian Geol. Surv., Mus. Bull.* 25.

Kuenen, Ph. H. (1953), Graded bedding, with observations on Lower Paleozoic rocks of Britain, *Verhandel. Koninkl. Ned. Akad. Wetenschap., Afdel. Natuurk.*, vol. 20, no. 3, pp. 1–47.

Menard, H. W. (1952), Deep ripple marks in the sea, *J. Sediment. Petrol.*, vol. 22, pp. 3–10.

Rich, J. L. (1950), Flow markings, groovings, and intra-stratal crumplings as criteria for the recognition of slope deposits, with illustrations from Silurian rocks of Wales, *Bull. Am. Assoc. Petroleum Geol.*, vol. 34, pp. 717–741.

Shrock, R. R. (1948), *Sequence in layered rocks*, New York, McGraw-Hill, pp. 131, 162–166.

Stokes, W. L. (1947), Primary lineation in fluvial sandstones: a criterion of current direction, *J. Geol.*, vol. 45, pp. 52–54.

Stokes, W. L. (1953), Primary sedimentary trend indicators as applied to ore finding in the Carrizo Mountains, Arizona and New Mexico, *U.S. Atomic Energy Comm.*, RME-3043 (Pt. 1).

Tansey, V. O. (1953), Para-ripples in limestone with special reference to occurrences in the Mississippian Boone formation, *J. Sediment. Petrol.*, vol. 23, pp. 62–64.

Trow, J. W. (1948), *The Sturgeon quartzite of the Menominee district, Mich.*, Univ. of Chicago, Ph.D. dissertation (unpublished).

Twenhofel, W. H., and others (1932), *Treatise on sedimentation*, 2d ed., Baltimore, Williams and Wilkins, pp. 726–755.

van Bertsbergh, J. W. B. (1940), Richtungen der Sedimentation in der rheinischen Geosynkline, *Geol. Rundschau*, vol. 31, pp. 328–364.

DEFORMED, DISRUPTED, AND DESTROYED BEDDING

Introduction

Bedding may be deformed or disturbed prior to consolidation of the materials; in many cases the deformation occurs prior to the deposition of the next overlying bed; it always takes place prior to uplift and consolidation.

Such "soft-sediment" deformation includes folding, faulting or brecciation, and mobilization of the bed in question, followed by flow or injection of the mobile materials into adjacent beds. Injection (autointrusion) or subaqueous flow obviously destroys the earlier-formed internal structures of the bed affected and produces new and characteristic structures.

The discrimination between soft-sediment flow and deformation and deformation induced by postconsolidation tectonic forces is generally not difficult although some deformation is of uncertain origin (Miller, 1922). The preconsolidation structures are confined to particular beds, some of which may be but a fraction of an inch in thickness. Unlike drag folds, they bear no relation to the larger structures or to the tectonic pattern of the region. Notable is the absence of vein fillings either in the microfaults or in the interstices of the breccias. In most cases the folds produced are small-scale and commonly they are truncated or beveled by a bedding-plane, showing that they were formed and partially eroded before deposition of the overlying bed. All preconsolidation structures are presumed to be due to a gravitational force directed down slope.[9] If so they become a criterion of slope direction quite equal to any downslope current structure and accordingly they should be carefully observed and mapped. The paleogeographic significance of these features has been pointed out by Kuenen (1952) and others (Rich, 1950, p. 733).

The angle of slope needed to induce movement and deformation no doubt varies with the nature and water content of the materials involved. In some cases it is very low, perhaps no more than two degrees (Grabau, 1913, p. 780).

It seems probable that soft-sediment movements, the so-called contemporaneous deformation, and the resulting structures are all aspects of the same problem, namely, the behavior of unconsolidated or semiconsolidated sands and clays under stress. Movement may occur without loss of internal structure, such as folding or brecciation, or movement may occur with complete loss of the internal structures by the production of a slurry capable of flow or injection. Contrary to what one might expect, the sands seem to be most capable of complete mobilization and injection; the clays are more tenacious and yield fragments which become included in the mobilized sands. Clay seams, however, may function as slip surfaces.

The many factors involved in preconsolidation movement of sediments are only partially known. Some understanding of the properties of unconsolidated and semiconsolidated materials and their behavior under stress has been gained from the fields of soil mechanics, ceramics, and related tech-

[9] Some soft-sediment folds, and so forth, have been attributed to shove by grounded icebergs, shore ice, etc. Although soft-sediment deformation is common in glaciolacustrine deposits, such features are equally abundant in deposits where iceberg action is highly improbable. The author's view is that gravitational action is adequate and common enough to produce virtually all the soft-sediment structures.

nologies. The interested reader is referred to the standard works in these fields (Terzhagi, 1943; Krynine, 1947; Houwink, 1937) and to papers dealing with the geological aspects of rheology (Boswell, 1951).

Contemporaneous Folding

Soft-sediment folding is common in many sediments. It is most conspicuous in the thin-bedded sand-shale sequences (Pl. 5, top).

As noted by Rich (1950) the folds are of several contrasting types. One variety is confined to a single siltstone or sandstone layer and was obviously produced by an intrastratal flowage confined to the layer in question. In such folds the stratum affected is not itself folded but maintains instead a uniform thickness throughout. The folds, involving only internal laminations, are disordered; they die out near the margins of the bed and may be flattened against the top as well as the bottom of the bed. In some cases the anticlines are pinched off and form closed structures superficially resembling concretions. The origin of these "internal" or "involute" folds is very puzzling. They are formed *after* deposition of the overlying bed as the boundary effects on the structures indicate. The maintenance of uniform thickness of the bed containing the folds and the restriction of such structures to the fine sand- or siltstone beds precludes large-scale movement due to external forces. Perhaps these folds are a record of internal flowage or readjustment and are not due to lateral translation or slump.[10]

A second type of folding involves more than one sedimentation unit—in contrast to the above-described structures. Folding of this type, described and well illustrated by Hadding (1931), affects many interbedded siltstone-shale layers and seems to be the result of a mass flowage of these materials which if long-continued leads from partial to complete disruption of the bedding and the production of a "pseudoconglomerate." The first stages are a crumpling of the beds and a noticeable pinch-and-swelling of the siltstone layers. The interbedded shaly partings or seams maintain their thickness and continuity whereas the associated siltstone shows marked "boudinage." Continued flowage produces squeezed-out lumps of sand or silt, some of which have a spiral structure. The final result is a disordered "pseudoconglomerate" consisting of irregular, somewhat rounded lighter-colored siltstone or sandstone "fragments" embedded in a darker claystone matrix.

Both the above types of folding seem to be the result of flowage; in one case confined to a single sharply defined layer and in the other involving many thin layers. In both cases it seems to be the sand- or siltstone layers that display mobility.

Crumplings and bucklings on a somewhat larger scale in which boudinage

---

[10] This view is supported by the occurrence of such "folds" in horizontal beds, or beds with initial dip of less than one degree. Apparently Ongley and Macpherson reached a similar conclusion (Hills, 1941, plate I).

is inconspicuous or absent are also known and have been described from many places including Wales (Kuenen, 1948; Challinor, 1949; Rich, 1950). These structures seem to be produced by actual downslope movement of somewhat more competent layers. They are analogous to the intrastratal crumplings observed in many varved glaciolacustrine clays.[11] Although the folding is intense, with recumbency common, the layers maintain their continuity and are not pulled apart or otherwise disrupted.

Sandstone Dikes, Sills, and Autointrusions

Injection or intrusion of sand into sedimentary and other rocks is a characteristic feature of certain sedimentary assemblages. Sandstone dikes, sills, and related bodies have been described many times (Pl. 5, bottom). They were early reported by Diller (1890) and Newsom (1903) in this country. More recent descriptions of these phenomena are given in papers by Monroe (1950a, 1950b) and Vitanage (1954). A short but comprehensive review of the subject is given by Shrock (1948).

Typical of such structures are the California dikes described by Diller (1890). These dikes are vertical or near-vertical, wall-like masses of sandstone, ranging from a mere film to a maximum of 8 feet in width and from a few yards to over 9 miles in length. They are parallel to the jointing in the Cretaceous shales which they cut, though locally they may show a zigzag or offset course. They contain a few inclusions of shale. The sandstone fillings are feldspathic and micaceous and in most respects similar to the sandstones interbedded with the shales which they cut. Similar dikes are reported from other California localities by Newsom (1903) who has also compiled an exhaustive record of such dike phenomena from the earlier literature.

Of interest are the sandstone sills commonly found with sandstone dikes. These are similar in all respects to the dikes but they are parallel instead of discordant to the bedding. The sills are difficult to distinguish from a sandstone interbed except, unlike some sandstone interbeds, they are not stratified, cross-bedded, or the like, and locally they cross the bedding and continue at a higher stratigraphic level. No doubt some sandstone beds are themselves sills of a sort injected at the mud-water interface by the underflow of a dense slurry. The similarity in microtexture of these beds and the true dikes and sills is a substantial argument for their origin from a turbidity underflow (see Pl. 18; compare C with D or other parts of Pl. 18).

As noted by Diller and others (Vitanage, 1954) the mica and other heterodimensional grains or fragments in the vicinity of the dike wall tend to be oriented parallel to these surfaces. This feature, plus the deformation

---

[11] Glacial varves also show two types of folds, namely, the disorderly flowage of the faint laminations within a single thick silty or sandy varve and the folding involving many varves.

of the wall rocks near some dikes and the dike apophyses and related sills parallel to the bedding, indicates forcible intrusion or injection of the dike filling. The latter obviously did not accumulate grain by grain in an open fissure but instead was injected as a slurry under considerable hydrostatic pressure. In some of the larger dikes the injection was multiple (Vitanage, 1954).

It is significant, perhaps, that the slurry that is injected is sand, not mud. The shales commonly interbedded with the sands do not become mobilized; the sands apparently do and carry pieces of the shale along as inclusions.

In most cases there is much uncertainty as to whether the injection was downward from above or upward from below. In some cases one or the other of these two alternatives can be established. The sandstones dikes in the Pikes Peak granite (Cross, 1894; Vitanage, 1954) certainly came from above. In a few cases injection upward from a lower stratum can be demonstrated.

Why sandstone dikes are common in some sedimentary terranes—especially in the thick, even-bedded, and interbedded sandstone-shale sequences —is not clear. The fissuring has been attributed to earthquakes; the injection to movement under hydrostatic pressure of water-saturated sands which are "quick" or capable of mobilization. Fairbridge (1946) has pointed out the association of sandstone dikes with slump structures, intraformational breccias, and other features indicative of disturbance of the beds. He considered the dikes and the associated structures to be indicative of a particular facies and environment of sedimentation, namely, the tectonically unstable "foredeep areas of geosynclinal belts."

Disrupted Bedding

In addition to folding or to mobilization and injection with loss of structure, beds may be broken and undergo varying degrees of dislocation. Such disruption may consist only of fissuring transverse to the beds—mud cracking, for example—to brecciation in which the fragments of the beds are completely dislocated, rotated, and even overturned. Such fragmentation, if contemporaneous with sedimentation, leads to the formation of the so-called intraformational breccias or conglomerates (p. 276).

Fissuring and fragmentation imply some degree of induration of the sediment in order that the materials cohere well enough to form fragments. In most cases it is the shaly materials that cohere and constitute the fragments. Fragmentation may be due to desiccation; it may be due also to stresses induced by sliding or slumping and to sand injection.

Desiccation cracking and fragmentation is perhaps most common. Mud cracks form an irregular checkered polygonal pattern. Both size of the polygons and breadth of the cracks vary widely. The polygons may be but a few millimeters in diameter separated by narrow cracks under 1 millimeter in width or they may be something over 30 centimeters broad and separated by cracks 3 to 5 centimeters wide. The coarseness of the network probably is related in some way to the thickness of the desiccating seam.

Normally the cracks taper downward and ultimately pinch out. They are commonly filled by sand or coarser materials. If the drying seam is relatively thin (a few millimeters), the cracks may extend through the clay bed. The polygonal fragments thus formed may become slightly displaced, rotated, or even overturned and transported a short distance by the next sand-depositing torrent. Thus originate some of the flat shale-pebble conglomerates with a sand matrix.

Because mud cracks are formed by the shrinkage of a rock on drying, they cannot be formed in pure sand, since the latter undergoes little or no decrease in volume on drying. The mud cracks proper are not themselves preserved but are usually represented only by their fillings ("casts"). The cracked clayey rock generally crumbles, but in the overlying sandstone bed the entire crack system is preserved as a polygonal network of elevated ridges on the underside of the bed.

The polygonal crack system is presumed to be due to shrinkage upon loss of water. Almost invariably this implies subaerial drying. Even though this takes place most commonly in the intertidal zone, it is unlikely that most mud cracks originate in this realm. Barrell (1906) concluded that ". . . mud cracks form one of the surest indications of the continental origin of argillaceous deposits." [12]

In addition to desiccation, bedding may be disrupted by mass movement or slump. Such has been believed to be the origin of some intraformational breccias.

Bedding may be partially effaced by boring organisms. The borings proper are filled with structureless sediment. If such borings are numerous the original stratification planes are largely destroyed and only vestiges remain. Complete eradication of bedding is possible and has probably occurred in some sediments.

Armored Mud Balls, Clay Galls, and Related Structures

Armored mud balls are large, subspherical balls of clay that are coated or armored with fine gravel. Clay galls are small, somewhat flattened pellets of clay which are generally embedded in a sandy matrix. Clay galls are both similar and related to clay flakes and shavings.

The morphology and origin of armored mud balls have been investigated

[12] The possibility that some mud cracks were formed under water cannot be completely ruled out. The shrinkage cracks of septaria must be so formed. The volume decrease in the latter case must be due to crystallization of an amorphous and gelatinous, highly watery mass. The formation of cracks in a bed in an analogous manner has not been demonstrated but may be possible.

by Bell (1940) who records their occurrence in the Las Posas barranca, Ventura County, California. The size of mud balls varies from a fraction of an inch in diameter to approximately twenty inches; those two to four inches in diameter were the most common (Pl. 6).

Well-formed mud balls are highly spherical; nearly 60 per cent of those studied by Bell exceeded 0.90, 32 per cent were over 0.95, 12 per cent exceeded 0.99, and nearly 7 per cent have a sphericity of 1.00. The mean sphericities of balls that had traveled ¼ mile, 1 mile, and 2¾ miles were 0.784, 0.839, and 0.898, respectively. These data indicate the sphericity to vary nearly as the cube root of the distance traveled.

The larger mud balls are coated with coarser gravel than were the smaller. The weight of the armor varied from 17.1 per cent to 44.0 per cent of that of the whole ball. The total quantity of armor materials was found to be a power function of the surface area, varying approximately as the 1.54 power of the area, or approximately as the linear function of the ball diameter. Whereas the armor consists of a poorly graded (nine size classes) mixture of sand and gravel, the interior consists of relatively pure clay and silt.

Field relations, as well as the character of the mud balls themselves, proved rather clearly that the mud balls originated as clay chunks which had been released by rapid bank erosion and undercutting and which, upon rolling downstream, had acquired a gravel armor. Sand grains and pebbles were impressed into the softened exterior. As soon as the surface became well covered, it was sealed against further accretion. The growth of the ball is determined more by its structural strength than by either the size of the clay chunks available or by the transporting ability of the current. The maximum size represents a balance between the forces of cohesion and the destructive forces of impact. Both theoretical and experimental observations led to the conclusion that the velocity with which a ball may move with safety in a stream is inversely proportional to the diameter. For the Las Posas mud balls the relations are given by Bell as follows:

Diameter (inches)	Velocity of Stream (feet per second)
2	32
4	16
8	8
12	5

Bell noted also that in general the clay balls are considerably larger than the other debris of the bed load of the stream.

Mud balls, though a minor and uncommon constituent of sediments, furnish means of estimating the maximum velocities of ancient streams, the nature of the bed material, the approximate distances to source material, and the kind of water body which formed them. Mud balls are known from torrential sediments of various ages. Those which occur in some Pleistocene glacial deposits are "till balls" because their core is made of till.

Clay galls, shale flakes, and chips are much more common than mud balls. These objects are markedly flattened fragments, somewhat rounded to sub-angular in outline. They are especially abundant at the base of heavy sand beds. Like mud balls they record contemporaneous channeling and erosion of the intercalated shales. In some cases they may arise from the desiccation and breaking up of a thin mud parting. The mud polygons may curl up, be blown a few feet, and be buried in sand (see p. 277).

REFERENCES CITED AND BIBLIOGRAPHY

Barrell, J. (1906), Relative importance of continental, littoral, and marine sedimentation, *J. Geol.*, vol. 14, pp. 524–568.

Bell, H. S. (1940), Armored mud balls—their origin, properties and role in sedimentation, *J. Geol.*, vol. 48, pp. 1–31.

Boswell, P. G. H. (1951), The trend of research on the rheotropy of geological materials, *Science Prog.*, No. 156, pp. 608–622.

Challinor, John (1949), The origin of certain rock structures near Aberystwyth, *Proc. Geol. Assoc. London*, vol. 60, pt. 1, pp. 48–53.

Cross, C. W. (1894), Intrusive sandstone dikes in granite, *Bull. Geol. Soc. Amer.*, vol. 5, pp. 225–230.

Diller, J. S. (1890), Sandstone dikes, *Bull. Geol. Soc. Amer.*, vol. 1, pp. 411–442.

Emery, K. O. (1950), Contorted Pleistocene strata at Newport Beach, California, *J. Sediment. Petrol.*, vol. 20, pp. 111–115.

Fairbridge, R. W. (1946), Submarine slumping and location of oil bodies, *Bull. Am. Assoc. Petroleum Geol.*, vol. 30, pp. 84–92.

Fairbridge, R. W. (1947), Possible causes of intraformational disturbances in the Carboniferous rocks of Australia, *J. Proc. Roy. Soc. New South Wales*, vol. 81, pp. 99–121.

Grabau, A. W. (1913), *Principles of stratigraphy*, New York, A. G. Seiler and Co., pp. 780–785.

Hadding, A. (1931), On subaqueous slides, *Geol. Fören. i. Stockholm Förh.*, vol. 53, pp. 378–393.

Hills, E. S. (1941), *Outlines of structural geology*, New York, Nordeman, pp. 12–19.

Houwink, R. (1937), *Elasticity, plasticity and structure of matter*, Cambridge, Cambridge Univ. Press.

Jenkins, O. P. (1925a), Mechanics of clastic dike intrusion, *Eng. Mining-J. Press*, vol. 120, p. 12.

Jenkins, O. P. (1925b), Clastic dikes of eastern Washington and their geologic significance, *Am. J. Sci.*, ser. 5, vol. 10, pp. 234–246.

Krynine, D. P. (1947) *Soil mechanics*, New York, McGraw-Hill.

Kuenen, Ph. H. (1948), Slumping in the Carboniferous rocks of Pembrokeshire, *Quart. J. Geol. Soc. London*, vol. 104, pp. 365–385.

Kuenen, Ph. H. (1952), Paleogeographic significance of graded bedding and associated features, *Proc. Koninkl. Ned. Akad. Wetenschap.*, ser. B, vol. 55, pp. 28–36.

Miller, W. J. (1922), Intraformational corrugated rocks, *J. Geol.*, vol. 30, pp. 587–610.

Monroe, J. N. (1950), Origin of the clastic dikes of the Rockwell area, Texas, *Field & Lab.*, vol. 18, pp. 133–143.

Monroe, J. N. (1951), Woodbine sandstone dikes of northern McLennan county, Texas, *The Woodbine and Adjacent Strata*, Dallas, Southern Methodist Univ., pp. 93–102.

Newsom, F. F. (1903), Clastic dikes, *Bull. Geol. Soc. Amer.*, vol. 14, pp. 227–268.

Rich, J. L. (1950), Flow markings, groovings, and intrastratal crumplings, etc., *Bull. Am. Assoc. Petroleum Geol.*, vol. 34, pp. 717–741.

Shrock, R. R. (1948), *Sequence in layered rocks*, New York, McGraw-Hill, pp. 212–220.

Terzaghi, Karl (1943), *Theoretical soil mechanics*, New York, Wiley.

Van Houten, F. B. (1954), Sedimentary features of Martinsburg slate, northwestern New Jersey, *Bull. Geol. Soc. Amer.*, vol. 65, pp. 813–818.

van Straaten, L. M. J. U. (1949), Occurrence in Finland of structures due to subaqueous sliding of sediments, *C. R. Soc. geol. Finlande*, no. 22, pp. 9–18.

Vitanage, P. W. (1954) Sandstone dikes in the South Platte area, Colorado, *J. Geol.*, vol. 62, pp. 493–500.

CHEMICAL ("SECONDARY") STRUCTURES

Introduction

Chemical action penecontemporaneous with sedimentation or subsequent thereto is responsible for various sedimentary structures. Some of these are the result of solution, such as stylolites, corrosion zones, "oolicasts," and vugs; other are the result of precipitation or segregation of mineral matter and include such structures as nodules, concretions, geodes, septaria, and the like.

Mineral Segregations, Definitions, and Classification

Various accretionary bodies, though a minor feature of most sedimentary rocks, are very common. These structures are segregations of the rarer constituents of the rock.

So many features obviously of diverse origins have been collectively dubbed "concretions" that this term has no exact meaning. It has been used interchangeably with the term "nodule" likewise without precise meaning.[13] If certain pseudoconcretionary forms, such as armored mud balls (p. 193, Pl. 6), certain "lime mud balls" (Croneis and Grubbs, 1939), and certain algal structures (p. 222, Pl. 26) be excluded, then the various mineral segregations fall into four groups, namely (1) nodules, (2) spherulites, rosettes, and other regular crystal growths, (3) concretions in a restricted sense, and (4) veins, geodes, septaria, and other forms related in that they have a partially or wholly filled interior cavity.

These four fundamentally different types of bodies are unlike in their structure and manner of origin. The *nodules*, such as those of chert and flint, are wholly irregular in form and normally without any internal structure. They are primarily the result of postdepositional replacement of the host rock. The crystal aggregates are irregular to spherical, coarsely crystalline aggregates, having a radial structure (spherulites) or a radial symmetry (rosettes), or a less regular intergrowth of coarse crystals (sand crystals). Some include and some exclude the matrix in which they grew. True concretions are normally subspherical, though commonly very oblate, to irregular bodies formed generally by orderly precipitation of mineral matter in the pores of a sediment adjacent to a nucleus. The fourth and last class of structures includes veins, geodes, conchilites, and other structures having a more or less filled central cavity. These are not all alike and do not constitute a homogeneous group.

Origin

It is significant that the various structures defined above are all segregations of the minor constituents of the rock in which they are found. They are the silica of the carbonate host rock, the lime carbonate of the shale or sandstone, the iron sulfide of the black shale, and the like. Introduction of foreign matter does not seem necessary for the precipitation of these aggregates. The only requirement is a segregation process. As noted by Ramberg (1952, p. 222) owing to surface energy differences, the free energy will be less if these constituents occur in clusters rather than finely divided and disseminated; hence aggregates will tend to form in the course of time.[14] The segregations thus produced may replace the host rock, fill openings, such as vugs or fractures, or be deposited in available pores, or form by thrusting aside the enclosing matrix.

[13] Recognizing the need for better definitions and terminology, Todd (1903) proposed four terms: accretion, intercretion, excretion, and incretion, based on mode of growth. The first type grows from the center outward in a regular manner; intercretions are the septaria which form by irregular and interstitial growth; excretions are those growing from the exterior inward; incretions are the cylindrical forms with a hollow core. Todd's proposals seem not to be generally followed.

[14] Analogous action is the growth in grain size of some precipitates in the chemical laboratory, such as barium sulfate, with digestion.

PLATE 7

MINERAL SEGREGATIONS I

Top: Calcareous concretions ("marlekor"), about half size.

Center: Hollow iron-oxide concretions. Length of largest about four inches. Essentially cemented shell of sand.

Bottom: Chert nodule. Length of nodule about five inches. Dense black "flint" with veneer of white "cotton" rock.

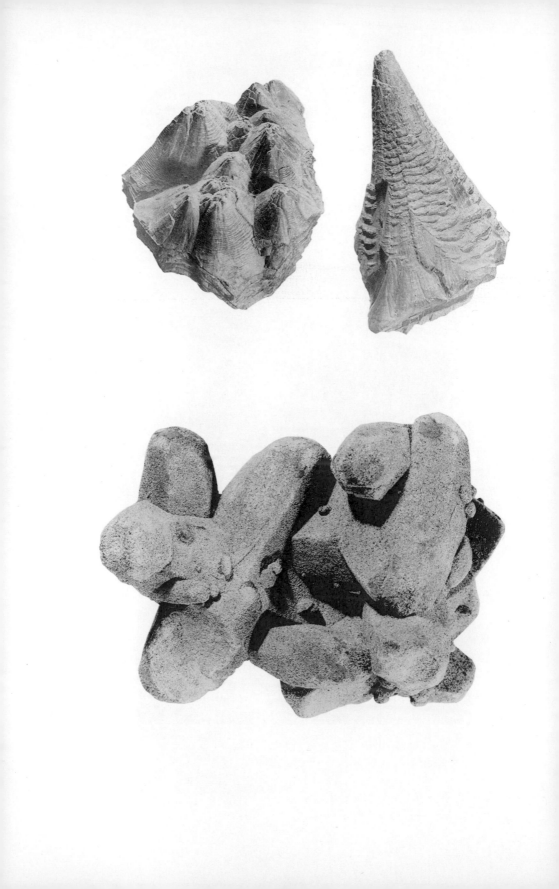

PLATE 8

MINERAL SEGREGATIONS II

Top: Cone-in-cone specimens showing transverse ridges and longitudinal striations. Note concave surface of cone on right. Length of largest cone three inches.

Bottom: Sand crystals, Miocene sandstone, Bad Lands, S.D. Scalenohedral calcite loaded with included sand grains. Length of specimen about six inches.

There remain many unexplained observations. Some segregations replace their matrix whereas others do not. Some segregations form true concretions whereas others form crystal aggregates or even single crystals. Some segregations include the matrix; others do not.

What determines the size, number, and spacing of the segregations? In many cases, as in the calcareous concretions of shale, the locus of deposition is a bit of organic matter such as a leaf or a fish. Many concretions are renowned for the excellent fossils which they enclose. As noted by Weeks (1953), the ammonia generated by decomposing matter may have locally altered the pH so that deposition of calcium carbonate took place which was elsewhere inhibited. The localization of chert nodules, barite rosettes, and the like, probably cannot be so explained.

Some writers have concluded that segregations are syngenetic, i.e., formed essentially on the sea floor (Tarr, 1921; Trefethen, 1947). In some cases certainly, the enclosed fossils unlike those in the matrix are not crushed, are full-bodied, and suggest therefore the early formation of the enclosing concretionary body. The passage of the bedding planes through other concretionary structures without distortion at the concretion matrix interface suggests a late postconsolidation origin for such structures. A postconsolidation age of others is clearly shown by the deformation of the enclosing rock as a result of the growth of the concretionary body (Daly, 1900).

Nodules

Nodules are irregular tuberous bodies of mineral matter unlike that of the host rock in which they occur. Their surface may be warty or knobby. They are commonly elongated parallel to the bedding, and if abundant, may coalesce into somewhat continuous layers.

By far the most common nodules are chert or flint; they are found typically in limestone or chalk (Pl. 7). They are more numerous along certain bedding planes or in certain beds than elsewhere. The spacing of such layers of nodules may be rhythmic (Richardson, 1919b). In some exposures they are said to be more abundant near the surface than in the deeper parts of the section.

Chert or flint nodules are nearly pure silica, though some are slightly calcareous (Table 37). Under the microscope they are structureless microcrystalline aggregates of chalcedonic quartz. The nodule is dense and most commonly devoid of any structure, radial or concentric. In a few, however, are silicified fossils, oolites, and a sparse scattering of spicule-like bodies of small size. Other nodules are marked by a concentric structure which has been interpreted as shrinkage (syneresis) cracks (Taliaferro, 1934).

Clearly the nodule is not an ordinary concretionary growth. The flint and chert nodules seem to be irregular replacements of the host rock by silica, although some writers have contended that they were original gelatinous precipitates of silica (Tarr, 1917, 1926; Trefethen, 1947). The chert problem is discussed in more detail on page 439.

Collophane also occurs in nodular form. Such phosphatic nodules have been described and reported from many places (see page 473).

TABLE 37. Chemical Composition of Nodules, Concretions, and Related Structures

	A	B	C	D (per cent)	E	F	G	H
SiO₂	70.78	23.92	13.1	36.99	3.46	1.80^d	1.16	9.08
TiO₂	0.03	0.62	....	....	0.26	....	....	0.12
Al₂O₃	0.45	6.82	35.1	5.36	n.d.	....	0.33	1.87
Fe₂O₃	0.02	1.12	4.7	0.82⎫	⎰....	⎰....	....	5.03
FeO	0.30	2.57	....	....⎭	6.78		3.21	....
Fe	....	....	....	....	....	45.80	....	....
MnO	0.02	0.93	....	....	0.07	....	T	0.50
MgO	1.88	2.26	....	0.03	0.43	....	0.88	13.80
CaO	12.90	31.35	22.9	0.51	42.98	....	36.16	27.29
BaO	....	....	....	35.76	....	....	....	....
Na₂O	0.05	1.16	....	....	....	....	....	....
K₂O	0.06	1.84	....	....	....	....	....	....
H₂O+	0.48	2.04	....⎫	0.27	⎰1.47	....⎫	0.31	⎰....
H₂O−	0.32	0.64	....⎭		⎱0.52	....⎭		⎱0.20
P₂O₅	0.16	0.36	....	....	30.91	....	T	T
CO₂	12.04	24.24	18.0^a	....	3.37	....	29.00	38.83
SO₃	T	....	....	19.20	0.19	....	0.15^f	....
FeS₂	0.27	....	....	....	3.48^c	....	21.58	....
C	0.33	....	....	0.32^b	....	....	7.20^g	2.25
S	....	....	....	....	....	51.10	....	0.67
Total	100.14	99.87	93.8	99.26	93.92	98.70^e	99.98	99.65

A. "Nodular chert," Delaware limestone (Devonian), Ohio. Downs Schaaf, analyst (Stout, 1945).
B. "Imatra Stone," a calcareous concretion in Late Glacial clay, East Finland. L. Lokka, analyst (Eskola, 1932).
C. Septarian nodule, partial analysis of interior matrix, from Lias shale, England (Richardson, 1919a).
D. Barite rosette, Oklahoma (Nichols, 1906).
E. Phosphatic "pebbles," basal Platteville limestone, St. Paul, Minnesota. Pettijohn (1926).
F. Pyrite nodules, marine clay, Torquay, Victoria, Australia. F. D. Drews, analyst (Edwards and Baker, 1951, p. 44).
G. Calcareous nodule ("coal ball") from coal, Lower Coal Measures, England (Stocks, 1902).
H. Concretion from Ohio shale (Devonian), Ohio. D. J. Demorest, analyst (Stout, 1944, p. 14).
  ^{a} Calculated from CaO.
  ^{b} "Organic matter."
  ^{c} S.
  ^{d} "Insoluble."
  ^{e} Deficiency is carbonate.
  ^{f} "Sulfuric acid."
  ^{g} "Organic matter and undetermined."

Spherulites, Rosettes, and Sand Crystals

Spherulites are more or less spherical bodies, varying in size from pellets visible only under the microscope to objects several inches or more in diameter. These rounded bodies are called spherulites if the constituents are arranged radially around one, or in some cases several, centers. The larger spherulites have been termed *spherulitic concretions*, or simply *nodules*, or *concretions*. The smaller spherulites resemble very closely oolites and pisolites with radial habit; but unlike true oolites, the spherulitic bodies were formed in the place where they are now found.

The outer surfaces of most spherulites are approximately circular in section, although some are irregular, especially where several coalesce. Between crossed nicols, simple spherulites show dark crosses resembling uniaxial interference figures (Pl. 40, C). The dark bars are parallel to the cross hairs if the extinction angles of the individual mineral crystals are zero. As the stage is turned, successive needles come into parallel position; consequently the cross remains stationary.

The spherulites of sedimentary rocks consist of many minerals. Noteworthy are the minute spherulites of chalcedony present in certain limestones (Pl. 40, C), the large dahlite (carbonate-apatite) spherulites of the Thermopolis formation (Upper Cretaceous) of Wyoming (McConnell, 1935), the aragonite spherulites of the Etchegoin formation (Pliocene) of California (Reed, 1926), and the extraordinarly large spherulitic carbonate concretions in the shales of Kettle Point, Ontario (Daly, 1900).

The spherical form has been attributed to primary precipitation as a colloidal gel. The internal radial structure therefore would be a late feature related to the crystallization of the gel. However, microspherulites with radiating crystalline structure can readily be made in the laboratory by ordinary chemical reaction and precipitation. No gel stage is required.

Another symmetrical growth form assumed by some accretionary bodies is the *rosette*. Barite, marcasite, and pyrite take this form in some rocks; best known are the barite rosettes from the red Permian sandstones of Oklahoma (Tarr, 1933; Nichols, 1906; Pogue, 1911; Shead, 1923). These rosettes are clusters of large crystals of barite, somewhat symmetrically disposed. They are similar to *sand crystals*, which are a poikiloblastic development of calcite also found in some sandstones (Pl. 17, D). Sand crystals, like the barite rosettes, include much sand; they occur as large euhedra or clusters of euhedra. Best known are the sand crystals of Fontenbleau, France (Cayeux, 1929, p. 154) and those of the Arikeree formation (Tertiary) in the badlands of South Dakota (Barbour, 1901). The formation of sand crystals is related to "luster mottling" seen in some sandstones, and to the cementation of sandstone, a topic which is discussed at some length in the chapter on lithification (see Pl. 8, bottom).

Spherulitic aggregates of marcasite in limestone have been figured and described (Diller, 1898, p. 110).

Both large and small crystalline aggregates of marcasite and pyrite occur in some clays and shales. Unlike calcite and barite, the iron sulfides seem able to exclude their matrix during growth. It is thought that pyrite is formed in a neutral or alkaline environment (in most cases marine), whereas marcasite is a product of an acid environment (fresh water) (Edwards and Baker, 1951).

Concretions

As noted, the term "concretion" is loosely applied to some or all of the objects here treated under the general heading of "mineral segregations." After the irregular nodules, spherulitic and other regular crystal aggregates, septaria, and related bodies have been removed from the general category, there still remains a large number of objects best termed "concretions." These structures are the product of accumulation of mineral matter in the pores of the sediment about a nucleus or center.

The concretions are normally spherical, spheroidal, or disk-shaped, though diverse shapes arise by fusion of two or more simple forms or by deposition about an object of elongate or irregular form. Though many do not have a nucleus, in others something—most commonly a shell, leaf, or bone—serves as a center around which the concretion is built. The concretion may have a concentric structure.

Concretions vary in size from small pellet-like objects to great spheroidal bodies as much as 10 feet in diameter (such as those in the Cretaceous Cannonball formation of Kansas). Certain sandstones or shales are characterized by numerous cannonball-like forms. The size seems to be in part determined by the permeability of the host rock. The concretions of sandstones are commonly larger than those of shales. In interbedded siltstones and shale, the concretions normally are confined to the former.

The mineral constituents of concretions are those which normally play the role of cement in the rocks in which these structures occur. Silica, calcite, and iron oxide are therefore the most common. Most concretions contain a good deal of rock matter. The bedding planes of the host rock pass through most concretionary structures, which indicates that these bodies were formed after deposition of the enclosing sediment. Especially is this true of the concretions of shales and sandstones. The substances of which the concretions are made were evidently collected from the surrounding rock and redeposited around the precipitating nucleus.

Of common occurrence and many times described in the literature are the calcareous concretions of certain Late Glacial clays (Pl. 7, top). These structures variously called *imatra stones* or *marlekor* occur in the varved lake clays of Finland, Sweden, and Norway, where they were early observed, and in similar deposits in North America, especially in the clays of the Connecticut valley (Tarr, 1935), in the Ottawa region (Kindle, 1923) and in the Espanola area (Quirke, 1917).

The most complete description of these structures is that given by Tarr (1935). The concretions occur primarily in the silt layers; they are flattened, parallel to the bedding, generally disk-shaped, and characterized by the passage of the bedding laminations through the concretion. Although generally small, 1 to 2 inches in diameter and a half inch or less in thickness, and of simple form, some are larger and irregular. These complex forms are due mainly to coalescence of simple types producing dumbbell-shaped pairs and in part due to warty outgrowths and other irregular overgrowths which defy description and in other cases produce a strange bilaterally symmetrical body.

The concretions are highly calcareous (Table 37, col. B) although all contain a large content of silt. Those of the Connecticut valley were about 50 per cent carbonate, mainly $CaCO_3$, and 50 per cent clayey silt. The percentage of carbonate is approximately that required to fill the pores of a freshly deposited silt.

It is clear, therefore, that the form, structure, and composition of these concretions is the result of localized precipitation of calcium carbonate in the pores of the silt beds. Tarr attempted to elaborate in some detail the mechanism of the process.

Geodes

The significant features of geodes are (1) their subspherical shape, (2) the hollow interior, (3) the outer chalcedonic silica layer, (4) the inner drusy lining of inward projecting crystals, and (5) the evidences of growth by expansion.

Geodes are hollow, globular bodies, varying in size from an inch or two to a foot or more in diameter. They tend to be slightly flattened with their equatorial plane parallel to the bedding. Geodes are characteristic of certain limestone beds, but are rarely found in shales. Geodes are marked by a thin outermost layer of dense chalcedony (Diller, 1898, p. 112). The layer is incomplete in some geodes and is lost in others by the erosion of the exterior.

Most geodes are more or less filled. Hence on the inner surface of the chalcedonic layer are younger, usually crystalline materials. Most commonly these are inward projecting quartz crystals, although in many geodes drusy coatings of scalenohedral calcite or rhombohedral dolomite are known. Less commonly associated with these are many minor and rarer constituents, which include aragonite, ankerite, magnetite, hematite, pyrite, millerite, chalcopyrite, sphalerite, kaolin, and bitumen (Van Tuyl, 1916). No constant order of succession holds for all geodes, although the outer shell is invariably chalcedony. In most cases, this shell is followed directly by calcite. In many geodes there is a later or second generation of chalcedony. The metallic sulfides, if present, are most generally the last-deposited minerals.

Most singular and most significant feature of geodes is the incontrovertible evidence that they have grown by expansion. Notable is the "exploding-bomb" structure. As Bassler (1908) has clearly shown, geodes originate in the cavities of fossils, and upon growth of the geode the fossil bursts. Upon further growth the fragments of the fossil adhering to the geode become widely separated. Ultimately the fragments are dissolved or absorbed by the growing geode and are lost.

The prime problem is to explain the origin of the pressure which is the cause of the remarkable expansion.[15] As Bassler's collection clearly shows, an initial cavity is a necessary prerequisite for the formation of a geode. The unfilled space within a crinoid calyx, a bivalve, or any similar opening will suffice. Nothing is present in the initial cavity except fluid, presumably connate salt solution. Inasmuch as the outer wall of the true geode is chalcedony, the initial deposit must have been a layer of gelatinous silica. The formation of this layer isolates the salt solution. If, in the course of time, the waters outside the cell thus created freshen, osmosis will begin and build up internal pressures.[16] This pressure is directed outward against the cell wall. Hence the geode will tend to expand. Expansion may occur at the expense of the surrounding limestone by solution at the silica-limestone interface. Or if the geode forms prior to consolidation, the surrounding lime mud may be simply pushed aside. Expansion continues until the cell volume is much increased and the salt concentration of the containing fluids reduced to such value that the expansive force becomes negligible. The geode has reached maturity. Ultimately the silica gel dehydrates and crystallizes. Shrinkage and cracking follow. Mineral-bearing waters enter and deposit the usual drusy geode lining over the primary chalcedonic layer.

Voidal "Concretions"

A somewhat different type of concretion is the voidal or hollow iron oxide bodies most commonly found in sands and sandstones and in some clays (Pl. 7). They are common in Pleistocene sands but are also reported from older Tertiary and even Cretaceous sands.

Like other concretions, they vary in size and shape but unlike most other concretions many are large and tubelike (Willcox, 1914) and all have a central void or cavity. The rim is a hard dense limonitic layer. The interiors are partially filled with a ferruginous sand which rattles when the concre-

[15] The origin of this pressure has been attributed to the "force of crystallization" but as some geodes contain no crystals this hypothesis is untenable.

[16] A mechanism suggested by Tanton (1944) for the growth of conchilites which are peculiar small, bowl-shaped objects of limonite or goethite growing in an inverted position on mineralized bedrock in a Canadian lake.

PLATE 9

MINERAL SEGREGATIONS III

The "box work" (melikaria) consists of vein fillings which have weathered out from a septarian nodule. Length of specimen about five inches.

A   B   C

PLATE 10

STYLOLITES

A: Stylolites in sandstone, Allegheny formation (Pennsylvanian), Garret County, Maryland, showing two stylolitic seams; the core has parted or separated along the upper stylolitic surface. Diameter of core about two inches.

B: Stylolites in sandstone, Allegheny formation (Pennsylvanian), Garret County, Maryland. Diameter of core about two inches. Dark coaly matter along stylolitic seam.

C: Portion of stylolitic column from Salem limestone (Mississippian), Indiana. Shows grooves or striations. Length of specimen about four inches.

tion is shaken ("klapperstein"). In a few the core is compact and consists of clay which may be slightly separated from the walls.

Hollow ferruginous concretions have been explained by "intergranular secretion of limonite" (Smith, 1948), by partial replacement of limestone pebbles by iron compounds (Shaw, 1917), oxidation of "claystone pebbles" (Leroy, 1949) or by oxidation of sideritic concretions (Bates, 1938; Todd, 1903). The latter explanation seems to be the correct one inasmuch as oxidation of jointed siderite beds turns each joint block into a hollow or partially filled limonitic "box" (Taylor, 1949, p. 90). The clay core of some ironstone concretions appears to be in part unoxidized sideritic clay. These structures therefore are a product of weathering and should not be found below the water table. The presumed evidence of expansion seen in thin section of the limonitic rim is only a record of corrosion and partial replacement of the quartz grains by siderite—a common phenomenon in siderite-cemented sands.

Septaria

Septaria are large (3 to 36 inches) nodules characterized by a series of radiating cracks that widen toward the center, which is crossed by a series of cracks concentric with the margins (Fig. 61). Uniformity of pattern is the

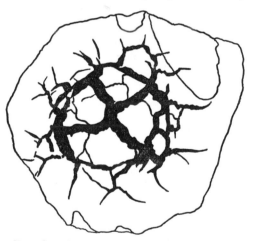

Fig. 61. Septarian structure. Length of specimen, about five inches.

exception and great irregularity generally prevails. The crack system, in section, more commonly appears polygonal, although near the margins the radial arrangement persists. Whereas the width of the cracks in general is independent of position in the nodules, those near the margin do wedge out toward the perimeter; marginal cracks rarely penetrate to the outside. The cracks are almost invariably filled with a crystalline deposit, most commonly calcite. Many septaria, released from their shale matrix, weather and are so eroded that the interior vein system may be seen ("turtle backs"). The vein system may be wholly freed of all adhering material (Pl. 9). Such structures have been termed *melikaria*. They are said to form in some shales and not be related to nodule development (Burt, 1928).

The septarian nodules, except the vein fillings, are normally impure argillaceous carbonate bodies, enclosed in shale. According to Richardson (1919a) the central part is more aluminous than the margins (Table 37, col. C).

A peculiarity of many septarian nodules is the shell of cone-in-cone which surrounds some of these bodies.

The formation of the septarian nodule involves (1) formation of a body of aluminous gel, (2) case-hardening of the exterior, dehydration of the interior, and formation of shrinkage crack pattern, and (3) partial or complete filling of the cracks with precipitated mineral matter, thereby producing the vein network of the nodule. The mechanism involved in forming an aluminous gel is the most obscure and seems to be in part an expansive process, as the peripheral cone-in-cone testifies. The mechanism involved in case-hardening, dehydration, and shrinkage cracking is irreversible chemical desiccation.[17] The mechanism of vein filling does not require elaboration.

Apparently related to the septarian nodules are the smaller *loess-kindchen* which are simple to compound nodules found in the loess. These bodies differ from septaria in having a thin calcareous outer shell, their compound character, and the lack of vein filling of their cracked interiors. Their formation is not well understood (Todd, 1913) but like true septaria, there seems to have been a case-hardening of the shell and shrinkage of the clay-filled interior.

Cone-in-Cone

Calcareous cone-in-cone layers are minor features of some shales (shales with "beef"). These layers, generally 1 to 6 inches thick, are characterized by an abundance of right circular cones (Pl. 8). These stand in an inverted position, i.e., base upward, apex down, and with the cone axis normal to the bedding. Apical angles vary widely but fall most commonly between 30 and 60 degrees. The diameter of the circular base therefore varies from near equality with, to about one-third of the height of the cone. In some cases the cones have flaring bases. The sides of the cones are usually ribbed or grooved and many are marked also by annular depressions and ridges which are most pronounced near the base of the cone and which become finer and more obscure near its apex.

[17] The relative roles of expansion and contraction in the formation of septaria have been debated (Davies, 1913; Todd, 1913; Crook, 1913).

Internally, the cones are fibrous calcite (Pl. 30, C) although cones in siderite (Hendricks, 1937) and gypsum (Tarr, 1932, p. 722) have been found. The fibers tend to be parallel with the axis of the cone, and hence are normal to the surface of the cone-in-cone layer, although there are exceptions. The fibrous material antedates the formation of the cones inasmuch as the cone structure transgresses the fibers and normally extends across the fibrous seam. That the fibrous character is not essential to the structure is further shown by the distinct, though rare, cone-in-cone structure shown by some coal (Bartrum, 1941).

Cone-in-cone occurs most commonly in thin layers in some flat-lying shales. It is also known to occur in the peripheral zone of some large accretionary bodies, especially some septarian nodules.

Although various theories have been formulated to explain cone-in-cone, most geologists agree that pressure is involved. The structure is in some ways analogous to percussion cones. The fibrous carbonate layers, in which the cone-in-cone is most commonly found, are flat, bedding-plane veins, not original carbonate beds. This conclusion is well supported by the observation that cone-in-cone seams may separate the upper and lower carapaces of trilobites or the upper and lower impressions of fish remains (Brown, 1954). The calcite fibers, set perpendicular to the layer, are comparable to those of fibrous vein quartz, the fibers of chrysotile veinlets, fibrous gypsum veins, and the fibrous ice crystals in the frost-heaved soils. The pressure built up by the growth of the fibrous layers, according to Richardson (1923) is responsible for the conical shearing. Tarr (Twenhofel, 1932, p. 729), however, attributes the pressure to the weight of the superincumbent beds. This view is untenable, however, because the usual inverted position of the cones indicates that the active forces came from lower rather than upper strata. If the pressure does not originate in the cone-in-cone layer itself, then the pressures built up by growth of other such layers in the formation might result in rupturing and conical shearing in the first-formed carbonate layers. Such pressure, which is analogous to that causing frost heaving, is directed upward. The cone-in-cone on the exterior of concretionary bodies would be related to expansive pressures of epigenetic concretionary action.

Because the cone-in-cone layers are generally carbonate, solution is prone to take place under pressure along the conical shear surfaces. Such solution is responsible for both the annular corrugations and the clay films between the concentric cones. These features are related in character and manner of origin to stylolites.

Veins, Vugs, and Geode Fillings

Small veins or veinlets are commonly seen in thin section and the nature of the fillings of these structures as well as those of vugs and geodes would be familiar to the student. Most common fillings are quartz (Adams, 1920) and calcite (Grout, 1946). Of special interest are the flat-lying fibrous veins of calcite ("beef") and gypsum which have been discussed in the section on cone-in-cone.

REFERENCES CITED AND BIBLIOGRAPHY

Adams, S. F. (1920), A microscopic study of vein quartz, *Econ. Geol.*, vol. 15, pp. 623–664.

Barbour, E. H. (1901), Sand crystals and their relations to certain concretionary forms, *Bull. Geol. Soc. Amer.*, vol. 12, pp. 165–172.

Bartrum, J. A. (1941), Cone-in-cone and other structures in New Zealand coals, *New Zeal. J. Sci. Technol.*, vol. 22, pp. 209B–215B.

Bassler, R. S. (1908), The formation of geodes, with remarks on the silicification of fossils, *U.S. Nat. Museum, Proc.*, vol. 35, pp. 133–154.

Bates, R. L. (1938), Occurrence and origin of certain limonite concretions, *J. Sediment. Petrol.*, vol. 8, pp. 91–99.

Brown, Roland (1954), How does cone-in-cone material become emplaced? *Am. J. Sci.*, vol. 252, pp. 372–376.

Burt, F. A. (1928), Melikaria: vein complexes resembling septaria veins in form, *J. Geol.*, vol. 36, pp. 539–544.

Burt, F. A. (1932), Formative processes in concretions formed about fossils as nuclei, *J. Sedimentary Petrol.*, vol. 2, pp. 38–45.

Cayeux, L. (1929), *Les roches sedimentaires de France, Roches silicieuses*, Paris, Imprimerie nationale.

Croneis, Carey, and Grubbs, D. M. (1939), Silurian sea balls, *J. Geol.*, vol. 47, pp. 598–612.

Crook, T. (1913), Septaria: A defence of the 'shrinkage' view, *Geol. Mag.*, vol. 10, pp. 514–515.

Daly, R. A. (1900), The calcareous concretions of Kettle Point, Lambton County, Ontario, *J. Geol.*, vol. 8, pp. 135–150.

Davies, A. M. (1913), The origin of septarian structure, *Geol. Mag.*, vol. 10, pp. 99–101.

Diller, J. S. (1898), The educational series of rock specimens, *U.S. Geol. Survey, Bull.* 150.

Edwards, A. B. and Baker, G. (1951), Some occurrences of supergene iron sulphides in relation to their environments of deposition, *J. Sediment. Petrol.*, vol. 21, pp. 34–46.

Emery, K. O. (1950), Ironstone concretions and beach ridges of San Diego County, California, *Calif. J. Mines Geol.*, vol. 46, pp. 213–221.

Eskola, P. (1932), Conditions during the earliest geological times, *Ann. Acad. Sci. Fennicae*, ser. A, vol. 36, no. 4.

Grout, F. F. (1946), Microscopic characters of vein carbonates, *Econ. Geol.*, vol. 41, pp. 475–502.

Hanna, M. A. (1936), Barite concretions from the Yazoo Clay, Eocene, of Louisiana, *J. Sediment. Petrol.*, vol. 6, p. 28–30.

Hendricks, T. A. (1937), Some unusual specimens of cone-in-cone in manganiferous siderite, *Am. J. Sci.*, vol. 33, pp. 458–561.

Kindle, E. M. (1923), Range and distribution of certain types of Canadian Pleistocene concretions, *Bull. Geol. Soc. Amer.*, vol. 43, pp. 614–617.

Leroy, L. W. (1949), A note on voidal concretions in the El Milagro formation of western Venezuela, *J. Sediment. Petrol.*, vol. 19, pp. 39–42.

McConnell, Duncan (1935), Spherulitic concretions of dahlite from Ishawooa, Wyoming, *Am. Mineralogist*, vol. 20, pp. 693–698.

Martens, J. H. C. (1925), Barite and associated minerals in concretions in the Genesee shale, *Am. Mineralogist*, vol. 10, pp. 102–104.

Mathias, H. E. (1928), Syngenetic origin of pyrite concretions in the Pennsylvanian shales of north-central Missouri, *J. Geol.*, vol. 36, pp. 440–450.

Merrill, G. P. (1894), The formation of sandstone concretions, *U.S. Nat. Mus., Proc.*, vol. 17, pp. 87–88.

Nichols, H. W. (1906), New forms of concretions, *Field Columbian Mus. Geol. Publ.*, vol. 3, pp. 25–54.

Pettijohn, F. J. (1926), Intraformational phosphate pebbles from the Twin City Ordovician, *J. Geol.*, vol. 34, pp. 361–373.

Pogue, J. E. (1911), On sand-barites from Kharga, Egypt, *U.S. Nat. Mus. Proc.*, vol. 38, pp. 17–24.

Quirke, T. T. (1917), Espanola district, Ontario, *Geol. Survey Canada, Mem.* 102, pp. 56–58, Pl. V.

Ramberg, H. (1952), *The origin of metamorphic and metasomatic rocks*, Chicago, Univ. Chicago Press, pp. 220–225 and pp. 232–233.

Reed, R. D. (1926), Aragonite concretions from the Kettleman Hills, *J. Geol.*, vol. 34, pp. 829–833.

Revelle, Roger and Emery, K. O. (1951), Barite concretions from the ocean floor, *Bull. Geol. Soc. Amer.*, vol. 62, pp. 707–724.

Richardson, A. W. (1919a), On the origin of septarian structure, *Mineralog. Mag.*, vol. 18, pp. 327–338.

Richardson, A. W. (1919b), The origin of Cretaceous flint, *Geol. Mag.*, vol. 56, pp. 535–547.

Richardson, A. W. (1921), The relative age of concretions, *Geol. Mag.*, vol. 58, pp. 114–124.

Richardson, A. W. (1923), Petrology of the shales with "beef," *Quart. Jour. Geol. Soc. London.*, vol. 79, pp. 88–99.

Shaub, B. M. (1937), The origin of cone-in-cone and its bearing on the origin of concretions and septaria, *Am. J. Sci.*, vol. 34, pp. 331–334.

Shaw, E. W. (1917), The Pliocene history of northeastern and central Mississippi, *U.S. Geol. Surv. Prof. Paper* 108, pp. 138, Pl. L.

Shead, A. C. (1923), Notes on barite in Oklahoma with chemical analyses of sand barite rosettes, *Proc. Oklahoma Acad. Sci.*, vol. 3, pp. 102–106.

Smith, L. L. (1948), Hollow ferruginous concretions in South Carolina, *J. Geol.*, vol. 56, pp. 218–225.

Stocks, H. B. (1902), On the origin of certain concretions in the Lower Coal Measures, *Quart. J. Geol. Soc. London*, vol. 58, pp. 46–58.

Stout, W. W. and Schoenlaub, R. A. (1945), The occurrence of flint in Ohio, *Bull. Geol. Survey Ohio*, 46.

Taliaferro, N. L. (1934), Contraction phenomena in cherts, *Bull. Geol. Soc. Amer.*, vol. 45, pp. 189–232.

Tanton, T. L. (1944), Conchilites, *Trans. Roy. Soc. Can.*, 3rd ser., vol. 38, sec. 4, pp. 97–104.

Tarr, W. A. (1917), Origin of the chert in the Burlington limestone, *Am. J. Sci.*, vol. 44, pp. 409–452.

Tarr, W. A. (1921), Syngenetic origin of concretions in shale, *Bull. Geol. Soc. Amer.*, vol. 32, pp. 373–384.

Tarr, W. A. (1926), The origin of chert and flint, *Univ. Missouri Studies*, vol. 1, pp. 1–54.

Tarr, W. A. (1933), The origin of the sand barites of the Lower Permian of Oklahoma, *Am. Mineralogist*, vol. 18, pp. 260–272.

Tarr, W. A. (1935), Concretions in the Champlain formation of the Connecticut valley, *Bull. Geol. Soc. Amer.*, vol. 46, pp. 1493–1534.

Tarr, W. A. (1932), in Twenhofel, W. H. and others (1932), *Treatise on sedimentation*, Baltimore, Williams and Wilkins.

Taylor, J. H. (1949), Petrology of the Northampton sand ironstone formation, *Mem. Geol. Survey G. Brit.*

Todd, J. E. (1903), Concretions and their geological effects, *Bull. Geol. Soc. Amer.*, vol. 14, pp. 361–362.

Todd, J. E. (1913), More about septarian structure, *Geol. Mag.*, vol. 10, pp. 361–364.

Trefethen, J. M. (1947), Some features of the cherts in the vicinity of Columbia, Missouri, *Am. J. Sci.*, vol. 245, pp. 56–58.

Van Tuyl, F. M. (1916), The geodes of the Keokuk beds, *Am. J. Sci.*, ser. 4, vol. 42, pp. 34–42.

Weeks, L. G. (1953), Environment and mode of origin and facies relationships of carbonate concretions in shales, *J. Sediment. Petrol.*, vol. 23, pp. 162–173.

Willcox, O. W. (1914), Iron concretions of the Redbank sands, *J. Geol.*, vol. 14, pp. 243–252.

Stylolites and Other Solutional Structures

Definitions

A stylolitic seam is a surface marked by interlocking or mutual interpenetration of the two sides. The teethlike projections of one side fit into sockets of like dimension on the other. In cross section the stylolitic surface resembles a suture (Ger.: Drucksuturen) or the tracing of a stylus—an oscillogram. Stylolitic seams are exceeding common in certain types of rock. Sections of such surfaces are elegantly displayed on the polished surface of marble and limestone panels used in many public buildings.

Properties and Occurrence

The relief on a stylolitic surface varies from a fraction of a millimeter (microstylolites) to ten or twenty centimeters. Most commonly, perhaps, the amplitude is about one centimeter. The width of the teeth or columns and the corresponding sockets into which they fit, varies with the height or amplitude of the structures. The larger columns have a proportionately greater width. The larger and better-developed columns (Pl. 10) are commonly striated, the striations being parallel to the column axis and indicating movement of the column into the socket in which it occurs. Very rarely the column is slightly curved.

The stylolitic seam proper is traceable for varying distances—a few centimeters to several meters. The seams commonly overlap and may even split into two subparallel branches.

The stylolitic surface itself is marked by a thin deposit of relatively insoluble material—material which is a very minor constituent of the rock in which the stylolite occurs. The residue on the seams in carbonate rocks is largely clay, in part carbonaceous and in part ferruginous. Particles of quartz silt or fine sand tend to collect along the seam (Pl. 30, F). The stylolites of some sandstones have a parting of coaly matter; those of quartzites are marked by iron oxide.

Stylolites are most commonly parallel to the bedding though there are stylolites which are transverse, even perpendicular to the bedding plane (Heald, 1953; Rigby, 1953; Stockdale, 1943). In general the columns are normal to the stylolitic surface, though there are a few cases in which the columns are vertical even though the seam is inclined.

Most significant are the relations of the stylolite to other structures. The stylolitic penetration of fossils has been described many times (Stockdale, 1922; Dunnington, 1954) as has the penetration of oolites (Bastin, 1951). Of special interest, too, is the relation of stylolites to veins (Dunnington, 1954; Conybeare, 1949; James, 1951, p. 256). The stylolites both cut and are cut by veinlets. Oblique veins that are cut by the stylolitic surface, show an *apparent* displacement by the stylolite proper (Conybeare, 1950).

Stylolites occur in many kinds of rocks. They are very abundant in the carbonate rocks and are found in many limestones, dolomites, and bedded siderites (James, 1951). They are present in the metamorphosed carbonates, especially the marbles. Stylolites are known to occur also in the noncarbonate rocks. They are reported from sandstones (Stockdale, 1936; Heald, 1953) and from quartzites (Conybeare, 1949). In the quartzites, in particular, they commonly occur normal to the bedding rather than parallel to it. Stylolites also occur in gypsum and probably in anhydrite and salt.

In all cases the stylolites occur only in relatively "pure" or homogeneous rocks. The quartzites are high silica quartzites; the limestones and marbles are high carbonate rocks. Stylolites do not occur in the "dirty" quartzites or "impure" carbonate rocks. It is significant that they have never been reported from shales. Apparently chemical homogeneity is a prerequisite for their formation.

Origin

Although there are some uncertainties connected with the origin of stylolites, there is no doubt that they are a pressure-solution phenomenon and were formed in the consolidated rock.[18] Stockdale (1922) has presented an extensive review of this subject; a shorter and more recent review was published by Dunnington (1954). The author agrees with both these writers that the geometrical relations between stylolite and such structures as fossils, oolites, bedding, and veins, demand removal of considerable rock material. Inasmuch as the stylolites transect structures that were indurated (shells and the like) and as they may be transverse to the bedding and as they cut postconsolidation features (veins and the like), there can be no doubt that they were formed by postconsolidation solution. That pressure is involved is shown by the evidences of movement between columns and sockets (i.e., the striations) and the orientation of the stylolite. The stylolitic surface is horizontal (normal to the gravitational field) or near-vertical (parallel to the axial plane of the fold) or otherwise correlated with a pressure-induced joint system.

Though a solution-pressure origin is a well-established conclusion, the mechanism by which solution, acting under directed pressure, makes a stylolite is far from clear. Stockdale believed that zones of differentially soluble limestone distributed laterally along both sides of a parting subject to solution would soon produce an undulatory surface; pressure would become greatest on the crests and troughs of these undulations and least on the sloping sides "since pressure is important in increasing the solubility of certain solids in liquids the rock opposite the top and bottom of adjacent undulations will succumb to a greater rate of solution, producing (a) a deepening of the interpenetrating parts, (b) a further decrease in pressure (and consequent dissolving of the rock) on the sides of the undulation, and (c) a possible final development of vertical columns with a decided concentration of pressure and accompanying solution at the ends" (Stockdale, 1926). Though admitting that stylolites can be produced only by differential solution and directed pressure, Dunnington does not consider Stockdale's mechanism as satisfactory. He proposes, however, no substitute.

[18] There appear to be, as always, some who dissent (Shaub, 1939, 1949, 1950, 1953; Prokopovich, 1952).

Significance

Stylolites abound in the carbonate rocks and are a record, therefore, of extensive intrastratal solution. In a few cases it is possible to estimate the volume of rock dissolved in the production of a stylolite seam.[19] Such estimates show that the thickness of the layer removed may be several times the amplitude of the seam itself. Even if the amplitude is taken as a measure of the minimum quantity removed, the aggregate reduction in thickness of a carbonate bed may be as much as 40 per cent of the original thickness (Stockdale, 1926).

As pointed out by Dunnington, solution along the stylolitic surface is almost certainly concomitant with precipitation from the same solutions elsewhere in the rock. The transfer of materials from stylolite to pores or other openings in the rock is thus a kind of large-scale application of Riecke's principle of simultaneous solution at points of pressure and reprecipitation in adjacent places of lower pressure. Heald (1953) has in fact suggested that such a mechanism may be the means by which sandstones become cemented. (The solution-reprecipitation theory had earlier been applied only to solution at points of contact between grains and precipitation in an adjacent pore—a very small-scale example of Riecke's principle). As noted by Ramsden (1952) and by Dunnington (1954) such stylolitic solution (and pore filling) would result in wholesale expulsion of pore fluids.

This theory of stylolitic solution and concurrent precipitation of the dissolved materials in the rock pores would, of course, demand that such cements be chemically similar to the host rock and that they be abundant only in relatively pure or chemically homogeneous rock systems. And if, as suggested by Dunnington, there is some critical pressure required before stylolitic solution begins, the cementation should be restricted to rocks subjected to some minimum load.

As noted above, stylolites may be formed at several times in the history of the rock. Some may be early postconsolidation; others may be later and oriented with reference to tectonic pressures. The early generated seams may now be tilted and differently oriented from those of a later stage.

Miscellaneous Solutional Structures

Other structures indicative of intrastratal solution include corrosion zones, vugs, "oolicasts," and crystal molds.

Corrosion zones are modified bedding surfaces which occur only in carbonate sediments and are presumed to result from cessation of lime deposi-

---

[19] Based on the relations between the concentration of quartz sand grains in the seam and their concentration in the host rock; also upon the amount of apparent displacement of an oblique vein by a cross-cutting stylolite.

tion and resorbtion of some of the previously deposited materials. Such a surface is characterized by minor irregularities, a black manganiferous stain, irregular rounded corroded limestone slabs likewise stained, and a concentration of relatively insoluble materials including quartz grains, phosphatic shells, and perhaps phosphatic pebbles and nodules (Sardeson, 1914; Pettijohn, 1926; Weiss, 1954).

Vugs are irregular openings related in origin to the "phreatic" passages produced by ground water action. They are most common in carbonate rocks but small vugs may occur in any rock. Commonly they are partially filled by precipitated mineral matter.

"Oolicasts" are small subspherical openings found only in oolitic lime-stones. They are obviously produced by the selective solution of the oolitic bodies in preference to the matrix. Perhaps the oolitic bodies are aragonitic and the matrix calcite (Wherry, 1915). The porosity produced by removal of the oolites may be significant in the movement and storage of rock fluids (Imbt and Ellison, 1946).

A feature which, though rarely seen, may be very significant, is crystal molds. These molds are cavities in the rocks left by the solution of crystals of salt, ice, and the like. Salt signifies very saline waters and aridity of climate. Such cubical voids are not to be confused with similar cavities formed by removal of pyrite cubes.

REFERENCES CITED AND BIBLIOGRAPHY

Bastin, E. S. (1933), Relations of chert to stylolites at Carthage, Missouri, *J. Geol.*, vol. 41, pp. 371–381.

Bastin, E. S. (1940), A note on pressure stylolites, *J. Geol.*, vol. 48, pp. 214–216.

Bastin, E. S. (1951), A note on stylolites in oolitic limestone, *J. Geol.*, vol. 59, pp. 509–510.

Blake, D. B. and Roy, C. J. (1949), Unusual stylolites, *Am. J. Sci.*, vol. 247, pp. 779–790.

Conybeare, C. E. B. (1949), Stylolites in pre-Cambrian quartzite, *J. Geol.*, vol. 57, pp. 83–85.

Conybeare, C. E. B. (1950), Microstylolites in pre-Cambrian quartzite: A reply, *J. Geol.*, vol. 58, pp. 652–654.

Dunnington, H. V. (1954), Stylolite development post-dates rock induration, *J. Sediment. Petrol.*, vol. 24, pp. 27–49.

Goldman, M. I. (1940), Stylolites, *J. Sediment. Petrol.*, vol. 10, pp. 146–147.

Heald, M. T. (1955), Stylolites in sandstones, *J. Geol.*, vol. 63, pp. 101–114.

Imbt, W. C. and Ellison, S. P., Jr. (1946), Porosity in limestone and dolomite, *Drilling and Production Practice*, pp. 364–372.

James, H. L. (1951), Iron formation and associated rocks in the Iron River district, Michigan, *Bull. Geol. Soc. Amer.*, vol. 62, p. 263.

Pettijohn, F. J. (1926), Intraformational phosphate pebbles of the Twin City Ordovician, *J. Geol.*, vol. 34, pp. 361–373.

Price, P. H. (1934), Stylolites in sandstone, *J. Geol.*, vol. 42, pp. 188–192.

Prokopovich, N. (1952), The origin of stylolites, *J. Sediment. Petrol.*, vol. 22, pp. 212–220.

Prouty, C. E. (1952), Unusual stylolites in Ordovician limestones of eastern Pennsylvania, *The Compass*, vol. 30, pp. 11–14.

Ramsden, R. M. (1952), Stylolites and oil migration, *Bull. Am. Assoc. Petroleum Geol.*, vol. 36, pp. 2185–2186.

Rigby, J. K. (1953), Some transverse stylolites, *J. Sediment. Petrol.*, vol. 23, pp. 265–271.

Sardeson, F. W. (1914), Characteristics of a corrosion conglomerate, *Bull. Geol. Soc. Amer.*, vol. 25, p. 269.

Shaub, B. (1939), The origin of stylolites, *J. Sediment. Petrol.*, vol. 9, pp. 47–61.

Shaub, B. (1949), Do stylolites develop before or after the hardening of the enclosing rock? *J. Sediment. Petrol.*, vol. 19, pp. 26–36.

Shaub, B. (1950), Microstylolites in pre-Cambrian quartzite: A discussion, *J. Geol.*, vol. 58, pp. 650–652.

Shaub, B. (1953), Stylolites and oil migration, *J. Sediment. Petrol.*, vol. 23, pp. 260–264.

Sloss, L. L. and Feray, D. E. (1948), Microstylolites in sandstone, *J. Sediment. Petrol.*, vol. 18, pp. 3–13.

Stockdale, P. B. (1922), Stylolites: the nature and origin, *Indiana Univ. Studies*, vol. 11, pp. 1–97.

Stockdale, P. B. (1926), The stratigraphic significance of solution in rocks, *J. Geol.*, vol. 34, pp. 399–414.

Stockdale, P. B. (1936), Rare stylolites, *Am. J. Sci.*, ser. 5, vol. 32, pp. 129–233.

Stockdale, P. B. (1943), Stylolites: primary or secondary? *J. Sediment. Petrol.*, vol. 13, pp. 3–12.

Wagner, G. (1913) Stylolithen und Drucksuturen, *Geol. paleont. Abhandl.*, new ser., vol. 11 (15), no. 2.

Weiss, Malcolm P. (1954) Corrosion zones in carbonate rocks, *Ohio J. Sci.*, vol. 54, pp. 289–293.

Wherry, E. T. (1915) A peculiar oolite from Bethlehem, Pennsylvania, *U.S. Nat. Mus., Proc.*, vol. 49, pp. 153–156.

ORGANIC STRUCTURES (FOSSILS)

Definitions

Organic structures found in rocks are *fossils*. Such structures, which are an integral part of the rock, are familiar to all students of the sedimentary deposits. Fossil organic structures may be a minor feature of the sediments or, as in the case of some limestones, the fossils may be the dominant structure present. Our task here is to inquire neither into the biological aspects of the fossil form—morphology and taxonomy—nor into its stratigraphic aspects, but rather to consider fossils as component parts of the rock. The petrologist should be able to recognize fossils in thin section and should, from their composition, preservation, and manner of occurrence, secure further pertinent data concerning the origin of the rock containing the fossils.

Composition and Mode of Preservation

Fossils are any evidences of past life. They may be buried but relatively unaltered remains such as the more resistant organic structures—bones, teeth, shells. Most shells and similar structures are originally calcium carbonate, but even these show a varied composition in terms of magnesium content and the minor elements (see page 385). Others are phosphatic, or siliceous, or chitinoid.

The organic remains may be altered in varying degrees. Some of the carbonate shells are leached; others have been recrystallized with loss of internal structure; the bones and like materials may be enriched in fluorine. The organic materials, such as cellulose—may be much degraded and in the oldest rocks consist only of a carbonaceous film. This is true of plant tissues, some chitinous materials, and even soft-bodied animal matter may be so altered. Such fossils are little more than carbon films, left after the loss of the volatile constituents of the original organic material which were driven off under anaerobic conditions. Carbonized plant fossils are abundant in shales associated with many coal beds. Numerous bits of carbonized wood are also found in both shales and sandstones. In a few cases, as in "mineral charcoal" (fusain) and in "coal balls" (Stopes and Watson, 1909), the cell walls are carbonized, but the cells themselves are filled with mineral matter, usually calcite (Pl. 36, D). Some of the most exquisitely preserved plant remains known are so preserved. The graptolite fossils of some Ordovician slates and black shales are preserved as carbon films.

Organic structures may be completely replaced so that the present composition of the fossils bears no relation to its original composition. Such replacements (petrifactions) are in truth segregations of the minor mineral constituents of the rock and have therefore the same geochemical significance as concretions, nodules, etc. Silica, carbonate, and iron sulfides are among the replacing materials. Such replacements may take place with preservation of considerable detail. Mineral pseudomorphs are in some cases very perfect; in other cases less so.

In many cases neither the original organic structure nor its replacement is present. Instead are found cavities, called *molds*, formed by the removal in solution of the original structures. The molds show the form and ornamentation of the original object. Should the mold be filled with foreign matter, the filling so formed is properly termed a cast.[20] A *cast*, like a true petrifaction, faithfully reproduces form and ornamentation, but unlike a petrifaction, it does not retain any of the internal structure of the object replaced.

Any structure produced by an organism is a fossil. Hence tracks, trails, and burrows are properly classed as such. *Tracks* are impressions left in soft materials by the feet of birds and other animals. *Trails* are the more or less continuous markings left by an organism as it moves over the bottom. The more complex trails are marked by transverse grooves. Some trails, cylindrical in form, may transect the bedding plane. Such trails are more properly termed *burrows*. They are generally attributed to mud-eating worms. Presumably, as the burrows are preserved in loose sand, they must have had a certain solidity, i.e., the animal must have constructed a tube. Such may have been the dwelling place of the animal for some time. *Scolithus* is an example of a tubelike burrow. *Scolithus* tubes are at right angles to the bedding surfaces and usually are straight. The filling in some of these tubes is more ferruginous than the matrix; in other tubes the converse is true (Hadding, 1929). *Arenicolithes* and *Diplocraterion* are similar structures that today are interpreted as being sand-filled burrows of marine worms. Similarly, *Arthrophycus* and related structures, once thought to be plant fossils, may also be worm burrows (Shrock, 1948, p. 176).

Faecal pellets or organic excreta (mainly of invertebrates) are present in many modern marine deposits and in some sedimentary rocks where they have been fossilized (Moore, 1939; Dapples, 1942). In many cases a large part of the deposit, 30 to 50 per cent, is composed of such materials. The pellets are commonly transformed to glauconite, replaced by pyrite, or they may serve as centers for the accumulation of phosphate. Most abundant are those of simple ovoid form and of small size—1 millimeter or less in length. These have been reported by several workers from ancient sediments, although they have not always been interpreted as fossil excreta. Rarer, but more clearly of faecal origin, are rod-shaped bodies with either longitudinal or transverse sculpturing, or both. Most faecal pellets are devoid of internal structure and in many cases have been overlooked or assigned to an inorganic origin.

Coprolites, of origin analogous to that of faecal pellets, are larger structures ($\frac{1}{2}$ to 6 inches in length) and are characterized by light to dark-brown or black color, ovoid to elongate form, and surface marked by annular convolutions. Longitudinal striae or grooves are rarely present. The brown

---

[20] A mold which preserves the exterior form and markings of a shell is an exterior mold, whereas one which shows the interior form and markings of such an object is an internal mold. An internal mold sometimes is called incorrectly a "cast of the interior." It can be so called only if the shell itself be regarded as a mold. Such internal molds may be composed of either mud or other fine grained sediment that filtered into the shell at the time of burial, or may be mineral matter precipitated after entombment.

vitreous material of many coprolites is phosphatic—optically isotropic and
with refractive index near that of collophane (1.58–1.62). Bradley (1946)
has shown that the coprolites of the Bridger formation (Eocene) of Wyoming are probably a carbonate-apatite (francolite). Coprolites are a relatively
rare constituent of sedimentary rocks.

Petrology of Fossils

Calcareous Algae

The calcareous algae deposit either aragonite or calcite. Certain genera
(*Halimeda*) are aragonitic and others (*Lithothamnion*) are calcitic.

Algae contribute large and important quantities of lime carbonate to present reefs, and therefore to the clastic lime deposits that are derived from
such reefs (Table 77). Algae also made important contributions to ancient
limestone deposits. Some algae, however, are believed not to be agents of
lime deposition but are, instead, agents for the entrapment of precipitated
carbonate (and also finer noncarbonate detritus). The algal colony is a sediment-binding structure. Many of the so-called algal structures, found in rock
of all ages from Precambrian to the Recent are believed to be produced by
blue-green algae of the sediment-binding type.

Among the structures ascribed to algal action are the *stromatolites* (Cloud,
1942). These appear to be laminated, are of varied form, and are produced
by an assemblage of blue-green algae. The resulting stromatolite is without
organic structures and is not a fossil of a specific organism. The various
generic names given to these structures are apparently invalid, since the
names apply only to various forms assumed by the accumulated entrapped
sediment and may not be directly related to specific organisms.

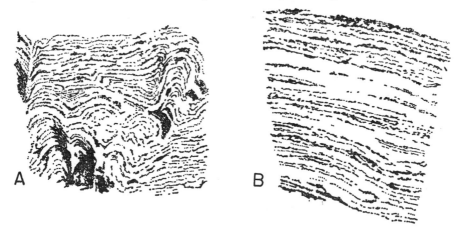

FIG. 62. Algal bedding. A: Early Paleozoic limestone, Nova Scotia; about three-
quarters natural size. B: Brighton limestone, Australia.

The algal structures vary from small pseudopisolitic forms and crusts to biscuit- and cabbage-like heads of considerable size (Pl. 26 and Fig. 62). The pseudoconcretionary forms attributed to algae are small (0.5 to 1.0 centimeter in diameter) subspherical bodies which show an irregular concretionary structure. The larger pisolites have thicker and more irregular outer coatings. Commonly, the growth is not equal in all directions, except in the earliest stages. Later growth is most active on the upper surface, and if perchance the pisolite was rolled over, the new growth may be on the side opposite to that which earlier received the greatest deposit. Some pisolites are composite, i.e., formed of several small masses grown together and enveloped by later growth layers. The nuclei of these structures may be a bit of foreign substance or in some cases a piece of algal material. Larger structures of a similar type are algal balls, also variously called "girvanella" and "pycnostroma."

The algal crusts are simple laminated, and commonly crinkled crusts which grade into irregular nodular masses having mammillary surfaces. The crusts may be nearly flat, essentially parallel to the bedding ("weedia" type stromatolite), or they may be slightly arched, several inches or more in diameter and but an inch or less in height—or more hemispherical to cabbage-like in form with a height equal to or greater than the equatorial diameter. The less convex forms have been called "collenia"; the more arched structures which expand somewhat above their base have been termed "cryptozoon." Some of the cryptozoon types are complex in that small mammillary outgrowths occur on the surface of the cryptozoon head. Another common type resembles a series of stacked inverted thimbles, or, if large, of soup bowls similarly arranged. These form vertical columns, usually several in number. The upright columns or fingers commonly split into two or more in the upward direction. These finger-like or digitate forms have been termed "gymnosolen" stromatolites.

Some of the complex algal structures attain a large size: they may be up to 10 feet high and as much as 15 or more feet in transverse diameter. They are thus veritable algal "reefs."

The algal structures are, in short, modified bedding, bedding modified by blue-green algal mats which under different conditions assume different forms. Under the microscope the only structure visible is a lamination parallel to the surface of the algal structure. The laminations are thin, a fraction of a millimeter thick, and are marked by a greater or lesser concentration of carbonate and other debris. Even grains of quartz silt may be trapped in the laminations.

The algal structures are of uncertain significance. They have been successfully used as a criterion of stratigraphic order in vertical and overturned beds. They also imply water shallow enough to allow light penetration and growth of the algae responsible for their formation. As the crinkling shown by the algal laminations has been attributed to drying, the water may have been exceedingly shallow—perhaps intertidal (Ginsburg, 1955). Algae seem not to be restricted either as to salinity or as to temperature of the waters. The close association of oolites and flat pebble conglomerates with algal structures further suggests very shallow waters.

Foraminifera

Although both calcareous and agglutinated Foraminifera are found in sediments, the calcareous forms are the ones most commonly seen in thin section. They commonly occur entire and are readily recognized under the microscope, although in some cases the chambers are detached (Pl. 27, E). In some genera the tests are composed of calcite, whereas in others aragonite is the mineral component. In the older rocks aragonite has been converted to calcite. The Foraminifera are important rock builders and their remains may constitute the bulk of the rock (certain fusilinid and nummulitic limestones).

The interior of the foraminiferal test may be filled with crystalline calcite, in some cases with a radial arrangement of fibers normal to the walls, so that the fibers present a black cross under crossed nicols. Glauconite is also deposited within the foraminiferal test and by removal of the latter is left in the form of interior molds or casts. According to some writers this is the origin of the glauconite granules common in many sediments.

Sponges

The spicules of siliceous sponges are a common constituent of some sediments. They are most prominent in some Paleozoic and Cretaceous cherts where they appear as clear, slender, curved structures of chalcedonic silica.

Corals

Most corals, according to Sorby (1897) consist of little fibers or, in other cases, granules of aragonite. Calcite occurs, however, in some forms, notably in those inhabiting the deep sea. The modern reef-building forms are chiefly aragonite. In general fossils originally aragonite have been converted to a mosaic of calcite with consequent destruction of original structural details.

Echinoderms

The hard parts of the echinoderms are most singular in that each plate or joint is a single crystal of calcite. The larger ones clearly show the calcite cleavage to the unaided eye, and the limestone composed primarily of such remains accordingly has a marked crystalline appearance. The crinoidal limestones are commonly described as "crystalline limestones" and "encrinites" and in many places in the building trade pass as "marbles." In most such cases the ossicles and plates have been cemented with clear calcite in crystallographic continuity with the crinoid fragment. The original fragment is distinguished by a dusty area showing the usually circular or elliptical (in oblique sections) outline with internal canals. The original fragment, however, is traversed by cleavage cracks that pass unbroken into the secondary cement and the fragment and adjoining cement extinguish as a unit between crossed nicols (Pl. 28, A).

Bryozoa

Bryozoa are common in many limestones. Their cell-like colonial structure makes their identification under the microscope easy. They may be either aragonite or calcite and they commonly consist of fibers set tangentially.

Brachiopods

The brachiopods, excepting only the phosphatic forms, are chiefly calcite. Their shells are built up of bundles of prisms, the prisms of each bundle being parallel and having a quadrangular cross section. The prisms do not have straight extinction. The bundles are arranged obliquely to the shell and adjacent bundles abut upon one another and in part are interlocking.

Mollusks

Mollusk shells are chiefly aragonite, and hence now appear as a mosaic of calcite (Pl. 27, B). Some exceptions, however, are noteworthy. Some pelecypod shells have an inner layer of aragonite that is protected by an outer layer of calcite. In some genera (notably Ostrea, Pecten, and Inoceramus) the whole shell consists of calcite arranged in two layers. The outer and principal layer has a prismatic structure in which the calcite prisms—unlike those of the brachiopod—are perpendicular to the shell surface. The inner pearly layer has a fine lamellar structure. Similarly, most gastropods have an aragonite shell, but a few exhibit a two-layer structure consisting of an inner aragonite layer covered by an outer calcite layer. The cephalopod shells are aragonite, though the aptychi of some of the ammonites were calcite. The guard of the belemnites is calcite, with the calcite fibers set radially about an axis.

Organisms as Documents of Milieu

Heretofore, fossils have received the attention of paleontologists as documents of time; today the student of sedimentary rocks is also concerned with organisms as documents of milieu. Because organisms are rock builders and indices of environmental conditions (Chapter 13), the sedimentary petrologist is interested in organisms and their fossilized remains. Payne (1942) has written an exceptionally good review of this topic, as have others (Hadding, 1933; Becker, 1935).

Although the study of fossils as indices of environment requires some knowledge of paleontology, the field geologist can make many pertinent observations. Paleontologist and petrologist alike can and should note the presence or absence of fossils, their abundance, manner of preservation, size, growth form, external conditions (breakage and wear), space arrangement and orientation.[21] The paleontologist should determine in addition the taxonomic position (class, genus, species, etc.) of the forms present. The size of the fossil remains may be a product of current sorting, as in the case of the crinoid debris of some limestones and some so-called "dwarf" faunas, or it may be indicative of abnormalities of the environment (Tasch, 1953). The growth form is of special interest in some cases, notably the colonial corals. Certain genera, *Favosites*, for example, will develop colonies of high domal form in the cores of reefs, whereas in the flanking beds they form broad tabular bodies (Payne, 1942, p. 1732).

Fossils shed light on the presence or absence of bottom currents, current strength, and direction and depth of water. The criteria of interpretation are by no means complete or agreed upon. Thick massive molluscan shells, for example, are said to be indicative of shallow agitated waters, whereas in the tranquil deeper waters the shells tend to be thin and fragile. The burrowing habit of many forms living on shallow sandy bottoms may be a defense against the strong scour of such areas. The presence or absence of currents is also suggested by the position of the fossil structure. As has been pointed out before, graptolites, *Tentaculites*, fusilinids, and even high-spired gastropods and the orthocerid cephalopods show preferred orientations in response to current action (Chenowith, 1952). Sorting of the fossil detritus, or lack of it, and articulation or disarticulation may be clues to the effectiveness of current action. Fragile forms, still intact and not broken or disarticulated, are indicative of a still-water environment. The stage of disarticulation is also a function of the rate of sedimentation. Very slow sedimentation leads to greater disassociation of the skeletal elements than does more rapid burial (Lowenstam, 1948).

The temperature, salinity, and depth requirements of the organisms, if known, are valuable indices of the depositional environment. Unfortunately these are not always certainly known for fossil forms. Few shells or skeletal structures show any features which can be interpreted as an adaptation to these environmental factors. Most interpretations of fossil organisms, therefore, have been based on analogy with living related forms (for example, no fresh-water crinoids or brachiopods are known) or by association, e.g., some

[21] An extensive German literature exists on these topics. For a brief summary of some of it, the reader is referred to a review by Becker (1935).

fossil types are never found with known or presumed marine faunas; others, like the trilobites, for example, are never found with a fresh-water assemblage. This is the principle of mutually exclusive relations. Analogy with living forms is subject to much uncertainty. Is it true that reef-building corals required the same restrictive conditions of temperature and salinity that modern reef-builders require? Could not the earlier forms have become adapted to different habitats? All too often the character of the environment in which the form lived must be deduced from the sediment itself.

That there is a relation between the fossil content of a stratum and its lithology has been pointed out by many workers. The expression "black shale fauna," for example, is a recognition of such relationships. The less obvious relations are seldom noticed and even more rarely investigated.

Care must be taken in all studies of fossils to discriminate between indigenous forms and those which have been displaced and introduced into an environment alien to that in which they grew. Although the redeposition of faunas has been known for some time as have the criteria for distinguishing between "rolled" fossils and those indigenous to the sediment, the importance and extent of such displacement of faunas has only recently been appreciated. Recent work has shown that modern assemblages have been transported many miles and deposited in waters of abyssal depths by turbidity flows. Similar displacement of faunas in the older sediments is now well established.

Fossils and Geochronology

The value of fossils as documents of time is known to every student of geology. Less well appreciated, however, are the difficulties involved in the use of fossils for correlation. Inasmuch as this is a matter for the specialist, no extended discussion of the problem can be given here.

The continuity of lithologic units can be shown by field mapping and by subsurface data, but that units so determined are precisely contemporaneous is rarely proved.[22] It is known that lithic boundaries cross horizons of identical age but the means for recognizing the latter are largely unknown. Though fossils have been used to establish contemporaneity of beds, it is not commonly realized that faunal zones also cross time planes. Moreover, the value of paleontologic methods decreases as the scale of correlation becomes refined. The classification of units into systems, series, etc., is reasonably valid. But in the smaller units successive faunas are so similar as to be essentially indistinguishable. Moreover, faunas from different beds of similar lithology within a limited area bear greater likeness to one another than do

[22] Except by catastrophic events such as an ash fall or an equally short-lived turbidity flow or by the uniquely climate-controlled variations in thickness of the Late Glacial varves.

contemporaneous faunas from different provinces and habitats. In other words, at the smallest scale, variations in population in synchronous beds are likely to be as great as contrasts in successive beds.

The failure of paleontologic methods at the smallest scale is due to the fact that forms present in any population are affected not only by the evolutionary development with time, but also by the habitat (reflected by the lithology) and paleogeographic factors controlling migration (isolation). Hence precise correlation by means of fossils is only rarely possible of attainment. Greater precision, however, can be achieved if account is taken of some of the complicating factors. The two faunas compared should be from lithologically similar beds (same lithofacies) and from beds which have similar organisms (same biofacies). Correlations will be improved, as pointed out by Kay (1947), if those who use fossils are aware, not only of the possibilities of their methods, but of the limitations also.

REFERENCES CITED AND BIBLIOGRAPHY

Becker, H. (1935), German contributions to the work on sediments, 1930–1933, *Bull. Nat. Research Council*, no. 98, pp. 34–35.

Bradley, W. H. (1946), Coprolites from the Bridger formation of Wyoming: Their composition and microörganisms, *Am. J. Sci.*, vol. 244, pp. 215–239.

Chenowith, P. A. (1952), Statistical methods applied to Trentonian stratigraphy in New York, *Bull. Geol. Soc. Amer.*, vol. 63, pp. 521–560.

Cloud, P. E. (1942), Notes on Stromatolites, *Am. J. Sci.*, vol. 240, pp. 363–379.

Dapples, E. C. (1942), The effect of macro-organisms upon near-shore marine sediments, *J. Sediment. Petrol.*, vol. 12, p. 123.

Ellison, S. P. (1951), Microfossils as environment indicators in marine shales, *J. Sediment. Petrol.*, vol. 21, p. 214–225.

Ginsburg, R. N. (1955), Recent stromatolitic sediments from south Florida, (abstract), *J. Sediment. Petrol.*, vol. 25, p. 129.

Hadding, Assar (1933), The pre-Quaternary sedimentary rocks of Sweden, Part V, On the organic remains of the limestones, *Lunds Univ. Ārsskrift.*, N.F., Avd. 2, Bd. 29, Nr. 4, pp. 7–93.

Hadding, Assar (1929), The pre-Quaternary sedimentary rocks of Sweden. Part III. The Paleozoic and Mesozoic sandstones of Sweden, *Lunds Univ. Ārsskrift.*, N.F., Avd. 2, Bd. 25, Nr. 3.

Kay, Marshall (1947), Analysis of stratigraphy, *Bull. Am. Assoc. Petroleum Geol.*, vol. 31, pp. 162–168.

Lowenstam, H. A. (1948), Biostratigraphic studies of the Niagaran inter-reef formations in northeastern Illinois, *Illinois State Museum, Sci. Papers*, vol. 4.

Moore, H. B. (1939), Faecal pellets in relation to marine deposits, in *Recent Marine Sediments*, Tulsa, Amer. Assoc. Petroleum Geologists, pp. 516–524.

Payne, T. G. (1942), Stratigraphical analysis and environmental reconstruction, *Bull. Am. Assoc. Petroleum Geol.*, vol. 26, p. 1728.

Shrock, R. R. (1948), *Sequence in layered rocks*, New York, McGraw-Hill.

Sorby, H. D. (1879), Presidential Address, *Quart. J. Geol. Soc. London*, vol. 35, pp. 56–77.

Stopes, M. C. and Watson, D. M. S. (1909), On the present distribution and origin of the calcareous concretions in coal-seams, known as coal balls, *Phil. Trans. Roy. Soc.*, ser. B, vol. 200, pp. 167–218.

Tasch, Paul (1953), Causes and paleoecological significance of dwarfed fossil marine invertebrates, *J. Paleontology*, vol. 27, pp. 356–444.

5

Classification and Nomenclature

OBJECTIVE AND PRINCIPLES OF ROCK CLASSIFICATION

THE classification and nomenclature of the sedimentary rocks is a problem on which much thought has been expended (see bibliography, p. 240) and one for which no mutually satisfactory or complete solution has been found as yet. It is appropriate, therefore, to inquire into the objectives of rock classifications and to examine more closely the principles involved in their construction. Many authors fail to make these objectives and principles explicit although there has been some discussion of the philosophy underlying the classification of sedimentary rocks (Grabau, 1904; Wadell, 1938; Pettijohn, 1948; Lombard, 1949; Rodgers, 1950).

As noted by Rodgers, the problem of classification inevitably entails the problem of terminology or nomenclature. Scientific names denote a group or class of objects and hence imply a classification. And classification is basically an attempt to group the objects of concern into classes or categories to which names can be given. The first purpose of a classification, then, is to provide such groups and appropriate names which can substitute for a description of the objects so classified. Only by the aid of such names or categories can individuals communicate effectively with one another. To be successful, therefore, a system of nomenclature and classification must have general agreement of those who have need of a system.

But, as noted by Grabau, precision in classification leads to precision in thought and so is of great value as a mental discipline. A classification embodies in shorthand form our knowledge about a subject. The construction of a classification, therefore, is an attempt to organize our knowledge. In short, its second objective is the schematic representation of ideas or concepts.

The definition of a class requires the choice of limiting parameters. The choice of parameters may be governed by convention or usage or simply by agreement (among the interested parties). But as genesis is the ultimate aim of any study of rocks, the parameter chosen should be genetically meaningful or significant.[1] In biology the basis of all sound taxonomic work must be the selection of significant characters for classificatory purposes and avoidance of irrelevant peculiarities. Not all organisms with wings, for example, should be grouped together. Difficulties in classifying sedimentary rocks stem in large part from failure to recognize the basic differences between clastic (exogenetic) and chemical (endogenetic) rocks. The significant properties of one group are not the significant properties of the other. Thus to apply the same textural terms to all carbonate rocks, which are in fact polygenetic, obscures rather than elucidates their natural history.

A rock is, after all, a complex of properties of which only two or three will be chosen for purposes of classification. It is not possible to construct a classification based on all known or knowable properties. A workable classification will take into account two or three and ignore all others. Such choice requires that the (defining) properties be not only genetically significant but that they be the most significant. All properties no doubt have some meaning but many are much less relevant than others. The magnetic susceptibility of a sandstone surely is genetically less important than its grain size. In general, too, the properties chosen should be readily observable and not such as to require long and complex methods of detection or measurement. Chemical analyses are important and useful but hardly usable for a working classification of sedimentary rocks.

What are the significant properties? Those chosen as such will be the ones believed meaningful in light of our present concepts and knowledge. New ideas and discoveries may render our choice obsolete and hence require revision of our system of classification and nomenclature. Such instability of nomenclature is disturbing but it is the penalty for progress and is only

---

[1] Some authors would advocate a "purely descriptive" classification. What they have in mind is a classification that one can apply without prejudging the origin of the rock. A classification devoid of any genetic connotation is difficult if not impossible to make. One cannot call a rock "sedimentary" without some commitment as to origin. A "sandstone," for example, is a clastic, sedimentary rock. Are there any rock names without genetic implications? Let one try to discriminate between granite and arkose without reference to origin.

another proof that classifications are a codification of ideas or concepts which are subject to constant revision.

Many classifications, however, are partial or incomplete in that they are based on but one property. Such are the textural classifications involving primarily grain size. Such classifications (see Fig. 14) though useful are too limited in character to satisfy the general needs of sedimentary petrology.[2]

The boundaries between classes may be set in several ways. They may be placed where tradition or usage dictates.[3] A class once established cannot be expanded or reduced without engendering confusion. Redefinition of terms is to be undertaken only with care and then only to sharpen the term rather than radically alter its meaning. The term "graywacke," for example, has been defined to include much more than that traditionally included or has been redefined so as to greatly alter its meaning. The result has been much misunderstanding (McElroy, 1954).

A common tendency in defining classes has been to place limits on them which make the classes subequal and which make their graphical representation symmetrical. A good example is the division of the sand-gravel binary system into four equal classes (Fig. 11, A). This makes the nomenclature and class definitions easy to remember and simple to diagram. In the example given, however, the definitions thus set up do not correspond to usage (Willman, 1942). Definitions which conform to field usage (Fig. 11, B) would make the class limits unequal and the diagram asymmetrical. Conformity to usage makes necessary many such unequal classes and a shift of the division point between such classes nearer to one "end type" than the other.[4]

In some cases the distinction between classes is based neither on an arbitrary symmetrically placed line of division nor one dictated by usage but on a supposed "natural" boundary. Winchell (1924), for example, noted the scarcity of certain sand-calcite mixtures, and it has been suggested that the division between sandstone and limestone accordingly be placed at such a natural boundary. Wentworth (1933) likewise argued that there were natural boundaries which corresponded to those chosen between gravel, sand, silt, and clay.

The defining parameters are presumed to be independent of one another. Such, for example, is the case in the igneous rocks where grain size (and

---

[2] Classifications can be made, of course, based on other than genetically significant properties. For engineering and other technological purposes, classifications based on behavioral characteristics may be more useful but the petrologist will be satisfied with nothing less than a classification which correlates closely with origin.

[3] Wentworth (1922), for example, defined the limits of the several size terms by means of a questionnaire sent to active workers in the field of sedimentation.

[4] See, for example, silt-shale classification, p. 377; mudstone-sandstone classification, p. 284.

uniformity of grain size) and mineral composition are the parameters usually chosen. The sedimentary petrologist has been urged to profit by the experience of the igneous petrographer and define his various rock groups on the basis of textures and mineral composition also (Folk, 1954). This advice cannot be accepted without reservations. Not only do the textural and compositional properties of clastic sediments have a different genetic meaning than do these properties in the case of the igneous rocks, but they are not independent of one another. The correlation between grain size and both chemical and mineralogical composition is very close (see p. 113).

A defect of some classifications is the erection of classes or categories for nonexistent rocks. If a set of defining parameters is decided upon, all possible combinations are explored and for some of these combinations there may not be any known rocks. It seems unsatisfactory to have a system with many such unfilled pigeonholes.

HISTORICAL

Most classifications of sedimentary rocks are traditional and like Topsy "just growed." There have been several efforts to standardize the nomenclature of sedimentary rocks—to redefine terms, to set quantitative limits and to weed out poor and obsolete terms.[5] Few efforts have been made, however, to review the whole problem and find a single integrated solution such as those proposed for the classification of the igneous rocks.

Space does not permit a detailed review of all the classifications or partial classifications proposed or used for sedimentary rocks. This has been done in some measure by Lombard (1949). It is even difficult to review properly those papers that deal specifically with the classification problem. Inasmuch as the classification of the several subgroups or families of sediments is treated in their respective sections of this book, only that material will be here reviewed which illustrates the several types of classification and their underlying principles.

Nearly all classifications used have been in part genetic. Most divide sediments into clastic and nonclastic; many distinguish between the clastic and chemical components when both are present in the same rocks—as they commonly are. All these distinctions imply a particular process of deposition and presuppose the existence of valid criteria for making the decisions neces-

---

[5] See for example the various reports of the Committee on Sedimentation on the nomenclature of the pyroclastic sediments (Wentworth and Williams, 1932), the coarse clastics (Wentworth, 1935), the medium-grained clastics (Allen, 1936), the fine-grained clastics (Twenhofel, 1937), and the siliceous sediments (Tarr, 1938). Rodgers (1954) has reviewed the nomenclatural problems of the carbonate rocks. Other efforts have been made to standardize the terms denoting size classes (Lane, et al., 1947; Niggli, 1935; Wentworth, 1922; Alling, 1943; Shepard, 1954).

sary to place the sediment in its proper class. In many cases the discrimination required are difficult or impossible to make.[6]

One of the most elaborate and ambitious attempts to classify and name rocks—especially the sedimentary rocks—was that of Grabau (1904, 1913). Grabau divided all rocks into two groups, namely, endogenetic and exogenetic. The endogenetic rocks owe their origin to forces within matter ("chemical affinity") whereas the exogenetic rocks owe their origin chiefly to forces acting from without. The first group are formed by "solidification, precipitation, or extraction of the mineral matter from the states of igneous fusion, aqueous solution or vaporization." The sediments belonging to this group are the nonclastic or chemical and biochemical sediments. The sediments belonging to the second group are the clastic or mechanical sediments.

TABLE 38.   Exogenetic or Clastic Rocks (simplified from Grabau)

Subclass	Composition	Rudaceous	Arenaceous	Lutaceous
Pyroclasts	Chiefly complex silicates	Pyrorudyte (volcanic breccia)	Pyrarenyte (volcanic tuff)	Pyrolutyte (volcanic ash)
Autoclasts	Varied	Autorudyte Autosilicirudyte Autocalcirudyte	Autoarenyte Autosilicarenyte Autocalcarenyte	Autolutyte Autosilicilutyte Autocalcilutyte Autoargillutyte
Atmoclasts	Varied; generally complex	Atmorudyte Atmosilicirudyte Atmocalcirudyte	Atmoarenyte Atmosilicarenyte Atmocalcarenyte	Atmolutyte Atmoargillutyte Atmocalcilutyte
Anemoclasts	Siliceous Calcareous Argillaceous	....	Anemosilicarenyte Anemocalcarenyte	Anemosilicilutyte Anemocalcilutyte Anemoargillutyte
Hydroclasts	Siliceous Calcareous Argillaceous	Hydrosilicirudyte Hydrocalcirudyte	Hydrosilicarenyte Hydrocalcarenyte	Hydrosilicilutyte Hydrocalcilutyte Hydroargillutyte
Bioclasts	Varied	Biorudyte (concrete)	Bioarenyte	Biolutyte (cement, plaster, and the like)

Grabau, however, went somewhat farther than most writers and attempted to discriminate, in each of the two major groups, the agent and to incorporate this distinction in the name of the rock. Consider the exogenetic or clastic rocks. One commonly makes the distinction between the pyroclastic, cataclastic (autoclastic) and epiclastic deposits. Grabau, in addition, would subdivide the latter into atmoclastic, anemoclastic, hydroclastic, and bio-

[6] For example, is lithographic limestone chemical or biochemical?; is a calcarenite clastic, chemical, or biochemical?

clastic categories. Grabau, like most students of the subject, employs texture (grain size) and composition in his classification. Unlike most writers Grabau abandons the common terms gravel, sand, and clay and uses instead rudyte (*rudus*, rubble), arenyte (*arena*, sand), and lutyte (*lutum*, mud).[7] The composition is expressed by use of the proper prefix, the common ones being *silic*(*i,a*)–, *calc*(*a,i*)–, and *argil*–. Thus a highly quartzose sandstone would be a *silicarenyte*; a quartz conglomerate would be a *silicirudyte*; a calcareous sand is a *calcarenyte*, etc. To complete the name the agent of fragmentation is added, thus: *hydroclastic calcarenyte* (see Table 38).

The nonclastic or endogenetic rocks are likewise subdivided into groups which give recognition to the agent of formation. Rocks may be pyrogenic (igneous), atmogenic (atmospheric sublimates), hydrogenic (aqueous precipitates) or biogenic (phytogenic if plant-formed and zoogenic if animal-formed) (Table 39). Only the hydrogenic and biogenic rocks are important as sediments. The terms denoting grain size to be applied to these constructional but nonclastic sediments, are *spheryte*, *granulyte*, and *pulveryte*. They correspond to the terms rudyte, arenyte, and lutyte applied to the clastic rocks. Compositional prefixes, such as *silic*-, *calc*-, may also be used. Hence a calcareous oolite, for example, would be a *hydrocalcigranulyte*; a diatomaceous earth would be a *biosilicipulveryte*.

TABLE 39. Endogenetic Rocks (simplified from Grabau)

Pyroliths	The Igneous Rocks				
Atmoliths	Snow	Snow-Ice (Névé or Firn)			
Composition	*Alkalious*	*Calcareous*	*Siliceous*	*Ferruginous*	*Carbonaceous*
Hydroliths	Rock salt Soda	Chemical limestones Gypsum Anhydrite	Vein quartz Siliceous sinter Flint, chert	Bog iron ore Siderite Limonite	
Bioliths		Organic limestones	Siliceous organic ooze	Organic limonite	Peat Lignite Bituminous coal Oil, gas Asphalt
	Phosphate rocks				

Grabau's classification differs from the usual or traditional classifications in several important respects. Although most workers attempt to discriminate between volcanic (pyroclastic), tectonic (autoclastic), and normal

[7] Spelled with an *i* instead of y in modern usage; Grabau, however, reserved the ending -ite for minerals and used -yte or -lith for rocks.

(epiclastic) sediments, Grabau carries this effort further and makes finer discriminations and *systematically incorporates these discriminations in his nomenclatural system*. Although most workers also recognize the importance of grain size and composition and utilize these in defining the various rock types, Grabau expresses both properties *in the rock name*. Grabau's system is unique in its complete abandonment of the terms commonly employed to name and describe sedimentary rocks and the use of wholly new nomenclature derived from the classical languages.

Grabau's system is complete and logical. Yet it has not found favor, primarily because of the considerable number of unfamiliar rock names employed. Despite the relatively few basic terms and rather simple rules for compounding these terms, geologists have on the whole avoided using them, preferring the common-language terms however unsatisfactory these might be. Some of Grabau's terms represent a real improvement. To call a rock a calcarenite, i.e., one formed of carbonate particles of sand size, aptly describes many of the clastic limestones. The use of Grabau's system requires abandonment of such wastebasket terms as "limestone" and makes necessary a closer study and analysis of these and other polygenetic rocks. Thus for some more common rocks Grabau has given us better and more specific terms. On the other hand, the names applied by Grabau to some rocks, such as arkose or chert, are more cumbersome and seem less satisfactory than those now in common use. In short then, Grabau's classification is in principle orthodox but in nomenclature it is novel and unique.

Some older classifications were based on the agent and/or environment of deposition. Trowbridge (1914), for example, classified sediments as eolian, fluvial, pluvial, talus, glacial (ice-laid and fluvioglacial), lacustrine (nearshore and still-water), and marine (shallow-water and deep-water). Such classifications are not in truth classifications of sedimentary rocks but are an attempt to establish criteria for the identification of the depositional environments and formative agents of such rocks. Inasmuch as valid criteria do not yet exist for many environments or agents, such "classifications," though laudable, are not workable. This approach to the problem of classification reappears in modern form in the writings of Tercier (1940), who has attempted to classify the major sedimentary facies or associations rather than the petrographic entities of which they are composed (see p. 632).

The primary differences between the older and the newer classifications, however, are not in the details of placement of class limits, but rather in choice of defining textural and compositional attributes. The choice, as stated elsewhere, should be made in terms of the genetic significance of the measure to be used. If the sediments are considered as chemical entities, the chemical behavior of the dominant elements may be the guiding principle used. If the sediments are washed residues—as are the clastic rocks—the textural and compositional maturity of the rock may dictate the choice of parameters.

Krynine (1942, 1945, 1948), for example, attempted to formulate a mineralogical classification of the clastic or detrital sediments which is presumed to correlate closely with the major tectonic and geomorphic cycle. This classification is predicated on the notion that the maturity of the detritus shed by a land mass is a function of the rate of erosion of that area which is, in turn, determined by the relief of that area—an expression of the balance between rates of downcutting and uplift. High relief and consequent rapid erosion produces ill-sorted sediment with poorly rounded grains and containing an abundance of unstable minerals; low relief and slow erosion permit prolonged reworking prior to final burial and produces well-sorted, highly rounded, and mineralogically mature sands and other coarse clastics. In other words, the later stages of the geomorphic cycle will be accompanied by the production of mature sediments—that is to say those approaching the stable end state toward which they evolve. Krynine, therefore, divides the sedimentary rocks into three classes or suites each of which is associated with a different stage of the geomorphic cycle. Each group has clastic representatives ranging from coarse conglomerates or breccias to the fine-grained muds and clays (Table 40). Because the medium-grained clastics—the sands—are most readily studied, they give the name to their respective groups or suites. These are the orthoquartzite suite, the graywacke suite, and the arkose suite which are presumed to correlate with the peneplanation stage, the stage of moderate deformation, and the orogenic stage, respectively.

As originally presented (Krynine, 1941, 1942) the feldspar content was considered to be the measure of the "tectonism" of the source area (see p. 328) and only in the final maximal stages of the tectonic cycle did feldspar appear in quantity in the sediments (arkose). It seems probable, however, that the feldspar content is also a matter of provenance and in some cases the graywackes are highly feldspathic.[8] But the difference between graywacke and arkose is also textural and hence not a question only of composition dependent on relief or even on provenance, but also a difference dependent on the manner of transport and distribution of the sands and muds (see p. 329). Hence the notion that graywacke and arkose are indicative of two different intensities of deformation is debatable.

Although the correlation of the three sandstone types and their associated suites with the three stages of the geomorphic cycle has been questioned and even though there is some confusion between provenance and maturity and no published data to support the presumed mineralogical character of the associated shales, the concept advanced by Krynine has proved a fruitful

[8] This was noted by Krynine in later writings (1945, 1948) and led him to subdivide the graywackes into "high" and "low" rank categories.

one. As a result of Krynine's work there have come a series of papers dealing with problems of provenance and maturity and sediment classification. Such studies have led to significant advances in the classification of sandstones (Tallman, 1949; Dapples, Krumbein and Sloss, 1953; Folk, 1954; Pettijohn, 1954; Packham, 1954; Bokman, 1955). The classification of sandstones can be readily extended to include the conglomerates also.

TABLE 40.   Generalized Classification of Sediments (after Krynine, 1945)

Composition		Quartz ± Chert	Quartz + Chert + Micas + Chlorite		Quartz + Feldspar ± Clay
			− Feldspar	+ Feldspar	
Texture		Quartz conglomerate	Graywacke conglomerate		Arkosic conglomerate
Detrital Rocks (Clastic Texture)	Coarse Conglomerates		Low rank	High rank	
	Medium Sandstones	Quartzite and quartzose sandstone	Graywacke		Arkose
			Low rank	High rank	
	Fine Shales	Quartzose shale	Micaceous shale	Chloritic shale	Kaolinitic and feldspathic shale
Chemical Rocks	Sandy (clastic)	Limestone, Dolomite, Chert, Salt, Gypsum, etc.			
	Pure (crystalline)				

Sediments may also be considered as chemical entities. The external geochemical cycle (Rankama and Sahama, 1950) is a complex of processes which tends to yield products of contrasting chemical nature. These processes fractionate and purify the materials supplied by weathering. The process has been likened to a colossal chemical separation in the course of a semiquantitative analysis of rock material (Barth, 1952, p. 38). The results of this natural analysis are not always perfect inasmuch as nature uses poor methods, but the over-all result is surprisingly good—witness the extraordinary concentration of certain elements, such as silicon, carbon, sulfur, phosphorous, calcium, etc., in certain sedimentary rocks. No magmatic or metamorphic processes can so effectively isolate these elements. Goldschmidt therefore classes the sediments as resistates, hydrolysates, oxidates, carbonates and evaporates. The resistates are enriched in silicon, the hydrolysates are notably aluminous, the oxidates are primarily ferruginous, the carbonates are concentrations mainly of magnesium and calcium, the evaporates are notably rich in sodium. The order given above is primarily the order of separation by the analyst and is essentially a "mobility" order—the most "refractory" or "insoluble" elements being concentrated in the resistates, the most fugitive elements appearing only in the rarer evaporates. Thus the classification of sediments, as chemical entities, on the basis of "oxide mobility" (p. 499) is meaningful and appropriate. It is somewhat the inverse of the order of "weatherability" or "weathering potential" (Reiche, 1950).

Oxide mobility or "weatherability" is related to mineral stability. Hence the Krynine classification, and others like it, based in part on the ratio of labile to stable minerals (quartz/feldspar ratio, for example) is but another expression of the general geochemical trend of enrichment of the residue sediments in the "felsic" constituents and impoverishment in the "mafic" components (Green and Poldervaart, 1955).

CONCLUSIONS

Any attempt to impose a single classification scheme on all sediments encounters difficulties owing to the polygenetic nature of the sedimentary materials. If a scheme is to be based on the genetically significant properties, it follows that those properties significant for one group of sediments may be inappropriate for another group of different origin. The maturity concept, for example, is a fundamental one, but it can be applied only to those sediments which are residues derived by weathering from a metastable source rock. It has no meaning (in a compositional sense) if applied to pyroclastic materials or to the chemical sediments as a group. Similarly the concepts of provenance basic to the understanding of the textural and compositional nature of the clastic sediments have little or no meaning if applied to the chemical sediments. Hence it is difficult to build an all-embracing classification of the sedimentary rocks.

It is, however, possible to build partial classifications—classifications appropriate for certain groups of sediments—classifications which are rational and based on observable properties which properties are closely correlated with fundamental concepts of origin. It is now possible to build a classification for the residue group of sediments—the sands and gravels and their consolidated equivalents. Such a classification is based on compositional and textural properties relevant to the concepts of maturity, provenance, and fluidity of the depositing medium. In considerable part the maturity, and to a lesser extent the provenance, are closely correlated with the relief of the source area and basin of deposition which in turn is determined by the tectonic stability or instability of these areas. Hence it follows that there is a correlation, in a general way, between petrology and tectonics.

The correlation of the parameters of provenance and maturity and stages in the tectonic cycle cannot be readily carried over to the chemical and biochemical sediments except by their association and the study of their clastic contaminants. In general, of course, these rocks accumulate, free of clastic debris, only under conditions of low relief and tectonic stability. In general, too, these rocks tell us little or nothing concerning the paleogeography of the past, and little or nothing about the nature of the source rocks or source region. On the other hand, unlike the residue sediments, they tell us a great deal about the chemical milieu in which they were deposited. A classification of the chemical sediments therefore will not be based on properties related to maturity, provenance, or fluidity of the depositing medium. They will instead be based on properties indicative of the acidity or alkalinity, the oxidation-reduction potential, and other chemical properties of the medium from which they were precipitated. Inasmuch as the stability of some of the most common minerals is determined by these parameters, the classification of the chemical and biochemical sediments is primarily mineralogical (and therefore chemical).

The argillaceous group of sediments is unlike either the residue group or the chemical group. It is a hybrid class containing both washed residues and chemical or biochemical contaminants as well as the clay-mineral materials which characterize this group. The latter are reactive and hence subject to change depending on the chemical milieu. Hence the shales cannot be classified on the same basis as either the residue or the chemical group of sediments. A satisfactory classification of these materials, yet to be worked out, must contain elements of both classifications.

In this book the sedimentary rocks are grouped according to prevailing usage. This is done for convenience only. A chapter each is devoted to the conglomerates (and breccias), the sandstones (and tuffs), and the shales (and siltstones). This arrangement is justified, perhaps, by the fact that the most conspicuous and first observed property of a clastic rock is its grain size. This classification or grouping, however, cuts across a more fundamental one, namely, one based on composition, which is closely correlated with provenance and maturity. Hence each textural group is subdivided or classified according to a composition scheme.

The inclusion of all limestones (and dolomites) in a single chapter, despite the polygenetic nature of this group of rocks, is again justified by prevailing usage. Moreover, despite the clastic textures and structures shown by many limestones, they are intrabasinal in provenance so that the concept of compositional maturity as applied to the other clastic rocks has no meaning if applied to the carbonate rocks.

The remaining sediments are entirely nonclastic and have been placed together in a single chapter because of the relatively minor volume of such sediments in the crust of the earth and by the common problems in the origin of many of these deposits. Furthermore, considerable difficulty is encountered deciding whether these rocks are original precipitates or diage-

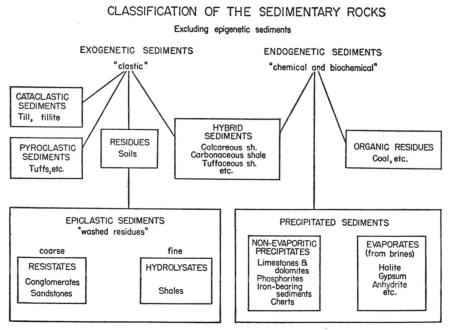

FIG. 63. Classification of sedimentary rocks.

netic (or epigenetic) replacements. In view of these uncertainties, a classification and separate treatment of the chemical precipitates, the biochemical precipitates, and the epigenetic replacements would be unwise.

Since it would be repetitious to discuss here the subdivisions of the several rock groups, the reader is referred to each of the chapters dealing with the respective sedimentary rock groups and to Fig. 63 for details concerning their subdivision and classification.

REFERENCES CITED AND BIBLIOGRAPHY

Allen, V. T. (1936), Terminology of medium-grained sediments, *Rept. Comm. Sed. 1935–1936*, Nat. Research Council (mimeographed), pp. 18–47.

Alling, H. L. (1943), A metric grade scale for sedimentary rocks, *J. Geol.*, vol. 51, pp. 259–269.

Barth, T. F. W. (1952), *Theoretical petrology*, New York, Wiley.

Bokman, John (1955), Sandstone classification: relation to composition and texture, *J. Sediment. Petrol.*, vol. 25, pp. 201–206.

Dapples, E. C., Krumbein, W. C., and Sloss, L. L. (1953), Petrographic and lithologic attributes of sandstones, *J. Geol.*, vol. 61, pp. 291–317.

Filipesco, M. G. (1934), Un essai de classification des roches sedimentaires, *Bul. Labor. de Min. al Univ. din Bucuresti*, vol. 1 (review in *J. Sediment. Petrol.*, 1935, vol. 5, p. 151).

Fischer, G. (1933), Gedanken zur Gesteinssystematik, *Jahrb. preuss. geol. Landesanstalt*. Berlin, vol. 54, pp. 553–584.

Folk, R. L. (1954), The distinction between grain size and mineral composition in sedimentary rock nomenclature, *J. Geol.*, vol. 62, pp. 344–359.

Grabau, A. W. (1904), On the classification of sedimentary rocks, *Am. Geol.*, vol. 33, pp. 228–247.

Grabau, A. W. (1913), *Principles of stratigraphy*, New York, Seiler.

Green, Jack and Poldevaart, Arie (1955), Petrochemical trends, *Bull. Geol. Soc. Amer.*, vol. 66.

Juan, V. C. (1947), Suggestions for a quantitative mineralogical classification of sedimentary rocks, *Bull. Geol. Soc. China*, vol. 27, pp. 205–228.

Krynine, P. D. (1942), Differential sedimentation and its products during one complete geosynclinal cycle, *Annals of the First Pan-Am. Congr. of Min. Eng. Geol.*, vol. 2, pt. 1, pp. 537–561.

Krynine, P. D. (1945), Sediments and the search for oil, *Producers Monthly*, vol. 9, pp. 12–22.

Krynine, P. D. (1948), The megascopic study and field classification of the sedimentary rocks, *J. Geol.*, vol. 56, pp. 130–165.

Lane, E. W. and others (1947), Report of the sub-committee on sediment terminology, *Trans. Am. Geophys. Union*, 1947, pp. 936–938.

Lombard, A. (1949), Critères descriptifs et critères génétiques dans l'étude des roches sédimentaires, *Bull. soc. belge géol.*, vol. 58, pp. 214–271.

McElroy, C. T. (1954), The use of the term "graywacke" in rock nomenclature in New South Wales, *Australian J. Sci.*, vol. 16, pp. 150–151.

Niggli, P. (1935), Die Charakterisierung der klastischen Sedimente nach der Kornzusammensetzung, *Schweiz. mineralog. petrog. Mitt.*, Bd. 15, pp. 31–38.

Niggli, P. (1938), Zusammensetzung und Klassifikation der Lockergesteine, *Schweiz. Archiv. f. angewandte Wissensch. und Tech.*, vol. 4.

Packham, G. H. (1954), Sedimentary structures as an important factor in the classification of sandstones, *Am. J. Sci.*, vol. 252, pp. 466–476.

Pettijohn, F. J. (1948), A preface to the classification of the sedimentary rocks, *J. Geol.*, vol. 56, pp. 112–118.

Pettijohn, F. J. (1954), Classification of sandstones, *J. Geol.*, vol. 62, pp. 360–365.

Rankama, K., and Sahama, T. (1950), *Geochemistry*, Chicago, Univ. Chicago Press, p. 189.

Reiche, Parry (1950), A survey of weathering processes and products, *Univ. New Mexico Publ. Geol.*, no. 3, 95.

Rodgers, John (1950), The nomenclature and classification of sedimentary rocks, Am. J. Sci., vol. 248, pp. 297–311.

Rodgers, John (1954), Terminology of limestones and related rocks: an interim report, J. Sediment. Petrol., vol. 24, pp. 225–234.

Shepard, F. P. (1954), Nomenclature based on sand-silt-clay ratios, J. Sediment. Petrol., vol. 24, pp. 151–158.

Shrock, R. R. (1946), Classification of sedimentary rocks, Bull. Geol. Soc. Amer., vol. 57, p. 1231.

Shrock, R. R. (1948), Classification of sedimentary rocks, J. Geol., vol. 56, pp. 118–129.

Tallman, S. L. (1949), Sandstone types: their abundance and cementing agents, J. Geol., vol. 57, pp. 582–591.

Tarr, W. A. (1938), Terminology of the chemical siliceous rocks, Rept. Comm. Sed. 1937–1938, Nat. Research Council, pp. 8–27 (mimeographed).

Tercier, J. (1940), Dépôts marins actuels et séries géologiques, Eclogae Geol. Helv., vol. 32, pp. 47–100.

Tieje, A. J. (1921), Suggestions as to the description and naming of sedimentary rocks, J. Geol. vol. 29, pp. 650–666.

Trefethen, J. M. (1950), Classification of sediments, Am. J. Sci., vol. 248, pp. 55–62.

Trowbridge, A. C. (1914), Classification of common sediments and some criteria for identification of the various types, J. Geol., vol. 22, pp. 420–436.

Twenhofel, W. H. (1937), Terminology of the fine-grained mechanical sediments, Rept. Comm. Sed. 1936–1937, Nat. Research Council (mimeographed), pp. 81–104.

Wadell, H. (1938), Proper names, nomenclature and classification, J. Geol., vol. 46, pp. 546–568.

Wentworth, C. K. (1922), A scale of grade and class terms for clastic sediments, J. Geol., vol. 30, pp. 377–392.

Wentworth, C. K. (1933), Fundamental limits to the sizes of clastic grains, Science, vol. 77, pp. 633–634.

Wentworth, C. K. (1934), The terminology of coarse sediments, Bull. Nat. Research Council, no. 98, pp. 225–246.

Wentworth, C. K. and Williams, Howel (1932), The classification and terminology of the pyroclastic rocks, Bull. Nat. Research Council, no. 89, pp. 19–53.

Willman, H. B. (1942), Geology and mineral resources of the Marseilles, Ottawa, and Streater quadrangles, Illinois State Geol. Survey, Bull. 66, pp. 343–344.

Winchell, A. N. (1924), Petrographic studies of limestone alterations at Bingham, Trans. Am. Inst. Mining Met. Engrs., vol. 70, pp. 884–902.

6

Gravels, Conglomerates, and Breccias

GENERAL CHARACTERISTICS

Definitions

A *gravel* (German: *Schotter*, for coarse gravel; *Kies*, for fine gravel; French: *gravier*) is an unconsolidated accumulation of rounded fragments larger than sand. The lower size limit is variously set, generally 2 millimeters (Wentworth, 1922a; 1935) or 5 millimeters (Cayeux, 1929). Material in the 2 to 4 millimeter range has been termed *granule gravel* by Wentworth or *very fine gravel* (Lane et al, 1947). There is no general agreement on the percentage of gravel-sized fragments that must be present before the aggregate warrants the term gravel. Actual analysis shows that the field geologist is prone to call a deposit gravel even if pebbles and like sizes form less than one-half of the whole. Some rocks, such as tillite or indurated boulder clay containing less than 10 per cent of gravel-sized fragments, are designated, none the less, as conglomerates. Willman (1942) suggested the following definitions which were thought by him to correspond to prevailing field usage: *gravel* contains 50 to 100 per cent pebbles; *sandy gravel* contains 25 to 50 per cent pebbles and 50 to 75 per cent sand; *pebbly sand* contains a conspicuous number of pebbles but less than 25 per cent; *sand* must contain 75 to 100 per cent sand (Fig. 10, B). Folk (1954) would apply the term gravel only to mixtures containing 30 or more per cent of the gravel size and would apply the adjective "gravelly" to sands and muds containing 5 to 30 per cent of pebbles or larger fragments. Other proposals for naming mixtures include those of Wentworth (1922a) and Krynine (1948).

Shapes of Gravel Bodies

Gravel and conglomeratic bodies are rarely of wide extent; most are local accumulations of one form or another. Many are, for example, *shoestring* bodies which are generally channel fillings. As such, they are very restricted in width and thickness but have a considerable length. Though generally straight they may meander and branch.

Common also are *wedges* or wedge-shaped deposits ("prisms" of Krynine, 1948) deposited as aprons or fans or compound aprons and fans ("fanglomerates" of Lawson, 1925) adjacent to an escarpment or ice front. They are characterized by a considerable persistence parallel to the depositional strike but by a rapid down-dip thinning. Most of the great conglomerates of the geologic record belong to this group.

Common also, but less impressive, are *blanket* conglomerates. Such sheets were deposits of gravel spread out by an advancing or transgressive beach. These deposits are notably thin and patchy; low areas may collect several tens of feet of gravel whereas the intervening higher areas may be devoid of any gravel accumulation.

Of somewhat uncertain character are the gravels or breccias—pseudotills or pebbly mudstones—deposited by subaqueous turbidity flows. Knowledge of these at present is very sketchy so that the extent and shape of such bodies is unknown. Some breccias of this origin appear to be of uniform thickness and widespread.

The term *conglomerate* (German: Konglomerat; French: conglomerat) is applied to indurated gravels. As in the case of gravel, the terms *pebble*, *cobble*, or *boulder* (see p. 20) may be prefixed according to the dominant fragment size.

The term *rubble* has been applied to an accumulation of angular rock fragments coarser than sand; the term *scree* may be applied if the blocks are large. *Breccia* (German: Bresche; French: breche; Spanish: brecha) is the consolidated equivalent of rubble. The term breccia is applied to nonsedimentary rocks also. Various terms have been proposed for several sizes of fragments of which rubble and breccias are composed (Woodford, 1925; see page 27).

To what extent must the fragments be rounded before the terms gravel or conglomerate rather than rubble or breccia is used? Usage is variable but most workers would apply the term breccia only to rocks the fragments of which are angular; conglomerate is used for subangular and better-rounded materials. The term *roundstone* (Fernald, 1929) and the term *sharpstone* (Shrock, 1948) have been used to distinguish between rounded and angular fragments; hence the terms *sharpstone conglomerate* and *roundstone conglomerate* have been proposed as substitutes for sedimentary breccias and conglomerates, respectively.

The term *conglomerite* (Willard, 1930) has been suggested for conglomerates which have reached the same stage of induration as a quartzite. It has, however, been little used; a deformed conglomerate or one otherwise altered by metamorphic changes is more commonly called a *metaconglomerate*.

Textures and Structures of Gravels

A gravel consists of a *framework* and *voids*. The framework is composed of the gravel-sized materials (*phenoclasts:* pebbles, cobbles, boulders); the voids are the openings between these framework elements. In the normal case the clastic elements touch one another and form a structure stable in the gravitational field. The voids are rarely empty; they are generally filled with detritus, sand, or smaller sizes, and with introduced precipitated cements. Gravels with unfilled voids have been termed *openwork* gravels, the significance of which is not clear. In most gravels the matrix material completely fills the voids; it forms, therefore, about one-third of the whole rock volume. In some conglomerates the matrix greatly exceeds this figure so that the framework is partially to completely disrupted, and the pebbles and the like are isolated and are scattered throughout the matrix.

It is significant, perhaps, that modern beach gravels, many of which are openwork, seem to be unimodal, whereas most of the fluvial gravels are bimodal (Table 41 and Fig. 64). The cause of the bimodal character has been discussed elsewhere (page 44).

Alluvial or river gravels are commonly bimodal even when great care is taken to secure samples of single beds. In general it is the coarse gravels that are bimodal. The bimodal gravel generally has its chief mode in the gravel class and its secondary mode in the sand grades. These maxima are 4 to 5 grades apart on the average. The chief ingredient, therefore, has a diameter 16 to 32 times that of the material in the secondary mode (Udden says 16 times for water deposits). In alluvial gravels the quantity of material in the modal class is small. Such gravels in California (Conkling, Eckis, and Gross, 1934), 92 per cent of which are bimodal, had but 15 to 25 per cent in this class, whereas in the unimodal gravels of beaches the chief ingredient may contain as much as 90 per cent of the whole sample. The secondary mode contains even less material—half that of the maximum class or roughly 5 to 10 per cent. A large range, 9 to 10 grades or even 12 grades with 1 per cent or more, is common. The modern gravels of the San Gabriel and the Arroyo Seco of California, for example, fall into 9 to 11 Udden size grades; the modal class has 15 to 35 per cent (average 20 per cent) of the total. Eighty-five per cent of the samples (35) have more than one mode (Krumbein

PLATE II

GRAVELS

Top: Pleistocene glacial outwash gravel, Cary, Illinois. Note tendency toward imbricate structure. Current flowed from right to left.

Bottom: Lake Michigan beach gravel, Little Sister Bay, Wis. Note absence of interstitial sand (compare with outwash shown above). (Krumbein and Griffith, *Bull. Geol. Soc. Amer.*, vol. 49, 1938, pl. 1.) Size analyses of these gravels shown in Fig. 64.

PLATE 12

CONGLOMERATES

Top: Pleistocene conglomerate, Cary, Illinois. Length of specimen approximately six inches.

An outwash gravel composed of limestone pebbles cemented by calcite. Pebbles in contact with one another; matrix very subordinate.

Bottom: Intraformational conglomerate, Gallatin (Cambrian) formation, Teton Mountains, Wyoming. Length of specimen about five inches.

Consists of flat pebbles of laminated calcilutite in a matrix of lime mud.

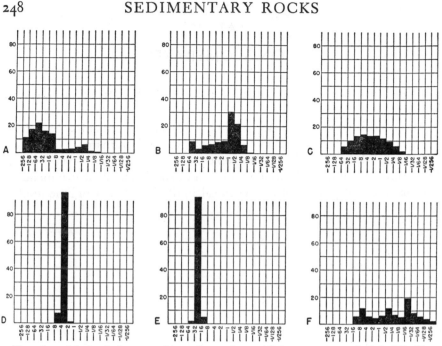

Fig. 64. Mechanical composition of gravels. **A**: Pleistocene outwash (glacial) Cary, Ill.; see Pl. 11. **B**: Mississippi River gravel, LaGrange, Missouri, from commercial dredge (Lugn, 1927). **C**: Flood gravel, Arroyo Seco, Calif. Represents deposit near maximum current velocity and turbulence (Krumbein, 1942). **D**: Lake Michigan beach gravel, Kenilworth, Ill. **E**: Lake Michigan beach gravel, Little Sister Bay, Wis. (Krumbein and Griffith, 1938). See Pl. 11. Note lack of interstitial material in this gravel; compare with **A**. **F**: Pleistocene till, composite sample, Cary, Ill.

1940, 1942). Glacial outwash gravels, even those of *single layers*, are characterized by 7 to 12 or more Udden classes; most of these are bimodal (Kurk, 1941). The quantity in the chief mode ranges from 14 to 35 per cent and averages 28 per cent. All but 1 of 37 samples of Lafayette gravel (fluvial, Pliocene?) from Kentucky (Potter, 1955) are bimodal. In 23 samples the principal mode is in the gravel fraction. The number of Udden grades (with over 1 per cent) ranged from 7 to 11; the quantity in the modal class varied from 19 to 40 per cent (average 26).

Present-day beach gravels, like the beach sands, are characterized by their good sorting (Fig. 64 and Pl. 11). They are generally better sorted than fluvial gravels of comparable coarseness (Table 41) (Emery, 1955). Unlike river gravels, beach gravels are almost all unimodal. They have 2 to 9 Udden grades that contain 1 per cent or more of the material. The average number of such grades is 4 or 5 although two or three classes may contain over 90 per cent of the distribution. Fifty to 60 per cent of the whole distribution usually falls in the modal class, although in some cases 90 per cent of the total falls in this grade.

TABLE 41. Size Characteristics of Modern Gravels

Gravel Type	No. Samples	No. Size Classes > 1% Range	No. Size Classes > 1% Average	% Bimodal	% Modal Class Range	% Modal Class Average
Beach[a]	26	2 to 9	4 to 5	3	35 to 95	55
Beach[b]	38	2 to 3	2½	none	54 to 96	79
Flood[c]	35	9 to 11	10	85	14 to 35	20
Glacial Outwash[d]	19	7 to 12	9	52	14 to 35	28
Alluvial[e]	37	7 to 11	9	97	19 to 40	27
Terrace[f]	23	9 to 11	10	87	14 to 33	23

[a] Miscellaneous sea and lake beaches (Udden, 1914, and others).
[b] Lake Michigan beach gravel, Wisconsin (Krumbein and Griffith, 1938).
[c] Flood gravels of the San Gabriel canyon and the Arroyo Seco, California (Krumbein, 1940, 1942).
[d] Pleistocene outwash, Illinois (Kurk, 1941). *Single layers* only.
[e] Lafayette formation (Pliocene?), western Kentucky and adjacent states (Potter, 1955).
[f] Pleistocene terrace gravels, Black Hills, S. D. (Plumley, 1948).

In many fluvial gravels the maximum size present is some function of the mean size present (Fig. 65). Because of this relation it is possible to substitute the more easily determined "largest size" for the mean size in facies mapping.

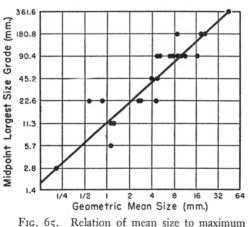

FIG. 65. Relation of mean size to maximum size of outwash gravel (data from Kurk).

The shape, roundness, and surface textures of the pebbles, cobbles, and the like, of conglomerates and breccias may aid in determination of the agent responsible for the transport and deposit of the gravel. Distinctive pebble shapes and markings include the faceted and snubbed ice-shaped cobble, the wind-faceted ein- and dreikanter, the striations and scars produced by ice action, the chink facets of some beach pebbles, the percussion marks and spalls of the pebbles of high-velocity streams, and so forth (see pages 54 and 68). The shape of a pebble is generally more dependent on the shape of the original fragment than on the agent or transport history. The shape of the original fragment is a function of the jointing, bedding, and cleavage of the source rock. Hence flatness is largely a function of lithology (Cailleux, 1945); slates and thin-bedded rocks yield flat pebbles, whereas massive rocks, like granite, shed more equidimensional fragments. The effects of the agent or environment are much less clear. It has been said that beach pebbles are flatter than river pebbles, and this statement has been supported by the observations of Landon (1936) and Cailleux (1945) but disputed by Gregory (1915), Wentworth (1922b), and by the observations of Grogan (1945) (see page 62).

Gravels and conglomerates have various internal structures. The kind and character of the bedding is an important attribute. Bedding is generally large-scale and varies from well defined to obscure or absent. In general cross-bedding, if present, is of the large-scale fore-set type. The clastic elements of a gravel tend to have a fabric or preferred orientation. Commonly the water-deposited stone shows an up-current dip or imbrication. The long axes of the pebbles are said to be oriented in the direction of current flow (Krumbein, 1939, 1940, 1942; Kopstein, 1954) or transverse to the same (Lane, 1954; Fraser, 1935; Twenhofel, 1947, p. 121) (see page 78). Even till, ice-deposited, tends to have a preferential orientation of the till stones parallel to the ice-flow (Richter, 1932; Krumbein, 1939; Holmes, 1941). The orientation of pebbles of ancient conglomerates may enable one to determine both direction of current flow and the angle of initial dip of the bed (White, 1952).

TABLE 42. Significant Characteristics of Marine and Fluviatile Gravels
According to Cailleux (1945)

Characteristic	Fluviatile	Marine
Inclination of pebbles in section		
Flatness 1.5	16° to 36°	2° to 7°
Flatness 3.5	7° to 33°	1° to 5°
Flatness of carbonate pebbles of 5 cm length	1.6 to 3.4	2.4 to 3.0
Asymmetry of carbonate pebbles 3 to 3.5 cm	0.559 to 0.585	0.545 to 0.558

Most complete investigation of the structures of gravels is that made by Cailleux (1945) (Table 42). Study of 4000 pebbles from 52 formations, both ancient and recent, showed that the average original inclination (dip) of the pebbles in fluviatile formations is about 15 to 30 degrees, whereas that of marine deposits is about 2 to 12 degrees. The actual inclination is affected by form, those notably flat are less steeply inclined; by the contiguity, pebbles in contact with one another are more steeply inclined than those isolated in sands; by the size, the position of the smallest pebbles in a deposit is atypical by reason of the influence of the larger stones; and by the topographic situation. The apparent angle of dip or inclination is affected, of course, by the orientation of the section observed. The section showing the maximum values should be investigated.

The conclusions of Cailleux have not been fully verified. Krumbein (1940, 1942), who investigated the fabric of both outwash and flood gravels, found the mean dip of the c pebble axes (normals to the maximum projection plane ab) of outwash gravel to be 54 degrees, indicating an average inclination of the maximum projection plane of 36 degrees. On the other hand, the mean dip of the c axes of beach pebbles is 44 degrees (Krumbein and Griffith, 1938) indicating an average inclination of the maximum projection plane of 46 degrees—a figure much higher than the 2 to 12 degrees for the inclinations of marine beach pebbles reported by Cailleux. The sample studied, however, was abnormal in its steepness of imbrication. White (1952) observed the dip of the apparent long axes [1] of pebbles in a Keweenawan conglomerate presumed to be fluvial in origin. The mean inclination of 388 pebbles of greater than average flatness was about 8 degrees. This is about the same as the 13½ degrees for the San Gabriel pebbles and the 6½ degrees for the pebbles from the flood gravels of the Arroyo Seco. [2] Owing to the different methods of collecting data and the uncertainties of converting one set of data into another, all that we can be certain of is that there is an imbrication of both beach and fluvial gravels. Whether the angle of dip of such imbrication is diagnostic is not known. The direction of dip of the fluvial gravels, at least, is significant in that it is upcurrent.

PROVENANCE OF GRAVELS AND CONGLOMERATES

The rock types present in a gravel are dependent not only on the character of the rocks in the source area, but also upon the geomorphic and climatic environment of that area. Under certain conditions some rocks yield blocks readily; others do not. Vein quartz and chert, for example, are common as pebbles. Granite, on the other hand, tends to disintegrate and become an arkosic sand (gruss); limestone tends to dissolve and leave no gravelly detritus (other than its insoluble chert). But both granite and limestone yield

---

[1] The conglomerate was too well indurated to extract the pebbles, and the dips measured are those of the long axes in the plane of the section studied.

[2] Krumbein did not compute the mean inclination. The figures quoted are those calculated from Krumbein's data by White. The reader is referred to White's paper for the discussion of the basis used in the calculations. The upstream dip of the long axes is clearly much less than the upstream dip of the ab plane of the outwash gravels.

blocks if conditions are such that disintegration and solution are inhibited or subordinated. Such conditions are those marked by high relief and consequent rigorous climate with its attendant rapid erosion and accelerated frost action, or, more rarely, by glacial conditions (Pleistocene gravels of some areas) which, even in regions of low relief, are productive of gravels of mixed character rich in metastable rock fragments.

In support of these theoretical considerations there seems to be a correlation between the abundance of conglomerate and the maturity of the associated sandstones. Geologic sections characterized by thick arkoses are notably conglomeratic. The average of several such sections (page 629)

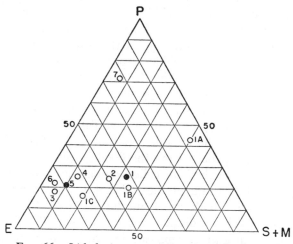

FIG. 66. Lithologic composition of conglomerates. *E,* eruptive (greenstone); *P,* plutonic (granite, gneiss, quartz porphyry); *S + M,* sedimentary and metamorphic (chert, jasper, iron formation, quartz). Numbers denote composition of various Archean conglomerates (from Pettijohn, 1943).

shows 10 to 20 per cent of conglomerate. The graywacke and subgraywacke suite has 1 to 5 per cent conglomerate; the orthoquartzite clan is marked by but 1 per cent or less conglomerate. In summary, the proportion of gravel increases with increasing immaturity of the associated sands, both of which appear to be functions of relief and climate and hence of tectonism.

Unlike sands and finer-grained sediments, the provenance of a gravel can be determined with the unaided eye. The kind and proportions of the larger clastic elements are readily determined by pebble counts. The several kinds and their proportions indicate both the source rocks and the distance of transport. Owing to the varying block-forming capacities of the several source rocks, however, and owing also to the varying resistance to abrasion of these rocks, the proportions present in a gravel are not a direct reflection of the relative abundance of the several rocks in the source area.

The composition of a gravel or conglomerate can be represented by grouping the rock types into extrusive igneous (E), plutonic igneous and meta-igneous (P), sedimentary (S), and metamorphic (M). Commonly these are plotted as a triangular diagram with sedimentary and metamorphic taken together (Fig. 66). As in the case of the sandstones, it seems desirable to distinguish between supracrustal and plutonic provenance. Such a distinction is in some degree a measure of the extent of uplift of the source area and the dependent depth of erosion—both functions of tectonism.

Of exceptional provenance are those conglomerates and breccias which derive their fragments from within rather than without the basin of deposition. In most such cases, fragmentation is contemporaneous with deposition. Such are the so-called intraformational conglomerates. These belong in a separate class and may be but a special case of disrupted or deformed bedding. Also exceptional are the coarse pyroclastic rocks, the agglomerates and tuffs, the fragments of which are contributed by volcanic action.

MATURITY OF GRAVELS AND CONGLOMERATES

As noted above, the gravelly residues derived from a land surface vary in their character as a result of varying conditions of relief and climate of that source area. Under conditions of low relief the gravel yield is both small and mature i.e., the materials are chemically inert residues. Only vein quartz, quartzite, and chert remain; the bulk of the source rocks are reduced to sands and clays. High relief and rapid erosion produce coarse, immature gravels. Unlike sand, stream transport produces marked downcurrent changes in the character of the gravels. The mechanically less durable materials are rapidly reduced and the proportions of the durable materials are increased (see Fig. 139). As shown by Plumley (1948) this change is appreciable even in relatively short distances of stream transport. Since quartz, quartzite, and chert are also mechanically durable as well as chemically inert, they tend to be further concentrated during transport. A mature gravel therefore is one consisting primarily of these materials; their percentage is therefore an appropriate measure of maturity (Plumley, 1948, p. 574).[3]

_____

[3] A gravel achieves maturity much more rapidly than does a sand under the same conditions. The gravels become rounded and compositionally mature as a result of short transport. Hence mature gravels may be associated with submature or even immature sands. The Mississippian Pocono, for example, contains orthoquartzitic conglomerates but the associated sands are protoquartzites and subgraywackes. Likewise the conglomerates within the Lorrain (Precambrian) of Ontario consist wholly of well-rounded vein quartz, quartzite, and chert; the associated sands are commonly subarkoses.

CLASSIFICATION OF GRAVELS AND CONGLOMERATES

Conglomerates and gravels have been classified in various ways. They may be classified in a purely descriptive sense based on their textures (boulder conglomerate, cobble conglomerate, etc.) or composition of their fragments (granite conglomerate, slate conglomerate, etc.) or their cement (ferruginous conglomerate, calcareous conglomerate, etc.). Commonly also they are classed according to the agent or to the environment responsible for their formation, such as beach conglomerate, fluviatile conglomerate, glacial conglomerate, or in broader terms, marine, littoral, or continental conglomerates. Only in the case of the present-day gravels can one be certain of the class to which a gravel deposit should be assigned. Also proposed is a classification based on the agent or process responsible for the fragmentation, hence epiclastic, cataclastic, and pyroclastic conglomerates or breccias. Here also assignment of ancient conglomerates to one or another class requires discriminating criteria which are not infallible.

Conglomerates, the coarser residues, are associated with finer but related residues—the sands. A classification appropriate for one group of materials should be appropriate or at least logically related to that used for the other group. Accordingly the classification here used for the gravels and conglomerates is the same in principle as that used for the sands and sandstones. In both cases the fundamental objective of the classification is to enable one to assign a gravel or conglomerate to a *genetically* significant group on the basis of *observable* properties. The properties or parameters used in the classification are those described in the preceding section, namely, texture, maturity, and source rock (provenance).

For reasons noted before, it is important to distinguish between "openwork" and "closed-work" gravels and between those gravels with an intact framework and those with a disrupted framework. Openwork and closed-work correspond to unimodal and bimodal distributions, and intact and disrupted framework correspond, in a general way, to the position of the dominant and the subordinate modes. Gravels collected by ordinary water currents have an intact framework; these are the *orthoconglomerates*. Those deposited by subaqueous turbidity flows and slides, and by glacial ice or other modes of mass transport have a disrupted framework—one notable for the greater excess of matrix over gravel-sized fragments (Table 43); these are the *paraconglomerates* or *conglomeratic mudstones*. Observations of the grain/matrix ratio is not enough; important also is the ratio of the size of the two modes in bimodal distributions. The orthoconglomerates have a principal mode in the gravel range and a lesser mode in the sand grade; normally these modes are 4 to 5 grades apart. In the conglomeratic mudstones, however, the principal mode is in the silt or clay range and the other in the gravel class.

Such extreme disparity in sizes denotes an unusual history and indicates deposition from media of high density and/or viscosity or postdepositional infiltration of fines into an openwork gravel. In the former case the principal mode is in the fines; in the latter case it is in the gravel range.

Some orthoconglomerates consist of a single rock type, vein quartz, for example, because all other debris has been eliminated by weathering or by long transport. Such conglomerates are supermature. Others have a mixed composition (petromict) and contain many unstable materials (granite, basalt, limestone, etc.). These are immature gravels. The maturity factor therefore must also be taken into account in the classification and the interpretation of the conglomeratic sediments.

TABLE 43. Classification of Consanguineous Clastics

Group	Conglomerates	Sandstones
Epiclastic, Extraformational Orthoconglomerates	1. Orthoquartzitic conglomerates (oligomictic)	1. Orthoquartzites
	2. Petromict conglomerates (polymictic)	2. Arkosic sandstones
		3. Lithic sandstones
Paraconglomerates (Conglomeratic Mudstones)	3. Tilloid ("Geröllton")	4. Graywackes and gritty mudstones
	4. Tillite[a]	
Epiclastic, Intraformational	5. Intraformational conglomerates	5. Calcarenites, etc.
Pyroclastic	6. Volcanic conglomerates and breccias	6. Tuffs and tuffogeneous sediments

[a] In one sense a cataclastic deposit analogous to gouge.

A third parameter is the provenance factor. The primary division is between an extra- and intrabasinal origin of the debris; hence extra- and intraformational conglomerates. For the more common extraformational conglomerates it is important to note the ratio of supracrustal to plutonic materials. A conglomerate composed of both is indicative of profound uplift and deep erosion. One composed only of pebbles of but a single rock type may record only a minor interlude or break in the sedimentary record. The variety and complexity of composition is, therefore, an important character.[4]

Gravels and conglomerates may be grouped as shown in Table 43.

[4] Those conglomerates composed of a single rock type have been termed oligomict (oligo- from *oligos* (Gr.): few + -mict from *miktos* (Gr.): mixed) whereas those containing many rock types are termed polymict (poly- from *polys* (Gr.): many + -mict from *miktos* (Gr.): mixed) (Schwetzoff, 1934).

ORTHOCONGLOMERATES

The orthoconglomerates are those with an intact framework of pebbles and coarse sands and characterized by a mineral cement. They were deposited from highly turbulent waters—either high-velocity streams or the surf. They are therefore strongly current-bedded and associated with coarse cross-bedded sands.

The orthoconglomerates may be divided into two groups, namely, (1) the orthoquartzitic conglomerates and (2) the petromict conglomerates. The first are the mature or supermature residues, mainly vein quartz and chert, whereas the second are the immature gravels characterized by an assortment of metastable rock fragments.

Orthoquartzitic (Oligomict) Conglomerates

These conglomerates are characterized by their simple composition. The pebbles are materials very resistant to wear and decomposition—such as quartz, quartzite, or chert or a mixture of these materials. There may be several types of quartzite or chert, and the varieties present—especially the fossiliferous cherts—may be the best clue to the provenance of these gravels.

In general the orthoquartzitic conglomerates are not coarse. Pebbles several inches in diameter are common, but those less than an inch in size are more typical. The debris, even the chert, is well-worn and rounded.

Orthoquartzitic gravels do not form any great deposit. They occur as sporadic pebbles, or pebbly layers and lenses interbedded with strongly cross-bedded orthoquartzitic and protoquartzitic sands.[5] These pebbly layers may occur mainly at the base of the sandstone or they may recur at several levels within the formation. The basal gravels constitute a "blanket type" deposit of varying thickness, commonly very thin or absent.

The gravels are well sorted and in places approach the character of a concentrate similar to some modern beach gravels. Many of these conglomerates probably are the deposits of a transgressive beach over a surface of low relief. Nearly everywhere the lowermost Cambrian is marked by a few inches, or more exceptionally, a few feet of such conglomerate. Such basal conglomerates, however, are more likely to be contaminated with locally derived subjacent metastable materials than are the conglomerates which recur at higher levels in the same section. The sporadic gravels scattered through the Mississagi and the Lorrain quartzites (Huronian) of Ontario are typical examples. The latter formation contains the justly famous red jasper-bearing conglomerate found in nearly all rock collections. A conglomerate of substantially

---

[5] As observed by Plumley (1948) and Schlee (1956), gravels achieve compositional maturity very quickly—much more rapidly than associated sands. Hence mature gravels may be found with submature sands.

similar nature and origin is that found in both the Mississippian (Pocono) and Pennsylvanian (Pottsville) of the Appalachian and Eastern Interior basins. These gravels are perhaps fluvial in origin rather than basal marine. Gravels similar in character are the Lafayette gravels of western Kentucky (Potter, 1955) and the Brandywine gravels of Maryland (Schlee, 1955) which are upland gravels consisting almost wholly of chert and vein quartz and quartzite. These gravels, a thin blanket deposit, were the product of stream deposition—the Tennessee and the Potomac rivers, respectively, during an earlier cycle of alluviation.

Petromict (Arkosic and Lithic) Conglomerates

The great conglomerates of the past belong to this group. In general these are thick, wedge-shaped, basin-margin accumulations of gravel that were shed from sharply elevated highlands. These gravels form a conspicuous part of the sequence to which they belong. They may be basal or they may be intercalated at several horizons.

Petromict (polymict) conglomerates are the coarse-grained representatives of the lithic and arkosic sandstone families. Although their composition is varied, all are marked in that the chief constituents are metastable rocks—generally of several kinds. The most common type is a mixture of pebbles or cobbles of plutonic (P), eruptive (E), and sedimentary and metamorphic rocks (S + M) (see Fig. 66). In many cases, however, one type or class of pebbles predominates.

Granite pebbles play the same role in these coarse sediments that the feldspars do in the sands. Accordingly, granite-bearing conglomerates are associated with feldspar-bearing sands. The converse, however, is not true, since some subarkoses are associated with orthoquartzitic conglomerates for reasons given elsewhere. Because of the limited block-forming capacity of much granite, however, the granite conglomerates are likely to be chiefly arkose with scattered pebbles of granite, or at best lenses of granitic gravel in arkose. Granite-bearing conglomerate is the coarse-grained equivalent of arkose. Both record rapid erosion of the crystalline basement. Accordingly the appearance of granitic debris in a sediment denotes major uplift; conglomerates devoid of granite may record only a minor interlude in the sedimentary history of a basin.

Exceptional in character are the limestone conglomerates. Such deposits must record unusual conditions which permitted the erosion of limestone as gravel rather than the usual removal by solution with resultant accumulation of chert. This implies sharp uplift and locally high relief—best achieved along a fault scarp—as the limestone conglomerates of the Triassic of Maryland and Pennsylvania testify. Extensive limestone gravels may be also a product of glaciation as exemplified by the limestone outwash gravels of parts of Illinois and Wisconsin derived by the ice from the Niagaran bed-rock of that region.

In regions of active volcanism, lavas may yield extensive gravels. In general these gravels are prone to consist of fragments of the felsitic lavas even though the bulk of the associated flows are basic. Apparently the gravel-forming capacity and the survival ability of the former are greater than the latter. The principle is well illustrated by the conglomerates of the Kewee-nawan composed mainly of felsitic fragments associated with the Keweenawan lavas which are largely basaltic. The volcanic gravels may be very thick (up to 5000 feet thick), are more or less contemporaneous with the lavas, and unlike the granite-bearing gravels, record no great uplift or erosional break.

The mechanical composition of these gravels is much the same (see Fig. 65). Characteristic of these deposits are (1) their coarseness, (2) the large number of grades in the coarser deposits, (3) polymodal character of the gravels and the deficiency of materials in the granule (2 to 4 mm) class, (4) general unimodal character of the interbedded sands, (5) the log normal character of the size distribution of the sands, (6) correlation between size of the material and thickness of the beds.

These conglomerates are marked by their coarseness (Pl. 11, top). Al-though boulders up to several feet or even several yards in diameter are com-mon, the mean size seldom exceeds 6 to 12 inches. In general, the mean size is one-tenth the maximum size (p. 249). Downdip size decrease is the rule; hence the maximum pebble size should be recorded and mapped. Sorting is fair to poor as the interstices of the deposit are filled with sandy materials.

In general the rounding of these gravels is fair to good, though exception-ally the rounding is very poor and the rock may be described as a breccia. The rounding of the larger cobbles is in marked contrast to the very poor rounding shown by the associated sands.

The bedding varies from near horizontal, characteristic of the torrential gravels to cross-bedded, mostly found in associated lenses of sand and pea-sized gravels. Most beds probably had a small initial dip. Only the sands are well-bedded and clearly cross-laminated. Many outcrops of the coarse gravels fail to show any bedding structure except a rude parallelism of the clasts in some cases expressed as a kind of false bedding owing to an upstream dip or imbrication of the flatter pebbles (Pl. 11, top).

Notable examples of conglomerates in this group include many of the early Precambrian (Archean) conglomerates of the Lake Superior region (Pettijohn, 1934; 1943) most of which are granite-bearing (see Fig. 66), the Keweenawan conglomerates of late Precambrian age in Michigan (White, 1952) which are primarily felsitic, the Franks limestone conglomerate and others of Pennsylvanian age in the Arbuckle Mountains of Oklahoma (Ham, 1954), the Triassic conglomerates of the Newark series in the Connecticut valley (Krynine, 1950) and the related conglomerates in the other Triassic basins of the eastern United States including the limestone conglomerates of Maryland ("Potomac marble") and Pennsylvania, the Roxbury and associated conglomerates of the Boston Bay area (Mansfield, 1906), the San Onofre "breccia" of Miocene age in California (Woodford, 1925), the Price River conglomerate of Cretaceous age in the Wasatch Plateau of Utah, and the Wasatch conglomerate (Eocene) itself. All of these conglomerates are notably thick, locally 5000 feet or more, all have a considerable along-strike persistence, and all wedge out rapidly down dip; many are related to or associated with contemporaneous faulting.

REFERENCES CITED AND BIBLIOGRAPHY

Barrell, J. (1925), Marine and terrestrial conglomerates, Bull. Geol. Soc. Amer., vol. 36, pp. 279–342.

Cailleux, Andre (1945), Distinction des galets marins et fluviatiles, Bull. soc. géol. France, vol. 15, ser. 5, pp. 375–404.

Cailleux, A. (1946), Granulometrie des formations a galets, Géol. terrains recents, Bruxelles, Soc. belges géol., p. 109.

Cayeux, L. (1929), Les roches sedimentaires de France, Paris, Imprimerie Nationale, p. 9.

Conkling, H., Eckis, R., and Gross, P. J. K. (1934), Ground water storage capacity of valley fill, Calif. Div. Water Resources, Bull. 45.

Emery, K. O. (1955), Grain size of marine beach gravels, J. Geol., vol. 63, pp. 39–49.

Fernald, F. A. (1929), Roundstone, a new geologic term, Science, vol. 70, p. 240.

Folk, R. L. (1954), The distinction between grain size and mineral composition in sedimentary-rock nomenclature, J. Geol., vol. 62, pp. 344–359.

Fraser, H. J. (1935), Experimental study of the porosity and permeability of clastic sediments, J. Geol., vol. 43, pp. 910–1010.

de Freitas, R. O. (1945), O conglomerado do Bau, Univ. de S. Paulo, Boletim L, Geol. No. 2, pp. 35–115.

Gregory, H. E. (1915), Notes on the shapes of pebbles, Am. J. Sci., vol. 39, pp. 300–304.

Gregory, H. E. (1915), The formation and distribution of fluviatile and marine gravels, Am. J. Sci., vol. 39, pp. 487–508.

Grogan, R. M. (1945), Shape variation of some Lake Superior beach pebbles, J. Sediment. Petrol., vol. 15, pp. 3–10.

Hadding, A. (1927), The pre-Quaternary rocks of Sweden. II. The Paleozoic and Mesozoic conglomerates of Sweden, Lunds Univ. Årsskr., Avd. 2, vol. 23, no. 5, pp. 43–171.

Kopstein, F. P. H. W. (1954), Graded bedding of the Harlech Dome, Thesis (Ph.D.), Rijksuniversiteit Groningen.

Krumbein, W. C. (1939), Preferred orientation of pebbles in sedimentary deposits, J. Geol., vol. 47, pp. 673–706.

Krumbein, W. C. (1940), Flood gravel of San Gabriel Canyon, California, *Bull. Geol. Soc. Amer.*, vol. 51, pp. 639–676.

Krumbein, W. C. (1942), Flood deposits of Arroyo Seco, Los Angeles County, California, *Bull. Geol. Soc. Amer.*, vol. 53, pp. 1355–1402.

Krumbein, W. C., and Griffith, J. S. (1938), Beach environment in Little Sister Bay, Wisconsin, *Bull. Geol. Soc. Amer.*, vol. 49, pp. 629–652.

Krynine, P. D. (1948), The megascopic study and field classification of sedimentary rocks, *J. Geol.*, vol. 56, pp. 130–165.

Krynine, P. D. (1950), Petrology, stratigraphy, and origin of the Triassic sedimentary rocks of Connecticut, *Connecticut State Geol. Nat. Hist. Survey, Bull. 73.*

Kurk, E. H. (1941), *The problem of sampling heterogeneous sediments*, Thesis (M.S.), University of Chicago.

Landon, R. E. (1930), An analysis of beach pebble abrasion and transportation, *J. Geol.*, vol. 38, pp. 437–446.

Lane, E. W., and Carlson, E. J. (1954), Some observations on the effect of particle size on movement of coarse sediments, *Trans. Amer. Geophysical Union*, vol. 35, pp. 453–462.

Lawson, A. C. (1925), The petrographic designation of alluvial fan formations, *Univ. Calif. Publ. Dept. Geol. Sci.*, vol. 7, pp. 325–334.

Leuchs, K. (1933), Über Breccien, *Geol. Rundschau*, vol. 24, pp. 273–284.

Mansfield, G. R. (1906), The origin and structure of the Roxbury conglomerate, *Harvard Mus. Comp. Zoology, Bull.* 49, pp. 91–271.

Mansfield, G. R. (1907), The characteristics of various types of conglomerate, *J. Geol.*, vol. 15, pp. 550–555.

Norton, W. H. (1917), A classification of breccias, *J. Geol.*, vol. 25, pp. 160–194.

Pettijohn, F. J. (1934), The conglomerate of Abram Lake, Ontario, and its extensions, *Bull. Geol. Soc. Amer.*, vol. 45, pp. 479–506.

Plumley, W. J. (1948), Black Hills terrace gravels: a study in sediment transport, *J. Geol.*, vol. 56, pp. 526–577.

Potter, P. E. (1955), The petrology and origin of the Lafayette Gravel. Part 1. Mineralogy and petrology, *J. Geol.*, vol. 63, pp. 1–38.

Reynolds, S. H. (1928), Breccias, *Geol. Mag.*, vol. 65, pp. 97–107.

Richter, K. (1932), Die Bewegungsrichtung des Inlandeises rekonstruiert aus den Kritzen und Längsachsen der Geschiebe, *Z. Geschiebeforschung*, vol. 8, pp. 62–66.

Schlee, J. (1956), *Sedimentological analysis of the upland gravels of southern Maryland*, Thesis (Ph.D.), The Johns Hopkins Univ., Baltimore, Md.

Schwetzoff, M. S. (1935), *Petrography of sedimentary rocks*, Moscow (Review in *J. Sediment. Petrol.*, vol. 5, 1935, p. 106).

Shrock, R. R. (1948), A classification of sedimentary rocks, *J. Geol.*, vol. 56, pp. 118–129.

Twenhofel, W. H. (1947), The environmental significance of conglomerates, *J. Sediment. Petrol.*, vol. 17, pp. 119–128.

Udden, J. S. (1914), Mechanical composition of clastic sediments, *Bull. Geol. Soc. Amer.*, vol. 25, pp. 655–744.

Wadell, H. (1936), Volume, shape, and shape position of rock fragments in openwork gravel, *Geog. Ann. 1936*, pp. 74–92.

Wentworth, C. K. (1922), A scale of grade and class terms for clastic sediments, *J. Geol.*, vol. 30, pp. 377–392.

Wentworth, C. K. (1922b), The shapes of beach pebbles, *U.S. Geol. Survey, Prof. Paper 131-C*, pp. 74–83.

Wentworth, C.K. (1935), The terminology of coarse sediments (with notes by P. G. H. Boswell), *Nat. Research Council Bull.* 89, pp. 225–246.

White, W. S. (1952), Imbrication and initial dip in a Keweenawan conglomerate bed, *J. Sediment. Petrol.*, vol. 22, pp. 189–199.

Willard, B. (1930), Conglomerite, a new rock term, *Science*, vol. 71, p. 438.

Willman, H. B. (1942), Geology and mineral resources of the Marseilles, Ottawa, and Streater quadrangles, *Ill. State Geol. Survey, Bull.* 66, pp. 343–344.

Woodford, A. O. (1925), The San Onofre breccia, *Univ. Calif. Publ. Dept. Geol. Sci.*, Vol. 17, no. 7, pp. 159–280.

PARACONGLOMERATES (CONGLOMERATIC MUDSTONES)

These rocks, which contain more matrix than clasts, are in reality mudstones with a sparse to liberal sprinkling of pebbles or cobbles. In many examples the pebbles form 10 per cent or less of the rock. However, the deposits are more commonly described as conglomerates rather than as mudstones.

No satisfactory terms have been proposed for this interesting though relatively uncommon group of rocks. It seems that most terms that can be applied to these rocks—applicable at the hand specimen or outcrop level and not implying genesis—are either inaccurate or inconveniently long.[6] The designation *paraconglomerate* is therefore proposed. As the term implies, something is amiss or aberrant. These rocks are not the product of normal aqueous flow. Some of the pebbly or cobbly mudstones are boulder clays, a term which although supposedly descriptive is generally considered synonymous with till. The latter is a particular kind of boulder clay—namely a deposit made by glacial ice. The term *geröllton* has been applied to the nonglacial pebbly mudstones (Ackermann, 1951); the term *tilloid* has also been used. The term *mudstone conglomerate* is more commonly used for a conglomerate in which the fragments (rather than matrix) are mudstone.

There are two basic types of pebbly mudstone: one has a stratified matrix; the second has an unstratified mudstone matrix.

[6] For a discussion of the problem of nomenclature of rocks of this group see Miller (1953).

PLATE 13

TILL AND TILLITE I

Top: Pleistocene till, Bull Lake, Wind River Range, Wyoming. Photograph by C. D. Holmes.

Bottom: Sturtian tillite, Adelaide Series, Precambrian (?) near Adelaide, Australia. Photograph by R. T. Chamberlin.

PLATE 14

TILL STONES AND TILLITE

Top: Till stones, Pleistocene, Illinois.

Note striations, faceting, and snubbed edges and corners. Largest cobble is about five inches in diameter.

Bottom: Gowganda (Huronian) tillite, Ontario, Canada.

Note sparsity of pebbles and dominance of dark matrix. Length of specimen is eleven inches. For thin-section appearance see Pl. 15, **B**.

Laminated Pebbly Mudstones

These relatively rare rocks are very distinctive in character. They consist of delicately laminated argillites or slates in which are thinly scattered phenoclasts—some no larger than sand grains; others full-sized cobbles or even boulders. The laminations are distorted near the larger clasts and bend down beneath them as well as lap upon or arch over them (Fig. 67; Pl. 23, bottom).

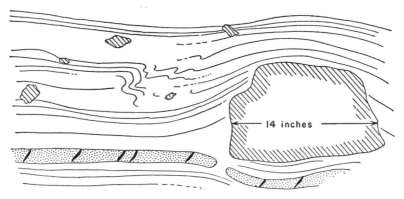

FIG. 67. Sketch showing ice-rafted pebbles and cobble. Fern Creek formation (Precambrian), Norway, Mich.

The conglomeratic laminated lutites are obviously produced by dropping of coarse blocks into still bottom waters in which the finest silts and muds were accumulating. This normally is the product of raft action—most commonly by glacial ice although cobble-sized fragments may be carried in the roots of floating trees, by river or shore ice, or even be dropped into quiet waters by volcanic explosions. The latter case is most probable if the fragments are mainly volcanic rocks and the matrix is rich in volcanic admixtures especially glass.

In general, laminated argillites with rafted blocks (conglomeratic pellodites) are glacial in origin and are closely associated with tillites and are themselves characterized by a varved structure. Rafted erratics occur in the glaciolacustrine clays of the Pleistocene of Scandinavia and Canada. Conglomeratic rocks of this type occur also in the Fern Creek beds of Precambrian age in Michigan (Pettijohn, 1952), in the Gowganda (Cobalt) of Huronian age in Ontario,[7] in the Tapley Hill slates of the Adelaide Series of Australia, etc. (Kulling, 1938; Caldenius, 1938).

[7] Plate 10 of Memoir 143 (Collins, 1925) of the Geological Survey of Canada is an excellent illustration of three fundamentally unlike conglomeratic rocks occurring in one and the same formation.

Tilloid ("Geröllton")

The conglomeratic mudstones with nonlaminated matrices are in part glacial (till and tillite) and in part nonglacial (tilloid). The latter are probably more common and have often been erroneously ascribed to glacial action.

The nonglacial conglomeratic mudstones or tilloids vary from a chaotic unassorted assemblage of coarse materials set in a mudstone matrix to a mudstone with sparsely distributed cobbles. The matrix may be either subordinate to the large clasts or it may be dominant. These conglomerates may lack any internal structure; in other cases large-scale grading and a preferred orientation of the long axes of the pebbles may be present. Cross-bedding and other evidences of normal current action are generally absent. These till-like beds are associated with graded graywackes and grits and with fine-grained siltstones and lutites which, in the younger sequences, may carry a deep-water marine fauna. The conglomeratic beds are commonly uniform in thickness. Unlike till, there may be gradations between these tilloids and the coarse but otherwise normal gravels. The associated still-water shales, though rhythmically interbedded, do not contain the ice-rafted erratics which characterize the glacial sequences. Unlike till also, the conglomeratic mudstones may be thin, a foot or two thick, and may be many times repeated in a section.

Conglomerates belonging to this class have been described from various places. Parts of the Haymond formation (Carboniferous) in the Marathon area of Texas are conglomeratic rocks with a graywacke matrix consisting of gritty, dark olive-green to black unstratified matrix in which are sparsely distributed small and large erratics (Baker, 1932). These materials are apparently similar to some phases of the Flysch (wildflysch) of the Alps. The Levis conglomerates (Ordovician) of the Quebec region which have a lime-mud matrix and the Squantum conglomerates (Sayles, 1914) are conglomeratic mudstones of similar character; here also belong some rubble beds in the Tertiary (Talara formation) of Peru (Dorreen, 1951) and perhaps the so-called "Johns Valley shale" (Carboniferous) in the Ouachita mountains (van der Gracht, 1931).

These tilloids have been explained in various ways. Perhaps they are polygenetic but even the same deposit has been interpreted differently by different authors. These rocks have been attributed to catastrophic flash floods of the arid regions, to deposition from glacial ice, to rafting and deposition from icebergs, to landslides and mud flows, to solifluction, and to subaqueous mudstreams and turbidity flows. Although deposits formed in any of the above ways might be pebbly mudstones and all perhaps may be represented in the stratigraphic record, it now seems probable in light of our knowledge of turbidity currents and related mudstreams, that most of these abnormal conglomerates are the product of subaqueous mudstreams or *slurries*. The interbedding with finely laminated argillites and graded-bedded graywackes replete with structures produced by soft-sediment deformation, the dark color of the fresh materials, their close association with marine fossils—not uncommonly deep-water forms—precludes a terrestrial origin. Desert alluvium, landslide, terrestrial mud flows, solifluction deposits, and the like are ruled out. The absence of ice-rafted debris in the associated argillutites excludes a glacial origin and the absence of volcanic glass and related materials precludes a volcanic origin.

The observed mudstreams which traveled a remarkable distance seaward along the floor of certain Norwegian fjords (Ackermann, 1951), the extraordinary extent and vigor of the presumed turbidity flow in the Grand Banks area (Heezen and Ewing, 1952), and the theoretical properties of turbidity flows and subaqueous mudstreams (Kuenen, 1951) make it clear that these agents are fully capable of producing the conglomeratic mudstones (tilloids) and make unnecessary appeal to any other agent.

There are some conglomerates, less appropriately called conglomeratic mudstones, which have also been ascribed to subaqueous slumping and turbidity flows. These deposits are not too different from the more poorly sorted immature terrestrial gravels, such as the fanglomerates, but the associations of these beds and other considerations require an extraordinary mode of transport and deposition. The conglomerates are intercalated with marine shales and show no evidence of channeling, small-scale cross-bedding, erosion, and terracing of previous deposited shales, all of which would be expected of near-shore or terrestrial gravels. Such conglomerates are common in Upper Cretaceous beds of the San Joaquin Valley in California (Briggs, 1953) and in the Pliocene of the Ventura Basin where they are believed to have accumulated in no less than 4000 to 5000 feet of water (Natland and Kuenen, 1951).

Till and Tillite

Introduction and Definitions

Although at present till is a rather common deposit over a large area in northern Europe and in the northern part of the United States and a large part of Canada, it is a relatively rare deposit elsewhere, except very locally, and its consolidated equivalent (tillite) is a very rare rock indeed. Nevertheless, because of its widespread occurrence in certain regions today and because of the great importance of tillite as a record of a major climatic event, considerable space is here devoted to both till and tillite.

The term *till* is properly applied only to unstratified and unsorted *ice-laid* materials. It is equivalent to the somewhat more descriptive term *boulder clay*. To the lithified tills, Penck applied the term *tillite*. Though composed dominantly of fine-grained materials, these deposits are here included with the gravels and conglomerates. Because of the conspicuous role played by the boulders or cobbles which they contain, they would generally be termed conglomerates by the field geologist.

Textures and Structures

The most striking characteristic of till and tillite is the great preponderance of their fine-grained and structureless matrix in which are sparsely distributed cobbles and boulders (Pl. 13). In the tills analyzed by Krumbein

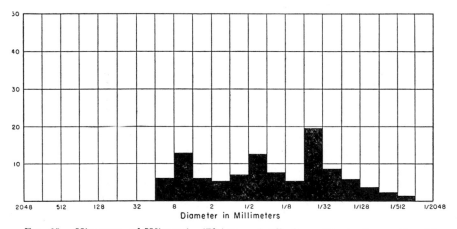

Fig. 68.   Histogram of Wisconsin (Pleistocene) till, Cary, Illinois. Composite of ten samples.

(1933) the matrix constitutes four-fifths to nine-tenths of the total and only one-fifth to one-twentieth of the whole falls in the gravel range. In most cases silt and clay forms half to two-thirds of the deposit. The median in most cases falls between three and ten microns. These tills are obviously clay tills (see Fig. 68).[8]

The sorting of till is notably poor. All of Krumbein's 48 analyzed tills had 12 or more grades containing 1 per cent or more of material. No very large amount of material, however, is present in any one size class. The largest modal class in the tills analyzed contained only 20 per cent by weight of the whole sample; obviously the modal class is inconspicuous. Though some

[8] These tills have, perhaps, an abnormally high clay content owing to the soft shales and limestones of the Paleozoic bedrock of the area from which they were derived. No doubt tills of other areas would contain a greater proportion of silt and sand but the general predominance of fine-grained matrix in which coarse-grained sand and gravel is dispersed is universally characteristic of till.

of the tills analyzed appear to have but a single modal class, most have two such maxima and a few have three or more such grades. The secondary mode, however, is very feeble at best, and it may be regarded as anomalous for reasons given below. Both the principal mode and the secondary mode showed a strong preference for certain grades. Sixty-two per cent (of 48 samples) had the secondary mode in the fine sand class ($\frac{1}{4}$ to $\frac{1}{8}$ mm); 54 per cent had the chief ingredient in the $\frac{1}{64}$ to $\frac{1}{128}$ millimeter class. With more than a dozen grades present, such a preference for these two grades shown by well over half the samples is significant.

Although composed predominantly of fine materials, till and tillite may contain very large boulders. Boulders one meter in diameter are rare but not unknown. As much material is one micron or smaller in size, till has therefore a millionfold size range and is one of the poorest sorted of all sediments.

Von Engelen (1930) maintained that glacial cobbles and pebbles tended to have a unique form which was diagnostic of glacial action. According to him the characteristic form was that of a striated and faceted flatiron. In detail the features of such a cobble are (1) the roughly triangular shape in plan with the facet of largest area and that which is flattest down, (2) the pointed but scour-snubbed nose at the apex of the narrowest angle of the bottom facet, (3) an only slightly scoured or hackly back side above the base line of the bottom triangle, (4) a tendency to hump form of the top side of the flatiron with (5) lateral facets running off toward the snubbed point, (6) chipping or nicking on the underside or at the apex of the point, (7) a tendency of the striations on the lateral facets to be directed diagonally downward toward the point, and (8) indication that the variations from the norm or the failure to develop one of these features in the well-processed pebble are due to a particular, and still obvious, configuration of the original fragment or the nature, rock structure, and composition of the specimen.

Von Engelen's description of the end form toward which glacial action tends to shape rock fragments was supported by quantitative data collected by Wentworth (1936) who analyzed 626 glacial cobbles. Three hundred, selected for perfection of glacial action, were studied in detail. The cobbles were classified according to the general shape as shown in Table 44. Clearly the dominant shape is tabular owing in part to the original tabular shape of the fragments and the sustained abrasion on the two initially opposed principal faces.

Study of the marginal profiles (as observed when the pebble lies on its most stable face, i.e., the profile normal to the shortest axis) shows the pentagonal outline to be the most common (Table 45). Approximately two-thirds of the margins might be described as pentagonal, quadrangular, triangular, polygonal, trapezoid, or reniform. The most characteristic shape of a

TABLE 44. General Shapes of 300 Glacial
Cobbles (after Wentworth, 1936)

Shape Classification	Number
Parallel Tabular	98.0
Wedge Tabular	47.0
Semitabular	29.5[a]
Subtabular	2.5
Roof-Shaped	27.5
Wedge-Shaped	10.0
Single Lens	4.0
Double Lens	10.0
Pyramid	10.0
Double Pyramid	7.0
Prism	41.0
Nodular	12.5
Ellipsoid	1.0

[a] In several cases cobbles were classified as intermediate between two types and were assigned half to each; this accounts for the fractions.

TABLE 45. Marginal Profiles of 300 Glacial Cobbles
(after Wentworth, 1936)

Type of Margin	Pure	Mixed
Parallel-Sided	5	4
Circular	2	6
Reniform	11	17
Lenticular	15	0
Bilenticular	6	0
Oval	14	11
Triangular	34	13
Rectangular	12	1
Quadrangular	36	4
Rhombic	1	0
Trapezoidal	15	1
Pentagonal	66	16
Hexagonal	14	3
Heptagonal	8	1
Polygonal	19	7

glacial cobble, therefore, is parallel tabular with a pentagonal outline. The flatiron shape noted by von Engelen is verified by actual count. Typical profiles are shown in Fig. 69.

In size the cobbles studied varied from 5 to 100 centimeters in diameter. The largest number had their maximum diameter between 10 and 20 centimeters. The average cobble studied was a slab having a length 1.4 times its width and 2.25 times its thickness. A few cobbles were four times as long as they were thick and over twice as long as wide. One hundred twenty-eight had well-rounded margins, 116 moderately-rounded margins, and 56 were

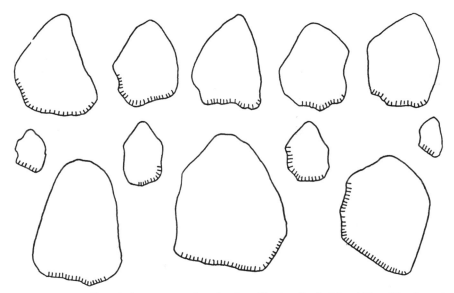

Fɪɢ. 69.   Profiles of the pentagonal and other "flat-iron" glacial cobbles. The largest is about 18 cm long. Stoss end at top of cut; margin showing snub scars hachured (from Wentworth, 1936).

rough and broken. By far the majority, therefore, showed definite evidence of superficial shaping of the margins by abrasion. The characteristic "push-off" ends and edges of the cobbles, termed snub-scars by Wentworth, were strongly marked on 43 cobbles, clearly present on 107, and faintly seen on 42. Though not seen on 108, these lee-end pressure spalls are sufficiently abundant to be considered a characteristic feature of glacial cobbles.

The typical till stone is striated, though such striations are more common on certain rock types than others and as a whole are by no means so abundant as is commonly supposed. Wentworth's study of striations (Wentworth, 1936) showed that in his material only 10 per cent of the limestones and only 1 per cent of all other rocks were found to show striations (Fig. 70). Wentworth found these striations to be subparallel to one another and to be generally parallel to the long axis of the till stone (see Table 46). The difficulty of removing cobbles intact and the scarcity of striations on typical glacial materials, as shown by Wentworth's data, explain the common failure to find striated stones in many ancient tillites.

Though till as a whole appears structureless and devoid of bedding, studies by Richter (1932), Holmes (1941) and others have shown that there is a weak but distinct tendency of the embedded rock fragments to lie with their longest axes nearly parallel to the direction of ice flow at the time the de-

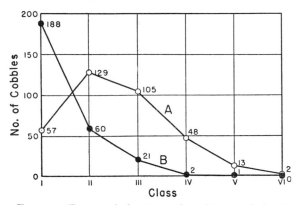

FIG. 70. Degree of shaping and marking in 626 pebbles and cobbles from Wisconsin (Pleistocene) drift near Baraboo, Wis. A: Limestones. B: All other rocks. Class I, no striae or facets; II, faint striations; III, clear striations on one side; IV, clear striations on two sides or grid on one side; V, grid on two sides; VI, grid on several sides (after Wentworth, 1936).

TABLE 46.   Classification of Striation Characteristics (after Wentworth, 1936)

	Parallel Pattern	Subparallel Pattern	Scatter Pattern	Grid Pattern	Moulded Pattern	Pattern Parallel to Axis
Character Strongly Developed	0	211	45	2	28	189
Character Partially Developed	2	57	111	14	18	74
Index of Occurrence per 1000 Cobbles[a]	3	791	335	30	123	753

[a] Counting partial development at one-half and strong development at one and transforming to rate per 1000.

posit was formed (Fig. 71). Such tendency is revealed by plotting the orientation of at least 100 till stones at any one locality. The results are expressed by means of the usual fabric diagrams (see page 76). Such studies make possible the determination of the direction of ice movement in the absence of exposed striae or other evidence (see page 80).

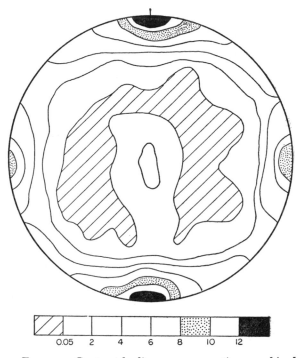

FIG. 71. Contoured diagram representing combined till-fabric pattern from ten places (1180 stones). Each individual pattern was superposed by placing its recorded ice-flow direction in "north-south" position. The direction from which the ice approached is indicated by dot above the diagram (from Holmes, 1941).

Composition of Till and Tillite

Although the composition of till and tillite is highly variable, nearly all are characterized by an assortment of unweathered blocks and till stones in a matrix or paste of unweathered materials ("rock flour"). The till stones though composed most commonly of material of the underlying basement are also in part of materials foreign to the area. All types of rocks, sedimentary, metasedimentary, and both plutonic and effusive igneous rocks, may be present. The matrix of till, if fresh, is usually a dark bluish gray; if oxidized it is buff. The usual tillite matrix is dark gray to greenish black. It closely resembles a graywacke—which it perhaps is—and under the microscope it appears to consist of fresh, angular grains of quartz, feldspar, and rock fragments set in a "paste" of fine grain (Pl. 15). In the tillites proper, the latter appears to be richly chloritic and micaceous, and is probably the product of low-grade metamorphism of the original clay component of the till. Triturated carbonate is common in tills of limestone regions and renders such deposits strongly calcareous.

The chemical analyses are much like those of graywackes and related rocks (Table 47). Normally these materials, like other immature sediments, are rich in lime and soda. Tills of limestone regions are notably calcareous.

TABLE 47.   Chemical Composition of Till and Tillite

	A	B	C	D	E
			(per cent)		
SiO_2	61.98	64.59	80.34	59.32	60.49
TiO_2	0.60	0.47	0.42	0.55	0.42
Al_2O_3	17.20	14.66	7.66	12.34	12.62
Fe_2O_3	1.42	2.89	1.39	2.29⎱	7.80
FeO	4.49	3.55	0.72	3.72⎰	
MnO	0.10	0.08	....	0.45	....
MgO	3.27	3.83	0.83	4.01	3.68
CaO	1.00	0.46	1.51	5.20	3.87
Na_2O	5.27	1.60	2.13	1.80	2.17
K_2O	2.04	5.86	1.94	2.52	2.53
H_2O+	2.70	1.66⎱	2.63[a]	7.76[a]	5.90[a]
H_2O-	0.10	0.08⎰			
P_2O_5	....	0.22	T	0.30	....
CO_2	....	0.31	....	....	....
C	....	0.07	....	....	....
S	....	0.01	....	....	....
	100.15	100.35	99.59	100.27	99.48

A. Cobalt tillite, Huronian (Collins, 1925).
B. Fern Creek tillite, "Huronian," Dickinson County, Michigan. B. Bruun, analyst.
C. Ipanema tillite, Permo-Carboniferous, Sao Paulo, Brazil. M. Fontoura, analyst (Leintz, 1937).
D. Barra Bonita tillite, Permo-Carboniferous, Parana, Brazil. M. Fontoura, analyst (Leintz, 1937).
E. "Red drift" (Late Pleistocene till), Coon Creek, Minn. F. F. Grout, analyst (Grout, 1919).

[a] Loss on ignition.

Geologic Occurrence and Associations

Tills and tillites record relatively rare events. But since glaciations are commonly multiple it follows that one till or tillite is likely to be associated with other such deposits.

Some, but by no means all, tillites and tills are found to rest on a striated pavement. This is characteristic only of the first or lowest till or tillite in a sequence. Higher and younger tills may be interbedded with glaciolacustrine and fluvioglacial beds.

An almost universal and a most significant associate of till or tillite is varved clay and its lithified equivalent (pellodite).[9] These materials show exceptionally even laminations which represent seasonal deposition of clay and slate in quiet freshwater lakes. Abundant rafted angular blocks of both

[9] A term attributed to J. B. Woodworth (Leintz, 1937).

small and large size which are embedded in these beds constitute the strongest evidence for ice action, excepting only perhaps the striated stones from the till itself (Pl. 23). Conversely the absence of such rafted cobbles casts great doubt on many ancient deposits attributed to glacial action. Even in thin section, coarse, angular grains of quartz will be observed in the finest siltstone or slate laminae, which is indicative of rafting on a microscopic scale (Pl. 24, B).

The fluvioglacial beds or "outwash" deposits are more or less normal stream-laid sands and gravels (Pl. 12, top). They differ in no important respect from such deposits.

Tillites belong to no particular time or place. Coleman (1926) has summarized the known and the problematic occurrences of glacial beds.

Precambrian tillites are known from several localities. The Fern Creek tillite of Michigan (Pettijohn, 1952), the well-known Gowganda tillites (Pl. 15, B) of the Huronian Cobalt series of Ontario and Quebec (Wilson, 1913), and the tillites of the Wasatch Range of Utah (Blackwelder, 1932) are excellent examples. The Gowganda tillite, in particular, which extends over an area of several thousand square miles has yielded striated stones and is associated with varved argillites bearing rafted blocks (Pl. 23, bottom).

The Sturtian tillite of Australia (Pl. 15, D) and other tillites of the Adelaide series (Howchin, 1908; Browne, 1940; Mawson, 1949) and the Permo-Carboniferous Dwyka tillite (Pl. 15, C) of South Africa (DuToit, 1921) are perhaps the most famous tillites known. The Carboniferous tillites of Brazil also display well the characteristics of glacial beds (Leintz, 1937) as do the sub-Cambrian tillites of northern Europe (Wegmann, 1951; Kulling, 1939). Although the Squantum beds of the Boston Bay area (Devonian?) have been said to contain tillites (Sayles, 1914) and do in fact resemble tillite in many respects, they lack many critical features and are probably nonglacial in origin.

Origin and Geologic Significance

Although much has been written on till, the mechanism of its formation is not wholly understood. The origin of the fabric displayed by till stones has been discussed by Holmes (1941). The relation between the composition of till and the subjacent bedrock has been studied both here (Holmes, 1952) and abroad (Lundquist, 1935). The size distribution of tills has not been fully explained though some study of the subject was made by Krumbein (1933) and by Krumbein and Tisdel (1940).

The geologic significance of tillite, however, is self-evident. Though conceivably related only to local glaciers of Alpine nature, the tillites of the past, especially those of considerable areal extent, record periods of intense and widespread refrigeration. The cause of such a drastic climatic change and the reason for the occurrence of many ancient tillites in very low latitudes is as yet unknown. Apparently, from the earliest times, the earth has been subjected to widespread glaciations as it has in the recent past and at the present.

Every chaotic deposit with large blocks embedded in a clayey matrix is not a tillite and great caution should be exercised in discriminating between true tillite and other materials which resemble it. Mudflows, landslide and solifluction deposits, and some volcanic tuffs or breccias closely resemble till. These materials, excepting the volcanic materials, are local and restricted and all these deposits lack the characteristic faceted and striated stones, and what is most important, are not associated with the laminated argillites *with rafted blocks.*

REFERENCES CITED AND BIBLIOGRAPHY

Ackermann, Ernst (1951), Geröllton, Geol. Rundschau, vol. 39, pp. 237–239.

Baker, C. L. (1932), Erratics and arkoses in the Middle Pennsylvanian Haymond formation of the Marathon area, Trans-Pecos, Texas, J. Geol., vol. 40, pp. 577–603.

Blackwelder, Eliot (1932), An ancient glacial formation in Utah, J. Geol., vol. 40, pp. 289–304.

Briggs, L. I. (1953), Upper Cretaceous sandstones of Diablo Range, California: Univ. Calif. Publ. Geol. Sci., vol. 29, pp. 417–452.

Browne, W. R. (1940), Late Proterozoic (?) glaciation in Australia, XVII Intern. Geol. Congress, vol. 6, pp. 57–63.

Caldenius, C. (1938), Carboniferous varves, measured at Paterson, N.S.W., Geol. Fören. i Stockholm Förh., vol. 60, pp. 349–364.

Coleman, A. P. (1926), Ice-ages, recent and ancient, New York, Macmillan.

Collins, W. H. (1925), North Shore of Lake Huron, Can. Geol. Survey, Memoir 143, pp. 63–67, Pls. X and XI.

Doreen, J. M. (1951), Rubble bedding and graded bedding in Talara formation of northwestern Peru, Bull. Am. Assoc. Petroleum Geol., vol. 35, pp. 1829–1849.

DuToit, A. L. (1921), The Carboniferous glaciation of South Africa, Trans. Geol. Soc. S. Africa, vol. 23, pp. 188–227.

Grout, F. F. (1919), The clays and shales of Minnesota, U.S. Geol. Surv. Bull. 678.

Heezen, B. C. and Ewing, M. (1952), Turbidity currents and submarine slumps and the 1929 Grand Banks earthquake, Am. J. Sci., vol. 250, pp. 849–873.

Holmes, C. D. (1941), Till fabric, Bull. Geol. Soc. Amer., vol. 52, pp. 1299–1354.

Holmes, C. D. (1952), Drift dispersion in west-central New York, Bull. Geol. Soc. Amer., vol. 63, pp. 993–1010.

Howchin, W. (1908), Glacial beds of Cambrian age in South Australia, Quart. J. Geol. Soc. London, vol. 64, pp. 234–259.

Krumbein, W. C. (1933), Textural and lithologic variations in glacial till, *J. Geol.*, vol. 41, pp. 382–408.

Krumbein, W. C. and Tisdel, F. W. (1940), Size distributions of source rocks of sediments, *Am. J. Sci.*, vol. 238, pp. 296–305.

Kulling, Oskar (1938), Notes on varved boulder-bearing mudstone in Eocambrian glacials in the mountains of northern Sweden, *Geol. Fören. i Stockholm Förh.*, vol. 60, pp. 393–396.

Kuenen, Ph. H. (1951), Properties of turbidity currents of high density, *Soc. Econ. Paleon. Min., Special Publ.*, No. 2, pp. 14–33.

Leintz, Viktor (1937), Estudos sobre a glaciacao permo-carbonifera do sul do Brasil, *Brazil Serv. Foments Prod. Min., Boletim* 21, 55 pp.

Lundquist, G. (1935), Blockundersokningar, Historik och Metodik, *Sveriges Geol. Undersökn.*, ser. 3, no. 390.

Mawson, Douglas (1949), The Late Precambrian Ice-Age and glacial record of the Bibliando dome, *J. Proc. Roy. Soc. New South Wales*, vol. 82, pp. 150–174.

Miller, D. J. (1953), Late Cenozoic marine glacial sediments and marine terraces of Middleton Island, Alaska, *J. Geol.*, vol. 61, pp. 17–40.

Natland, M. L. and Kuenen, Ph. H. (1951), Sedimentary history of the Ventura Basin, California, and the action of turbidity currents, *Soc. Econ. Paleon. Min., Special Publ.*, No. 2, pp. 76–107.

Pettijohn, F. J. (1952), Precambrian tillite, Menominee district, Michigan, *Bull. Geol. Soc. Amer.*, vol. 63, p. 1289.

Richter, Konrad (1932), Die Bewegungsrichtung des Inlandeises rekonstruiert aus den Kritzen und Längsachsen der Geschiebe, *Z. Geschiebeforschung*, Bd. 8, pp. 62–66.

Sayles, R. W. (1914), The Squantum tillite, *Harvard Mus. Comp. Zool., Bull.*, vol. 66 (geol. ser. vol. 10), pp. 141–175.

van Waterschoot van der Gracht, W. A. J. M. (1931), The pre-Carboniferous exotic boulders in the so-called "Caney shale" in the northwestern front of the Ouachita Mountains of Oklahoma, *J. Geol.*, vol. 39, pp. 697–714.

von Engelen, O. D. (1930), Type form of facetted and striated glacial pebbles, *Am. J. Sci.*, ser. 5, vol. 19, pp. 9–16.

Wegmann, E. (1951), Subkambrische Tillite in der herzynischen Faltungszone, *Geol. Rundschau*, vol. 39, pp. 221–234.

Wentworth, C. K. (1936), An analysis of the shapes of glacial cobbles, *J. Sediment. Petrol.*, vol. 6, pp. 85–96.

Wilson, M. E. (1913), The Cobalt Series: its character and origin, *J. Geol.*, vol. 21, pp. 121–141.

INTRAFORMATIONAL CONGLOMERATES AND BRECCIAS

An intraformational conglomerate or breccia is a rudaceous deposit formed by penecontemporaneous fragmentation and redeposition of the stratum in question (Walcott, 1894; Field, 1916). Such fragmentation and redeposition is but a minor interlude in the deposition of the formation and in some cases may be wholly subaqueous. The debris is always of very local origin, has undergone very little or no transportation and is but slightly worn.

Though fragmentation conceivably can be the result of several different processes, most commonly it appears to be caused by shoaling and temporary withdrawal of the waters followed by desiccation and mud cracking. Subsequent flooding of the mud-cracked layers disturbs the fragments which may be slightly shifted and deposited together in a thin, though persistent conglomerate of flat pebbles. In some few cases the fragmentation has been attributed to subaqueous gliding or slump, and the brecciated zone can be traced into sharply folded and much contorted strata. The desiccation conglomerates, on the other hand, show no such relationship to contemporaneous deformation and are associated instead with mud-cracked zones and other strand line features.

Two types of intraformational conglomerates are very common. One is a slate or shale-pebble conglomerate (or breccia) in which thin or tabular pieces of shale or slate are embedded in a sandy matrix. Such flat-pebble conglomerates are common in formations composed of alternating beds of shale and sandstone. Mudstone breccias such as these occur at the base of the sandy beds. The fragments may be a few scattered chips or flakes of shale or even an appreciable number of pieces, one or two inches across, confined to the lower two or three inches of the sandy member. If these shale pebbles occur in red-bed sequences, as they commonly do, they are probably desiccation fragments. If they are found in interbedded graywacke-shale sequences, the shale pieces may be a product of subaqueous fragmentation—perhaps "pull-aparts" produced by turbidity flows (Kuenen and Natland, 1951, p. 90).

A second common type of intraformational deposit is found in limestones and dolomites especially those which are sandy and oolitic. The fragments of such conglomerates or breccias are flat, generally small, pieces of limestone (or dolomite) embedded in a limestone or sandy limestone (or dolomite) matrix (Pl. 12, bottom). As is probably the case with the mudstone conglomerates, such breccias are probably in part the product of desiccation and induration of the lime muds and redeposition in a matrix of similar composition and in part the product of subaqueous fragmentation and transport by turbidity flows. The former, local in character, would be associated with mud-cracked beds and other strand line features (such as algal structures) and be characterized by a sandy matrix; the latter would be very widespread, unrelated to the strand line, have a mud matrix and be associated with graded beds or other turbidity-current features.

The flat pebbles of some limestone conglomerates stand on edge and are packed together to form the enigmatic "edgewise" conglomerates. Such structure is apparently the result of the tabular form of the fragments and the more-than-normal agitation by waves and currents.

A type of intraformational breccia and conglomerate differing from the above, in that it has larger fragments and is more restricted in extent, is the limestone breccias and conglomerates that flank limestone reefs. Steep initial bedding and association with reef structure makes identification of this type possible.

In summary, it may be said that intraformational conglomerates, though common, are not indicative of any great break in sedimentation. They are characterized by their thinness; the flat-pebble form, the edgewise arrangement in some cases; the restricted composition of the fragments (shale or limestone only); the association of some with mud-cracked beds; or in the cases of the less common types, the relation to subaqueous folds and graded beds, or to reef structures. Those generated by subaqueous slump and turbidity flows are significant in that the deposit so formed, even though very thin, may be widespread and be a precise time line as the event producing such a conglomerate or breccia is that of but a few hours' duration.

Intraformational conglomerates sometimes may be confused with true riebungsbreccias of tectonic origin or with some rare true interformational conglomerates consisting dominantly or solely of limestone fragments.

So common are intraformational conglomerates and breccias that only a few can be cited as examples. They abound in the lowest Paleozoic limestones and dolomites of the Appalachian region. Well-known are the desiccation features and the associated conglomerates near Bellefonte, Pennsylvania (Walcott, 1894); conglomerates of similar character, age, and origin occur in the Conococheague (Ordovician) of Maryland (Long, 1953). At the top of the Gros Ventre and at the base of the Gallatin formation (Cambrian) of west-central Wyoming is an excellent example of a flat-pebble conglomerate (Pl. 12, bottom). The exceptionally wide extent of this conglomerate as well as its chaotic nature and mud matrix suggests that it might be the product of a turbidity flow and hence be a precise time line. The flat-pebble conglomerates of the Muav limestone (Cambrian) of the Grand Canyon area are apparently similar in nature. They were believed to have formed in comparatively deep water a very considerable distance from the shore (McKee, 1945). Since single beds of but slight thickness can be traced for more than 60 miles normal to the presumed strand line and seaward of the shale belt, these flat-pebble beds can hardly be strand line or intertidal features.

The Precambrian "slate breccia," which is a thin but widespread marker bed, in the Iron River-Crystal Falls district of Michigan consists of small sparsely distributed slate fragments in a dense pyritic mudstone matrix. It is believed to be a product of a catastrophic turbidity flow.

Examples of the shale-pebble conglomerates are provided by the Grinnell argillite (Belt Series) in Glacier Park, Montana, by some of the Juniata beds (Ordovician) near State College, Pennsylvania, and by the mud pellet conglomerates of the Moenkopi formation (Triassic) of Arizona (McKee, 1954, p. 45).

REFERENCES CITED AND BIBLIOGRAPHY

Fairbridge, R. W. (1946), Submarine slumping and location of oil bodies, *Bull. Am. Assoc. Petroleum Geol.*, vol. 30, pp. 84–92.

Field, R. M. (1916), A preliminary paper on the origin and classification of intraformational conglomerates and breccias, *Ottawa Naturalist*, vol. 30, pp. 29–36, 47–52, 58–66.

Foerste, A. F. (1917), Intraformational pebbles in the Richmond Group, at Winchester, Ohio, *J. Geol.*, vol. 25, p. 304.

Hyde, J. E. (1908), Desiccation conglomerates in the Coal Measures limestones of Ohio, *Am. J. Sci.*, ser. 4, vol. 25, pp. 400–408.

Long, Miner B. (1953), *Origin of the Conococheague limestone*, Ph.D. thesis, The Johns Hopkins University, Baltimore, Md.

McKee, E. D. (1945), Cambrian history of the Grand Canyon region: part I. Stratigraphy and ecology of the Grand Canyon Cambrian, *Carnegie Inst. Wash., Publ.*, 563, pp. 65–70.

McKee, E. D. (1954), Stratigraphy and history of the Moenkopi formation of Triassic Age, *Geol. Soc. Amer., Mem.* 61, p. 45.

Natland, M. L., and Kuenen, Ph. H. (1951), Sedimentary history of the Ventura Basin, California, and the action of turbidity currents, *Soc. Econ. Paleon. Min., Special Publ.* No. 2, pp. 76–107.

Norton, W. H. (1920), Wapsipinicon breccias of Iowa, *Iowa Geol. Survey*, vol. 27, pp. 355–547.

Walcott, C. D. (1894), Paleozoic intra-formational conglomerates, *Bull. Geol. Soc. Amer.*, vol. 5, pp. 191–198.

PYROCLASTIC CONGLOMERATES AND BRECCIAS

The coarse pyroclastic deposits form a group apart from the normal sediments, although they may be interbedded with or grade into the usual clastic sediments. The term *agglomerate* is applied to these materials if their fragments are over 32 millimeters in diameter. Wentworth and Williams (1932) would restrict the term, however, to deposits formed primarily of *bombs* or lava which solidified in flight, and would reserve the term *volcanic breccia* for those pyroclastic deposits composed of previously consolidated materials, i.e., lava fragments or other rocks through which the volcanic vent passes. The former materials are "cognate"; the latter noncognate or "accidental."

The coarse pyroclastics are poorly bedded, or lack bedding altogether—particularly the products of the *nuées ardentes* type of eruptions. They weather readily, and accordingly present a rusty weathered appearance in outcrop. The tuffaceous matrix, rich in volcanic glass, serves to identify these materials.

Like the sedimentary conglomerates, some volcanic breccias and tuffs show well-defined stratification and sorting; others are without either. The first type are those deposited slowly from air currents; the second type is a product of the *nuées ardentes* type of eruption and is formed by a single, short-lived event. The *nuées ardentes* deposits are analogous to those formed by the heavy subaqueous mudstreams and turbidity flows. The cinder-laden cloud is in fact a density current consisting of gas plus solid instead of water plus solid.[10]

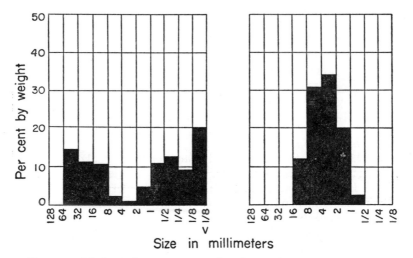

Fig. 72. Mechanical composition of tuffs. Right, normal; left, nuées ardentes deposit, Crater Lake area, Oregon (data from Moore, 1934).

Less easy to recognize are those deposits which were formed by the reworking of land-deposited pyroclastic materials or by the infall of tuffaceous materials into water. Both types of formation exhibit a mixing of normal sedimentary and pyroclastic materials. Metamorphism and shearing may further render difficult a proper identification of these rocks.

REFERENCES CITED AND BIBLIOGRAPHY

Moore, B. N. (1934), Deposits of possible *nuée ardente* origin in the Crater Lake region, Oregon, *J. Geol.*, vol. 42, pp. 358–375.
Wentworth, C. K. and Williams, Howel (1932), The classification and terminology of the pyroclastic rocks, *Rept. Comm. Sed., 1930–1932, Nat. Research Council, Bull.*, No. 89, pp. 19–53.

[10] The mechanical composition of the deposits of *nuées ardentes* and the more usual wind-transported land-deposited tuffs are quite different (Moore, 1934). See Fig. 72.

CATACLASTIC BRECCIAS AND CONGLOMERATES

In the cataclastic rocks ("autoclastic" of Grabau, 1904) the fragmentation was accomplished by movement of large masses of rock past one another. The boundary materials are literally ground up. The movement that occurs along a fault surface gives rise to fault breccias and to gouge. If the fault is an overthrust sheet the deposit created is a thin blanket along the sole of such an overthrust. In one sense till is such a cataclastic deposit—essentially an extensive gouge caused by the grinding along the base of an overthrust ice sheet.

Normally considered here are the *fault breccias, fold breccias* ("ricbungs-breccia"), and *crush conglomerates.* The fault breccias are distinguished by their cross-cutting relations and by the presence of gouge. Blackened, slicken-sided blocks, and shaly matter that is marked by similar evidences of shearing usually serve to identify these materials. The "tectonic moraines" or boulders and similar materials that are incorporated in the base or sole of an over-thrust mass, are more readily mistaken for normal rudaceous beds, inasmuch as they have a local concordant relation to the associated strata. Some of the "Caney shale" ("Johns Valley shale") with its great exotic blocks found in the Ouachita Mountains in Oklahoma has been interpreted as such a forma-tion (van Waterschoot van der Gracht, 1931; see also p. 265).

More common are the fold breccias, or riebungsbreccias, which are the result of sharp folding of thin-bedded brittle layers between which are in-competent plastic beds. Interbedded chert and shale are likely to form a rie-bungsbreccia on sharp folding. Such breccias are local, are confined to sharply folded strata, and are likely to pass into unbroken beds.

The crush conglomerates are produced by deformation of brittle, closely jointed rocks. Rotation of the joint blocks and granulation and crushing may produce a rock that closely simulates a normal conglomerate. The lozenge shape of the fragments, the similarity in composition of the fragments and matrix, and the restricted composition of both (generally one rock type) are distinguishing features of these rocks. Crush conglomerates are most likely to be confused with the "recomposed" basal conglomerates (see p. 325), which may have been deformed following their deposition.

PSEUDOCONGLOMERATES

A few rocks simulate conglomerates and may be so misinterpreted by the novice. Such rocks, if metamorphosed, might confuse even an experienced worker.

Diabases and related rocks weathered *in situ* yield large rounded *boulders of exfoliation* which, if still in place and surrounded by clayey weathering products, may bear a superficial resemblance to a conglomerate. A sandstone packed with many rounded concretionary bodies might also bear a likeness to a conglomerate. As pointed out on page 281, shearing of close-jointed brittle rocks rounds off the joint blocks and produces a gouge-like matrix and a tectonic conglomerate which may easily be mistaken for a normal sedimentary conglomerate.

7

Sandstones

PROPERTIES AND CLASSIFICATION OF SANDSTONES

Textures of Sandstones

A sand consists primarily of a *framework*,[1] which is the detrital sand fraction, and *voids*, which are the pores or empty spaces in the framework. The voids may, of course, be partially or completely filled. The study of a sand or sandstone therefore centers on the framework, its character and make-up, and on the nature and volume of the voids and void filler.

The framework is formed of the sand-sized materials, $\frac{1}{16}$ to 2 millimeters in diameter. Normally these are packed together in such a way that each grain is in contact with its neighbors so that the whole framework is a mechanically stable structure in the gravitational field. In such a sand, the framework elements of which are reasonably uniform in size and closely packed, there are approximately 0.85 contacts per grain in the plane of any given cross section— in a thin section, for example (Gaither, 1953) (Fig. 170). The nature and number of grain contacts is an important attribute of any sandstone. The framework of some sands has undergone a "condensation" so that the grains are brought into a closer contact with one another. In such sandstones the number of contacts per grain in a thin section rises to 5 or more (Taylor, 1950). In some sandstones, on the other hand, the framework is disrupted or broken and many grains appear not to be in contact with each other. The condensation or the disruption may be the result of several processes.

The size distribution of the elements of the framework fraction can be defined by the statistical measures of size and uniformity of size. These characteristics are related to the specific hydraulic regimen that governed

[1] An appropriate term suggested by Nanz (1954).

the deposition of the sand. The interpretation of such size analyses is discussed elsewhere (pp. 38–51). A rough measure of the uniformity of size, or sorting, is given by the ratio of the diameters of the largest to the smallest present. A well-sorted sand has three or fewer Udden size classes, and the maximum diameter therefore is 8 or fewer times the smallest. Sands with 4 to 6 grades, inclusive, may be said to show fair sorting. In these, the diameter of the largest grain does not exceed that of the smallest by more than a factor of 64. Sands with a size range in excess of this have 7 or more grades and are poorly sorted.

The voids form 30–35 per cent of the normal sand (p. 86). In a sandstone these may be empty or nearly so, or partially to wholly filled with some type of void filler. Void-filling materials may be either (1) finer detritus (silt and clay) or (2) precipitated mineral cements. In the case of interstitial detritus, the distinction between framework and matrix may be arbitrary if there is a complete gradation from largest to smallest size.[2] On the other hand, the size distribution may be bimodal—especially so if the void-filling detritus was introduced *after* deposition of the sand.

The grain/matrix ratio is an important characteristic. If the voids are completely filled with interstitial debris, the latter forms about one-third (30–35 per cent) of the whole rock. If the matrix exceeds this figure, the sand fraction forms a disrupted framework, and as the proportion of matrix increases, the rock passes over into a gritty mudstone. The division between such a mudstone and a sandstone (of the graywacke type) is arbitrarily set at 75 per cent matrix and 25 per cent sand. In other cases the matrix may only partially fill the voids—the balance being empty or filled with a precipitated cement. Sands deposited from most rivers and subaqueous currents contain little or no fines. If the fines reach an appreciable figure—15 per cent, for example—they are significant. Accordingly, the figure 15, as well as 30, and 75 are the critical percentages of matrix materials in the classification and interpretation of sandstones.

Precipitated mineral cements are most common. The origin of these and problems of cementation and decementation are described in detail elsewhere (p. 651). The kinds and relations of the precipitated cements to the framework should be noted. The cement may be deposited in crystallographic continuity with the detrital grains (as quartz on quartz or calcite on calcite), or it may be deposited on the detrital grains as drusy coatings, or as a microcrystalline mosaic in the voids. Exceptionally the carbonate cements may be coarsely crystalline and envelop one or more of the detrital grains as inclusions within these crystalline units ("crystal sandstone" and "sand

[2] Pettijohn (1943) defined the upper limit of "matrix" detritus at 0.02 mm; Gilbert (Williams, Turner, and Gilbert, 1954, p. 297) also placed the limit at 0.02 mm; Briggs (1954, p. 426) considered the limit to be about 0.05 mm.

crystals," Pl. 8, Fig. 167). Some of the cements, especially the carbonate cements, show encroachment on the framework and partially replace portions of it. Such replacement leads to partial disruption of the framework. Rarely, and in a small degree, the cementing carbonate may mechanically disrupt the grains of the framework.

The sands vary appreciably in their textural maturity, and since the sandstone classification is in part dependent on textural as well as mineralogical maturity, close attention to the maturity factors is necessary. The grain/matrix ratio, if a primary characteristic, is a partial measure of such maturity. So also is the rounding of the grains. A high degree of sorting (approach to uniform size) coupled with a high degree of rounding characterizes a mature sand. If the grains are well rounded but interstitial clay is present, the situation is anomalous and may be indicative of postdepositional introduction of clay.

Structures of Sandstones

Sandstones vary from well-bedded to massive in character. If thin and interbedded with shales, the sandstone is flaggy. In general the coarser the sandstone, the thicker the bedding units.

The internal structure of the bedding unit is most significant. Commonly the unit shows cross-bedding, the scale of which is some function of both the coarseness of the sand and the thickness of the sedimentation unit. Cross-bedded sands are also commonly ripple-marked.

The sedimentation unit may have a graded internal structure. Such sands are rarely cross-bedded, and as noted elsewhere (p. 164), graded-bedding and cross-bedding, more or less mutually exclusive, are indicative of two quite different sandstone facies. The one is indicative of shallow, turbulent waters at or above the profile of equilibrium; the other is indicative of deposition below wave base and is characteristic mainly of deep-water sandstones.

Sandstones commonly have concretionary bodies, especially those which are calcareous or ferruginous. The calcareous concretions appear to be largely postdepositional as the bedding planes normally pass through them. Structures due to solution are less conspicuous in sandstones than in carbonate rocks but they are by no means rare. Stylolites are found in many sandstones, especially the pure quartzitic varieties (Pl.10). They are commonly present along joints, perpendicular to the bedding and are perhaps less common along bedding planes. The highly friable sandstones of the older geological periods may owe their friability to wholesale leaching of their carbonate cements. Such solution, however, takes place without disruption of the framework of the rock and hence without production of any megascopic structures.

Classification and Nomenclature

At the present time the properties of a sandstone which seem significant are those which reflect the character of the source rocks (provenance), those which measure the approach of the sand debris to the ultimate end product to which it has been driven by the formative processes operating on it (maturity) and those which reflect the fluidity (density and viscosity) of the medium from which the sand was deposited. Many of the older workers used a nomenclature and classification that was in some degree indicative of one or another of these fundamental concepts. Some of the more recent papers on the subject are attempts to formalize these intuitive concepts and to organize or order our knowledge so as to provide a more rational classification of sandstones.

Provenance Factors

The provenance factors will be considered first. Sands may be produced by disintegration with or without much decomposition of the plutonic crystalline rocks—most especially the quartz-bearing plutonic rocks such as granite. In fact these rocks must be the *ultimate* source for all or nearly all the quartz which is the dominant constituent of most sandstones. Sands may also be derived from the supracrustal rocks, such as pre-existing sediments, low-grade metamorphic rocks, and from eruptive igneous rocks. These rocks are capable of yielding rock particles of sand size and these particles may form a significant part of some sandstones and be the dominant constituents in others.

Owing to the difference in grain size of the plutonic and supracrustal rocks the plutonic contributions are mineral grains, notably quartz and feldspar, whereas the supracrustal contributions are *rock particles*, either lavas or low-grade metamorphic or sedimentary rocks. The ratio of feldspar to the rock particles is therefore a provenance or source rock index and a measure of the relative importance of the contributions of the two fundamental groups of rocks.[3]

Maturity Factors

Maturity may be compositional and expressed in chemical or mineralogic terms. The ultimate sand is a concentration of pure quartz. This mineral is

[3] Other "source rock indices" have been proposed. Dapples, Krumbein, and Sloss (1953) used the ratio of feldspar to rock fragments plus "clay" matrix. This index is hybrid measure involving both provenance and sorting. It would seem undesirable to use a parameter compounded of unlike and unrelated items. Folk (1954) attempted to discriminate between a metamorphic and an igneous provenance and accordingly determined the ratio of feldspar (igneous) to metamorphic rock fragments, micas, and metamorphic quartz. This parameter is also a mixed one. The mixing of labile and stable components in a source rock index means that this index is subject to variations unrelated to source rocks, namely modifications related to climate and relief and mineral response to these factors.

the only chemically and physically durable constituent of plutonic rocks common enough to be accumulated in great volume. A measure of the mineralogical maturity of a sand, therefore, is given by its quartz content. As most of the quartz was originally plutonic and closely associated with feldspar, the maturity may also be expressed by the disappearance of the feldspar, or as earlier proposed (Pettijohn, 1949, p. 382), by the quartz/feldspar ratio.

The quartz/feldspar ratio is not appropriate for sands the sources of which were feldspar-poor, such as the supracrustal suite, namely, the low-grade metamorphic and sedimentary rocks. The paucity of feldspar would lead to a deceptively high quartz/feldspar ratio. The sands derived from a supracrustal complex would contain rock particles none of which, except chert, has both chemical and mechanical stability. The ratio of chert/noncherty rock fragments would be an appropriate maturity index for such sands.[4] Inasmuch as most sands have a complex source, the maturity indices might best be combined so that the influence of source rocks be eliminated. The index therefore would be quartz plus chert/feldspar plus rock fragments.

The maturity index, based essentially on the concentration of quartz and chert, does not indicate how this concentration was achieved. The index is only a measure of the effectiveness of the processes which are both chemical and mechanical.[5]

The compositional maturity of a sandstone can also be expressed in chemical terms. The percentage of silica would be a good measure if it were not augmented or diminished (relatively) by the introduction of the various chemical cements. Immature sands commonly are high in alumina, soda, and potash. Unfortunately, some ill-sorted sediments, otherwise mature, may also be high in some of these components.

Compositional maturity is rarely attained without a corresponding achievement of textural maturity. The latter may be defined in terms of uniformity of size of the clastic elements ("sorting") and perfection of rounding. Though to some degree independent, statistically the best sorted sands are also the best rounded (Dapples, Krumbein, and Sloss, Fig. 10). The correlation is poor, however, perhaps because sorting is achieved very quickly under normal conditions, whereas rounding requires prolonged abrasion. Both experimental studies and field observations show that sand, unlike gravel, is rounded with extreme slowness. Rivers do round sand, as demonstrated by

[4] Essentially similar to maturity index devised by Plumley (1949, p. 574) for gravels.
[5] Most other attempts at a rational classification of sands have recognized the significance of the high quartz content. Dapples, Krumbein, and Sloss expressed this as a quartz *index* which is a ratio, much like that of the author's, except that the clay matrix, if any, is added to the labile feldspar and rock fragments. Clay is not a labile constituent but is instead a very stable one. The index so modified is a hybrid involving both compositional maturity and sorting. Nanz (1952) on the other hand, rightly grouped the rock fragments with the feldspar and the chert with the quartz.

Plumley's studies in the Black Hills (1949) but do so so slowly that the movement of sand from the continental interior to the sea is insufficient to produce a high degree of rounding. Yet brief transport is normally all that is needed to achieve a reasonably good sizing. Glacial outwash sands, which have traveled for only a very short distance and for a very brief time may be well sorted though they remain highly angular.

Fluidity Factor

The effectiveness of the sorting process is dependent *mainly* on the density and viscosity of the transporting medium. If the density difference between solid carried and the transporting fluid is great, the separation is rapid and complete; if small, the separation is incomplete or lacking. Obviously, if the fluid and solid had the same density no separation whatever would take place. Settling in fluids of high viscosity is also greatly retarded, so that separation is commonly very poor (Kuenen, 1951, pp. 25–26). A deposit, therefore, in which the sand is not separated from the silt or clay must be either formed from a medium of high density or high viscosity or the time must have been too brief for completion of the normal sorting action. Inasmuch as the latter is achieved even by ephemeral streams as a result of a very brief and short transport, the mixed sediments or "wackes" must be mainly the products of deposition from media of high density or viscosity. The only such media in nature are those in which the sediment/fluid ratio is very high. Such a medium behaves in all essential respects like a heavy fluid. It will transport large fragments or blocks, even at very low velocities, will deposit all sizes without effective sorting, will underflow fluids of more normal densities, and will even flow on slopes of zero inclination. A very high sediment/fluid ratio results in both high density and high viscosity. The flow behavior of these media are more like semisolid bodies than fluids.

The presence or absence of a detrital clay-sized matrix in a sand is an index of the effectiveness of the sorting ability of the transporting medium and therefore to the sediment/fluid ratio of that medium.

Sands and sandstones may be divided into two major groups on the basis of the binding material. One group is held together by a mineral cement, i.e., an introduced precipitated material which fills the pore space between the grains and holds them together. The other group is bonded together by a fine-grained primary interstitial detritus or matrix of claylike nature or the authigenic derivatives therefrom. The first group therefore is the normal "clean" sands deposited by fluids of low density. As Lane (1938) has noted, the bed deposits of rivers, even those like the Mississippi, the chief burden of which is silt and clay, are clean sands. Also the glacial outwash sands, deposited from the silt-laden glacial waters ("glacial milk") after a brief and short transport are relatively clean. The analyses of the deposits of littoral and other shore currents show these materials also to be normal clean sands (Fig. 73).

The second group, therefore, probably owes its detrital matrix or "paste" to deposition from fluids with higher sediment/fluid ratios. Such media are

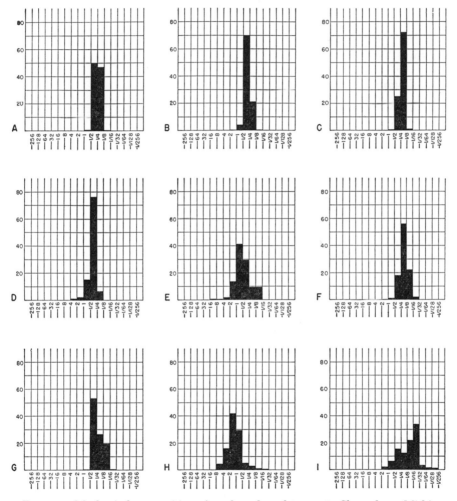

FIG. 73. Mechanical composition of sands and sandstones. A: Shore dune, Michigan City, Ind. B: Lake beach, Michigan City, Ind. C: Sea beach, San Francisco, Calif. D: Calcareous sea beach sand, Christmas Island (Wentworth and Ladd, 1931), chiefly foraminiferal tests and shell debris. E: Calcareous sand, Pearl and Hermes Reef (Thorp, 1936), bottom sample near center of lagoon. F: Jordan sandstones, Cambrian, Minneiska, Minn. (Graham, 1930), a friable orthoquartzite. G: St. Peter sandstones, Ordovician, Minneapolis, Minn., a friable orthoquartzite. H: Fluvial (glacial outwash) sand, Dundee, Ill. I: Fluvial ("Spokane flood") sand, carbonate-free basis.

the subaqueous turbidity flows found in some lakes and in many marine environments and their atmospheric analogues.[6]

Not all sandstones with a clay matrix, however, are products of turbidity flows or similar media. The clay matrix of some sandstones may be introduced *after* deposition of the sand fraction either by mechanical infiltration or perhaps even by precipitation from solution. Even though the interstitial clay may be polygenetic, it is desirable to set apart those sandstones with such a matrix from those with empty voids or with the ordinary precipitated cements.

Classification

It seems necessary, therefore, to define sandstone on the basis of those parameters which are the indices of provenance, maturity, and fluidity of the depositing medium. These are the "source rock index" or ratio of feldspar

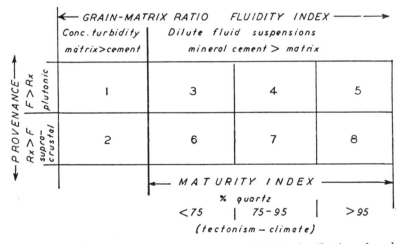

FIG. 74. Diagram to show the principles utilized in classification of sandstones. The numbers refer to the sandstone types shown in Table 48.

(plutonic) to rock fragments (supracrustal), the "maturity index" or ratio of quartz (plus chert) to feldspar plus rock fragments, and the "fluidity index" or ratio of sand detritus to the interstitial detrital matrix. On the basis of these three parameters sandstones may be grouped into four major classes and several lesser ones (Fig. 74). The major groups are the graywackes, the lithic sandstones, arkosic sandstones, and the orthoquartzites.

---

[6] Although most media of high density are subaqueous and responsible for a large and important class of sands—the graywackes—some terrestrial deposits are formed from such media. These are generally rare and can be distinguished from the product of subaqueous turbidity flows by other criteria than their lack of assortment.

TABLE 48.   Classification of Sandstones[a]

Cement or Matrix		Detrital Matrix Prominent (over 15%) to Predominant. Chemical Cement Absent	Detrital Matrix Absent or Scanty (under 15%) Voids Empty or Filled with Chemical Cement			
Sand or Detrital Fraction	Feldspar Exceeds Rock Fragments	*GRAYWACKES* Feldspathic graywacke	*ARKOSIC SANDSTONES* Arkose	Subarkose or feldspathic sandstone	*ORTHOQUARTZITES*	Chert < 5%
	Rock Fragments Exceed Feldspar	Lithic graywacke	*LITHIC SANDSTONES* Subgraywacke	Protoquartzites		Chert > 5%
	Quartz Content	Variable; generally < 75%	< 75%	> 75% < 95%		> 95%

[a] Volcanic tuffs and intraformational calcarenites not included.

These major groups are defined and related to each other as shown in Table 48 and Fig. 75.

The graywackes, as shown in the table, are the sandstones with high detrital matrix content and no chemical cement. These rocks are divided into two subgroups dependent on dominance of feldspar over rock fragments or vice versa and are named feldspathic and lithic [7] graywackes, respectively. The arkosic sandstones are defined as those rocks with considerable feldspar. They differ from graywackes in the absence of a significant quantity of interstitial matrix. Arkoses contain 25 per cent or more of labile particles, half or more of which are feldspar; subarkoses are similar but with a smaller proportion of labile components (5–25 per cent).[8] Sandstones in which rock particles exceed feldspar, but which do not have a detrital matrix and have instead a mineral cement, are the lithic arenites or sandstones of which there are two types, namely, subgraywackes and protoquartzites.[9] The former is

[7] The adjective "lithic" has long been applied by petrographers to certain tuffs to denote a high content of rock particles.
[8] Note that although feldspar may constitute 25 or more per cent of the arkose, it might form as little as 12.5 per cent of the detrital fraction.
[9] A term used by Krynine (in Payne, 1951).

analogous to arkose in that the labile fragments exceed 25 per cent (of which more than half are rock particles); in the protoquartzites these materials constitute 5 to 25 per cent of the detrital fraction. Orthoquartzites are the "pure" sandstones, 90 per cent or more quartz. These may be derived from the lithic arenites or from the arkosic sandstones. In the former case they will be characterized by metamorphic quartz and chert particles; in the latter case chert is absent or nearly so (under 5%) and the quartz is igneous quartz.

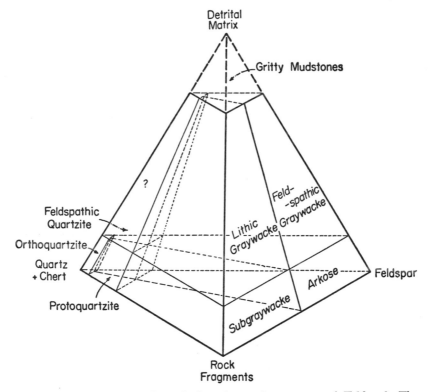

FIG. 75. Compositional tetrahedron for sandstone types of Table 48. The composition is expressed in terms of four detrital components (after L. D. Clark).

There are two groups of sands not properly accounted for by the above classification. These are the volcanic sands or tuffs and the calcareous sands. The volcanic sediments may be classified in terms of the matrix/grain ratio and the feldspar/rock fragment ratio. The quartz/feldspar ratio, however, has no relation to maturity as it does in the epiclastic sands. In fact the maturity concept has no meaning in the case of the pyroclastic materials. The quartz content might, however, be some measure of the acidity of the generating lava or a measure of contamination by normal epiclastic materials.

The chaotic unsorted tuffs laid down by the *nueés ardentes* are related to the graywackes in their manner of deposition and hence have similar textures and structures. Many tuffs, both airborne and water-laid, are reasonably well sorted and without appreciable interstitial materials. Crystal tuffs are the volcanic equivalent of arkose; lithic tuffs correspond to lithic arenites.

The calcareous sands are of intraformational origin and the terms *provenance index* and *maturity index* as applied to the "extraformational" sands have no meaning for intraformational debris. The provenance of the carbonate sands may be biogenic or chemical and only in a textural sense can they be mature.

Although the classification here presented is based on what arc believed to be genetically significant properties, the classification is not genetic. A knowledge of the origin is not necessary to name or classify the sandstone. The classification is based upon simple observable characters.

Although the defining properties are best seen under the microscope the classification is not without value to the field geologist. With a little experience the principal types can be recognized in the hand specimen, since each is generally characterized by distinctive secondary properties such as color, internal structures, associations, and the like which are closely correlated with the defining parameters.

Relative Abundance of Principal Sandstone Groups

If the calcarenites be grouped with the limestones and the volcanic arenites be excluded, we may regard the arenites as belonging to three principal families, namely, the graywackes (and subgraywackes), the arkoses (and subarkose), and the orthoquartzites and protoquartzites. Examination of about 100 randomly chosen thin sections of sandstones in the collection of The Johns Hopkins University shows that 50 are graywackes and subgraywackes, 30 are orthoquartzites and protoquartzites, and 15 are arkoses and subarkose. Because the percentage of feldspar in each of these three groups averages about 15, 0, and 25 per cent, respectively, the average sandstone should have 11 or 12 per cent of feldspar. As Clarke (1927) has estimated the normative feldspar content of the average chemically analyzed sandstone at 11.5 per cent, it seems probable that the relative abundance of the principal types in The Johns Hopkins collections approximates their abundance in nature. The modal feldspar percentage, 12.5, based on 74 published analyses, is also in reasonable agreement with the computed value. The results may be checked also by considering the other most important constituent, namely, quartz. If the percentage of quartz in the three groups averages 45, 91, and 60 per cent, respectively, then the average sandstone should contain about 63 per cent of quartz. This agrees reasonably well with the 67 per cent calculated by Clarke.

Krynine (1948) has placed the proportions of graywacke (including sub-graywacke as here defined), orthoquartzite, and arkose at 45, 23, and 32, respectively (Fig. 76). Tallman (1949) assembled a sample of about 275 sandstones with wide geographic and stratigraphic distribution. He gives the percentage of graywacke, orthoquartzite, and arkose as 38, 45, and 17, respectively. The differences between the various estimates of Krynine, Tallman,

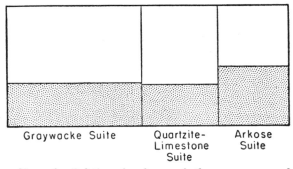

Graywacke Suite   Quartzite-Limestone Suite   Arkose Suite

FIG. 76. Relative abundance of the common sandstones and the three principal families of sediments. Abundance proportional to area. Based on data by Krynine (1945).

and the author probably result in part from differences in the definitions of the several rock types and also the differences in the samples on which the estimates were made. As noted by Tallman, graywacke occurs in thin beds intercalated with shales or slates and is not as a rule in mappable stratigraphic units, and since they have no economic worth as well as no stratigraphic name, they are not likely to appear in collections so commonly as are the orthoquartzites. Averages therefore are likely to be weighted too heavily with orthoquartzites and to be deficient in graywackes.

REFERENCES CITED AND BIBLIOGRAPHY

Briggs, L. I., Jr. (1953), Upper Cretaceous sandstones of Diablo Range, California, *Univ. Calif. Publs. Geol. Sci.*, vol. 29, pp. 417–452.

Clarke, F. W. (1927), Data of geochemistry, *U.S. Geol. Survey, Bull.* 770, p. 33.

Dapples, E. C., Krumbein, W. C., and Sloss, L. L. (1953), Petrologic and lithologic attributes of sandstones, *J. Geol.*, vol. 61, pp. 291–317.

Folk, R. L. (1954), The distinction between grain size and mineral composition in sedimentary rock nomenclature, *J. Geol.*, vol. 62, pp. 344–359.

Gaither, A. (1953), A study of porosity and grain relationships in experimental sands, *J. Sediment. Petrol.*, vol. 23, pp. 180–195.

Kuenen, Ph. H. (1951), Properties of turbidity currents of high density, *Soc. Econ. Paleon. Mineralogists, Special Publ.*, No. 2, pp. 14–33.

Krynine, P. D. (1948), Sediments and the search for oil, *Producers Monthly*, vol. 9, fig. 8.

Lane, E. W. (1938), Notes on the formation of sand, *Trans. Am. Geophys. Union*, 19th Ann. Meeting, pp. 505–508.

Nanz, R. H., Jr. (1952), *Personal communication.*

Nanz, R. H., Jr. (1954), Genesis of Oligocene sandstone reservoir, Seeligson field, Jim Wells and Kleberg counties, Texas, *Bull. Am. Assoc. Petroleum Geol.*, vol. 38, p. 108.

Payne, T. G., and others (1951), The Arctic slope of Alaska: *U.S. Geol. Survey, Oil and Gas Invest.*, Map OM 126, Sheet 2.

Pettijohn, F. J. (1943), Archean sedimentation, *Bull. Geol. Soc. Amer.*, vol. 54, pp. 1955–1972.

Pettijohn, F. J. (1949), Sedimentary rocks, 1st ed., New York, Harper & Brothers, pp. 382–383.

Pettijohn, F. J. (1954), Classification of sandstones, *J. Geol.*, vol. 62, pp. 360–365.

Plumley, W. J. (1949), Black Hills terrace gravels: A study in sediment transport, *J. Geol.*, vol. 56, pp. 526–577.

Tallman, Sefton (1949), Sandstone types: Their abundance and cementing agents, *J. Geol.*, vol. 57, pp. 582–591.

Taylor, Jane (1950), Pore-space reduction in sandstones, *Bull. Am. Assoc. Petroleum Geol.*, vol. 34, pp. 701–716.

Williams, Howel, Turner, F. J., and Gilbert, C. M. (1954), Petrography, San Francisco, Freeman.

ORTHOQUARTZITES

Definitions

The orthoquartzites constitute a group of sandstones, characterized by their high quartz content, for which there is no wholly satisfactory name. They have been variously called "pure quartz sandstone," "siliceous sandstone," and "quartzose sandstone." Grout (1932) suggested that they be called "siliceous quartz sandstones" if silica cemented and "calcareous quartz sandstones" if carbonate-bound. Wentworth and Allen (Allen, 1936) suggested that these types be designated "silicanate siliceous sandstone" and "calcarinate siliceous sandstone," respectively. Because "calcarinate" is too much like Grabau's "calcarenite" it is likely to engender much confusion.

Krynine (1948) proposed the term *orthoquartzite* for those quartzites of sedimentary origin and closely related rocks.[10] Quartzite usually denotes a sandstone completely and solidly cemented by secondary quartz, so that the rock breaks across the grains. As noted by Krynine, however, even the hardest and most siliceous quartzite may contain some carbonate as an additional

[10] The term *metaquartzite* is reserved for those quartzites produced by metamorphic recrystallization.

component, and as the proportions of this nonsiliceous cementing material increase, the orthoquartzites begin to show more diversification and less cohesiveness. Although the term seems less appropriate for these more calcareous and more friable varieties, it has been retained for the family or group of sandstones in which the framework fraction is essentially pure quartz. One may, if he so wishes, apply the term *calcareous orthoquartzite* to those varieties which contain a large proportion of calcareous cement and a relatively small content of secondary silica.

In general to warrant the name orthoquartzite, the framework fraction must consist of at least 90 per cent quartz; some authors would require that it be 95 per cent quartz and/or chert. The cement consists of silica, usually as a secondary overgrowth, or silica and carbonate in varying proportions. The volume of secondary silica may vary from just enough to hold the rock together to complete filling of the voids.

Mineral Composition

The chief detrital constituent is, by definition, quartz. The quartz may be ultimately either of igneous or metamorphic derivation but much of it is probably derived from earlier sandstones. The quartz is remarkably well rounded and sorted and may, in the less well-cemented varieties, show a frosted surface, which, under the binocular microscope, looks like ground glass. Very commonly, however, the individual grains have a reconstructed crystal form and show brilliant crystal facets (Pl. 1, C, Fig. 168) which are the result of regeneration of the crystal form of quartz by deposition of secondary quartz in crystallographic continuity with the quartz of the worn grains. If this process of regeneration is carried to completion, however, the adjacent grains grow together to form an interlocking aggregate of anhedral quartz grains, and the rock is indeed a quartzite—a product of hydrous metamorphism.

Many sandstones and orthoquartzites contain small amounts of clastic chert but in a few chert is a prominent or even dominant constitutent. In the latter case, the orthoquartzite is in considerable part derived from preexisting sediments. Proof of such derivation lies not only in the chert debris but also in the worn rims of secondary quartz within which is an earlier detrital nucleus. The secondary quartz, in turn, may be enlarged by secondary growth so that two generations of secondary quartz appear in the same grain.

Other detrital constituents are rare in the most typical orthoquartzites. Transitional types may contain feldspar up to 10 per cent; such types are then called feldspathic sandstones or subarkose. Though any kind of feldspar may be present, the acid feldspars, particularly the potash-bearing varieties, are most common. They may show secondary rims of limpid feldspar deposited in crystallographic continuity on the worn, more clouded, detrital core (Pl. 40, E, F). Slight differences in chemical composition may give the core a slightly different extinction point than that of the nucleus. With the appearance of detrital sand-size rock fragments other than chert and of detrital mica, the orthoquartzites pass into protoquartzites. The transition is characterized also by a lesser rounding of the quartz grains.

The orthoquartzites and related sandstones are but sparingly fossiliferous. Unless they are richly calcareous, well-preserved carbonate shells are rare. Scattered aggregates of dolomite and calcite may be present. In the latter case these aggregates have been interpreted as dissolved and reprecipitated shelly matter. The effect of partial solution of shells, notably the thinning of the shell, and the complete cementation of the sand *within* the shell by calcite, have been noted by Krynine (1940). Most commonly, unless the shells were phosphatic, the fossils of the orthoquartzites are preserved only as molds and casts.

The quartzose sandstones are notably impoverished in both variety and quantity of heavy minerals. Species present are limited to the most stable, notably tourmaline and zircon, though some other slightly less stable species, such as garnet, may occur in some cases. These minerals, like the quartz, show evidence of extensive abrasion and are markedly rounded (Pl. 1, F).

The cement of the orthoquartzites is primarily silica, usually quartz, deposited, as noted above, in optical and crystallographic continuity with the detrital quartz grains. Chert, and rarely opal, have also been reported as cements. Common carbonates, both calcite and dolomite, are present in addition to quartz, and in many cases, especially in the younger sandstones, they may be the dominant cement. Normally each pore is filled—or partly filled—by a single carbonate crystal. In exceptional and rare cases, the carbonate crystals are large and envelop a number of detrital grains. These are the luster-mottled or crystal sandstones. As noted elsewhere (p. 653), the carbonate cement may encroach upon and corrode the detrital quartz grains.

Chemical Composition

As shown in Table 49, the orthoquartzite and related sandstones are exceedingly high in silica. These rocks, if silica cemented, may contain less than 0.5 per cent of other oxides. In such cases they constitute a commercial source of silica and even may be suitable for the manufacture of glass. Those species which have appreciable carbonate cement will contain, of course, a significant quantity of lime and magnesia, and will show a corresponding reduction in the per cent of silica. The finer-grained varieties, transitional to siltstone, and those which verge on subarkose or protoquartzite, will have appreciable amounts of alumina, alkalies, and alkaline earths.

TABLE 49. Chemical Composition of Orthoquartzitic Sandstones
(per cent)

	A	B	C	D	E	F	G	H	I
SiO_2	95.32	99.45	98.87	97.80	99.39	93.13	61.70	99.58	93.16
TiO_2	....	....	....	....	0.03	....	....	....	0.03
Al_2O_3	2.85	....	0.41	0.90	0.30	3.86	0.31	0.31	1.28
Fe_2O_3	0.05⎫	0.30	⎧0.08	0.85	0.12	0.11	0.24	1.20⎫	0.43
FeO	....⎭		⎩0.11	....	....	0.54	....	....⎭	
MgO	0.04	T	0.04	0.15	None	0.25	....	0.10	0.07
CaO	T	0.13	....	0.10	0.29	0.19	21.00	0.14	3.12
Na_2O	0.30	....	⎧0.80	0.40	....	....	⎧0.17	0.10⎫	0.39
K_2O			⎩0.15				⎩....	0.03⎭	
H_2O+	1.44[a]	....	0.17	....	0.17	1.43[a]	....	0.03[a]	0.65
H_2O-									
CO_2	....	....	....	....	....	....	16.10	....	2.01
	100.00	99.88	99.91	100.21	100.30	99.51	99.52	99.62[b]	101.14

A. Lorrain (Huronian), *Can. Geol. Survey, Mem.* 143, 1925, p. 68, M. F. Conner, analyst.
B. St. Peter (Ordovician), *U. S. Geol. Survey, Min. Resources,* 1911, pt. 2, pp. 624–630, R. E. Lyons, analyst.
C. Mesnard (Precambrian), *U. S. Geol. Survey, Mono.* 52, 1912, p. 257, R. D. Hall, analyst.
D. Tuscarora (Silurian), *Penn. Geol. Survey, Bull M3,* ser. 4, Moore and Taylor, 1924, p. 17.
E. Oriskany (Devonian), *Penn. Geol. Survey, Prog. Rept.* 12, 1919, Fettke, p. 164.
F. Berea (Mississippian), *U. S. Geol. Survey, Bull.* 818, 1931, p. 110, N. W. Lord, analyst. Probably a protoquartzite.
G. "Crystalline sandstone," Fontainebleau, France (after Cayeux).
H. Sioux (Precambrian), *S. Dakota State Geol. Survey, Rept. Invest.* No. 63, 1949, p. 17.
I. Average of A–H, inclusive.
  [a] Loss on ignition.
  [b] Includes SO_3, 0.13 per cent.

Textures and Structures

The orthoquartzites are clean white sandstones in outcrop. They are commonly marked by cross-bedding and ripple-marking. The cross-bedding varies from festoon to torrential in type and may be present on a fairly large scale. Both oscillation and current ripples may be present. Though well sorted, many orthoquartzites contain coarser pebble zones or at least a scattering of well-rounded quartz pebbles near the base of the thicker beds.

In hand specimen and in thin section most orthoquartzites are characterized by the excellence of the sorting and rounding of the detrital quartz. These sands are indeed the best-sorted and best-rounded sands known and are the equal of many beach and dune sands, which they may in fact be.

Occurrence, Associations, and Distribution

The orthoquartzites and related sands are typically blanket sands, i.e., they have a great areal extent in proportion to their thickness. Although generally thin, a few hundred feet thick or less, some attain a thickness of several thousand feet. The most remarkable feature of all is the scarcity of any interbedded shaly materials.

The orthoquartzites are commonly associated with or grade into limestones and dolomite. Many dolomites are sandy. The contained sands are similar in rounding and frosting to the constituents of the associated ortho-quartzites. By increase in proportion of quartz sand and diminution of the carbonate materials, the rock grades into typical orthoquartzites. The inter-bedding of quartzose sandstone and carbonate rock and the absence or scarcity of shale seem to be typical of some stratigraphic sections.

Orthoquartzites are known from many places and are of many ages, though most of these sandstones seem to occur in the late Precambrian and in the older Paleozoic. The oldest Precambrian or Archean seems not to contain much orthoquartzite. This rock is common, however, in the younger Precambrian of many places. The Huronian of the north shore of Lake Huron contains much orthoquartzite. The Mississagi quartzite in the Bruce Mines area is an excellent example, although it is a feldspathic quartzite in its lower portion. The Lorrain quartzite of the same area is an extraordinarily thick formation (6000–7000 feet) of typical orthoquartzitic nature. Both the Mississagi and Lorrain abound in ripple marks and cross-bedding. In Michi-gan the Sturgeon quartzite, about 1000 feet thick, and its correlative, the Mesnard, are typical orthoquartzites. The Baraboo and the Waterloo quartz-ites of Wisconsin, the Barron quartzite of the same state and the Sioux quartzite of Iowa, Minnesota, and South Dakota, perhaps all of the same age, are good orthoquartzites. They appear to be approximately 5000 feet thick and consist almost solely of clean, cross-bedded and ripple-marked orthoquartzite (Pl. 2, top, and Pl. 2, center; also Pl. 16, A). The Uinta quartzite (Cambrian or Precambrian) of Utah is also said to be an ortho-quartzite. It is about 10,000 feet thick and one of the greatest examples of quartz accumulations known.

The older Paleozoic in North America abounds in orthoquartzitic sand-stones. The Potsdam (Cambrian), the St. Peter and Simpson (Ordovician), the Tuscarora (Silurian), and the Oriskany and Sylvania (Devonian) of the eastern United States are typical widespread blanket sands of high purity. The Tensleep sandstone (Pennsylvanian) of Wyoming and the Coconino (Permian) of Arizona are orthoquartzitic sands of later Paleozoic age. The Berea (Mississippian) of Ohio is a borderline rock and is perhaps a proto-quartzite.

Orthoquartzitic sands are less common and less widespread in the Meso-zoic, though the Dakota (Cretaceous) is a typical orthoquartzitic deposit.

Origin and Geologic Significance

The high quartz content and the excellent sorting and rounding exhibited by the orthoquartzitic sandstones is indicative of a high degree of textural and mineralogical maturity. These rocks are obviously the end product of protracted and profound weathering, sorting, and abrasion. In order that there be sufficient time to achieve these results, it is imperative either that the source area and site of deposition be tectonically very stable or that the sand go through several cycles of sedimentation.

Under tectonically stable conditions—i.e., at or near base level—chemical decomposition of the source rocks is complete so that the only material of sand grade is quartz. The repeated washing and winnowing of this material in the shore zone will give rise to a supermature quartz sand. Transgression of the shore zone might therefore produce a first-cycle blanket deposit of an orthoquartzitic sand. Only locally, as near granitic monadnocks or near the underlying granitic basement, would any feldspar appear in the sandstone. It is noteworthy that the best examples of orthoquartzites are associated with some of the most profound base leveling that the North American continent has undergone.

As has been pointed out elsewhere, prolonged abrasion will slowly eliminate the feldspar and round the quartz. A second cycle sand therefore should achieve a higher degree of maturity than its predecessor. Some orthoquartzites appear to be such multicyle sands. Worn overgrowths on the quartz, and detrital chert grains constitute some of the evidence of their derivation from pre-existing sediments.

Locally winnowing or washing may "clean up" some of the graywacke and subgraywacke sands. Such sands, like the typical orthoquartzites, will be well sorted and enriched in quartz. Unlike the orthoquartzites proper, the grains will not be well rounded. These cleaned-up graywackes are essentially local products and do not form extensive blankets. They are the shoestring sands of some sections and are commonly associated with subgraywackes and other poorly differentiated sediments. The Venango sand (Krynine, 1941) and the Hartshorne sandstone are examples of this type. To this group of sands Krynine (Payne and others, 1951) has given the name *protoquartzite*.

REFERENCES CITED AND BIBLIOGRAPHY

Allen, V. T. (1936), Terminology of medium-grained sediments, *Rept. Comm. Sedimentation 1935–1936*, Nat. Research Council, pp. 18–47.

Grout, F. F. (1932), *Petrography and petrology*, New York, McGraw-Hill, p. 275.

Krynine, P. D. (1940), Petrology and genesis of the Third Bradford Sand, *Penn. State College Mineral Inds. Expt. Sta., Bull.* 29, fig. 8.

Krynine, P. D. (1941), Paleogeographic and tectonic significance of sedimentary quartzites (abstract), *Bull. Geol. Soc. Amer.*, vol. 52, pp. 1915–1916.

Krynine, P. D. (1948), The megascopic study and field classification of sedimentary rocks, *J. Geol.*, vol. 56, pp. 130–165.

Payne, T. G. and others (1951), Geology of the Arctic slope of Alaska, *U.S. Geol. Survey, Oil Gas Invest.*, Map OM 126.

GRAYWACKES

Definition

The term *graywacke* was applied by field geologists to certain rocks of Devonian and early Carboniferous age in the Harz Mountains of Germany. By 1808, the name was used for similar rocks of Lower Paleozoic age in the Southern Highlands of Scotland. The original graywackes were probably so named because of their resemblance to the partially weathered residues (wackes) from basalt and related rocks.[11] The similarity, however, is superficial and misleading, since the Harz graywackes consist of angular to subrounded grains of quartz and small fragments of siliceous slate, phyllite, and other rocks, and in many cases feldspars, all bound together by a fine-grained matrix which imparts a great toughness and hardness to the rock (Naumann, 1858, p. 663). These graywackes are obviously not derived by disintegration of basalts or related rocks, but are composed of debris derived from both acid plutonic crystalline rocks and a metamorphic and sedimentary terrane.

The term graywacke is today applied to essentially the same type of rock as that for which it was originally used. Although present students of the subject so apply the term, they have not reached agreement on a quantitative definition of graywacke. Inasmuch as graywacke has a complex composition and several unique textural features, difficulties in framing a suitable definition which expresses these characteristics are to be expected. As would be expected, too, there is disagreement as to precise location of the boundaries between graywackes and other rocks into which they grade.[12]

Examination of representative graywackes and a review of the literature on the subject shows that graywackes, like those of the Harz, are characterized by (1) a varied assemblage of unstable materials (25 per cent or more) including both feldspar grains and sand-sized rock fragments, and (2) interstitial matrix (15 per cent or more) which takes the place of the chemical or mineral cement characteristic of normal sandstones. Rocks without the detrital matrix (which has the mineral composition of a slate) are arkoses

---

[11] Apparently because of the mistaken notion that graywackes were in fact indurated "wacke," there have been some attempts (Twenhofel, 1950, p. 317) to define graywacke as the basic equivalent of an arkose, i.e., to consider it derived by the disintegration, without decomposition, of the basic igneous rocks. This definition does not fit either the original graywacke nor the many graywackes described by field workers during the past 150 years.

[12] The term *graywacke* has proved one of the most troublesome, and some writers have even recommended its abandonment, without proposing a substitute term for the important group of rocks which have been and still are called graywackes. The term is unquestionably needed. It does not seem profitable here to trace in detail the origin of the term or the various definitions proposed. The interested reader is referred to the literature (Allen, 1936; Bailey, 1930, 1936; Edwards, 1947a, 1947b; Fischer, 1933; Folk, 1954; Helmbold, 1952; Krynine, 1940, 1941, 1948; McElroy, 1954; Naumann, 1858; Pettijohn, 1943, 1950, 1954; Tyrrell, 1933).

if they are primarily feldspathic, and lithic arenites (subgraywackes) if they are feldspar-poor and rich in rock particles.

Textures and Structures

Graywackes occur in relatively thin beds—a few inches to a few feet thick. Most beds lack any internal stratification and are commonly massive. Because of their chaotic disordered structure they are tough and break with a subconchoidal fracture. Because of their dark color, absence of stratification and subconchoidal fracture, they may be mistaken both in outcrop and in hand specimen for a basic igneous rock. Although not usually stratified, graywackes do commonly show graded bedding. It is important to note that the grading is expressed by a gradual diminution in the larger sizes from the base of the bed upward. The finer sizes, however, are present throughout the bed, even at the base (see Fig. 60, B). A rhythmic alternation of the graywacke and slate or shale is commonplace. In such cases the graywacke generally grades abruptly upward into slate. The heavier, more massive beds may enclose randomly oriented fragments of shale or slate presumably derived from the associated slates.

Associated with the interbedded graywackes and shales or slates, may be graywacke dikes and sills. These are similar in all microscopic details to the concordant beds except that they are not graded. This similarity in microstructure is significant in that it implies a similar or related manner of origin. Since the dikes are presumably formed by injection of a thick slurry, the beds also must be deposited from such a medium (Pl. 18; compare C with rest of plate).

The underside of the graywacke beds may be irregular. The irregularities, which are small downward protuberances of the sand beds, have been called "lobate rill marks," also "flow casts" (Shrock, 1948, pp. 131 and 156). They have been variously explained, but since they are elongated and the long axes of these structures are parallel, they must be related to the flow responsible for the graywacke itself (Kuenen, 1953, p. 24; Rich, 1950) (see Pl. 3).

Cross-bedding is conspicuous by its general absence. If present, it is on a very small scale and is confined to layers only two or three inches thick. Fragments of carbonized wood are common in the younger graywackes; fossils of other kinds are rare. Contemporaneous folding and slump structures are common in the finer laminated beds of the graywacke suite.

Of the two definitive properties of the graywackes, texture and composition, texture is the most significant, since it alone distinguishes graywacke from all other sandstones. It may indeed be the only defining property (Payne, 1948; Pettijohn, 1950). Graywacke, whether it be Archean or Tertiary, is both uniform and distinctive in appearance. It is gray to black on fresh fracture. Scattered, small, vitreous, detrital quartz grains are evident to the unaided eye. Under the microscope, the rock is marked by sharp, angular, sliver-like quartz, together with equally angular feldspar and rock particles. These constituents are set in a paste, which in some graywackes equals or exceeds the volume of the larger detrital grains. The paste or matrix is a microcrystalline aggregate of quartz, feldspar, chlorite, and sericite which in places is replaced by a carbonate. Sheared graywackes are marked by an alignment of the folia of sericite and chlorite, which impart a rude schistosity to the rock. The typical graywackes, even many of Archean age, are massive and devoid of any mineral orientation either primary or pressure induced. Though foliation is by no means rare, since graywackes are typical of deformed belts, the chaotic and random orientation of the mica flakes, slate fragments, etc., is the rule. Most striking features are therefore the dark color of the fresh rock, the preponderance of the matrix in many specimens, the extreme angularity of the quartz and feldspar, and the chaotic and random distribution of the components. The term microbreccia is most appropriate.

Mineral Composition

Tyrrell (1933) recognized the complex composition of the graywackes. The coarse components fall into three groups: first, the minerals of plutonic rocks, which, in addition to quartz and feldspar, include augite, hornblende, serpentine, and iron ores; second, the fragments of low rank metamorphic and sedimentary origin—slate, phyllite, siltstone, quartzite, and chert; and third, the fragments of aphanitic flow rocks, especially of the greenstone and spilitic suite. Some graywackes are characterized by a preponderance of one class or group of materials, but most commonly the graywackes have a mixed composition and therefore a mixed origin.[13]

Those with mixed compositions appear to be the most common. As shown in Table 50, the average graywacke, however, is mainly quartz and feldspar (two-thirds), and therefore, like arkose, is derived mainly from acid plutonic rocks.[14] It has, in addition, some materials of sedimentary and metamorphic origin. To those graywackes in which feldspar (plutonic provenance) exceeds rock fragments (supracrustal provenance) the term feldspathic graywacke may be applied. A few graywackes, on the other hand, are quartz-poor and contain hornblende and igneous rock fragments. Some of these, such as the Miocene graywackes of Papua (Edwards, 1947a) (Table 50, E) are undoubtedly contaminated with or derived from basic tuffs. Such graywackes may grade into and be difficult to distinguish from water-laid basic tuffs. True

[13] Krynine (1943) originally defined graywacke as a feldspar-poor rock (1–2 per cent on average) but later (1948) recognized the feldspar-rich character (20 per cent average) of some graywackes and applied the term low-rank and high-rank to the two groups, respectively.

[14] Taliaferro (1943) believed the Franciscan graywackes were derived from crystalline rocks having the general composition of a granodiorite.

tuffs would, of course, contain some glass or devitrified glass with shard structures. Graywackes with materials primarily of sedimentary or low-rank metamorphic origin are less common than the other types, but they are by no means rare. These might best be called lithic graywackes because, as in the lithic tuffs, rock particles exceed the feldspar in quantity. Some of the gray sandstones of the Siwalik series with little or no feldspar and 40–45 per cent of metamorphic rock fragments—mainly phyllite and schist—may be graywackes of this type (Krynine, 1937). The graywackes of the Squantum series near Boston are apparently lithic graywackes.

TABLE 50. Mineralogical Composition of Graywacke
(per cent)

Mineral	A	B	C	D	E	F
Quartz	45.6	46.0	24.6	9.0	tr	34.7
Chert	1.1	7.0	. . . .	. . . .	. . . .	. . . .
Feldspar	16.7	20.0	32.1	44.0	29.9	29.7
Hornblende	. . . .	. . . .	. . . .	3.0	10.5	. . . .
Rock Fragments	6.7	. . . .[a]	23.0	9.0	13.4	. . . .
Carbonate	4.6	2.0	. . . .	. . . .	. . . .	5.3
Chlorite-Sericite	25.0	22.5	20.0[b]	25.0	46.2[d]	23.3
	99.7	97.5	99.7	90.0[c]	100.0	96.0

A. Average of six (3 Archean, 1 Huronian, 1 Devonian and 1 Late Paleozoic).
B. Krynine's average "high-rank graywacke" (Krynine, 1948).
C. Average of three Tanner graywackes (Upper Devonian-Lower Carboniferous) (Helmbold, 1952).
D. Average of four Cretaceous graywackes, Papua (Edwards, 1947b).
E. Average of two Miocene graywackes, Papua (Edwards, 1947a).
F. Average of two parts average shale and one part average arkose.
   [a] Not separately listed.
   [b] Includes 2.8 per cent "limonitic substance."
   [c] Balance is glauconite, mica, chlorite, iron ores.
   [d] "Matrix."

The distinctive character of a graywacke is the matrix, which, as long noted, *has the composition of a slate* (Bailey, 1930) and imparts both the distinctive color and general toughness to the rock. Like a slate, the matrix consists of a fine-grained mixture of white mica, chlorite, and quartz. Under the microscope in ordinary light, the matrix is seen to contain a great abundance of green flakes or folia, blades, and irregular shredlike plates of chlorite. In some specimens no prevailing orientation is discernible; in others a faint foliation may be seen. In many places the fine and irregular folia of chlorite pass out from the surrounding matrix and penetrate the body of the quartz grains. The original waterworn boundaries of the quartz, in these cases, have wholly disappeared, and the existing boundaries therefore are composed of a kind of a *chevaux de frise* of acicular green chlorite projecting into clean quartz (Fig. 77) (Greenly, 1897).

It is manifest therefore that the constituents of the graywackes have undergone considerable readjustment such that chemical interaction between matrix and sand grains and also reorganization within the matrix have taken place. The degree of reorganization varies greatly in the different specimens seen by the author, but some recrystallization seems to be the rule as friable graywackes are quite exceptional. The recrystallization is probably the result of deep burial and folding to which nearly all graywackes have been subjected.

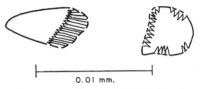

FIG. 77. Camera lucida drawing showing replacement of quartz by authigenic sericite (Krynine, 1940).

The origin of the matrix has been explained in several ways. Irving and Van Hise (1892) consider it to be the product of the "micaceous and chloritic alteration of the feldspar," though some source extraneous to the feldspar fragments is needed to provide the magnesium and the iron in the chlorite. Krynine (1945) considered the materials finely chopped up quartz, chlorite, sericite, and the like; he thus apparently regarded these constituents as original detrital components though, as observed by Krynine, some of the sericite and chlorite must be authigenic, since it is seen to replace detrital quartz (Krynine, 1940). It seems most probable that all the matrix minerals are, indeed, authigenic and are the result of reorganization of an original interstitial mud. This view is supported by the observed reorganization of muds into just such an assemblage of minerals (in slates, for example). It is further supported by the over-all chemical composition of a graywacke, which is about equivalent to two parts average shale and one part average arkose (see Table 50, also Table 52).

Two minor constituents of graywackes deserve special mention, namely, the pyrite and the carbonates, both apparently the product of authigenesis. The pyrite is scattered throughout the graywackes and associated slates. In general it occurs in euhedral cubes which appear to replace the matrix in which they are embedded. The pyrite is perhaps the product of penecontemporaneous diagenesis and either the product of sulfate-reducing bacteria or the product of decomposition of sulfur-bearing organic matter. The presence of sulfides and the generally reduced state of the iron in the graywackes are indicative of deposition in a reducing rather than an oxidizing environment. The carbonate is probably an ankerite rather than calcite or dolomite as both its indices are above Canada balsam. It replaces both matrix and coarser detrital grains and may also be a diagenetic product of the reducing environment.

TABLE 51. Chemical Composition of Graywackes
(per cent)

	A	B	C	D	E	F	G
SiO_2	68.20	63.67	62.40	61.52	69.69	60.51	65.05
TiO_2	0.31	....	0.50	0.62	0.40	0.87	0.46
Al_2O_3	16.63	19.43	15.20	13.42	13.53	15.36	13.89
Fe_2O_3	0.04	3.07	0.57	1.72	0.74	0.76	0.74
FeO	3.14	3.51	4.61	4.45	3.10	7.63	2.60
MnO	0.30	....	....	....	0.01	0.16	0.11
MgO	1.30	0.84	3.52	3.39	2.00	3.39	1.22
CaO	2.45	3.18	4.59	3.56	1.95	2.14	5.62
Na_2O	2.43	2.73	2.68	3.73	4.21	2.50	3.13
K_2O	2.33	1.34	2.57	2.17	1.71	1.69	1.41
P_2O_5	0.23	....	....	....	0.10	0.27	0.08
SO_3	0.13	....	....	....	....	....	....
CO_2	0.05	....	1.30	3.04	0.23	1.01	2.83
H_2O+	1.75⎱	2.29[a]	⎰1.56	2.33	2.08	3.38	2.30
H_2O-	0.55⎰		⎱0.07	0.06	0.26	0.15	0.28
S	....	....	....	....	....	0.42	0.05
	99.84	100.06	99.57	100.01	100.01	100.24	99.77

TABLE 51. Chemical Composition of Graywackes (Continued)
(per cent)

	H	I	J	K	L	M
SiO_2	68.05	73.04	69.11	53.30	65.18	68.56
TiO_2	0.33	0.15	0.60	0.84	0.90	0.08
Al_2O_3	11.43	10.17	11.38	18.33	13.85	12.50
Fe_2O_3	4.06	0.56	1.41	2.41	1.30	2.80
FeO	1.09	4.15	4.64	2.36	5.43	1.87
MnO	0.12[b]	0.18	0.17	0.08	0.22	0.05
MgO	1.45	1.43	2.06	2.62	1.87	3.29
CaO	1.94	1.49	1.15	5.88	0.72	0.83
Na_2O	3.13	3.56	3.20	2.18	1.48	4.33
K_2O	2.48	1.37	1.76	1.72	1.60	1.78
P_2O_5	0.15	0.23	0.03	0.28	0.38	0.06
SO_3	....	....	....	0.08	0.90	....
CO_2	2.51	0.84	0.00	1.00	tr	0.52
H_2O+	1.17⎱	2.36[a]	⎰4.13	3.14	3.94	2.38
H_2O-	....⎰		⎱0.05	5.74	2.10	0.80
S	[c]	0.10	....	....	....	0.08
	100.43	99.80[d]	99.69	99.99[e]	100.08[f]	99.93

A. Paleozoic (Devonian?), Mungo River, New Zealand (Morgan, 1908, p. 95).
B. Trias-Jura (average of 3), Balclutha area, New Zealand (Marshall, 1918, p. 36).
C. Archean (average of 3), Minnesota (Grout, 1929, p. 997).
D. Archean, Kirkland Lake, Ontario (average of 3) (Todd, 1928, p. 20).
E. Franciscan (Jurassic?) (average of 3), California (Taliaferro, 1943, p. 136).
F. Archean, Manitou Lake, Ontario. B. Brunn, analyst.
G. Eocene, Olympic Mountains, Washington, B. Brunn, analyst.
H. Keewatin, Casummit Lake, Ontario (Horwood, 1937, p. 24).
I. Kulm (Carboniferous), Steinbach, Frankenwald, Germany (Eigenfeld, 1933, p. 58).
J. Rensselaer (Ordovician?), Spencertown, N. Y. (Balk, 1953, p. 824).
K. Aure (Miocene), Papua (Edwards, 1950, p. 139).
L. Cretaceous, Papua (Edwards, 1950, p. 169).
M. Tanner (average of 3) (Upper Devonian-Lower Carboniferous) (Helmbold, 1952, p. 256).
   [a] Loss on ignition.
   [b] Reported as MnO_2.
   [c] FeS_2 0.56 and FeAsS 1.96.
   [d] Includes 0.17 C.
   [e] Includes 0.03 Cl.
   [f] Includes 0.16 Cl.

Chemical Composition

The chemical composition of graywackes (Table 51) necessarily reflects their complex mineralogical composition. Graywacke is lower in silica than the average sandstone (Table 20) and much of the silica present is combined in silicates. Free silica as detrital quartz, though usually dominant, may be only a minor constituent. The content of alumina is high, as is the content of lime, soda, and potash. In these respects graywackes differ in no essential particular from arkose, except that soda exceeds potash. They differ notably from arkose in the high content of magnesia, combined water, and in both the high content and reduced state of the iron. These constituents are contained mainly in the fine-grained, hydrous aluminum silicates of iron and magnesia of the chlorite type. These materials, probably present in the muddy interstitial matrix of the original sediment as amorphous hydroxides of iron and alumina, reacted during authigenesis with the magnesium carbonate to yield the observed chlorite.

TABLE 52. Chemical Composition of Average Graywacke
(per cent)

	A	B	C
SiO_2	64.7	68.1	64.2
TiO_2	0.5	0.7	0.6
Al_2O_3	14.8	15.4	13.8
Fe_2O_3	1.5	3.4[a]	3.4
FeO	3.9	3.4	2.0
MnO	0.1	0.2	....
MgO	2.2	1.8	1.7
CaO	3.1	2.3	2.5
Na_2O	3.1	2.6	1.5
K_2O	1.9	2.2	3.8
P_2O_5	0.2	0.2	0.2
SO_3	0.4	....	....
CO_2	1.3	....	1.9
H_2O+	2.4 ⎫	2.1	3.6
H_2O-	0.7 ⎭		
S	0.2		
	101.0	102.4[a]	99.2

A. Average of 23 graywackes in Table 51.
B. Average of 30 graywackes. After Tyrrell (1933).
C. Average of 2 parts average shale (Table 61) and 1 part average arkose (Table 56).
   [a] Probably in error; Fe_2O_3 probably should be 1.4 and the total should be 100.0.

The chemical composition of graywacke most closely resembles that of a slate (see Table 61). In fact the composition of a graywacke can be closely approximated by taking about two parts of average shale and one part average arkose. The result differs from normal graywacke in that the iron of the graywackes is more highly reduced and the potash is greater than soda instead of the reverse. The latter difference means that graywacke is the product of incomplete weathering as well as incomplete sorting. Graywacke is not, therefore, just a shaly sandstone.

Chemically graywacke resembles many igneous rocks. Edwards (1947a) has noted the resemblance of Papua Miocene graywackes to andesites. The graywackes of the Franciscan approach a granodiorite in composition (Taliaferro, 1943). Owing to the varied provenance of graywackes such resemblance and variations are to be expected. The sodic nature of graywacke is not so readily explained. Neither incomplete weathering nor incomplete sorting can account for the prevalence of soda over potash.

Occurrence and Associations

Graywackes are widely distributed in time and space. They are the most characteristic sedimentary rock in many Archean terranes (Pettijohn, 1943) (Fig. 78). Ninety per cent of the so-called Temiskaming and similar series found in Ontario is graywacke. Apparently the pre-Karelidic deposits of Finland are likewise characterized by graywackes (Simonen, 1953, pp. 23–25). Associated with these early sediments, which basically are no different from their younger counterparts, are slate, some conglomerate (locally very conspicuous), pillow lavas (greenstones) and tuffs, and a small volume of nonproductive iron formation. Some of the later Precambrian sections are also characterized by thick sequences of graywacke and slate. The Tyler and parts of the Michigamme formations of Michigan and Wisconsin contain many graywacke beds. Associated with these are slates, some tuffs and greenstones, and some lean iron-bearing formations.

The graywacke suite is typical of the Lower Paleozoic section of Great Britain in the Caledonian geosyncline of Wales, the Lake District of England, and the Southern Highlands of Scotland, where it is associated with pillow lavas and cherts (Jones, 1938). The Ordovician of the Taconic region of New York and Vermont contain excellent graywackes (Rensselaer grit) (Balk, 1953). Many of the sandstones of the Stanley shale (Carboniferous) of the Ouachita Mountains of Oklahoma and Arkansas are typical graywackes (Bokman, 1953), as are the rocks of equivalent age in the Marathon region of Texas. Graywackes occur in the Boston Bay group of Devonian or Carboniferous age where they are associated with slates, conglomerates, and some volcanics. They also occur associated with pillowed greenstones in the Devonian of southwestern Cornwall, in the Armorican geosyncline, and in the Devonian and Lower Carboniferous of the Harz Mountains in Germany.

Extensive and thick graywackes characterize the Franciscan (Jurassic or Cretaceous) of California and similar rocks also associated with greenstones

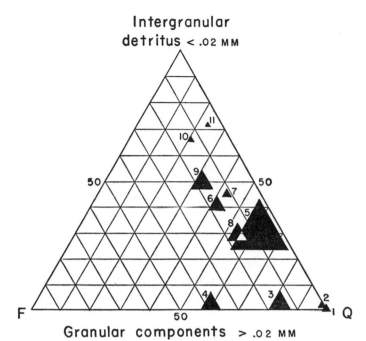

Intergranular
detritus < .02 MM

Granular components > .02 MM

FIG. 78. Mineral composition of representative sandstones. *F*, feldspar; *Q*, quartz. Intergranular detritus is mainly authigenic chlorite with little authigenic ankerite and sericite with some detrital or authigenic quartz and feldspar. Precipitated mineral cements are excluded. Only detrital constituents or their authigenic derivatives shown. Size of black triangle denotes proportion of other detrital materials, chiefly rock particles (including chert).

(1) Potsdam (Cambrian) orthoquartzite, (2) Ajibik (Precambrian) quartzite, (3) Serpent feldspathic quartzite (Huronian), (4) Portland arkose (Triassic), (5) Graywacke (Late Paleozoic) from Saxony, (6) Ladock graywacke (Devonian) from Cornwall, (7) Hurley graywacke (Precambrian), Wisconsin, (8) Feldspathic graywacke (Archean), (9) Manitou graywacke (Archean), Canada, (10) Graywacke (Archean), Canada, (11) Gowganda tillite (Huronian), Canada (from Pettijohn, 1943).

and cherts appear in rocks of equivalent age in Oregon and Washington and in many parts of Alaska. The Alpine Tertiary Flysch is a graywacke deposit as is much of the Siwalik (Tertiary) of northwestern India. The graded sandstones of Pliocene age in the Ventura Basin of California are in part graywackes. Typical graywacke also occurs in a thick Eocene sequence interbedded with shales and greenstones in the Olympic peninsula of Washington.

In summary, it can be said that graywacke belongs to no particular age. It is extensive only in the folded mountain chains, where it is typically inter-

PLATE 15

TILL AND TILLITE II

A: Pleistocene (Wisconsin) glacial till, Illinois, ordinary light, $\times$16.

Large rock fragments are fossiliferous and dolomitic limestone; smaller fragments mainly are clear angular quartz, some feldspar, and many smaller limestone grains, together with a few pieces of shale (black). Matrix is a paste of calcareous silt and clay.

B: Gowganda (Cobalt) tillite, Huronian, from Bruce Mines, Ont., Canada, ordinary light, $\times$15.

Largest fragments are granite; small ones are quartz (clear), and feldspar (clouded with inclusions). Matrix is an intimate pastelike intergrowth which when resolved under high power is found to be rich in chlorite and sericite.

C: Dwyka tillite, Permian, South Africa, ordinary light, $\times$42.

Rock fragments are granite, composed of microcline (dusty and traversed by cleavage cracks), and quartz (clear blebs); sand grains mainly are clear quartz and dusty feldspar. Matrix is a fine paste of indeterminate character.

D: Sturtian tillite, Adelaide series, Australia, ordinary light, $\times$12.

Largest fragments are pieces of granite or feldspar (inclusion-filled) and quartz (clear).

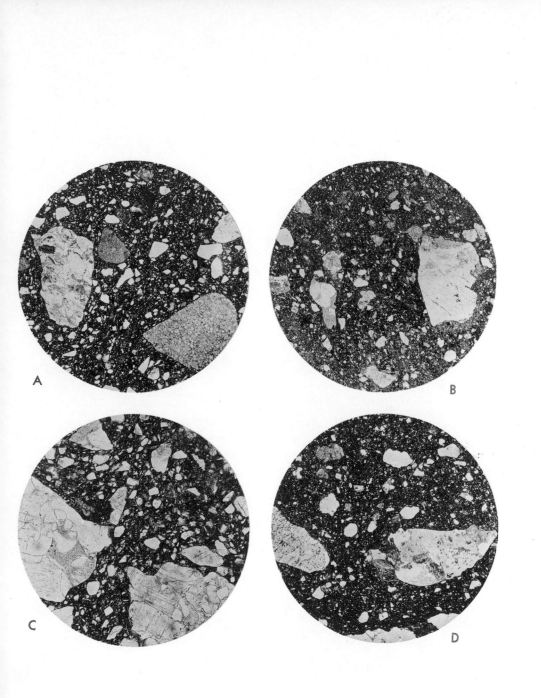

A

B

C

D

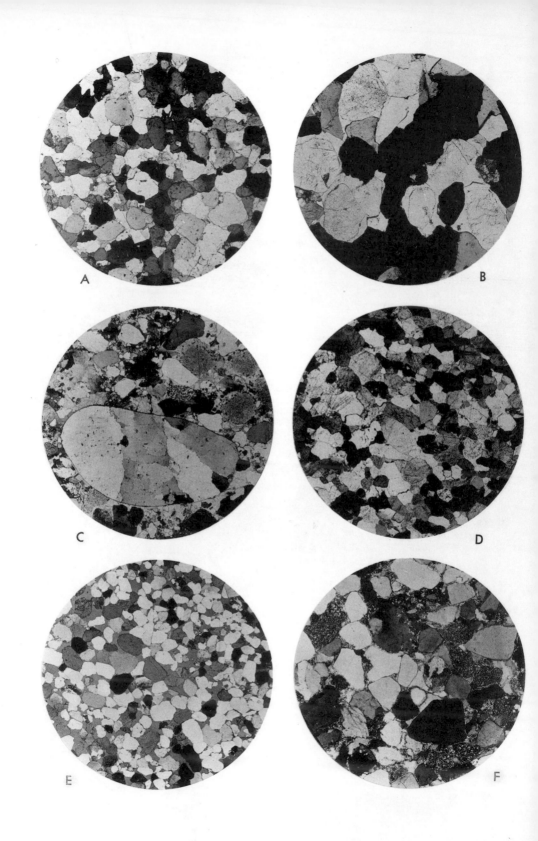

PLATE 16

ORTHOQUARTZITES I

A: Sioux quartzite, Precambrian, South Dakota. Crossed nicols, ×14.
Primarily a mosaic of quartz produced by cementation of detrital quartz
with quartz. Note well-rounded outline of original detrital quartz.

B: Tuscarora quartzite, Silurian, Bald Eagle Mountain, Penna. Crossed
nicols, ×42.
Essentially all quartz (95 to 98 per cent) cemented by quartz in optical
continuity with the detrital grains, thus welding the whole rock into a dense
quartzite. Quartzite fragments in coarser facies indicate a second-cycle origin.
Outlines of inclusion-filled, original grains clearly visible.

C: Conglomeratic sandstone from Coldwater (Devonian) shale, Mich.
Crossed nicols, ×13.
Vein quartz pebble (largest fragment), quartz, carbonate debris ("dusty")
and chert (aggregates) cemented by carbonate. Authigenic pyrite granules in
ringlike arrangement around detrital carbonate.

D: Oriskany sandstone, Devonian, Maryland. Crossed nicols, ×12.
A somewhat condensed orthoquartzite showing some microstylolitic contacts between quartz grains.

E: Hinckley sandstone, Cambrian, Minnesota. Crossed nicols, ×14.
A supermature quartz sand slightly cemented by quartz. Unlike the Sioux
quartzite, cementation is slight and porosity high.

F: Malvern quartzite, Cambrian, Malvern, England. Crossed nicols,
×14.
Detrital chert (microcrystalline aggregates, 20 per cent) and quartz (80
per cent) cemented by silica. Note well-rounded character of both chert and
quartz. A second-cycle orthoquartzite.

bedded with marine shales (or slates) and is associated with submarine flows (greenstones) and ferruginous or radiolarian cherts. In places it is associated with and grades into submarine basic tuffs. Its association with greenstone has been noted before and the significance of this association has been discussed (Tyrrell, 1933). It is rarely associated with limestone and if so the limestone is likely to be thin, dark, and siliceous. Graywacke is almost never associated with thick "pure quartz" sandstones of the orthoquartzitic clan.

Origin and Geologic Significance

Graywackes are characterized by certain attributes and associations, that distinguish them from other sandstones, and which must be properly explained. These are the graded character which most of them show, the absence of a chemical cement in place of which is the detrital matrix, the compositional and textural immaturity of these rocks, their association with bedded cherts and with pillowed greenstones and their general confinement to orogenic belts.

Woodland (1938) regarded the graywackes of the Cambrian Harlech grits of Wales as a product of marine sedimentation. He was particularly impressed by the closely intermixed relations of the sandy and muddy debris. It is clear that these two materials are normally deposited separately to form sands and shales. In the graywackes there was little or no separation of the two phases by the ordinary means of grading or lateral transportation. Woodland presumed therefore that the fine-grained matrix, once a colloidal suspension of clayey aluminous and siliceous materials, was subject to constant flocculation, thereby becoming a constant component of all rocks in this group. As the matrix forms upward of 50 per cent of even the coarse grits, it would follow that the flocculation must have been rapid and complete. Salt water was believed to be the precipitating agent. Kuenen (1951), however, has shown that the settling of sand grains is greatly retarded and even completely inhibited in concentrated clay suspensions. If the clay concentration is great enough there will be little or no size fractionation of much of the suspended materials including even coarse sand. The textures of the deposits made from such media resemble in all essential details those of the graywackes (Kuenen and Migliorini, 1950). Since most modern marine sands, even those in deltaic areas, seem to be reasonably clean despite the flocculating action of salt water, it seems more probable that the graywacke-type sands are the products of deposition from turbid media rather than the result of concurrent flocculation of the clay materials.

The graded bedding, so characteristic of many graywackes, is a most significant property. Bailey (1930, 1936) regarded graded bedding and current bedding as the distinguishing marks of two different sandstone facies. Current-bedded sandstones are obviously the products of bottom currents, whereas graded-bedded sandstones are the products of settling in comparatively still bottom waters. He concluded therefore that current-bedded sandstones "belong to relatively shallow water (or to the air), and graded-bedded sandstones belong to relatively deep water." The association of some graywackes with radiolarian cherts and with shales carrying deep-water faunas strongly supports this view. Bailey was uncertain how the coarse sands and grits reached deep water. He suggested, however, that submarine earthquakes were "intermittent distributors of sand and mud." According to him the deposits of sand and mud probably formed unstable accumulations on the border of the geosyncline and were periodically dislodged by submarine temblors and thrown into suspension to settle out with the graded internal structure. That Bailey was in a large measure correct is borne out by Kuenen's experimental work on turbidity flows (Kuenen and Migliorini, 1950). Turbidity-current deposits are typically graded, and study of these currents shows that they are indeed capable of carrying coarse materials into deep waters and there depositing their burden in company with bathyl to abyssal materials. That the graywackes were the product of turbidity flows was suggested by Payne (1948) and restated by others (Pettijohn, 1950).

If the theory of deposition of graywackes by submarine-generated turbidity flows is correct, it is clear why such deposits have never been observed to form despite the fact that graywackes are a relatively common type of sandstones found in all geologic ages. Each graywacke bed is the record of a single semicatastrophic event—a short-lived episode which is completely hidden from ordinary observation.

Turbidity flows might be generated by submarine slumps, triggered by seaquakes, or they may form by other means, but as Bailey (1936), Fairbridge (1946), and others have noted, such slumps and resultant deposits are probably characteristics of certain unstable tectonic environments. It is not surprising, therefore, to find them associated with other products characteristic of such unstable belts, namely the tuffs and submarine lava flows.

That graywackes are indicative of a special tectonic environment was a concept advanced by various writers, notably Jones, Tyrrell, Fischer, Krynine, and Pettijohn. Fischer (1933), for example, regarded graywacke as a "poured-in" type of sediment characteristic of geosynclinal sedimentation. Krynine (1941) regarded graywackes as the normal arenaceous sediment of the middle to late stages of the geosynclinal cycle. Pettijohn (1943) regarded graywackes as the earmark of sedimentation in tectonically unstable regions especially in eugeosynclinal belts. Their distribution in time and space seems to support this concept, though some other sediments, notably arkose, may also be the product of sedimentation in orogenic belts. Arkoses, however, are primarily current-deposited sediments, more commonly terrestrial than marine, whereas graywackes are transported and deposited subaqueously by submarine turbidity flows.

Graywackes appear to have no climatic significance. They require only an environment in which erosion, transportation, and deposition are so rapid that complete chemical weathering of the materials does not take place. Because graywacke is not confined to the Precambrian or even to the pre-Devonian, the absence of a plant cover does not seem to be a requirement for its formation, as has been thought by some. The carbonized wood fragments in the Franciscan and other graywackes demand a plant cover for at least part of the source area.

Most graywackes are certainly marine. The reducing environment implied by their dark color, the pyrite, the ankeritic carbonate, their association with submarine pillow lavas, and their association with radiolarian-bearing cherts and with shales containing graptolites or marine microfossils all bear out the marine nature of the graywackes. The soda-rich character of the greenstones and albitization of these rocks has been attributed to the sodium of the sea water or to that in the connate waters of the associated sediments. Whether extensive or important nonmarine graywackes exist is uncertain, although some of the graywackes of the Siwalik (Tertiary) series of India were said to be nonmarine (Krynine, 1937). It is doubtful whether much graywacke is nonmarine though many of the subgraywackes may be so.

REFERENCES CITED AND BIBLIOGRAPHY

Allen, V. T. (1936), Terminology of medium-grained sediments, *Rept. Comm. Sed.*, 1935–1936 (mimeographed), National Research Council, pp. 18–47.

Bailey, E. B. (1930), New light on sedimentation and tectonics, *Geol. Mag.*, vol. 67, pp. 86–88.

Bailey, E. B. (1936), Sedimentation in relation to tectonics, *Bull. Geol. Soc. Amer.*, vol. 47, pp. 1716–1718.

Balk, R. (1953), Structure of graywacke areas and Taconic Range, east of Troy, New York, *Bull. Geol. Soc. Amer.*, vol. 64, pp. 811–864.

Bokman, John (1953), Lithology and petrology of the Stanley and Jackfork formations, *J. Geol.*, vol. 61, pp. 152–170.

Davis, E. F. (1918), The Franciscan sandstone, *Univ. Calif. Publ., Bull. Dept. Geol.*, vol. 11, pp. 6–16.

Diller, J. S. (1898), The educational series of rock specimens, etc., *U.S. Geol. Survey, Bull.* 150, pp. 84–87.

Edwards, A. B. (1947a), The petrology of the Miocene sediments of the Aure Trough, Papua, *Proc. Roy. Soc. Victoria*, vol. 60 (n.s.), pp. 123–148.

Edwards, A. B. (1947b), The petrology of the Cretaceous graywackes of the Purari Valley, Papua, *Proc. Roy. Soc. Victoria*, vol. 60 (n.s.), pp. 163–171.

Eigenfeld, R. (1933), Die Kulmconglomerat von Teuschnitz im Frankenwalde, *Abhandl. math. phys. Kl. sächs. Akad. Wiss.*, vol. 42, no. 1, p. 58.

Fairbridge, R. W. (1946), Submarine slumping and location of oil bodies, *Bull. Am. Assoc. Petroleum Geol.*, vol. 30, pp. 84–92.

Fischer, Georg (1933), Die Petrographie der Grauwacken, *Jahrb. preuss. geol. Landesanstalt*, vol. 54, pp. 320–343.

Fischer, Georg (1932), Die Culmgrauwacke, *Jahrb. preuss. geol. Landesanstalt*, No. 53, Sitzungber., vol. 8.

Folk, R. W. (1954), The distinction between grain size and mineral composition in sedimentary rock nomenclature, *J. Geol.*, vol. 62, pp. 344–359.

Greenly, E. (1897), Incipient metamorphism in the Harlech grits, *Trans. Edinburgh Geol. Soc.*, vol. 7, pp. 254–258.

Grout, F. F. (1933), Contact metamorphism of the slates of Minnesota by granite and by gabbro magmas, *Bull. Geol. Soc. Amer.*, vol. 44, p. 997.

Helmbold, R. (1952), Beitrag zur Petrographie der Tanner Grauwacken, *Heidelberger Beitr. Mineral Petrog.*, vol. 3, pp. 253–288.

Horwood, H. C. (1937), Geology of the Casummit Lake area and the Argosy Mine, *Ontario Dept. Mines, Ann. Rept.*, vol. 46, pt. 7, p. 24.

Irving, R. D. and Van Hise, C. R. (1892), The Penokee iron-bearing series of Michigan and Wisconsin, *U.S. Geol. Survey, Mon.* 19, pp. 206f.

Jones, O. T. (1938), On the evolution of a geosyncline, *Proc. Geol. Soc. London*, vol. 94, pp. lxii–lxvi.

Krynine, P. D. (1937), Petrography and genesis of the Siwalik series, *Am. J. Sci.*, ser. 5, vol. 34, pp. 422–446.

Krynine, P. D. (1940), Petrology and genesis of the Third Bradford Sand, *Penn. State Coll. Mineral Inds. Expt. Sta., Bull.* 29, pp. 50–51.

Krynine, P. D. (1941), Graywackes and the petrology of Bradford Oil Field, Pennsylvania, *Bull. Am. Assoc. Petroleum Geol.*, vol. 25, pp. 2073–2074.

Krynine, P. D. (1942), Paleogeographic and tectonic significance of graywackes (abstract), *Bull. Geol. Soc. Amer.*, vol. 52, p. 1916.

Krynine, P. D. (1943), *Diastrophism and the evolution of sedimentary rocks*, Am. Assoc. Petroleum Geol. Distinguished Lecture series. Mimeographed notes privately distributed.

Krynine, P. D. (1945), Sediments and the search for oil, *Producers Monthly*, vol. 9, pp. 12–22.

Krynine, P. D. (1948), Megascopic study and field classification of sedimentary rocks, *J. Geol.*, vol. 56, pp. 130–165.

Kuenen, Ph. H. (1951), Properties of turbidity currents of high density, *Soc. Econ. Geol. Paleon., Special Publ.* No. 2, pp. 14–33.

Kuenen, Ph. H. (1953), Graded bedding, with observations on Lower Paleozoic rocks of Britain, *Verhandel. Koninkl. Ned. Akad. Wetenschap. Afdel. Natuurk.*, vol. 20, pp. 1–47.

Kuenen, Ph. H. and Migliorini, C. I. (1950), Turbidity currents as a cause of graded bedding, *J. Geol.*, vol. 58, pp. 91–127.

McElroy, C. T. (1954), The use of the term "graywacke" in rock nomenclature in New South Wales, *Australian J. Sci.*, vol. 16, pp. 150–151.

Marshall, P. (1918), The geology of the Tuapeka district, Central Otago Division, *New Zealand Geol. Surv., Bull.* 19, p. 36.

Morgan, P. G. (1908), The geology of the Mikonui subdivision, North West-land, *New Zealand Geol. Surv., Bull.* 6, p. 95.

Naumann, C. F. (1858), *Lehrbuch der Geognosie,* vol. 1, Leipzig, Engelman, p. 663.

Payne, T. G. (1948), *Personal communication.*

Pettijohn, F. J. (1943), Archean sedimentation, *Bull. Geol. Soc. Amer.,* vol. 54, pp. 941–943.

Pettijohn, F. J. (1950), Turbidity currrents and graywackes: A discussion, *J. Geol.,* vol. 58, pp. 169–171.

Pettijohn, F. J. (1954), Classification of sandstones, *J. Geol.,* vol. 62, pp. 360–365.

Rich, J. L. (1950), Flow markings, groovings, and intrastratal crumplings, etc., *Bull. Am. Assoc. Petroleum Geol.,* vol. 34, pp. 717–741.

Shrock, R. R. (1948), *Sequence in layered rocks,* New York, McGraw-Hill.

Simonen, Ahti (1953), Stratigraphy and sedimentation of the Svecofennidic, early Archean supracrustal rocks in southwestern Finland, *Bull. Comm. géol. Finlande,* No. 160.

Taliaferro, N. L. (1943), Franciscan-Knoxville problem, *Bull. Am. Assoc. Petroleum Geol.,* vol. 27, pp. 136–138.

Todd, E. W. (1928), Kirkland Lake gold area, *Ontario Dept. Mines, Ann. Rept.,* vol. 37, pt. 2, p. 20.

Twenhofel, W. H. (1950), *Principles of sedimentation,* 2d ed., New York, McGraw-Hill, p. 317.

Tyrrell, G. W. (1933), Greenstones and greywackes, *C. R. réunion intern. pour l'étude du Précambrien* 1931, pp. 24–26.

Udluft, Hans (1931), Versuch einer Charakteristik und Definition devonischer Grauwacken, Sandsteine, und Quartzite, *Sitzber. preuss. geol. Landesanstalt,* 6, pp. 128–136.

SUBGRAYWACKE AND PROTOQUARTZITE (LITHIC SANDSTONES)

Definition and Nomenclature

Those sandstones in which the rock fragments exceed feldspar particles are called *lithic sandstones* (in the same way in which tuffs with an abundance of rock fragments are called lithic tuffs). If the labile components exceed 25 per cent, the rock is a *subgraywacke.* Sandstones with a lesser content (10 to 25 per cent) are quartzose subgraywackes or *protoquartzites* (Pettijohn, 1954).

The subgraywackes are the most common types of sandstones in the geologic column. Because these rocks have many properties in common with the graywackes to which they bear superficial resemblance and because they are intermediate in composition between graywackes and orthoquartzites, they were named *subgraywackes* (Pettijohn, 1949). Subgraywackes are characterized by (1) an abundance of unstable materials, feldspars and rock fragments (over 25 per cent), (2) an excess of rock fragments over feldspar, and (3) *an excess of voids or of mineral cement or both over detrital matrix.* The detrital matrix therefore is quite small, generally under 10 per cent.[15] Subgraywackes thus differ from arkose in the subordinate role of feldspar and differ from graywackes in the subordinate role of the matrix.

Krynine has applied the term graywacke to both true graywacke and to the subgraywackes. In fact as first defined by Krynine (1943), the term graywacke could be applied only to the subgraywackes. Later Krynine (1945) redefined the term, and two types, namely, *low-rank graywacke* and *high-rank graywacke* were recognized. The latter contained important quantities of feldspar, whereas the low-rank types were feldspar-poor. In the writer's opinion the extension of the term graywacke to include arenites that are intermediate in character between true graywackes and orthoquartzites is undesirable. The end types or "poles" should be recognized and named, but the intermediate types should be differently designated. As originally defined, the author's subgraywacke was more or less the same as Krynine's low-rank graywacke. As redefined, however, this is not true. Subgraywacke differs from graywacke *not* in the feldspar content but rather in the grain/matrix ratio.

Subgraywacke, as redefined by Dapples, Krumbein, and Sloss (1953), differs only slightly from the author's present use of the term. The difference is mainly in the choice of an appropriate source *rock factor.* On the other hand, Folk (1954), like Krynine, ignores the sorting factor in his definition of the term, and defines subgraywacke solely in terms of mineral composition.

Mineral and Chemical Composition

By definition subgraywacke contains 25 per cent or more of labile materials, including both feldspar and rock fragments. The rock fragments must exceed the feldspars or otherwise the rock would be termed an arkose or subarkose. Further by definition the subgraywacke has only a small quantity of interstitial detrital materials; less than one-half of the voids are so filled. Normally, therefore, there is no more than 10 to 15 per cent of such matrix material. The balance of the void volume is either empty—and the rock therefore porous—or partially or completely filled with a precipitated mineral cement. The latter is most commonly carbonate.

[15] As originally defined, subgraywacke contained 0 to 10 per cent feldspar and 20 to 75 per cent detrital matrix (largely sericite and chlorite). This definition, however, has proved quite unsatisfactory. Even the best examples, such as the Bradford sand of Devonian age and the Oswego sandstone of Ordovician age, which are indeed excellent subgraywackes, do not wholly conform to the definition. As a result there have been several attempts to redefine the term. (Tallman, 1949; Dapples, Krumbein, and Sloss, 1953; Pettijohn, 1954.)

Inspection of Table 53 shows that normal subgraywackes have a quartz content ranging from 30 to 65 per cent. Detrital chert is very common and may constitute as much as 30 per cent of the total. Other rock fragments— most usually sedimentary or metasedimentary—form 10 to 50 per cent of the whole rock. Feldspar, by definition, is a subordinate and in most examples varies from 1 to 10 per cent. Detrital micas vary from a few grains to 5 per cent or more. Some graywackes are typical micaceous sandstones.

TABLE 53. Mineral Composition of Typical Subgraywackes
(per cent)

	A	B	C	D	E	F	G
Quartz	30.9	36.3	32.0	33.0	60	60–65	50
Chert	14.5	15.0	28.0	20.0	....	....	....
Feldspar	10.0	2.2	2.2	5.5	2–10	1.5	3–5
Micas	1.0[a]	tr	0.2	0.1	up to 5	2–3	....
Rock Fragments	18.8	32.6	15.2	21.0	up to 15[b]	30[b]	40[b]
"Clay"	5.5	10.1[c]	8.9[c]	9.2[c]	20[d]	5–10	10
Silica cement	....	1.3	1.8	tr	tr	....	....[e]
Calcite cement	19.2	3.7	13.0	26.5	5–20[f]	2–18	....

A. Frio, Oligocene, Texas. (Average of 22 samples) (Nanz, 1954).
B. "Normal graywacke," Cretaceous, Torok, Alaska. (Average of 3 samples) (Krynine in Payne, 1951).
C. "Calcareous graywacke," Cretaceous, Torok, Alaska. (Average of 3 samples) (Krynine in Payne, 1951).
D. "Calcareous graywacke," Cretaceous, Topagoruk, Alaska. (Average of 7 samples) (Krynine in Payne, 1951).
E. Trivoli, Pennsylvanian, Illinois (Siever, 1949).
F. Bradford, Devonian, Pennsylvania (Krynine, 1940).
G. Oswego, Ordovician, Pennsylvania (Krynine and Tuttle, 1941).
  [a] Includes iron ores.
  [b] Includes chert.
  [c] Chlorite, sericite, montmorillonite, kaolinite.
  [d] Chlorite, illite, kaolinite.
  [e] 5–10 per cent, author's observations.
  [f] Includes some siderite.

The intergranular space is filled by a combination of clay materials and mineral cement. Unlike typical graywackes, chemical cements, especially carbonate, are common and may fill most of the voids. Subgraywackes are therefore commonly calcareous. Some, like many orthoquartzites, contain silica precipitated in optical continuity with the detrital quartz grains, though in general carbonate rather than silica is the normal cement. Many are only partially cemented and are therefore porous and, unlike graywackes, may function as a reservoir for fluids.

As can be seen by inspection of Table 54, the subgraywackes are intermediate in composition between the graywacke and orthoquartzite. Silica therefore ranges from 65 to 85 per cent of the whole; alumina lies between 5 and 15 per cent; iron oxides and magnesia together make 3 to 6 per cent; the alkalies together with lime form about 4 per cent except in the calcareous varieties which have 10 or more per cent lime and a corresponding content of carbon dioxide. In the carbonate-rich varieties the silica percentage is somewhat depressed, though on a lime-free basis it is essentially like the other subgraywackes. In brief, the chemical composition of subgraywackes reflects their high concentration of quartz and chert, their lesser clay content, and the carbonate cement characteristic of so many of these rocks.

TABLE 54.   Chemical Composition of Subgraywackes and Protoquartzite
(per cent)

	A	B	C	D	E
SiO_2	74.43	76.84	65.0	82.15	93.13
TiO_2	0.83	....	....	0.35	....
Al_2O_3	11.32	11.76	9.6	5.37	3.86
Fe_2O_3	0.81	0.55	1.6	1.47	0.11
FeO	3.88	2.88	1.1	1.08	0.54
MnO	0.04	tr	....	....	....
MgO	1.30	1.39	0.4	2.22	0.25
CaO	1.17	0.70	10.1	1.85	0.19
Na_2O	1.63	2.57	2.1	1.84	....
K_2O	1.74	1.62	1.4	1.09	....
H_2O+	2.15	1.87[a]	0.8	0.74⎱	1.43
H_2O-	0.20	....	0.2	0.07⎰	
P_2O_5	0.18	....	....	....	....
CO_2	0.48	....	6.9	....	....
C	0.17	....	0.1	....	....
S	0.12	....	0.2	....	....
	100.45	100.18	98.23	99.6	99.51

A. Subgraywacke from Stanley shale (Carboniferous) near Mena, Arkansas. B. Brunn, analyst. (See Pl. 19, A).
B. Subgraywacke from Tyler slate (Precambrian), near Hurley, Wisconsin. H. N. Stokes, analyst (Diller, 1898, p. 87).
C. Frio sandstone (Oligocene), Seeligson Field, Texas. Averages of 10 analyses (Nanz, 1954).
D. "Graywacke phase" of the Rove formation (Animikie, Precambrian), Loon Lake, Minnesota. D. M. Davidson, analyst (Grout and Schwartz, 1933, p. 22).
E. Berea (Mississippian), a protoquartzite.
   [a] Ignition loss.

Textures and Structures

Because of their content of rock particles—shales, slates, and similar materials—subgraywackes tend to be gray in color though they are not so dark as are typical graywackes.[16] The lighter-colored varieties are commonly speckled and constitute a *salt-and-pepper* sandstone. Subgraywackes are notably better sorted than graywackes—witness their high porosity, content of mineral cement, or both. The detrital grains are notably better rounded as well as better sorted.

[16] Fresh cored rock is light gray; outcrop materials are buff or sandcolored. The color difference is probably due to oxidation of interstitial iron-bearing carbonates.

Subgraywackes may be well stratified, are commonly cross-bedded, and are locally ripple-marked.

They are commonly interbedded with shales and form considerable sand bodies commonly of irregular lenticular form. Some are shoestring sands.

Occurrence and Distribution

The total volume of subgraywackes is very large and probably greatly exceeds that of graywacke proper. Krynine (1948) and Pettijohn (1949) have estimated graywacke and subgraywacke to form 45 per cent of all sandstones. Graywacke proper (Krynine's high-rank graywacke) forms about 10 per cent of the total. Subgraywacke, therefore, is at least three times as abundant as graywacke and forms roughly one-third of all sandstones.

Subgraywackes are found throughout the geologic section. The Oswego sandstone (Ordovician) (Krynine and Tuttle, 1941) and the Bradford (Devonian) (Krynine, 1940) of Pennsylvania are typical subgraywackes (see Table 53 and Pl. 19). The Trivoli sandstone (Pennsylvanian) of Illinois is another excellent example (Siever, 1948). Many of the sands in the Atoka (Carboniferous) of Arkansas and Oklahoma and the Pocono (Mississippian) of Maryland and Pennsylvania are apparently subgraywackes. Many of the Lower Cretaceous sandstones of the Alaskan coastal plain are typical subgraywackes (Krynine in Payne, 1951). Some of the Tertiary sandstones of the Oligocene and Miocene of the Gulf Coast are subgraywackes. An excellent example is the Frio Oligocene sandstone (Nanz, 1954). The Molasse sandstone seems to be typical subgraywacke.

Origin and Geologic Significance

Because of their lamination, cross-bedding, and generally fair sorting, most subgraywackes, unlike graywackes, were evidently deposited by normal subaqueous currents. Unlike the orthoquartzites, they are immature sediments as their content of feldspar and labile rock fragments testify. Unlike the arkoses, they are derived mainly from sedimentary and low-rank metamorphic terranes.

The conditions under which these rocks formed are not fully understood. As they are commonly found in coal measures, they are in part nonmarine or at least closely associated with nonmarine beds. Those better known from close study seem to be a product of *paralic sedimentation*, i.e., they accumulated on floodplains or in deltas in the coastal plains or in closely associated marine environments.

In some cases, despite their low content of interstitial silt or clay, subgraywackes display graded bedding and are rhythmically interbedded with shales in a manner similar to that shown by the graywackes proper. Such sandstones, unlike others of similar composition, may be the product of turbidity flows appreciably below wave base. The basis for discrimination between such deposits and those of normal currents lies not in their composition, or even their microtextures, but rather in their internal structures and their grosser features and associations. The Modello sandstone (Upper Miocene) of the Los Angeles basin and some of the Upper Cretaceous sandstones of the Diablo Range, California, seem to be subgraywackes of the kind here discussed.

As noted later many subgraywackes appear late in the orogenic cycle along with coal beds. They vary somewhat in their maturity. The more mature varieties are the protoquartzites of Krynine (Payne, 1951) and perhaps record periods of greater stability which permitted cleaning up of the sands and increased concentration of the quartz.

REFERENCES CITED AND BIBLIOGRAPHY

Dapples, E. C., Krumbein, W. C., and Sloss, L. L. (1953), Petrographic and lithologic attributes of sandstones, *J. Geol.*, vol. 21, pp. 291–317.

Diller, J. S. (1898), The educational series of rock specimens collected and distributed by the United States Geological Survey. *U.S. Geol. Survey, Bull.* 150.

Folk, R. L. (1954), The distinction between grain size and mineral composition in sedimentary rock nomenclature, *J. Geol.*, vol. 62, pp. 344–359.

Grout, F. F. and Schwartz, G. M. (1933), The geology of the Rove Formation and associated intrusives in northeastern Minnesota, *Minn. Geol. Survey Bull.* 24, 103 pp.

Krynine, P. D. (1940), Petrology and genesis of the Third Bradford sand, *Penn. State Coll. Bull.* 29.

Krynine, P. D. (1943), *Diastrophism and the evolution of sedimentary rocks* (mimeographed), Am. Assoc. Petroleum Geol. Lecture.

Krynine, P. D. (1945), Sediments and the search for oil, *Producers Monthly*, vol. 9, pp. 12–22.

Krynine, P. D. (1948), The megascopic study and field classification of sedimentary rocks, *J. Geol.*, vol. 56, pp. 130–165.

Krynine, P. D., and Tuttle, O. F. (1941), Petrology of Ordovician-Silurian boundary in central Pennsylvania, *Bull. Geol. Soc. Amer.*, vol. 52, pp. 1917–1918.

Nanz, R. H., Jr. (1954), Genesis of Oligocene sandstone reservoir, Seeligson field, Jim Wells and Kleberg Counties, Tevas, *Bull. Assoc. Petroleum Geol.*, vol. 38, pp. 96–117.

Payne, T. G., and others (1951), The Arctic slope of Alaska, *U.S. Geol. Survey Oil and Gas Invest.*, Map OM 126, Sheet 2.

Pettijohn, F. J. (1949), *Sedimentary rocks* (1st ed.), New York, Harper & Brothers, pp. 255–257.

Pettijohn, F. J. (1954), Classification of sandstones, *J. Geol.*, vol. 62, pp. 360–365.

Siever, Raymond (1949), Trivoli sandstones of Williamson County, Illinois, *J. Geol.*, vol. 57, pp. 614–617.

Tallman, S. F. (1949), Sandstone types: Their abundance and cementing agents, *J. Geol.*, vol. 57, pp. 582–591.

ARKOSE AND SUBARKOSE (FELDSPATHIC SANDSTONES)

Definitions and Nomenclature

The term *arkose* is an old one, the derivation of which is uncertain. It has been attributed to Brongniart (Oriel, 1949), who wrote one of the first comprehensive papers on arkose and its geological significance (Brongniart, 1826). The meaning of arkose as originally defined has changed very little. It is a sandstone, generally coarse and angular, moderately well sorted, composed principally of quartz and feldspar, and presumably derived from a granite or rock of granitic composition. Quartz is generally the dominant mineral, although in some arkoses feldspar exceeds quartz. Other constituents are very subordinate (Table 55).

Arkose may, and generally does, resemble granite, and if it has been welded by mild metamorphism it may be mistaken for granite or granite gneiss. It is commonly but not universally pink or reddish in color. Some arkoses are pale gray.

There has been no general agreement on how little feldspar a sandstone can contain and still be designated arkose. Allen (1936) placed the lower limit at 25 per cent; Krynine (1940) suggested 30 per cent but later (1948) showed 25 per cent to be the *average* feldspar content of arkose.[17] Pettijohn (1949) accepted the 25 per cent lower limit and proposed to restrict the term *feldspathic sandstone* to those sandstones having a feldspar content of 10 to 25 per cent (of their detrital fraction). Owing to the ambiguous character of the term *feldspathic*, the name *subarkose* was proposed for these sandstones—a term independently suggested by Folk (1954) for very similar rocks. Arkose was redefined (Pettijohn, 1954) as a rock characterized by 25 per cent or more of labile constituents (feldspar and rock fragments) of which feldspar forms half or more. Arkose might therefore contain as little as 12.5 per cent feldspar. Subarkose would contain 10 to 25 per cent of labile constituents, and might have as little as 5 per cent feldspar.

Most difficulty is encountered with those sandstones which, though highly feldspathic, are neither arkose nor subarkose. Many of these have been designated arkose; more commonly they are called impure arkose, or dirty

---

[17] Many authors did not indicate whether the percentage stated was of the whole rock (including cement or voids) or of the detrital fraction only. Krynine's figure is for the whole rock, including voids or their filling.

arkose. Very probably many of these rocks are graywackes; others may be lithic arenites.[18]

Mineralogical and Chemical Composition

As can be seen from Table 55, arkoses are composed primarily of feldspar and quartz (80 to 95 per cent). The quartz generally, though not always, exceeds the feldspar. The feldspar is largely potash feldspar—usually microcline. Other constituents form 5 to 15 per cent of the rock and are mainly micas; both biotite and muscovite, and some clay—said to be kaolinitic (Krynine, 1950). In the transitional types, arkoses may approach the

TABLE 55. Mineral Composition of Arkose
(per cent)

	A	B	C	D[a]	E[a]	F[a]	G
Quartz	57	51	60	57	35	28	48
Microcline	24	30	34⎫	35[b]	59[b]	64	43
Plaglioclase	6	11	....⎭				
Micas	3	1	....	....	....	....	2
Clay	9	7	....	....	....	....	8
Carbonate	c	c	....	c	2	....	c
Other	1	....	6[d]	8[e]	4[e]	8[e]	c

A. Pale arkose (Triassic) Conn. (Krynine, 1950, p. 85).
B. Red arkose (Triassic) Conn. (Krynine, 1950, p. 85).
C. Sparagmite (Precambrian) Norway (Barth, 1938, p. 60).
D. Torridonian (Precambrian) Scotland (Mackie, 1905, p. 58).
E. Lower Old Red (Devonian) Scotland (Mackie, ibid., p. 58).
F. Portland (Triassic) Conn. (Merrill, 1891, p. 420).
G. Average A–F, inclusive.
  [a] Normative or calculated composition.
  [b] Modal feldspar, given by Mackie as 55 and 60, respectively.
  [c] Present in amounts under 1 per cent.
  [d] Chlorite.
  [e] Iron oxide (hematite) and kaolin.

lithic arenites in composition. In such cases rock particles become common and form an important part of the detrital materials. In arkoses the cement is commonly scanty. In some cases it is calcite; in others both the quartz and feldspar show overgrowths which knit the rock together; in still others iron oxide forms the cement. Except for the meta-arkoses, which are thoroughly welded rocks, the arkoses are rarely as well cemented as either the orthoquartzites or the graywackes.

Arkoses are typically light pink or light gray—unlike the dark greenish gray or black of the graywackes.

[18] See, for example, Davis (1918) and Taliaferro (1943), who designated the Franciscan of California as *arkosic sandstone*. All outcrops and specimens seen by the author are graywackes. The Jurassic "arkose" of Edwards and Baker (1942) appears to be a graywacke or subgraywacke, judging from the descriptions and analyses given.

As can be seen from Table 56, typical arkose contains less silica than an orthoquartzite, is rich in alumina, lime, potash, and in many cases, soda. Unlike graywacke, potash exceeds soda and lime greatly exceeds magnesia. Moreover, in the unmetamorphosed arkoses ferric oxide exceeds the ferrous oxide. The subgraywackes and other lithic arenites are less clearly distinguished chemically from arkose. In general they have less potash, more magnesium, and ferrous rather than ferric oxide.

TABLE 56.   Chemical Composition of Arkose
(per cent)

	A	B	C	D	E	F
SiO_2	69.94	82.14	75.57	73.32	80.89	76.37
TiO_2	....	....	0.42	....	0.40	0.41
Al_2O_3	13.15	9.75	11.38	11.31	7.57	10.63
Fe_2O_3	2.48	{ 1.23	0.82	3.54	2.90	2.12
FeO		{	1.63	0.72	1.30	1.22
MnO	0.70	....	0.05	T	....	0.25
MgO	T	0.19	0.72	0.24	0.04	0.23
CaO	3.09	0.15	1.69	1.53	0.04	1.30
Na_2O	3.30	0.50	2.45	2.34	0.63	1.84
K_2O	5.43	5.27	3.35	6.16	4.75	4.99
H_2O+	1.01	0.64[a]	{1.06}	0.30[a]	1.11	0.83
H_2O-			{0.05}			
P_2O_5	....	0.12	0.30	....	....	0.21
CO_2	....	0.19	0.51	0.92	....	0.54
	99.10	100.18	100.00	100.20	99.63	100.94

A. Portland stone, Triassic, Conn. (Merrill, 1891, p. 420).
B. Torridon sandstone, Precambrian, Scotland (Mackie, 1905, p. 58).
C. Torridonian arkose (average of three analyses) (Kennedy, 1951, p. 258).
D. Lower Old Red Sandstone, Devonian, Scotland (Mackie, op. cit.).
E. Sparagmite (unmetamorphosed), Engerdalen region (Barth, 1938, p. 58).
F. Average of A–E, inclusive.
   [a] Loss on ignition.

Textures and Structures

Arkoses are typically coarse; perhaps on the average, the coarsest of the sandstones. Although bedding commonly is obscure, arkoses do show some stratification and may be coarsely cross-bedded. Porosity may be high both due to fair sorting and to incomplete cementation. The detrital grains are characteristically angular or subangular.

Associations and Occurrence

Arkose occurs either as a thin blanket-like residuum at the base of a sedimentary series that overlies a granitic terrane, or as a very thick wedge-shaped deposit interbedded with much coarse granite-bearing conglomerate and deposited with a lesser quantity of red shale and siltstone. Chemical precipitates, such as chert or limestone, are not associated with the wedge-type of arkose except in very minor proportions.

Basal arkose, owing to its thin and discontinuous character, is seldom of large volume. Examples from the geologic record are very common. A few feet of such material, for example, appear at the base of the LaMotte sandstone (Cambrian) of the Ozark area where this formation rests on Precambrian granite (Pl. 20, A).

Basal arkose is a slightly reworked feldspathic residuum. Encroachment of the sea on a land area that is underlaid by granitic rocks results in reworking of the arkosic mantle rock. Reworking of this material and removal of the more completely decayed and finer portions leave a feldspathic residue which, upon consolidation, may be called an arkose or subarkose depending upon the feldspar content. Such material is restricted to the base of the formation or to intercalated wedges of granite wash near the base or near buried hills of granite. In some cases the residuum is so little reworked and so little decomposed that upon cementation the deposit looks very much like the granite itself. It is then termed *recomposed* or *reconstituted* granite. Such rocks can be readily misidentified in the field, and especially so if one can examine only cuttings from the drills. It may be difficult, in the latter case, therefore, to know whether the "basement" has been reached or whether the bit has penetrated only a tongue of granite wash. Even in outcrop, especially in some Precambrian and similar terranes where the rocks are welded by metamorphism, controversy has arisen as to whether the meta-arkose is in truth an arkosic sediment, or a granite, or a granitized sediment. Such contacts between granite and the overlying meta-arkose may be gradational, and if truly sedimentary, the relations have been appropriately termed *graded unconformity*.

The criteria for discrimination between the true granite and its recomposed equivalent are numerous but commonly difficult to apply. True granite may exhibit a faint gneissic foliation, which is lost upon complete disintegration and the slightest reworking. True granite is also cut by aplites and other complementary dikes. The recomposed granite, upon extended search of the outcrop, usually will contain a few granite fragments or pebbles and some faint bedding. Under the microscope the recomposed granite exhibits an unusual range of sizes of grain. This characteristic of recomposed granite is in contrast to the even-grained nature of granite or the porphyritic textures of some intrusives. The recomposed rock has a greater percentage of quartz than is normal for granite. A slight rounding of the feldspars (not to be mistaken for resorbed phenocrysts) is also probable. Well cuttings offer fewer criteria, though the slight rounding and the abundance of quartz, characteristic of sediments, are probably the most useful.

The thicker and better-known deposits of arkose include the Fountain

PLATE 17

ORTHOQUARTZITES II

A: Whitehorse sandstone, Permian, Okla., crossed nicols, ×40.

Calcareous orthoquartzite composed of well-rounded quartz together with a little feldspar set in a carbonate matrix. Quartz shows some etching by the carbonate cement.

B: Dakota formation, Upper Cretaceous, Lincoln, Kansas, crossed nicols, ×42.

A calcareous orthoquartzite showing "luster mottling" in hand specimen, composed of rounded quartz grains markedly etched and corroded by the carbonate cement which binds them together. The cement is coarsely crystalline and single crystals enclose many detrital quartz grains.

C: Concretion from Dakota sandstone, Upper Cretaceous, Ellsworth County, Kansas, ordinary light, ×42.

A "spotted" sandstone, each spot of which is a small area cemented by limonite (black) derived by oxidation of siderite cement. Some unaltered siderite is still present in center of one of the limonite-cemented areas.

D: Barite-cemented sandstone, basal Cretaceous sand (Kiowa or lower), McPherson County, Kansas, crossed nicols, ×42.

Barite cement occurs in large optically continuous patches. Note cleavage in barite cement.

E: Opal-cemented sandstone, Ogallala "quartzite," Pliocene, Kansas, ordinary light, ×16.

A coarse sandstone composed of quartz together with a little feldspar cemented by opal.

F: Lower Greensand, Foringdon, Berkshire, England, ordinary light, ×15.

Fossiliferous orthoquartzite composed chiefly of quartz cemented by carbonate. Two bryozoan (?) colonies present in field of view.

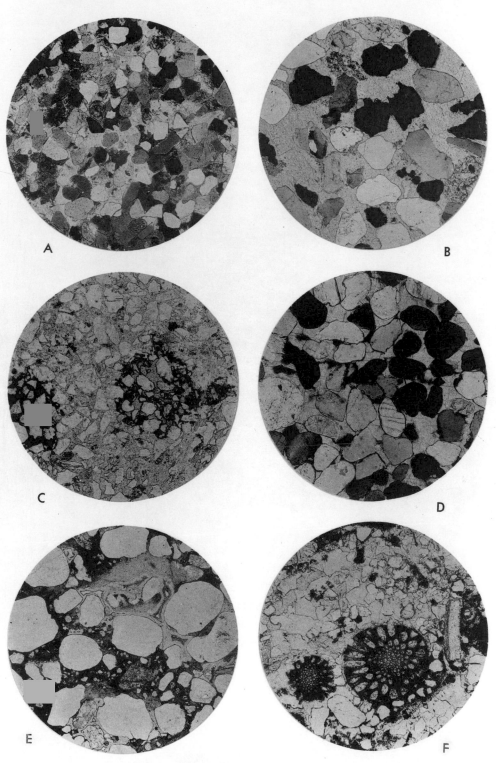

A

B

C

D

E

F

A

B

C

D

E

F

PLATE 18

GRAYWACKES

A: Manitou graywacke, Archean, Manitou Lake, Ont., Can. Crossed nicols, ×15.

Clear quartz (57 per cent), plagioclase feldspar (twinned and with sericite inclusions, 30 per cent), and chert and other rock fragments (fine-grained aggregates, 10 per cent) in matrix of which about two-thirds is chlorite and sericite. Ratio of grains to matrix is fifty-three to forty-seven. A feldspathic graywacke.

B: Harz graywacke, Harz Mountains, Germany. Crossed nicols, ×14.

The "type" graywacke consisting of quartz (clear), feldspar (twinned and untwinned), and rock particles (fine-grained aggregates) in about equal proportions set in a matrix consisting of an aggregate of chlorite and sericite particles.

C: Sandstone (graywacke) dike cutting Espanola (Huronian) formation, near Espanola, Ont., Canada. Crossed nicols, ×14.

Consists of quartz, feldspar, and rock fragments set in chlorite-sericite paste. See Pl. 5.

D: Silurian graywacke, near Balashiels, Scotland. Crossed nicols, ×42.

Quartz (clear), feldspar, and mica. Note subparallel arrangement of mica flakes. Not apparent in photomicrograph are shreds of chlorite and chloritized biotite, also in parallel arrangement.

E: Devonian graywacke, Ladock, Cornwall, England, ordinary light, ×44.

Principally quartz (65 per cent); subordinately feldspar (25 per cent), and mica (5 per cent), together with chloritized and sericitized rock fragments (5 per cent) in fine paste of chlorite and sericite.

F: Franciscan (Jurassic ?) graywacke, near Garberville, Calif. Crossed nicols, ×16.

Chiefly quartz (clear) and feldspar (twinned and clouded), and a few rock fragments in fine-grained chloritic and sericitic matrix.

arkose (Carboniferous) of Colorado and Wyoming (Knight, 1929), the New Haven, Portland and other arkoses of the Newark Series (Triassic) in Connecticut and other eastern states (Krynine, 1950), and many of the sandstones of Keweenawan age in the Lake Superior region (Irving, 1883). Also famous among arkoses are the *sparagmites* of Norway and Sweden (Barth, 1938; Hadding, 1929) and the presumed equivalent, the Torridonian, of Scotland (Kennedy, 1951). Much of the "Old Red Sandstone" (Devonian) of Great Britain is also arkose.

Origin and Geologic Significance

The problem of the arkoses is twofold. The first question is the significance of the feldspar; the second is the significance of arkose as distinct from and unlike other highly feldspathic sediments, such as the feldspathic graywackes.

The feldspar problem has been reviewed at some length elsewhere in this volume (pp. 126, 639). In summary, feldspar is not a normal component of sands; it is virtually absent in mature sands. The arkoses and other immature feldspathic sands owe their feldspar content to interruption or retardation of the weathering processes in the source region. The escape of feldspar from the area of provenance is promoted by a rigorous climate—either extreme cold or extreme aridity—or by exceptionally high relief. The low temperature and the absence of water inhibit chemical decomposition of the feldspar or prevent the formation of an effective plant cover, the absence of which leads to accelerated erosion. Accelerated erosion, whether the result of absence of vegetation or of high relief, leads to interruption of the weathering processes and promotes the escape of feldspar. High relief alone, and consequent rapid erosion—especially in the deeply incised canyons—will produce feldspathic sands even under a warm and humid climate. As shown by Barton (1916), Reed (1928), and Krynine (1935) many ancient arkoses and some present-day arkosic sands have formed under such climatic conditions. It seems probable, therefore, that arkose does not necessarily signify, as commonly supposed, a climatic extreme; it may denote instead only high relief and vigorous erosion of granitic and other feldspathic rocks.

More controversial is the significance of arkose, a sandstone type which should be distinguished from the feldspathic graywackes.[19] The latter, though containing much feldspar, were formed under quite different conditions. Some graywackes, of course, are feldspar-poor and hence of a different provenance. Others, however, are feldspar-rich (feldspathic or high-rank

---

[19] Much confusion has been engendered by lack of agreement on the definition or petrologic differences between arkose and graywacke and were agreement reached on the defining parameters no doubt most of the conflict on the significance of these rocks would be resolved.

graywacke) and must therefore be in considerable part derived from granitic and other feldspar-bearing source rocks. Krynine (1948) related arkoses "to the stage of maximum deformation of the diastrophic cycle (orogenic stage)" and believed they were "formed either during or immediately after that stage." He believed they were generally of continental origin, and therefore red, and were commonly associated with large-scale block faulting. On the other hand, the graywackes, according to Krynine, were formed earlier in the geosynclinal cycle and were related to moderate deformation and normally deposited under reducing conditions (hence their dark color).

Gilbert (Williams, Turner, and Gilbert, 1954) has taken issue with the concept that arkose and graywacke are indicative of contrasting tectonic environments. According to Gilbert these two rock types cannot be strictly compared nor distinctly contrasted, as they are defined according to different criteria. Graywacke, according to Gilbert, is basically a textural type of rock and may have many compositions and hence may be derived from any source. Arkose, on the other hand, has a particular composition and a particular source but may have any texture. As thus defined it is indeed difficult to ascribe arkose to a particular depositional environment.

Folk (1954), on the other hand, has attempted to distinguish between graywacke and arkose solely on their mineralogy and recognizes no textural differences. Hence, according to him, arkose is of igneous (granitic!) provenance, whereas graywacke is of metamorphic derivation (both low- and high-rank metamorphic source rocks).[20]

The author agrees with Gilbert that texture is a distinctive attribute of graywackes (Pettijohn, 1950)—in fact it may be the only distinctive attribute of these rocks. He would, however, place a textural restriction on the term arkose. Arkose must be moderately well sorted; it must have less than 15 per cent interstitial detritus (p. 291). For those rocks which Gilbert calls *arkosic wacke*, the author would reserve the term *feldspathic graywacke* (Krynine's high-rank graywacke); rocks of similar composition but texturally more mature would be arkose proper. As thus defined, graywackes and arkoses are indicative of differing physical environments. The graywackes are the products of deposition from media incapable of effective separation of clay, silt, and sand; arkoses are the products of fluids which deposit relatively clean sands (both, of course, are mineralogically immature). The former are most characteristically the products of deposition from submarine turbidity flows; the latter are most characteristically the product of deposition of fluvial and near-shore currents of normal character. Graywackes are therefore generally

[20] Folk in effect is reviving the concept that arkose and graywacke differ only in their provenance—earlier expressed in the notion that arkose was derived from a granite, whereas graywacke was the basic equivalent of an arkose (i.e., derived from a basic igneous rock). Folk substitutes the metamorphic suite for the basic igneous rock.

deep-water deposits accumulated in a reducing environment; arkoses are continental or neritic deposits formed in a turbulent oxidizing environment. Krynine is probably therefore essentially correct in his view that graywackes are geosynclinal sediments, whereas arkoses are largely postorogenic terrestrial accumulations. No doubt there are exceptions to these concepts but the finding of an exception does not invalidate the general theory. One swallow does not make a summer.

As pointed out elsewhere the influence of provenance is recognized by dividing graywackes into low-rank and high-rank or lithic and feldspathic graywackes, respectively. An analogous distinction between arkoses proper and sediments deposited under similar conditions but of differing provenance is made by the use of the terms arkosic sandstones (arkose and subarkose) and lithic sandstone (subgraywacke and protoquartzite).

REFERENCES CITED AND BIBLIOGRAPHY

Allen, V. T. (1936), Terminology of the fine-grained mechanical sediments, *Rept. Comm. Sedimentation, 1935–1936*, Nat. Research Council, pp. 18–47.

Barth, T. F. W. (1938), Progressive metamorphism of sparagmite rocks of southern Norway, *Norsk Geol. Tidsskr.*, vol. 18, pp. 54–65.

Barton, D. C. (1916), The geological significance and genetic classification of arkose deposits, *J. Geol.*, vol. 24, pp. 417–449.

Brongniart, A. (1826), De l'arkose, caractères minéralogiques et histoire géognostique de cettes roches, *Ann. sci. nat.*, vol. 8, pp. 113–163.

Davis, E. F. (1918), The Franciscan sandstone, *Univ. Calif. Publ., Bull. Dept. Geol.*, vol. 11, pp. 6–16.

Edwards, A. B. (1943), Jurassic arkose in southern Victoria, *Proc. Roy. Soc. Victoria*, vol. 55, pp. 195–228.

Folk, R. W. (1954), The distinction between grain size and mineral composition in sedimentary rock nomenclature, *J. Geol.*, vol. 62, pp. 344–359.

Hadding, Assar (1929), The pre-Quaternary sedimentary rocks of Sweden III. The Paleozoic and Mesozoic sandstones of Sweden, *Lunds Univ. Arsskr.*, N.F., Avd. 2, Bd. 25, Nr. 3.

Irving, R. D. (1883), The copper-bearing rocks of Lake Superior, *U.S. Geol. Survey Mono.* 5, pp. 127–133.

Kennedy, W. Q. (1951), Sedimentary differentiation as a factor in Moine-Torridonian correlation, *Geol. Mag.*, vol. 88, p. 258.

Knight, S. H. (1929), The Fountain and Casper formations of the Laramie basin; a study on genesis of sediments, *Univ. Wyoming Publ. Sci., Geol.*, vol. 1, no. 1.

Krynine, P. D. (1935), Arkose deposits in the humid tropics. A study of sedimentation in southern Mexico, *Am. J. Sci.*, ser. 5, vol. 29, pp. 353–363.

Krynine, P. D. (1940), Petrology and genesis of the Third Bradford Sand, *Penn. State Coll. Bull.* 29, p. 50.

Krynine, P. D. (1941), Paleogeographic and tectonic significance of arkoses (abstract), *Bull. Geol. Soc. Amer.*, vol. 52, pp. 1918–1919.

Krynine, P. D. (1948), The megascopic study and field classification of sedimentary rocks, *J. Geol.*, vol. 56, pp. 130–165.

Krynine, P. D. (1950), Petrology, stratigraphy and origin of the Triassic sedimentary rocks of Connecticut, *Connecticut State Geol. Nat. Hist. Survey, Bull.* 73.

Mackie, Wm. (1899), The felspars present in sedimentary rocks as indications of the conditions of contemporaneous climate, *Proc. Edinburgh Geol. Soc.*, vol. 7, pp. 443–468.

Mackie, Wm. (1905), Seventy chemical analyses of rocks (chiefly from the Moray area), *Proc. Edinburgh Geol. Soc.*, vol. 8, p. 58.

Merrill, G. (1891), *Stones for building and decoration*, New York, Wiley, p. 420.

Oriel, Steven S. (1949), Definitions of arkose, *Am. J. Sci.*, vol. 247, pp. 824–829.

Pettijohn, F. J. (1950), Turbidity currents and graywackes—A discussion, *J. Geol.*, vol. 58, footnote 3.

Pettijohn, F. J. (1954), Classification of sandstones, *J. Geol.*, vol. 62, pp. 360–365.

Reed, R. D. (1928), The occurrence of feldspar in California sandstones, *Bull. Am. Assoc. Petroleum Geol.*, vol. 12, pp. 1023–1024.

Taliaferro, N. L. (1943), Franciscan-Knoxville problem, *Bull. Am. Assoc. Petroleum. Geol.*, vol. 27, pp. 109–219.

Williams, H., Turner, F. J., and Gilbert, C. M. (1954), *Petrography*, San Francisco, Freeman.

TUFFS AND TUFFACEOUS SANDSTONES

Definitions and Terminology

The pyroclastic deposits, or pyroclasts, are those detrital materials which have been expelled aerially from a volcanic vent. Materials so ejected may fall upon the land or into a body of standing water. The land-laid deposit is prone to be eroded and redeposited in a water body. Either the original water-laid pyroclast or the reworked and redeposited materials may be mingled with ordinary sedimentary detritus so that the final deposit, with its introduced cement, may be a very complex rock.

Volcanic ejecta vary greatly in size and composition. These materials may be divided into agglomerates and breccias if the fragments (bombs and blocks) are over 32 millimeters in diameter; lapilli tuff if the particles (cinders) are four to 32 millimeters in diameter; tuff if composed of particles (ash) ¼ to 4 millimeters in size; and fine tuff if the detritus be smaller than ¼ millimeter (Wentworth and Williams, 1932).

The character of the material is also to be taken into account. The coarse pyroclasts (32 mm) are either agglomerates or breccias. Agglomerates are composed of bombs which are masses of magmatic material which solidified in flight. Breccias are composed of blocks or fragments of rock material that were solid at the time of ejection. If the fragments are the erupting lava, they are termed essential; if they are debris of earlier lavas and pyroclasts of the same cone, they are accessory; if the fragments are other rocks, they are termed accidental. The material of the deposits of finer grain size are vitric, crystal, or lithic according as they are glass, crystal debris, or rock particles.

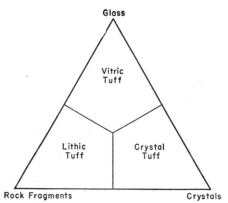

FIG. 79. Nomenclature and classification of the tuffs.

The tuffs (of coarse or fine ash) may be essential, accessory, or accidental, according to the source of the materials of which they are composed. They may also be classed according to the proportions of glass, crystal, or rock debris which they contain. In most tuffs, glass and crystal detritus are called vitric tuff, vitric-crystal tuff, crystal-vitric tuff, and crystal tuff according to the proportion of each component (Figs. 79, 80).

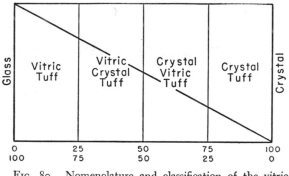

FIG. 80. Nomenclature and classification of the vitric and crystal tuff.

The hybrid rock, in which nonvolcanic debris is mixed with volcanic ejectamenta, may be called tuffaceous sand and sandstone, tuffaceous clay and shale and the like, if the sedimentary materials exceed the volcanic. If the converse be true, the mixtures may be called sandy tuff, clayey tuff, and so forth.[21] The alteration of some volcanic tuff or ash leads to the formation

[21] Hay (1952) would call the reworked tuffs volcanic sandstones, although he also applies the term tuffaceous sandstone if the volcanic debris is less than 50 per cent of the whole rock.

of special products, such as bentonite, which is a rock (plastic clay) composed of claylike material—usually montmorillonite, less commonly beidellite—which has been formed by the devitrification and attendant chemical alteration of glassy igneous material.

Textures and Composition

As Correns and Leinz (1933) have pointed out, many pyroclasts formed by a volcanic eruption are *porphyritic*. Relatively large crystals and rock fragments lie in a matrix of much finer debris (Pl. 21, D). This disparity in grain size also reflects a hiatus in composition. The larger fragments are chiefly crystal debris, whereas the finer materials are mainly glass (Table 57). If the glass is present as pumice fragments, however, it may be more

TABLE 57.   Composition of Tuff with "Porphyritic" Texture
(after Correns and Leinz, 1933)

Mechanical Composition		Mineralogical Composition (%)			
Size Classes (mm)	Per Cent	Mineral Component	Coarse Fraction	Fine Fraction	Total
> 0.5	21.8	Quartz	40	31	34
0.5 to 0.2	12.8	Sanidine	35	15	21
0.2 to 0.06	51.2	Plagioclase	....	3	2
< 0.06	14.2	Biotite and hornblende	3	3	3
		Glass	22	48	40

TABLE 58.   Size and Composition of Crater Lake Tuffs
(after Moore, 1934)

Size Classes (mm)	Whole Sample %	Pumice Fraction (78.9% of total)	Crystal Fraction (21.1% of total)
8 to 16	9.9	12.6	....
4 to 8	24.2	31.0	....
2 to 4	26.0	33.0	....
1 to 2	19.2	20.1	16.3
½ to 1	16.8	2.8	66.9
¼ to ½	3.6	0.2	15.8
⅛ to ¼	26.0	....	1.0

abundant in the coarser grades (Table 58). Owing to the low effective density of the porous pumice, the crystal grains tend to settle with the large pumice fragments. Some of the most poorly sorted tuffs and breccias closely resemble till, landslide, and mud-flow deposits. The deposits of *nuées ardentes* in particular are exceedingly poorly sorted. The size composition of such deposits has been shown to follow Rosin's law of crushing (Krumbein

PLATE 19

LITHIC ARENITES (SUBGRAYWACKE AND PROTOQUARTZITES)

A: Graywacke from Stanley shale (Carboniferous), near Mena, Arkansas, crossed nicols, ×40.

This figure and the two which follow are a series that show the relations between true graywacke, subgraywacke, and a "washed" graywacke or protoquartzite. **A** is essentially a graywacke composed dominantly of sliver-like, irregular quartz grains, together with a lesser amount of feldspar, and slaty or phyllitic rock fragments embedded in a chloritic and sericitic matrix. The latter forms a large and significant part of the rock shown.

B: Atoka formation (Carboniferous), near Mena, Arkansas, crossed nicols, ×48.

This subgraywacke differs from the graywacke of **A** in that the matrix is subordinate, the sorting is improved, and fewer phyllitic fragments are present.

C: Atoka formation (Carboniferous), near Mena, Arkansas, crossed nicols, ×46.

This rock is a protoquartzite formed by the elimination of fine interstitial detritus. Only quartz remains, which shows distinct rounding. Such a rock, if not thoroughly cemented, constitutes a potential oil sand. The graywacke to which it is related, such as shown in **A**, is plugged tight with a paste and is impermeable.

D: "Third Bradford Sand" (Devonian), Pennsylvania, crossed nicols, ×47.

The mineral composition is about 60 to 65 per cent quartz, one to two per cent feldspar, 30 per cent rock fragments (quartzite and low-rank metamorphic argillites), 5 to 10 per cent fine-grained sericitic and argillaceous "paste." The specimen illustrated has fewer rock fragments than the average and is essentially the same in character and origin as the "washed graywacke" of **C**.

E: Frio (Oligocene) subgraywacke, Seeligson field, Texas, crossed nicols, ×14.

Consists of about 30 per cent quartz, feldspar about 10 per cent, rock fragments about 35 per cent, calcite cement about 20 per cent and 5 or 6 per cent interstitial clay (Nanz, 1954).

F: Berea (Mississippian) protoquartzite, Ohio, crossed nicols.

Composed of detrital quartz and chert with silica cement.

334

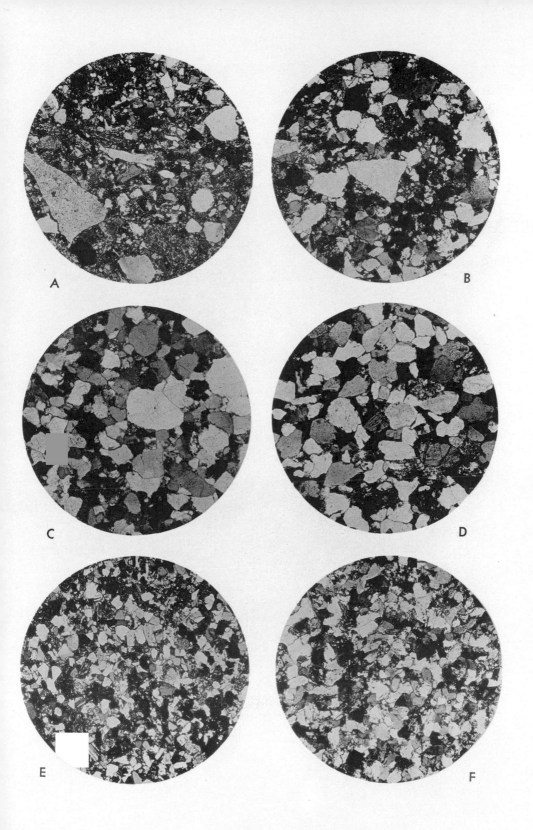

A

B

C

D

E

F

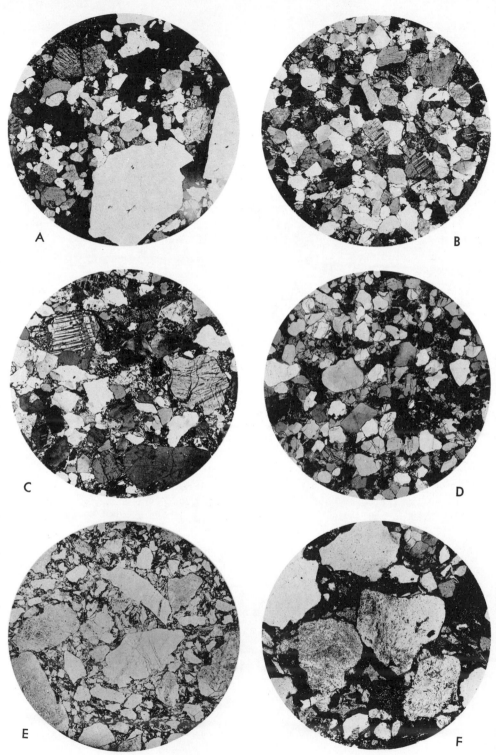

A

B

C

D

E

F

PLATE 20

ARKOSIC SANDSTONES

A: LaMotte sandstone, Cambrian, Jonca Creek, Mo. Crossed nicols, ×25.

A basal arkose, restricted to lower part of formation near contact with underlying Precambrian granite. Consists of large, poorly-rounded fragments of quartz (clear) and feldspar (clouded), together with small well-rounded quartz grains. Abnormal size-roundness relations (p. 64) indicate local source (a granite) for the coarse angular debris and a distant source for well-rounded smaller grains.

B: Torridonian, Precambrian, Assynt, Sutherland, Scotland. Crossed nicols, ×17.

Consists of moderately rounded quartz and feldspar. The latter varies from brilliantly fresh to markedly clouded. This is an unusual arkose in that it contains rounded grains and is cemented with secondary quartz.

C: Fountain arkose (Pennsylvanian), Colorado. Crossed nicols, ×14.

A coarse reddish sandstone consisting of angular to poorly rounded quartz (clear) and feldspar (clouded and showing multiple twinning).

D: Kome sandstone, Cretaceous, western Greenland. Crossed nicols, ×17.

A subarkose or feldspathic sandstone consisting chiefly of a quartz (85 to 90 per cent) with a lesser amount of feldspar (10 to 15 per cent) cemented by carbonate. Note shattering and fracturing of grains. Cement in places has eaten into and replaced the detrital grains, especially the feldspars.

E: Newark arkose, Triassic, Mt. Tom, Mass. Ordinary light, ×17.

Chiefly angular quartz (clear), and feldspar (clouded), together with a little mica in ferruginous and calcareous matrix.

F: Portland arkose, Newark series (Triassic), Conn. Ordinary light, ×15.

Consists of quartz (55 per cent), feldspar (36 per cent) and rock fragments (6 per cent) poorly cemented by calcite.

and Tisdel, 1940). Under the microscope the texture of these deposits resembles rather closely that of the graywackes and also certain tillites (see Pls. 15, 18, 21, D).

In composition the tuffs and tuffaceous sediments are marked by their constituents of volcanic origin, namely glass, crystals, and rock particles. The finest volcanic glass shows a peculiar structure and characteristic form (Pl. 21, A) owing to immense numbers of gas bubbles drawn out into capillary tubules. As a result, the glass fragments are elongated and longitudinally striated. Also present are the curved shards of crescentic and spicule-like form. The glass particles are isotropic—unless devitrified—and are colorless, except in the case of the basic glasses, which are pale yellow or brown. The glass particles may be charged with magnetite dust.

The crystals usually are broken euhedra of the common phenocrysts of lavas. Hence they commonly show marked zoning. They may be sheathed in an envelope of glass. It is said that the crystals commonly are oriented with their long axes vertical, roughly perpendicular to the bedding. As would be expected, zoned feldspars are common; notable also are the volcanic amphiboles and pyroxenes.

The rock fragments, less common than glass or crystal debris, are chiefly acid aphanitic igneous rocks, although basic tuffs contain andesitic and basaltic particles. Both the rock particles and the matrix of the tuff may contain an abundance of microlites.

Also characteristic of tuffs are pellets, small ovoid to subspherical bodies with concentric structure.

As might be expected, the tuffs have a chemical composition similar to that of the igneous rocks of the same family.

Alteration

The alteration of tuffs is promoted by their loose porous character, their fine state of division and large surface area, the unstable nature of glass, and to a lesser degree the metastable character of the crystal detritus. The feldspathic tuffs readily alter to clay. One of the earliest changes in tuffs is the deposition in them of hydrated silica-opal and chalcedony. Complete silicification leads to conversion of the friable, porous tuff to a dense flinty rock which closely resembles rhyolite, novaculite, jasper, and so forth. Tuffs may be mistaken for such rocks in the field. In thin section, however, the vitroclastic character may remain and this feature together with the composition and form of the associated crystals and their chemical composition will serve to prove their pyroclastic origin. Other tuffs are indurated thoroughly by carbonate.

Devitrification commonly accompanies the alteration. The result is that between crossed nicols the whole rock appears to be composed of a mosaic of feebly polarizing particles (Pl. 21, B). Careful study in ordinary light may disclose shards, threads, cusps, vesicles, and the like, of the original glass. The devitrification produces a montmorillonite clay.

Metamorphism superimposed on other alterations may completely obscure the original nature of the deposit.

Association and Distribution

Tuffs grade imperceptibly into tuffaceous sandstones which, in turn, may grade into sandstones that are free of any volcanic admixtures. Tuffs commonly, though not always, are associated with contemporaneous flows.

The close association of graywacke and greenstone in certain geosynclinal belts has led some workers to conclude that graywackes were in large part waterlaid basic tuff. Tyrrell (1933) says that "graywackes may grade into tuffs by increase in the amount of igneous rock fragments, or into sandstone by diminution and disappearance of this material." He believed that submarine eruptions contributed large amounts of greenstone debris to the sea, which mingled with sand and mud and ". . . became sorted with regard to grain size, and settled so as to form graded sediments which have the composition of graywacke." The presence in some graywackes of particles of volcanic rock, especially of the greenstones and spilites, lends weight to this view. The mineral composition of some Papuan graywackes strongly resembles that of tuffs, and these rocks may be tuffaceous graywackes (Table 50).

The recognition of fragmental volcanic materials in fresh surficial deposits is relatively easy. These deposits, however, are readily altered and if they have been buried under later sediments and metamorphosed, the task of identifying them becomes one of the most difficult encountered by the petrographer. All field, petrographic, and chemical data available may not lead to conclusive results. The difficulty of identification is increased by the mingling of the volcanic materials with normal sedimentary detritus. Thus every degree of transition into ordinary sandstones and shales is to be expected. A most helpful elementary treatment of the microscopical characteristics of these deposits is that of Pirsson (1915).

Origin

Tuffs and related rocks are by definition products of explosive volcanic origin. But they vary widely in textures and structures depending on the mode of transport and site of deposition. Some are the products of a nueé ardente, the aerial counterpart of a turbidity flow; others are the normal air-borne fall-out products. These two types differ in their textures and structures as do the turbidity-current-deposited graywackes and tilloids and the normal-current-deposited arenites (Table 60). Deposition or redeposition in lakes and streams may also modify the character of the tuffs. Correns and Leinz (1933) have discussed the relations between the textures and structures of these deposits and their mode of transport and place of deposit. Their conclusions are summarized in Table 59.

TABLE 59. Classification, Textures, and Structures of the Pyroclastic Arenites
(after Correns and Leinz, 1933)

Type	I. Transport	I. Place of Deposit	II. Transport	II. Place of Deposit	Texture	Structure
A 1	Volcanic explosions	Terrestrial	....	....	Porphyritic	Without bedding
A 2		Lacustrine	....	....		Bedded with parallel structure
B 1		Terrestrial	Fluvial	Lacustrine	Uniform grained	
B 2			By the surf	Littoral		Without bedding

TABLE 60. Comparison of Pyroclasts and Hydroclasts and Mode of Transport
(after Pettijohn, 1950)

Composition	Water and Sediment (hydrosol)		Gases and Volcanic Ejectamenta (aerosol)	
	Concentrated	Dilute	Concentrated	Dilute
Type	Mudflows and turbidity currents	Normal water currents	Nueés ardentes	Normal air currents
Product	Tilloids and graywackes	Orthoarenites and con- glomerates	"Ignimbrites" or welded tuffs	Bedded tuffs and ash

REFERENCES CITED AND BIBLIOGRAPHY

Blyth, F. H. (1940), The nomenclature of clastic deposits, Volconologique Bull. 6, ser. 2, pp. 145–156.

Correns, C. W., and Leinz, Viktor (1933), Tuffige Sedimente des Tobasees (Nordsumatra) als Beispiele für die sediment-petrographische Bedeutung von Struktur und Textur, Centr. Mineral., Geol., 1933, Ab. 4, pp. 382–390.

Hay, Richard, L. (1952), The terminology of fine-grained detrital volcanic rocks, J. Sediment. Petrol., vol. 22, pp. 119–120.

Krumbein, W. C., and Tisdel, F. W. (1940), Size distributions of source rocks of sediments, Am. J. Sci., vol. 238, pp. 296–305.

Moore, B. N. (1934), Deposits of possible nueé ardente origin in the Crater Lake region, Oregon, J. Geol., vol. 42, pp. 358–375.

Pettijohn, F. J. (1950), Turbidity currents and graywackes—A discussion, J. Geol., vol. 58, pp. 169–171.

Pirsson, L. V. (1915), The microscopical characters of volcanic tuffs—a study for students, Am. J. Sci., ser. 4, vol. 40, p. 191–211.

Ross, C. S. (1928), Altered volcanic materials and their recognition, Bull. Am. Assoc. Petroleum Geol., vol. 12, pp. 143–164.

Ross, C. R., Miser, H. D., and Stephenson, L. W. (1929), Water-laid volcanic rocks of early Upper Cretaceous age in southwestern Arkansas, southeastern Oklahoma, and northeastern Texas, U.S. Geol. Survey, Prof. Paper 154-F, pp. 175–202.

Tyrrell, G. W. (1933), Greenstones and greywackes, C. R. réunion internationale pour l'étude du Précambrian, pp. 24–26.

Waters, A. C., and Granger, H. C. (1953), Volcanic debris in uraniferous sandstones, etc., U.S. Geol. Survey, Circular 224.

Wentworth, C. K., and Williams, H. (1932), The classification and terminology of the pyroclastic rocks, Rept. Comm. Sed., Nat. Research Council, Bull. No. 89, pp. 19–53.

8

Shales, Argillites, and Siltstones

INTRODUCTION

OF the common sediments, shales are the most abundant. They form about half of the geologic column, being estimated at 44 per cent by Schuchert (1931), 46 per cent by Leith and Mead (1915), and 56 per cent by Kuenen (1941). On the basis of certain geochemical considerations (see p. 10) the shales are calculated to constitute 70 (Holmes, 1937) to 80 (Clarke, 1924) per cent of all the sediment produced throughout geologic time.

Despite their abundance they are not so well exposed as are the more resistant limestones and sandstones. And because of their fine grain they are not so well known as the other sedimentary materials. Their fine grain makes thin-section study difficult. Many of the constituents are not readily resolved under the microscope, so that they cannot be identified by the usual optical means. Recourse must be had to analyses of gross chemical composition or to special techniques of identification such as x-ray and differential thermal analyses. For these reasons the description, classification, and interpretation of the shales and argillites are inadequate and incomplete at present writing.

DEFINITIONS AND TERMINOLOGY

A *clay* had been defined as a natural plastic earth (though some clays are nonplastic), composed of hydrous aluminum silicates (the "clay minerals"), and of fine grain (a clay is a sediment with grains less than 0.002 or 1/256 mm in diameter). The definition based on grain size is least satisfactory because most commercial clays are not clays by this definition. The definition based on mineral composition errs in that the clay minerals form only a small part of the total material (one-third or less). Twenhofel (1937) says that the small particles should be dominantly clay minerals and that clay should have an excess of particles (over 50 per cent) of clay size. The clay minerals therefore must form at least one-fourth of the total.

Claystone is indurated clay. If possessed of bedding cleavage or fissility approximately parallel to the bedding, claystone is also a shale. However, some writers (Flawn, 1953; Shrock, 1948) would use the term claystone for a rock less indurated than a shale.

Shale is a laminated or fissile claystone or siltstone. This term is generally restricted to buried deposits. To those claystones which are neither fissile nor laminated but are blocky or massive, the term *mudstone* may be applied.

The terms claystone and mudstone have also been defined in a more restricted manner by Ingram (1953), who defined claystone as a massive rock in which clay predominates over silt (whereas siltstone is used for massive rocks in which silt exceeds clay). Ingram applied the term mudstone to materials of massive character in which the proportions of clay and silt are not known or specified. The terms *clay shale, silt shale,* and *mud shale* were proposed for the correlative *fissile* rocks. As pointed out below, most shales contain more silt than clay, so that in effect Ingram would call a rock shale if it were fissile and siltstone if massive.

Twenhofel would extend, rather than restrict, the term mudstone and would define it to include clay, silt, siltstone, claystone, shale, and argillite.[1] This term is used where the precise nature of a sample is in doubt or to characterize the whole family, of which the above-mentioned types are members. Ingram would so apply the term *mudrock*, and like most writers would reserve the term *mudstone* for a rock of clay or silt size, grade, and composition if the rock were without laminations or fissility.[2]

Silt is the material between 1/16 and 1/256 millimeter in diameter or a sediment in which 50 per cent of the particles fall in this range. *Siltstone* is indurated silt. If possessed of bedding plane fissility the rock might be termed silty shale or shaly siltstone. Though many, if not most shales, contain 50 or more per cent silt they are not siltstones. Siltstones, unlike shales,

[1] The term *mud* has also been defined as a silt-clay mixture (Shepard, 1954; Folk, 1954). Mudstone therefore is a better term than claystone for the shale or argillite group or clan.

[2] Shrock (1948) would use the term *mudstone* for partly indurated muds which slake upon wetting and the term *claystone* for "very fine-grained, somewhat unctuous, conchoidally fracturing sedimentary rocks composed largely of clay material." It is clear that some agreement on the nomenclature of the argillaceous sediments would be desirable. Clark's (1954) useful summary of the problems of shale nomenclature has appeared since this chapter was written.

are commonly bonded by chemical cements, are cross-bedded on a small scale, show evidence of intrastratal flowage and injection, and so forth.

The term *argillite* is also of uncertain meaning. Twenhofel applies the term to a rock derived from a siltstone or shale that has undergone a somewhat higher degree of induration than is usually present in those rocks. It is thus intermediate in character between a shale and a slate. Grout (1932) uses the term *argillite* for a clay or shale hardened by recrystallization, and applies the term *slate* to a similar rock if it possesses a secondary cleavage. Flawn (1953) would use the term in much the same sense as defined by Twenhofel and would use the term *meta-argillite* for the more completely recrystallized rocks. Both terms, however, would be restricted to rocks without cleavage or parting.

For the relations between the several types of argillaceous materials see Fig. 81.

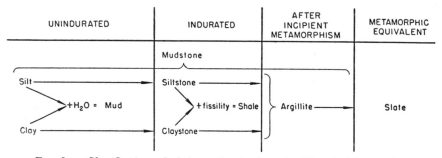

Fɪɢ. 81.   Classification of shales and related rocks (Twenhofel, 1937).

COMPOSITION OF SHALES AND ARGILLITES

Chemical Composition

The chemical analysis remains the chief source of information about the composition of the shales.

Silica is the dominant constituent of all clays and shales. It is present as a part of the clay mineral complex, as undecomposed detrital silicates, and as free silica both detrital and biochemically precipitated silica (radiolaria, diatoms, spicules). Alumina is an essential constituent of the clay mineral complex as well as a component of unweathered detrital silicates—primarily the feldspars. Exceptionally high alumina content suggests free aluminum hydrate (diaspore) or bauxitic materials. The iron of clays and shales is present as an oxide pigment, as a part of the chloritic matter present, and exceptionally as pyrite or marcasite, siderite, or iron silicate. The state of oxidation of the iron greatly affects the color of the shale. Magnesia occurs in the chlorite complex, or as a component of dolomite. Lime in the shales occurs chiefly as the carbonate, although in some shales it is present in larger amounts than necessary to form carbonates, and therefore must be contained in unweathered detrital silicates. Lime is also present in the form of gypsum in some shales. The alkalies occur in unweathered detrital silicates (especially feldspar) or, as in the case of potash, are adsorbed to the clay mineral constituent or form a part of the authigenic derivatives (clay mica) of such materials. Minor constituents are titania (as rutile), manganese, phosphorus, and organic matter.

The interpretation of chemical analyses of shales is fraught with considerable difficulty, for, as pointed out elsewhere (p. 100), the analysis is dependent upon grain size, the maturity of the sediment, and the restoration by chemical or biochemical processes of many of the constituents removed during the provenance of the sediment.

The effect of grain size has been discussed at some length elsewhere (p. 101). It is well illustrated by comparison of the analysis of the fine winter clay of a glacial varve with the analysis of the silty summer fraction of the same varve (Table 62). Here the maturity and postdepositional histories of the materials are identical, so that the composition differences are due wholly to differences in grain size. As can be seen from Table 62, the coarser fraction is richer in silica, whereas the finer materials are richer in alumina, iron, potash, and water. These differences reflect, no doubt, the enrichment of the silt in detrital quartz and the finer fraction in the clay minerals—potash-bearing hydrous aluminum silicates and iron-rich magnesium-bearing chlorites.

The silica/alumina ratio is therefore generally a good index of the grain size—the higher the silica content (and the lower the alumina) the coarser the grain size.

The composition of the average shale (Table 61, Col. A) differs materially in character from a typical residual clay. The differences are in part due to grain size. Inspection of Grout's analyses of the several size fractions present in shales (Table 19, p. 101) would suggest that the average shale is about two parts silt and one part clay. Such a mixture would have a composition approximating that of the average shale. Close comparison of the analyses of the average shale and those of residual clays (Table 69) show differences other than those produced by the addition of silt. The residual clays are extremely low in alkalies and alkaline earths, whereas the average shale contains a notable content of these elements. In other words, the average shale is not just a transported residual clay. Not only is it a mixture of clay and silt, but in the clay fraction some of the constituents removed by weathering have been partially restored during the sedimentation process. Potash, in particular, and to some extent magnesium also, are apparently taken up by the clay mineral complex and built into authigenic sericites and

TABLE 61. Chemical Composition of Average Shale, Average Mississippi Delta
Sediment, and Related Materials
(per cent)

Constituent	A	B	C	D	E	F
SiO₂	58.10	55.43	60.15	60.64	56.30	69.96
TiO₂	0.65	0.46	0.76	0.73	0.77	0.59
Al₂O₃	15.40	13.84	16.45	17.32	17.24	10.52
Fe₂O₃	4.02	4.00	4.04	2.25	3.83⎱	3.47
FeO	2.45	1.74	2.90	3.66	5.09⎰	
MnO	....	T	T	....	0.10	0.06
MgO	2.44	2.67	2.32	2.60	2.54	1.41
CaO	3.11	5.96	1.41	1.54	1.00	2.17
Na₂O	1.30	1.80	1.01	1.19	1.23	1.51
K₂O	3.24	2.67	3.60	3.69	3.79	2.30
H₂O+⎱	5.00	⎧3.45	3.82	3.51	3.31	1.96
H₂O−⎰		⎨2.11	0.89	0.62	0.38	3.78
P₂O₅	0.17	0.20	0.15	....	0.14	0.18
CO₂	2.63	4.62	1.46	1.47	0.84	1.40
SO₃	0.64	0.78	0.58	....	0.28	0.03
Cl	....	....	....	....	....	0.30
Organic	0.80[a]	0.69[a]	0.88[a]	....	1.18[a]	0.66
Misc.	....	0.06[b]	0.04[b]	0.38[c]	1.98[c]	0.32
Total	99.95	100.48	100.46	99.60	100.00	100.62

A. Average shale (Clarke, 1924, p. 24) (based on cols. B and C).
B. Composite sample of 27 Mesozoic and Cenozoic shales, H. N. Stokes, analyst (Clarke, 1924, p. 552).
C. Composite sample of 51 Paleozoic shales, H. N. Stokes, analyst (Clarke, 1924, p. 552).
D. Unweighted average of 36 analyses of slate (29 Paleozoic, 1 Mesozoic, 6 early Paleozoic or Precambrian) (Eckel, 1904).
E. Unweighted average of 33 analyses of Precambrian slates (Nanz, 1953).
F. Composite analysis of 235 samples of Mississippi delta, Geo. Steiger, analyst (Clarke, 1924, p. 509).
[a] Carbon.
[b] BaO.
[c] FeS₂.

chlorites. The lime is not normally so added but may be fixed by biochemical action. Sodium alone is not restored. Hence the alumina-soda ratio is perhaps the best index of maturity.

The chemical composition of a shale therefore is dependent on grain size, maturity, and selective chemical or biochemical restoration of certain elements. To untangle the effects of each on the gross composition is a rather difficult task.

The chemical composition of some shales is notably aberrant.[3] Nonsilty shales with abnormally high silica (the siliceous shales) are likely to be diatom-rich or to contain silica from volcanic ash. Those notably low in silica and abnormally high in alumina are either exceptionally fine-grained or are enriched in residual materials—i.e., are bauxitic. Exceptionally iron-rich shales or slates probably contain iron sulfide (pyrite) if black or are

[3] The recognition of "abnormal" or "aberrant" composition is not easy. Some knowledge of what is normal and of the expected range of composition for any constituent is required. Statistical studies of chemical composition are few and until such studies are commonplace one must rely on experience and judgment gained from the study of many chemical analyses.

siderite-rich or contain appreciable quantities of iron silicate. The iron silicate-bearing shales grade into chamositic and related mudstones. The so-called "ferruginous shales" are simply red shales, and they may not contain any abnormal quantity of iron (see p. 347); they are characterized by the ferric rather than ferrous compounds of iron. Shales abnormally high in lime and magnesia are most likely calcareous and contain calcite or dolomite. A high content of CO_2 will substantiate such a conclusion. If the lime exceeds that required by the CO_2 some unweathered silicates are probably present. Exceptionally, shales may be gypsiferous, in which case the high lime content is associated with a high sulfate content.

Potash nearly always exceeds soda in shales and slates. The few shales in which soda exceeds potash must be those which contain the products of abrasive action rather than the clay minerals. Some glacial clays and silts are thus characterized (Table 62). Shales which have important volcanic admixtures and some shales associated with graywackes have a higher than normal soda content; the soda may exceed potash.

The potash content of the average shale is very nearly the same as that of the average igneous rock. Yet weathering of the latter tends to form potash-poor residual clays. Apparently the potassium removed by weathering is somewhat restored to the shales. Potassium in shales may be present as

TABLE 62.   Chemical Composition of Late-Glacial Varved Sediments and Pellodites (per cent)

Constituent	A	B	C	D	E
SiO_2	59.20	50.33	52.00	62.74	66.87
TiO_2	1.20	1.13	....	....	0.47
Al_2O_3	16.14	19.17	16.11	16.94	15.36
Fe_2O_3	4.36	6.50}	4.69	{5.07	2.81
FeO	3.24	2.52}	4.69	{1.59	1.89
MnO	0.09	0.13	....	....	0.05
MgO	3.14	3.77	4.10	3.05	2.40
CaO	2.52	1.43	8.26	1.39	0.34
Na_2O	3.82	1.78	2.76}	6.07	{1.21
K_2O	1.97	4.03	1.74}	6.07	{6.60
P_2O_5	0.17	0.14	....	....	0.23
CO_2	....	....	....[a]	....	0.28
H_2O+	1.16	4.87	....	3.20[b]	1.35
H_2O-	1.15	3.74	9.64[b]	0.36	none
SO_3	....	....	0.09	....	....
C	1.94	0.41	....	....	0.04
Total	100.10	99.95	99.39	100.41	99.93

A. Summer silt, late-glacial varved sediment, Leppakosi, Finland. L. Lokka, analyst (Eskola, 1932).
B. Winter clay, same as A.
C. Varved clay, north end Lake Timiskaming (Miller, 1905, p. 27).
D. Argillite, Cobalt series (Precambrian), Cobalt District, Ontario (Miller, 1905, p. 42).
E. Argillite, Fern Creek formation (Precambrian), Dickinson County, Michigan. B. Bruun, analyst.
 [a] Included in ignition loss.
 [b] Loss on ignition.

(1) unweathered detrital silicates, (2) be adsorbed by the clay minerals or be an essential constituent of the authigenic derivatives thereof, (3) or be contained in glauconite, or (4) as potash-rich organic matter (marine plant debris). Potassium apparently is selectively removed from seawater by the clays as it is present in river waters with sodium in the ratio of 1 to 4, whereas in sea water the ratio is 1 to 30 (Clarke, 1924, p. 140). Conway (1945) has attributed the potassium restoration wholly to glauconitization, a process for which he believed organic matter was necessary. Hutchinson (1944) has taken exception to this view and has presented cogent evidence against it.

Highly carbonaceous shales are those which have accumulated slowly under anaerobic conditions. Such shales will be rich also in sulfide sulfur. Some are also phosphate-rich.

As shown by Eckel (1904), Nanz (1953) and others, metamorphism of shales and conversion to slate (or even phyllite) does not appreciably change the gross chemical composition (compare cols. C and D, Table 61). Normally the only appreciable changes are the reduction of the iron (by organic matter) and loss of hygroscopic water. Presumably some of the organic matter is lost as CO_2 as a result of reduction of the ferric iron.

Color

More emphasis is placed on the color of shales than on most sedimentary rocks. Field geologists, in particular, are likely to describe a shale or slate in terms of its color such as black shale, red slate, etc.

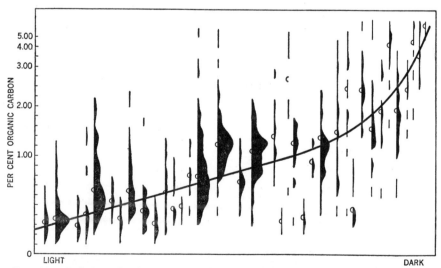

FIG. 82.   Relation of color to carbon content of sediments (after Trask and Patnode, 1936).

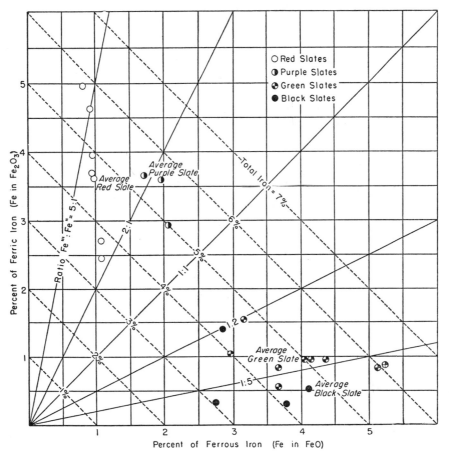

FIG. 83.   Relation of ferrous ferric iron content to color of slates. Note that the red slates contain no more *total* iron than the black slates (redrawn from Tomlinson, 1916).

The color of shales and slates generally results from a pigmentation of some kind. The darker the shale, the higher the content of organic matter (Trask and Patnode, 1936) (Fig. 82). The black shales, in particular, are rich in carbonaceous materials (Table 70). As shown by Tomlinson (1916) (see Fig. 83), the red slates contain no more iron than do those which are black, gray, or green. The color differences reflect only the state of oxidation of the iron (MacCarthy, 1926, Table 1). Red shales are so colored because of the presence of finely divided ferric oxide (hematite). In the green and black shales the iron is largely in the ferrous state. The siderite-bearing shales tend to be gray to bluish on wholly fresh surfaces, such as cores, but owing to the instability of siderite they become brown or buff in the outcrop even after a very brief period of exposure.

Mineral Composition

Although the chemical composition of clays and shales is readily determined by analysis, mineral composition is not so easily ascertained. Fineness of grain makes uncertain identification of the component minerals. Under the microscope only the larger grains (over 0.01 mm) can be identified with certainty. These prove to be the same as the grains found in the silts and finer sandstones. The residue is a paste which cannot be resolved. On the assumption that the finer fraction consists of the same minerals as the coarser portions, though in different proportions, it is possible to calculate the probable composition of the clay or shale from its chemical analysis. Such calculations show that the finer fraction is richer in the clay minerals, the clay micas, chlorite, and the hydroxides of iron. The coarser part, on the other hand, contains more quartz and feldspar (see Table 21, p. 113).

TABLE 63.　Calculated Mineral Composition of Average Shale

Constituent	Average Shale (Leith and Mead, 1915)		(Clarke, 1924)	
Quartz	32		22.3	
		32		22.3
Kaolinite and Clay Minerals	10		25.0[a]	
Sericite and Paragonite	18		....	
Chlorite and Serpentine	6		....	
		34		25.0
Limonite, Hematite, and Pyrite	5		5.6[b]	
Calcite and Dolomite	8		5.7	
Feldspars	18		30.0	
Titanite and Rutile	1		....	
Carbonaceous Matter	1		....	
Other Minerals	....		11.4	
		33		52.7

[a] Probably sericite in part. In that case the feldspar figure becomes lower.
[b] Limonite only.

The mineral composition of the average shale thus determined (Table 63) shows that it consists of about one-third quartz, one-third clay minerals (kaolin, sericite, chlorite), and one-third miscellaneous (carbonates, iron oxides, etc.). The high detrital quartz content of the average shale further substantiates the view that silt is the dominant constituent of most shales and supports Krynine's statement (Krynine, 1948, p. 154) that shales are in reality mechanical mixtures of approximately 50 per cent silt, 35 per cent "clay or fine mica fraction," and 15 per cent chemical or authigenic materials.

Because modal analyses of shales are very difficult to make, very few have ever been published. An exception is the study of the Perry Farm shale (Pennsylvanian?) of Missouri (Keller and Ting, 1950). Though a plastic shale, this rock contained 74 per cent by weight of fine sand and silt and but 14 per cent clay-sized materials. The balance was acid-soluble carbonate, etc. Excepting perhaps the studies of Millot (1949), the author knows of no other complete analysis of shales. Millot's work further supports the conclusion reached by chemical data that silt-sized material is a large and important constituent of most shales and that the clay mineral fraction rarely forms more than one-third of the whole rock.

Owing to fineness of grain, clays are particularly susceptible to authigenic change. Examples of such changes are the conversion of the clay minerals (especially montmorillonite) to the clay mica, braivisite, or illite. Apparently also the amorphous matter of the clay—such as the iron hydroxides, colloidal silica, and perhaps some hydrous aluminum silicates—react with magnesium-bearing solutions and are built up into chlorite. Such internal rearrangement probably is the main reason for the induration of shale. The chlorite is most conspicuous where crystalline reconstruction is most advanced, as in the slates and most graywackes. The chlorite of these rocks is intergrown intimately with sericite. The amorphous iron sulfide is recrystallized as scattered pyrite cubes or rosettes. Some of the other minor and diffuse components are collected into concretions and similar bodies.

TEXTURES AND STRUCTURES

Grain Size

The particle size distribution or "mechanical composition" of clays and shales has been extensively investigated. Size analyses of such materials, however, are subject to marked limitations. Owing to their fineness of grain, the particle size of clays is usually determined by methods based on differential settling velocities. These velocities are notably affected by the shape and specific gravity of the particles as well as their size. The analytical results, therefore, are misleading in that the size values computed are based on the premise that the particles are spheres of quartz (Krumbein and Pettijohn, 1938, p. 96). The analyzed sample, moreover, is fully dispersed prior to the initiation of the settling period. Such dispersal, achieved by physical or chemical agents, probably destroys the original size distribution or at least profoundly modifies the grading curve. Many clays, especially those which accumulate in marine waters, are in a state of partial or complete flocculation at the time of deposition. The grading curves, as determined by analysis, may be quite unlike those of the original sediment. A more serious limitation is encountered in the older shales, owing to the effect of diagenesis on the size distribution. Because of the fine state of division of the materials and the resulting large total surface of the grains, as well as the instability of some clay minerals, these materials are prone to diagenetic change. Such reorganization must alter greatly the size distribution. For the foregoing reasons, therefore, size analyses of clays and shales must be interpreted with great caution.

The most significant result of size analyses is the disclosure that most clays and shales—certainly the more common types found in the geologic column —contain a very large proportion of silt. The Perry Farm shale, cited above, contained 74 per cent fine sand and silt. A marine Pennsylvanian shale in Illinois (Krumbein, 1938) contained 68 per cent silt. These analyses appear to be typical. Shales therefore are about two parts silt to one part clay as the chemical analyses suggested. They are, in composition, not much different from the average material forming the Mississippi delta (Table 64).

TABLE 64.   Composite Mississippi Delta Sediment[a]
(after Russell and Russell, 1939)

Size Grade	Diameter (mm)	Per Cent	
Coarse Sand	1.0 to 0.5	Trace	
Medium Sand	0.5 to 0.25	Trace	
Fine Sand	0.25 to 0.125	6 ⎱	
Very Fine Sand	0.125 to 0.0625	23 ⎰	29
Silt	0.0625 to 0.312	30 ⎱	
	0.0312 to 0.0156	16 ⎱	
	0.0156 to 0.0078	7 ⎰	60
	0.0078 to 0.0039	7 ⎰	
Clay	Under 0.0039	11	
		100	

Many textural analyses of the finer clastics show a relation between the size of grain and the skewness of the size distribution. The silts and clays (muds), unlike the sands, tend to be notably skewed (see Table 65). Normally the fine fraction constitutes a long "tail" on the distribution curve. These observations have been described from the present-day bottom muds of Buzzard's Bay, Cape Cod Bay, Barataria Bay, and the Atlantic continental shelf. Not only are the finer sediments markedly skewed but they are more poorly sorted than the associated sands.

The reasons for the poorer sorting and skewed distributions are not fully understood. They may be related to the processes of transport and deposition (Inman, 1949) or they may be analytical, i.e., introduced by the dispersion procedure used. As noted by Rubey (1930), if the lack of sorting shown by the finer grades means that these sizes were coagulated and deposited as floccules at the time of deposition, then it might be possible to distinguish between such flocculated and nonflocculated clays by their sorting. In general the former would be marine and the latter would be fresh water.

TABLE 65.   Size Characteristics of Cogenetic Coarse and Fine Sediments
(after Hough and others)

Type	Location	Median Diam (mm)	Sorting Coef	Log Skewness
Sand	Cape Cod Bay	0.210	1.32	+0.008
	Barataria Bay	0.139	1.18	−0.040
	Continental Shelf	0.210	1.35	+0.020
Silt	Cape Cod Bay	0.0365	2.22	−0.236
	Barataria Bay	0.040	2.33	−0.390
	Continental Shelf	0.034	2.82	−0.340

A feature of some clays is pellet structure (Allen and Nichols, 1943; Grim and Allen, 1938). Pellets are small rounded aggregates of clay minerals and fine quartz scattered through a matrix of the same materials. The pellets may be separated from the matrix by a shell of organic material. In size the pellets are 0.1 to 0.3 millimeter in diameter and in a few cases several millimeters in length. The pellets have been ascribed to the action of water currents.

Fissility

Compaction with concomitant recrystallization is in part the cause of fissility which most shales and related rocks possess. In some degree, however, that property is due to parallel orientation of the micaceous constituents at the time of deposition. Under the microscope the tendency to parallelism can be readily seen. Many of the individual crystals do not lie exactly parallel to the bedding. In all sections cut normal to that structure most micaceous minerals will be approximately parallel to the bedding. Because such minerals have the slow ray vibrating parallel to their cleavage they show parallel extinction. Thin sections that are cut normal to the bedding therefore show an aggregate positive elongation and mass extinction very much as if the slide were cut from a single crystal.

In a few clays, however, the clay mineral crystals show a random orientation (Keller, 1946). The random orientation has been interpreted as the result of authigenic crystal growth in place.

TABLE 66.   Fissility Scales

(Alling, 1945)	(Ingram, 1953)	(McKee and Weir, 1953)
Massive	Massive	Massive
Platy-Flaggy		Blocky
Heavy-Bedded	Flaky	Slabby
Thin-Bedded		Flaggy
Fissile	Flaggy	Shaly; platy
		Papery

Alling (1945) attempted to establish a scale of fissility (Table 66) and to relate fissility to the composition of the shale (Fig. 84). Ingram (1953) also undertook the study of the relation of composition to the fissility of mudrock. Ingram described the splitting of such rocks as flaggy, flaky, or

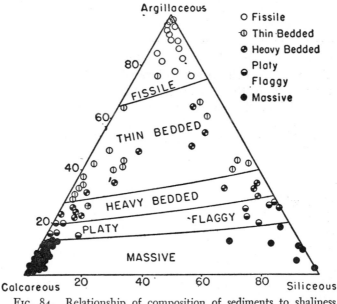

FIG. 84.   Relationship of composition of sediments to shaliness and ease of splitting (from Alling, 1945).

massive (Table 66). As noted by both Alling and Ingram, an increasing content of siliceous or calcareous matter decreases the fissility of a shale. As stated by Rubey (1930), the fissility of a shale seems to bear an inverse relationship to the calcium carbonate content. Shales rich in organic matter, on the other hand, seem to be exceptionally fissile.

Rubey has also noted that fissility is not everywhere parallel to the bedding; that it is more pronounced in the older beds of any given section; and that those rocks which have the steepest dip and the most pronounced aggregate orientation show the most pronounced fissility. Possibly the fissility is in part a secondarily induced structure brought about by rotation or growth of the micaceous "clay minerals" by pressure. Such certainly is the case of the slates where rock cleavage is commonly at high angles with the bedding.

More puzzling, perhaps, are the argillites, which though finely laminated are not materially different in composition from normal shales or slates, are without fissility, either parallel to the bedding or otherwise.

Laminations

The laminations of shales range from 0.05 to 1.00 millimeter in thickness, with most laminations in the range of 0.1 to 0.4 millimeter. The laminations appear to be of three kinds: (1) alternations of coarse and fine particles, such as silt and clay, (2) alternations of light and dark layers distinguished only by their organic content, which is responsible for their color, (3) alternations of calcium carbonate and silt. These alternations of the various materials seem to be due to differential settling rates of the several constituents or differing rates of supply of these materials to the basins of deposition.

The laminations may be due to storms or floods or other more or less capricious or accidental causes. Or they may be due to fluctuations in supply that are seasonally controlled (Rubey, 1930; Bradley, 1931a, 1931b). If the very thinnest laminations are persistent and show no effects of scour, it seems likely that storms, or bottom currents which arise from them, can hardly be responsible for these laminations. As many laminations are of the right order of thickness, as shown by the rates of sedimentation estimated for times past or observed at the present time, and have a structure similar to the year-laminations now forming, it seems probable that many are of an annual nature (varves) and depend on the yearly climatic cycle (Pl. 23). This cycle affects temperature, salinity, and the silt content of the waters as well as the seasonal production of plankton.

The absence of laminations, which is rather common, is in some ways more remarkable than the laminations themselves. Extremely uniform sedimentation over a very long time may produce a structureless sediment; more probable cause of such sediment is the reworking and ingestion of the mud by scavenging benthonic organisms (Dapples, 1942).

Porosity

The porosity of a freshly deposited clay is very large. It may be 50 per cent or even more (Trask, 1931). The porosity of shale is notably less. Although the average clay has a porosity of 27 per cent, the porosity of the average shale is only 13 per cent. The decrease in porosity accompanying conversion of a mud to a shale is the result of compaction. Such compaction results from the pressure of the superincumbent beds. Athy (1930) and others (Hedberg, 1926; Jones, 1944) have shown that the porosity is a function of the thickness of the overlying strata (Table 67). Rubey (1930) has at-

TABLE 67.　Porosity of Shales in Relation to Overburden (after Athy, 1930)

Depth Below Surface (ft.)	Porosity %
0 to 100	50
1000	30
2000	23
3000	18
8000	8

tempted to express the relation between porosity and depth below the surface in algebraic form: $P = 100C/(B + C + D)$, where P is the porosity, B is the thickness of rocks eroded away, from above the surface, C is a constant, and D is the depth below the surface. The porosity-depth relations are complicated by two other factors, namely, textures and deformation. In general, fine-grained rocks tend to be more compacted than coarse-grained rocks, and therefore if other things are equal, they will show larger decreases in porosity for a given depth of burial.

TABLE 68.　Effect of Deformation on Porosity of Black Hills Shales (after Rubey, 1929)

Sample	Degree of Dip	Porosity %
E	1	37.6
C	4	33.3
A	5	32.5
I	5[a]	26.0
K	7[a]	25.4
H	10[a]	25.4
F	33	23.8
J	45	35.8
G	50	25.3

[a] Near faults.

Deformation also induces a decline in porosity, as was shown by Rubey, who expressed the relations between deformation and porosity as $P_u = 100 -$

cos $d(100 - P_p)$, where P_u is the porosity of the untilted rock, d is the present angle of dip, and P_p is the present porosity.

Concretions and Related Structures

Shales and siltstones commonly contain concretionary bodies. Calcareous concretions, flattened parallel to the bedding and with bedding planes passing through them, are common in many clays and shales. They are more prominent in the silt or siltstone interbeds. Black shales are prone to contain cone-in-cone layers. Not uncommon in many shales are septarian nodules and clay ironstone concretions.

CLASSIFICATION AND ORIGIN OF SHALES

Clays and shales can be classified as residual or transported. The residual clays formed in place and are, in fact, a soil or a product of the soil-forming processes. Although some such clays have important commercial uses, they are seldom encountered in the older strata except rarely as "fossil" soils at unconformity surfaces. But because most clays and shales contain materials of residual origin, it is important to know what these materials are like in order to recognize the presence of such material and to correctly interpret its significance. The residual clays therefore are briefly described.

Residual Clays

Residual soils (*regolith* of Merrill; *saprolith* of Becker; *sathrolith* of Sederholm) are the products of weathering formed *in situ*. The character of these deposits is dependent upon climate, drainage, and parent-rock materials. In mature soils (normal or zonal types) the climate is the more important factor. In the immature soils (intrazonal and azonal) the effects of drainage and the nature of the parent rock are readily discernible. That essentially similar end products are formed from diverse source rocks is well shown by comparison of analyses A, B, and C (Table 69) which are residual clays formed from basalt, limestone, and granite gneiss, respectively.

In general in humid regions the residual materials are enriched in the hydroxides of aluminum and ferric iron (pedalfers) and impoverished in lime, magnesia, and the alkalies. Under most favorable conditions even the silica is removed (analysis E, Table 69), so that the end product will consist of little else than alumina and iron oxide. These residual materials are the *laterites*. Laterization requires both the high rainfall and the high temperatures of the tropical regions. Laterites, both ferruginous and bauxitic, are marked by concretionary structures, pisolites, and larger bolster-like bodies.

In the arid regions the soils are enriched in lime (pedocals). A *caliche* or *duricrust* (Woolnough, 1928) may be formed. A duricrust is a peculiar type of deposit which is formed on a peneplain that is marked by sharply defined alterations of saturation and desiccation. It is an armor-like deposit produced by upward capillary migration of ground waters during the arid period. From these ground waters are precipitated aluminous, ferruginous, siliceous, or calcareous materials.

TABLE 69. Chemical Composition of Residual Clays
(per cent)

Constituent	A	B	C	D	E	F
SiO_2	40.7	55.42	55.07	44.80	9.28	48.00
TiO_2	7.3	T	1.03	2.44	3.78	1.00
Al_2O_3	30.9	22.17	26.14	38.84	69.76	34.56
Fe_2O_3	8.7[a]	8.30	3.72	0.36[a]	1.14[a]	1.54[a]
FeO	....	T	2.53	....	....	....
MnO	....	....	0.03	....	....	....
MgO	....	1.45	0.33	0.10	0.15	0.35
CaO	1.0	0.15	0.16	0.05	0.40	0.23
Na_2O	0.4	0.17	0.05	0.30	0.40	0.51
K_2O	0.3	2.32	0.14	0.23	0.95	0.59
H_2O+	11.0[b]	7.76	9.75	13.62[c]	13.37[c]	12.30
H_2O-	....	2.10	0.64	....	....	1.30
P_2O_5	....	T	0.11	....	....	....
SO_3	....	....	T	....	....	....
CO_2	....	....	0.36	....	....	....
BaO	....	....	0.01	....	....	....
S	....	....	0.04	....	....	....
	100.3	99.84	100.11	100.74	99.23	100.38

A. Residual clay from basalt, Spokane County, Wash. (Scheid, 1945).
B. Residual clay from dolomite, Morrisville, Ala., W. F. Hillebrand, analyst (Russell, 1889).
C. Residual clay from Morton gneiss, Redwood Falls, Minn., S. S. Goldich, analyst (Goldich, 1938).
D. White flint clay, Phelps County, Mo., R. T. Rolufs, analyst (Allen, 1935).
E. Diaspore clay, same location as "D," R. T. Rolufs, analyst (Allen, 1935).
F. Plastic Ione clay, Jones Butte, Calif. (Allen, 1929).
[a] Total iron.
[b] Ignition loss.
[c] Total water.

For a more detailed treatment of soils, their properties and origin, the reader is referred to the standard works (Glinka, 1927; Byers, Kellogg, Anderson and Thorpe, 1938; Reiche, 1950).

The examination of an unconformable contact should include observation on an undisturbed residuum which may be present on such a surface and on the freshness or degree of alteration of the rocks below the unconformity. The character of such a residuum in part will be those of a soil but in part it will also be due to changes since burial. These changes are diagenetic and are a reversal of the soil-forming processes.

"Fossil" soils may not be present at all places, because of their removal before deposition of the younger beds. A "fossil" regolith is characterized by its ill-sorted nature. The textures and structures of the parent rocks have been obliterated largely without being replaced by textures and structures that characterize a normal sediment. The regolith may grade downward into the unaltered source rock and may also grade upward into the overlying sedimentary rock. Such graded unconformities commonly occur where arkose overlies granite. The arkosic residuum may be indurated by later cementation, so that it constitutes a recomposed granite (p. 325).

Because the residuum mainly is the product of chemical decay, it should be marked by certain chemical features. The residuum contains a notably higher content of ferric oxide and alumina than does the parent rock and is deficient in the more fugitive oxides, such as soda. Moreover, if the residuum is a mature soil it will show a soil profile or zonal arrangement, as do present-day soils. The profile may be incomplete owing to removal of the upper zones by the advancing sea; or incomplete owing to the climatic conditions under which it formed. Most fossil soils probably are azonal or intrazonal. The original profile in any case will be more or less altered by the authigenesis which has taken place since burial.

"Fossil" soils have been given cursory field and laboratory study, so that the nature of the postburial alterations are not well understood. The criteria for recognizing such materials need to be worked out because such criteria are also the means for recognizing an unconformity (Sharp, 1940; Grim and Allen, 1938). The student must exercise caution in studying unconformity surfaces to be sure that the rock alterations, if any, were not the product of the present day. Such surfaces may be zones of accelerated ground-water flow and leaching.

Transported Shales and Mudstones

The transported clays and shales derived their constituents from three sources (Fig. 85). They are composed in varying proportions of (1) the products of abrasion (mainly silt), (2) the end products of weathering (residual clays), and (3) chemical and biochemical additions. These chemical additions either are materials precipitated from solution and deposited concurrently with the accumulating clays, such as lime carbonate, or they are materials added by reaction or exchange with the surrounding medium (normally sea water) such as potassium or magnesium. The several varieties or subclasses of shales are dependent in the main on the relative importance of the several contributing sources. The kind and proportion of mechanically derived silts are dependent on the relief and climate of the source area. If mechanically derived materials are absent or rare, the mudstones are enriched in the residual materials, and under appropriate conditions they are enriched in the chemical precipitates such as calcite, aragonite, siderite, chamosite, silica, and in some cases in organic matter. The shales and related rocks therefore range widely in composition and show responses to the tectonic and geomorphic nature of the basin of accumulation, as do the associated arenites of the same family.

Theoretically under conditions of peneplanation, little other than ionic and colloidal materials should be removed from the land area and reach the basin of deposition. Under such conditions both silica and iron migrate and may accumulate in favorable sites as chemical or biochemical deposits. Slight uplift should lead to partial destruction of the regolith. Sedimentation fol-

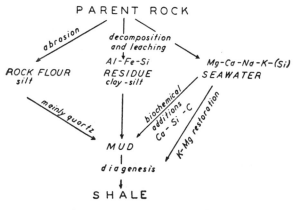

FIG. 85.   Provenance of shale.

lowing such slight rejuvenation therefore should be marked by the deposition of highly aluminous shales. More marked elevation and consequent higher relief interrupts the soil-forming processes at midcycle, so that both weathered and unweathered products are delivered to the basin of deposition. Less mature sands and muds would be deposited.

The concept of shales and mudstones of varying degrees of residual character was advanced by Vogt (1927) and more recently by Kennedy (1951). It has been investigated also by Nanz (1953), who undertook the study of the chemical composition of shales or slates associated with the several unlike types of sandstone. Because of the small number of analyses available, the relations between maturity of the sandstone and that of the associated shales are uncertain. Clearly, however, the shales or lutites are much less differentiated chemically than are the associated sands or arenites. The meager data suggest that, as expected, the shales associated with the more mature sands are themselves more mature than those associated with the immature sediments (arkose and graywacke). The average Al_2O_3/Na_2O ratio of two lutites associated with orthoquartzites was 125, whereas the corresponding average of two lutites of graywacke affinities was 11.

Krynine (1948, Table 4) states that the mineral compositions of the shales associated with the several sandstone types differ. The shales associated with the highly mature sands (orthoquartzites) were said to be quartzose; those affiliated with low-rank graywackes are micaceous; those found with high-rank graywackes are chloritic, and those associated with arkoses were said to be kaolinitic. Krynine, however, did not present the data on which these conclusions were based nor did he give any reasons for the associations claimed.

A somewhat more elaborate attempt to classify shales with respect to their associations and especially with reference to the tectonic stability of the site of deposition is that of Krumbein (1947). Krumbein utilized all the characteristics of the sediment, including texture, color, composition, and associations.

The concepts of shale types advanced by Vogt, Kennedy, Nanz, and probably Krynine and Krumbein are essentially attempts to classify shales according to their maturity and to relate them to certain environments of provenance—primarily to the relief of the source region, which is itself a function of tectonism. More effort, perhaps, has been expended in an attempt to determine the nature of the environment of deposition. The latter presumably determines the kind of chemical or biochemical constituents present, the pH of the shale, and the clay mineral composition itself.

Of special interest is the recent work on the stability fields of the iron-bearing minerals in terms of the oxidation-reduction potential (Eh) of the environment of deposition (Krumbein and Garrels, 1952; James, 1954). Iron sulfide, mainly pyrite, iron carbonate (siderite), iron silicates (iron-rich chlorites, chamosite, glauconite), and iron oxide (hematite) constitute a mineral series correlated with increasing oxidation potential. The presence of these minerals, even in small amounts, if they be truly contemporaneous with the sedimentation, is indicative of the oxidation state of the environment of deposition. Even the ferric-ferrous iron ratio, as shown by chemical analysis, is indicative in a general way of the oxidation potential of the depositional environment. As the ferric-ferrous oxide ratio is rather closely correlated with color (MacCarthy, 1926, Table 1), the color itself is a guide to nature of the environment. Red shales (and purple also) are indicative of an oxidizing environment; blue, green, gray, and black are indicative of a reducing environment.[4]

The pH of the shale (determined by an aqueous suspension of the ground material) is believed to be the same as that of the waters of the depositional environment (Shukri, 1942; Millot, 1949). The freshwater shales are said

---

[4] As pointed out by Keller (1953) and Grim (1951), some clay minerals are green but nonetheless have a high ferric iron content. Despite this observation, the observations of Tomlinson (1916) and MacCarthy (1926) that the color of most clays, shales, and slates is closely correlated with the ferrous-ferric oxide ratio is correct.

to have a mean pH of about 4.7, whereas the mean pH of shales deposited in marine, lagoonal, or lime-depositing lakes is about 7.8

Because of the marked differences in pH within the depositional environment, there are believed to be corresponding differences in the clay mineral formed in such environments (Millot, 1949; Grim, 1951). Kaolin is believed to be stable or formed only in an acid fresh-water environment in which the alkalies and alkaline earths are vigorously removed by leaching. In alkaline environments, especially if magnesium and potash are available, as in sea water, the clay micas or closely related clay minerals (illite, glauconite, chlorite, etc.) are stable. According to Millot, Grim, and others, the character of the clay mineral in many clays and shales bears out this concept. The shales presumed to be of fresh-water origin were largely kaolinitic; those of lagoons and alkaline lakes were devoid of kaolin and rich in the micaceous minerals. Marine clays are somewhat intermediate in character. A study of the clay fraction (less than 0.006 mm) of some Molasse sediments did not seem to bear out these conclusions (Lemcke, et al., 1953, p. 56). The proportions of illite, chlorite, kaolinite, and montmorillonite in fresh brackish and marine beds did not show any significant variations related to the environment of deposition.

If the shales of a marine origin are characterized by illite and chlorite they should be richer in these materials than the shales of fresh-water origin and should show a corresponding enrichment in K_2O and MgO. Most published data seem to bear out this conclusion. Millot's marine (and lagoonal) shales were notably richer in potash and magnesia than those of fresh-water origin. Lagoonal shales, however, were richer in both potash and magnesia than the marine shales, which occupy an intermediate position. Some recent work tends to show a progressive increase in potash and magnesia in muds with increasing distances from the shore (and with presumed increasing salinity of the waters). There is a corresponding increase in chlorite and illite at the expense of montmorillonite, although the results are far from conclusive.

In conclusion it seems probable that, aside from faunal criteria, the chemical and mineralogical character of the clay mineral complex, and the chemical or biochemical additions to the shales, will prove the most useful guides to their environment of deposition.

Hybrid Shales and Mudstones

Under conditions of great crustal stability and low relief, the land-derived detrital material reaches a minimum. Under these conditions the sedimentation in adjoining basins will be chiefly chemical. Under conditions of less perfect peneplanation the supply of terrigenous clastics, though small, is appreciable, but the rate of accumulation is very slow. Although the resulting sediment may be a shale or mudstone, it will be richer than ordinary in chemically or biochemically precipitated materials or in materials of volcanic derivation. The hybrid rocks thus formed have a distinctive chemical composition by which they may be recognized. Normally they are richer in one or more constituents than the average shale. If rich in lime they are cal-

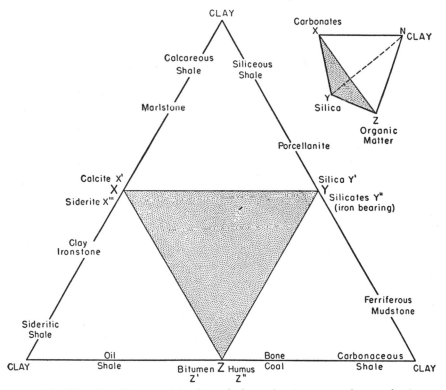

Fig. 86. "Developed" compositional tetrahedron, showing nomenclature of mixtures of clay and nonclastic materials.

careous shales or marls; if rich in iron they are ferriferous shales and mudstones; if rich in carbon they are carbonaceous shales; if rich in silica, they are siliceous shales, and the like (Fig. 86). Such hybrid rocks are here briefly described. If the chemical component is deducted from the rock, the residue will be found to be a more or less normal shale.

Black Shales (Carbonaceous Shales)

Black shales are fissile and many readily split into thin semiflexible sheets of large size. They are exceptionally rich in organic matter (Table 70). They tend also to be rich in iron sulfide, usually pyrite, which replaces fossils, forms nodules, or occurs in disseminated grains. The black shales rarely contain any fossils, or at best have a sparse, depauperate, and restricted fauna. Except for the phosphatic forms present, the organisms are preserved only as a graphitic or carbonaceous film or as pyrite replacements. Concretionary carbonate layers or nodules, commonly showing cone-in-cone structure and septarian nodules, are abundant locally in some black shales.

TABLE 70. Chemical Composition Carbonaceous Shales
(per cent)

Constitutent	A	B	C	D	E	F
SiO_2	51.03	60.65	36.67	58.03	63.09	33.15
TiO_2	....	0.62	0.39	0.64	0.99	....
Al_2O_3	13.47	11.62	6.90	15.00	18.58	17.3
Fe_2O_3	8.06	0.36	....[a]	3.67	2.17⎱	2.6[b]
FeO	....	....	2.35[a]	5.82	2.73⎰	
MnO	....	0.04	0.002	0.09	0.22	0.25[c]
MgO	1.15	1.90	0.65	1.64	2.67	1.0
CaO	0.78	1.44	0.13	0.26	1.11	10.4
Na_2O	0.41	0.60	0.26	3.52	4.54	1.0
K_2O	3.16	3.10	1.81	3.60	0.54	3.0
H_2O+⎱ H_2O-⎰	0.81	⎰3.77 ⎱1.19	1.25 0.55	3.46⎱ 0.84⎰	2.69	1.7
P_2O_5	0.31	0.18	0.20	0.16	0.12	....
CO_2	....	1.65	....	0.03	....	9.24
S	7.29	3.20[d]	....	0.04	T	2.31
C	13.11	9.20	7.28	3.27	....	9.06[e]
FeS_2	....	....	38.70	....	....	....
V_2O_5	....	....	0.15	....	....	....
Total	102.90[f]	99.52	100.21	100.24[g]	99.45	91.01

A. Black shale (Devonian), Dry Gap, Walker County, Georgia. L. G. Eakins, analyst. Includes 3.32 hydrocarbons (Diller, 1898).
B. Ohio shale (Devonian) Logan County, Ohio. Downs Schaaf, analyst (Lamborn, Austin and Schaaf, 1938, p. 20).
C. "Graphitic slate," Wauseca member Dunn Creek slates (Precambrian) 10th level Buck Mine, Iron River district, Michigan. C. M. Warshaw, analyst (James, 1951, p. 255).
D. Black slate, Dunn Creek slates (Precambrian), Crystal Falls district, Michigan. R. H. Nanz, Jr., analyst (Nanz, 1953).
E. Nonesuch shale (Keweenawan), Michigan (Lane, 1911).
F. Kupferschiefer, Mansfeld, Germany (Stelzner and Bergerat, 1904).
   [a] Direct determination not possible because of organic matter; iron in excess of pyrite reported as FeO.
   [b] Iron.
   [c] Manganese.
   [d] FeS₂.
   [e] Bitumen.
   [f] Less O = S; total loss becomes 100.17.
   [g] Includes 0.14 SO₃.

The faunas of black shales are remarkably uniform. Littoral and benthonic forms, of the usual warm-water facies, are missing. The brachiopods are represented only by the phosphatic, inarticulate shells, such as *Lingula* or *Discina*, which are ubiquitous and hardy types capable of survival under adverse conditions. The mollusca are all thin-shelled and as a rule, depauperate. Among them are byssiferous pelecypods which are as likely to attach themselves to floating as to fixed objects. The noncalcareous black shale fauna is very unlike that of the limestones and calcareous shales that are found in the same area (Ruedemann, 1934). The conodonts, rare fish remains, and spores and spore cases complete the list of organic remains found in black shales. The black shales of the Ordovician and Silurian, however, are marked in addition by the graptolitic remains preserved as carbon films.

Black shales contain an unusual amount of carbonaceous matter, in part distillable, and sulfide sulfur. Whereas the average shale has about 1 per cent carbon, the carbonaceous shale contains from 3 to 15 per cent. Some are also noted for the unusual concentration of certain trace elements (V, U, Ni, Cu). The oxidation of the iron sulfides produces a swelling and disintegration of the rock in outcrops and covers the surface with a white efflorescence (melanterite or iron sulfate).

The paper-thin bedding so characteristic of many black shales has been ascribed to the colloidal nature of the materials, which have shrunk and have been compressed perhaps to only one-fifth of the original thickness.

Black shales occur in many places and formed at many times during the geologic past. Most notable examples are the Precambrian black shales of Michigan (James, 1951; White and Wright, 1954), the Ordovician black shales of the Taconic region (Ruedemann, 1934), the Devonian black shales (Chattanooga, etc.) (Rich, 1951, and others), and the black shales of the Pennsylvanian coal measures. The latter seem not to be of the same origin as those of the earlier times. As pointed out by James (1954), black shales and related products of strongly reducing environment seem to appear in the geosynclinal cycle just after the sediments formed on the aerated shelf and those derived from the rising geanticlinal island arc. The rise of the latter, prior to emergence within the geosyncline, produces the semi-isolation required for black shale deposition.

The origin of black shales has been much debated. Certainly they were deposited under anaerobic conditions. How such conditions were achieved is less certain. The stagnated water body may have been deep and sealed off from the atmosphere by a density stratification of the waters produced by a layer of relatively fresh water overlying more saline waters as in the present Black Sea (Androussow, 1897) or in certain Norwegian fiords (Ström, 1936). Some writers contend that the black shales were deep-water marine sediments; others have postulated comparatively shallow waters either marine or lagoonal. Ruedemann (1934), Twenhofel (1939), and Rich (1951) have reviewed the black shale problem. For further discussion of it see page 622.

Siliceous Shales

Siliceous shales have an abnormally high content of silica. Whereas average shale has 58 per cent of silica, siliceous shales may contain as much as 85 per cent (Table 71). Other constituents, notably ferrous iron and carbonates, are absent or very minor. Calculation of the norm, assuming silicate minerals with the highest probable silica ratios, shows at least 70 per cent of the rock is uncombined silica. Such highly siliceous shales, as might be expected, are hard, durable rocks that resist disintegration.

TABLE 71. Chemical Composition of Siliceous Shales and
Related Materials
(per cent)

Constitutent	A	B	C
SiO_2	84.14	73.71	84.45
TiO_2	0.22	0.50	0.35
Al_2O_3	5.79	7.25	4.14
Fe_2O_3	1.21	2.63	1.48
FeO	....	0.44	0.51
MnO	....	....	....
MgO	0.41	1.47	0.52
CaO	0.31	1.72	1.25[a]
Na_2O	0.99	1.19	0.46
K_2O	0.50	1.00	0.64
H_2O+	5.56	6.94	3.11
H_2O-		2.88	3.25
P_2O_5	....	0.24	0.28
CO_2	none	T?	[a]
SO_3	....	0.16	0.18
S	....	....	....
C	....	0.00	0.12
Total	100.03	100.13	100.74[b]

A. Siliceous shale, Mowry, Cretaceous, Black Hills, S. D. F. G. Fairchild, analyst (Rubey, 1929).
B. Diatomaceous shale, Modelo formation (Miocene), California. J. G. Fairchild, analyst (Hoots, 1938, p. 108).
C. Cherty shale, Modelo formation (Miocene), Mulholland Highway, Santa Monica Mountains. J. G. Fairchild, analyst (Bramlette, 1946, p. 13).
[a] CO_2 and a corresponding proportion of CaO to combine as $CaCO_3$ calculated out of the composition.
[b] $CaCO_3$ calculated as 5.16 not included in total.

The siliceous character seems not to be due to large quantities of detrital quartz but rather to be derived from amorphous silica, such as opal, or from volcanic ash. Rubey (1929) estimated the siliceous Mowry shale (Cretaceous) to be one-third cryptocrystalline quartz derived from opaline (chemically precipitated) silica. More or less devitrified ash (rhyolitic) also forms a major part of the shale and accounts for its peculiar chemical composition.

Rubey concluded that the Mowry shale owed its highly siliceous character to the volcanic ash with which it is closely associated. Chemical decomposition of slowly accumulated very fine-grained, highly siliceous, volcanic ash in the presence of decaying organic matter, provided the silica which was precipitated concurrently with the accumulation of the normal shale constituents.

Goldstein and Hendricks (1953) reached similar conclusions respecting the siliceous shales of the Stanley, Jackfork, and Atoka (Carboniferous) formations of Arkansas and Oklahoma. The silica of these shales was thought to be derived from submarine weathering (halmyrosis) of volcanic ash. The restricted fauna of these shales (linguloid and orbiculoid brachiopods, conodonts, radiolaria, and sponge spicules) suggest waters rich in silica and poor in lime. The fine laminations suggest quiet waters and a slow rate of deposition.

Bramlette (1946) concluded that the siliceous shales of the Monterey formation (Miocene) of California, called porcelaneous shale and porcellanite or cherty shale (Table 71) by him, were produced by the addition of biochemical silica to normal shale at the time of formation of the deposit. Infalls of volcanic ash may have been a source of the silica utilized by the abundant microorganisms.

High-Alumina Shales

The average shale contains 15.4 per cent alumina (Table 61). Those with an abnormal content of silt will be lower, whereas those of finer grain will have a higher than average content of alumina. Unlike residual clays, few shales or slates contain more than 20 per cent alumina. A shale or slate may be said to be a high-alumina rock if the content of this constituent exceeds 22 per cent. Probably less than 5 per cent of the shales will have this much or more alumina.

The origin of high-alumina shales is not clear. If the material were largely of residual origin the alumina content might be high (Table 69), but since most shales are a mixture of both residual clays and detrital silt (mainly quartz), the alumina content is depressed. If the residual materials are bauxitic rather than kaolinitic, the alumina content is augmented. A high-alumina shale, therefore, is either a shale containing such bauxitic materials or a shale exceptionally low in silt and hence rich in kaolin or similar clay mineral.[5]

Clay Ironstones, Chamositic, and Other Ferriferous Mudstones

The average shale contains 6.47 per cent of the iron oxides (4.02 per cent of Fe_2O_3; 2.45 per cent FeO) (Clarke, 1924, p. 34). The average slate of late Precambrian age contains 8.92 per cent iron oxides; the average Paleozoic slate contains 5.91 per cent of these constituents (Nanz, 1953). In the slates, unlike the shales, ferrous oxide exceeds ferric oxide. It is clear that the normal pelitic sediment has 6 to 8 per cent iron oxide. As is apparent from

[5] Excluded from consideration are the clays, such as fire clays, which owe their high alumina content to postdepositional weathering and leaching (Allen, 1946).

PLATE 21

TUFFS AND TUFFACEOUS SANDSTONES

A: Wasatch tuffaceous sandstone, Eocene, Jackson Hole, Wyoming, ordinary light, ×42.

Quartz and feldspar sand grains (clear) and numerous glass fragments (shards) in a carbonate matrix. Note bedding plane separating finer tuff with few mineral grains from coarser bed with many mineral grains. Mineral grains concentrated near base of bed.

B: Hatton tuff member, Stanley shale, Carboniferous, near Mena, Ark., ordinary light, ×41.

A much altered tuff or tuffaceous sandstone, associated and interbedded with shales and graywacke (Pl. 19, **A**). Angular quartz (clear), much sericitized feldspar (clouded), and devitrified glass (large shard) in chloritized and sericitized matrix.

C: Volcanic ash from Brule formation, Oligocene (?), Morrill County, Nebr., ordinary light, ×35.

Contains an abundance of glass shards plus a few small angular quartz and feldspar grains (clear) in a clay paste. The latter contain a little carbonate.

D: Rhyolite tuff, Ixtopan, Mexico, crossed nicols, ×15.

Large quartz grains set in fine matrix composed of comminuted mineral grains and devitrified glass. In contrast to **A** above, this tuff shows no stratification or sorting; it resembles the tills (Pl. 15) and some of the graywackes (Pl. 18) and may be deposited from the atmospheric analogue of the turbidity or mud flow.

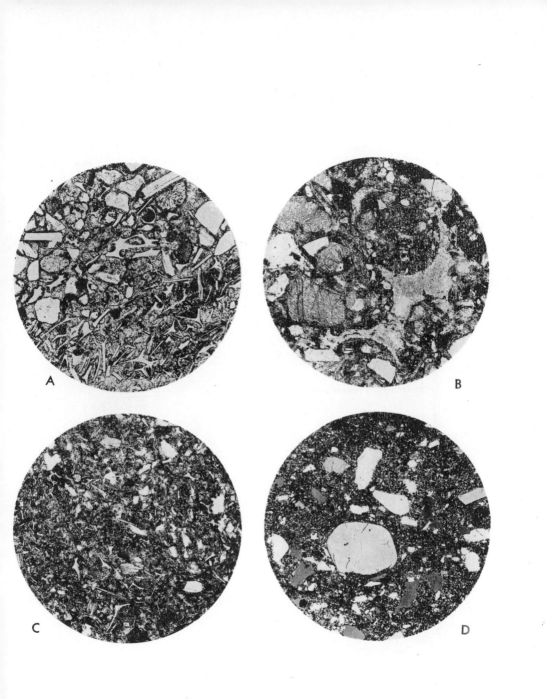

A

B

C

D

PLATE 22

SHALE AND SILTSTONE

Left: Brecciated siltstone, Precambrian, Spies Mine, Iron County, Mich. Diameter of core 1½ inches. U.S. Geological Survey photograph.

Brecciation was contemporaneous with sedimentation; a pseudoconglomerate.

Center: Shale and siltstone, Upper Pennsylvanian, Cumberland County (Kentucky). Diameter of core is two inches.

Shows bedding typical of zone of intermittent turbulence. Silt layers (light) broken into planoconvex segments; shale (dark) laminations unbroken.

Right: Siltstone and slate, Precambrian ("footwall"), Hiawatha Mine, Iron County, Mich. Diameter of core approximately one inch. James, U.S. Geological Survey photograph.

Shows graded bedding. Silt (light-colored) grades upward into slate (dark). Bedding characteristic of zone of no turbulence.

Fig. 87, an iron oxide content in excess of 12 per cent is unusual and certainly if more than 15 per cent is present the shale or slate is ferriferous.[6]

Such iron-bearing rocks grade into true ironstones—rocks with at least 15 per cent metallic iron (about 20 per cent of iron oxides). The high iron content of a shale or mudstone is indicative of the presence of iron sulfide, iron carbonate, iron silicate, or an iron oxide. Inspection of the analyses should disclose the nature of the iron-bearing mineral. Such rocks are evidently mixed sediments produced by cosedimentation of fine argillaceous sediment and a precipitated iron-bearing mineral. The petrology of the ironstones is covered elsewhere (page 449).

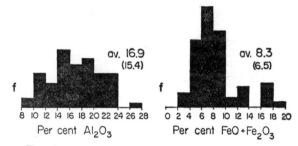

FIG. 87. Distribution of alumina and the iron oxides in 60 Paleozoic and Precambrian slates. The average content of these oxides is also given; numbers in parentheses indicate the content of these oxides in Clarke's average shale.

Clay ironstone is an old term for a mudstone rich in siderite. Such rocks occur as thin beds and nodules in the Coal Measures of both the United States and Great Britain. The chamositic or chloritic mudstones are mixtures of chamosite or chlorite and clay. These relatively rare rocks are associated with sideritic mudstones and bedded siderites in some iron-bearing districts, notably the Cleveland area of Great Britain (Taylor, 1949) and the Iron County area of Michigan (James, 1951).

Calcareous Shales and Marls

The lime carbonate content of most shales is small. The average shale has a CO_2 content of 2.63, equivalent to about 6 per cent calcite. As the carbonate content is increased the rock loses its fissility and effervesces in acid and may be properly termed a calcareous shale. No agreement exists on how much carbonate must be present before the rock is properly called calcareous. Twenty per cent carbonate will materially alter the character of the rock

[6] Ferruginous would be a better term, but this term is often used for rocks of a red color but with normal iron content.

and may be taken as a minimum carbonate content for a calcareous shale or marl.

Marls, proper, are semifriable mixtures of clay materials and lime carbonate. The better-indurated rocks of like composition are *marlstones* or *marlite* and are more correctly an earthy or impure limestone rather than a shale. Marl has been defined as a rock with 35 to 65 per cent carbonate and a complementary content of clay (see page 410).

The carbonate in a calcareous shale may consist of finely precipitated materials or small particles of organically fixed carbonate (microfossil tests, and the like).

Potassic Shales

The average shale, according to Clarke (1924, p. 34) contains 3.24 per cent potash. The average slate of late Precambrian or Paleozoic age contains about 3.6 per cent potash. As can be seen from Fig. 88, a potash content of

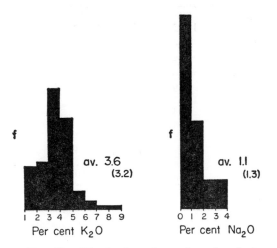

Fig. 88. Distribution of potash and soda in 66 Paleozoic and Precambrian slates. The average content of these oxides is also given; numbers in the parentheses indicate the content of these oxides in Clarke's average shale.

2 to 5 per cent is normal for about 80 per cent of all shales. Only about one shale in twenty has 5 or more per cent potash. Such shales are high-potash shales.

Illustrative of such shales is the Ordovician Decorah shale of Minnesota (Table 72, col. B, C) once considered as a possible potash reserve (Schmitt, 1924), and the Glenwood shale, also Ordovician, of the same region (Table

72, col. A). These shales have potash contents of 5.96 and 10.85 per cent, respectively.

According to Gruner and Thiel (1937) the potash of these rocks is believed to be present in orthoclase thought by them to be of authigenic origin. These conclusions do not explain the reason for the high potash content. Perhaps a related problem is the feldspathization of a Cambrian sandstone described by Berg (1952) who ascribed the feldspar of this rock to reaction between clay minerals and seawater. Potassium restoration in shales by such a reaction is a normal process. The problem therefore is to explain why this reaction was carried so exceptionally far.

TABLE 72.   Chemical Composition of Potash-Rich Shales
(per cent)

Constituent	A	B	C
SiO_2	56.29	37.87	52.93
TiO_2	0.64	0.45	0.63
Al_2O_3	19.22	14.23	19.89
Fe_2O_3	4.39	2.97	4.15
FeO		1.63	2.29
MgO	1.65	3.29	1.62
CaO	0.09	14.73	0.00
Na_2O	0.19	0.43	0.60
K_2O	10.85	5.96	8.33
H_2O+	2.04	2.67	3.73
H_2O-	3.54	1.25	1.75
P_2O_5	....	2.83	3.95
CO_2	....	13.94	0.00
SO_3	0.72	....	....
S	....	0.10	0.14
Total	99.62	99.50	100.01

A. Glenwood shale, Ordovician, Minn., R. B. Ellestad, analyst (Gruner and Thiel, 1937).
B. Decorah shale, Ordovician, Minnesota (Schmitt, 1924).
C. Decorah shale (recalculated on a carbonate-free basis).

REFERENCES CITED AND BIBLIOGRAPHY

Allen, V. T. (1929), The Ione formation of California, Univ. Calif. Publ., Dept. Geol. Sci., Bull., vol. 18, pp. 347–448.

Allen, V. T. (1935), Mineral composition and origin of Missouri flint and diaspore clays, Missouri Geol. Survey and Water Resources, 58th Biennial Rept., Appendix IV.

Allen, V. T. (1946), Sedimentary and volcanic processes in the formation of high alumina clay, Econ. Geol., vol. 41, pp. 124–138.

Allen, V. T. and Nichols, R. L. (1945), Clay-pellet conglomerates of Hobart Butte, Lane County, Oregon, J. Sediment. Petrol., vol. 15, pp. 25–33.

Alling, H. L. (1945), Use of microlithologies as illustrated by some New York sedimentary rocks, Bull. Geol. Soc. Amer., vol. 56, pp. 737–756.

Androussow, N. (1897), La mer noire, Guide des excursions du VII congres géol. internat., vol. 29.

Athy, L. F. (1930), Density, porosity, and compaction of sedimentary rocks, Bull. Am. Assoc. Petroleum Geol., vol. 14, pp. 1–35.

Berg, R. R. (1952), Feldspathized sandstone, J. Sediment. Petrol., vol. 22, pp. 221–223.

Bradley, W. H. (1929), The varves and climate of the Green River epoch, U.S. Geol. Survey, Prof. Paper 158-E.

Bradley, W. H. (1931), Non-glacial marine varves, Am. J. Sci., ser. 5, vol. 22, pp. 318–330.

Bramlette, M. N. (1946), The Monterey formation of California and the origin of its siliceous rocks, U.S. Geol. Survey, Prof. Paper 212.

Byers, H. G., Kellogg, C. E., Anderson, M. S., and Thorp, James (1938), Formation of soil, in Soils and Men: U.S. Dept. Agric., Yearbook, 1938, pp. 948–978.

Clark, T. H. (1954), Shale: a study in nomenclature, Trans. Roy. Soc. Can., vol. 48, ser. 3, sec. 4, pp. 1–7.

Clarke, F. W. (1924), Data of geochemistry, U.S. Geol. Survey Bull. 770, p. 140.

Conway, E. J. (1945), Mean losses of Na, Ca, etc., in one weathering cycle and potassium removal from the ocean, Am. J. Sci., vol. 243, pp. 583–605.

Correns, C. W. (1938), Die Tone, Geol. Rundschau, vol. 29, pp. 201–219.

Dapples, E. C. (1942), The effect of macro-organisms upon near-shore marine sediments, J. Sediment. Petrol., vol. 12, pp. 118–126.

Diller, J. D. (1898), The educational series of rock specimens collected and distributed by the United States Geological Survey, U.S. Geol. Survey Bull. 150.

Eckel, E. C. (1904), On the chemical composition of American shales and roofing slates, J. Geol., vol. 12, pp. 25–29.

Eskola, Pentti (1932), Conditions during earliest geological times, Ann. Acad. Sci. Fennicae, ser. A, vol. 36, p. 16.

Folk, R. L. (1954), The distinction between grain size and mineral composition in sedimentary-rock nomenclature, J. Geol., vol. 62, pp. 344–359.

Flawn, P. T. (1953), Petrographic classification of argillaceous sedimentary and low-grade metamorphic rocks in subsurface, Bull. Am. Assoc. Petroleum Geol., vol. 37, pp. 560–565.

Glinka, K. D. (1927), The great soil groups of the world and their development (trans. C. F. Marbut), Ann Arbor, Mich., Edwards Bros.

Goldstein, A., Jr., and Hendricks, T. A. (1953), Siliceous sediments of Ouachita facies in Oklahoma, Bull. Geol. Soc. Amer., vol. 64, pp. 421–442.

Goldich, S. S. (1938), A study in rock-weathering, J. Geol., vol. 46, pp. 17–58.

Grim, R. E. (1942), Modern concepts of clay materials, J. Geol., vol. 50, pp. 225–275.

Grim, R. E. (1951), The depositional environment of red and green shales, *J. Sediment. Petrol.*, vol. 21, pp. 226–232.

Grim, R. E. and Allen, V. T. (1938), Petrology of the Pennsylvanian underclays of Illinois, *Bull. Geol. Soc. Amer.*, vol. 49, pp. 1485–1513.

Grout, F. F. (1925), Relation of texture and composition of clays, *Bull. Geol. Soc. Amer.*, vol. 36, pp. 393–416.

Grout, F. F. (1932), *Petrography and petrology*, New York, McGraw-Hill, p. 365.

Gruner, J. W. and Thiel, G. A. (1937), The occurrence of fine grained authigenic feldspar in shales and silts, *Am. Mineralogist*, vol. 22, pp. 842–846.

Holmes, A. (1937), *The age of the earth*, London, Nelson, p. 75.

Hedberg, H. D. (1926), The effect of gravitational compaction on the structure of sedimentary rock, *Bull. Am. Assoc. Petroleum Geol.*, vol. 10, pp. 1035–1072.

Hoots, H. W. (1938), Geology of the eastern part of the Santa Monica Mountains, Los Angeles County, Calif., *U.S. Geol. Survey, Prof. Paper 165-C.*

Hutchinson, G. E. (1944), Conway on the ocean: An appreciation and a criticism, *Am. J. Sci.*, vol. 242, pp. 272–280.

Ingram, R. L. (1953), Fissility of mudrocks, *Bull. Geol. Soc. Amer.*, vol. 64, pp. 869–878.

Inman, D. L. (1949), Sorting of sediments in the light of fluid mechanics, *J. Sediment. Petrol.*, vol. 19, pp. 51–70.

James, H. L. (1951), Iron formation and associated rocks in the Iron River district, Iron County, Michigan, *Bull. Geol. Soc. Amer.*, vol. 62, pp. 251–266.

James, H. L. (1954), Sedimentary facies of iron-formation, *Econ. Geol.*, vol. 49, pp. 236–293.

Jones, O. T. (1944), The compaction of muddy sediments, *Quart. J. Geol. Soc. London*, vol. 100, pp. 137–160.

Keller, W. D. (1946), Evidence of texture on the origin of the Cheltenham fire clay of Missouri and associated shales, *J. Sediment. Petrol.*, vol. 16, pp. 63–71.

Keller, W. D. (1953), Clay minerals in the type section of the Morrison formation, *J. Sediment. Petrol.*, vol. 23, pp. 93–105.

Keller, W. D. (1953), Illite and montmorillonite in green sedimentary rocks, *J. Sediment. Petrol.*, vol. 23, pp. 3–9.

Keller, W. D. and Ting, C-P. (1950), The petrology of a specimen of the Perry Farm shale, *J. Sediment. Petrol.*, vol. 20, pp. 123–132.

Kennedy, W. Q. (1951), Sedimentary differentiation as a factor in Moine-Torridonian correlation, *Geol. Mag.*, vol. 88, pp. 257–266.

Krumbein, W. C. (1938), Size frequency distributions of sediments and the normal phi curve, *J. Sediment. Petrol.*, vol. 8, pp. 84–90.

Krumbein, W. C. (1947), Shales and their environmental significance, *J. Sediment. Petrol.*, vol. 17, pp. 101–108.

Krumbein, W. C. and Garrels, R. M. (1952), Origin and classification of chemical sediments in terms of pH and oxidation-reduction potentials, *J. Geol.*, vol. 60, pp. 1–33.

Krumbein, W. C. and Pettijohn, F. J. (1938), *Manual of sedimentary petrography*, New York, Appleton-Century.

Krynine, P. D. (1948), The megascopic study and field classification of sedimentary rocks, *J. Geol.*, vol. 56, pp. 130–165.

Kuenen, Ph. H. (1941), Geochemical calculations concerning the total mass of sediments in the earth, *Am. J. Sci.*, vol. 239, pp. 161–190.

Lamborn, R. E., Austin, C. R., and Schaaf, Downs (1938), Shales and surface clays of Ohio, *Geol. Survey Ohio*, ser. 4, Bull. 39, p. 20.

Lane, A. C. (1911), The Keweenaw series of Michigan, *Mich. Geol. Survey Div. Publ.* 6 (geol. ser. 4).

Leith, C. K. and Mead, W. J. (1915), *Metamorphic geology*, New York, Holt, pp. 60; 316–319.

Lemcke, K. von Engelhardt, Wolf, and Fuchthauer, Hans (1953), Geologische und sedimentpetrographische Untersuchungen im Westteil der ungefalteten Molasse des suddeutschen Alpenvorlandes, *Beihefte Geol. Jahrb.*, vol. 11, pp. 56–57.

MacCarthy, G. R. (1926), Colors produced by iron in minerals and the sediments, *Am. J. Sci.*, ser. 5, vol. 12, pp. 17–36.

McKee, E. D., and Weir, G. W. (1953), Terminology for stratification and cross-stratification in sedimentary rocks, *Bull. Geol. Soc. Amer.*, vol. 64, pp. 381–390.

Miller, W. G. (1905), The cobalt-nickel arsenides and silver deposits of Temiskaming, *Ontario Dept. Mines, Ann. Rpt.*, vol. 14, pt. 2.

Millot, G. (1949), Relations entre la constitution et la genèse des roches sédimentaires argileuses, *Bull. assoc. ing. geol. univ. Nancy*, II, 2–3–4.

Nanz, R. H. (1953), Chemical composition of pre-Cambrian slates with notes on the geochemical evolution of lutites, *J. Geol.*, vol. 61, pp. 51–64.

Picard, M. D. (1953), Marlstone—a misnomer as used in Uinta Basin, Utah, *Bull. Am. Assoc. Petroleum Geol.*, vol. 37, pp. 1075–1077.

Reiche, Parry (1950), A survey of weathering processes and products, *Univ. New Mexico Publ. Geol.*, no. 3.

Rich, J. L. (1951), Probable fondo origin of Marcellus-Ohio-New Albany-Chattanooga bituminous shales, *Bull. Am. Assoc. Petroleum Geol.*, vol. 35, pp. 2017–2040.

Rubey, W. W. (1929), Origin of the siliceous Mowry shale of the Black Hills region, *U.S. Geol. Survey Prof. Paper*, 154 D.

Rubey, W. W. (1930), Lithologic studies of fine-grained Upper Cretaceous sedimentary rocks of the Black Hills region, *U.S. Geol. Survey Prof. Paper* 165 A.

Ruedemann, R. (1934), Paleozoic plankton of North America, *Geol. Soc. Amer., Mem.* 2.

Rukhin, L. B. (1944), Genetic significance of granulometric composition of clayey sediments, *Compt. rend. acad. sci. U.R.S.S.*, vol. 43, no. 6, pp. 260–262.

Russell, I. C. (1889), Subaerial decay of rocks and origin of the red color of certain formations, *U.S. Geol. Survey, Bull.* 52, p. 25.

PLATE 23

VARVED SEDIMENTS

Top: Varved clay, Pleistocene, Baraboo, Wisconsin.

Five varves or year-layers are present. Darker bands are clay; laminated and thicker layers are silt. Length of specimen about 2½ inches.

Bottom: Varved argillite, Precambrian (Cobalt), Ontario, Can.

About eighteen year-layers are present. Rafted pebble of granite shown. Distortion of layers about pebble largely due to compaction. Length of specimen visible about eight inches.

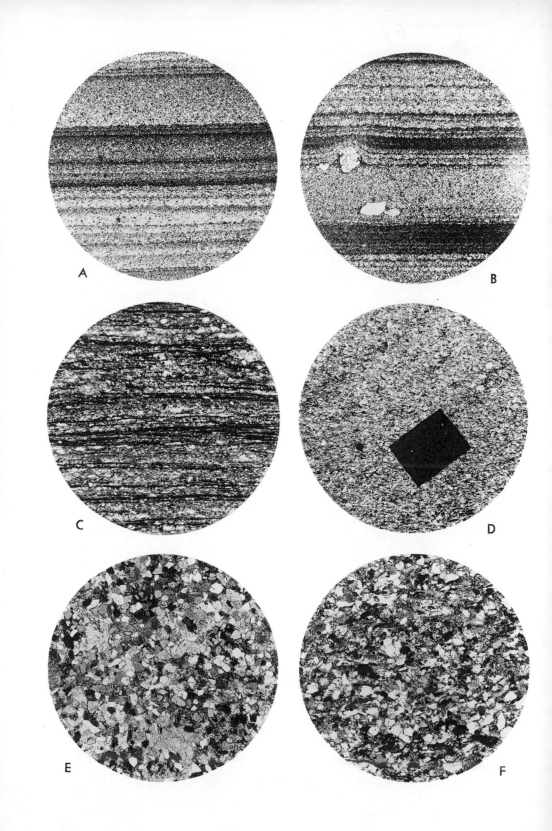

PLATE 24

ARGILLITE, SHALE, AND SILTSTONE

A: Cobalt argillite, Upper Huronian, Cobalt, Ontario, Canada. Ordinary light, ×45.

Laminations chiefly composed of angular bits of quartz and feldspar of silt size plus interstitial chlorite interbedded with layers of finer detritus of similar composition but much richer in chlorite. Note micrograded bed.

B: Cobalt argillite, Upper Huronian, Cobalt, Ontario, Canada. Ordinary light, ×45.

Similar to **A** but showing coarse ice-rafted sand grains and a rock fragment. Laminations bend up over the latter.

The banding is probably seasonal; three dark winter layers and three coarser summer silts are shown. Minor sublamination records subseasonal freshets. This glacial argillite closely associated with tillites (see Pls. 14 and 23).

C: Green River oil shale, Eocene, (Colorado), ordinary light, ×45.

Consists of organic-rich laminations (black), and laminations containing some organic matter (gray) and much carbonate (white). The latter forms one-third to one-half of the total. A very little detrital quartz and authigenic analcite is also present.

D: Archean slate, Minnitaki Lake, Ontario, Canada. Ordinary light, ×15.

A fine-grained slate containing large cube of pyrite (black). Note that the boundaries of the pyrite crystal lie athwart the structure of the slate.

E: Dolomitic silt, Sly Gap formation (Devonian) San Andres Mountains, N. Mex. Crossed nicols, ×38.

Angular quartz and feldspar of coarse silt or fine-grained sand set in calcite matrix. Abundant, though not clearly shown in figure, are rhombic dolomite euhedra.

F: Devonian siltstone, Pennsylvania. Crossed nicols, ×33.

Mainly angular quartz, and some detrital micas in a chloritic and sericitic matrix. Typical flagstone.

Russell, R. J. and Russell, R. D. (1939), Mississippi River delta sedimentation in *Recent Marine Sediments*, Tulsa, Amer. Assoc. Petroleum Geologists, pp. 153–177.

Scheid, V. E. (1945), Preliminary report on Excelsior high-alumina clay deposit, Spokane County, Washington, *Unpublished report*, U.S. Geol. Survey (see Allen and Nichols, 1946).

Schmitt, H. A. (1924), Possible potash production from Minnesota shale, *Econ. Geol.*, vol. 19, pp. 72–83.

Schuchert, C. (1931), The age of the earth, *Nat. Research Council, Bull.* 80, pp. 10–64.

Sharp, R. P. (1940), Ep-Archean and ep-Algonkian erosion surfaces, *Bull. Geol. Soc. Amer.*, vol. 51, pp. 1235–1270.

Shepard, F. P. (1954), Nomenclature based on sand-silt-clay ratios, *J. Sediment. Petrol.*, vol. 24, pp. 151–158.

Shrock, R. R. (1948), A classification of sedimentary rocks, *J. Geol.*, vol. 56, pp. 118–129.

Shukri, M. N. (1942), The use of pH-values in determining the environment of deposition of some Liassic clays and shales, *Bull. Fac. Sci., Fouad I Univ.*, 24, pp. 61–65.

Ström, K. M. (1936), Land-locked waters; Hydrography and bottom deposits in badly-ventilated Norwegian fjords with remarks upon sedimentation under anaerobic conditions, *Skrifte Norske Videnskaps. Akad. Oslo, Mat. Natur. Kl.*, vol. 1, no. 7, pp. 1–85.

Taylor, J. H. (1949), Petrology of the Northampton sand ironstone formation, *Mem. Geol. Survey G. Brit.*

Tomlinson, C. W. (1916), The origin of red beds, *J. Geol.*, vol. 24, pp. 153–179.

Trask, P. D. (1931), Compaction of sediments, *Bull. Am. Assoc. Petroleum Geol.*, vol. 15, pp. 271–276.

Twenhofel, W. H. (1937), Terminology of the fine-grained mechanical sediments, *Rept. Comm. on Sedimentation for 1936–1937*, National Research Council, pp. 81–104.

Twenhofel, W. H. (1939), Environments of origin of black shales, *Bull. Am. Assoc. Petroleum Geol.*, vol. 23, pp. 1178–1198.

Urbain, P. (1937), Texture microscopique des argiles, *Bull. soc. géol. France*, ser. 5, vol. 7, pp. 341–352.

Urbain, P. (1942), Logique des roches argileuses, *Bull. soc. géol. France*, ser. 5, vol. 12, pp. 97–112.

Vogt, T. (1927), Geology and petrology of the Sulitelma district, *Norges Geol. Undersökelse*, Nr. 121.

White, W. S. and Wright, J. C. (1954), The White Pine copper deposit, Ontonagon County, Michigan, *Econ. Geol.*, vol. 49, pp. 675–716.

Woolnough, W. G. (1928), Origin of white clays and bauxite, and chemical criteria of peneplanation, *Econ. Geol.*, vol. 23, pp. 887–894.

SILTSTONES

Although silt seems to be very abundant in nature, forming, for example, 60 per cent of the material deposited in the Mississippi delta, siltstone appears not to be so common a rock as either sandstone or shale. Silt occurs primarily as a constituent of shales rather than as siltstone. In some geologic sections, however, siltstones are common as thin flags interbedded with more abundant shales or slates. Siltstones rarely, if ever, form beds of any considerable thickness and almost never constitute a "formation."

Silt has been defined as material $\frac{1}{16}$ to $\frac{1}{256}$ millimeter in diameter (also 0.05 to 0.005 mm and 0.1 to 0.01 mm). Siltstone is consolidated silt. The content of silt in a siltstone is not generally specified, but since shales *normally* contain at least 50 per cent of silt, it seems reasonable to define siltstone as a rock of which at least two-thirds is material of silt size. Rocks having this much silt would probable have the grosser properties characteristic of siltstones. Siltstones tend to be flaggy, that is, they are hard, durable layers, generally thin, which weather in relief on the outcrop. They may show small-scale cross-bedding and various primary current structures, notably striation and flow casts, rib-and-furrow, and primary current lineation. Silts when water-saturated tend to be "quick," and siltstones therefore may show evidence of intrastratal flowage and soft-sediment boudinage. The associated clays, on the other hand, are tenacious and not prone to flow.

Silt particles are angular rather than round like sand grains. The siltstones are in part cemented with a mineral cement and in part simply bonded by recrystallization of the component clay materials.

In composition silt and siltstone are intermediate in character between sandstones and shales. They are richer in silica, poorer in alumina, potash, and water than a shale but generally not so rich in silica as are the more mature sands. Siltstones rarely, if ever, consist of pure quartz silt (unless, perhaps, some *ganister* is such a rock).[7] Most siltstones contain an abundance of mica, or micaceous clay minerals and chlorite. Because of their fineness of grain, rock particles are virtually absent.

In general the study of siltstones has been somewhat neglected. No subdivision or classification of siltstones has been attempted.

The siltstone flags of the Devonian (especially the Portage group) of New York state are among the best known examples of these rocks (Pl. 24, F).

Loess

A silt of very special character is *loess*. Loess (Dutch, loess; German, loess, löss) is an unconsolidated silt commonly buff in color (locally gray, yellow,

---

[7] Milner gives the average grain size of ganister as 0.05 to 0.15 mm, which is part silt and part fine sand.

brown or red) characterized by its lack of stratification and remarkable ability to stand in a vertical slope. It is generally highly calcareous.

Loess is essentially a silt. Udden's analyses of loess from the upper Mississippi valley show the $\frac{1}{16}$ to $\frac{1}{32}$ millimeter (0.06 to 0.03 mm) grade to be the modal class and to contain about 60 per cent of the whole size distribution (Udden, 1914). The material was well sorted; very little sand or clay is present. The Chinese loess is said to have an average grain size of about 0.01 mm (Barbour, 1927); the Dutch loess consists mainly of materials 0.01 to 0.05 mm in size (Doeglas, 1949); western European and Kansan loess is mostly $\frac{1}{16}$ to $\frac{1}{32}$ millimeter in size (Swineford and Frye, 1955).

TABLE 73. Chemical Composition of Loess
(per cent)

Constituent	A	B	C	D	E
SiO_2	64.61	60.69	74.46	59.30	72.77
TiO_2	0.40	0.52	0.14	0.60	1.79
Al_2O_3	10.64	7.95	12.26	11.45	7.09
Fe_2O_3	2.61	2.61	3.25	2.32	2.98
FeO	0.51	0.67	0.12	1.55	....
MnO	0.05	0.12	0.02	....	....
MgO	3.69	4.56	1.12	2.29	1.02
CaO	5.41	8.96	1.69	9.78	5.33
Na_2O	1.35	1.17	1.43	1.80	1.04
K_2O	2.06	1.08	1.83	2.17	1.64
H_2O+ $\atop$ H_2O-	2.05	1.14	2.70	0.96	5.76[a]
P_2O_5	0.06	0.13	0.09	0.20	0.10
CO_2	6.31	9.63	0.49	7.41	....
SO_3	0.11	0.12	0.06	....	T
C, organic	0.13	0.19	0.12	....	....
Cl	0.07	0.08	0.05	....	....
Total	100.06	99.62	99.83	98.73	99.52

A. Loess, near Galena, Illinois. R. B. Riggs, analyst (Clarke, 1924, p. 514).
B. Loess, Vicksburg, Miss. R. B. Riggs, analyst (Clarke, 1924, p. 514).
C. Loess, Kansas City, Missouri. R. B. Riggs, analyst (Clarke, 1924, p. 514).
D. Loess, Kansu, China (Barbour, 1927, p. 283).
E. Loess, Landen-Liege, Belgium. R. Runnels, analyst (Swineford and Frye, 1955, p. 6).
  [a] Loss at 1000° C.

The Muscatine, Iowa, loess has quartz as its chief constituent (Diller, 1898). Other components are orthoclase, plagioclase, hornblende, occasional biotite, some carbonate and clay colored by iron oxide. Loess from St. Charles, Missouri (Oefelein, 1934) contains quartz and feldspar (in the ratio 72 to 28 to 57 to 43) and a clay mineral (beidellite). Heavy minerals form 0.05 to 0.20 per cent and are mainly green and brown hornblende, garnet, tourmaline, zircon, and epidote. In less quantity were augite, apatite, rutile, titanite, limonite, biotite, chlorite, and leucoxene. Loess from the lower Mississippi valley is similar and contains mainly hornblende, zircon, garnet, epidote, and opaques (Doeglas, 1949). The essential similarity of the heavy minerals of both the Mississippi valley and the Dutch loesses to those of the associated glacial deposits was pointed out by Doeglas (1949, 1952). Swineford and Frye (1955), however, have shown that despite close similarity of gross properties, loess from different localities shows a wide range in mineral composition. They attribute the differences to variations in the source materials.

The chemical composition of loess is given in Table 73. As can be seen from the table, loess is an oxidized immature silt.

Loess occurs primarily as a thin blanket deposit (generally under 100 feet thick) of Pleistocene age in central Europe, especially in the Netherlands and Germany, in the Mississippi valley, in the Pacific northwest, and in portions of China. In the upper Mississippi valley there are several loessial deposits closely associated with the Pleistocene glacial beds. The most recent is closely related in position and thickness to the larger streams. The loess thins rapidly and regularly eastward from these streams (Krumbein, 1937; Smith, 1942; Simonson and Hutton, 1954). No lithified pre Pleistocene loess has been positively identified in the geologic record.

Loess is presumed to be an aeolian silt though it has been interpreted as a product of *eluviation*. The reader interested in the "loess problem" is referred to the recent literature on the subject (Russell, 1944; Thwaites, 1944; Doeglas, 1949, 1952; Krynine, 1937).

REFERENCES CITED AND BIBLIOGRAPHY

Barbour, E. F. (1927), The loess of China, Ann. Rept. Smithsonian Inst. 1926, pp. 279–296.

Clarke, F. W. (1924), Data of geochemistry, U.S. Geol. Survey Bull. 770, p. 514.

Correns, Carl W. (1953), Die Anteil des Staubes an der Bildung der Sediment-gesteine, Z. Ver. deut. Ing., vol. 95, pp. 293–296.

Diller, J. S. (1898), The educational series of rock specimens, etc., U.S. Geol. Survey Bull. 150, p. 65.

Doeglas, D. J. (1949), Loess, an eolian product, J. Sediment. Petrol., vol. 19, pp. 112–117.

Doeglas, D. J. (1952), Loess, an eolian product, J. Sediment. Petrol., vol. 22, pp. 50–52.

Krumbein, W. C. (1937), Sediments and exponential curves, J. Geol., vol. 45, pp. 577–601.

Krynine, P. D. (1937), Age of till on "Palouse Soil" from Washington, Am. J. Sci., vol. 33, pp. 205–216.

Oefelein, R. T. (1934), A mineralogical study of loess near St. Charles, Missouri, *J. Sediment. Petrol.*, vol. 4, pp. 36–44.

Russell, R. J. (1944), Lower Mississippi Valley loess, *Bull. Geol. Soc. Amer.*, vol. 55, pp. 1–40.

Simonson, R. W., and Hutton, C. E. (1954), Distribution curves for loess, *Am. J. Sci.*, vol. 252, pp. 99–105.

Smith, G. D. (1942), Illinois loess-variations in its properties and distribution, *Illinois Agr. Expt. Sta. Bull. 490.*

Swineford, Ada, and Frye, J. C. (1951), Petrography of the Peoria loess in Kansas, *J. Geol.*, vol. 59, pp. 306–322.

Swineford, Ada (1955), Petrographic comparison of some loess samples from western Europe with Kansas loess, *J. Sediment. Petrol.*, vol. 25, pp. 3–23.

Thwaites, F. T. (1944), Review of R. J. Russell's article on loess, *J. Sediment. Petrol.*, vol. 14, pp. 246–248.

Udden, J. A. (1898), Mechanical composition of wind deposits, *Augustana Library Publ. no. 1.*

Udden, J. A. (1914), The mechanical composition of clastic sediments, *Bull. Geol. Soc. Amer.*, vol. 25, pp. 655–744.

9

Limestones and Dolomites

INTRODUCTION

To THE lime manufacturer, *limestone* is a general term for that class of rocks which contains at least 80 per cent of the carbonates of calcium or magnesium and which, when calcined, gives a product that slakes upon the addition of water. Although this perhaps is the literal meaning of the term limestone, geologists now use it to embrace a larger group of rocks.[1] The suitability of the rock for the manufacture of lime is not an essential characteristic.

In general the term limestone is applied only to those rocks in which the carbonate fraction exceeds the noncarbonate constituents. If, for example, clastic quartz is present in excess of 50 per cent, the term calcareous sandstone would be more appropriate.[2] Likewise rocks in which shaly matter exceeds the carbonate fraction are calcareous shales rather than limestones (Fig. 6).

Normally the term limestone is used for those rocks in which the carbonate fraction is composed primarily of calcite and the term dolomite is

[1] The term "carbonatite" has also been used for these rocks (Kay, 1951, p. 5) although more commonly this term is applied to certain nonsedimentary rocks (Barth, 1952, p. 216).
[2] Winchell (1924) has observed, however, that although all possible mixtures of clastic quartz and calcite are known, some are much less common than others. Study of 600 samples of sandy carbonate rocks at Bingham, Utah, showed that a mixture of 82 per cent carbonate and 18 per cent quartz is most rare. This proportion might accordingly be taken as the natural dividing line between sandstone and limestone instead of the arbitrary 50–50 division suggested above. Such a convention probably would more closely approximate actual usage because it is likely that many rocks with less than 50 per cent quartz are termed calcareous sandstones by field workers (Fig. 89).

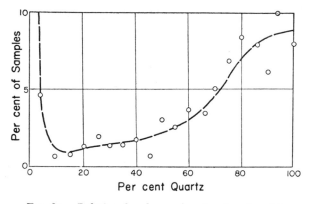

FIG. 89. Relative abundance of sand-carbonate mixtures
(after Winchell, *Trans. A.I.M.E.*, vol. 70, 1924, p. 885).

reserved for those rocks which are composed primarily of the mineral dolomite.[3]

In many ways the term limestone is not suitable. Limestones are a polygenetic group of rocks (Fig. 90). Some are fragmental or detrital and are mechanically transported and deposited; others are chemical or biochemical

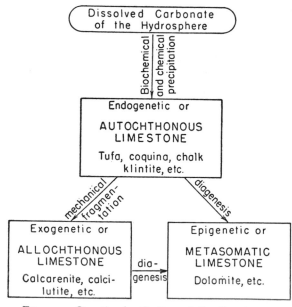

FIG. 90. Genetic classification of the limestones.

[3] Dolomites are, of course, lime-bearing rocks and as such are limestones. The problem of dolomite-limestone nomenclature and the naming of rocks of intermediate composition is further elaborated in the section on dolomite, page 416.

precipitates and grew in place. Both types may be profoundly modified by various postdepositional changes so that the original characters are obscured or erased. That rocks of such diverse origins are all designated limestone is to obscure rather than elucidate their history. It is, no doubt, for this reason that Grabau (1904) would abandon the term limestone altogether and designate the clastic carbonates as calcarenite, and so forth, and the carbonate precipitates as calcigranulites, and the like. The term limestone has persisted and will no doubt continue in use as a trade or commercial term and perhaps as a field term. Established usage is difficult to change, although abandonment of the term would result in closer observation and better understanding of the lime-bearing strata.

COMPOSITION

Chemical Composition

The chemical composition of limestones, as might be expected, reflects rather closely their mineral composition. The limestones are primarily calcite, hence the content of both CaO and CO_2 is extremely high (Table 74) forming in some cases more than 95 per cent of the whole. Other constituents which commonly become important include MgO, which, if it exceeds 1 or 2 per cent, probably indicates the presence of the mineral dolomite. Magnesian limestones are those containing 1 to 2 per cent MgO.[4]

The magnesium content is a function of both the magnesium content of the skeletal debris in the limestone and of postdepositional chemical changes. Normally magnesium is added by the dolomitization processes, although some studies suggest that the ancient rocks containing less magnesium than that demanded by the organic debris of which they are made may have lost magnesium (Chave, 1954b, p. 598). Although the average limestone contains 7.90 per cent MgO, equivalent to 16.5 per cent $MgCO_3$, most limestones contain either much less magnesia or much more (Fig. 91). Most limestones have less than 4 per cent or over 40 per cent $MgCO_3$ equivalent. Rocks with intermediate composition are uncommon. Clarke's average limestone is therefore an average carbonate rock—not a limestone— and includes dolomites as well as limestones.

Silica, if excessive, indicates the presence of much noncarbonate detritus or the presence of chert (Table 74, cols. C and D). If alumina is high also, the silica is probably a constituent of contaminating shaly matter. With the

---

[4] Rodgers (1954) would restrict the term magnesian limestone to those rocks containing several per cent MgO but without the mineral dolomite. Except in calcite deposited by living organisms no more than 2 per cent $MgCO_3$ (less than 1 per cent MgO) in solid solution is possible. The solid solution is unstable, so that fossil calcite invariably contains less than 1 or 2 per cent of magnesium carbonate (Chave, 1952).

advent of such argillaceous materials, the potash and the combined water also are higher than normal (Table 74, col. F).

TABLE 74. Chemical Composition of Representative Limestones
(per cent)

Constituent	A	B	C	D	E	F	G	H
SiO_2	5.19	0.70	7.41	2.55	1.15	13.80	2.38	0.09
TiO_2	0.06	....	0.14	0.02	....	....	....	....
Al_2O_3	0.81	0.68	1.55	0.23	0.45	7.00	1.57[a]	
Fe_2O_3	0.54	0.08	0.70	0.02	....	4.55	0.56	0.11
FeO		....	1.20	0.18	0.26	....	....	
MnO	0.05	....	0.15	0.04	....	0.29	....	....
MgO	7.90	0.59	2.70	7.07	0.56	1.32	0.59	0.35
CaO	42.61	54.54	45.44	45.65	53.80	38.35	52.48	55.37
Na_2O	0.05	0.16	0.15	0.01	0.07	2.61	....	....
K_2O	0.33	none	0.25	0.03		0.86	....	0.04
H_2O+	0.56[b]	....	0.38	0.05	0.69	....	....	0.32
H_2O-	0.21	....	0.30	0.18	0.23	....	....	
P_2O_5	0.04	....	0.16	0.04	....	0.25	none	....
CO_2	41.58	42.90	39.27	43.60	42.69	31.31	41.85[c]	43.11
SO_3	0.05	0.06	0.02	0.03	none	....	....	0.44
Cl	0.02	....	....	....	....	....	....	....
S	0.09	0.25	0.25[d]	0.30[d]	....	none	none	....
BaO	....	....	none	0.01[e]	....	....	....	....
SrO	....	....	none	0.01	....	....	....	....
Li_2O	T	....	....	....	....	....	....	....
Organic	....	T	0.09[f]	0.04[f]	....	....	....	0.17
Total	100.09	99.96	100.16	100.04	99.90	100.34	98.84	100.10

A. Composite analysis of 345 limestones. H. N. Stokes, analyst (Clarke, 1924, p. 564).
B. "Indiana limestone" (Salem, Mississippian). A. W. Epperson, analyst (Loughlin, 1929, p. 150).
C. Crystalline, crinoidal limestone (Brassfield, Silurian, Ohio). Downs Schaaf, analyst (Stout, 1941, p. 77).
D. Dolomitic limestone (Monroe formation, Devonian, Ohio). Downs Schaaf, analyst (Stout, 1941, p. 132).
E. Lithographic limestone (Solenhofen, Bavaria). Geo. Steiger, analyst (Clarke, 1924, p. 564).
F. Argillaceous limestone (natural cement rock), Lower Freeport limestone, Columbiana Co., Ohio. P. J. Demarest, analyst (Stout and Lamborn, 1924, p. 195).
G. Chalk (Fort Hays, Cretaceous), Ellis County, Kansas (Runnels and Dubins, 1949).
H. Travertine, Mammoth Hot Springs, Yellowstone. F. A. Gooch, analyst (Clarke, 1904, p. 323).
   [a] Includes TiO_2.
   [b] Includes organic matter.
   [c] Calculated from MgO and CaO (ignition loss, 40–1000° C given as 40.95).
   [d] Calculated as pyrite.
   [e] Constituent does not exceed figure given.
   [f] Organic carbon.

Exceptionally a limestone may be notably rich in a minor constituent such as phosphorus or iron oxide or sulfide.

Since many limestones are composed of skeletal structures or debris derived therefrom, the composition of such rocks is an expression of the bulk composition of the skeletal constituents. The composition of shell and other hard parts varies with the nature of the organism and the conditions under which it lived. The chemical composition of the inorganic constituents of

TABLE 75. Inorganic Constituents of Marine Invertebrates (data from Clarke and Wheeler, 1922)

Class[a]	No. Analyses	CaCO₃ (%)	MgCO₃ (%)	Ca₃P₂O₈ (%)	SiO₂ (%)	(Al, Fe)₂O₃ (%)	Remarks (%)
Foraminifera	7	77.0 to 90.1	1.8 to 11.2 avg. 8.2	T[b]	T to 15.3	T to 4.0	····
Calcareous Sponges	4	71.1 to 85.0	4.6 to 14.1	? to 10.0	T to 7.8	1 to 5.7	····
Corals							
Madreporaria	30	97.6 to 99.7	0.1 to 0.8	0 to T	0 to 1.2	0 to 0.6	····
Alcyonaria	22	73.0 to 98.9	0.3 to 15.7 avg. 11.1	T to 8.3	0 to 1.7	T to 1.0	0.5 to 5.4 CaSO₄
Echinoderms							
Crinoids	24	83.1 to 91.5	7.9 to 13.7 avg. 10.8	T to 1.1	T to 2.0	0.1 to 1.4	····
Echinoids	14	77.9 to 91.7	6.0 to 13.8	T to 1.8	T to 9.9	0.1 to 5.2	T to 2.6 CaSO₄
Bryozoa	13	63.3 to 96.9	0.2 to 11.1	T to 2.9	0.2 to 16.7	0.1 to 2.2	····
Brachiopods							
Calcareous	5	88.6 to 98.6	0.5 to 8.6	T to 0.6	0.1 to 0.5	T to 0.5	····
Phosphatic	4	? to 8.3	1.7 to 6.7	74.7 to 91.7	0.5 to 0.9	0.3 to 1.2	? to 8.4 CaSO₄
Mollusks							
Pelecypods	11	98.6 to 99.8	0 to 1.0	T to 0.4	0 to 0.4	T to 0.5	····
Gastropods	20	96.6 to 99.9	0 to 1.8	T to 0.8	0 to 2.2	T to 1.9	····
Cephalopods	3	93.8 to 99.5	0.2 to 6.0	T	0 to 0.2	T to 0.1	····
Crustaceans	13	28.6 to 82.6	3.6 to 16.0	6.6 to 49.6	0 to 1.1	T to 8.8	····
Algae, Calcareous	16	73.6 to 88.1	10.9 to 25.2 avg. 17.4	T to 0.4	T to 3.5	T to 1.6	····

[a] Clarke and Wheeler also give analyses of hydroids, annelids, starfishes, ophiurans, scaphopods, and amphineurans, all of which make minor contributions to the sedimentary rocks.
[b] T stands for "trace," or less than 0.1 per cent.

marine invertebrates has been investigated by Clarke and Wheeler (1922). As can be seen from Table 75, even though each phylogenetic group shows

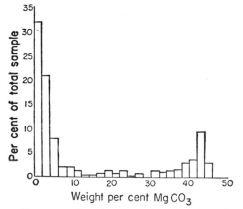

a range in composition, there are differences between groups. The calcareous algae, for example, are notably richer in $MgCO_3$ than are the mollusks; the carapaces of the crustaceans are notably phosphatic, and so forth. Chave (1952, 1954a, 1954b) has made a special study of the magnesium content of the carbonates of the marine invertebrates. He found magnesium to decrease with the level of organization of the organism, those of the higher phyla being less rich in MgO. The content of magnesium was also a function of the temperature of formation and was generally

FIG. 91. Distribution of magnesium in 317 quarried Paleozoic limestones from Illinois (based on data by Krey and Lamar, 1925).

higher in the shells living in the warmer waters. Most important factor was the shell mineralogy. Aragonitic shells are poor in magnesia; calcitic shells commonly are rich in this constituent.

It is clear from inspection of Chave's data that simple accumulation of skeletal materials will not explain the distribution of $MgCO_3$ in the older limestones. The high-magnesium-bearing rocks must either be inorganic precipitates of dolomite or skeletal accumulations which have been enriched in this substance. The most common type of limestone, i.e., that with less than 4 per cent $MgCO_3$, must either be an inorganic precipitate of calcite (or aragonite), an accumulation of organic detritus of only those organisms which secrete magnesium-poor skeletons, or the material, if produced by other organisms, has lost its magnesia.

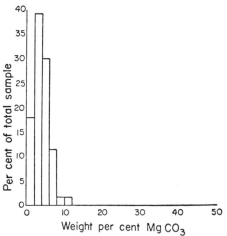

FIG. 92. The distribution of magnesium in modern calcareous sediments (after K. E. Chave, Aspects of the biogeochemistry of magnesium, J. Geol., vol. 62, 1954).

The last possibility seems proved in those cases where the organic debris is of a type known to be magnesium-rich at the present time—such as the crinoidal lime-stone (compare C, Table 74, for example, with Crinoids, Table 75). Comparison of Figs. 91 and 92 might lead one to conclude that the carbonate of the average skeletal detritus, containing $MgCO_3$ in solid solution, had unmixed and produced two end members, one calcitic and one dolomitic. If, so, however, the magnesia has moved out of the deposit in which it formed and is segregated in separate beds.

Mineralogical Composition

Since the limestones are carbonate rocks, the essential minerals are the carbonates calcite, aragonite, and dolomite.[5] Rock-building organisms use both calcite and aragonite in their skeletal structures (see page 221). Some skeletal materials are exclusively aragonite, others are calcite and some are in part aragonite and in part calcite. The factors responsible for these differences have been studied by Lowenstam (1954).

Aragonite is an unstable form of calcite and is found therefore only in recent materials. Even the aragonite of recent shell materials may change into calcite in the course of a few years (Lowenstam, 1954, p. 288). The visible effect of this transformation is a loss of detailed internal structure and the formation of an anhedral crystalline mosaic (Pl. 27, B). Aragonite is also presumably precipitated as minute needles, since it is now found in many calcareous muds. It is also precipitated as oolites. These undergo a recrystallization as do the aragonitic shells, and are converted to a mosaic of calcite with loss of much or all of the original internal structure (Ginsburg, 1954).

Most dolomite appears to be a postdepositional product and shows replacement relations with calcite. Although it occurs as isolated rhombs transecting the primary structures of the rock, it more commonly occurs as patchy anhedral or subhedral mosaics. In the dolomites proper the entire rock is such a mosaic of dolomite crystals. In part the dolomite may be a product of the unmixing of the solid solution, calcite-dolomite, found in the hard parts of many marine invertebrates (Chave, 1952); in part it is the product of reaction of magnesium-bearing waters with the original carbonate.

Siderite is a rare and generally a very minor constituent of some limestones. Ferrous iron is commonly present in the mineral dolomite, but in a few cases it occurs as scattered siderite rhombs. Slight oxidation results in breakdown of the siderite, which is then readily detected by the heavy iron oxide stains along both the cleavage and grain boundaries.

Silica, usually as chalcedony, is a common constituent of many limestones.

[5] $CaCO_3$ also crystallizes as vaterite, which, however, is very unstable and changes to calcite in a few days time.

Although it may be disseminated throughout the rock, it is more commonly segregated into large nodules—the chert or flint nodules of many limestones and dolomites. The chalcedonic silica is fine-grained, and if disseminated it is difficult to detect in thin section. It may occur also as small spherulites (Pl. 40, C) or as a filling between the dolomitic rhombs of some dolomitized rocks. In the latter case solution of the dolomite leaves a spongy porous residue of dolocastic chert (Ireland, 1936; McQueen, 1931). Such material is most conspicuous in the acid-insoluble residues of such rocks. Silica also occurs as small quartz euhedra which transect primary structures and are therefore authigenic. Many limestones and dolomites, especially those which are calcarenites, contain detrital quartz grains (p. 402).

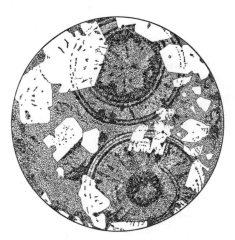

FIG. 93. Feldspathized oolite, Siyeh limestone (Precambrian), Glacier Park, Montana (drawing based on Hatch, Rastall, and Black, *Petrology of the sedimentary rocks*, Allen & Unwin, 1938, Fig. 58).

Feldspar, as authigenic euhedra, is a common minor constituent of many limestones and dolomites (see section on feldspars, page 665) although in rare cases feldspar may form as much as 40 per cent of the whole rock (Fig. 93).

Clay materials are one of the most common contaminants of the carbonate rocks. Clay is not conspicuous in thin section because of its fine grain and disseminated state, but it is readily apparent in the acid-insoluble residues prepared from many limestones. The nature of the clay minerals is determined only with difficulty. In Illinois limestones and dolomites illite is most common; kaolinite is found in some; no montmorillonite has been reported (Grim, Lamar, and Bradley, 1937).

Other minor constituents of limestones include glauconite, collophane, and pyrite. Glauconite occurs as larger rounded granules and locally may be an abundant component (Pl. 29, E, F). Collophane occurs primarily as phosphatic skeletal debris: shells of the linguloid brachiopods, fishbones, and similar materials. Although usually a subordinate constituent it, too, locally may be important and the limestone may be properly described as phosphatic. Pyrite is nearly ubiquitous as small scattered grains, which upon oxidation of the rock are converted to limonite. Exceptionally a limestone is rich enough in pyrite to warrant the description pyritic. The pyrite may occur principally along the borders of fossil debris.

Bituminous matter is common enough in some limestones to impart a dark color to the rock and a fetid odor when the rock is broken.

TEXTURES AND STRUCTURES

Because of the polygenetic origin of the carbonate rocks—in part detrital, in part chemical and biochemical, and in part metasomatic—they exhibit a variety of textures and structures unequalled by any other group of rocks. For this reason a detailed description of these features is given only in the sections dealing with the several carbonate rock families.

The mechanically deposited limestones, as might be expected, show the same textures and structures as do the noncarbonate clastic sediments. Current sorting and stratification, cross-bedding, both large- and small-scale, and even graded bedding (Carozzi, 1952) are well displayed in many limestones. The lime muds, silts, and sands behave in much the same manner as their noncarbonate counterparts in a given hydrodynamic regimen.

The biochemically formed carbonates have a distinctive assemblage of textures and structures. Notable are the biohermal and reef structures, which may be of great size, the sediment-binding framework which characterizes the reef structures, and the numerous modifications of bedding produced by the sediment-secreting and sediment-binding algae—the so-called "algal structures" and algal bedding (see p. 224).

Some of the chemically deposited limestones have distinctive textures—such as the pisolitic and oolitic textures—and unique structures, notably the banding of some travertines and the spongework of some tufas.

Superimposed on these primary textures and structures are various features produced by solution and replacement. The carbonate rocks are particularly susceptible to solution. Hence they show innumerable solution features—stylolitic seams, microstylolitic contacts between the clastic elements and at the boundaries of fossil structures. The metasomatic carbonates, principally the dolomites, have the usual granoblastic textures of rocks recrystallized in the solid state. Relict textures and structures of the rock replaced may still be visible.

The fabric of limestones (and dolomites) has been briefly studied. Both limestones and dolomites are reported to show markedly anisotropic crystallographic fabrics (Hohlt, 1948). Later work (Johnson, 1951) seems not to bear out this observation and discloses only a randomly scattered distribution of calcite or dolomite axes. The detrital carbonate rocks may show a dimensional (rather than crystallographic) fabric like other mechanically deposited materials. The crystallographic fabrics reported by Sander (1951) seem to be largely those produced by deposition of crystals on internal surfaces.

PLATE 25

LIMESTONES

Top: Coquina, Recent, Florida. Note fragmental character of shell debris, absence of matrix and uniformity of size.

Center: Coquinoid limestone. Note that many fossils are entire, that the matrix is fine-grained, the lack of assortment, and the diversity of the types represented.

Bottom: Calcareous tufa, Recent. Calcareous material deposited on plant stems. Note high porosity and spongy character.

All photographs about natural scale.

PLATE 26

ALGAL LIMESTONES

Top: Algal limestone, ×3. Polished transverse section of algal reef rock showing alternate algal and inorganic layers. The irregular light-colored layers consist of the molds of *Chlorellopsis coloniata* and typical spongy algal deposit. The black and gray finely banded layers are of inorganic origin and owe their dark color to disseminated pyrite. U.S. Geological Survey photograph. (Bradley, *U.S. Geol. Survey, Prof. Paper*, 54, pl. 45.)

Bottom: Algal pisolite ("algal structure"), ×5. Polished specimen showing details of internal structure. These bodies consist of layers of spongy algal deposit and thin, dense inorganic layers. Between the algal pebbles are small oolite grains mixed with fine limy sand. U.S. Geol. Survey photograph. (Bradley, *U.S. Geol. Survey, Prof. Paper* 154, pl. 47.)

CLASSIFICATION

The classification of the carbonate rocks, like that of all other rocks, has a genetic basis. As noted in the preceding portions of this chapter, the carbonates are in part clastic—lime gravels, lime sands, and lime muds. Unlike the noncarbonate counterparts, these materials, though characterized by textures and structures similar to those of the usual clastic sediments, are not the waste products of a landmass undergoing erosion. Instead, the debris of which they are composed is derived from within the basin in which they are accumulating. They are therefore in a sense intraformational—certainly intrabasinal—deposits. Although most of the detritus is of clastic origin—broken pieces of reefrock, fragmented and worn shell debris—some of it is unbroken and biochemical or chemical in origin. Many of the lime sands contain entire foraminiferal tests; others are rich in or dominantly oolites. All these materials, as well as the fragmental constituents, are current-sorted and deposited and have the textures and structures of a normal clastic rock. For this reason these mechanically deposited limestones are treated as a separate group despite the fact that in a strict sense they are not wholly clastic.[6] Since the material has been transported and redeposited these limestones may be called *allochthonous* (without roots).

A second group of limestones are formed *in situ* by an accumulation of organic structures. These biochemical rocks have not been subject to current transport and redeposition. They are therefore not sorted or bedded as are current-laid materials. In part these limestones were consolidated during the deposition process and in such cases may have formed wave-resistant masses or reefs. In other cases the accumulating lime carbonate was not so consolidated. These limestones which grow in place by biochemical action may be termed accretionary or *autochthonous* limestones. If of restricted extent they are *biohermal* limestones; if of extended character they are *biostromal*.

Not all autochthonous limestones are biochemical accumulations. Some rather minor varieties such as travertine, caliche, and calcareous tufa are also formed in place. These are purely chemical precipitates from supersaturated solutions and are the products of localized precipitation in springs and lakes or in the soil profile. Moreover, even in those autochthonous limestones rich in skeletal materials, there may be, as in the case of the transported limestones, important additions directly precipitated from sea water without any evident biological cause.

Commonly the distinction between allochthonous and autochthonous deposits is easy. But this is not always so. The criteria for distinguishing be-

---

[6] Although one should discriminate carefully between the several types of materials found in these calcarenites, etc., a nomenclature discriminating between clastic, detrital, fragmental, and mechanical seems unnecessary. Most calcarenites are of mixed derivation.

tween these types of limestone are related to the sorting, to current structures, to the state of articulation of the skeletal materials, and to the content and size of the noncarbonate detritus (see Table 76).

TABLE 76. Criteria for Distinguishing between Autochthonous and Allochthonous Limestones

Autochthonous Limestone	Allochthonous Limestone
1. Associated with shales.	1. Associated wtih orthoquartzites.
2. Grades into calcareous shales and mudstones.	2. Grades into and is interbedded with orthoquartzites (calcareous sandstones).
3. Interstices between fossils filled with lime muds.	3. Interstices filled with clear calcite cement.
4. Bryozoan-incrusted fossils.	4. Contains rolled fossils.
5. Unsorted as to size.	5. Sorted as to size.
6. Fossils articulated.	6. Fossils disarticulated.
7. Reef structures.	7. Cross-bedded.

Any given limestone formation may be a composite of the two fundamental types. The Maastrichian limestone (Andrée, 1915), for example, consists of three parts regularly repeated: (1) crinoidal limestone, (2) coral limestone, and (3) bryozoan limestone. Number 1 is transported, whereas numbers 2 and 3 are sedentary. In the Conococheague (Ordovician) of Maryland, there are alternating beds of detrital limestone (calcarenite and calcilutite) and algal limestones which formed *in situ*.

Any of the above limestones, both those transported and those formed in place, may be greatly altered by replacement by dolomite. Such dolomitized rocks constitute a separate group or class of carbonates, and therefore are discussed in a separate section. Dolomite is, of course, not the only replacing material. Limestones may be replaced by chert, by phosphate, by hematite, etc. Such replacement rocks are not usually of great extent and are distinguished with some difficulty from original or primary precipitates of these same materials. They are, therefore, considered in some detail in the next chapter.

AUTOCHTHONOUS (ACCRETIONARY AND BIOCHEMICAL) LIMESTONES

As the autochthonous limestones form by the direct extraction of $CaCO_3$ from sea water by either organic or inorganic means, they are in a sense the *primary* carbonate deposits. It is from these deposits that much or most of the transported or redeposited (allochthonous) limestones are derived.

Role of Organisms in Limestone Formation

The relative importance of the various organisms as rock builders varies widely in time and place. Certain forms, however, are important rock builders whereas others are rarely so.

Analysis of modern limy sediments shows that only a few types of organisms make large contributions (Tables 77 and 78). Noteworthy at the present time is the importance of the lime-secreting algae (Thorp, 1936).

TABLE 77. Quantitative Biologic Composition of Modern Reef Sediments
(after Thorp, 1936)
(per cent)

Constituents	A	B	C	D
Algae, Calcareous	48.5	25.1	18.0	42.5
Mollusks	17.8	17.5	12.2	15.2
Corals, Madreporarian	16.6	9.3	8.2	34.6
Foraminifera	6.3	9.0	17.3	4.1
	89.2	60.9	55.7	96.4
Constituent Ratios				
Algae/Coral	2.92	2.70	2.20	1.23
Algae/Mollusk	2.72	1.43	1.47	2.79
Algae/Foraminifera	7.70	2.80	1.04	10.03
Mollusk/Foraminifera	2.82	1.94	0.71	3.71
Mollusk/Coral	1.07	1.88	1.49	0.44
Coral/Foraminifera	2.64	1.01	0.47	8.44

A. Pearl and Hermes Reef.
B. Southeastern Florida.
C. The Bahamas.
D. Murray Island, Australia (after Vaughn, 1917).

Notable also is the relatively subordinate position of the corals even in the so-called coral reefs. The order of abundance of the organisms that contribute to the Funafuti reef was found to be (1) *Lithothamnion*, (2) *Halimeda*, (3) *Foraminifera*, and (4) the corals. Although quantitative studies of the ancient limestones have not been made, it is clear that the leading role played by the algae was not recently acquired (Fenton and Fenton, 1939; Johnson, 1951). The algae were important rock builders in the Precambrian and may have been the dominant limestone builders throughout all time.[7]

[7] Although algal structures are ubiquitous, one cannot conclude that the algae precipitated the limestone in which their structures are found. Some algae appear to function only as a sediment-binding agent, whereas others actively precipitate calcium carbonate (Ginsburg, 1955). The sediment-binding algae merely modify the bedding of the accumulating carbonate mud or silt formed by purely mechanical or chemical agents.

Some ancient limestones, however, are marked by the preponderance of the calcareous structures of one or another organism (Hadding, 1933). Notable are the foraminiferal limestones composed of nummulitic (Pl. 27, F) and fusilinid (Pl. 27, E) remains and the crinoidal limestones or encrinites of the Paleozoic (Pl. 27, C). Less common are the coralline (Pl. 27, D) and the molluscan limestones (Pl. 27, B).

The chemical composition of the limy structures of the common rock-builders was given in Table 75.

TABLE 78. Percentage Distribution of Constituents of Modern Lime-Bearing
Sediments (after Thorp, 1936)
(per cent)

Constituent	A	B	C
Organic Constituents			
Algae, Calcareous	22.8	25.1	18.0
Mollusks	15.8	17.5	12.2
Foraminifera	11.7	9.0	17.3
Coral	9.0	9.3	8.2
Spicules, Total	3.6	4.3	2.1
Worm Tubes	1.8	1.4	3.0
Crustacea	1.2	1.4	0.7
Bryozoa	0.3	0.4	T
Other Constituents			
Silt	13.2	13.9	11.7
Clay (with aragonite needles)	10.2	7.8	14.8
Minerals (mostly quartz)	2.8	3.9	0.5
$CaCO_3$ (unidentifiable forms)	5.5	5.3	6.0
Oolites	0.8	0.4	1.6
Pellets (faecal ?)	1.3	T	3.8
Aggregates	0.2	....	0.8
	100.2	99.7	100.7

A. Average of 50 samples from Florida and 24 samples from the Bahamas.
B. Average of 50 Florida samples.
C. Average of 24 Bahama samples.

Bioherms and Biohermal Limestones

The term *bioherm* has been defined by Cumings and Shrock (1928) as any domelike, moundlike, lenslike, or otherwise circumscribed mass; built exclusively or mainly by sedentary organisms and enclosed in a normal rock of different lithologic character. By some, bioherm has been considered synonymous with reef, inasmuch as the structures to which the term was first applied were reefs (Lowenstam, 1950). If a reef is defined as a wave-resistant structure (or having potential wave resistance), then some bioherms were indeed reefs whereas others were not.

Bioherms vary in size and shape, and as to the types of constituent organic remains. They may be composed in part or entirely of algal colonies, stromatoporoid colonies, coral colonies, crinoid remains, brachiopod remains, and the like. They may be merely small mounds measurable in inches or they may be impressive structures several thousand feet across and a hundred or more feet thick.

If the organisms responsible for the bioherm were sediment-binding, the structure may have been somewhat wave-resistant, and have stood somewhat above the surrounding bottoms.[8] It might, in fact, have been emergent and have been in part subaerial. In this case the bioherm is a true reef. On the other hand, the organisms responsible for the bioherm may not be sediment-

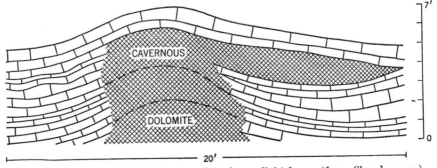

Fig. 94. Limestone reef. This is a relatively small bioherm (from Shrock, 1939).

binding, so that the structure was not wave resistant, and did not therefore ever reach the surface or even rise appreciably above the surrounding bottoms. The bioherm in this case is essentially a facies, much restricted in area, which persisted through time, so that a body of rock markedly different from the surrounding materials came into being.

The Silurian bioherms of Indiana (Cumings and Shrock, 1928), Illinois (Lowenstam, 1950), and Wisconsin (Shrock, 1939) are perhaps typical biohermal reefs. Such structures consist of a massive central mound of uneven textured, fossiliferous dolomite—the reef core—surrounded by a relatively narrow zone—the reef flank—consisting of well-bedded, granular, porous, and sparsely fossiliferous strata which lap against and grade into the core and which commonly show steep dips away from the core (Fig. 94). The distal flanking beds grade imperceptibly into the horizontal and relatively unfossiliferous rock of the interreef region. Upon erosion the massive core commonly remains as a prominent knob or hill, known as a klint.

[8] It should be emphasized that such structures or reefs are the product of a community of organisms which changed with the growth of the structure. But essential to the maintainance of the structure against wave and current action is the sediment-binding character of some of the elements of the ecologic complex (Lowenstam, 1950; Newell, 1955).

The rock composing such klints may be termed *klintite*. This rock is a loosely knit, reticulating network of dense dolomite, which is hard and tough, and which because of its rigid framework gives the biohermal mound its strength and resistance to denudation. The reef core may contain lenses or irregular masses of dolomitized coquina which, though well-cemented, is still very porous. Half the volume of the rock may be voids and coated cavities. The cavities have a drusy lining of calcite crystals. The larger cavities are coated with explanate masses of thinly laminated onyxlike calcite which resemble the flowstone of caves. A few of the larger pockets have been filled with a laminated or massive shale. Some of the cavities appear to be original voids in the reef; others show by their shape that they are openings left by the solution of fossils; still others are irregular solution cavities not related to organic forms. Some of the reef rock has the appearance of a rude breccia.

In general the central part of the core is devoid of bedding or related structures except for a *Stromatactis* framework. The peripheral portion, on the other hand, shows a crude stratification which grades radially outward into the well-defined bedding of the inclined flanking beds.

The core rock may be exceptionally fossiliferous, but in other cases, extensive dolomitization and solution seem to have destroyed all organic forms. In general the fossils mainly are internal and external molds, casts, and impressions.

There is, in some of the larger reefs, a slight downward flexure under part of the core, as though the underlying strata had been bent downward somewhat from the weight of the overlying rock.

The flanking strata form a narrow zone that is concentric with the core. In these strata the well-bedded porous dolomite dips away from the core at angles up to 50 degrees or more. These inclined beds pass into the core on the one side and grade outward into the interreef limestone of the surrounding area. The high dips of some of the flanking strata are attributed to steepening by slumping and compaction.[9] The material of the flanking strata is well-bedded, even-textured, porous, or cavernous granular dolomite with few fossils. This material has the appearance of a poorly cemented calcareous sand. It is, in fact, the detritus formed by the grinding up of the biohermal core material. In places, large fragments of the rough, nonfossiliferous and porous reef rock are embedded in the flanking beds. If these fragments are numerous enough, the term reef breccia may be applied.

[9] The compaction of lime-mud has been shown to be nearly as great as that of many clays (Terzhagi, 1940). Because the core itself is nearly incompressible, the compaction of the surrounding interreef muds would leave the core a structural "high." A similar process might produce quaquaversal dips on the borders of biohermal rock masses which never were reefs and never stood above the surrounding bottoms. The porosity of the core and dip of the flanking beds makes the bioherm a potential trap for oil and gas (see for example Lowenstam and DuBois, 1946).

The reefs were islands of intense vital activity. They grew primarily from the calcareous material deposited by the inhabiting organisms (mainly benthonic). Almost immediately after initiation the reefs rose above the surrounding bottoms. With entrance into the zone of wave-generated turbulence, they shed debris which formed the flanking beds, the deposition of which broadened the reef platform. The growing core commonly expanded and overgrew the flanking detrital apron. The surrounding bottoms were never heavily populated and seem to have been built up slowly by the fine calcareous muds and silts derived by erosion of the growing bioherm and perhaps also by carbonate precipitated directly from sea water.[10] The high porosity of the reef rock proper favored dolomitization, which greatly modified the reef rock and in some cases destroyed most of the organic structures characterizing the reef. Today such reef structures appear as irregular bodies of massive dolomite that interrupt the uniform bedding of the regional stratigraphic sequence.

The dip of the flanking strata diminishes away from the reef core and ultimately is reversed, in the case of the very large reefs. The gentle reverse dip and the peripheral sag which it bounds are interpreted as the response of the strata to sinking of the heavy reef structure and compensatory upbulging of the surrounding strata (Shrock, 1939).

Since reef-building organisms seem to be limited by depth and temperature, reefs will be formed only under conditions which permit the growth of the reef community. Reefs seem to occur in belts which are mainly depth-controlled. Shifting of the strandline related to transgression or regression of the sea, will result in migration of the reef belt (Link, 1950). Not uncommonly the lagoons between the reef belt and the shoreline proper become hypersaline and even the site of salt deposition.

Biostromal Limestone

The term *biostrome* is applied to deposits formed by sedentary organisms (shell beds, crinoidal limestone, algal beds, and so forth) which are stratiform and not swelling into moundlike or lenslike form. Obviously, all strata are lenses and the distinction between bioherm and biostrome is somewhat arbitrary.

Biostromal limestones vary from those which are crowded with easily recognized fossils to those which contain few fossil structures. Some biostromal beds, especially those interbedded with the shales (such as the limestone beds in the Eden and Maysville beds of southwestern Ohio) are veritable museums of past life (Pl. 25, center). They are coquina-like deposits, but if unsorted and nontransported they may be described as coquinoid

---

[10] Except perhaps in the proximity of the reef where reef-induced turbulence inhibited deposition of interreef materials, with the result that interreef strata tend to thin in the proximity of the reef (Lowenstam, 1950).

limestones. In some limestones such highly fossiliferous layers are inter-bedded with fine-grained nonfossiliferous limestone. Subsequent dolomitiza-tion of the rock may obscure the character of the biostromal beds, which appear only as a rough porous layer characterized by ill-preserved and obscure fossil structures. The cavities, like those in reef rock proper, acquire drusy linings of dolomite.

Biostromal shelly beds may originate in several ways. (1) They may record periods in which no clastic material was deposited. (2) They may be lag deposits, i.e., represent a coarse residue left by removal of the once asso-ciated fines. In this case the fossils are a concentrate from a thicker stratum through which they were once scattered. (3) They may record wholesale destruction of life, such as might occur by fouling of the waters with hydro-gen sulfide.

Some limestones also properly classed as biostromal contain few obvious fossils. These are the algal biostromes. They vary from beds a few inches thick to those several feet thick, crowded with typical stromatolites with pycnostromid, collenia, or cryptozoon-type structures (Fig. 62, A). Algal limestone, lacking the typical stromatolite forms, may be difficult to recog-nize (Fig. 62, B). Characteristic of some modern carbonate sediments is a delicate lamination. This lamination may be minutely crinkled, broken, and deformed in various ways. In some cases the crinkling is superimposed upon larger irregularities. At the present time these structures are produced by desiccation of a mat of blue-green algae which occur in the intertidal waters of Florida (Ginsburg, 1955). The algal mat appears primarily to be a sedi-ment-binding rather than a sediment-producing structure. The living mat is somewhat spongy and elastic but infilling with detrital and precipitated carbonate tends to solidify the structure. The resulting deposit is laminated but devoid of any other microstructures.

In some rocks the algal laminations are very indistinct. Precipitated calcite infillings produce a bird's-eye limestone, such as the McLish (Ordovician) of Oklahoma (Ham, 1954), the algal origin of which had been long over-looked. Some nonlaminated nodular and bolster-like masses found in other-wise well-bedded limestones are probably of algal origin although they show none of the features usually attributed to algae. So also some limestones exhibit an irregular bedding, which in cross section appears as an anasto-mosing network of stratification planes. This has been described as a *weedia-*type stromatolite and attributed to algal action (Richardson, 1949; Cloud, 1942). The lamination or stratification planes bifurcate and join in an irregular manner. Since this structure bears some resemblance to bedding irregularities seen in noncarbonate silts and muds, it may not be algal, but as in the noncarbonate deposits, may be a product of hydroplastic or soft-sediment boudinage.

Algal limestones are very common in the Precambrian (Fenton and Fenton, 1939; Richardson, 1949; Young, 1935) and early Paleozoic especially in the Cambro-Ordovician of the Appalachian region (Sando, 1953; Long, 1953), the Arbuckle Mountains of Oklahoma (Ham, 1954; Johnson, 1951), and the Teton Mountains (Blackwelder, 1915).

Pelagic Limestones

Normally biochemical limestones are produced by bottom-living (benthonic) organisms. Some biochemical limestones, however, are formed chiefly by the accumulation of the tests of pelagic or floating organisms. Such organisms are usually microscopic and the carbonate accumulation produced by the "rain" of their tests upon the sea floor is very fine-grained. The resulting limestones are rather poor, as a rule, in megascopic fossils, particularly those of benthonic habit.

The Foraminifera are chiefly responsible for these pelagic carbonate deposits. But as the lime-secreting habit was not acquired by the pelagic Foraminifera until the Cretaceous, deposits of this type are Cretaceous or younger in age. Pelagic limestones may be the product of lime-carbonate deposition in relatively deep water (though not necessarily abyssal).[11]

Pelagic limestones are relatively rare. They seem to be most characteristic of the geosynclinal belts, where they occur as thin and commonly siliceous beds (Sloss, p. 112, 1947). Limestone of this type is reported from the Alps.

There are in addition widespread carbonate deposits known as *chalk* which formed mainly by the accumulation of the tests of planktonic calcareous microorganisms, chiefly Foraminifera. Chalk is a porous, fine-textured, and somewhat friable material. Normally it is white and consists almost wholly of calcium carbonate (Table 74, col. G) as calcite. The carbonate content varies from 90 to 98 per cent in the French chalk; the Kansas chalk is 88 to 98 per cent carbonate (average 94 per cent) (Runnels and Dubins, 1949). Under the microscope, chalk consists of the tests of microorganisms composed of clear calcite set in a structureless matrix of fine-grained carbonate. In the Kansas chalk the microfossils form 17 to 34 per cent of the rock; the balance was the matrix. *Globigerina*, *Textularia*, and other Foraminifera are the most conspicuous. Also present in chalk are spikes and cells of planktonic algae known as *rhabdoliths* and *coccoliths*, together with a few sponge spicules and radiolarian tests.

The best known chalks seem to be of Cretaceous age. Most famous chalk is that exposed in cliffs on both sides of the English Channel, the type locality of the Cretaceous (Lt: cretaceus: chalk) system. In North America

---

[11] Oceanic surveys show that the calcareous oozes are absent from the ocean floors in depths exceeding 3000 fathoms. The deeper waters seem to be able to dissolve the carbonate.

chalk occurs extensively in beds of Cretaceous age in Alabama, Mississippi, and Tennessee (Selma chalk) and in Nebraska and adjoining states (Niobrara chalk). The Fort Hays chalk of Kansas has been described in some detail (Runnels and Dubins, 1949).

Chalk is a friable carbonate. Although it may contain chert nodules, in some cases in rhythmically spaced layers (Richardson, 1919), it is an almost unaltered deposit. That solutions moving through such a porous and easily alterable material have affected so little change is indeed remarkable. It has been suggested that unlike other lime-carbonate deposits, the chalk was precipitated as calcite instead of aragonite, and owing to the greater stability of this substance, no reorganization took place as it would have done if the original precipitated carbonate were aragonite. It failed therefore to become a dense, hard rock.

DETRITAL (ALLOCHTHONOUS) LIMESTONES

Calcarenites and Calcirudites

Calcarenite (Grabau, 1904) is a general term used to describe those mechanically deposited carbonate rocks of sand-grain size ($\frac{1}{16}$ to 2 mm in diameter) that are composed of 50 per cent or more of carbonate detritus. If the fragments are over 2 millimeters in diameter, the term *calcirudite* may be applied to the rock. The calcarenites and calcirudites are cemented by clear calcite.

The carbonate detritus is of subaqueous origin [12] and consists mainly of fossil materials, both entire and broken, pebbles, and granules of calcilutites and of oolites. Some of the detritus is therefore biofragmental, some strictly clastic, and in part both biochemical and chemical carbonate. All of it, however, is current transported and sorted and mechanically deposited so that the accumulation has the structure of a detrital sediment.

The distinction between materials of biofragmental, fragmental, and even chemical origin is arbitrary. Some of the fossil debris is coated with one or more layers of precipitated carbonate; many of the oolites proper have nuclei of detrital carbonate or quartz. Moreover, calcarenites vary greatly in the importance of the contributing materials. Some are nearly all oolites; others wholly fossil debris. Still others consist mainly of granules of calcilutitic material and contain only a few scattered oolites or recognizable fossil materials.

Those detrital limestones consisting wholly or nearly so of sorted fossil debris are *coquinas* of one kind or another. The term coquina is most commonly applied to the more or less cemented coarse shell debris (Pl. 25, top).

---

[12] Some limestone *conglomerates* are of terrestrial derivation and are not intraformational or intrabasinal as are most calcarenites and associated calcirudites.

For the finer shell detritus of calcarenite grade, the term *microcoquina* is more appropriate.[13]

Most common of the microcoquinas are the crinoid coquinas to which the term *encrinite* has been applied (Pl. 28, A). These crinoidal limestones have been also called *organogenic conglomerates* (Hadding, 1933). They consist almost exclusively of disks and plates that are detached from one another. These materials commonly are worn and are sorted into beds that differ in the size of the constituent fragments. Well-preserved crowns and long stems are not found in these rocks; they occur in the marlstones. The latter, which are crinoid-bearing rocks but not encrinites, were formed in more tranquil waters than are the crinoid coquinas, so that after the death of the animals the remains were entombed more or less intact in the bottom mud. The marls having scattered but well-preserved articulate crinoid remains, and the encrinites that are built up of sorted and washed crinoid ossicles, are indices of two contrasting facies of lime deposition. Hadding (1933) attributed removal of muds and concentration of crinoid debris to bottom currents upon uplift of the sea bottom and the shoaling of the waters.

◨ Oolites
▢ No oolites
◼ Quartz sand
⊢⎯ 10%

Vertical scale: 1" = 20'

FIG. 95. Co-occurrence of carbonate oolites and detrital quartz grains in Greenbriar (Mississippian) of West Virginia (after G. Rittenhouse, Bulletin, American Assoc. Petrol. Geologists, vol. 33, 1949).

The calcarenites in which oolites are the chief ingredient are the *oolites* or oolitic calcarenites (see page 95 for definition of terms oolite and so forth). The oolitic texture almost certainly is a primary feature that is characteristic of shallow, strongly agitated waters. The uniformity of size of the oolites, the association of oolites and quartz sand grains (Fig. 95), the cross-bedded character of many oolitic rocks, and the clear crystalline carbonate cement (and absence of fine interstitial carbonate mud) are supporting evidence for this interpretation.[14] Observations on the calcareous oolites of the Bahamas led Illing (1954, p. 43) to the conclusion that these oolites

[13] A distinction should be made between true coquinas and *coquinoid* limestones. The former is a true detrital rock, whereas coquinoid limestones are autochthonous deposits consisting of coarse shelly materials which have accumulated in place (compare Pls. 27, D, and 28, E) and generally with a fine-grained matrix.

[14] The clear crystalline matrices of some oolitic limestones, however, have been attributed to recrystallization of an original fine-grained interstitial mud (Bonet, 1951, p. 172).

were precipitated where "the fresh oceanic waters sweeping on the shallow Banks have been sufficiently warmed and stirred up" and thus become supersaturated with calcium carbonate. According to Illing "oolitic accretion depends fundamentally on the movement of the sand grains under the impetus of marine currents."

In addition to organic detritus and oolites, calcarenites contain small, sand-sized grains which are fine-grained and without any internal structure, organic or otherwise. Such rounded nonskeletal grains have been called pellets, granules, false oolites, pseudo-oolites, and so forth. In some calcarenites these grains greatly exceed either recognizable organic debris or oolites proper.

These grains may indeed be pellets—a term applied to the small ovoid bodies which are produced by various marine organisms. Examples of such faecal pellets have been described (Moore, 1933; Eardley, 1938; Illing, 1954). Although pellets of faecal origin are rather common they probably are rarely quantitatively important and the majority of the nonskeletal grains are formed in some other manner.

These microcrystalline sand grains have been attributed to subaqueous erosion of previously consolidated calcilutites. There is no fundamental difference in character between the larger flat pebbles of many intraformational conglomerates and the smaller pebbles found in some calcarenites and the sand-sized debris of the calcarenites themselves. Hence some writers (Long, 1953) have regarded all the structureless carbonate clasts as mechanical in origin.

Illing (1954, pp. 27–35), however, believed these grains to be in large part a product of a penecontemporaneous aggregation process. These cemented aggregates were thought to form in a calcareous silt or mud as irregular to botryoidal bodies (lumps, grapestone, and the like). Currents tend to winnow these grains, round them, and deposit them with organic debris and oolites of the same size grade. Conceived in this manner the calcarenites are sands built up from calcareous silts and muds and are somewhat analogous to the lithic arenites which contain shale, slate, and argillite sand grains, and are thus rebuilt argillites (Fig. 96). They differ, however, in that the reconstitution process in the one case is penecontemporaneous, whereas in the other it is mainly epigenetic and in some cases metamorphic (though, of course, the mud pellets and mudstone conglomerates are a product of penecontemporaneous compaction and induration of noncalcareous muds).

The proportions of organic detritus, oolites, and nonskeletal sand grains may vary greatly. They may be mixed with noncarbonate sand, mainly clastic quartz, in varying proportions. A suggested classification of the possible mixtures is given in Figs. 97 and 98. The nomenclature of these rocks

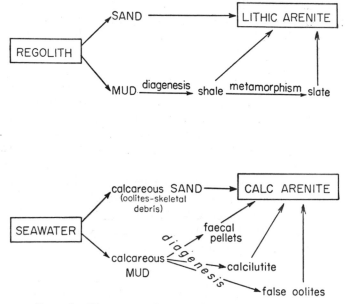

FIG. 96. Diagram to show similarity in provenance of calcarenites and lithic arenites.

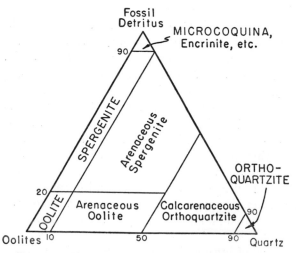

FIG. 97. Classification of the calcarenites and related rocks based on the composition of the detrital fraction.

has not been worked out or agreed upon. If the oolitic materials predominate, the term oolite may be applied to the rock; or the rock may be called an oolitic limestone (or better, an oolitic calcarenite). If the fossil debris predominates, the rock may be termed a microcoquina. If the calcarenites consist largely of nonskeletal sand grains (essentially fragments of calcilutites or calcisiltites) the rock is a lithic arenite of a very special sort, namely, a lithic calcarenite. For rocks containing all these materials, no one perhaps dominant, there is no suitable name. The Salem (or Spergen) limestone of Mississippian age of Indiana is a rock of this type (Pl. 28, E). This rock is widely used as a building stone ("Bedford" or "Indiana oolitic limestone") (Loughlin, 1929). Such a rock therefore might be designated spergenite.

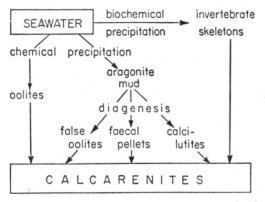

Fig. 98. Diagram showing provenance of calcarenites.

The calcarenites are closely associated with the orthoquartzites. Not only are they interbedded with one another, but they grade into each other (Pl. 28, C and D). The clastic carbonate and clastic quartz are mingled in all proportions. Even formations that commonly are termed limestone may contain a significant volume of detrital quartz (Winchell, 1924; Long, 1953; Merritt, 1928; Rittenhouse, 1949). With increasing proportions of detrital quartz the calcarenite becomes an arenaceous limestone (arenaceous spergenite or arenaceous oolite). If the quartz exceeds 50 per cent the term calcarenaceous orthoquartzite may be applied.[15] The larger conspicuous quartz grains are remarkably well rounded. In some cases the quartz forms the nuclei of the calcareous oolites.

Secondary enlargement of the quartz is very common although not uni-

[15] The term calcareous orthoquartzite would be inappropriate because it refers to an orthoquartzite with some introduced carbonate cement, not to a sandstone consisting of mixed quartz and carbonate detritus.

PLATE 27

FOSSILIFEROUS AND OTHER AUTOCHTHONOUS LIMESTONES

A: Limestone bed from Decorah shale, Ordovician, St. Paul, Minn. Ordinary light, ×15.

Shell debris—brachiopods and bryozoa—in a fine-grained lime mud.

B: Shell limestone ("Purbeck Marble"), Purbeck, Purbeckian, Dorsetshire, England. Ordinary light, ×15.

A veritable coquina. Note crystalline mosaic replacing mollusk shells. Also note angular quartz sand trapped within broken shell. A fresh-water limestone with both gastropod and pelecypod remains.

C: Crinoidal limestone, Carboniferous, Matlock, England. Ordinary light, ×15.

Unlike most encrinites, the crinoid debris is unsorted and is embedded in fine-grained lime mud. Compare crinoidal limestone of Pl. 28, **A**.

D: Coral limestone, Silurian, Wenlock, Shropshire, England. Ordinary light, ×15.

Entire brachiopod shell and debris from echinoderms embedded in lime mud.

E: Dolomitic (?) limestone, Burlescombe, Carboniferous, Somerset, England. Ordinary light, ×38.

Foraminiferal and other shell debris embedded in crystalline mosaic of calcite.

F: Foraminiferal limestone, Eocene (?) from the Pyramids, Ghizeh, Egypt. Ordinary light, ×18.

Several entire *Nummulites* (?) tests, embedded in a lime mud which contains much comminuted fossil debris.

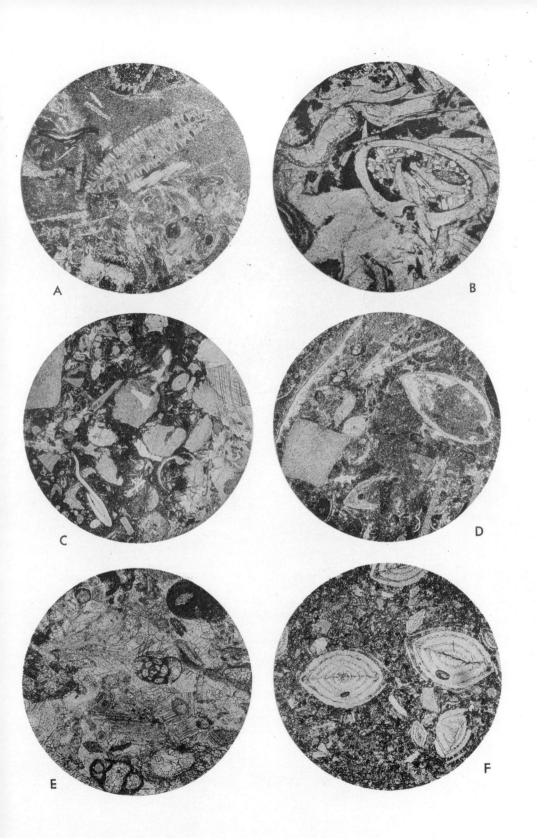

A

B

C

D

E

F

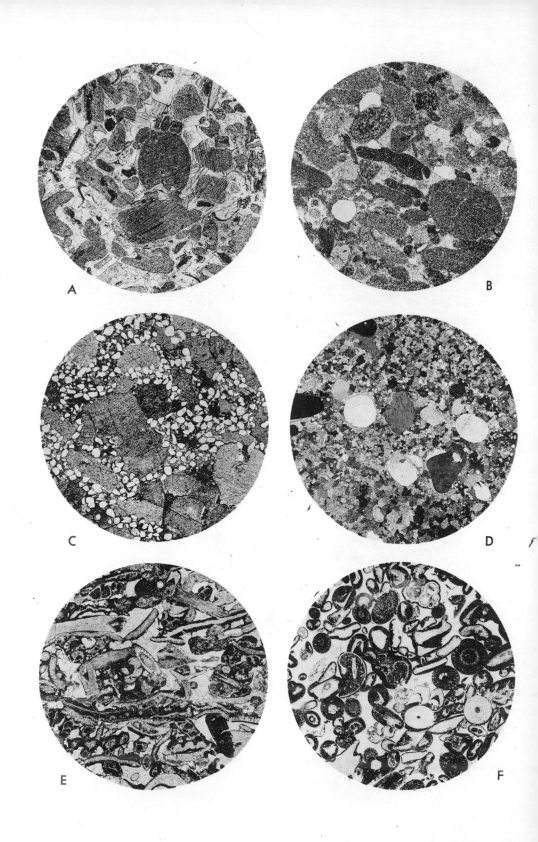

A

B

C

D

E

F

PLATE 28

CALCARENITES

A: Crystalline limestone, Fernvale, Ordovician, Carter County, Okla. Ordinary light, $\times 14$.

Consists almost wholly of crystalline crinoid debris cemented by calcite. Cement deposited in crystallographic continuity with detritus. Note cleavage which passes without interruption from dusty detrital grain into clear cement. Properly called a calcarenite, variety microcoquina (encrinite).

B: Altyn limestone, Belt Series, Precambrian, Glacier National Park, Montana. Ordinary light, $\times 15$.

A calcarenite consists mainly of rounded carbonate detritus associated with a little detrital quartz, feldspar, particles of granite and chert. Not shown in photograph are outgrowths on feldspar (see Pl. 40, **D**) and quartz and calcareous oolites.

C: Grand Tower limestone, Devonian, Ozora, Missouri. Ordinary light, $\times 16$. Photograph by T. G. Payne.

Coarse crinoidal debris (75 to 80 per cent), and fine well-rounded quartz sand (8 to 10 per cent) cemented by calcite (5 to 10 per cent). Illustrates mingling of debris from two unlike sources.

D: St. Louis limestone, Mississippian, Beardstown quadrangle, Illinois. Crossed nicols, $\times 13$.

Large rounded quartz, quartzite, and chert grains, together with small silt-sized particles of quartz in a carbonate matrix. Matrix dominant. Hand specimen shows limestone pebbles.

E: Salem ("Bedford") limestone, Mississippian, Indiana. Ordinary light, $\times 15$.

A microcoquina or spergenite cemented by clear calcite. Consists of sorted fossil debris, including bryozoan fragments and a few entire Foraminifera (*Endothyra*), together with carbonate detritus of unknown origin.

F: "Oolitic" limestone, Mississippian, Anna, Illinois. Ordinary light,

A spergenite composed of detrital carbonate, fossil debris, some entire Foraminifera, and some oolites bound together by a clear calcite cement.

versal. The authigenic overgrowth may restore the crystal form of the quartz. The detrital core is marked by a ring of included carbonate particles (Pl. 39, C, D, and E). The quartz euhedra cut across and replace various primary structures, such as the oolites (Henbest, 1945). The silica was therefore introduced after consolidation of the rock.

Calcarenites may contain some glauconite. Many glauconitic limestones belong to this group and are better described as glauconitic calcarenites.

The normal cement of the calcarenites is calcite (except where it is later dolomitized). In some calcarenites the carbonate appears both as a comb-like fringe on the detrital grains and as a clear coarsely crystalline mosaic between the grains. That carbonate detritus, which is crystallographically a unit, such as echinoderm ossicles, plates, and spines, invariably is surrounded by cementing carbonate in crystallographic (and optical) continuity. The original fragment is distinguished only by the abundance of the dusty inclusions that it contains (Pl. 28, A). Thus by enlargement of the crinoid debris in the encrinites the so-called *crystalline limestones* or sedimentary *marbles* are formed. In the Fredonia oolite, however, Graf and Lamar (1950) regard the clear calcite cement as a second-generation cement, the first being a finely crystalline brown calcite. The earlier cement was believed to have been largely removed by solution prior to the deposition of the clear calcite. Bonet (1951, p. 174), however, regarded the clear calcite cement of the calcarenites as a product of recrystallization of an original microcrystalline interstitial carbonate mud. This interpretation, however, was considered and rejected for the calcarenites associated with the Scurry reef (Permo-Carboniferous) of Texas (Bergenback and Terriere, 1953). In the absence of a cement, calcarenites may have about the same porosity as a sandstone, and like sandstones they may function as reservoirs for natural gas and oil. In rare but interesting cases the oolites may be removed by solution but the cement remain intact. Such rocks are also porous and may constitute a reservoir for fluids.

In the field calcarenites resemble the noncarbonate sandstones. They are commonly current bedded with the cross-bedding similar in scale and structure to that found in the ordinary sandstones. They also show scour-and-fill structures. They grade into and are associated with both normal and noncarbonate sandstones and with finer-grained calcareous siltstones and calcilutites.

Calcilutites

By decrease in grain size the calcarenites grade into carbonate silts (calcisiltites) and into carbonate muds, which if consolidated are the *calcilutites*. If the calcilutites are exceptionally fine-grained, dense, homogeneous, and exhibit conchoidal or subconchoidal fracture, they are termed *lithographic limestones* because at one time the best-quality stone of this sort was used in lithography.

Calcareous muds, however, are not of a single origin. Although some may indeed be the finer productions of marine attrition—as the calcarenites are the coarser detritus formed by such action—some of the calcareous mud may be instead a chemical or biochemical precipitate. Bacterial action has been thought responsible for some of the fine impalpable lime muds (drewite) (Drew, 1914; Bavendam, 1931, 1932). The bacteria responsible are those which produce ammonia, which reacts with carbonates to form ammonium carbonate. The ammonium carbonate reacts with the calcium sulfate of sea water to precipitate calcium carbonate. The fine-grained nonfossiliferous Precambrian limestones have been thus explained (Daly, 1909). Although there is some uncertainty as to whether sea water is saturated with calcium carbonate (Sverdrup, Johnson, and Fleming, 1946, pp. 997–1001), there can be no doubt that very shallow marine waters, partially isolated, may become saturated and from such waters carbonate may be precipitated as aragonite. Under turbulent conditions oolites may form; in tranquil waters aragonite is precipitated as minute acicular crystals. The aragonite needles found in the muds of shallow lagoons in the Bahamas have been regarded as evidence of direct precipitation of calcium carbonate. In other cases the fine-grained limestones have been explained as accumulations of coccoliths or as "algal dust" (Wood, 1941).

The origin of the fine-grained, dense, and structureless limestones is certainly a moot question. Though commonly called calcilutites they may not be true trituration products. These aphanitic limestones are very common and although seldom forming a whole rock, they form the bulk of many limestone beds. And as noted by Illing (1954) these fine-grained materials may be rebuilt into coarse-grained calcarenites. The latter commonly consist mainly of nonskeletal sand grains of calcilutite.

MISCELLANEOUS CHEMICAL LIMESTONES

Tufa and *travertine* are limestones formed by the evaporation of spring and river waters. Tufa is a spongy, porous rock which forms a thin, surficial deposit about springs and seeps and exceptionally in rivers. The carbonate of lime is deposited on growing plants and therefore commonly bears the imprint of leaves and stems. It has a reticulate to explanate structure; much of it is weak and semifriable. Tufa is seldom extensive and is restricted mainly to Recent or Quaternary deposits. Lithoid tufa deposited in extinct lakes Lahonton and Bonneville occurs as large domes.

Travertine is a more dense, banded deposit especially common in limestone caverns where it forms the well-known *flowstone* and *dripstone*, including stalactites and stalagmites (Allison, 1923). Like tufa it forms relatively small deposits of no great geologic importance and is primarily Quaternary or Recent in age.

   Caliche is a lime-rich deposit formed in the soils of certain semiarid regions. Capillary action draws the lime-bearing waters to the surface where, by evaporation, the lime-rich caliche is formed. Old caliches are likely to be

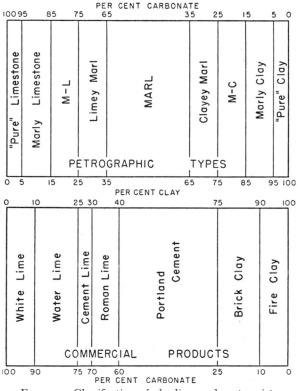

FIG. 99.   Classification of clay-lime carbonate mixtures; top, petrographic classification; bottom, classification based on commercial use (after Barth, Correns, and Eskola, 1939).

well indurated. Some are marked by large, concentrically banded, bolster-like masses. In some regions caliche forms the cap rock of mesas and buttes (Price, 1933; Bretz and Horberg, 1949). Caliche, if found in the geologic record, is important as a climatic index. It forms only in regions of limited rainfall.

   Marl is a term of varied meanings. It has been applied to glauconitic greensands but is used most commonly to designate certain friable carbonate earths accumulated in Recent or present-day fresh-water lakes (Davis, 1900).

Certain plants, notably *Chara* (stonewort) are able to obtain carbon dioxide for photosynthesis from calcium bicarbonate. Calcium carbonate therefore is precipitated as a crust on the leaves and stems of the plant. This deposit is sloughed off in time and accumulates on the bottom of the lake. Fresh-water limestones as thus formed will be characterized by a pseudobrecciation. Small angular chips or flakes of calcium carbonate are embedded in a mud of similar composition. To the material thus produced may be added carbonate precipitated by microorganisms (Williams and McCoy, 1934) and that secreted by fresh-water mollusks. The fresh-water marls are somewhat argillaceous and are commonly used as an ingredient in the manufacture of Portland cement (see Fig. 99).

Fresh-water limestones of the geologic record are characterized by lack of a marine fauna; they contain *Spirorbis*, various ostracods, and occasional mollusks. Many are algal and show algal structures. Some are nodular. The nodule-like masses show calcite filled syneresis cracks. Under the microscope the rock has a clotted appearance, being made up of rounded clotlike masses of dense fine-grained carbonate held together with clearer coarser-textured carbonate (Pl. 30, A and B).

Marlstone (also marlite) is a term applied to better indurated rocks of about the same composition as marl. The marlstones are less fissile than the shales, and like mudstones, have a blocky subconchoidal fracture. The term marlstone has been extended to include other calcareous rocks—a practice which has been criticized (Picard, 1953).

DIAGENESIS OF LIMESTONES

More than any other rock, perhaps, limestone is prone to alterations, both pre- and postconsolidation. Most profound are those changes in texture and composition which lead to the formation of dolomite (page 421) and to replacement by silica, phosphate, and so forth (pages 439, 471, and 432). In some cases these replacements involve the introduction of foreign materials into the rock; in others the changes involve only rearrangements of materials already present—a diagenetic differentiation.

Of major importance also is the conversion of the original carbonate, such as vaterite or aragonite, to calcite. This change is rapid and spontaneous. As noted elsewhere, this recrystallization, like dolomitization, leads to loss of textural detail. Aragonitic oolites or shells lose their internal structure and are converted to a coarse calcite mosaic with only faint or ghostlike relics of their original structure. Such recrystallization is controlled by the original mineral composition, i.e., those elements of the rock, such as the oolites or particular shelly materials that were aragonitic, are recrystallized; the calcitic portions are not affected.

On the other hand, a pervasive recrystallization is commonly found in some limestones. The recrystallized areas are not controlled by the original composition. The end results are patches of coarsely crystalline carbonate which invade in an irregular way, shell debris, oolites, and matrix alike. The unrecrystallized areas remaining dark, dense, and fine-grained, are finally surrounded by the water-clear coarse crystalline calcite. Such a rock has a clotted or grumous texture (Bonet, 1951, p. 172).

The distinction between recrystallization which is selective, and that which is pervasive and not selective, is not sharp. Nor is the difference between carbonate produced by selective recrystallization and that precipitated in the intergranular voids always clear. Bonet (1951) attributes the clear calcite cement of some calcarenites to recrystallization of an interstitial carbonate mud instead of precipitation of vein calcite in the voids.

Even a fine-grained or cryptocrystalline limestone may be reorganized by recrystallization and become a coarse-grained crystalline rock. If this reorganization is incomplete so that the rock is a grumous limestone, it superficially resembles a calcarenite with crystalline matrix. The cryptocrystalline elements of the rock, however, are irregular patches with hazy borders unlike the sharply defined clasts and other detritus of the true calcarenites.

Most conspicuous in limestones are the effects of solution. Such effects, though also seen in noncarbonate sandstones, are most prominent in the limestones. Microstylolitic contacts between fossils, between fossils and their matrix, and more continuous stylolitic seams are very common in the purer carbonate rocks. The net effect of this internal solution is to remove an appreciable volume of material—40 per cent or more in some cases (Stockdale, 1926) and greatly to alter or to modify the primary textures and structures. Selective solution may remove the fossils and leave voids (external molds) or may remove oolites but leave their matrix intact (oolicasts); stylolites may produce apparent offsets of oblique veins and be in turn cut by later veins.

REFERENCES CITED AND BIBLIOGRAPHY

Allison, V. C. (1923), The growth of stalagmites and stalactites, *J. Geol.*, vol. 31, pp. 106–125.

Andrée, K. (1915), Ursachen und Arten der Schichtung, *Geol. Rundschau*, Bd. 6, H 7/8, pp. 351–397.

Bavendamm, W. (1932), Die mikrobiologische Kalkfällung in der tropischen See, *Arch. Mikrobiol.*, vol. 3, pp. 205–276.

Bavendamm, W. (1931), The possible rôle of micro-organisms in the precipitation of calcium carbonate in tropical seas, *Science*, vol. 73, pp. 597–598.

Bergenback, R. E., and Terriere, R. T. (1953), Petrography of Scurry reef, Texas, *Bull. Am. Assoc. Petroleum Geol.*, vol. 37, pp. 1014–1029.

Blackwelder, E. (1915), A fully exposed reef of calcareous algae (?) in the Middle Cambrian of the Teton Mountains, Am. J. Sci., ser. 4, vol. 39, pp. 646–650.

Bonet, Frederico (1952), La facies Urgoniana del Cretacico Medio de la region de Tampico, Bol. Assoc. mexicana geol. petroleros, vol. 4, pp. 153-262.

Bretz, J Harlen, and Horberg, Leland (1949), Caliche in southeastern New Mexico, J. Geol., vol. 57, pp. 491–511.

Carozzi, A. (1949), Sur une particularité des calcaires pseudo-oolithiques de l'Urgonien (Nappe de Morcles), Arch. sci. Genève, vol. 2, pp. 348–350.

Carozzi, A. (1952), Tectonique, courants de turbidité et sédimentation. Application au Jurassique supérieur des chaines subalpines de Haute-Savoie, Rev. gén. sci., vol. 59, pp. 229–245.

Cayeux, Lucien (1935), Les roches sédimentaires de France: Roches carbonatées, Paris, Masson.

Chave, K. E. (1952), A solid solution between calcite and dolomite, J. Geol., vol. 60, pp. 190–192.

Chave, K. E. (1954a), Aspects of the biogeochemistry of magnesium. 1. Calcareous marine organisms, J. Geol., vol. 62, pp. 266–283.

Chave, K. E. (1954b), Aspects of the biogeochemistry of magnesium. 2. Calcareous sediments and rocks, J. Geol., vol. 62, pp. 587–599.

Clarke, F. W. (1904), Analyses of rocks, U.S. Geol. Survey Bull. 228.

Clarke, F. W. (1924), Data of geochemistry, U.S. Geol. Survey Bull. 770.

Clarke, F. W. and Wheeler, W. C. (1922), The inorganic constituents of marine invertebrates, U.S. Geol. Survey Prof. Paper 124.

Cloud, P. E. (1942), Notes on stromatolites, Am. J. Sci., vol. 240, pp. 363–379.

Cumings, E. R. and Shrock, R. R. (1928), Niagaran coral reefs of Indiana and adjacent states and their stratigraphic relations, Bull. Geol. Soc. Amer., vol. 39, pp. 579–620.

Daly, R. A. (1909), First calcareous fossils and the evolution of limestone, Bull. Geol. Soc. Amer., vol. 20, pp. 153–170.

Davis, C. A. (1900), A contribution to the natural history of marl, J. Geol., vol. 8, pp. 485–497.

Decker, C. E. and Merritt, C. A. (1928), Physical characteristics of the Arbuckle limestone, Oklahoma Geol. Survey, Circular No. 15, p. 49.

DeFord, R. K. (1946), Grain size in carbonate rocks, Bull. Am. Assoc. Petroleum Geol., vol. 30, pp. 1921–1928.

Drew, G. H. (1914), On the precipitation of calcium carbonate in the sea by marine bacteria and on the action of denitrifying bacteria in tropical and temperate seas, Carnegie Inst. Wash., Publ. no. 182, pp. 7–45.

Eardley, A. J. (1938), Sediments of Great Salt Lake, Utah, Bull. Am. Assoc. Petroleum Geol., vol. 22, pp. 1305–1411.

Evans, J. W. (1900), Mechanically formed limestones from Junagarh (Kathiwar) and other localities, Quart. J. Geol. Soc. London, vol. 56, pp. 559–583.

Fenton, C. L. and Fenton, M. A. (1939), Pre-Cambrian and Paleozoic algae, Bull. Geol. Soc. Amer., vol. 50, pp. 89–126.

Ginsburg, R. N. (1954), Early diagenesis and lithification of carbonate sediments in south Florida, *Special Public. No. 4, Soc. Econ. Paleon. and Mineralogists.*

Ginsburg, R. N. (1955), Recent stromatolitic sediments from south Florida, *J. Sediment. Petrol.*, vol. 25, p. 129.

Grabau, A. W. (1904), On the classification of sedimentary rocks, *Am. Geol.*, vol. 33, pp. 228–247.

Graf, D. L. and Lamar, J. E. (1950), Petrology of Fredonia oölite in southern Illinois, *Bull. Am. Assoc. Petroleum Geol.*, vol. 34, pp. 2318–2336.

Graf, D. L. and Goldsmith, J. R. (1952), Stability of magnesian calcites, *Bull. Geol. Soc. Amer.*, vol. 63, p. 1256 (abstract).

Grim, R. E., Lamar, J. E., and Bradley, W. F. (1937), The clay minerals in Illinois limestones, *J. Geol.*, vol. 45, pp. 829–843.

Hadding, Assar (1933), The pre-Quaternary sedimentary rocks of Sweden, V. Limestones, *Lunds Univ. Arrsk.*, N.F., Avd. 2, Bd. 29; nr. 4.

Hadding, Assar (1941), The pre-Quaternary sedimentary rocks of Sweden, VI. Reef Limestones, *Medd. Lunds Geol. Mineral. Inst., Lunds Univ. Arsskr.*, N.F. Avd. 2, Bd. 37, nr. 10.

Haldane, Gee (1932), Inorganic marine limestone, *J. Sediment. Petrol.*, vol. 2, pp. 162–166.

Ham, W. E. (1954), Algal origin of the "birdseye" limestone in the McLish formation, *Proc., Oklahoma Acad. Sci.*, vol. 33, pp. 200–203.

Henbest, L. G. (1945), Unusual nuclei in oolites from the Morrow group near Fayetteville, Arkansas, *J. Sediment. Petrol.*, vol. 15, pp. 20–24.

Hohlt, R. B. (1948), The nature and origin of limestone porosity, *Colo. School Mines Quart.*, vol. 43, no. 4.

Illing, L. V. (1954), Bahaman calcareous sands, *Bull. Am. Assoc. Petroleum Geol.*, vol. 38, pp. 1–95.

Ireland, H. A. (1936), Use of insoluble residues for correlation in Oklahoma, *Bull. Am. Assoc. Petroleum Geol.*, vol. 20, pp. 1086–1121.

Johnson, F. A., Jr. (1951), *Fabric of limestones and dolomites*, Ph.D. thesis, Univ. of Chicago.

Johnson, J. Harlan (1951), An introduction to the study of organic limestones, *Colo. School Mines Quart.*, vol. 46, no. 2.

Kay, Marshall (1951), North American geosynclines, *Geol. Soc. Amer. Mem. 48.*

Link, T. A. (1950), Theory of transgressive and regressive reef (bioherm) development and origin of oil, *Bull. Am. Assoc. Petroleum Geol.*, vol. 34, pp. 263–294.

Loughlin, G. F. (1929), Indiana oolitic limestone, *U.S. Geol. Survey Bull.* 811-C, pp. 113–202.

Long, M. B. (1953), *Origin of the Conococheague limestone*, Ph.D. thesis, The Johns Hopkins Univ.

Lowenstam, H. A. (1950), Niagaran reefs of the Great Lakes area, *J. Geol.*, vol. 58, pp. 430–487.

Lowenstam, H. A. (1954), Factors affecting the aragonite:calcite ratios in carbonate-secreting marine organisms, *J. Geol.*, vol. 62, pp. 284–322.

Lowenstam, H. A. and DuBois, E. P. (1946), Marine pool, Madison County, *Illinois State Geol. Survey, Rept. Invest.,* no. 114.

McQueen, H. S. (1931), Insoluble residues as a guide to stratigraphic study, *Missouri Bur. Geol. 56th Bien. Rept. Appendix.*

Moore, H. B. (1939), Faecal pellets in relation to marine deposits, in *Recent Marine Sediments,* Tulsa, Amer. Assoc. Petroleum Geologists, pp. 516–524.

Newell, N. D. (1955), Depositional fabric in Permian reef limestones, *J. Geol.,* vol. 63, p. 301–309.

Pia, J. (1933), Die rezenten Kalksteine, *Z. Krist. Mineral. Petrog.,* Abt. B, Erganzungsband.

Picard, M. D. (1953), Marlstone—a misnomer as used in Uinta Basin, Utah, *Bull. Am. Assoc. Petroleum Geol.,* vol. 37, pp. 1075–1077.

Price, W. A. (1933), Reynosa problem of south Texas and origin of caliche, *Bull. Am. Assoc. Petroleum Geol.,* vol. 17, pp. 488–522.

Richardson, E. S. (1949), Some Lower Huronian stromatolites of northern Michigan, *Fieldiana,* vol. 10, pp. 47–62.

Richardson, W. A. (1919), The origin of Cretaceous flint, *Geol. Mag.,* vol. 56, pp. 535–547.

Rittenhouse, Gordon (1949), Petrology and paleogeography of Greenbriar formation, *Bull. Am. Assoc. Petroleum Geol.,* vol. 33, pp. 1704–1730.

Rodgers, John (1954), Terminology of limestone and related rocks: an interim report, *J. Sediment. Petrol.,* vol. 24, pp. 225–234.

Runnels, R. T., and Dubins, I. M. (1949), Chemical and petrographic studies of the Fort Hays Chalk in Kansas, *Geol. Survey Kansas Bull.* 82, part I.

Sander, Bruno (1951), *Contributions to the study of depositional fabrics (Rhythmically deposited Triassic limestones and dolomites).* Translated by Eleanora Bliss Knopf. Tulsa, Am. Assoc. Petroleum Geologists.

Sando, W. F. (1953), *The stratigraphy and paleontology of the western belt of the Beekmantown group in Maryland,* Ph.D. thesis, The Johns Hopkins Univ.

Schwarzacher, W. (1946), Sedimentpetrographische Untersuchungen kalkalpiner Gesteine—Hallstatterkalke von Hallstatt und Ischl, *Jahrb. geol. Bundesanstalt* (Austria), vol. 91, pp. 1–47.

Shrock, R. R. (1939), Wisconsin Silurian bioherms (organic reefs), *Bull. Geol. Soc. Amer.,* vol. 50, pp. 529–562.

Sloss, L. L. (1947), Environments of limestone deposition, *J. Sediment. Petrol.,* vol. 17, pp. 109–113.

Stockdale, P. B. (1926), The stratigraphic significance of solution in rocks, *J. Geol.,* vol. 34, pp. 399–414.

Stout, Wilber (1941), Limestone and dolomite of western Ohio, *Bull. Geol. Survey Ohio,* 42.

Stout, Wilber and Lamborn, R. (1924), Geology of Columbiana County, *Bull. Geol. Survey Ohio,* 28.

Sverdrup, H. U., Johnson, M. W., and Fleming, R. H. (1946), *The oceans,* New York, Prentice-Hall.

Terzhagi, R. D. (1940), Compaction of lime mud as a cause of secondary structure, *J. Sediment. Petrol.,* vol. 10, pp. 78–90.

Thorp, E. M. (1936), The sediments of the Pearl and Hermes Reef, *J. Sediment. Petrol.*, vol. 6, pp. 109–118.

Vaughan, T. W. (1914), Preliminary remarks on the geology of the Bahamas with special reference to the origin of the Bahaman and Floridian oolites, *Carnegie Inst. Wash., Publ.*, 182.

Vaughan, T. W. (1917), Chemical and organic deposits of the sea, *Bull. Geol. Soc. Amer.*, vol. 28, pp. 933–944.

Williams, F. T. and McCoy, Elizabeth (1934), On the role of microorganisms in the precipitation of calcium carbonate in the deposits of fresh water lakes, *J. Sediment. Petrol.*, vol. 4, pp. 113–126.

Winchell, A. N. (1924), Petrographic studies of limestone alterations at Bingham, *Trans. Am. Inst. Mining Met. Engrs.*, vol. 70, pp. 884–902.

Wood, A. (1941), Algal dust and the finer-grained varieties of Carboniferous limestone, *Geol. Mag.*, vol. 78, pp. 192–200.

Young, R. B. (1935), A comparison of certain stromatolitic rocks in the dolomite series of South Africa with modern algal sediments in the Bahamas, *Trans. Geol. Soc. S. Africa*, vol. 37, pp. 153–162.

DOLOMITE

Composition and Nomenclature

Dolomites are those varieties of limestone containing more than 50 per cent carbonate, of which more than half is dolomite. The term dolomite (Fr: dolomie) was first applied to certain carbonate rocks of the Tyrolean Alps. Since it is also used as a mineral name, its abandonment as a rock term has been advocated (Shrock, 1948) and the term *dolostone* proposed as a substitute. Despite the possible ambiguity arising from the use of the same term for both a rock and a mineral, the term has persisted and will probably continue to be used for both.[16]

Rocks intermediate in composition between limestone (*sensus strictus*) and dolomite have been variously named. In general those in which calcite exceeds dolomite are called dolomitic limestone and those in which dolomite exceeds calcite are called limy, calcitic, calciferous, or calcdolomites. The precise line of division between these mixed rocks and the more homogeneous end members has not been agreed upon. As suggested above, the predominance of calcite over dolomite or vice versa is taken as the basis of the division between limestone and dolomite. The limestone end member is called a *high-calcium limestone* if it contains only a little magnesium. If it contains appreciable magnesium it is a *magnesian limestone*, and if dolomite

---

[16] Some writers (Grout, 1932, p. 288) would restrict the term *dolomite* to the mineral and use the term *dolomite limestone* for the rock. The latter is so similar to dolomitic limestone used by Cayeux (1935, p. 339) for a rock consisting of a mixture of dolomite and calcite that further confusion would be engendered by its use.

is conspicuous it is a *dolomitic limestone*. If the content of magnesium is small, this element is present as $MgCO_3$ in solid solution in the calcite and no dolomite is present. Calcite, however, ordinarily can contain only 1 or 2 per cent $MgCO_3$ in solid solution. A magnesian limestone therefore will contain an appreciable, though small, amount of dolomite. As inspection of

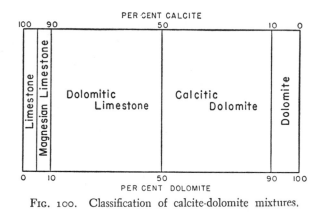

Fig. 100.   Classification of calcite-dolomite mixtures.

Fig. 91 and Table 79 will show, carbonate rocks with more than 10 but less than 90 per cent dolomite (less than 90 but more than 10 per cent calcite) are comparatively rare.[17] If the boundary between the dolomite end member and the mixed calcite-dolomite rock is placed at 90 per cent dolomite and that between limestone and the mixed rocks is placed at 10 per cent dolo-

TABLE 79.   Relative Abundance of Limestones and Dolomites[a] (based on data by Scobey, 1940)

Per Cent Dolomite[b]	Number of Samples
0 to 10	48
10 to 50	8
50 to 90	5
90 to 100	97
	158

[a] In the Cedar Valley, Wapsipinicon, Gower, and Hopkinton formations (Silurian and Devonian) of Iowa.
[b] Petrographically determined.

[17] The scarcity of rocks of intermediate composition was early noted by Steidtman (1917). This observation, though challenged (Cloud and Barnes, 1948, p. 92), is supported by data of Goldich and Parmalee (1947), Chave (1954b) and others.

TABLE 80. Nomenclature of Sedimentary Calcitic and Dolomitic Carbonates

Type	Per Cent Dolomite	Approx. MgO Equivalent Per Cent	Approx. MgCO$_3$ Equivalent Per Cent
Limestone			
High-calcium ⎫	0 to 10[a]	⎧ 0 to 1.1	0 to 2.3
Magnesian ⎭		⎩ 1.1 to 2.1	2.3 to 4.4
Dolomitic Limestone	10 to 50	2.1 to 10.8	4.4 to 22.7
Calcitic Dolomite	50 to 90	10.8 to 19.5	22.7 to 41.0
Dolomite	90 to 100	19.5 to 21.6	41.0 to 45.4

[a] Dolomite not present in high calcium limestone; magnesium carbonate is in solid solution in calcite.

TABLE 81. Chemical Composition of Dolomites
(per cent)

Constituent	A	B	C	D	E	F
SiO$_2$	....	2.55	7.96	3.24	24.92	0.73[a]
TiO$_2$	....	0.02	0.12	....	0.18	....
Al$_2$O$_3$	....	0.23	1.97	0.17	1.82	0.20
Fe$_2$O$_3$	....	0.02	0.14	0.17	0.66	....
FeO	....	0.18	0.56	0.06	0.40	1.03[b]
MnO	....	0.04	0.07	....	0.11	....
MgO	21.9	7.07	19.46	20.84	14.70	20.48
CaO	30.4	45.65	26.72	29.58	22.32	30.97
Na$_2$O	....	0.01	0.42	....	0.03	....
K$_2$O	....	0.03	0.12	....	0.04	....
H$_2$O+	....	0.05	0.33 ⎫	0.30	0.42 ⎫	....
H$_2$O−	....	0.18	0.30 ⎭		0.36 ⎭	....
P$_2$O$_5$	....	0.04	0.91	....	0.01	0.05
CO$_2$	47.7	43.60	41.13	45.54	33.82	47.51[c]
SO$_3$	....	0.03	....	....	0.01[d]	....
S	....	0.30[e]	0.19	....	0.16[e]	....
BaO	....	0.01[d]	none	....	none	....
SrO	....	0.01[d]	none	....	none	....
Organic	....	0.04[f]	....	....	0.08[f]	....
Total	100.0	100.06	100.40	99.90	100.04	100.97

A. Theoretical composition of pure dolomite.
B. Dolomitic limestone, Monroe formation (Devonian), Downs Schaaf, analyst (Stout, 1941, p. 564).
C. Niagaran dolomite (Silurian), Joliet, Ill. D. F. Higgins, analyst (Fisher, 1925, p. 34). MgO dolomite equivalent is 89.5 per cent.
D. "Knox" dolomite (Cambro-Ordovician), Morrisville, Ala. W. F. Hillebrand, analyst (Russell, 1889, p. 25). MgO dolomite equivalent is 96.5 per cent.
E. Cherty dolomite, Niagaran group (Silurian) Highland County, Ohio. Downs Schaaf, analyst (Stout, 1941, p. 82).
F. Randville dolomite (Precambrian), Dickinson County, Michigan. E. E. Brewster, analyst (Bayley, 1904, p. 215). MgO dolomite equivalent is 94.5 per cent.
  [a] Residue (mostly silica).
  [b] Calculated from reported iron.
  [c] Calculated from ferrous iron, magnesia, and lime.
  [d] Constituent does not exceed figure given.
  [e] Calculated as pyrite.
  [f] Organic carbon.

mite, the bulk of the carbonate rocks are either limestones or dolomites. The suggested nomenclature is summarized in Table 80.[18]

In chemical composition dolomites resemble limestones except that (by definition) MgO is a large and important constituent (Table 81). The magnesium content of the sedimentary carbonates appears to show a secular trend (Table 118, p. 686). The older carbonate rocks are higher in magnesia than those of the later geologic times (Daly, 1909, p. 165).

Textures and Structures

The dolomites closely resemble limestones in their grosser aspects. Close inspection, however, shows many differences. General dolomitization, like other types of metamorphism, tends to destroy earlier textures and structures. Therefore the clastic textures found in many limestones may be largely obliterated. In some cases only scattered grains of detrital quartz bear witness to the original clastic nature of the rock. In other cases the original clastic character is suggested by a ghostlike pattern faintly outlining the original debris. Dolomitized oolites and fossils also appear as faint shadows outlining the original shapes, but largely without any internal detail. Although dolomites are characteristically unfossiliferous, in some examples fossil remains are visible to the unaided eye as internal and external molds. The preservation of detail is poor and such cavities tend to be lined with drusy dolomite.

Dolomitization involves large-scale recrystallization. The end result is a granoblastic texture. Complete recrystallization produces a medium to coarsely crystalline mosaic in which, however, many of the dolomite crystals tend to show euhedral form. In general the dolomitic rocks are more even-grained than the limestones. In general also they are not so fine-grained. Incomplete dolomitization produces either a scattering of dolomite euhedra (porphyroblasts) in an unaltered calcitic matrix or a mottled rock with a patchy distribution of dolomite. The mottled appearance of the rock is primarily shown on the weathered surface. Mottled dolomite has been described in several places (Van Tuyl, 1916; Griffin, 1942; Beales, 1953; Sando, 1953) and probably is rather common. The dolomite areas in such rocks are very irregular in shape and form an anastomosing network. Few patches of dolomite are wholly isolated. They have been interpreted as a product of arrested dolomitization produced by the migration of magnesian solutions

---

[18] The nomenclature here recommended is much like that of Cayeux (1935, p. 339) and Rodgers (1954) but differs from usage of others. Cooper (1945), for example, classifies the carbonates as high calcium limestone (over 95 per cent $CaCO_3$), magnesian limestone (5 to 20 per cent $MgCO_3$), dolomite (20–46 per cent $MgCO_3$). The chief difficulty seems to be the term magnesian limestone, used by some for rocks with some MgO but containing no dolomite, by others for rocks with dolomite subordinate to calcite and by still others for all possible mixtures of dolomite and calcite.

through the rock (Griffin, 1942; Beales, 1953). The lack of control by bedding or other structures and the isolation of some dolomitic patches, however, are difficult to explain. Perhaps the mottling is a product of diagenetic differentiation resulting from unmixing of a solid solution of magnesium and calcium carbonate. The exsolved magnesium carbonate might form dolomite which would tend to be reorganized into segregations of relatively pure dolomite. The quantity of dolomite, some 20 to 30 per cent (on the average) in the Platteville limestone and 10 to 40 per cent in the Palliser (Devonian) of Alberta is approximately that to be expected by reorganization of algal limestone which is notably rich in magnesia. The incompleteness of the dolomitization and its uniformity over vast areas and great thickness are further evidence of an internal source for the magnesium.

The dolomite rhombs seen in partially altered limestones and in many dolomites are commonly zoned. The central portion may be clouded with inclusions whereas the peripheral part is relatively clear. In a few cases the crystals show alternately clear and clouded zones. In other rhombs the central part is calcite and the exterior is dolomite. The dolomite rhombs in some arenaceous dolomites may enclose small grains of detrital quartz.

The dolomite is automorphic against calcite. The rhombs transect primary structures such as fossils, oolites, and glauconite grains (Pl. 29, F), and the dolomite therefore is a replacement product.

The relations between dolomitic carbonate and precipitated silica (chert) are contradictory. In some rocks dolomite appears to be the earliest and to have been replaced by later silica, as chert pseudomorphs of dolomite (Pls. 32, F and 40, B). The evidence for the converse is less clear. Dolocastic chert is a common constituent of insoluble residues from many limestones. It is a chert in which there are many rhomb-shaped cavities that were left by the solution of dolomite. Were the original dolomite rhombs metacrysts in the chert? If so, they must have replaced the chert. They might also have been dolomite crystals trapped in a primary silica gel, or they may have been formed by selective replacement of the calcite matrix in which there were numerous dolomite crystals.

Occurrence and Associations

Dolomite occurs in rocks of all ages, although as noted above it is more common among the older rocks. It is closely associated with limestone, with which it may be interbedded. Beds of dolomite a foot or two in thickness or several tens of feet thick may be interbedded with limestone of like orders of thickness. In some places, however, the dolomite-calcite boundary crosses the stratigraphic planes. In some such cases the distribution of the dolomite seems to be controlled by structures such as faults (Ham, 1951) or folds (Landes, 1946).

It is not rare for dolomite to grade laterally into limestone. Such facies changes may be abrupt. Although not much is yet known about the paleogeography of dolomite, it appears that dolomite is more commonly a near-shore facies, and limestone is the product of off-shore and deeper-water sedimentation. Dolomite may characterize the back-reef areas whereas limestone forms in the reef or seaward thereof (King, in Cloud and Barnes, 1946, p. 92). The dolomites of the lower Silurian seem to be geographically distinct from the coexisting limestones (Amsden, 1955).

In the field dolomite is commonly a buff-weathering rock. This characteristic, which serves in some cases to distinguish between limestone and dolomite, is the result of oxidation of the iron carbonate. Ferrous carbonate occurs in solid solution in dolomite but not in calcite.

Origin

The origin of dolomite has been much debated and the literature on the subject is extensive (Van Tuyl, 1916a, 1916b; Steidtmann, 1911, 1917; Linck, 1937; Weynschenk, 1951; Canal, 1947; Skeats, 1905, 1918) (Fig. 101). Most dolomites are clearly replaced limestones. The evidence for replacement includes the automorphic boundaries of dolomite against calcite, even against clastic quartz and glauconite, the inclusion of clastic quartz in dolomite euhedra, the transection by the dolomite euhedra of oolites, fossil structures,

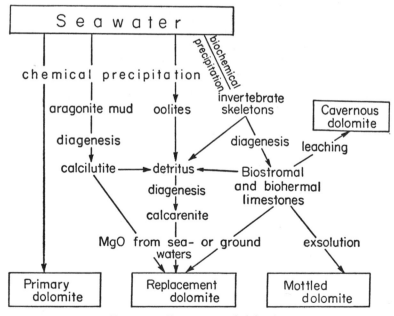

FIG. 101.   Provenance of dolomite.

PLATE 29

DOLOMITIC LIMESTONES AND DOLOMITES

A: Bruce limestone, Huronian, near Bruce Mines, Ont., Canada. Crossed nicols, ×17.

Chiefly carbonate showing polysynthetic twinning, plus a small amount of detrital quartz (see Pl. 39, **B**). Originally a calcarenite which has been recrystallized and in some degree dolomitized.

B: Dolomitic limestone, Rochester, N.Y. Ordinary light, ×40.

A coquinoid limestone, composed chiefly of brachiopod shells (*Leptocoelia*) now fibrous calcite. The calcareous mud between the brachiopod shells has been converted to coarse dolomite crystals.

C: Dolomitic encrinite, Lockport, N.Y. Ordinary light, ×40.

Shows incipient dolomitization of crystalline limestone composed largely of echinoderm debris.

D: Dolomitic limestone, Minn. Ordinary light, ×42.

Zoned porphyroblasts of dolomite scattered throughout anhedral mosaic of calcite.

E: Glauconitic dolomite, Cambrian, Colorado. Ordinary light, ×31.

A coarsely crystalline dolomite (gray rhombs) with glauconite granules (black) and some scattered detrital quartz (white). Not well shown in picture are overgrowths on quartz.

F: Bonneterre dolomite, Cambrian, Missouri. Ordinary light, ×15.

Fine-grained anhedral mosaic of dolomite in which are numerous glauconite grains and a little detrital quartz. Glauconite granules show partial destruction and replacement by dolomite. Evidently a glauconitic, arenaceous calcarenite which has been profoundly dolomitized.

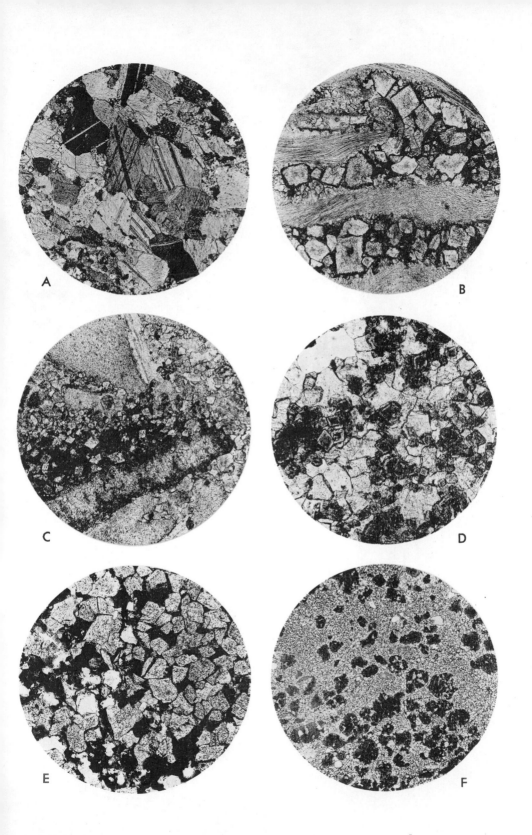

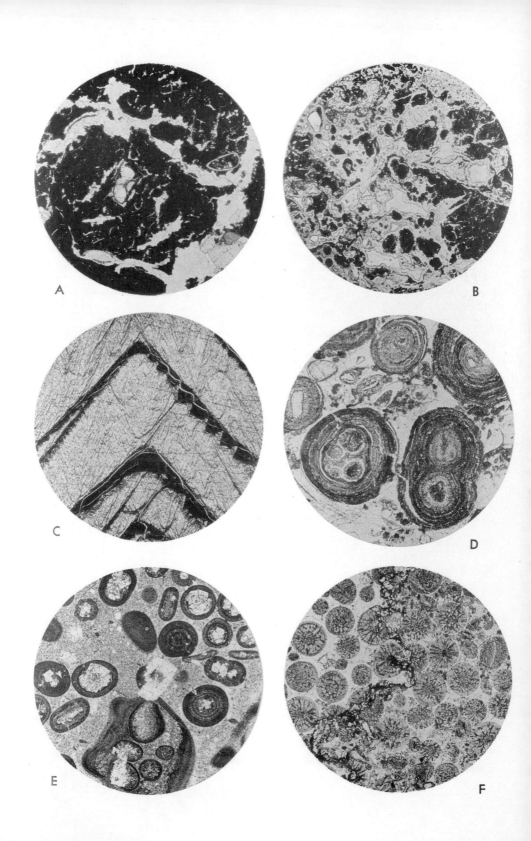

PLATE 30

CHEMICAL AND MISCELLANEOUS LIMESTONES

A: Greenbush limestone, Pennsylvanian, Ill. Ordinary light, $\times18$.

An exceedingly fine aggregate of carbonate (black) in which are embedded a few shell fragments (clear lemniscate areas) cut by irregular cracks and openings filled with vein calcite and microcrystalline silica (clear). A fresh-water limestone.

B: Ogallala limestone, Tertiary, Kansas. Ordinary light, $\times17$.

Fine-grained aggregate of carbonate in clotlike areas (black) bound together by opaline silica showing agate-like banding (gray to clear areas). A fresh-water limestone (lacustrine? or caliche?)

C: Cone-in-cone limestone. Ordinary light, $\times17$.

D: Calcareous pisolite, Silurian, Malvern, England. Ordinary light, $\times17$.

Note composite character of several of the pisolites. Structure is chiefly concentric. Algal pisolites?

E: Arbuckle limestone, Cambro-Ordovician, Okla. Ordinary light, $\times17$.

A calcareous oolite. Note wide separation of oolitic bodies and the large porphyroblasts of carbonate which in places have destroyed the oolitic structure.

F: Warrior limestone, Cambrian, State College, Penna. Ordinary light, $\times17$.

A calcareous oolite composed of oolites with radial and concentric structure cemented by carbonate. Note stylolite seam along which ferruginous clay (black) and bits of detrital quartz (white) have been concentrated. The amount of solution involved in the formation of the stylolite is indicated by the concentration of the quartz silt which is very sparsely distributed throughout the rock.

and the like, the shadowy palimpsest patterns of original clastic, bioclastic or oolitic textures, and the structural control of the distribution of dolomite and the transgression of stratigraphic planes by the calcite-dolomite boundary. Most compelling evidence of a replacement origin is the fact that no organisms secrete dolomite yet whole coquinas or coquinoid beds are now all dolomite.

Dolomite replacement appears to have been nearly volume for volume rather than molecule for molecule. The latter requires an over-all reduction in volume in the ratio of 100 to 88, with consequent increase in porosity. Steidtmann (1917) has shown that there is no significant difference in porosity between limestones and dolomite, although Landes (1946) has described a case in which only the dolomitized portion of a formation is porous (and productive of petroleum). The porosity of dolomites has been ascribed to the selective removal of calcitic constituents (Hall and Sardeson, 1895).

Although a replacement origin is clearly established for many, perhaps most, dolomites, the time or date of replacement is by no means clear. It can take place in the environment of deposition and before burial. The dolomitized old reef in the Funafuti boring is an example (Judd, 1904). The replacement, however, may take place after burial but before uplift, or it may take place after burial and uplift. Presumably earlier dolomitization is the result of reaction of the lime carbonate sediment and the magnesium-bearing sea water. Later replacement would be the product of reaction of the limestone and either magnesium-bearing connate brines or circulating meteoric waters. The principal argument for early replacement is the stratigraphic persistence of many dolomite beds. It is difficult to believe that a thin bed, extending over many square miles, would be dolomitized by circulating waters while the overlying and underlying beds remain unaffected. On the other hand, later dolomitization can be proved if the distribution of the dolomite is confined to the vicinity of faults or is otherwise structurally controlled. A further argument for later dolomitization is Daly's observation that the older the rock the more magnesium-rich it appears to be (Daly, 1909). The older the rock the greater the probability that it would come in contact with magnesium-bearing waters and become dolomitized.[19] No doubt dolomites are formed by both early and late replacement.

Dolomites are so commonly associated with salt and gypsum beds that high salinity and perhaps higher than normal temperatures promote dolomite formation. It may be that the waters of the basins that are partially isolated under conditions of aridity are enriched in magnesium by the con-

[19] Daly (1909) and Steidtmann (1911, p. 427) took the view that the composition of the early seas was different from that of later times and hence the earlier rocks were more dolomitic than the younger ones. This nonuniformitarian view has been challenged.

tinued inflow of normal sea water and by the precipitation of calcium carbonate and sulfate. Enrichment in this manner would favor the formation of magnesium carbonate or dolomite. It even may be that dolomite itself is precipitated under these conditions and that some dolomite is indeed a primary rock. That such is the case is the view of Sloss (1953), who attributes an evaporite origin to certain thinly laminated wholly unfossiliferous dolomites closely associated with bedded anhydrite. Sando (1953) reached a similar conclusion respecting thinly laminated dolomites interbedded with limestones of the Beekmantown (Ordovician) of Maryland. Although no anhydrite was present in the Beekmantown, the dolomite was found to enclose small pebbles of the underlying limestone. It is difficult to escape the conclusion that this dolomite is a primary precipitate. The interbedding of dolomite and limestone on a micro scale, the laminations being but a fraction of a millimeter thick, has been cited as evidence that some dolomite is a primary constituent (Sander, 1936).

The mottled dolomites, previously described, need not be either a primary precipitate or a postdepositional replacement. They may be, as suggested above, a product of diagenetic differentiation. Some algal limestone contains enough $MgCO_3$ (up to 24 per cent) in solid solution in calcite to produce such a mottled rock upon exsolution. Such exsolution would not of itself be sufficient to convert a limestone to dolomite. Two generations of dolomite are therefore implied in those cases where mottled dolomites are converted to solid dolomite.

REFERENCES CITED AND BIBLIOGRAPHY

Amsden, T. W. (1955), Lithofacies map of Lower Silurian deposits in central and eastern United States and Canada, Bull. Am. Assoc. Petroleum Geol., vol. 39, pp. 60–74.

Barth, T. F. W. (1952), Theoretical petrology, New York, Wiley.

Bayley, W. S. (1904), The Menominee iron-bearing district of Michigan, U.S. Geol. Survey Mono. 46.

Beales, F. W. (1953), Dolomitic mottling in Palliser (Devonian) limestone, Banff and Jasper National Parks, Alberta, Bull. Am. Assoc. Petroleum Geol., vol. 37, pp. 2281–2293.

Birse, D. J. (1928), Dolomitization processes in the Palaeozoic horizons of Manitoba, Trans. Roy. Soc. Canada, Sec. 4, vol. 22, pp. 215–221.

Canal, P. (1947), Observations sur les caracteres petrographiques de calcaires dolomitiques et des dolomies, Compt. rend. soc. géol. France, pp. 161–162.

Cayeux, L. (1935), Les roches sédimentaires de France. Roches carbonatées, Paris, Masson.

Chave, K. E. (1954b), Aspects of the biogeochemistry of magnesium. 2. Calcareous sediments and rocks, J. Geol., vol. 62, pp. 587–599.

Cloud, P. E. and Barnes, V. E. (1948), The Ellenburger Group of central Texas, *Univ. Texas Bur. Econ. Geol. Publ.* no. 4621.

Cooper, B. N. (1945), Industrial limestones and dolomites in Virginia: Clinch Valley district, *Virginia Geol. Survey, Bull.* 66, p. 9.

Daly, R. A. (1909), First calcareous fossils and the evolution of the limestones, *Bull. Geol. Soc. Amer.*, vol. 20, p. 165.

Fisher, D. J. (1925), Geology and mineral resources of the Joliet quadrangle, *Illinois State Geol. Survey Bull.* 51.

Goldich, S. S. and Parmalee, E. B. (1947), Physical and chemical properties of Ellenburger rocks, Llano County, Texas, *Bull. Am. Assoc. Petroleum Geol.*, vol. 31, pp. 1982–2020.

Griffin, R. H. (1942), Dolomitic mottling in the Platteville limestone, *J. Sediment. Petrol.*, vol. 12, pp. 67–76.

Grout, F. F. (1932), *Petrography and petrology*, New York, McGraw-Hill.

Ham, W. E. (1951), Dolomite in the Arbuckle limestone, Arbuckle Mountains, Oklahoma, *Bull. Geol. Soc. Amer.*, vol. 62, pp. 1446–1447 (abstract).

Hall, C. W. and Sardeson, F. W. (1895), Origin of the dolomites, *Bull. Geol. Soc. Amer.*, vol. 6, p. 198.

Judd, J. W. (1904), The atoll of Funafuti, *Rept. Coral Reef Comm., Roy. Soc., London*, pp. 364–365.

Landes, K. K. (1946), Porosity through dolomitization, *Bull. Am. Assoc. Petroleum Geol.*, vol. 30, pp. 305–318.

Linck, G. (1937), Bildung des Dolomits und Dolomitisierung, *Chemie der Erde*, Berlin, Borntraeger, vol. 11, pp. 278–286.

Rodgers, John (1954), Terminology of limestone and related rocks: an interim report, *J. Sediment. Petrol.*, vol. 24, pp. 225–234.

Russell, I. C. (1889), Subaërial decay of rocks, *U.S. Geol. Survey Bull.* 52, p. 25.

Sander, B. (1936), Beiträge zur Kenntniss der Ablagerungsgefüge rhythmische Kalk und Dolomit aus der Trias, *Mineralog. u. petrog. Mitt.*, vol. 48, pp. 27–139.

Sando, W. J. (1953), *The stratigraphy and paleontology of the western belt of the Beekmantown group in Maryland*, Ph.D. dissertation, The Johns Hopkins University, p. 18.

Scobey, E. S. (1940), Sedimentary studies of the Wapsipinicon formation in Iowa, *J. Sediment. Petrol.*, vol. 10, pp. 34–44.

Shrock, R. R. (1948), A classification of sedimentary rocks, *J. Geol.*, vol. 56, pp. 118–129.

Skeats, E. W. (1905), The chemical and mineralogical evidences as to the origin of the dolomites of southern Tyrol, *Quart. J. Geol. Soc. London*, vol. 61, pp. 97–1141.

Skeats, E. W. (1918), The formation of dolomite and its bearing on the coral reef problem, *Am. J. Sci.*, ser. 4, vol. 45, pp. 185–200.

Sloss, L. L. (1953), The significance of evaporites, *J. Sediment. Petrol.*, vol. 23, pp. 143–161.

Steidtmann, E. (1911), Evolution of limestone and dolomite, *J. Geol.*, vol. 19, pp. 323–345.

Steidtmann, E. (1917), Origin of dolomite as disclosed by stains and other methods, *Bull. Geol. Soc. Amer.*, vol. 28, p. 437.

Stout, Wilber (1941), Dolomites and limestones of western Ohio, *Bull. Geol. Survey Ohio*, 42 (ser. 4).

Van Tuyl, F. M. (1916a), The origin of dolomite, *Iowa Geol. Survey Bull.* 25, pp. 241–422.

Van Tuyl, F. M. (1916b), New points on the origin of dolomite, *Am. J. Sci.*, ser. 4, vol. 42, pp. 249–260.

Wallace, R. C. (1913), Pseudobrecciation in Ordovician limestones in Manitoba, *J. Geol.*, vol. 21, pp. 402–421.

Weynschenk, R. (1951), The problem of dolomite formation considered in the light of research on dolomites in the Sonnwendmountains (Tirol), *J. Sediment. Petrol.*, vol. 21, pp. 28–31.

10

Nonclastic Sediments
(Excluding Limestones)

INTRODUCTION

THE nonclastic sediments fall into three main categories, namely, primary precipitates, secondary segregations and metasomatites, and certain organic accumulations—the bioliths of Grabau.

The *primary precipitates* include the evaporites, which are deposits formed by the evaporation of saline solutions—principally sea water. The evaporites include the rock sulfates (mainly anhydrite), the chlorides (chiefly rock salt), some carbonates (principally dolomite), and various rare nitrates. A second group of precipitates is the result of chemical reactions. Such reactions may be between dissolved materials and the finest suspended clay sediment or may be the result of change in acidity or shift in the oxidation-reduction potential. Presumed to be included here are the various iron-bearing sediments including the bedded iron sulfides, carbonate ironstones, various iron silicate beds, and ferric oxide formations, the rock phosphates, and perhaps the bedded cherts.

The *segregations* and *metasomatites* are the products of chemical reactions which take place after deposition of the sediment. Included are those re-arrangements which take place *within* the sediment and which produce the segregations of the minor constituents of the rock. Such segregations constitute the nodules, concretions, and similar bodies of iron sulfide, iron carbonate, calcium carbonate, phosphates, and silica as well as the mineralogically more complex geodes and veins. Most important, but less certain products of such diagenetic differentiation, are the mottled dolomites and perhaps also the bedded cherts. The metasomatites (Berkey, 1924) are a group of rocks produced by chemical alteration of existing rocks. For the most part they are altered limestones that have been dolomitized, silicified, phosphatized, and so forth. In these rocks the changes are so profound that the introduction of material from *without* must have taken place. The source of the introduced materials may be sea water (as it is for many dolomites) or circulating waters, either meteoric or magmatic. Metasomatism is

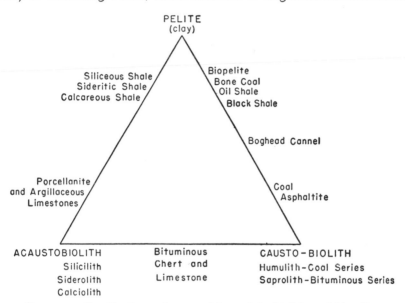

FIG. 102. Classification and nomenclature of the bioliths and biopelites.

a replacement process that forms new rocks, chemically unlike the parent rock, that retain in some degree the textures and structures of the original rock. The changes therefore are a species of metamorphism produced at relatively low temperatures and pressures.

The *bioliths*, or organic accumulations, do not form a homogeneous group but fall into two unlike subgroups, namely, the acaustobioliths and the caustobioliths, which are the noncombustible and combustible rocks, respectively (Fig. 102). Of the former the calciliths form an important part of the limestone group and therefore have been placed with these rocks and described elsewhere. The siliciliths (mainly diatomite) have been grouped with the cherts, to which they are closely related. The remaining acaustobioliths are relatively rare and unimportant. The combustible bioliths, including the coals and the bitumins, though relatively rare rocks, are of great economic and scientific interest. They have accordingly been given special treatment.

PLATE 31

BEDDED MONTEREY CHERT

Top: Calcareous concretion in cherty shale, San Luis Obispo County, Calif.

Bottom: Lateral uniformity of bedding in rhythmically bedded chert, Monterey formation (Miocene), Calif.

U.S. Geological Survey photographs. (Bramlette, *U.S. Geol. Survey, Prof. Paper* 212, pls. 6 and 10.)

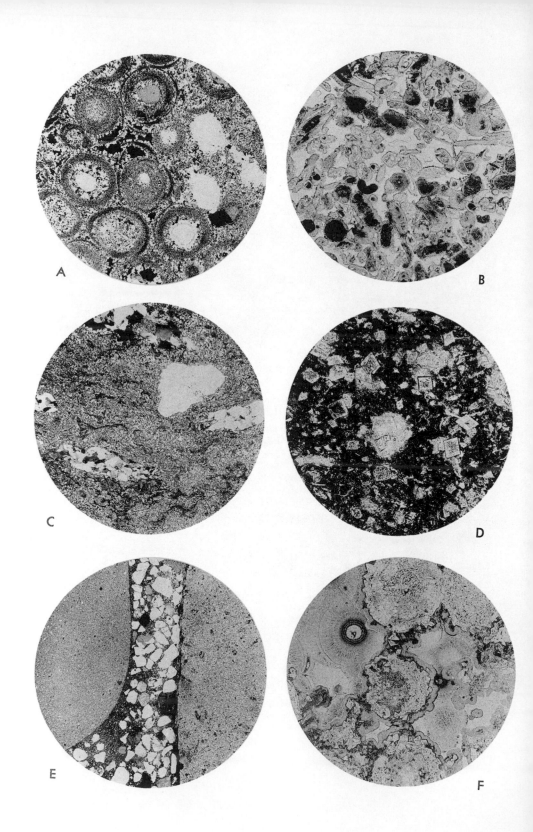

PLATE 32

SILICEOUS SEDIMENTS (CHERTS)

A: Siliceous oolite, Mines formation, Cambrian, State College, Penna. Crossed nicols, ×17.

This is the well-known "State College oolite." The oolites commonly have detrital quartz grains, usually secondarily enlarged, as nuclei (see Pl. 39, **F**). Silicification of calcareous oolite has destroyed much of the concentric structure and converted the carbonate to a microcrystalline mosaic of quartz. Quartz micromosaic surrounds and binds oolites together.

B: "Oolitic" chert, Osage (?) formation, Mississippian, Indiana. Ordinary light, ×17.

Composed wholly of silica but retaining much of the structure of the original limestone (spergenite) from which it was formed by silicification. Original rock contained detrital carbonate, fossil debris, and calcareous oolites. Compare with Pl. 28, **E**, which is an unaltered calcarenite.

C: Oneota chert, Ordovician, near Baraboo, Wis. Crossed nicols, ×17.

Fine-grained micromosaic of quartz in which are large fragments of Baraboo quartzite (coarse mosaic) and detrital quartz. Probably a silicified sandy calcarenite.

D: Huntersville chert, Devonian, Wood County, W.Va. Ordinary light, ×42.

A dense chert consisting of chalcedony with scattered rhombs of dolomite. Mottling of chert suggests texture of fossiliferous calcarenite which has been chertified.

E: Hertfordshire "puddingstone" conglomerate, Eocene, England. Crossed nicols, ×15.

Detail of two flint pebbles and enclosing matrix. Flint is exceedingly fine-grained mosaic of microcrystalline silica.

F: Shakopee oolitic chert, Ordovician, Utica, Ill. Ordinary light, ×45. Photograph by Chester Johnson.

Original calcareous oolites no longer show either concentric or radial structures. Under crossed nicols they now reveal a micromosaic of crystalline silica. Note silicified rhomb-shaped pseudomorphs of dolomite which lie within and without the oolites. A later generation of chalcedony has been deposited between the oolites. The chalcedony has assumed radial and concentric habit, and was deposited in part as conformal envelop around the silicified oolites.

In theory the differences between the segregations and metasomatites, the primary precipitates, and the bioliths are clear and unequivocal. The actual assignment of a particular deposit to one of these groups, on the other hand, may be difficult. Moreover many nonclastic rocks are polygenetic and form in more than one way. Chert, for example, may occur as a segregation (chert nodule) as a replacement (silicified limestone), as a modified biolith (silicified diatomite), and perhaps even as an original precipitate. Owing to such complexities of origin and to an economy of space which is thereby gained, the nonclastic sediments are grouped according to their chemical composition. The siliceous (free silica), ferruginous, phosphatic, saline (sulfates and chlorides), and carbonaceous (carbon residues) are recognized and separately treated. The calcareous group is the largest and most common, and for that reason is described in a separate chapter. The segregations are, for the most part, minor bodies of rock, and they are described therefore mainly in the chapter dealing with the structure of sediments.

CHERT AND OTHER SILICEOUS SEDIMENTS

Definitions and Classification

Tarr (1938) prepared a summary of the proper names of the chemical siliceous sediments; in the main, the usage here followed is that recommended by Tarr.

Chert and flint are the most common chemical siliceous sediments. Much confusion is current concerning the origin of these terms, their exact meaning, and the differences, if any, between them. Chert is a dense cryptocrystalline rock, composed of chalcedony (microcrystalline fibrous silica and microfibrous amorphous silica or opal)[1] and cryptocrystalline quartz. Chert has a tough splintery to conchoidal fracture. It may be white or variously colored gray, green, blue, pink, red, yellow, brown, and black. Flint (feuerstein) is a term widely used both as a synonym for chert and as a variety of chert. Tarr states that it is identical with chert, and the term therefore should be dropped or reserved for artifacts to which it is most often applied. Although the term flint antedates the term chert, usage favors the latter as the proper designation of the materials to which both terms have been applied.

Silexite, hornstone (hornstein), and phthanite have been used, in part, as synonyms for chert and in part for special kinds of chert. They are little used in the United States at the present time.

---

[1] Folk and Weaver (1952) state that chert consists of microcrystalline quartz and chalcedonic quartz. Opal or amorphous silica is said not to be present in chalcedony. This conclusion was also reached by Midgeley (1951).

Several special terms have been applied to the bedded cherts. These are mainly provincial and not universal in application. *Novaculite* is a very dense, even-textured, light-colored, cryptocrystalline siliceous rock. It is essentially a bedded chert characterized by dominance of microcrystalline quartz over chalcedony—a characteristic also of the Precambrian cherty rocks. Novaculite is a term little used outside of Arkansas and Oklahoma. *Jaspilite* is a term applied to the interbedded jasper and hematite of the Precambrian iron-bearing districts, especially those of the Lake Superior region. Jasper proper is a ferruginous chert characteristically red, although yellow, brown, and black cherts have also been called jasper. *Jasperoid* is a term applied to the cherty beds in the zinc-mining districts of Missouri, Oklahoma, and Kansas.

Porcellanite (porcelanite) is a term applied to dense, hard rocks having the texture and fracture of unglazed porcelain. Most commonly, though not always, such rocks are cherts with an abundance of included materials. These impure cherts are in part argillaceous and in part calcareous, or more rarely, sideritic. The argillaceous cherts grade into the siliceous shales; the calcareous cherts grade into the siliceous limestones. Some porcellanites are, however, silicified tuffs (halleflinta).

Not all siliceous sediments are dense and tough rocks; some are friable and porous. These are the siliceous earths including *diatomaceous earth* and *radiolarian earth*. They are composed of the opaline tests of diatoms and the latticelike skeletal framework of Radiolaria, respectively. They are usually white, or cream-colored; more rarely they are buff, red, or brown. These rocks are homogeneous, porous, friable, and have a dry earthy feel and appearance. Where there is infilling of the pores these materials become dense and chertlike. To these consolidated equivalents of diatomaceous earth and radiolarian earth, the terms *diatomite* and *radiolarite*, respectively, have been applied.[2]

Siliceous sinter is also a porous siliceous material, white or light-colored and light in weight, deposited by the waters of hot springs. *Geyserite* is merely a variety of siliceous sinter deposited by geysers.

Tripoli is another very porous, light-weight, siliceous rock (mainly chalcedony). It is white, or variously colored, gray, pink, buff, red, or yellow. It has a harsh, rough feel. Tripoli forms fairly large masses and, as it is confined to the earth's surface, Tarr considers it to be a product of weathering (leaching and hydration) of chert and siliceous limestones. Some writers consider tripoli to be an incompletely silicified limestone from which the carbonate has been leached. It includes rottenstone. Originally, and to some extent today, the term is applied to the diatomaceous and other siliceous earths which tripoli closely resembles.

[2] Not always is diatomite used in this sense; it may be applied to the less dense materials also (Bramlette, 1946, p. 13).

Composition of Cherts and Related Rocks

Chemically or biochemically precipitated silica consists mainly of opal, chalcedony, and quartz; rarely is it christobalite. One or more of the first three form the rock known as *chert* (or flint). Opal appears to be present only in the younger (Tertiary) cherts and in the biochemical precipitates of silica. The older cherts contain only quartz and chalcedony. Christobalite has been reported in some bentonite and bentonitic shales (Gruner, 1946). It is uncertain whether christobalite in sediments is a secondary product or was contributed as a detrital constituent. Folk and Weaver (1952) state that cherts are composed primarily of microcrystalline quartz and chalcedony. The former appears as equant grains; the latter as radiating fibers. Although there has been some uncertainty as to the nature of chalcedony, these authors regard it as a form of quartz. Submicroscopic water-filled cavities lower the refractive index of the chalcedonic quartz.

Constituents other than the forms of silica listed above are rare in cherts. Some of the less common "impure" cherts contain calcite, dolomite, or siderite. Even some common cherts contain scattered dolomite rhombs (Pl. 32, D). Although pure chert and pure carbonate appear to be more common than mixtures, analyses of many cherts and associated carbonate rocks in southern Illinois show all possible mixtures of silica and carbonate (Wyant, personal communication, 1955). A few cherts contain large detrital quartz grains (Pl. 32, C). Chemical analyses of others suggest other impurities.

As would be expected from the mineral composition, cherts are highly siliceous rocks. Many, as shown by Table 82, are 95 or more per cent silica. The cherts with carbonate admixtures contain CaO, MgO, FeO, and CO_2; those with admixtures of clay contain Al_2O_3. The younger opaline cherts contain the most water.

Siliceous Earths

Radiolarites and diatomites, if these terms be restricted to the somewhat friable and porous deposits, are confined to the younger strata. These earths are named according to the most prominent constituents. Diatom tests, composed of opaline silica, are the predominant constituent of the diatomites, but the remains of Radiolaria and silico-flagellates also are common. Sponge spicules usually are present. The proportions are different in the various radiolarites.

The porosity of the purer earths is very high because of the minute pore spaces within and between the skeletal remains. Air-dried samples of diatomite, for example, have a specific gravity of only 0.5. The silica content of pure diatomite is very high, but many of the diatomaceous rocks are impure

(Table 82, col. G). The average silica content of ten diatomaceous rocks from the Monterey formation of California is 71.8 per cent (Bramlette, 1946, p. 13).

TABLE 82. Chemical Composition of Cherts and Related Rocks
(per cent)

	A	B	C	D	E	F	G	H	I
SiO$_2$	93.54	98.93	99.47	82.69	70.78	43.43	73.71	85.78	93.75
TiO$_2$	....	0.005	....	....	0.03	....	0.50	....	0.00
Al$_2$O$_3$	2.26	0.14	0.17	1.76	0.45	11.25[a]	7.25	5.68	2.63
Fe$_2$O$_3$	0.48	0.06	0.12	1.00	0.02	0.18	2.63	2.92	1.43
FcO	....	0.08	....	0.31	0.30	21.00	0.44	2.09	0.00
MnO	0.79	0.01	....	0.01	0.02	....	....	....	0.02
MgO	0.23	0.02	0.05	1.08	1.88	1.39	1.47	0.25	T
CaO	0.66	0.04	0.09	2.93	12.90	0.70	1.72	0.48	1.36
Na$_2$O	0.37	T	0.15	0.50	0.05	1.21	1.19	0.68	....
K$_2$O	0.51	T	0.07	2.61	0.06	3.99	1.00	0.36	0.00
H$_2$O+	0.72[b]	0.17	0.12[b]	4.75[b]	0.32⎰	0.50	6.94⎰	1.88	0.00
H$_2$O−	0.21	0.27	....	....	0.48⎱		2.88⎱		
P$_2$O$_5$	....	T	....	0.21	0.16	....	0.24	....	0.00
CO$_2$	....	0.02	....	2.28	12.04	15.76	T?	....	1.00
SO$_3$	....	none	....	....	T	....	0.16	....	0.00
Cl	....	....	....	0.15	....	....	....	....	....
C	....	0.18	....	....	0.33	0.08	0.00	....	....
Total	99.86	99.92	100.24	100.28	100.14	99.45	100.13	100.13	100.19

A. Franciscan chert, Jurassic? (Davis, 1918, p. 268).
B. Vanport "flint," Carboniferous, Flint Ridge, Ohio. Downs Schaaf, analyst (Stout and Schoenlaub, 1945, p. 82).
C. Novaculite, Devonian, Rockport, Arkansas. R. N. Brackett, analyst (Clarke, 1924, p. 551).
D. Average of ten cherty rocks, Monterey formation, Miocene. California (Bramlette, 1946, p. 49).
E. Calcareous nodular chert, Delaware limestone, Devonian, Ohio. Downs Schaaf, analyst (Stout and Schoenlaub, 1945, p. 28).
F. Porcellanite, sideritic Precambrian, Iron County, Michigan. B. Bruun, analyst.
G. Diatomaceous shale, Hollywood, California. J. G. Fairchild, analyst (Hoots, 1931, p. 108).
H. Green chert, Notre Dame Bay, Newfoundland (Sampson, 1923, p. 580).
I. Bedded Ft. Payne (Mississippian), near Lafayette, Georgia. L. F. Turner, analyst (Hurst, 1953).
    [a] Includes P$_2$O$_5$.
    [b] Loss on ignition.

Petrography of Chert and the Like

Chert, the most extensive siliceous rock of chemical origin, occurs in two principal ways, namely, as nodular segregations in limestones and dolomites and as areally extensive bedded deposits.

The chert (or flint) nodules are very irregular, usually structureless, dense masses of microcrystalline silica. Such nodular masses vary from more or less regular disks an inch or two in diameter to large, highly irregular, and tuberous bodies a foot or so long. The shape of these objects is infinitely varied but the larger ones, though of rounded contour, are marked by warty or knobby exteriors (Pl. 7, bottom). In most cases the nodules are elongated parallel to the bedding and are commonly concentrated along certain bedding planes. In some limestones they are numerous enough to coalesce into more or less continuous layers. The chert-bearing layers in many cases seem to be rhythmically spaced (Richardson, 1919). In a given layer the chert forms an irregular two-dimensional network; if layers are close spaced, some connections or "bridging" between layers may occur, and the chert network becomes three-dimensional. Few limestones are so cherty; most are characterized only by scattered, discrete nodules.

Although generally structureless, some nodules have a dense black interior surrounded by a lighter, in some cases white, exterior ("cotton rock"). A few show traces of the bedding that is continuous with that of the host rock; still others are marked by a concentric structure (contraction spheroids). A few enclose patches of the host rock. Rather commonly cherts are fossiliferous, the fossils being either silicified or calcareous. In the latter case the carbonate may be dissolved leaving only a cavity or mold. Cherty nodules are widely distributed and are found in carbonate rocks of all ages. Best known, perhaps, are the cherts in the Mississippian limestones of the upper Mississippi Valley region, of the Niagaran (Silurian) of the Great Lakes area, and the flint nodules of the Cretaceous chalk of England and France.

The bedded cherts are the most impressive occurrences of precipitated silica. They not only make up whole formations but are both thick and areally extensive. Thicknesses of several tens of feet are common, although several hundred are by no means rare. The bedded cherts are rhythmically layered cherts. The layers, an inch or two thick, are separated by partings of shale, or less commonly by layers of siderite (cherty iron carbonates, p. 452). Although apparently even-bedded (Pl. 31) the chert layers may pinch and swell in an irregular manner, lens out, or even bifurcate. In most cases the chert beds make up the bulk of the formation; the partings form a lesser fraction of the deposit. As in the nodules, the chert is cryptocrystalline, dense, and subvitreous. The bedded cherts are brittle, close-jointed rocks.

The best-known bedded cherts include the Monterey chert (Miocene) of California, the cherts of the Franciscan (Jurassic?) of the same region, the Rex chert (Permian) of Idaho and adjoining states, the Woodford chert (Devonian) of Oklahoma and its correlatives—the Caballos novaculite of Texas and the famous Arkansas novaculite. Bedded chert is present in the Normanskill (Ordovician) of New York state. The jaspilites and cherty iron carbonates are Precambrian bedded cherts in the Lake Superior district with an abnormally high content of iron. Important European chert deposits occur in the Ordovician of the Caledonian geosyncline of southern Scotland; radiolarian cherts occur in the Carboniferous in the Armorican geosyncline of southern Wales. Best known of all, perhaps, are the Mesozoic radiolarian cherts of the Alps and Apennines.

Not all stratigraphic units called cherts are true bedded cherts. Some appear only to be exceptionally cherty limestones inasmuch as the chert is present as an anastomosing three-dimensional network rather than being rhythmically interbedded. The so-called Bigfork chert (Ordovician) of Oklahoma appears to be such a cherty limestone.

Typical chert, either nodular or bedded, is a hard dense rock that shows a smooth conchoidal fracture. The color varies with the impurities, and ranges from white to gray to black; or in other cases gray-green, yellow, brown, or red.

Under the microscope the chert is a colorless, exceedingly fine-grained microcrystalline aggregate (Pl. 32, E). In some cherts there are circular or elliptical clear areas which represent Radiolaria which, if these be not too much damaged by recrystallization of the matrix, show the spines or more rarely the internal lattice characteristic of these organisms. Siliceous sponge spicules are abundant in other cherts (spiculites). The individual grains of the chert, under the highest magnification, commonly show a fibrous wavy extinction which is different from that of the adjacent grains. Some younger cherts contain much isotropic material in which may be seen a few or many minute polarizing specks. Very possibly these polarizing specks are crystallites of quartz—the first step in the devitrification of the original amorphous silica gel. Like volcanic glass, the opaline silica becomes wholly crystallized with passage of time. The older cherts (all those of the Precambrian) now consist entirely of a fine-grained mosaic of quartz. Under the electron microscope some cherts show well-defined polyhedral blocks of quartz; others are less dense and contain numerous bubblclike holes—in some cases numerous enough to give the chert a scoriaceous aspect (Folk and Weaver, 1952). The holes are believed to have been filled with water.

Some cherts are relatively impure and under the microscope show carbonate disseminated throughout the body of the chert. Porcellanite, in particular, contains much such carbonate. That due to carbonate inclusions exhibits all gradations from a chert that contains a few scattered rhombs of calcite (or dolomite) to rocks in which the carbonate rhombs become so numerous as to touch one another and form a spongelike mesh, the interstices of which are filled with opal; or opal with chalcedony. The carbonate may be uniformly distributed throughout the chert; in other cases it may be concentrated in laminations which become accentuated by weathering. Siderite, rather than calcite or dolomite, may occur in some porcellanite (Table 82, col. F). Weathering of such material is accompanied by oxidation and conversion of the carbonate to a dense hard limonite, which forms a black crust over the whole of the rock and conceals its true nature.

Rocks consisting of a mixture of clay or silty clay and a large but variable proportion of opaline silica also are porcelaneous and have been termed porcellanite (Bramlette, 1946, p. 15). These grade into the siliceous shales, which consist of a mixture of the common constituents of shale with an exceptional amount of precipitated silica (see p. 363). The siliceous shales are flintlike in hardness and have a platy parting and subconchoidal fracture. The silica of the siliceous Mowry shale is thought to have been derived from associated fine volcanic ash. Decomposition of the glass in the sea water and concurrent precipitation of the silica by diatoms or other agents is believed to be the origin of this rock (Rubey, 1929). A similar explanation has been proposed for the origin of the siliceous shales in the Stanley (Carboniferous) beds of Oklahoma (Goldstein and Hendricks, 1953).

Sandy cherts are not common, although all gradations between chert, sandy chert, and sandstone with chert cement are known. In some cherts large, rounded sand grains are scattered sparsely through the body of the chert.

Closely related to the cherts and much like them in appearance are the silicified tuffs (p. 336). These rocks differ from true cherts by the inclusion of glassy materials—distinguished with some difficulty from isotropic opaline spicules and other curved structures. Devitrification of the glass may render recognition specially difficult.

In a special class are the oolitic cherts. Although a minor variety of chert, the siliceous oolites show most clearly the evidence of a replacement origin, and they are therefore of the greatest interest in connection with the chert problem. Best known are the siliceous oolites from State College, Pennsylvania (Diller, 1898, p. 95; Choquette, 1955; Krynine, Honess and Meyers, 1941). Under the microscope (Pl. 32, A) this chert shows numerous oolitic bodies, about 1 millimeter in diameter, composed of microcrystalline quartz and chalcedony of concentric structure. Most contain a well-rounded detrital quartz nucleus which is enclosed in an overlay of secondary quartz in optical continuity with the nucleus. The boundary between the original grain and the overgrowth is marked by carbonate inclusions. The interstices between the oolites are filled with a finely crystalline quartz mosaic. In some of the oolites the quartz nucleus is displaced to one side; others, lacking a quartz nucleus, show a geopetal fabric resulting from removal in solution of the central core of the oolite, leaving the insolubles displaced to the lower side followed by infilling with precipitated, coarsely crystalline quartz (Choquette, 1955).

Other siliceous oolites have similar characteristics. The oolitic chert from the Shakopee dolomite at Utica, Illinois, is noteworthy for the festoon-like deposits on the exterior of many of the oolites as well as the chert pseudomorphs of dolomite present both in the oolites and their matrix (Pl. 32, F). These oolites clearly are replacements of a calcareous oolite, and all stages of transformation may be seen in a properly collected suite of specimens.

Origin of Chert

The literature on the chert problem is very extensive. The various theories that have been advanced to explain these materials fall into two groups. According to one concept the silica is contemporaneous with the sedimentation; according to the other concept, the silica is a postdepositional replacement of the host rock, generally limestone. There are various modifications of each of these theories (Fig. 103).

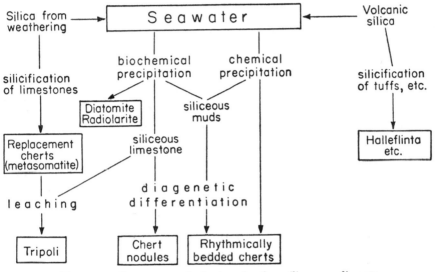

FIG. 103. Provenance of chert and other siliceous sediments.

Although there is no general agreement on the chert problem, majority opinion seems to incline toward an epigene formation of the nodular cherts and flints found in limestone and other carbonate rocks. A few writers, notably Tarr (1917, 1926) and some others (Trefethen, 1947) stoutly maintain the view that the nodular cherts are formed by the direct precipitation of masses of silica gel on the sea floor. The evidence for replacement (and therefore postdepositional origin) of the nodular cherts is abundant and clear. Van Tuyl (1918) has given a good résumé of the evidence bearing on this question. Supporting the epigenetic origin are (1) the occurrence of chert along fissures in limestone, (2) the very irregular shape of some chert nodules, (3) the presence of irregular patches of limestone within some nodules, (4) the association of silicified fossils and cherts in some limestones, (5) the presence of replaced fossils in some cherts (Pl. 32, B), (6) the preservation of textures and structures (especially bedding) in some cherts (Bastin, 1933; White, 1947), (7) the failure of some cherts to follow definite zones in limestone formations, and (8) the occurrence of silicified oolites formed by replacement of calcareous ones.

The first criterion, perhaps, is not one of replacement but rather one of age. Veinlets of chert place the formation of the chert in the postconsolidation period of the host rock. Chert veinlets are rather rare and Twenhofel (1950, p. 412) is quite correct in citing this observation as evidence that the chert is not generally introduced by circulating waters. Further evidence of a replacement and epigene origin is the observation of Bastin (1933) that some chert nodules have a stylolitic contact with the adjacent limestone. Only by replacement along one side of a stylolite seam is such a relation readily explained. In some cases seen by Bastin, the chert nodule antedates the stylolitic surface.

In conclusion it can be said that the replacement hypothesis for the nodular cherts is supported by a wealth of observations, both field and microscopic (see Fowler, Lyden, Gregory and Agar, 1935). Certainly the anastomosing two- or three-dimensional network of some cherts in a carbonate host rock is difficult to explain except by replacement.

The source of the replacing silica and the mechanics of nodule formation, however, is less clear. The principal problem is: Was the replacing silica introduced from without or was it derived from within the host bed? It has been suggested that the silica was precipitated concurrently with the deposition of the limestone perhaps by diatoms, Radiolaria, or sponges and then in time dissolved and reprecipitated as nodular masses which replace the matrix in which they occur (Sollas, 1880; Hinde, 1887; Richardson, 1919). The silica needed for nodule formation therefore is extracted from sea water by normal, widespread biochemical processes. No special supply of silica, nor abnormal concentrations, nor special conditions of precipitation are necessary. And as Ramberg (1952, p. 222) has given theoretical reasons why solution and reprecipitation of disseminated silica should occur, the concept of diagenetic differentiation is the most plausible explanation of the nodular cherts. Beds most susceptible to replacement would explain the concentration of the nodules in certain layers; greater ease of replacement parallel to the bedding explains the elongation of the nodules in the plane of the bedding. Field relations support this concept also. Lowenstam (1948, p. 36) has noted a definite relation between the type of chert and the state of preservation and distribution of siliceous sponges in the Niagaran dolomites of Illinois. He was led to the view that the silica of the cherts was derived from the sponges, a conclusion earlier reached respecting some Palestinian cherts (Lowenstam, 1942).

In those few cases where the chert constitutes a major part of the rock replaced, or even all of it, clearly redistribution of the silica within the bed will not explain the deposit. Introduction of silica seems inescapable.

It has been suggested that nodular chert is a product of silicification associated with weathering. But the stratigraphic continuity of most cherty zones and the distinctive character of the cherts of various beds indicates the chert to be unrelated to the present-day surface (and in most cases unrelated to unconformities) and to be related to the sedimentation responsible for the host rock itself.

The origin of the bedded cherts is a very controversial subject; many theories to explain these deposits have been advanced. Some workers consider the chert to be a consolidated or indurated siliceous biolith; it is, in other words, a lithified diatomaceous or radiolarian ooze or a lithified spiculite. As organisms are today forming pure siliceous deposits, the uniformitarian view requires that such deposits or their lithified equivalents be present in the geologic section. Other investigators, noting that the chert nodules are replacements of the host limestone, consider the bedded cherts to be formed by an extension of the process of replacement to the whole rock. Most students of bedded chert, however, reject both the biochemical and the metasomatic origins for these deposits and regard them as primary precipitates of silica gel.

Inasmuch as the remains of Radiolaria, diatoms, and siliceous sponge spicules are found in many cherts, and are very abundant in some, the conclusion that these organisms are responsible for the precipitation of the chert is not surprising. Some cherts, however, are barren of such remains. Either these delicate, relatively soluble structures were destroyed by recrystallization, or they were never present and the chert is a product of some nonbiological process. That the bedded cherts are lithified siliceous bioliths has been stated by various students of the deposits from time to time. Some of the cherts of the Phosphoria (Permian) formation of Montana have recently been ascribed to ". . . the accumulation and partial diagenetic reorganization of sponge spicules and other siliceous remains . . ." (Cressman, 1955, p. 25). Bramlette (1946) believed that the bedded Monterey chert (Pl. 31) was produced by addition of silica to diatomite. For the most part the silica was derived from the diatom materials themselves at an early stage in the formation of the rock. These cherts therefore are a product of diagenetic rearrangement of the silica of a diatomaceous ooze. The rhythmic bedding is a feature inherited from the unaltered diatomites and diatomaceous shales. Another line of evidence suggesting that the cherty rocks were thus formed is chemical. If pure silica and average diatomaceous shale are taken in equal proportions, the resulting rocks will have the composition substantially like that of the associated bedded cherts.

As noted elsewhere, the siliceous shales (such as those of the Carboniferous Stanley of Oklahoma and the Cretaceous Mowry of Wyoming) and associated porcellanites have been interpreted as a silica reinforcement of normal marine shale (Goldstein and Hendricks, 1953; Rubey, 1929). The silica has been attributed to infalls of volcanic ash. It is noteworthy, perhaps, that these siliceous shales and the cherty shales of the Monterey are quite impure cherts; on the other hand, many cherts are nearly pure silica and cannot have been formed merely by the addition of silica to a shale or similar rock.

The extraordinary thickness of these deposits and their great areal extent make it difficult to consider them merely a replacement of limestone or other carbonate rock. Postconsolidation replacement would yield a much more irregular pattern of distribution of the chert—essentially that observed in those limestones in which the chert nodules have grown and coalesced into an anastomosing three-dimensional network enclosing much unreplaced limestone. The uniformity and rhythmic nature of the bedding and the absence of evidence of replacement make the hypothesis of a metasomatic origin unlikely.

Many writers ascribe the bedded cherts to direct precipitation of silica (Davis, 1918; Sampson, 1923; Sargent, 1929; Aldrich, 1929, p. 135; Moore and Maynard, 1929; James, 1954). As noted by James (1954, p. 273) the chert layers in places are involved in slump structures and intraformational breccias; the chert therefore must be essentially contemporaneous with the sedimentation and be prelithification.

If the bedded cherts be primary, it is pertinent to inquire into the conditions which permit their formation. Although sea water contains but four parts per million of silica, organisms have been able to extract this material and in places form extensive deposits of nearly pure silica. Such deposits today are restricted to areas receiving little or no land-derived sediment and to waters too acid (too deep) for the deposition of calcareous sediment. Presumably these are the conditions necessary for accumulation of precipitated silica in times past. As shown by Correns (1950) where $CaCO_3$ is dissolved, SiO_2 can be precipitated and vice versa. The critical factor involved is the acidity or alkalinity (pH).[3]

The common association of siderite, black shale, or phosphorite with the bedded cherts suggests precipitation in a restricted basin. This basin has the attributes of a starved basin (Adams, Frenzel, Rhodes, and Johnson, 1951), i.e., one so situated as to receive little or no clastic materials and one too deep or otherwise unfavorable for normal benthonic organisms and with such a low pH that planktonic calcareous remains are taken into solution. Under such conditions sedimentation is exceedingly slow and is confined to the finest papery black shales and to the deposition of compounds of iron, phosphorus, and silicon.

[3] Krumbein and Garrels consider chert to be largely independent of either pH or Eh (1952, p. 19).

The depth of water in which bedded cherts form has been much debated. The radiolarian Normanskill and Deepskill (Ordovician) of New York were considered to be abyssal (12,000 feet) on the basis of paleontological evidence (Ruedemann and Wilson, 1936). Similar views have also been expressed respecting the Alpine cherts (Bailey, 1936). On the other hand, Davis (1916) and Taliaferro (1943) noted that the radiolarian cherts of the Franciscan (Jurassic?) of California are interbedded and closely associated with coarse clastics—sandstones and even conglomerates. Since the clastics were considered proof of shallow water, the cherts were deemed of shallow-water origin. However, this view was expressed before the concept of turbidity-current transport and deposition of coarse clastics was understood. Deposition of such materials, even at abyssal depths, has been demonstrated and makes unnecessary either the hypothesis of a shallow-water origin or that of frequent and radical changes in water depth for those sections containing both bedded chert and sandstone. Some of the iron-formation cherts are associated with hematite presumed to be primary. Since the hematite is in part oolitic, as is the chert also, an oxidizing and turbulent environment seems to be implied. Perhaps not all chert is of a deep-water origin.

Whether the chert is a product of flocculation of colloidal silica or of biochemical origin, it is necessary to inquire into the source of the silica and the concentrations implied. Silica is carried into the sea by river waters and although these contain more silica than do the waters of the ocean, the concentration of silica is not very great. Twenhofel (1950, p. 409) has attempted to correlate chert formation with the mouths of rivers. But such correlation is at best very tenuous and in many cases no such correlation can be proved. Moreover, Correns (1950) states that concentrations of silica substantially greater than that of present-day streams cannot be flocculated by any known agent and hence the silica of the cherts and related rocks must be biochemically deposited.

Others have appealed to volcanism to supply the silica and build up the concentration of this material to the point where inorganic precipitation is possible (Davis, 1918; Taliaferro, 1933; Van Hise and Leith, 1911, p. 516). Although some cherts are associated with submarine flows (greenstones) and tuffs, many bedded cherts have no known association either with flows or infalls of volcanic ash. Lacking such associations, volcanism cannot be appealed to for silica and that normally found in sea water must be adequate.

After deposition, the silica, be it gel or the opaline tests of organisms, undergoes some diagenetic changes. The silica gel tends to dehydrate and crystallize; the opal is converted to chalcedonic and microcrystalline quartz. The disseminated silica of the limestones is segregated into the familiar nodules. That deposited in the muds may be segregated into layers. Such diagenetic unmixing is the explanation given by Davis (1918) for the rhythmic bedding of the California cherts.[4]

In conclusion it can be said that the chert problem is not yet solved. Perhaps chert is a polygenetic rock for which no single mode of origin exists. Some cherts, the nodular cherts in particular, are diagenetic segregations; others are silica reinforcements of various rocks, or are, in other words, silicified diatomite, silicified tuff, or even silicified limestones; still other chert may be inorganically precipitated silica. The origin of a particular chert will have to be decided on the evidence at hand.

REFERENCES CITED AND BIBLIOGRAPHY

Adams, J. E., Frenzel, H. N., Rhodes, M. L., and Johnson, D. P. (1951), Starved Pennsylvanian Midland basin, Bull. Am. Assoc. Petroleum Geol., vol. 35, pp. 2600–2606.

Aldrich, H. R. (1929), The geology of the Gogebic iron range of Wisconsin, Wisconsin Geol. Nat. Hist. Survey, Bull. 71, pp. 143–153.

Bailey, E. B. (1936), Sedimentation in relation to tectonics, Bull. Geol. Soc. Amer., vol. 47, pp. 1713–1726.

Bastin, E. S. (1933), Relations of cherts to stylolites at Carthage, Missouri, J. Geol., vol. 41, pp. 371–381.

Berkey, C. P. (1924), The new petrology, N.Y. State Museum Bull. 251, pp. 105–118.

Bramlette, M. N. (1946), The Monterey formation of California and the origin of its siliceous rocks, U.S. Geol. Survey Prof. Paper 212, pp. 15–16.

Cayeux, L. (1929), Les roches sedimentaires de France: Roches siliceuses (Mem. carte geol. de France), Paris, Imprimerie nationale.

Choquette, P. W. (1955), A petrographic study of the "State College" siliceous oolite, J. Geol., vol. 63, pp. 337–347.

Clarke, F. W. (1924), Data of geochemistry, U.S. Geol. Survey, Bull. 770.

Conger, P. S. (1942), Accumulation of diatomaceous deposits, J. Sediment. Petrol., vol. 12, pp. 55–66.

Cornelius, H. P. (1951), Zur Frage der Absatzbedingungen der Radiolarite, Geol. Rundschau, vol. 39, pp. 216–221.

Correns, C. W. (1950), The geochemistry of diagenesis, Geochim. et Cosmochim. Acta, vol. 1, pp. 49–54.

Correns, C. W. (1924), Beitrage zur Petrographie und Genesis der Lydite (Kieselschiefer), Mitt. preuss. geol. Landesanstalt, Berlin, pp. 18–36.

Cressman, E. R. (1955), Physical stratigraphy of the Phosphoria formation in part of southwestern Montana, U.S. Geol. Survey Bull. 1027-A, p. 25.

Davis, E. F. (1918), The radiolarian cherts of the Franciscan group, Univ. Calif. Publ. Dept. Geol. Sci. Bull., vol. 11, pp. 235–432.

[4] Others have explained the rhythmic bedding as a product of seasonal deposition of chert (Sakamoto, 1950).

Diller, J. S. (1898), The educational series of rock specimens collected and distributed by the United States Geological Survey, *U.S. Geol. Survey Bull.* 150.

Folk, R. L. and Weaver, C. E. (1952), A study of the texture and composition of chert, *Am. J. Sci.*, vol. 250, pp. 498–510.

Fowler, G. M., Lyden, J. P., Gregory, F. E., and Agar, W. M. (1935), Chertification in the Tri-State mining district, *Trans. Am. Inst. Mining Met. Engrs.*, vol. 115, pp. 106–163.

Goldstein, A. Jr., and Hendricks, T. A. (1953), Siliceous sediments of Ouachita facies in Oklahoma, *Bull. Geol. Soc. Amer.*, vol. 64, pp. 421–442.

Gruner, J. W. (1940), Cristobalite in bentonite, *Am. Mineralogist*, vol. 25, pp. 587–590.

Harlton, B. H. (1953), Ouachita chert facies, southeastern Oklahoma, *Bull. Am. Assoc. Petroleum Geol.*, vol. 37, pp. 778–796.

Heald, M. T. (1952), Origin of chert in the Helderberg limestone of West Virginia (abstract), *Bull. Geol. Soc. Amer.*, vol. 63, p. 1261.

Hoots, H. W. (1931), Geology of the eastern part of the Santa Monica Mountains, Los Angeles County, California, *U.S. Geol. Survey Prof. Paper* 165-C.

Hurst, V. J. (1953), Chertification in the Fort Payne formation, Georgia, *Georgia Geol. Survey, Bull.* 60, pp. 215–238.

James, H. L. (1954), Sedimentary facies of iron-formation, *Econ. Geol.*, vol. 49, pp. 235–293.

Keller, W. D. (1941), Petrography and origin of the Rex chert, *Bull. Geol. Soc. Amer.*, vol. 52, pp. 1279–1298.

Krumbein, W. C., and Garrels, R. M. (1952), Origin and classification of chemical sediments in terms of pH and oxidation-reduction potentials, *J. Geol.*, vol. 60, pp. 1–33.

Krynine, P. D., Honess, A. P., and Myers, W. M. (1941), Siliceous oolites and chemical sedimentation, *Bull. Geol. Soc. Amer.*, vol. 52 (abstract), pp. 1916–1917.

Lowenstam, H. A. (1942), Geology of the eastern Nazareth Mountains, Palestine. I Cretaceous stratigraphy, *J. Geol.*, vol. 50, p. 813.

Lowenstam, H. A. (1948), Biostratigraphic studies of the Niagaran inter-reef formations in northeastern Illinois, *Illinois State Museum Sci. Papers*, vol. 4.

Midgley, H. G. (1951), Chalcedony and flint, *Geol. Mag.*, vol. 88, pp. 179–184.

Moore, E. S. and Maynard, J. E. (1929), Solution, transportation, and precipitation of iron and silica, *Econ. Geol.*, vol. 24, pp. 399–413.

Richardson, A. W. (1919), The origin of Cretaceous flint, *Geol. Mag.*, vol. 58, pp. 114–124.

Rubey, W. W. (1929), Origin of the siliceous Mowry shale of the Black Hills region, *U.S. Geol. Survey, Prof. Paper* 154, pp. 153–170.

Ruedemann, R. and Wilson, T. Y. (1936), Eastern New York Ordovician cherts, *Bull. Geol. Soc. Amer.*, vol. 47, pp. 1535–1586.

Sakamoto, Takao (1950), The origin of the Pre-Cambrian banded iron ores, *Am. J. Sci.*, vol. 248, pp. 449–474.

PLATE 33

SEDIMENTARY PYRITE AND PHOSPHORITE

Top: Pyritic black slate, Precambrian, Iron River, Mich. About natural size.

Pyritic layers appear light-colored on polished surface; unpolished specimens are dull and nearly black. (James, *Bull. Geol. Soc. Amer.*, vol. 62, 1951, pl. 1.)

Bottom: Phosphorite, Phosphoria formation (Permian), McDougals Pass, Salt River Range, Wyoming, ×3.

Nodular and oolitic phosphate rock. U.S. Geological Survey photograph. (Mansfield, *Prof. Paper* 152, pl. 63.)

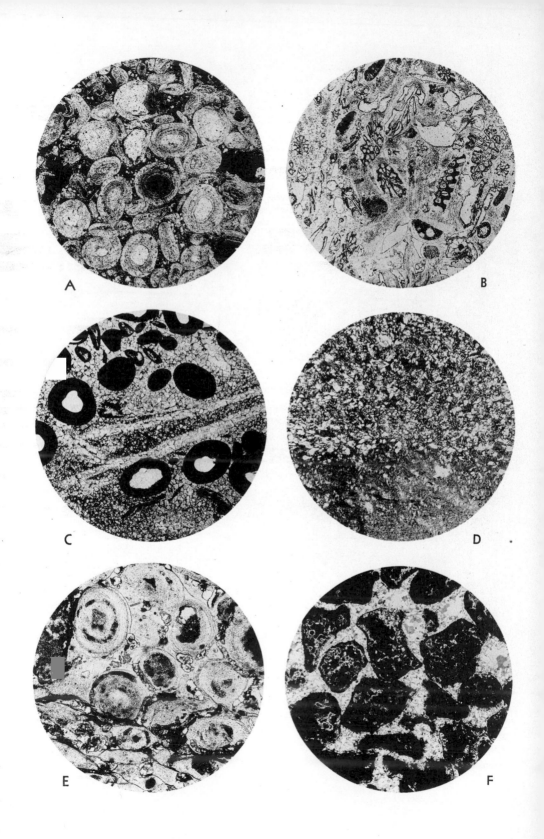

A

B

C

D

E

F

PLATE 34

IRON-BEARING SEDIMENTS

A: Clinton oolitic hematite ("flaxseed ore"), Silurian. Ordinary light, $\times 15$.

A nitrocellulose peel of polished surface of oolitic hematite. Many oolites apparently had quartz grains as nuclei. Note flattening of some oolitic bodies.

B: Clinton "fossil" ore, Silurian. Ordinary light, $\times 17$.

A nitrocellulose peel of polished surface of fossil ore. The fossil structures are well preserved in hematite.

C: Hematite oolites. Ordinary light, $\times 12$.

A thin section of hematite (black) oolites, some with detrital quartz nuclei (white), in a dolomite matrix. The dolomite shows some fossil structures.

D: Crystal Falls iron formation, Precambrian, Crystal Falls, Mich. Ordinary light, $\times 42$.

Consists of stilpnomelane (gray) in which are embedded numerous crystals of siderite (white). Bedding-plane contact between siderite-rich and siderite-poor layers.

E: Oolitic chamosite, Jurassic, Lorraine. Ordinary light, $\times 30$.

Mainly chamosite (oolites) with a few spherulites of siderite (clear granules with high relief).

F: Greenalite granules, Gunflint iron formation, Precambrian. Crossed nicols, $\times 30$. H. L. James photograph.

Greenalite granules in chert matrix. Greenalite shows peculiar mottling caused by recrystallization of chert. (James, *Econ. Geol.*, vol. 49, 1955, p. 292, fig. 27.)

Sampson, E. (1923), The ferruginous chert formations of Notre Dame Bay, Newfoundland, *J. Geol.*, vol. 31, pp. 571–598.

Sargent, H. S. (1921), The Lower Carboniferous chert formations of Derbyshire, *Geol. Mag.*, vol. 58, pp. 265–278.

Sargent, H. S. (1923), The massive chert formation of North Flintshire, *Geol. Mag.*, vol. 60, pp. 168–183.

Sargent, H. S. (1929), Further studies in chert, *Geol. Mag.*, vol. 66, pp. 272–303.

Storz, Max (1928), Die sekundare Kieselsaure in ihrer petrogenetischgeologischen Bedeutung, *Monograph z. Geol. u. Paleo.*, Ser II, vol. 4.

Stout, W. and Schoenlaub, R. A. (1945), The occurrence of flint in Ohio, *Bull. Geol. Survey Ohio*, No. 46, Ser. 4.

Taliaferro, N. L. (1933), The relation of volcanism to diatomaceous and associated siliceous sediments, *Univ. Calif. Publ. Dept. Geol. Sci., Bull.*, vol. 23, pp. 1–55.

Taliaferro, N. L. (1934), Contraction phenomena in cherts, *Bull. Geol. Soc. Amer.*, vol. 45, pp. 196–197.

Taliaferro, N. L. (1943), Franciscan-Knoxville problem, *Bull. Am. Assoc. Petroleum Geol.*, vol. 27, pp. 109–219.

Tarr, W. A. (1917), Origin of chert in the Burlington limestone, *Am. J. Sci.*, ser. 4, vol. 44, pp. 409–452.

Tarr, W. A. (1926), The origin of chert and flint, *Univ. Missouri Studies*, vol. 1, no. 2.

Tarr, W. A. (1938), Terminology of the chemical siliceous sediments, *Rept. Comm. Sed.*, 1937–1938, Nat. Research Council, pp. 8–27. (mimeographed)

Trefethen, J. M. (1947), Some features of the cherts in the vicinity of Columbia, Missouri, *Am. J. Sci.*, vol. 245, pp. 56–58.

Tromp, S. W. (1948), Shallow-water origin of radiolarites in southern Turkey, *J. Geol.*, vol. 56, pp. 492–494.

Twenhofel, W. H. (1950), *Principles of sedimentation*, New York, McGraw-Hill.

Van Hise, C. R., and Leith, C. K. (1911), The geology of the Lake Superior region, *U.S. Geol. Survey Monograph* 52.

Van Tuyl, F. M. (1918), The origin of chert, *Am. J. Sci.*, ser. 4, vol. 45, pp. 449–456.

Wenk, E. (1949), Die Association von Radiolarienhornsteinen mit ophiolithischen Erstarrungsgesteinen als petrogenetisches Problem, *Experientia*, vol. 5, pp. 226–232.

Wetzel, W. (1922), Sedimentpetrographische Studien, I. Fuerstein, *Neues Jahrb. Mineral.*, Beilage 47, pp. 39–92.

White, D. E. (1947), Diagenetic origin of chert lenses in limestone at Soyatal, state of Queretaro, Mexico, *Am. J. Sci.*, vol. 245, pp. 49–55.

IRON-BEARING SEDIMENTS

Definitions and General Introduction

Iron is one of the most abundant elements in the earth's crust, and few rocks indeed are iron-free. The average shale, for example, contains 6.47 per cent of FeO and Fe_2O_3. Hence in the broadest sense all sediments are likely to be iron-bearing. Generally, however, the term *iron-bearing* is reserved for those rocks which are much richer in iron than is usually the case. The term ferruginous would be appropriate, perhaps, had it not been applied to sandstones and shales colored red by ferric oxide. Such rocks, although called ferruginous, commonly have no more iron than similar strata not so colored (p. 347). Commonly the terms *iron formation* and *ironstone* are applied to the iron-rich rocks; less commonly these rocks are termed *ferriferous*.[5]

A precise definition of iron formation or ironstone is difficult to frame, since the term embraces a mineralogically and texturally diverse group of rocks (see Table 83). The only restriction is that the total iron content be higher than that of normal sediments. Usage in the Lake Superior district suggests that 15 per cent iron be present before the term iron formation be applied (James, 1954). This would correspond to 21.3 per cent Fe_2O_3 or 19.4 per cent FeO.

TABLE 83. Vadose Iron Compounds and Their Mineralogic Derivatives
(after Polynov, 1937, with modifications)

Sol or Solution	Iron-Bearing Mineral
1. Organomineral compounds of living matter (haemoglobin, etc.)	
2. Coagels with active humus	
3. Gels of ferric oxide	Turgite, etc. $Fe_2O_3 \cdot qH_2O$ Limonite, brown Iron ore: $FeO(OH) \cdot qH_2O$
4. Coagels with silica (ferrisilicic colloidal acids)	Nontronite $H_2Fe_2Si_3O_{10} \cdot 2H_2O$ Stilpnomelane (?)
5. The same with adsorbed cations	Glauconite, etc.
6. Coagels with silica and alumina	Chamosite: $Fe_3Al_2Si_2O_{10} \cdot qH_2O$
7. Gels with adsorbed phosphoric acid	Vivianite: $Fe_3(PO_4)_2 \cdot 8H_2O$
8. Ferrous ions in solution	Siderite: $FeCO_3$; ankerite; ferro-dolomite Copperas: $FeSO_4$ (melanterite)
9. Hydrotroilite $FeS \cdot nH_2O$	Pyrite, marcasite: FeS_2
10. Native vadose iron	

[5] The grouping of the iron-bearing sediments together is an illogical departure from the general compositional classification of the chemical sediments. Yet the iron-bearing sediments are related, one to the other, and usage favors a unified treatment of the group as a whole even though the other chemical sediments are classified on the anion rather than the cation constituents present.

Mineralogy and Classification

The iron-bearing sediments are classified best on the basis of the iron minerals present (see Table 83). These belong to four major groups: (1) the sulfides (mainly pyrite), (2) the carbonates (siderite), (3) the silicates (chamosite, greenalite, glauconite, etc.), and (4) the oxides (limonite, hematite, and magnetite). Many iron-bearing sediments are complex in that more than one type of iron-bearing mineral is present (Fig. 104). Laminations of

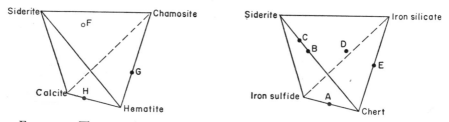

FIG. 104. The approximate mineral composition of the iron-bearing rocks, the analyses of which are given in Table 84. Minor constituents omitted.

iron silicate occur in the sideritic iron formations; magnetite is interlaminated with iron silicate, etc. Moreover other chemical sediments—notably chert—and the common clastic materials are mixed or interbedded with the iron-bearing minerals. In fact chert is considered by some to be an essential constituent of iron formation in the Lake Superior district. Like other sediments, the iron-bearing rocks undergo changes in mineral composition during diagenesis and metamorphism. The petrographers problem, as always, is to distinguish between the later-formed suite of minerals and those precipitated initially.

Bedded Iron Sulfides

The iron sulfides of sedimentary origin, marcasite and pyrite, are common minor accessory minerals in many sedimentary rocks, are abundant in a few such rocks, and are the chief constituent in more relatively minor beds. The sulfides may be disseminated throughout the rock, or they may be segregated into nodular crystalline aggregates and spherulites (p. 202) or they may be precipitated in geodic cavities and veins, or they may replace fossils and other structures.

The rocks in which iron sulfide is an important constituent or even the dominant one are uncommon and insignificant in volume. Beds of pyrite, six inchs to a little over a foot thick, interbedded with fissile black shale, occur in the Wabana district of Newfoundland in rocks of Ordovician age (Hayes, 1915). The pyrite beds are composed primarily of minute spherulites of pyrite together with both pyritized and unpyritized fossil fragments, all cemented by an extremely fine-grained siliceous groundmass. Pyrite forms about 65 per cent of these beds.

Similarly in some of the black slates associated with the bedded cherty iron carbonates of the Crystal Falls district, Michigan, there are interbedded layers of pyrite varying from a mere film to those one or two inches in thickness. The most important occurrence of sedimentary pyrite in this district, however, is the so-called "graphitic slate," a formation about fifty feet thick which, on the basis of a few samples, averages about 38 per cent pyrite. The pyrite in this rock is extremely fine-grained and the individual crystals are nearly invisible to the naked eye. The pyrite tends to be concentrated in

TABLE 84. Chemical Analyses of Ironstones
(per cent)

	A	B	C	D	E	F	G	H
SiO_2	36.67	28.86	24.25	31.84	61.90	8.51	12.59	8.71
TiO_2	0.39	0.20	....	0.12	none	0.36	0.27	....
Al_2O_3	6.90	1.29	1.71	2.09	0.37	6.12	5.71	3.67
Fe_2O_3	....	1.01	0.71	14.83	15.00	1.77	75.12	30.24
FeO	2.35	37.37	35.22	20.59	10.28	36.91	....	....
FeS_2	38.70	....	....	....	....	....	....	....
MnO	T	0.90	2.11	2.35	....	0.42	0.06	....
MgO	0.65	3.64	3.16	3.80	2.33	3.75	0.42	7.84
CaO	0.13	0.74	1.78	1.49	0.28	5.54	1.49	20.64
Na_2O	0.26	....	0.04	nd	none	0.05	....	....
K_2O	1.81	....	0.20	nd	none	0.03	....	....
H_2O+	1.25⎱	0.68[a]	⎰0.21⎱	1.80	⎰4.17	4.05	2.17[a]	....
H_2O-	0.55⎰		⎰....⎰		⎱2.50	10.00	0.52	....
P_2O_5	0.20	T	0.91	0.83	none	1.30	1.63	0.75
CO_2	....	25.21	27.60	19.40	2.04	20.70	....	24.78
SO_3	2.60	....	....	none	....	....	....	0.15
S	....	....	nd	0.33	....	0.05	none	....
C	7.60	....	1.96	....	....	0.27	....	....
Total	101.21[b]	99.90	99.86	99.47	99.54[c]	99.86	99.98	96.78

A. Sulfide iron-formation, Precambrian, 10th level Buck Mine, Iron River, Michigan (James, 1954, p. 250).
B. Cherty iron carbonate; Ironwood iron-bearing formation; Precambrian, Michigan. W. F. Hillebrand, analyst (Irving and Van Hise, 1892, p. 192). Approximately 29 per cent chert and 62 per cent siderite.
C. Cherty iron carbonate; Precambrian; Iron River district, Michigan. Leonard Shapiro, analyst (James, 1951, p. 257). About 24 per cent chert and 70 per cent siderite.
D. Cherty iron carbonate, Precambrian, Crystal Falls, Michigan. J. G. Fairchild, analyst (Pettijohn, 1952). About 20 per cent chert, 48 per cent siderite, and 23 per cent stilpnomelane.
E. Greenalite iron formation, Biwabik formation, Precambrian, Minnesota. George Steiger, analyst (Leith, 1903 X, p. 108). Approximately 50.4 per cent greenalite and 50 per cent chert.
F. Sideritic-chamositic mudstone, Cleveland ironstone, Great Britain. J. E. Stead, analyst (Hallimond, 1925, p. 51). About 34.2 per cent chamosite, 34.7 siderite.
G. Chamositic hematite, Dominion bed, zone 2 (Ordovician) Wabana, Newfoundland (Hayes, 1915, p. 45). About 65 per cent hematite and 24 per cent chamosite.
H. Hematite "fossil ore," Clinton (Silurian), Alabama. E. C. Sullivan, analyst (Burchard and others, 1910), p. 34). Hematite about 30 per cent, calcite 17 per cent, and dolomite 36 per cent.
[a] Ignition.
[b] Includes 0.15 per cent V_2O_5.
[c] Includes 0.64 per cent iron and aluminum oxides in soluble part.

certain layers and regularly interbedded with dark carbonaceous slate (Pl. 33, top). The iron sulfide content of these richer layers is about 75 per cent. The chemical composition of this rock is given in Table 84, col. A.

Pyrite also occurs in some limestones. Representative of such a limestone is a four-foot bed at the base of the Greenhorn formation (Upper Cretaceous) of Wyoming (Rubey, 1930). It consists of calcite, 45.4 per cent; pyrite, 25.2 per cent; gypsum (in part of secondary origin), 17.6 per cent; iron oxides, 6.1 per cent; organic matter, 2.6 per cent, and bone phosphate, 2.0 per cent. The Tully limestone (Devonian) of New York is notably pyritic and in places grades into a thin but widespread pyrite bed (Loomis, 1903). The Tully is closely associated with carbonaceous black shales. The association of pyrite with carbonates and with organic matter (or carbonaceous residues therefrom) is rather general. The black shales or slates have the most pyrite. This suggests that the source of the sulfur is the nitrogenous component of the organic matter; it is possible also that the association is due primarily to the reducing environment needed for the preservation of organic matter and the bacterial reduction of the sulfates of sea water. Rubey (1930) has noted the relationships between pyrite, organic matter, and carbonate in certain Cretaceous formations (Table 85).

TABLE 85.   Content of Pyrite, Organic Matter, and Carbonates in Black Hills Cretaceous Rocks (after Rubey, 1930)

	Carbonates Plus Organic Matter	Pyrite
Colorado group		
Average of five samples	2.3	0.4
Pierre shale		
Average of three samples	8.7	0.8
Calcareous parts of Greenhorn and		
Niobrara formations	42.7	9.1

Bedded Siderites (Cherty Iron Carbonate, Clay Ironstone)

The iron carbonates (siderite) occur intimately interbedded with chert (cherty iron carbonates) or mixed in all proportions with clay (clay ironstone).

Typical bedded cherty iron carbonate consists of fine-grained, light to dark-gray siderite and dense black chert. The constituents are rhythmically interbedded in layers a fraction of an inch to three or four inches thick. In the less cherty formations the chert occurs as small nodules. The proportions are variable but commonly the formation is one-fourth to one-third chert and one-half to two-thirds siderite. In places formations of this character reach a thickness of several hundred feet. The iron content of the rock as a whole is 20 to 30 per cent (50 to 70 per cent siderite).

The siderite layers may show paper-thin laminations of iron silicate or iron sulfide; they may be nearly pure carbonate. The latter are commonly stylolitic. The carbonate iron formation is generally free of detrital materials of any sort. Oolitic textures are absent.

The cherty iron carbonates are common in the Lake Superior district in the United States. This formation has been rather generally considered to be the major primary iron-bearing sediment of this district and most other types of iron formation were regarded as postdepositional modifications of this rock. Except for the truly metamorphosed cherty carbonate rocks, it now seems clear that the other types of iron formation (silicate and oxide) are themselves primary sedimentary facies and not oxidized (weathered) or silicated (metamorphosed) iron carbonate rocks (James, 1954). Primary bedded iron carbonate is the principal iron formation in the Crystal Falls-Iron River district of Michigan. It is present also in important volume in both the Gogebic and Marquette districts.

In some areas siderite appears as a constituent of limestone and in some cases the limestone bed appears to have undergone sideritization; a process akin to dolomitization and like some dolomitization appears to have taken place during early diagenesis while the materials were still unconsolidated and in their environment of deposition. In such rocks calcitic shell fragments are set in a matrix of calcite and siderite in varying proportions and are in part or completely replaced by siderite. Some of the Dogger ironstones of Great Britain, especially the marlstone of the Midlands, appear to be siderites of this type. In less common cases the siderite iron formation may be a hydrothermal replacement. Such is said to be the origin of the siderites of the Michipicoten district of Ontario (Hawley, 1942). This deposit is believed to be a replacement of a tuff bed.

Clay ironstone is the term applied to the argillaceous sideritic concretions and beds found in the coal measures of both Great Britain and the United States. Clay ironstone occurs as layers of nodules, many of which display a septarian structure, and as more or less continuous thin beds. Their color is dark gray to brown; less commonly black (blackband ore). Clay ironstones are fine-grained; the clay content varies from 1 to 30 per cent. The ironstone nodules or beds are found most commonly to overlie coal seams. Fossils are common.

Bedded Iron Oxides (Including Bog Iron)

Some iron formations consist largely of iron oxide. Of these hematite is the most important. The sedimentary hematities are best illustrated by the Clinton iron-bearing strata of Silurian age (Smyth, 1892; Alling, 1947).

These beds, several in number, are found throughout the Appalachian region and form important deposits of iron ore in the Birmingham district of Alabama (Burchard, 1910). The iron-bearing rock is either (1) fossil ore,[6] or (2) oolitic ore (Pl. 34, A and B). Fossil ore consists of broken and water-worn shell fragments which evidently were gathered by the action of waves and currents (calcarenites) and which subsequently were replaced and cemented together by hematite and carbonate. The oolitic ore consists of an aggregate of flattened hematitic oolites of uniform size and shape (flaxseed ore). The oolites consist of a nucleus of quartz which may be very minute or a not so small quartz sand grain, around which successive layers of iron oxides, and in many cases silica, were deposited.

That these hematites were early, perhaps contemporaneous replacements or original precipitates, is proved by their stratigraphic continuity, the distribution which is not related to either outcrop or unconformities, by the occurrence of fragments of ore in overlying beds of limestone of the same formation, by the presence of hematitic oolites in calcareous beds in which the matrix consists of dolomite or calcite, and by the occurrence of calcareous fossils enveloped in concentrically deposited shells of hematite.

The Mayville oolitic ores of Wisconsin also appear to be a primary ferric oxide precipitate (Hawley and Beavan, 1934).

The Wabana ores of Newfoundland are complex and contain hematite, iron silicate (chamosite), and less commonly siderite (Hayes, 1915). The hematite is oolitic; some oolites are themselves complex and consist of alternating layers of hematite and chamosite. Chamosite occurs as pure oolites and is present also in the matrix of the oolitic rocks. The average iron-bearing stratum consists of hematite, 50 to 70 per cent; chamosite, 15 to 25 per cent; siderite, zero to 50 per cent; calcium phosphate, 4 to 5 per cent; calcite, zero to 1 per cent; and quartz, zero to 10 per cent. The compositions of three typical iron-bearing beds (A, B, C) and a ferruginous sandstone (D) are shown in Fig. 105.

Hayes cites much evidence to establish the primary marine origin for the hematite oolites. The sorting, ripple marking, and cross-bedding of the oolitic members; the close association with marine fossils; the borings of marine worms into the oolitic layers which are filled with mud but which contain few oolites; the intraformational conglomerates holding pebbles of the hematite-chamosite beds—all point to this conclusion.

Bedded oolitic hematites occur also in the Lake Superior region. In this district hematite is rhythmically interbedded with jasper or red chert. The oolitic structure is most readily seen in some of the jaspers where the oolites consist mostly of silica but with the structure defined by the hematite. Oolites consisting more largely of hematite are also present and no doubt

[6] The term ore is used in a colloquial sense.

many of the hematite layers were once oolitic. More commonly, however, the hematite layers appear not to be oolitic. The rhythmically interbedded jasper and steel-gray hematite forms one of the most spectacular rocks in the Lake Superior district. Jaspilite, as it is termed, occurs in the Marquette, Menominee, and Gogebic districts of Michigan. It was once regarded as the product of premetamorphic weathering of a cherty iron carbonate. James (1954), however, considers it a primary sedimentary deposit. The preservation of exceeding fine bedding and knife-edged contacts between the

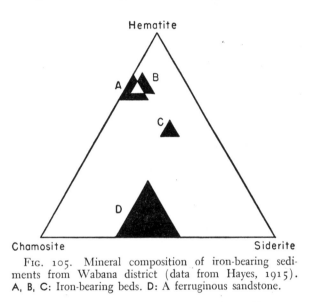

Fig. 105. Mineral composition of iron-bearing sediments from Wabana district (data from Hayes, 1915). A, B, C: Iron-bearing beds. D: A ferruginous sandstone.

hematite and jasper is not characteristic of weathered rocks. Moreover the presence of continuous, though thin, layers of hematite in unoxidized carbonate formation and the existence of primary hematites of younger age in other areas are evidence of a primary origin of the hematitic beds. Furthermore the close association of oolite and sand grains and the absence of such features in other facies of iron formation is further evidence of a primary origin in a turbulent environment.

Magnetite is, of course, a product of metamorphic reorganization and it is also a major constituent of black sands—a placer-like concentration of magnetite. Recognition of magnetite as a precipitated constituent of iron formation is relatively recent (James, 1954) although its supergene occurrence in sediments has been known for some time (Berz, 1922; Friedman, 1954). The abundance of magnetite in rocks that are essentially unmetamorphosed, as indicated by the fine grain of the chert, and the presence of low-grade iron silicates, are a valid criterion that should serve to separate the primary magnetite rock from magnetite-bearing rocks that are products of later metamorphism. The magnetite-banded rocks are typically, almost invariably, associated with the iron silicate facies of iron formation, and every gradation can be found between the two. Primary banded magnetite rocks are common in the Mesabi district of Minnesota and in the Gogebic district of Wisconsin and Michigan.

Limonite occurs in oolitic form in some iron formations. It is most characteristic, however, of bog iron ore. Bog ore is composed principally of an earthy mixture of yellow to dark brown ferric hydroxides. Such ore is deposited along the borders of certain lakes and in bogs. The lake ores consist mainly of flat disklike or irregular concretionary masses of ferric hydroxide, a foot or two thick, or as a layer of soft to hard porous yellow bedded limonite, or as a limonitic cement in sand. The bog ore proper occurs in the bog or marsh as a spongy mass mixed with peat. Some are tubular, others pisolitic, and still other deposits are nodular or concretionary bodies. A few form solid bodies, commonly rather thin and filled with sand and clay impurities.

Bog iron ores are abundant in the glaciated northern regions of North America and Europe. Iron dissolved from the drift is precipitated either chemically or biologically. Although they are rather small deposits, they are of great interest because they are the only iron-bearing sediments known to form at the present time.[7]

Bedded Iron Silicates (Except Glauconite)

The chief iron-bearing silicates are glauconite, chamosite, chlorite (aphrosiderite and thuringite), and stilpnomelane. In the Lake Superior districts greenalite and minnesotaite are found in addition to chlorite and stilpnomelane.

James (1954) recognized two major types of silicate iron formation. In one the silicate mineral is present as granules or as oolites; in the other the silicate is nongranular and is typically thinly bedded or laminated.[8] Greenalite and glauconite are characteristically granular; chamosite forms both oolites and granules. Although some granules have a microcrystalline and structureless interior others show an obscure mottling in thin section (Pl. 34, F). The typical granules are about 0.5 millimeter in diameter and are irregular to rudely elliptical in form. They may occur in a matrix of chert or of other silicate materials. The oolites vary from simple concentrically structured, subspherical forms one-half millimeter or less in diameter to

---

[7] Except perhaps some glauconite and iron sulfide which, however, are minor accessory constituents of the sediments in which they occur.

[8] A granule is a false oolite, i.e., it has a structureless or a nonconcentric and nonradial interior. An oolite has a radial and/or concentric internal arrangement.

much flattened bodies to those which are markedly deformed (spastoliths). Some, like those of the Wabana district, are composite and consist of alternating layers of silicate and hematite.

The second type of silicate iron formation—nongranular and nonoolitic—is thinly bedded or laminated. Characteristically these laminations are but a millimeter, or fraction thereof, in thickness. The variations in the FeO/Fe_2O_3 ratio in those composed of stilpnomelane, as indicated by the refractive indices, are good evidence that the present composition of the layers is essentially that of the primary rock. (If the silicate were a metamorphic product equilibrium would have been attained through a greater thickness of rock).

The composition of the silicate-rich iron formation varies within wide limits, chiefly because of the varying proportions of carbonate and iron oxide present in addition to the silicates (Table 84). The analyses fall into two groups, namely, those high in alumina and relatively low in magnesia and those low in alumina and high in magnesia. The greenalite- and minnesotaite-rich rocks belong to the first group; the stilpnomelane-, chamosite-, and chlorite-rich beds belong in the second group. There is considerable variation in the FeO/Fe_2O_3 ratio (even within the same group). The iron of minnesotaite seems to be mainly ferrous; that of glauconite largely ferric. The iron of stilpnomelane and chamosite shows a widely varying ferrous oxide/ferric oxide ratio.

The nongranular iron silicate rocks seem to have a high proportion of fine clastic materials. These are in many cases aptly described as chloritic mudstones, chamositic mudstones, etc. It may be that these silicate formations are essentially fine-grained mechanical sediments that were enriched in iron during deposition.

Silicate iron formations are a very common type of iron-bearing sediment. Glauconitic sandstones and limestones are common in the Cambrian and later times and some of these are rich enough in iron to qualify as an iron formation.[9] The chamosite-bearing beds are common in the Jurassic iron formations of Great Britain (Hallimond, 1925; Taylor, 1949), of France (Cayeux, 1909, 1922), and of Switzerland (Deverin, 1945). Chamosite is a minor constituent of the Clinton (Alling, 1947) and the Wabana (Hayes, 1915) iron-bearing beds. It seems not to be present in the Lake Superior formations; instead greenalite, stilpnomelane, minnesotaite, and aphrosiderite are the common iron silicates (Gruner, 1924, 1946; James, 1951, 1954). Greenalite is certainly primary; the others may be diagenetic or metamorphic in origin.

[9] Some of the New Jersey greensands (Cretaceous) are half or more glauconite and contain, therefore, about 20 or more per cent of FeO and Fe_2O_3 (Ashley, 1918, p. 31). Technically they are iron-bearing formations.

Origin of Ironstones

The origin of iron-bearing sediments has long been a controversial matter. The several aspects of the problem are (1) the source of the iron, (2) the manner of transport of the iron from source to site of accumulation, (3) the manner of precipitation, and (4) postdepositional alteration including diagenesis, metamorphism, and ore formation.

The most difficult problem has been to sort out and assess the importance of the results of original sedimentation, postdepositional diagenesis, and other changes, including metamorphism and weathering. Some have considered the formations as seen today to be essentially the same as those deposited; others regard the iron formation as a diagenetic or later replacement of an original nonferruginous bed, such as a limestone or a tuff. Still others regard some facies of iron formation as a weathered (and later metamorphosed) alteration of an originally different iron-bearing deposit. Others regard some facies as products of metamorphic changes, such as silication. There is some evidence for each of the views but only in recent years has our knowledge of iron-formation petrography and of the stability of iron-bearing minerals and the oxidation-reduction potential reached a stage that permits unraveling of the complex natural history of these interesting deposits.

The iron contained in the iron-bearing sediments has been considered to be derived either from the breakdown of ordinary rocks during the normal cycle of weathering or to have been contributed by hydrothermal waters or lavas (Fig. 106).

The theory that the deposition of iron formation is related to volcanism was set forth by Van Hise and Leith (1911, p. 516). The major factor which led these workers to the concept of a volcanic source for the iron was the presumed inadequacy of ordinary weathering to supply solutions of the proper type for precipitation of iron formation. More recent work by Gruner (1922), Gill (1927), and James (1954) has shown that under tropical or subtropical conditions, the iron and silica content of stream waters may be very high and sufficient to account for iron-formation deposition. As noted by Gruner (1922), the Amazon with an iron content of only three parts per million is competent to transport 1,940,000 million metric tons of iron in 176,000 years, an amount about equal to that contained in the Biwabik formation of Minnesota. And as James (1954) points out, the accumulation of an iron formation requires only that the chemical factors governing precipitation (Eh, pH) be just right; neither the concentration nor quantity of iron in the waters at a given time need be excessive. The enormous accumulation of lime carbonate on the Bahama Banks is a product of localized chemical (and biochemical) precipitation from sea water in which the Ca content differs but slightly from that in areas of nondeposition of this element.

Most of the later iron formations, and many, if not most, of the Precambrian iron formations, are not associated with volcanic rocks of contemporary age. Thus there is no compelling reason for ascribing the iron to volcanism and none is indeed needed.

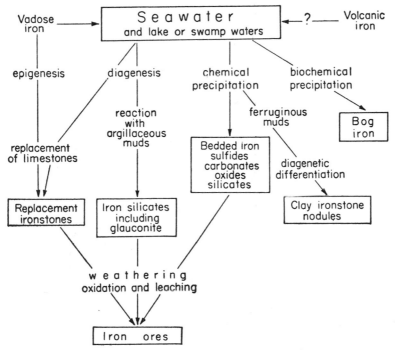

Fig. 106.   Provenance of the iron-bearing sediments.

The transportation of iron has been considered a problem. The ferric compounds are notably insoluble; iron oxides and hydroxides tend to form laterites—the insoluble residues of weathering. Although readily soluble ferrous salts are known, these are unstable in the presence of oxygen and tend to hydrolyze and be precipitated. As a result of these observations some authors have postulated a reducing atmosphere in order to explain the extensive transport and precipitation of sideritic iron in the Precambrian (see for example, Tyler and Twenhofel, 1952, p. 134). This extreme view seems quite unnecessary inasmuch as iron was transported and deposited in marine waters during the later geologic times when, as the fossil record shows, abundant fauna and flora requiring an aerobic environment were present.

Moore and Maynard (1929) have shown that iron is not carried as the bicarbonate in natural surface waters but rather is transported as ferric oxide hydrosol stabilized by organic colloids and in lesser quantity as salts of organic acids or adsorbed by organic colloids. As much as thirty-six parts per million ferric oxide can be held in colloidal solution by sixteen parts per million of organic matter. The form in which the iron is *precipitated*—even ferrous carbonate—is a function of the local environment of accumulation, not the manner in which the iron is *transported*. Local reducing conditions, despite an oxidizing atmosphere, are common today and even ferrous sulfide is known to be forming in these environments. A summary of the forms in which iron is transported and the mineral species assumed by the compounds precipitated is given in Table 83.

The compound of iron precipitated is primarily a function of the oxidation-reduction potential (redox or Eh). Experimental work by Casteno and Garrels (1950) (see also Krumbein and Garrels, 1952) and geological observations show that stability of the iron-bearing minerals is determined by the oxidation-reduction potential (see Fig. 155, p. 597). At the lowest potential only iron sulfide will form; at a slightly higher potential ferrous carbonate is precipitated. Under fully oxidizing conditions the ferric hydroxides are formed. The stability of the various iron silicates is less clear. Apparently they form over a considerable range of Eh values inasmuch as they show a varying FeO/Fe_2O_3 ratio within themselves. According to Teodorovich (Chilingar, 1955) the iron chlorites form in a neutral zone whereas glauconite forms in a weakly oxidizing environment.

The naturally occurring assemblages (mineral facies) support the experimental and theoretical considerations. Sulfides occur alone or in association with siderite; the silicates are associated with siderite and magnetite; the oxides occur alone or with the silicates (as in the case of magnetite). The oxides (and some silicates, such as glauconite) carry structures (oolites or granules) or have an association (quartz sand grains) which indicates turbulence—a condition more likely to be realized in an aerobic rather than an anaerobic environment. The absence of these associations or features in the sulfide and carbonate facies is significant.

Although bacteria are known to precipitate iron, there is no good evidence that they have played a major role in the formation of the iron-bearing strata. Harder (1919) has attributed many of the ferric hydroxide deposits to bacteria. These bacteria are of three types: (1) those which precipitate ferric hydroxide from solutions of ferrous carbonate and use the carbon dioxide liberated and the energy produced during oxidation for their life processes, (2) those which do not require ferrous bicarbonate for their life processes but which cause the deposition of ferric hydroxide if iron salts are present, and (3) those which attack organic iron salts, using the organic acid radicle as food and precipitate the ferric hydroxide, or basic ferric salts which yield the hydroxide.

Although some bog ores may be bacterial in origin, bacteria do not precipitate iron carbonate or the iron silicates. And because the primary constituents of the more important iron-bearing sediments are the carbonates and silicates, the role of bacteria in the formation of iron-rich deposits may be rather minor.

The sulfides may be in part the product of sulfate-reducing bacteria as suggested by Androussow (1897), Galliher (1933), and others. Bacterial sulfate reduction is known to take place (see Fig. 107) but the reaction of H_2S and iron may not involve any organisms.

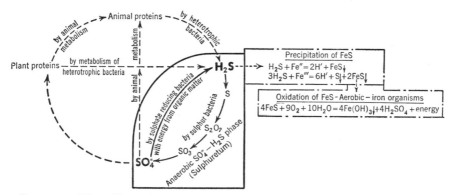

Fig. 107. The sulfur cycle in sediments with special reference to the reactions which are involved in the formation of ferrous sulfide sediments (from Galliher, 1933). Reactions are also given which relate to the oxidation of ferrous to ferric iron.

The principal problem of iron deposition seems to be to define those conditions which *permit* the deposition of iron compounds but inhibit the deposition of lime and retard or prevent introduction of clastic sediments into the basin of sedimentation. The absence or paucity of clastics is understandable if the relief of the land areas be extremely low; the absence of lime is perhaps a result of a delicate balance between pH and the ionic concentrations in the waters of the basin (James, 1954).

Most troublesome to recognize and interpret are the postdepositional changes which the iron-bearing sediment undergoes. Diagenetic reorganization, metamorphism, and weathering all produce marked changes in mineralogy and textures. The evidences of replacement—siderite replacing fossils, the hematitic fossil ore and the like prove that iron migrates and readily replaces calcium carbonate. The importance of these replacements was early recognized by Cayeux (1909, 1922) and more recently described by Deverin (1945). The studies of Cayeux in particular led to the conclusion that the

PLATE 35

COAL

Top: Nonbanded cannel coal.

Shows blocky structure, conchoidal fracture, and absence of stratification. U.S. Bur. Mines photograph. (Sprunk, *J. Geol.*, vol. 50, 1942, p. 414) (see Pl. 36, **A**.)

Bottom: Banded bituminous coal. No. 6 bed, Franklin County, Illinois.

Shows alternations of vitreous bright coal ("vitrain") with thinly laminated coal ("clarain"). U.S. Bur. Mines photograph. (Sprunk, *J. Geol.*, vol. 50, 1952, p. 413) (see Pl. 36, **F**.)

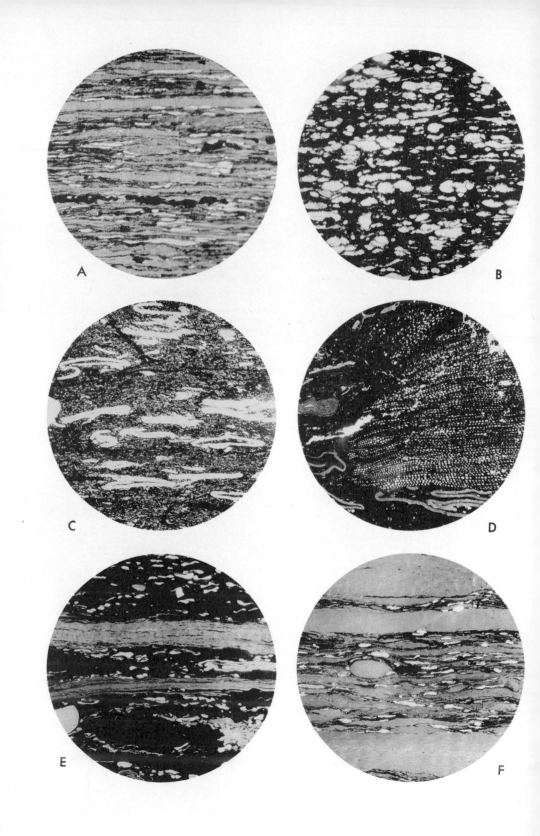

A

B

C

D

E

F

PLATE 36

CARBONACEOUS SEDIMENTS

A: Cannel coal. Ordinary light, ×155. Composed largely of fragmental woody debris. Some opaque matter and a few spores are distributed throughout the mass. U.S. Bur. Mines photograph. (Sprunk, *J. Geol.*, vol. 50, 1942, p. 414.)

B: Boghead coal. Ordinary light, ×155. The irregular light patches represent oil algae which are yellowish in color in the original thin section. U.S. Bur. Mines photograph. (Sprunk, *J. Geol.*, vol. 50, 1942, p. 415.)

C: Durain. Ordinary light, ×4. Low Main Coal, Nottingham, England. Chiefly opaque attritus with numerous collapsed megaspores.

D: Fusain. Ordinary light, ×40. Arley seam, Atherton, N. Manchester, England.

E: Dull or splint coal. Ordinary light, ×155. Composed mainly of opaque matter (micrinite). Note thin anthraxylon band and collapsed microspores. U.S. Bur. Mines photograph (Sprunk, *J. Geol.*, vol. 50, 1942, p. 413.)

F: Bright or glance coal. Ordinary light, ×155. Shows anthraxylon bands separated by translucent attritus. U.S. Bur. Mines photograph. (Sprunk, *J. Geol.*, vol. 50, 1942, p. 413.)

ironstones were essentially metasomatic replacements, and to rejection of the direct precipitation theory. The chamosite oolites were explained as replacements of crinoidal and other shelly debris. Deverin postulated an oolite origin at one place and deposition at another. According to Cayeux the original or primary calcite was altered to siderite, which in turn was replaced by chlorite (chamosite). Subsequent oxidation led to conversion to limonite and even to magnetite and hematite. This sequence of replacement is not inflexible. Deverin points out that the siderite usually replaced the chamosite and that in some rocks the hematite has directly replaced the calcite.

Hallimond (1925) and most other students of ironstones believe that the theory of a metasomatic origin of the various facies of ironstone must be abandoned. Hallimond noted the presence of unaltered calcite shells in a siderite matrix. In other cases sideritized shells and limestone pebbles, seen in a groundmass of clear calcite, were interpreted to mean that sideritization had taken place on the sea floor. The stratigraphic persistence of the iron-bearing beds, the varying facies of iron formation, the preservation of fine sedimentary features and the presence of each of the facies as fragments in intraformational breccias and clastic dikes make the replacement origin of iron formation seem very unlikely (James, 1951, p. 263).

The evidences of replacement (sideritized fossils and the like) cited above therefore are to be considered evidences of later reorganization—early diagenetic in most cases and metamorphic in a few cases. Siderite in particular seems to be prone to solution and redeposition as siderite spherulites and siderite metacrysts (Pl. 34, D and E) appear in the various silicate formations and as replacements of fossils in the calcareous ironstones.

Weathering and metamorphism may profoundly alter the iron-bearing strata. This is especially true of the formations in the Lake Superior district where the primary iron minerals are oxidized and converted to limonite or hematite and the silica—primarily the chert—has been removed by wholesale leaching, which converted the rock to ore. Metamorphism has converted the original rock to a complex grunerite-magnetite rock. It is not within the province of this book to discuss either the formation of the oxide ore bodies or the metamorphic derivatives of these strata. The interested reader is referred to the original works dealing with these subjects (Leith, Lund, and Leith, 1935; James, 1955).

REFERENCES CITED AND BIBLIOGRAPHY

Aldrich, H. R. (1929), The geology of the Gogebic iron range of Wisconsin, Wisconsin Geol. Nat. Hist. Survey, econ. ser. 24, Bull. 71.

Alling, H. L. (1947), Diagenesis of the Clinton hematite ores of New York, Bull. Geol. Soc. Amer., vol. 58, pp. 991–1017.

Androussow, N. (1897), La mer noire. Guide excursions VII congres geol. internat., vol. 29.

Ashley, G. H. (1917), Notes on the greensand deposits of the eastern United States, U.S. Geol. Survey Bull. 660-B, pp. 27–49.

Berg, Georg (1944), Vergleichende Petrographie oolithischer Eisenerz, Arch. Lagerstättenforsch., vol. 76.

Berz, K. C. (1922), Ueber Magneteisen in marinen Ablagerungen, Centr. Mineral. Geol., pp. 569–577.

Burchard, E. F. and others (1910), Iron ores, fuels, and fluxes of the Birmingham district, Alabama, U.S. Geol. Survey Bull. 400.

Casteno, J. R. and Garrels, R. M. (1950), Experiments on the deposition of iron with special reference to the Clinton iron ore deposits, Econ. Geol., vol. 45, pp. 755–770.

Cayeux, L. (1909), Les minerais de fer oolitique de France. I. Minerais de fer primaires, Paris, Imprimerie nationale.

Cayeux, L. (1922), Les minerais de fer oolitique de France. II. Minerais de fer secondaires, Paris, Imprimerie nationale.

Chilingar, G. V. (1955), Review of Soviet literature on petroleum source-rocks, Bull. Am. Assoc. Petroleum Geol., vol. 39, pp. 764–767.

Correns, C. W. (1947), Über die Bildung der sedimentaren Eisenerze, Forschungen u Fortschr., xxi/xxiii Jg., nr. 4/5/6.

Correns, C. W. (1952), Zur Geochemie des Eisens: Symposium sur les gisements de fer du monde, XIX Cong. géol. International, vol. 2, Alger, pp. 23–27.

Correns, C. W. (1952), Mineralogisches Untersuchungen an sedimentären Eisenerzen: Symposium sur les gisements de fer du monde, XIX Congr. géol. International, vol. 2, Alger, pp. 28–30.

Deverin, L. (1945), Etude petrographique des minerais de fer oolithique du Dogger des Alpes suisses, Beitr. Geol. Schweiz, Lieferung 13, vol. 2.

Edwards, A. B. and Baker, G. (1951), Some occurrences of supergene iron sulphides in relation to their environments of deposition, J. Sediment. Petrol., vol. 21, pp. 34–46.

Friedman, S. A. (1954), Low temperature authigenic magnetite, Econ. Geol., vol. 49, p. 101.

Galliher, E. W. (1933), The sulfur cycle in sediments, J. Sediment. Petrol., vol. 3, pp. 51–63.

Gill, J. E. (1927), Origin of the Gunflint iron-bearing formation, Econ. Geol., vol. 22, pp. 726–727.

Gruner, J. W. (1922), The origin of the sedimentary iron formations, Econ. Geol., vol. 17, pp. 417–458.

Gruner, J. W. (1923), Algae, believed to be Archean, J. Geol., 31, pp. 146–148.

Gruner, J. W. (1924), Contributions to the geology of the Mesabi Range, Minn. Geol. Survey, Bull. 19, pp. 45–64.

Gruner, J. W. (1946), Mineralogy and geology of the Mesabi Range, Iron Range Resources and Rehabilitation Commission, St. Paul, Minn.

Hallimond, A. F. (1925), Iron ores: Bedded ores of England and Wales, *Geol. Survey G. Brit., Spec. Rpts. Mineral Resources*, vol. 29.

Harder, E. C. (1919), Iron-depositing bacteria and their geologic relations, *U.S. Geol. Survey, Prof. Paper* 113.

Hawley, J. E. (1926), An evaluation of the evidence of life in the Archean, *J. Geol.*, vol. 34, pp. 441–461.

Hawley, J. E. (1942), Origin of some siderite, pyrite, chert deposits, Michipicoten district, Ontario, *Trans. Roy. Soc. Can.*, vol. 36, pp. 79–87.

Hawley, J. E. and Beavan, P. A. (1934), Mineralogy and genesis of the Mayville iron ore of Wisconsin, *Am. Mineralogist*, vol. 19, pp. 494–514.

Hayes, A. O. (1915), Wabana iron ore of Newfoundland, *Geol. Survey Canada, Mem.* 78.

Irving, R. D., and Van Hise, C. R. (1897), The Penokee iron-bearing series of Michigan and Wisconsin, *U.S. Geol. Survey, Mono.* 19.

James, H. L. (1951), Iron formation and associated rocks in the Iron River district, Michigan, *Bull. Geol. Soc. Amer.*, vol. 62, pp. 251–266.

James, H. L. (1954), Sedimentary facies of iron-formation, *Econ. Geol.*, vol. 49, pp. 235–293.

James, H. L. (1955), Zones of regional metamorphism in the Precambrian of northern Michigan, *Bull. Geol. Soc. Amer.*, vol. 66, pp. 1455–1458.

Jolliffe, F. J. (1935), A study of greenalite, *Am. Mineralogist*, vol. 20, pp. 405–425.

Krumbein, W. C., and Garrels, R. M. (1952), Origin and classification of chemical sediments in terms of pH and oxidation-reduction potentials, *J. Geol.*, vol. 60, pp. 1–33.

Leith, C. K. (1903), Mesabi iron-bearing district of Minnesota, *U.S. Geol. Survey, Mono.* 43.

Leith, C. K., Lund, R. J., and Leith, Andrew (1935), Pre-Cambrian rocks of the Lake Superior region, *U.S. Geol. Survey Prof. Paper* 184.

Loomis, F. B. (1903), The dwarf fauna of the pyrite layers of the horizon of the Tully limestone of western New York, *N.Y. State Museum Bull.* 69, pp. 892–920.

Moore, E. S. (1946), Origin of iron deposits of the "Lake Superior" type, *Trans. N.Y. Acad. Sci.*, vol. 9, ser. 2, pp. 43–51.

Moore, E. S. and Maynard, J. E. (1929), The solution, transportation, and precipitation of iron and silica, *Econ. Geol.*, vol. 24, pp. 272–303, 365–402, 506–527.

Newhouse, W. H. (1927), Some forms of iron sulphide occurring in coal and other sedimentary rocks, *J. Geol.*, vol. 35, pp. 73–83.

Pettijohn, F. J. (1952), Geology of the northern Crystal Falls area, Iron County, Michigan, *U.S. Geol. Survey Circ.* 153.

Polynov, B. B. (1937), *The cycle of weathering* (trans. A. Muir), London, Murby.

Rubey, W. W. (1930), Lithologic studies of fine-grained Upper Cretaceous sedimentary rocks of the Black Hills region, *U.S. Geol. Survey Prof. Paper* 165-A.

Smyth, C. H., Jr. (1892), On the Clinton iron ore, Am. J. Sci., ser. 3, vol. 43, pp. 487–496.

Tarr, W. A. (1927), Alternative deposition of pyrite, marcasite, and possibly melnikovite, Am. Mineralogist, vol. 12, pp. 417–422.

Taylor, J. H. (1949), Petrology of the Northampton sand ironstone formation, Geol. Survey G. Brit. Memoir.

Thiessen, R. (1920), The occurrence and origin of finely divided sulphur compounds in coal, Trans. Am. Inst. Mining Met. Engrs., vol. 63, pp. 913ff.

Tyler, S. A. and Twenhofel, W. H. (1952), Sedimentation and stratigraphy of the Huronian of upper Michigan, Am. J. Sci., vol. 250, pp. 1–27, 118–151.

GLAUCONITE

The glauconite-bearing sediments are closely related to the silicate iron formations. Since glauconite is more widespread in time and place than the other iron-bearing silicates, it is more commonly observed. It therefore deserves special consideration.

Glauconite is a microcrystalline mineral of the dioctahedral type rich in iron and potash. Roughly it is half silica, one-fourth iron oxides, one-tenth alumina and magnesia, and one-sixth potash and water. Glauconite forms granules, rudely elliptical, averaging one-half millimeter in diameter. These have no well-defined internal structure; they have, however, a polylobate outline. They are commonly shiny, bright to dark green in color (yellow brown if oxidized). Exceptionally glauconite forms an envelope or pellicle around grains of collophane, quartz and feldspar, micas, or even heavy minerals.

Glauconite granules occur in many quartz-rich sandstones; although found in some feldspathic sandstones, they do not seem to be characteristic of graywackes. They occur also in calcarenites and the dolomitic derivatives therefrom. Granular glauconite therefore seems to be deposited in a somewhat current-agitated environment. Glauconite is said to occur finely divided and disseminated in some shales. Our knowledge of the geology and distribution of glauconite has been summarized by Hadding (1932), Cloud (1955), and others (Galliher, 1935a, 1935b; Goldman, 1919; Takahashi, 1939; Schneider, 1927).

The greensands or greensand marls are the most important glauconite-bearing sediments. The term greensand has been applied to unconsolidated glauconite-rich sands. Under the hand lens the best greensands appear to be composed entirely of glauconite, less than 1 per cent being grains of quartz sand. More commonly quartz is the dominant constituent forming half or more of the whole. Sands composed mainly of glauconite are dark to light green; mixed sands have a salt and pepper appearance. Greensands are prominent in beds of Cretaceous and Eocene age in the Coastal Plain of the eastern United States—especially in New Jersey and Delaware (Ashley, 1918).

Although individual beds seldom exceed twenty-five feet in thickness, they are areally extensive and potentially an important source of potash (and iron and phosphorus).

Glauconite appears to be formed in marine environments at the present time. It has been recovered by dredging in waters of moderate depths (200–300 fathoms) (Murray and Renard, 1891) and in comparatively shallow water (5–60 fathoms) (Galliher, 1935a, 1939).

Much has been written on the origin of glauconite. The geological aspects of the problem have been recently reviewed by Cloud (1955). According to Cloud, glauconite is formed only in marine waters of normal salinity; it requires slightly reducing conditions (weakly oxidizing, according to Chilingar, 1955); its formation is facilitated by the presence of organic matter; it is mainly characteristic of waters 10 to 400 fathoms in depth; it is formed only in areas of slow sedimentation, and is chiefly formed from micaceous minerals or bottom muds rich in iron. As noted by Hadding (1932) and others, the place of formation of glauconite and the place of accumulation may not be the same. Some glauconite is reworked or transported.

Galliher (1935a, 1935b) concluded that glauconite was derived from biotite by a process of submarine weathering. He observed a series of transition grains that demonstrate this transformation. Galliher also noted that the biotite-rich sands near shore grade horizontally into mixed glauconite-mica silty sands offshore and thence progressively to glauconite muds at a depth of one hundred fathoms. Gruner (1935) has shown that the ionic arrangement and the structure of the unit cells of glauconite and biotite were very similar, if not identical, so that the transformation of biotite to glauconite requires no great change. Although Galliher's observations have been confirmed in other places (Edwards, 1945), some glauconite seems not to be formed from mica (Allen, 1937).

Takahashi (1939) says that,

Glauconitization is one of the processes of submarine metamorphism that gives rise to the mineral glauconite. The phenomenon is known only in marine sediments that are formed under anaerobic or reducing conditions. It is usually associated with the presence of iron sulfide, though subsequent reworking may cause the glauconite to be concentrated in sandy deposits without the presence of iron sulfide.

In summary, Takahashi says,

Glauconite seems to be formed under marine conditions by a process of hydration of silica and subsequent absorption of bases and loss of alumina. Glauconite may originate from a number of mother materials, such as faecal pellets, clayey substances filling cavities of foraminifera, radiolaria, and tests of other marine organisms, or from silicate mineral substances, such as volcanic glass, feldspar, mica, or pyroxene. The presence of organic matter seems to facilitate the formation of glauconite. In salt water . . . . the mother substances during glauconitization lose alumina, silica, and alkalies except potash, and gain ferric iron and potash. Sea water, therefore, seems essential. . . .

An interesting but not readily explained observation is the scarcity or apparent absence of glauconite in strata of Precambrian age.

REFERENCES CITED AND BIBLIOGRAPHY

Allen, V. T. (1937), A study of Missouri glauconite, Am. Mineralogist, vol. 22, pp. 842-846.

Ashley, G. H. (1918), Notes on the greensand deposits of the eastern United States, U.S. Geol. Survey Bull. 660-B, pp. 27-49.

Chilingar, G. V. (1955), Review of Soviet literature on petroleum source-rocks, Bull. Am. Assoc. Petroleum Geol., vol. 39, pp. 764-767.

Cloud, P. E., Jr. (1955), Physical limits of glauconite formation, Bull. Am. Assoc. Petroleum Geol., vol. 39, pp. 484-492.

Collet, L. W. and Lee, G. W. (1906), Recherches sur la glauconie, Proc. Roy. Soc. Edinburgh, vol. 26, pp. 238-278.

Dryden, A. L. Jr. (1931), Glauconite in fossil foraminiferal shells, Science, vol. 74, p. 17.

Edwards, A. B. (1945), The glauconitic sandstone of the Tertiary of East Gippsland, Victoria, Proc. Roy. Soc. Victoria, n.s., vol. 57, pp. 153-167.

Galliher, E. W. (1935a), Glauconite genesis, Bull. Geol. Soc. Amer., vol. 46, pp. 1351-1356.

Galliher, E. W. (1935b), Geology of glauconite, Bull. Am. Assoc. Petroleum Geol., vol. 19, pp. 1569-1601.

Galliher, E. W. (1939), Biotite-glauconite transformation and associated minerals, Recent Marine Sediments, Tulsa, Amer. Assoc. Petroleum Geologists, pp. 513-515.

Goldman, M. I. (1919), General character, mode of occurrence and origin of glauconite, J. Wash. Acad. Sci., vol. 9, pp. 501-502.

Goldman, M. I. (1922), Basal glauconite and phosphate beds, Science, vol. 56, pp. 171-173.

Gruner, J. W. (1935), The structural relationship of glauconite and mica, Am. Mineralogist, vol. 20, pp. 699-714.

Hadding, Assar (1932), The pre-Quaternary sedimentary rocks of Sweden: IV. Glauconite and glauconitic rocks, Medd. Lunds Geol.-Mineral. Inst., no. 51.

Hendricks, S. B. and Ross, C. S. (1941), Chemical composition and genesis of glauconite and celadonite, Am. Mineralogist, vol. 26, pp. 683-691.

Hutton, C. O. and Seelye, F. T. (1940), Composition and properties of some New Zealand glauconite, Am. Mineralogist, vol. 26, pp. 595-604.

Light, M. A. (1952), Evidence of authigenic and detrital glauconite, Science, vol. 115, pp. 73-75.

Murray, John, and Renard, A. F. (1891), Report on deep-sea deposits based on the specimens collected during the voyage of H.M.S. *Challenger* in the years 1872 to 1876: *Challenger Repts.*, pp. 378–391.

Prather, J. K. (1905), Glauconite, *J. Geol.*, vol. 13, pp. 509–513.

Ross, C. S. (1926), The optical and chemical composition of glauconite, *Proc. U.S. Nat. Museum*, vol. 69, Art. 2.

Schneider, H. (1927), A study of glauconite, *J. Geol.*, vol. 35, pp. 299–310.

Schumann, H. (1940), Ein mecklenburgischer Glaukonitsandstein, *Chemie der Erde*, Bd. 13, pp. 336–352.

Takahashi, J. (1939), Synopsis of glauconitization, *Recent Marine Sediments*, Tulsa, Amer. Assoc. Petroleum Geologists, pp. 503–512.

Takahashi, J. (1929), Peculiar mud-grains and their relation to the origin of glauconite, *Econ. Geol.*, vol. 24, pp. 838–852.

Takahashi, J. and Yagi, T. (1929), The peculiar mud-grains in the recent littoral and estuarine deposits, with special reference to the origin of glauconite, *Ann. Rept. Saito Ho-on Kai*, vol. 5, pp. 44–59.

PHOSPHORITE AND OTHER PHOSPHATIC SEDIMENTS

Definitions and Classification

Phosphorite, also called phosphate rock or rock phosphate, is a sedimentary deposit composed mainly of phosphate minerals. The term has not been rigorously defined. It has been used for those rocks composed only of apatite (collophane, fluorapatite, hydroxylapatite, etc.); it has also been extended to include all rock phosphates of calcium whether or not they are apatitic (McConnell, 1950, p. 18). Phosphorites may be comparatively free from contaminating minerals. In some, however, the phosphatic minerals form a cement for an assemblage of detrital minerals or the phosphatic constituent is mixed with other materials. Perhaps if the phosphatic mineral is a subordinate constituent the rock should be designated a phosphatic formation, such as a phosphatic limestone or shale.

Most important phosphorites are the bedded phosphates (Fig. 108) which are distinguished from other phosphate deposits by their great areal extent and interbedding with other marine sediments. A minor primary phosphate accumulation is *guano*, which is a rare deposit of bird excrement, more or less leached, found only on certain desert islands. *Bone phosphates* or "bone beds" are primary deposits which in one or two cases are large enough to warrant the designation phosphate rock.

Phosphatic sediments in some places are converted to a deposit of phosphate by secondary enrichment (Fig. 108). Such secondary phosphates in part are *residual phosphates* and in part transported phosphatic residues (respectively the "land-pebble" and "river-pebble" phosphates of Florida). Under some conditions phosphates may go into solution and be redeposited

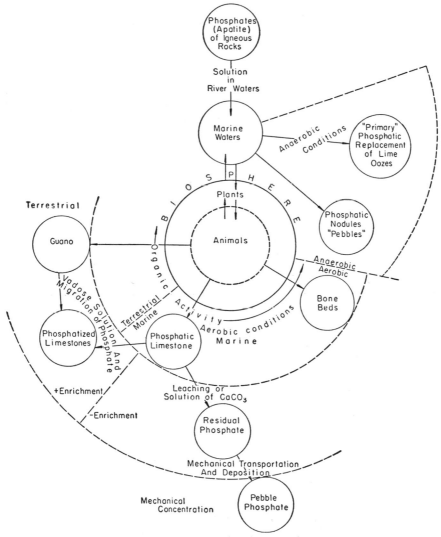

FIG. 108. The phosphorus cycle.

as a secondary phosphate accumulation. The deposits of Florida are residues from lean phosphatic limestones, whereas the phosphates of Tennessee in large part are secondary replacements of limestone.

Mineralogy and Composition

Various studies have shown the composition of the phosphorites to be complex (Lacroix, 1910; Schaller, 1912; Rogers, 1922, 1944; Hendricks, Jefferson and Mosely, 1932; Bushinsky, 1935; McConnell, 1950). The mineral components of the phosphorite are difficult to study because their submicroscopic crystals are admixed with fine-grained impurities. Crystal-structure studies show that many isomorphic replacements are common, which explains why the mineral composition of the phosphates is so poorly defined and understood. The term collophane (Rogers, 1922) applied to this mineral complex is probably not a true mineral species but may be no more than a convenient name for a group of closely related minerals.

McConnell lists thirty-eight phosphate minerals known in rock phosphates, many of which, however, are rare. Most common are the phosphates of calcium, especially the varieties of apatite such as francolite (carbonate fluorapatite) and dahlite (carbonate hydroxylapatite). The phosphate of the marine phosphorites of the Permian (Phosphoria formation) of the northwestern United States occurs as a cryptocrystalline or apparently amor-

TABLE 86. Chemical Composition of Phosphatic Sediments and Nodules (per cent)

Constituent	A	B	C	D
SiO_2	0.46	11.70	36.65	1.21
TiO_2	....	....	0.16	....
Al_2O_3	0.97	4.11	1.02	1.30
Fe_2O_3	0.40⎰	3.75	1.77	⎰ 8.36
FeO	....⎱			⎱ ....
MnO	....	....	0.04	....
MgO	0.35	0.84	0.50	0.10
CaO	48.91	40.96	29.43	40.38
Na_2O	0.97	....	1.01	T
K_2O	0.34	....	0.47	T
H_2O+	1.34	3.65[a]⎱	3.14[b]	⎰ ....
H_2O-	1.02	....⎰		⎱ 3.02
P_2O_5	33.61	23.54	17.14	21.44
CO_2	2.42	10.64	5.19	9.20
SO_3	2.16	1.39	1.48	none
Cl	T	....	....	T
F	0.40	....	2.08	1.52
S	0.40	....	0.05[c]	....
Organic matter	nd	....	0.58[d]	0.37
	95.97[e]	100.18	99.25	100.14[f]

A. Phosphate bed, Phosphoria formation (Permian), Cokeville, Wyoming. George Steiger, analyst (Clarke, 1924, p. 534).
B. Phosphate nodule from sea floor, 1900 fathoms. C. Klement, analyst (Murray and Renard, 1891, p. 383). Recalculated from separate analyses of soluble and insoluble portions.
C. Upper phosphorite stratum, Cenomanian, Briansk (Bushinsky, 1935, p. 90).
D. Oolitic phosphate, Modelo formation (Miocene), California. J. G. Fairchild, analyst (Hoots, 1931, p. 106).
[a] Ignition.
[b] Includes organic substances.
[c] FeS₂.
[d] Carbon.
[e] Includes 2.62 per cent insoluble.
[f] Includes 13.24 per cent insoluble in HCl.

phous material that varies in color, in thin section, from amber to black. Normally it consists of oolitic bodies which in some cases are surrounded by banded zones of crystalline fibers. According to Schaller (1912) the oolitic amorphous material is probably collophane, whereas the crystalline mineral is a metacolloid form of the hydrous, isotropic material. Chemical analyses show the material to be hydrous tricalcium phosphate with varying amounts of calcium carbonate and fluoride. Phosphate deposits contain abnormal concentrations of certain rare elements, notably vanadium, uranium, selenium, chromium, nickel, zinc, molybdenum, and silver. The chemical composition of phosphatic sediments and bedded phosphorite is summarized in Table 86.

Associated with the phosphate minerals are the common minerals of sediments including calcite, dolomite, chalcedony, and the clay minerals.

Petrology

Most of the bedded primary phosphates are black. Even the so-called "brown" phosphates of Tennessee have black phases. Secondary concentrations by meteoric waters, on the other hand, are white, yellow, and more rarely, brown.

In the bedded phosphorites, part of the phosphate is in the form of interstitial cement, and in a few layers the most of the phosphate is in phosphatized brachiopods and fish scales. The great bulk of the phosphatic material, however, is conglomerated into pellets and nodules. These are generally somewhat elliptical with the long axis parallel to the bedding. They range in diameter from 0.05 millimeter to more than 3 centimeters and are generally well sorted. Most are structureless granules but some of the larger ones are concentrically laminated (Pl. 33, bottom). Some of the larger nodules are compound, i.e., are themselves composed of cemented, fine-grained pellets.

The phosphatic rocks are generally well cemented with carbonate-fluorapatite, argillaceous matter, chert, calcite, or dolomite. In the Phosphoria formation the phosphatic layers range in thickness from a millimeter to two meters (McKelvey, Swanson, and Sheldon, 1953). Most of them are a few millimeters thick and are interbedded with less phosphatic mudstones or carbonate rocks.

Phosphatic nodules or pebbles are found not only in the phosphate deposits proper but are widely scattered in some limestones (Pettijohn, 1926) and especially in the Cretaceous chalk (Fisher, 1873). They occur also on the present sea bottom (Murray and Renard, 1891; Dietz, Emery, and Shepard, 1942). These objects vary from small granules to pebble-like objects several centimeters in diameter. Typically they are irregular in shape, black in color, and have a dense, hard shiny surface. The larger nodules contain much foreign matter, including sand grains, mica flakes, shell debris, and sponge spicules. The black color of the nodules is commonly most intense near the outer rim.

Hydrocarbons commonly are included in phosphorite and are responsible for the fetid odor when phosphorite is struck with the hammer.

Associations and Occurrence

Marine phosphorites commonly are associated with glauconite or green-sand. This is true of nodules now forming (Murray and Renard, 1891, p. 396) and of the Cretaceous nodules layers of the English chalk (Fisher, 1873) and of the Russian deposits (Bushinsky, 1935). It is also true of the Tennessee phosphates (Hayes, 1896) and the Cambrian nodules layers of southern New Brunswick (Matthew, 1893, p. 109). This association has been pointed out by Cayeux (1905) and Goldman (1922).

Bones, sharks' teeth, fish scales, and the remains of *Lingula* and trilobites —all of which are highly phosphatic—seem to be the only common fossil constituents other than diminutive rolled and phosphatized casts of certain gastropods and other invertebrates.

Phosphate beds have been said to occur at major and minor unconformities, and the phosphatic and glauconitic materials even have been cited as criteria for such surfaces (Grabau, 1919; Goldman, 1922). Pettijohn (1926) interpreted the zones of phosphatic limestone that are rich in phosphatic granules or pebbles as the residuum on a "corrosion surface" or diastemic plane due to submarine solution.

Phosphorite occurs in rocks of nearly all ages and probably is more common than has been supposed. Best known and most extensive are the bedded phosphates of the Permian Phosphoria formation of Utah, Idaho, Wyoming, Montana, and adjoining parts of Colorado and Nevada (Mansfield, 1927; McKelvey, Swanson, and Sheldon, 1953). Thin phosphorite beds (twenty or more) occur in the lower shale member of the Phosphoria. Their aggregate thickness is about 73 feet in southeastern Idaho. The thickest bed is 4 to 7 feet thick. The phosphatic shale with the interbedded phosphorites is overlain by a bedded chert (Rex chert); a little cherty limestone is also present.

Origin

Various theories have been promulgated to explain the phosphatic deposits. Most of these are inadequate and are of historic interest only. The phosphate beds have been considered, for example, as accumulations of coprolites of fish and higher animals. The deposit therefore would be a kind of submarine guano. Nondeposition caused by failure of land-derived sediments is invoked to explain the concentration of coprolitic materials. Other writers have supposed that unfavorable conditions for the formation of carbonate of lime permitted the accumulation of the phosphatic hard parts of organisms during a period of nondeposition (Miller, 1896). Hayes and Ulrich (1903) thought that the black Devonian phosphates of Tennessee were formed by the mechanical reworking by the sea of residual concentrations of the brown Ordovician phosphates in the same area. Fisher (1873) explained the coprolitic beds of the Gault of England as phosphatized sponges.

None of the above theories explains all the observed features of the areally extensive bedded phosphorites. Phosphate is known to be extracted from sea water by living organisms and concentrated within their hard parts. Abnormal concentration of such bones, teeth, fish scales, or phosphatic invertebrate hard parts has produced phosphate-rich beds. However, the relative role of biogenic versus abiotic precipitation of the phosphorus is not yet clear. The close association of phosphorites and organic matter, and the abundance of phosphatic skeletal structures suggests a cause and effect relation. On the other hand, the phosphorites and the organic materials, like the chert, may be only products of the same environment. The phosphatic granules and pellets have been ascribed to a faecal origin. But as noted by McKelvey and co-workers, their wide range in size, good sorting in individual layers, regional trends in average size, and the compound nature of the larger ones as well as the oolitic structure of some, do not favor an organic origin. It has been suggested that ammonium phosphate generated by the decay of pelagic organisms may be the agent of precipitation of the phosphate (Blackwelder, 1916, p. 293).

The fossils prove the phosphorites to be marine. The black color and commonly associated hydrocarbon materials indicate anaerobic conditions. The absence of fossils of sessile and bottom-living types and the presence of depauperized forms as well as the pyrite and associated black shales further confirm this interpretation. The associated glauconite likewise suggests subnormal aeration. The scarcity of carbonate of lime either in skeletal form or as precipitated carbonate and the presence of much chert suggest a pH slightly less than normal.

Kazakov (1937) observed that the phosphorites form mainly in the border zone between the shallow-water platform sediments and the deep-water geosynclinal accumulation. The platform phosphorites are nodular in habit, are associated with glauconite and arenaceous materials. The geosynclinal phosphorites are bedded, platy, richer in P_2O_5 and, as noted by McKelvey and others, associated with black shales and cherts.

Although phosphorus, like iron, is present only in very small quantities in sea water, it will be precipitated in important quantities locally if the conditions are favorable. At a particular Eh and pH either may accumulate relatively free of the deposits of calcium. The similarities of many micro-structures (granules and oolites) and the gross lithologic associations (bedded cherts and black shales), and the co-occurrence of iron silicates (glauconite) with some phosphatic deposits and the abnormal concentrations of P_2O_5 with some iron silicates and iron carbonates (see Table 84, Cols. F and G) suggests that the environments of phosphorite and ironstone deposition have many factors in common. Both seem to require a somewhat anaerobic milieu, one which has a slightly lower than normal pH, and one in which clastic sedimentation is exceedingly slow or completely inhibited. If these conditions are maintained long enough, circulation of oceanic waters will supply all the needed phosphorus or iron. The unusual conditions, namely, a basin with impeded convection and yet with adequate connection with and inflow from the ocean plus greatly restricted clastic influx and crustal stability for a long period of time, explain the relative scarcity of bedded deposits of both iron and phosphorus. Where these conditions are not fully achieved the iron is deposited in a scattering of glauconite granules and the phosphorus is precipitated in phosphatic invertebrate skeletal structures or is present as a few isolated nodules or pellets.

REFERENCES CITED AND BIBLIOGRAPHY

Blackwelder, Eliot (1916), The geologic role of phosphorus, Am. J. Sci., ser. 4, vol. 42, p. 293.

Branner, J. S. and Newsom, J. F. (1902), The phosphate rocks of Arkansas, Arkansas Agric. Expt. Sta. Bull. 74, pp. 68–69.

Bushinsky, G. I. (1935), Structure and origin of the phosphorites of the U.S.S.R., J. Sediment. Petrol., vol. 5, pp. 81–92.

Cayeux, L. (1905), Genese des gisements de phosphates de chaux, Bull. soc. géol. France, ser. 4, vol. 5, pp. 750–753.

Cayeux, L. (1939), Les phosphates de chaux sédimentaires de France, Serv. Carte Géol. Fr., vol. 1, Paris, Imprimerie nationale.

Charles, G. (1953), Sur l'origine des gisements de phosphates de chaux sedimentaires, Intern. Geol. Congr. 19th Sess., vol. 11, pp. 163–184.

Clarke, F. W. (1924), Data of geochemistry, U.S. Geol. Survey Bull. 770, pp. 523–534.

Dietz, R. S., Emery, K. O. and Shepard, F. P. (1942), Phosphorite deposits on the sea floor off southern California, Bull. Geol. Soc. Amer., vol. 53, pp. 815–847.

Fisher, Osmond (1873), On the phosphatic nodules of the Cretaceous rocks of Cambridgeshire, Quart. J. Geol. Soc. London, vol. 29, pp. 52–63.

Goldman, M. I. (1922), Basal glauconite and phosphate beds, Science, n.s., vol. 56, pp. 171–173.

Grabau, A. W. (1919), Prevailing stratigraphic relationships of the bedded phosphate deposits of Europe, North Africa, and North America (abstract), *Bull. Geol. Soc. Amer.*, vol. 30, p. 104.

Hayes, C. W. (1896), The Tennessee phosphates, *U.S. Geol. Survey, 17th Ann. Rept.*, part II, pp. 519–550.

Hayes, C. W. and Ulrich, E. O. (1903), Columbia folio: *U.S. Geol. Survey, Geol. Atlas U.S.*, No. 95, p. 6.

Hendricks, S. B., Jefferson, M. E., and Mosely, V. M. (1932), The crystal structure of some natural and synthetic apatite-like substances, *Z. Krist.*, vol. 81, pp. 353–369.

Hoots, H. W. (1931), Geology of the eastern part of the Santa Monica Mountains, Los Angeles County, California, *U.S. Geol. Survey Prof. Paper* 165C.

Kazakov, A. V. (1937), The phosphorite facies and the genesis of phosphorites, in *Geological Investigations of Agricultural Ores, Trans. Sci. Inst. Fertilizers and Insecto-Fungicides*, No. 142 (published for the 17th Sess. Intern. Geol. Congr.), Leningrad, pp. 95–113. (Summarized by McKelvey et al.).

Kazakov, A. V. (1950), Fluorapatite-system equilibria under conditions of formation of sedimentary rocks, *Akad. Nauk. S.S.S.R. Trudy Inst. Geol. Nauk,* Vyp., 114, Geol. Ser. No. 40, pp. 1–21.

Lacroix, A. (1910), Sur la constitution mineralogique des phosphates francais, *Compt. rend. soc. géol. France*, vol. 150, p. 1213.

McConnell, Duncan (1950), The petrography of rock phosphates, *J. Geol.*, vol. 58, pp. 16–23.

McKelvey, V. E., Swanson, R. W., and Sheldon, R. P. (1953), the Permian phosphorite deposits of western United States, *Intern. Geol. Congr. 19th Sess.*, vol. 11, pp. 45–64.

Mansfield, G. R. (1920), Geography, geology, and mineral resources of the Fort Hall Indian Reservation, Idaho, *U.S. Geol. Survey, Bull.* 713, p. 108–114.

Mansfield, G. R. (1927), Geography, geology, and mineral resources of part of southeastern Idaho, *U.S. Geol. Survey Prof. Paper* 152, pp. 75–78, 208–308.

Mansfield, G. R. (1940), The role of fluorine in phosphate deposition, *Am. J. Sci.*, vol. 238, pp. 863–879.

Matthew, W. D. (1893), On phosphate nodules from the Cambrian of southern New Brunswick, *Trans. N.Y. Acad. Sci.*, vol. 12, p. 109.

Miller, A. M. (1896), The association of the gastropod genus *Cyclora* with phosphate of lime deposits, *Am. Geol.*, vol. 17, pp. 74–76.

Murray, J., and Renard, A. F. (1891), Report on deep-sea deposits based on the specimens collected during the voyage of H.M.S. *Challenger* in the years 1872–1876, *Challenger Repts.*, p. 396.

O'Brien, M. V. (1953), Phosphatic horizons in the Upper Carboniferous of Ireland, *Intern. Geol. Congr. 19th Sess.*, vol. 11, pp. 135–143.

Pardee, J. T. (1917), The Garrison and Philipsburg phosphate fields, Montana, *U.S. Geol. Survey Bull.* 640-K, pp. 225–228.

Pettijohn, F. J. (1926), Intraformational phosphate pebbles of the Twin City Ordovician, *J. Geol.*, vol. 34, pp. 361–373.

Rogers, A. F. (1922), Collophane, a much neglected mineral, *Am. J. Sci.*, ser. 5, vol. 3, pp. 269–276.

Rogers, A. F. (1944), Pellet phosphorite from Carmel Valley, Monterey County, California, *Calif. J. Mines Geol.*, vol. 40, pp. 411–421.

Schaller, W. T. (1912), Mineralogical notes, series 2, *U.S. Geol. Survey Bull.* 509, p. 89–100.

SALINES AND OTHER EVAPORITES (EXCLUDING CARBONATES)

Definitions and Classification

The saline deposits are formed by the precipitation of salts from concentrated solutions or brines. Because concentration is brought about by evaporation, the saline deposits have been termed *evaporites*. Most common are rock salt (halite), gypsum, and anhydrite. Certain carbonates, especially travertine and caliche, and perhaps the oolitic carbonates and some dolomites, may also be precipitated by evaporation. Although these are chemical salts, they have been described elsewhere in this text and are excluded here.

Mineralogy and Composition

A great many salt minerals are known; over thirty have been identified in the Stassfurt deposits of Germany. Most such minerals are very rare and only halite, gypsum, and anhydrite are of importance (p. 151). Carbonates are sparingly present in some evaporite sections but may be dominant in others.

TABLE 87.   Chemical Composition of Evaporitic Sulfates
(per cent)

	A	B	C	D	E
SiO_2	2.12	0.40	....	0.10	....
Al_2O_3	0.20	2.97	....	0.12	
Fe_2O_3		0.77	....		0.14
MgO	2.11	1.53	....	0.33	0.24
CaO	36.76	30.76	41.2	32.44	38.46
Na_2O	....	....	....	....	0.07
K_2O	....	....	....	....	0.19
SO_3	36.11	43.70	58.8	45.45	39.53
CO_2	6.43	2.80	....	0.85	7.73
H_2O	16.27	17.53	....	20.80	12.69
Total	100.00	100.54	100.0	100.09	99.54[a]

A. Gypsum, Silurian, Caledonia, Ontario (Caley, 1940, p. 113). Gypsum calculated, 77.67%.
B. Gypsum, Silurian, New York. G. E. Willcomb, analyst (Stone *et al.*, 1920, p. 214). Gypsum calculated, 94.26%.
C. Anhydrite, theoretical.
D. Gypsum, Triassic, from east of Cascade, Black Hills, South Dakota. George Steiger, analyst (Stone *et al.*, 1920, p. 248).
E. Gypsum, Jurassic (?), Nephi, Utah. E. T. Allen, analyst (Clarke, 1924, p. 232). Calculated composition is calcite 17.5%, gypsum 60.5% and anhydrite 19.3%.
   [a] Insoluble, 0.45.

Neither halite (NaCl) nor gypsum ($CaSO_4 \cdot 2H_2O$) or anhydrite ($CaSO_4$) is found in nature in a state of absolute purity. Study of the water-insoluble residues of salt deposits sheds much light on their minor constituents. Salt from the salt domes of Louisiana (Taylor, 1937) contains 5 to 10 per cent of water-insoluble materials. Of the insolubles, 99 per cent is anhydrite in the form of cleavage fragments and euhedra. The carbonates are common as crystal euhedra, especially dolomite and calcite. Rarer constituents identified include pyrite, quartz crystals, limonite, hematite, hauerite, sulfur, celestite, marcasite, barite, kaolinite, gypsum, magnesite, danburite, and boracite. The residues of the Louisiana salt seem to differ somewhat from those of the Silurian and Permian salt deposits.

The chemical composition of the evaporitic sulfates is given in Table 87.

Petrography

Rock gypsum varies from coarsely crystalline to fine granular. The latter is most common. Gypsum may show distinct bedding planes or it may occur as a compact body lacking both bedding and joints. Anhydrite, like rock gypsum, occurs in beds which in some places are thick and extensive. It may be delicately laminated (Udden, 1924). Anhydrite is commonly finely granular, although fibrous and coarsely crystalline masses are also known. In some places crystals of gypsum are scattered throughout the anhydrite, thereby giving the rock a porphyritic appearance.

Under the microscope, anhydrite appears coarsely crystalline. Replacements by gypsum are seen in thin sections; the converse is perhaps less common although it is reported from the Salina beds of Michigan (Dellwig, 1955). Gypsum may have a pseudoporphyritic or pseudo-ophitic texture. A pseudoporphyritic texture is characterized by large prismatic crystals embedded in a finely crystalline groundmass of the same material; the pseudo-ophitic texture is marked by large platy crystals which enclose small, well-formed euhedra. The larger crystals, variety selenite, probably are of later origin than the matrix in which they are found. They are of a porphyroblastic character rather than being phenocrysts.

Gypsum commonly appears to be formed by hydration of anhydrite. The process involves an increase in volume of 30 to 50 per cent. The resultant swelling produces notable effects, such as the enterolithic folding of thin anhydrite layers enclosed in rock salt or other beds. Local crumpling and intense folding of the hydrated layers may take place without much effect on the enclosing strata.

Gypsum veins are common in rock gypsum and also in associated strata. These veins commonly show cross fibers and may exhibit cone-in-cone structure. Large gypsum euhedra and rosettes also occur in some muds and shales. These occurrences probably are authigenic and formed in the muds after deposition.

Halite or rock salt is a massive, coarsely crystalline material. It is without joints. In some deposits it is laminated. Layers of salt several centimeters thick are separated by partings of anhydrite or dolomite. In some cases layers of dark salt are interbedded with white salt; in other cases cloudy salt is interbedded with clear salt. The dark salt is filled with anhydrite inclusions; the cloudy salt is marked by an abundance of liquid inclusions. The salt crystals may be well-defined cubes; in other cases the crystals are hopper-shaped. According to Dellwig (1955) the hopper-shaped crystals were formed at the surface of the brine whereas the cubic habit is a product of growth at the depositional interface between the salt and the brine.

Study of the fluid inclusions and the enclosed bubbles in the Salina salt of Michigan indicates a temperature of crystallization of 32°C to 48.4°C (Dellwig, 1955). As these determinations were made only on inclusions in crystals presumed to have formed at the surface of the brine, they are indicative only of the temperature attained by such surface layer, which may be appreciably higher than that of the whole body of the brine.

Salt is a rock which is prone to flow at relatively low temperatures and pressures. Salt from a deeply buried stratum may rise as a piercement plug or salt dome. The adjacent strata are intruded by the salt, may be ruptured, and sheared. Salt domes are common on the Gulf Coast of Texas and Louisiana and are known also in Germany, Russia, and Iran. The salt plug is circular in plan, most commonly a half to two miles in diameter, and has a nearly vertical axis. The top tends to be flat or domical and is surmounted by a cap rock, which may exceed 100 feet in thickness, is composed of limestone, gypsum, and anhydrite (Brown, 1931). The salt within the domes displays an intricate system of large- and small-scale folds, lineation, etc., produced by its upward flow (Balk, 1953).

Although several theories have been advanced to explain salt domes, they are now generally regarded as intrusive bodies of salt. They are therefore a tectonic structure, and extended treatment of them is out of place here. The interested reader is referred to the extensive literature on these interesting and economically important structures (DeGolyer and others, 1926).

The evaporites are associated with the common sediments. Most usual associates are shales and dolomites. An association with red beds is common but is by no means universal.

Many evaporites are interbedded with, or rest upon, the carbonate rocks. Dolomite is more abundant than limestone. In some sections it is notably brown, probably owing to bituminous matter, and is thinly laminated. The rock actually may be fetid (stinkstein), although megascopic fossils are very rare indeed. Anhydrite is common in the dolomites and locally forms a large part of the rock. Very probably these dolomites are chemical precipitates (Sloss, 1953).

Shales also are associated with anhydrite and salt and may be intimately interbedded with them. They may or may not be red. Cross-cutting veins of rock salt and gypsum are common.

The absence of megascopic fossils from evaporite and associated rocks is nearly universal, although there are striking exceptions. The absence is not surprising, however, in view of the high salinity of the waters from which the deposits crystallized. Note has been made of the association of bitumen and the evaporites. It is present in the associated dolomites, may form laminations in the anhydrite itself, and may be found as inclusions in salt crystals. The bitumen probably owes its origin to planktonic organisms swept into the gulf of salt sea from the open ocean.

Occurrence of Evaporites

Although evaporite deposits in North America occur in every system from the Cambrian upward (Krumbein, 1951), the best-known occurrences are those of the Silurian salt basins of New York and Michigan and of the vast Permian salt basin of west Texas and New Mexico.

The New York Silurian (Salina) evaporites underlie about 10,000 square miles in western New York, Pennsylvania, eastern Ohio, and northern West Virginia (Alling, 1928). Single beds 40 to 80 feet thick are known. Seven salt beds which alternate with shales and total 250 feet in thickness, are reported from one section between depths of 1900 and 3130 feet. Salt and gypsum of Salina age also occur in the Michigan basin and adjoining parts of Ontario (Landes, 1945; Dellwig, 1955). The maximum aggregate thickness of the salt beds in Michigan is in excess of 1600 feet.

The most spectacular of the evaporite deposits is the Castile formation of Permian age which underlies an area roughly 200 miles in diameter in Texas, New Mexico, and adjoining parts of Mexico. More than 95 per cent of the formation is composed of salts deposited by evaporation of a brine (Kroenlein, 1939). The Castile formation has a maximum thickness of about 4000 feet, of which 1200 to 1500 feet are laminated anhydrite. It thus is one of the thickest evaporite deposits known in the world. The lower portion is chiefly delicately banded anhydrite, the laminations of which average 1.6 millimeters in thickness. A thin, brown, bitumen-rich film separates the laminations from one another. Udden (1924) interprets the laminations as annual layers or varves and has estimated that the precipitation of the laminated anhydrite took over 306,000 years. Near the outcrop the anhydrite is converted to gypsum. The upper part of the Castile is chiefly halite, although there are some potash-bearing salts, chiefly polyhalite, as well as some intercalated gypsum beds. The ratio of halite to anhydrite is about 1 to 1 instead of the 30 to 1 ratio that would be the case if the deposit were formed by the simple isolation and desiccation of sea water.

Origin of Evaporites

The origin of evaporites involves several problems. Was the calcium sulfate originally deposited as anhydrite or as gypsum? Was the original solution from which the salt-precipitating brine formed sea water? What were the conditions that led to concentration?

The relations between anhydrite and gypsum have been restudied by Posnjak (1938, 1940). Ordinary sea water is far from being saturated with calcium sulfate. On the basis of studies of the solubility of gypsum and anhydrite in sea water, Posnjak concluded that at 30°C and at a salinity 3.35 times that of normal sea water, gypsum will begin to precipitate. When the solution becomes 4.8 times as saline as normal sea water, that is, the volume is reduced to about one-fifth of the initial volume, direct precipitation of anhydrite takes place. Saturated solutions of NaCl, however, are not necessary in order that anhydrite form. Above 42°C only anhydrite will be precipitated even in the absence of any other salt. According to Posnjak, therefore, the vast anhydrite deposits commonly assumed to be primary either must be formed about 42°C (which is unlikely) or be derived from gypsum. Posnjak's conclusions, however, are based on pure calcium sulfate solutions. Thermodynamic calculations by MacDonald (1953) show that in a complex solution such as sea water, anhydrite will form at all temperatures above 34°C. Hence whether gypsum or anhydrite will form depends on both temperature and gross salinity—anhydrite alone being deposited from the most concentrated brines regardless of temperature.

The geological evidence indicates that the original material of many gypsum beds was anhydrite. Evidence supporting this view is the observation that gypsum beds at outcrop grade into anhydrite at depth, that gypsum occurs as veins and penetrates the anhydrite in an irregular manner, and that small isolated patches of anhydrite occur in gypsum. The porphyroblastic occurrence of selenite crystals further supports the view that the gypsum is later. Although it is possible that the initial gypsum was converted to anhydrite and then reconverted to gypsum, evidence to support this view is lacking. It has been suggested, however, that the original precipitate of gypsum might sink into a lower denser bottom brine and there be converted to anhydrite before burial (Hollingworth, 1948). Such anhydrite would be difficult to distinguish from that directly precipitated. In some deposits, anhydrite forms pseudomorphs after gypsum; hence the anhydrite is secondary and the original precipitate was gypsum.

In conclusion it can be said that anhydrite commonly is the first-formed precipitate and that following deposition it may remain unchanged or it may become hydrated and transformed to gypsum. In other deposits gypsum is first precipitated; it may remain unaltered but is most likely to be converted to anhydrite either by reaction with concentrated brines or by pressure (MacDonald, 1953). It cannot survive deep burial.

All salt deposits are formed by the evaporation of a brine. The ultimate source of such brines is normal sea water. The deposit may be formed directly from sea water by evaporation in a semi-isolated or wholly isolated arm of the sea in an arid region. Salt deposits may be formed also in interior basins of arid regions into which waters flow that derived their salt either from the connate waters of marine sediments ("fossil" sea water or trapped brine) or from older salt beds.

The evaporation of sea water and the course of crystallization that follows have been studied experimentally. Sea water contains about 3.5 per cent by weight of dissolved solids of which about four-fifths is sodium chloride. The average composition of these materials is given in Table 88.

TABLE 88. Composition of Oceanic Salts
(Clarke, 1924, p. 23)

Salt	Per Cent
NaCl	77.76
$MgCl_2$	10.88
$MgSO_4$	4.74
$CaSO_4$	3.60
K_2SO_4	2.46
$CaCO_3$	0.35
$MgBr_2$	0.22
	100.00

The experiments of Usiglio (1849) show that when the original volume of sea water is reduced to about one-half, a little iron oxide and some $CaCO_3$ are precipitated. When the volume is about one-fifth that of the original sea water, gypsum is formed. Upon reduction to approximately one-tenth the original volume, NaCl begins to crystallize. Further reduction in volume leads to the appearance of sulfates and chlorides of magnesium and finally to NaBr and KCl.

Although the order observed by Usiglio agrees in a general way with the sequence found in some salt deposits, many exceptions are known. Also many minerals known from salt beds did not appear in the experimentally formed residues. The crystallization of a brine is very complex, and depends not only on the solubility of the salts involved but also upon the concentration of the several salts present and the temperature. The reader interested in the phase relations is referred to the early work of van't Hoff (1905) and the more recent studies on brines.

Were all the salt of a 1000-foot column of sea water precipitated, it would form a deposit but 15 feet thick, of which about 0.4 feet would be calcium sulfate, 11.6 feet would be halite, and the remaining 3.0 feet would be the potassium and magnesium-bearing salts. Anhydrite beds several hundred feet thick, therefore, must require the evaporation of a very great volume of water. Deep water, however, is not implied. Indeed, deep water is improbable because of the association of anhydrite and salt beds with mud-cracking shales and because of ripple-marking of some salt beds indicating turbulent and shallow waters (Kaufmann and Slawson, 1950).

If the precipitation were carried to completion the salts deposited should appear in an order approximating that given by Usiglio and roughly in the proportions in which they are present in sea water. Moreover, once a salt has begun to precipitate, its crystallization should continue until the end stage is reached, unless it reacts with the residual liquid to form a different solid phase. Each succeeding evaporite layer therefore will become mineralogically more complex than its predecessor. Inasmuch as many evaporite deposits show marked exceptions to the above requirements, simple evaporation of sea water did not occur, and either the parent brine was not formed from sea water or the evaporation took place under special conditions that will explain the anomalies.

An extended discussion of salt deposits of various derivations is given by Grabau (1920) and Lotze (1938). Grabau has classed salt deposits of marine origin as marginal salt pans, marine salina, marginal lagoons, and relict seas. The first two are likely to form only small bodies of salt, and therefore are of little importance. The lagoonal theory of salt deposition has received much attention because of the association of fetid dolomite and salt beds and the possible role played by such barred basins in the formation of oil. Relict seas seem incapable of producing the thick salt deposits for reasons given above; a continued influx of marine waters is required to maintain the precipitation of salt.

Several modifications of the barred basin concept are needed to explain the stratigraphy of the various accumulations. The multiple-basin hypothesis (Branson, 1915), for example, postulates a succession of connected basins. The waters flow from the sea through the successive basins and become progressively more saline. In a second or third basin, perhaps, halite might be precipitated without a subjacent deposit of anhydrite or gypsum. Because this concept, however, requires a most complex arrangement of basins and concentrations, it is an improbable one. Fractional crystallization can be accomplished in a simpler manner. King (1947), for example, has advanced an ingenious explanation for the thick anhydrite deposits of the Permian Castile formation of Texas and New Mexico. He postulates deposition in a semi-isolated sea into which normal sea water flowed through a somewhat restricted channel. The concentrated brine of the Castile sea tended to sink to the bottom and in part return, by a sort of reflux action, to the sea. The salinity achieved was sufficient to precipitate calicum sulfate but not sodium chloride. The initial deposit would be gypsum, but King shows that the anhydrite stage would be reached in about $\frac{1}{1000}$th part of Castile time (assuming a temperature of $30°$ C). An evaporation of 114 inches per year is estimated to be necessary in order to produce the observed annual increment of anhydrite. Calculation shows that the rate of influx to reflux was about 10 to 1. Such a balance would lead to anhydrite precipitation with relatively little halite and would permit the more soluble salts to be carried out of the basin and back to the sea. Modern oceanographic studies of the circulation patterns in somewhat restricted lagoons or embayments provide support for the influx-reflux concept (Scruton, 1953).

Gypsum may form by reaction of sulfate-bearing waters on limestone. The oxidation of pyrite, especially the pyrite of the black shales, has led to the formation of large quantities of acid sulfate waters which react with limestone and convert large parts of it to gypsum. Most gypsum deposits, however, seem not to be of this origin.

Gypsum is found in some places as *gypsite*, which is gypsum earth. This material is an efflorescent deposit, found only in arid regions, which occurs over the ledge outcrop of gypsum or a gypsum-bearing stratum. Locally it is a source of gypsum.

REFERENCES CITED AND BIBLIOGRAPHY

Alling, H. L. (1928), The geology and origin of the Silurian salt of New York state, *N.Y. State Museum Bull.*, no. 275.

Balk, R. (1953), Salt structure of Jefferson Island salt dome, Iberia and Vermilion parishes, Louisiana, *Bull. Am. Assoc. Petroleum Geol.*, vol. 37, pp. 2455–2474.

Branson, E. B. (1915), Origin of thick salt and gypsum deposits, *Bull. Geol. Soc. Amer.*, vol. 26, pp. 231–242.

Brown, L. S. (1931), Cap rock petrography, *Bull. Am. Assoc. Petroleum Geol.*, vol. 15, pp. 509–530.

Caley, J. F. (1940), Paleozoic geology of the Toronto-Hamilton area, Ontario, *Geol. Survey Canada Mem.* 224.

Clarke, F. W. (1924), Data of geochemistry, *U.S. Geol. Survey Bull.* 770, pp. 218–260.

DeGolyer, E. L., and others (1926), *Geology of salt dome oil fields*, Chicago, Am. Assoc. Petroleum Geol.

Dellwig, L. F. (1955), Origin of the Salina salt of Michigan, *J. Sediment. Petrol.*, vol. 25, pp. 83–110.

Grabau, A. W. (1920), *Geology of the non-metallic mineral deposits*, Vol. I. *Principles of salt deposition*, New York, McGraw-Hill.

Hollingworth, S. E. (1948), Evaporites, *Proc. Yorkshire Geol. Soc.*, vol. 27, pp. 192–198.

Kaufmann, D. W., and Slawson, C. B. (1950), Ripplemark in rock salt of the Salina formation, *J. Geol.*, vol. 58, pp. 24–29.

King, R. H. (1947), Sedimentation in Permian Castile sea, *Bull. Am. Assoc. Petroleum Geol.*, vol. 31, pp. 470–477.

Kroenlein, G. A. (1939), Salt, potash, and anhydrite in Castile formation of southeastern New Mexico, *Bull. Am. Assoc. Petroleum Geol.*, vol. 23, pp. 1682–1693.

Krumbein, W. C. (1951), Occurrence and lithologic associations of evaporites in the United States, *J. Sediment. Petrol.*, vol. 21, pp. 63–81.

Landes, K. K. (1940), The Salina and Bass Island rocks in the Michigan Basin, *U.S. Geol. Survey, Oil and Gas Invest., Prelim. Map* 40.

Lotze, Franz (1938), *Steinsalz und Kalisalz Geologie*, Berlin, Borntraeger.

MacDonald, Gordon (1953), Anhydrite-gypsum relations, *Am. J. Sci.*, vol. 251, p. 884.

Posnjak, E. (1938), The system $CaSO_4$–H_2O, *Am. J. Sci.*, ser. 5, vol. 35, pp. 247–272.

Posnjak, E. (1940), Deposition of calcium sulfate from sea water, *Am. J. Sci.*, vol. 238, pp. 539–568.

Schaller, W. T. and Henderson, E. P. (1932), Mineralogy of drill cores from the potash field of New Mexico and Texas, *U.S. Geol. Survey Bull.* 833.

Scruton, L. P. (1953), Deposition of evaporites, *Bull. Am. Assoc. Petroleum Geol.*, vol. 37, pp. 2498–2512.

Sloss, L. L. (1953), The significance of evaporites, *J. Sediment. Petrol.*, vol. 23, pp. 143–161.

Stewart, F. H. (1949, 1951), The petrology of the evaporites of the Eskdale No. 2 Boring, East Yorkshire, *Mineralog. Mag.*, vol. 28, pp. 621–675; vol. 29, pp. 445–475, 557–572.

Stewart, F. H. (1953), Early gypsum in the Permian evaporites of northeastern England, *Proc. Geologists Assoc.*, vol. 64, pp. 33–39.

Stone, R. W., and others (1920), Gypsum deposits of the United States, *U.S. Geol. Survey, Bull.* 697.

Taylor, R. E. (1937), Water-insoluble residues in rock salt of Louisiana salt plugs, *Bull. Am. Assoc. Petroleum Geol.*, vol. 21, pp. 1268–1310.

Udden, J. A. (1924), Laminated anhydrite in Texas, *Bull. Geol. Soc. Amer.*, vol. 35, pp. 347–354.

Usiglio, J. (1849), Analyse de l'eau de la Mediterranee sur la cote de France, *Ann. chim. et phys.*, ser. 3, vol. 27, pp. 92, 172. (See Clarke, 1924, pp. 219–220.)

van't Hoff, J. H. (1905), *Zur Bildung der ozeanischen Salzablagerungen*, vol. 1, Braunschweig.

Wallace, R. C. (1914), Gypsum and anhydrite in genetic relationship, *Geol. Mag.*, n.s., dec. VI, vol. 1, pp. 271–276.

THE CARBONACEOUS ROCKS AND RELATED MATERIALS

Introduction

The organic compounds of living matter undergo combustion and are changed to CO_2 and water. This combustion does not cease on the death of the organism but is replaced by bacteriological decay or direct oxidation (Fig. 109). Depending on where they accumulate and the amount of oxygen

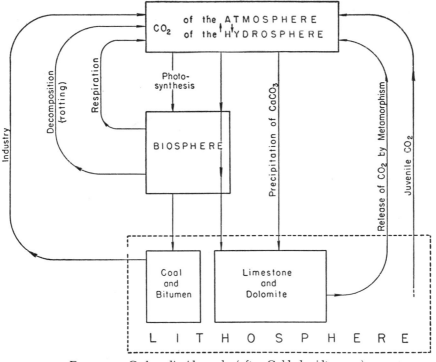

FIG. 109.   Carbon-dioxide cycle (after Goldschmidt, 1933).

available, the organic residues undergo incomplete oxidation, known as humification or putrefaction. Such incompletely oxidized products are CH_4, CO, H_2, and so forth. Some of the products which do not reach the end state (CO_2) are buried and preserved in the lithosphere where further changes take place.

The resistance to oxidation and decomposition of organic materials varies. Most susceptible to decomposition are the proteins, sugars, starches, and other food materials. Cellulose and fats decompose less readily; amber, the chitin of certain brachiopods and other forms, the resins, and waxes remain even in rocks of Cambrian age. The degradation of plant tissues is highly selective and not well understood (Barghoorn, 1952).

Forms of Organic Residues

The residues are of three main types: (1) humus, (2) peat, and (3) sapropel (Polynov, 1937).

Humus is the accumulation of organic residues in the uppermost part of the lithosphere, mainly in the soil. For the most part, this form of accumulation undergoes oxidation. In a normal soil therefore the humus consists of newly added organic matter and a large number of compounds representing various stages of decay. Some of the intermediate products, the so-called humic acids, are very active. These acids, in fact, are a colloid complex capable of adsorbing cations from solution. If sesquioxides and dissolved humus are prepared in certain proportions, mixed sols are formed. If the proportions are altered, coagels of humus with the hydrated oxides of iron and alumina are formed (Table 83).

Peat-forming conditions are nearly everywhere associated with fresh-water swamps. The organic residues may form from 70 to 90 per cent of the total accumulation. Mineral components become nil. Peat deposition takes place when there is (1) rapid growth and reproduction of the plants, (2) excessive development of such organic compounds as are difficult to decompose, and (3) development of such conditions in the medium that the life activity of microorganisms is reduced to a minimum or completely extinguished.

Plants vary in their peat-forming ability. Involved in peat formation are rushes, sedges, horsetails (*Equisetum*), various woody plants—notably certain species of pine, birch, black alder, and spruce—and most important of all, the peat mosses (*Sphagnum* and *Hypnum*).

The peat-moss accumulations may be tens of feet thick and cover many square miles. They are hygroscopic and absorb up to fourteen times their own volume of water. Peat mosses fulfill the conditions for peat accumulation because (1) they grow rapidly, (2) they consist largely of cellulose and waxy substances with little protein, and (3) the organic acids formed on putrefaction cannot obtain bases for their neutralization, hence the resulting acidity inhibits microorganisms.

Coalification follows on burial and proceeds without benefit of microbiological aid.

Sapropel is a silt that is rich in, or is composed wholly of, organic compounds which collect on the bottom of various water basins: lakes, lagoons, estuaries, and the like. The remains of phyto- and zooplankton are richer in fatty and protein substances than is peat. Hence decomposition (putrefaction) in the presence of a little oxygen takes place. Various types of hydrocarbons form, as do the reduced forms of iron (ferrous oxide and ferrous

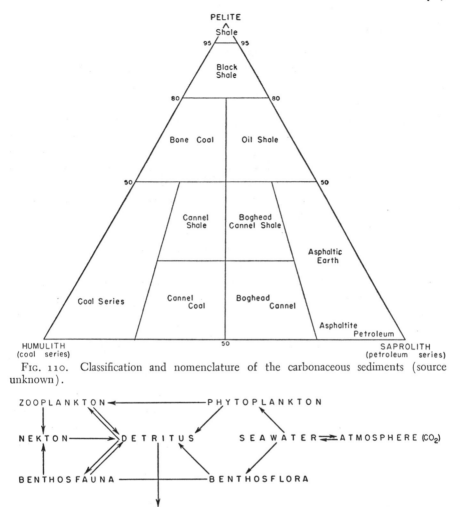

FIG. 110. Classification and nomenclature of the carbonaceous sediments (source unknown).

FIG. 111. Relation of carbon, organisms, and marine sediments. Nekton, active swimming surface forms; plankton, passive surface forms; benthos, bottom-living forms.

sulfide). The progressive accumulation of sapropel is governed largely by the rapid multiplication of the organisms responsible for it. Free organic acids are lacking, because the environment essentially is neutral. Such accumulations may not occur or may take place with considerable mixture of mineral matter; hence sapropelite (biopelite; also sapropsammite, Figs. 110 and 111).

Bituminization forms bituminous shale (oil shale) and eventually petroleum.

The Coal Series

General Characteristics and Classifications

Coal is a black, or brownish-black, solid, combustible mineral substance formed by the partial decomposition of vegetable matter without free access of air, under the influence of moisture, and in many cases, increased pressure and temperature.[10] Coal is an opaque (except in very thin slices) noncrystalline solid which varies in color from light brown to black. It is dull to brilliant in luster and has a low specific gravity (1.0 to 1.8). The hardness varies from 0.5 to 2.5. It is brittle and has a hackly to conchoidal fracture. The properties vary with the type and rank of coal.

Coal is classified according to (1) rank and (2) physical constitution. The first classification antedates the second and is based primarily on the degree of metamorphism of the coal. The second classification is biopetrologic and is based in large part on the microscopic study of coal.

The ranks of coal depend on the degree of coalification. More or less arbitrarily, although carefully selected chemical criteria are used to supplement the gross features which characterize each rank (Fig. 112). The commonly recognized ranks of coal are: (1) brown coal or lignite, (2) subbituminous, (3) bituminous, (4) semibituminous, (5) semianthracite, and (6) anthracite. In addition certain other coal types, not part of the usual graded series, are commonly recognized. These include cannel coal and bone coal.

Brown coal, or lignite, is a low-rank coal which is brown, brownish-black, but rarely black. It commonly retains the structures of the original wood. It is high in moisture, low in heat value, and checks badly upon drying. It burns readily with a smoky flame. Most lignite is Cretaceous or younger in age.

Bituminous coal is a higher-rank coal, i.e., contains a higher percentage of carbon and less water. It also burns readily, and does not disintegrate so easily on exposure. Most bituminous coals are banded (Pl. 5, top).

Anthracite coal is marked by its bright, almost submetallic luster and its conchoidal fracture. It is high in fixed carbon and low in volatile hydrocarbons. It ignites less readily than the lower ranks of coal and burns with a short flame which produces much heat and little smoke. It is relatively high in ash.

Subbituminous, semibituminous, and semianthracite coals are transitional coal types.

Cannel coal is a dull black coal of bituminous rank with a conchoidal fracture (Pl. 35, bottom). It burns readily with a long smoky flame. It is very high in volatile constituents. Bone coal is a very impure coal, high (33 per

[10] *Webster's New International Dictionary*, 2d ed., unabridged.

cent or more) in ash. To the various coal types should be added anthroxalite and graphitoid, which are coaly substances which have been metamorphosed beyond the anthracite stage.

Constituents of Coal

There are two schools of thought on the nomenclature and classification of the constituents of coal: the American and the British. The American or Thiessen nomenclature (Thiessen, 1920) is botanical and genetic and can be applied only after microscopic study. The British or Stopes classification (Stopes, 1919) is primarily megascopic and descriptive and hence applicable to the hand specimen. Each of these systems has its proponents; some attempts have been made to reconcile or to combine the two rival schemes (for a review of the subject see Cady, 1939, 1942; Dapples, 1942; Marshall, 1942).

Any specimen of common bituminous coal reveals, to the unaided eye, three or four varieties of coal, each having individual and characteristic features. These components, which are more or less segregated into bands, are the ingredients of coal and are designated as *vitrain, fusain, clarain,* and *durain* (Pl. 35, top).

To the naked eye *vitrain* forms thin horizontal bands up to 20 millimeters thick. It is a brilliant, vitreous or glassy-looking, jetlike coal which alternates with broader bands or other kinds of coal. Vitrain has a marked conchoidal fracture, is brittle, and is clean to the touch. To the naked eye it commonly appears homogeneous and structureless (eu-vitrain). In other cases it exhibits striations attributed to plant structure (pro-vitrain).

Fusain, or mineral charcoal, is most readily identified because of its resemblance to common charcoal. If not mineralized, it is very friable and highly porous. The pores are in some cases filled with calcite or with pyrite. In thin sections it is opaque and highly cellular (Pl. 36, D). In the hand specimen fusain forms irregular wedges lying on bedding planes at various angles.

Clarain is the term applied to those thin to thick bands, which unlike vitrain, are laminated. This coal type has a smooth fracture, marked glossy or shiny luster, which is especially distinguished by a silky luster that arises from the sublaminations. The silkiness of luster is distinctly different from the smooth brilliance of vitrain in the same coal.

Durain is a dull coal characterized by its lack of luster, its matte or earthy appearance, and black or lead-gray color. It occurs in solid bands which possess a close, firm texture. Stratification is generally absent.

Microscopic examination has led to refinement and subdivision of these megascopically defined terms (Table 89). The coal types are considered rock species made up of *macerals* (analogous to the *minerals* of the noncarbo-

TABLE 89. Classification of the Ingredients of Coal (Heerlen Committee, after Marshall, 1942)

Rock Types (Termination -ain)	Macerals (Termination -inite)		Notes
Vitrain	Vitrinite	{ Collinite { Telinite	May be subdivided if desired. May be subdivided according to botanical origin if desired.
	Semifusinite		Intermediate between vitrinite and fusinite.
Fusain	Fusinite		Opaque cellular tissue.
	Micrinite		Opaque residuum.
	Exinite	{ Sporinite { Cutinite	Spore material. Cuticle material.
Clarain	. . . .		Dominantly vitrinite with some exinite and other macerals.
Durain	. . . .		Dominantly micrinite wtih exinite.

naceous rocks). A maceral is an organic unit, that is, a single fragment of plant debris or material derived therefrom. The basic macerals are: vitrinite, consisting of collinite and telinite; fusinite; micrinite; and exinite, which consists of sporinite and cutinite. Collinite is a structureless jellified plant residue, whereas telinite is a translucent golden gel that retains some cell structure. Fusinite is the opaque-walled carbonized cell structure found in fusain. Micrinite is an opaque residuum which is the dominant constituent of durain. Exinite consists of sporinite and cutinite, which are spore remains and cuticular materials, respectively. The spores are yellow transparent bodies (in most cases collapsed) of both small and large spore bodies (microscopores and megaspores, Pl. 36, C). In addition small translucent and reddish resin bodies occur in some coals. The several types of coals consist of these materials in varying proportions.

Thiessen and some other American students of coal consider coal to consist of two fundamental constituents, namely *anthraxylon* and *attritus*. The proportions of the two determine the type of coal. Bright (glance) coal is composed primarily of anthraxylon, whereas dull (matte or splint) coal is chiefly attritus (Pl. 36, E and F). According to Thiessen, the bright layers were derived chiefly from the woody parts of plants (anthraxylon). The thicker bands represent branches or trunks of trees; the thinner ones are smaller branches or twigs. There are several types of anthraxylon, moreover, which are determined by the type of plant from which it formed. Anthraxylon is clearly translucent. Attritus, on the other hand, is applied to all materials not identified as anthraxylon. Attritus, unlike anthraxylon and fusain, which are masses of integrated plant tissue preserved as units, is macerated and degraded plant materials. It is both opaque and translucent.

The common coal types recognized are known as (1) bright coal, (2) semisplint, (3) splint, (4) cannel, and (5) boghead.

Under the microscope it appears that vitrain is primarily anthraxylon; clarain is composed of translucent attritus and thin shreds of anthraxylon. Durain, on the other hand, appears to be made up mainly of opaque attritus.

Cannel and boghead coals (Pl. 36, A and B) are clean, compact, block coals of massive structure and of uniform, fine-grained texture. They are normally gray to black, have a greasy luster, and have a prominent conchoidal fracture. Cannel coal is devoid of bedding. Under the microscope cannel coal appears to be made almost wholly of microdebris (Pl. 36, A) which consists of spores, resins, woody fragments, and opaque attritus. Boghead cannel contains large masses of oil algae.

Chemical Composition of Coal

Coal is composed chiefly of carbon, hydrogen, and oxygen. Nitrogen is a lesser constituent as is sulfur. Mineral matter (ash) is a variable constituent. The proportions of the several constituents vary with the rank of the coal. The variations of the chief constituents (C, H, N, and O), starting with wood and ending with anthracite, are given in Table 90. This table may be

TABLE 90. Average Composition of Wood, Peat, and Coals
(after Clarke, 1924, p. 773)
(per cent)

	Carbon	Hydrogen	Nitrogen	Oxygen
Wood	49.64	6.23	0.92	43.20
Peat	55.44	6.28	1.72	36.56
Lignite	72.95	5.24	1.31	20.50
Bituminous Coal	84.24	5.55	1.52	8.69
Anthracite	93.50	2.81	0.97	2.72

TABLE 91. Relative Proportions of Constituents of Wood, Peat, and Coals
(after Clarke, 1924, p. 773)

	Carbon	Hydrogen	Nitrogen	Oxygen
Wood	100	12.5	1.8	87.0
Peat	100	11.3	3.5	64.9
Lignite	100	7.2	1.8	28.1
Bituminous Coal	100	6.6	1.8	10.3
Anthracite	100	3.0	1.3	2.9

restated in different form so as to show the proportions of the hydrogen, nitrogen, and oxygen to 100 parts of carbon (Table 91). A steady decrease in hydrogen and oxygen thus becomes apparent. Furthermore, the proportional decrease in oxygen is greater than for hydrogen. In cellulose ($C_6H_{10}O_5$) these two elements exist in exactly the proportions in which they are found in water (1 to 8). In wood the hydrogen is slightly in excess of that ratio (1 to 7), and the excess steadily increases until in anthracite it is roughly 1 to 1. The changing composition, nitrogen neglected, is shown in Fig. 112.

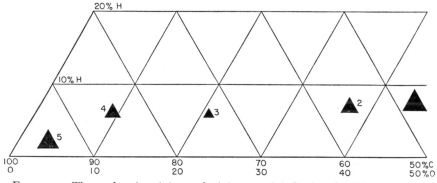

FIG. 112. The coal series. (1) wood, (2) peat, (3) lignite, (4) bituminous coal, (5) anthracite coal (data from Clarke, 1924, p. 773).

Occurrence of Coal

Coal is a relatively rare, though widely distributed, type of rock. Even in the coal measures, which contain the commercially valuable coals, it forms only 1 or 2 per cent of the whole section. The individual beds of coal vary from a mere film to over 400 feet in thickness. The average thickness, however, is 1 or 2 feet. Seams over 10 feet thick are very rare. The Pittsburgh seam which maintains a thickness of 6 to 10 feet over a wide area is exceptional. Individual seams, however, have a wide extent. The Pittsburgh seam, for example, underlies 22,000 square miles in western Pennsylvania, West Virginia, and Ohio and is of workable thickness beneath 6000 square miles. In any given coal-bearing section, numerous seams, both workable and nonproductive, are likely to be present. In western Illinois there are 18 coal seams; in part of Ohio and southwestern Pennsylvania over 40 seams are known; in Nova Scotia more than 70 beds have been recorded; and in the Westphalian field more than 90, aggregating 274 feet, are reported.

The coal occurs interbedded in a cyclical manner with ordinary sedimentary rocks (see p. 620) (Udden, 1912; Weller, 1930). In many places it rests on a clay of special character known as underclay. Some underclays are so low in iron and the alkalies as to constitute a fireclay.

Origin of Coal

The presence of organic structures in coal and the well-established coal series, beginning with wood and ending with anthracite, leaves no room for doubting the plant origin of coal (Jeffrey, 1915; White and Thiessen, 1913). There remains, however, to consider (1) the mode of accumulation of the vegetable matter and (2) its transformation into coal.

Two views have been held relative to transportation. Most students of coal suppose the organic matter to have accumulated in place, thereby giving rise to an autochthonous coal. Some investigators, however, have supposed the organic debris to have been transported from its place of growth to another place, where it accumulated to form an allochthonous coal seam. Coal undoubtedly has formed both ways, but the prevailing view favors accumulation in place in large fresh-water swamps. The uniformity of thickness, wide extent, and absence of admixtures of inorganic detritus favor this conclusion. Some of the cannel coals, however, may represent accumulations of transported organic detritus.

Normally, vegetable matter is oxidized to water and carbon dioxide. If the plant material accumulates under water, however, oxygen is excluded and decomposition is only partial. The plant residues are incompletely oxidized. Such incomplete destruction leads to the accumulation of an organic deposit—peat. Although some of the decomposition and change may be due to the action of bacteria, normally the toxic condition of the peat bog suppresses or extinguishes the activity of such microorganisms. The chemistry of the coalification processes involved in the change of peat to the various ranks of coal is not fully understood. Burial with consequent rise in pressure and temperature promotes the changes. Only in sharply folded beds is the anthracite rank reached. In the very old rocks (i.e., pre-Carboniferous) true coal is very rare, although certain graphitoids which are transformed coal have been reported from rocks as old as the Precambrian. Prior to the evolution of a land flora, such coal-like accumulations may have been algal (boghead cannel).

Sapropel, Petroleum, and Natural Gas

The origin of petroleum and natural gas is a subject which has been much discussed and upon which there is little unanimity of opinion. Adequate treatment of the problem and a digest of the vast literature on the subject cannot be given here. It is appropriate, however, to point out how the study of the sedimentary rocks bears on the problem of origin of the fluid hydrocarbons contained within them.

Most students of the subject now agree that petroleum and natural gas are generated from the organic matter trapped in the sediments at the time of their deposition. In general it is agreed that sapropelic rather than peaty materials were the parent substance.

The study of the origin of petroleum and natural gas involves not only a study of the organic matter in sediments and its transformation into petroleum, but also a study of the source beds and the ultimate reservoir rocks. Unfortunately there is no agreement on what are the source beds. Exhaustive study has been made of the source-bed problem and the establishment of chemical and other criteria for their recognition (Trask and Patnode, 1936). Although the reservoir rocks are better known, since they are more readily identified, there has been little systematic work on their petrology. Krynine (1945) has advanced the view that the reservoir rocks are specialized, somewhat atypical deposits. To date this concept has not been supported by adequate data although some attempt has been made to evaluate the idea by statistical scrutiny (Emery, 1955). Certainly, however, there are several different petrologic types of oil pools markedly distinct from one another.

It has been suggested by several writers that if the petrologic characters of the reservoir rocks were adequately known, it should be possible to predict where in time and space such characteristics would have their optimum development, so that oil prospecting could be put on a rational basis. Were the petroliferous zone closely delimited, the search for structural traps could then be carried out with the usual geological and geophysical tools at minimum expense and with maximum chances of success. In essence the problem is to frame a geological and petrological definition of the habitat of oil within a given basin.

The solution of this problem involves an analysis and understanding of the kind and character of sedimentary basins and the pattern of development displayed by the several types of basins. Several geosynclinal basins, for example, show similar histories, even though the sections involved are somewhat different in age. The parallelism in the evolution of these basins suggests that there is a normal geosynclinal cycle (p. 636), the stages of which are related to the filling of the basin. In this cycle there is a certain optimum period for the accumulation of organic matter. This seems to be early in the cycle. The first-deposited sands, however, are unfit as reservoir rocks because they are graywackes and have their interstitial voids plugged tight with clay-like materials. Later in the cycle the sands become cleaner washed, and hence are more porous (subgraywackes) and may be suitable reservoirs of oil and gas. Such sands normally would run parallel with the axis of the geosyncline. Successively younger beds would have their productive zones shifted somewhat as the geosyncline filled and overflowed with sediment, as it does late in its history. The latest beds involved in the filling are prone to be continental and coal-bearing rather than oil-bearing. The habitat of oil is far from understood but one can be certain only that the kind and character of the rocks of the basin are not unrelated to the kind of basin, stage of filling, and the occurrence of petroleum. All are products of one common tectonic cycle and hence are related one to the other.

REFERENCES CITED AND BIBLIOGRAPHY

Barghoorn, E. S. (1952), Degradation of plant tissues in organic sediments, *J. Sediment. Petrol.*, vol. 22, pp. 34–41.

Cady, G. H. (1939), Nomenclature of the megascopic description of Illinois coals, *Econ. Geol.*, vol. 34, pp. 475–494.

Cady, G. H. (1942), Modern concepts of the physical constitution of coal, *J. Geol.*, vol. 50, pp. 337–356.

Clarke, F. W. (1924), Data of geochemistry, *U.S. Geol. Survey Bull.* 770, pp. 756–783.

Dapples, E. C. (1942), Physical constitution of coal as related to coal description and classification, *J. Geol.*, vol. 50, pp. 437–450.

Emery, J. R. (1955), The application of a discriminant function to a problem in petroleum geology (Abstract), *J. Sediment. Petrol.*, vol. 25, p. 131.

Jeffrey, E. C. (1915), The mode of origin of coal, *J. Geol.*, vol. 23, pp. 218–230.

Krynine, P. D. (1945), Sediments and the search for oil, *Producers Monthly*, vol. 9, pp. 12–22.

Marshall, C. E. (1942), Modern conceptions of the physical constitution of coal and related research in Great Britain, *J. Geol.*, vol. 50, pp. 385–405.

Polynov, B. B. (1937), *The cycle of weathering* (trans. by A. Muir), London, Murby.

Stopes, M. C. (1919), On the four visible ingredients in banded bituminous coal. Studies in the composition of coal, *Proc. Roy. Soc. (London)*, ser. B., vol. 90, pp. 470–487.

Thiessen, R. (1920), Compilation and composition of bituminous coals, *J. Geol.*, vol. 28, pp. 185–209.

Trask, P. D. and Patnode, H. W. (1936), Means of recognizing source beds in *Drilling and production practice*, Amer. Petroleum Inst., pp. 368–384.

Udden, J. A. (1912), Geology and mineral resources of the Peoria quadrangle, *U.S. Geol. Survey Bull.* 506, pp. 45–70.

Weller, J. M. (1930), Cyclical sedimentation of the Pennsylvanian period and its significance, *J. Geol.*, vol. 38, pp. 97–135.

White, D., and Thiessen, R. (1913), The origin of coal, *U.S. Bur. Mines Bull.* 38.

11

Provenance
(and Mineral Stability)

INTRODUCTION

BASICALLY and fundamentally the clastic sediments are *residues*. These residues are the insoluble materials left after the chemical breakdown and disintegration of some pre-existing rock. The composition of the residue depends in part on the nature of the parent rock and in part on its maturity, which is a measure of the extent to which the decomposition processes were carried toward completion. The maturity is a function of the time through which the action is extended and of the intensity of that action. Time and intensity are dependent upon relief and climate, respectively.

But sediments are *washed* residues that have been subjected to a sorting action, as a result of which they have been fractionated into several size grades. These grades differ not only in size of grain but also in their mineralogical and chemical composition.

The task of the geologist is to examine the final fractionated residue or sediment and to determine whence it came (distance and direction of transport), to determine from what kind of rock or rocks the residue was derived, and to deduce from the maturity of the residue the nature of the climate and relief of the source area. The latter objectives constitute a study of the *provenance*, the subject of this chapter, whereas the former are dealt with in the next chapter on *dispersal*.

498

DEFINITIONS

The term provenance has to do with origin or birth, and as applied to a sedimentary deposit, has to do primarily with the source rocks from which these materials were derived. Each type of source rock tends to yield a distinctive suite of minerals which therefore constitute a guide to the character of that rock. But the composition of a sediment is not determined solely by the nature of the source rock; it is also a function of the climate and relief within the distributive province [1] which determines the maturity of the residues derived from such a province.

Erosion commonly interrupts the processes of weathering in mid-course, especially in districts of high relief. The material eroded will then include rock and mineral fragments that have escaped alteration or have been only partially altered. Likewise in certain climatic regimens the processes of chemical distintegration are greatly retarded or even inhibited. The composition of the residues of weathering and the resulting sediments is therefore the result largely of the combined effects of relief and climate on the source rocks, and any conclusions concerning these two factors, as well as the kind of source rocks, must be made from the chemical and mineralogical make-up of the sediments. To assay the maturity of a sediment one must know (1) something of the mobility of the several chemical constituents of which it is composed, and especially (2) the relative stability of the various rock-making minerals.

MOBILITY OF THE OXIDES

The chemical changes that take place during weathering are determined by comparison of the composition of the weathered residue with the fresh rock from which it was derived. The changes are well illustrated by the alteration of the Morton granite gneiss (Goldich, 1938). The fresh gneiss contains about 30 per cent quartz, 19 per cent potash feldspar, 40 per cent plagioclase, 7 per cent biotite, and the remaining 3 per cent is hornblende, magnetite, and minor accessories. The chemical composition of the unaltered gneiss is given in Table 92, Column A. That of the altered rock is shown in Column B. It is difficult, however, to determine by inspection of these two analyses the actual changes, because the results must, of course, total 100 per cent in both analyses. The change of alumina from 14.62 to 26.14, for example, does not mean alumina has been added, but that probably alumina has increased *relative* to the other constituents because some of these constituents actually were lost by leaching. Because alumina is rather inert and is less likely to migrate by solution than most other oxides, we may assume

[1] A term applied to the source region by Brammall (Milner, 1922).

that it remained constant. If so, 100 grams of fresh rock contain 14.62 grams of alumina. The residual products of weathering will also contain 14.62 grams of alumina if none of it is assumed to be lost. Because this amount is 26.14 per cent of the whole residue, the weight of the residual materials is $14.62/26.14 \times 100$, or 55.88 grams. This is the number of grams of altered rock which contains the same weight of alumina as 100 grams of fresh rock.

TABLE 92.   Analyses of Fresh and Weathered Morton Gneiss (after Goldich)

	A (per cent)	B (per cent)	C (grams)	D (grams)
SiO_2	71.54	55.07	30.83	−40.71
TiO_2	0.26	1.03	0.58	+0.32
Al_2O_3	14.62	26.14	14.62	0.00
Fe_2O_3	0.69	3.72	2.08	+1.39
FeO	1.64	2.53	1.43	−0.21
MgO	0.77	0.33	0.18	−0.59
CaO	2.08	0.16	0.09	−1.99
Na_2O	3.84	0.05	0.03	−3.81
K_2O	3.92	0.14	0.08	−3.84
H_2O+	0.30	9.75	5.40	+5.10
H_2O-	0.02	0.64	0.36	+0.34
CO_2	0.14	0.36	0.20	+0.06
	99.82[a]	99.92[a]	55.88	−43.94

A. Fresh Morton gneiss, Cold Spring Granite Company quarry, Morton, Minnesota. S. S. Goldich, analyst.
B. Residual clay from Ramsey Park, Redwood Falls, Minnesota. S. S. Goldich, analyst.
C. Grams of each constituent present in 55.88 grams of weathered material derived from 100 grams of fresh rock, assuming alumina to be constant.
D. Loss in grams of each constituent in conversion of 100 grams of fresh rock to 55.88 grams of altered material, alumina assumed to be constant (Col. A − Col. C).
   [a] Several minor constituents determined by Goldich omitted from totals.

This weight of residual material therefore will contain 55.88/100 of each item in Column B. Therefore the residue will contain 30.83 grams of silica, and so forth. By subtracting each item of Column C from the corresponding one in Column A, the gains or losses, assuming alumina constant, will be obtained (Column D). In the example given, there is an apparent gain of ferric oxide and titania; and a loss of silica, ferrous oxide, magnesia, lime, soda, and potash. Additions of water and carbon dioxide (from the atmosphere) are also evident.

It is not necessary to assume any oxide constant. If the percentage of each constituent in the fresh rock be divided by its percentage in the altered rock and the quotients, multiplied by 100, be plotted on a suitable scale, the *relative* gains and losses can be seen at a glance.[2] Figure 113 illustrates the

[2] So-called "gain-loss" or "straight-line" diagram (see Leith and Mead, 1915).

results when this procedure is applied to the analyses of the fresh and weathered Morton gneiss. This diagram may be interpreted as showing that 55.88 grams of altered rock contain as much alumina as 100 grams of fresh rock, but 120 of weathered residue are required to contain as much silica (71.54 grams) as in the fresh rock, and so forth. It is apparent that alumina has increased relative to silica or that silica has decreased relative to alumina. The latter is the more probable conclusion. Similarly all points which plot

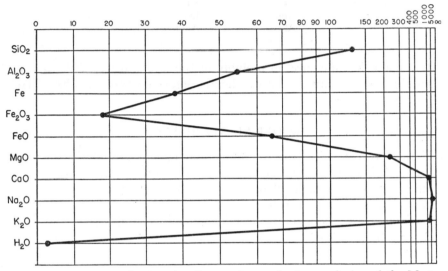

FIG. 113. Losses and gains of oxide constituents in the weathering of the Morton granite gneiss (data from Goldich, 1938).

to the left of the alumina represent gains relative to that oxide, whereas all those which fall to the right represent losses. The gains or losses relative to any other oxide can be deduced similarly from this diagram. Of the original oxide constituents in this rock, soda shows the greatest loss, whereas ferric iron displays the least. The order of loss is Na_2O, CaO, K_2O, MgO, SiO_2, Al_2O_3 and iron.

The average order of loss can be determined by study of the alteration of large numbers of rocks by similar treatment (or by comparing the average igneous rock and the average sediment). Students of weathering agree that all constituents except water are lost in prolonged weathering. The order in which the oxides are lost, as interpreted by several investigators, is given in Table 93. The variations in the orders given in this table probably result from sample inadequacies. Some differences might be expected in different rocks; more marked differences may be related to differences in climate (Reiche, 1950, p. 44).

TABLE 93. Average Order of Loss of the Oxides in Weathering

Order	Steidtmann (1908)	Leith and Mead (1915)	Goldich (1938)
1	CaO	CaO	Na_2O
2	MgO	Na_2O	CaO
3	Na_2O	MgO	MgO
4	K_2O	K_2O	K_2O
5	SiO_2	SiO_2	SiO_2
6	Iron	Iron	Al_2O_3
7	Al_2O_3	Al_2O_3	Iron

It is upon the differences in mobility of the several oxides that some indices of residue maturity (or of weathering potential) have been based (see page 507).

MINERAL STABILITY

If there is a definite order or differential rate of loss of the chemical oxides, it follows that the rock-forming minerals in which these constituents occur should exhibit different degrees of stability. The consistency of the findings, observed and experimental, recorded in the literature, support this conclusion. As a group, the mafic minerals are less stable than the alkali feldspars; the potash feldspars are more stable than the sodic feldspars, and so forth.

Definitions and Criteria of Stability

The stability of a mineral is its resistance to alteration. We are here concerned primarily with its chemical stability or resistance to solution and decomposition rather than mechanical stability or resistance to abrasion. Minerals are, at the time of their formation, presumably in equilibrium with their environment and therefore stable. But as they are brought into new environments, unlike those in which they formed, they are prone to go into solution or to be decomposed. Many rock-making minerals were formed within the earth at somewhat elevated temperatures and pressures. When these minerals are placed in the low-temperature, low-pressure, and aqueous environment such as that prevailing at the earth's surface, or near it, many are unstable and are taken into solution or decomposed. Such changes, which occur in the soils and in the sedimentary envelope of the earth, need to be understood in order to interpret properly the sedimentary rocks. The study of such changes has been aptly called "mineral pathology."

Evidences of stability or instability are of several kinds. "Pathologic" features such as etched surfaces and corroded borders are indicative of solution and hence instability. Conversely outgrowths or secondary enlargements are indicative of stability, since the mineral appears to be growing rather than disappearing. The disappearance of minerals or their absence in soils and other residua derived from rocks in which the minerals in question are present, is further evidence of their instability. To a limited extent the stability of a mineral can also be experimentally determined by measuring the solution losses under somewhat restricted and simplified conditions of leaching.

Stability Order

All minerals are not equally immune to solution and decay. There have been many attempts to determine the relative stability of minerals in soils and sediments. These have been reviewed by Milner (1940, p. 492), Boswell (1933, p. 37), Pettijohn (1941), Allen (1948), Reiche (1950), and Smithson (1950). In general there are two approaches to the problem. The first is to study soil profiles and to note the order of disappearance of the minerals as one passes from fresh to altered rock. The second approach is to determine frequency of occurrence of the several minerals species in recent and ancient sedimentary deposits on the premise that the frequency of occurrence is in some way related to the survival ability of the several species.

TABLE 94.   Mineral Stability Series in Weathering (after Goldich)

Olivine	
	Calcic plagioclase
Augite	
	Calcic-alkalic plagioclase
Hornblende	Alkalic-calcic plagioclase
	Alkalic plagioclase
Biotite	
Potash feldspar	
Muscovite	
Quartz	

Goldich (1938), as a result of quantitative studies of several soil profiles, arranged the common rock-making minerals in a "mineral stability series" which is nearly identical in arrangement with the reaction series of Bowen. This arrangement is not, however, to be interpreted as a reaction series. Olivine does not weather to a pyroxene which in turn alters to hornblende, and so forth. Rather, in a normal igneous rock that contains olivine and pyroxene, the rate of decomposition of the olivine may be expected to exceed that of the pyroxene, which in turn exceeds that of the hornblende, and so on. Similarly all other things being equal, a gabbro may be expected to decompose more readily and more rapidly than a granite.

Goldich dealt primarily with the common rock-making minerals. Other workers have studied the minor accessory minerals also and attempted to determine the stability order of the "heavy minerals." An example of such a study is that of Dryden and Dryden (1946) in which the heavy minerals in certain kinds of fresh rocks are compared with their weathering products

TABLE 95. The Stability of Heavy Minerals[a] (modified from Smithson)

Intrastratal Solution		Weathering (?)	Weathering (soil profile)	
Pettijohn (1941)	Smithson (1941)	Sindowski[b] (1949)	Goldich (1938)	L. and C. Dryden (1946)
Rutile				
Zircon	Zircon	⎧ Zircon		Zircon
	Rutile	⎨ Rutile		
Tourmaline	Tourmaline	⎩ Tourmaline		Tourmaline
	Apatite			
Monazite	Monazite			Monazite
Garnet	Garnet			
Biotite			Biotite	
Apatite				
Staurolite	Staurolite	⎧ Staurolite		
Kyanite	Kyanite	⎨ Kyanite		Kyanite
Hornblende		⎩ Hornblende[c]	Hornblende	Hornblende
	Ferro-magnesian minerals			Staurolite
		⎰ Garnet		Garnet
Augite		⎱ Augite	Augite	
Olivine		⎰ Apatite		
		⎱ Olivine	Olivine	

[a] The spacing is intended to draw attention to the similarities between the series. Minerals occurring in fewer than three of the five lists have been omitted.

[b] Sindowski does not arrange minerals in a continuous series but places them in groups indicated by the brackets in the above table; the minerals in each group are here arranged to show the maximum possible agreement with the other lists.

[c] Given as "amphibole" in original paper.

(Table 95). Sindowski and co-workers (Sindowski, 1949) grouped the heavy minerals into several groups in order of their resistance to weathering ('Table 95). The order was determined in part by comparison of the heavy mineral content of younger and older terraces of the Rhine. The older terraces were impoverished in their heavy mineral content.

As noted by Sindowski, the marked differences in the heavy mineral content of two sedimentary deposits of different ages may be the result of selective loss of certain mineral species *after* deposition rather than to a different provenance or differing weathering regimen *before* deposition. Loss following deposition is *intrastratal solution*, and in general, the results of such action are similar to those of solution in the weathering profile proper.

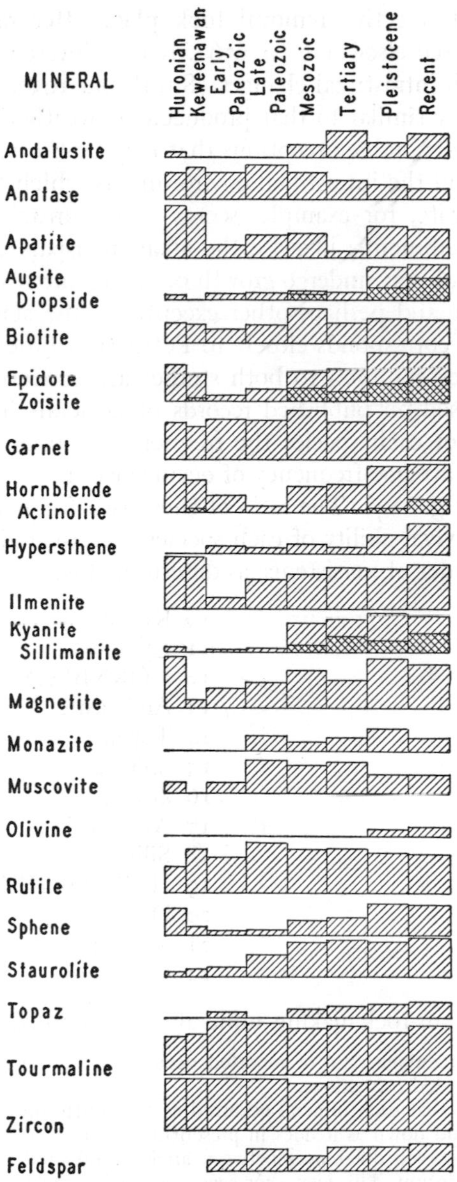

Fig. 114. Frequency of occurrence of detrital minerals in sandstones, based on presence or absence of the species shown. Height of columns proportional to the percentage of times present to total number of investigated formations of the age indicated (Pettijohn, 1941).

The evidence that selective removal took place after rather than before deposition is discussed elsewhere (p. 676). It is of interest to note, however, that studies of such intrastratal changes (Smithson, 1939, 1941, 1942) show an order of loss very similar to that produced by weathering proper (Table 95). There are some notable exceptions that may be the result of differences between the soil and the intrastratal environments which though similar are not identical. Apatite, for example, seems to be unstable in soils but is stable in ancient sediments; likewise the alkali feldspars decompose readily in the soil profile but may undergo growth or enlargement in the sedimentary rock. Despite these and perhaps other exceptions, the stability order determined by Goldich corresponds closely to Pettijohn's order of persistence in so far as the species common to both studies are concerned. The order of persistence was based on published records of minerals in sediments of all ages and places. For each species the frequency of occurrence [3] in Recent sediments and the average frequency of occurrence in non-Recent sediments was determined (Fig. 114). The ratio of these two frequencies is taken as a measure of the survival ability of each species investigated.[4]

The complete order of persistence as determined is:

−3 Anatase[5]	10 Kyanite
−2 MUSCOVITE[5]	11 Epidote
−1 Rutile[5]	12 HORNBLENDE
1 Zircon	13 Andalusite
2 Tourmaline	14 Topaz
3 Monazite	15 Sphene
4 Garnet	16 Zoisite
5 BIOTITE	17 AUGITE
6 Apatite	18 Sillimanite
7 Ilmenite	19 HYPERSTHENE
8 Magnetite	20 Diopside
9 Staurolite	21 Actinolite
	22 OLIVINE

The common igneous-rock-making minerals are capitalized.

[3] Defined as the percentage ratio of reported occurrence of the species in question to the number of investigated formations.

[4] Pettijohn assumed that each mineral occurred as frequently in ancient deposits at the time that they were laid down as it does in present-day deposits (a strictly uniformitarian view) and that the observed differences between ancient and modern sediments were the result of intrastratal solution. This view, however, was challenged by Krynine (1942) who attributed the impoverished suites of the older sediments to destruction of the less stable species in the distributive province. Except that the stability of a mineral in a soil differs from that within a sedimentary rock, it is immaterial which view is correct, since the problem here is determination of a stability series and not an explanation of the richness of the suite and geologic age.

[5] A negative sign indicates the mineral to be more abundant in ancient than in modern sediments.

There have been various attempts to calculate or predict the stability of minerals and rocks and to provide a theoretical basis for the empirically determined stability orders. Reiche (1943), for example, proposed a *weathering potential index* which can be computed either for a mineral or a rock from the usual chemical analysis. This index is defined as the mol percentage [6] ratio of the sum of the alkalies and alkaline earths, less combined water, to the total mols present exclusive of water, or

$$\frac{100 \times \text{mols } (K_2O + Na_2O + CaO + MgO - H_2O)}{\text{mols } (SiO_2 + Al_2O_3 + Fe_2O_3 + CaO + MgO + Na_2O + K_2O)}$$

This is roughly the percentage of the four oxides empirically found to be the most fugitive. In the case of rocks containing free silica (as the granites), the amount of free silica is excluded from the calculations. Where the amount of free silica cannot be ascertained readily, as in the case of the shales, total silica is used, but the results are misleading in some degree. Minerals or rocks of low stability will have a high index; those of great stability in general will have a low index or even a negative index (owing to deduction of mols H_2O). The weathering potential of certain common minerals is given in Table 96.

TABLE 96. Weathering Potential Index
(after Reiche, 1950)

Mineral	Average	Range
Olivine	54	45–65
Augite	39	21–46
Hornblende	36	21–63
Biotite	22	7–32
Muscovite	−10.7[a]	no data
Labradorite	20	18–20
Andesine	14	none
Oligoclase	15[a]	no data
Albite	13[a]	no data
Orthoclase	12[a]	no data

[a] Average computed from averaged analysis; no data on range.

The order of stability of the common rock-making minerals inferred from the weathering potential index corresponds fairly well with that empirically determined by Goldich. Chief exception is quartz (index for which is 0) and the relative stabilities of the whole feldspar group as compared to the mafic suite.

[6] The percentage of any constituent divided by its molecular weight.

The stability of minerals according to Fersman (Baturin, 1942) is related to certain thermodynamical principles.

The greater the amount of energy evolved by an ion during its passage into the crystalline state, the more stable is the crystal obtained, the more difficult it is to reduce it to a dispersed state, to dissolve and to melt, or to divide again the atoms of the lattice into free ions; the more stable is such a system of minerals, the higher is its ability to accumulate during natural process and the less is it subject to destruction, melting and dissolution. . . .

Furthermore, according to Baturin, studies in crystal chemistry have shown that lattices that are characterized by a medium coördination number of average symmetry and by a smaller radius of the ions display the greatest stability.

There have been other attempts to relate mineral stability to crystal structure. Fairbairn (1943), for example, attempts to correlate the rate or ease of alteration with the *packing index*. This index was defined as the ratio of the ion volume to the volume of the unit cell. Within certain groups of minerals some correlation is apparent. Of two minerals with the same composition, the mineral that has the higher packing index is the more stable. Muir (in Polynov, 1937) has also discussed the relation between crystal structure and mineral stability. Gruner (1950) also attempted to arrange the silicate minerals in the order of their stability. Gruner's arrangement was based on an "energy index" computed from electronegativities of the elements involved and the coördination coefficients. In a general way, Gruner's order agrees with Goldich's stability order and other empirically-determined orders.

MINERALOGICAL MATURITY

Indices of Maturity

The prime interest of the student of sedimentary rocks in the chemical mobility of the rock-making oxides and the stability of the rock-forming minerals is in the concept of sediment maturity. The maturity of a clastic sediment is the extent to which it approaches the ultimate end product to which it is driven by the formative processes that operate upon it. Reiche's weathering potential index is therefore also an index of maturity. The more mature a sediment, the less its weathering potential. This index cannot, however, be used indiscriminately. It is applicable—as a maturity index— only to the residues or their washed equivalents. It cannot be considered a maturity index for rocks of mixed mechanical and chemical origin. Sandstones with infiltrated carbonate cements have a high lime and magnesia content. Restoration of materials which had been removed during weathering raises the weathering potential and obscures the primary mature nature of the sediment to which it has been added.

Vogt (Kennedy, 1951) expressed maturity as the degree of residual character. Vogt assumed, with considerable justification, that the argillaceous sediments would tend to be enriched in alumina as they became more mature. The true enrichment of alumina, however, may be obscured by a change in the amount of the independent quartz component present, with the result that clay sediments with different residual character may contain the same amount of alumina, and vice versa. To eliminate the masking effect of silica, which fluctuates with texture, Vogt recalculated the chemical analysis to the sum of 100, excluding SiO_2 (and TiO_2). In general the three oxides, MgO, CaO, and Na_2O decrease gradually and regularly with increasing residual character, whereas K_2O, SiO_2, and TiO_2 increase. Iron tends to remain constant over a large range in composition.

Alumina perhaps is the least mobile oxide, whereas Na_2O is the oxide most readily removed and at the same time (unlike lime, magnesia, or potash) is not restored to the sediment in the ordinary cycle of sedimentation. The alumina-soda ratio therefore may be used as an abbreviated chemical index of maturity. The maturity of sandstones may also be expressed in mineralogical terms. Quartz is the only chemically and physically durable mineral constituent of the plutonic rocks common enough to be accumulated in great volume. The mineralogical maturity of a sand therefore is expressed by its quartz content. As most of the quartz was originally associated with feldspars, the maturity may also be expressed by the disappearance of the feldspar or by the quartz/feldspar ratio.

TABLE 97. Maturity Indices of Sandstones

Rock Type	Quartz/Feldspar Ratio	Alumina/Soda Ratio	Quartz plus Chert/Feldspar plus Rock Fragments
Average arkosic sandstone	1.1	5.7	1.1
Average graywacke	2.7	4.8	1.2
Average lithic sandstone	9.8	4.5 [a]	2.3
Average orthoquartzite	over 10.0	20.4	....
Average sandstone (Clarke)	5.8	9.6	....

[a] Based on 4 analyses only.

The quartz/feldspar ratio is not so appropriate for the sands derived from feldspar-poor rocks. The paucity of feldspar would lead to a deceptively high quartz/feldspar ratio. The sands derived from a supracrustal complex would contain rock fragments of which none, except chert, have both chemical and mechanical stability. The ratio of chert/noncherty rock fragments would be an appropriate maturity index for such sands. Inasmuch as most sands have a mixed source, the maturity index of most general application would be quartz plus chert/feldspar plus rock fragments. The chemical and mineralogical maturity indices of some of the principal types of sandstone are given in Table 97.

Significance of Maturity

It is not sufficient to measure the maturity of a sediment knowing something of the mobilities of the oxides and the stabilities of the rock-forming minerals; more important is the significance or geological meaning of maturity. Under what conditions are highly mature sediments produced? What does immaturity indicate?

Since maturity is the measure of the approach of a clastic sediment to the stable end type toward which it is driven by the formative processes operating on it, the maturity is also therefore a combined record of the *time* through which such processes have operated and the *intensity* of their action. If the time is brief the end product will be immature regardless of the intensity. If the intensity of action (input of energy per unit time) be low, the end product is immature no matter how long the time. On the other hand, if the intensity is high and the time is long enough, the end product will be mature.[7]

What, in geologic terms, determines the time or duration of action and the intensity of that action? It seems probable that the time or duration is determined largely by *relief*. The rapidity of erosion is a function of relief. High relief promotes a high rate of erosion, whereas low relief is associated with a retarded rate of erosion. Under conditions of rapid erosion, the soil-forming processes lag behind those of transportation, and much incompletely weathered material finds its way into the streams. Under conditions of retarded erosion, the weathering goes to completion, so that only the most stable residues appear in the sediments. In areas of high relief but with youthful topography, some relatively level interstream areas remain. As noted by Krynine (1949), erosion of these areas yields maturely weathered detritus, whereas the sharply incised canyons are the sources of fresh, unweathered materials. Therefore the erosion of such an area will yield both mature and immature products of weathering. In general, the mature products are fine-grained and accumulate mainly in the shale, whereas the immature products are coarse-grained and appear in the sandstones. The separation, however, is never complete nor perfect.

The effects of *climate* are more complex and have been of concern to the

[7] The time-intensity concept was briefly outlined by Krynine (1945); somewhat related ideas were expressed by Folk (1951), Payne (1950), and Keller (1954).

students of soils for many years. On the basis of rainfall, there are two types of climate, namely, arid and humid. Hilgard (1906) reports that the most striking difference between the residues formed in arid and in humid regions is the relative percentages of insoluble materials. The proportion of insolubles is highest in the humid regions where the soils are subjected to thorough leaching. The insoluble material in the average of 696 analyses of soils from humid regions is 84 per cent; it is 69 per cent in an average of 573 analyses of soils from arid regions. Lime tends to accumulate in the soils of arid or semiarid regions. The soils of humid regions, on the other hand, are enriched in alumina and iron. Presumably the finer-grained sediments derived from such soils might show similar differences. Moreover, as the absence of water tends to retard chemical action, the coarser residues produced under arid conditions might contain many unstable minerals.

Temperature is also presumed to influence the rate of weathering and therefore the kind of residues produced. High temperature promotes chemical reactions, although in the absence of water these reactions may be inhibited. Under tropical conditions, where temperature is high and moisture most abundant, weathering appears to be most rigorous, and the residues formed are notably enriched in the oxides of iron and alumina and consequently relatively deficient in silica. The laterites and bauxites are the end products of such tropical soil-forming processes. The shales derived from such parent materials would be alumina-rich, perhaps bauxitic. In general it may be said that the warmer, more humid climates lead to a more complex decomposition of the source rock, whereas a colder or more arid climate is marked by products of lesser maturity.

The actual composition of a sedimentary deposit, however, is the result of interaction or the combined effects of relief and climate on the source rock. A composition that indicates maturity, such as high quartz-to-feldspar and high alumina-to-soda ratios, most likely is the product of a warm humid climate in an area of low relief. Mixtures of stable and unstable materials, such as feldspathic sandstone associated with high alumina and low soda shales, suggest a warm, humid climate in regions of high relief with youthful topography. If the sediment contains only immature products, the area of provenance either is very high in relief with a mature topography or is a region of rigorous climate. In the former case the sands and silts will contain numerous bits of carbonized wood. In general, according to Barrell (1908), the character of the fine fluviatile or wash detritus in the region of its origin may be taken as an index of the climate. The size or abundance of the coarser materials, on the other hand, is a measure of the rapidity of erosion, and hence a measure of topographic relief. As relief is dependent on the balance between uplift and erosion, the character of the coarser materials is therefore also an index to *tectonism*.

MINERALS AND SOURCE ROCKS

The student of clastic sedimentary deposits would like to know the nature and character of the source rock or rocks from which the sediment was derived. Such knowledge might, in part, enable him to identify the source region. Fragments of a distinctive rock or an unusual mineral in the sands might make such identification certain and thus contribute to the understanding of the paleogeography of the ancient times. In addition, events outside the basin of sedimentation influence the kind and character of the sediments accumulating in the basin. Sharp uplift and erosion in the source region will release a flood of new minerals not heretofore present; volcanism outside the basin will be registered by influx of a new and distinctive mineral assemblage. It is necessary, therefore, to know and recognize the mineral suites distinctive and characteristic of the contrasting source rocks.

It is obviously important to know if a sediment is a first-cycle sediment derived from a crystalline rock or whether it is second cycle and is derived from earlier sediments. Many properties, such as roundness, may be inherited from earlier cycles of abrasion, so that interpretation of the history of a given sediment is complex. The average sandstone, according to Krynine, consists of about 30 per cent reworked material, about 25 per cent of new material of igneous derivation, and 45 per cent of materials derived from metamorphic sources.

The distinction between first cycle and multicycle materials is fundamental; the distinction between an igneous and a metamorphic origin of the debris is less significant. More important, however, is the distinction between a plutonic and a supracrustal origin. The *depth* from which the material comes is something of a measure of the magnitude of uplift responsible for the debris. Accordingly the gneisses and plutonic igneous rocks are grouped together as are the low-rank metamorphic and sedimentary rocks. The plutonic rocks are coarse-grained and yield quartz and feldspar, which constitute the bulk of most sands. The supracrustal rocks yield quartz (second-cycle) and rock particles of sand grade. The feldspar/rock fragment ratio has been used (see chapter on sandstones) as a provenance index of the sands and is a measure of the relative contributions of the plutonic and supracrustal zones, respectively. As might be expected, the sediments of supracrustal derivation greatly exceed those of plutonic descent. Subgraywackes and related sandstones loaded with rock particles are more common than the arkosic sandstones.

Both the light and the heavy minerals have been used as guides to provenance although most reliance has been placed on the latter.

As noted elsewhere (p. 120) the type of quartz is a guide to the nature of the source rock. In general, metamorphic quartz is characterized by min-

TABLE 98. Detrital Mineral Suites Characteristic of Source Rock Types[a]

REWORKED SEDIMENTS

Barite	Rutile
Glauconite	
Quartz (esp. with worn overgrowths)	*Tourmaline, rounded*
Chert	*Zircon, rounded*
Quartzite fragments (orthoquartzite type)	
Leucoxene	

LOW-RANK METAMORPHIC

Slate and *phyllite* fragments	*Quartz* and *quartzite* fragments (meta-quartzite type)
Biotite and muscovite	
Chlorite (if clastic)	*Tourmaline* (small pale brown euhedra carbonaceous inclusions)
Feldspars generally absent	
	Leucoxene

HIGH-RANK METAMORPHIC

Garnet	*Staurolite*
Hornblende (blue-green variety)	*Quartz* (metamorphic variety)
Kyanite	Muscovite and biotite
Sillimanite	Feldspar (acid plagioclase)
Andalusite	*Epidote*
	Zoisite
	Magnetite

ACID IGNEOUS

Apatite	Sphene
Biotite	*Zircon,* euhedra
Hornblende	*Quartz* (igneous variety)
Monazite	*Microcline*
Muscovite	Magnetite
	Tourmaline, small pink euhedra

BASIC IGNEOUS

Anatase	*Leucoxene*
Augite	Olivine
Brookite	*Rutile*
Hypersthene	Plagioclase, intermediate
Ilmenite and magnetite	Serpentine
Chromite	

PEGMATITE

Fluorite	*Monazite*
Tourmaline, typically blue (indicolite)	*Muscovite*
Garnet	Topaz
	Albite
	Microcline

[a] Italicized species are more common.

eral inclusions, wavy extinction, and other strain effects, and an elongate form. Igneous quartz contains no inclusions or only liquid and gas inclusions, is relatively strain-free, and is more nearly equidimensional. Of sedimentary provenance is highly rounded and frosted quartz, quartz with overgrowths, and chalcedonic forms of silica (chert). Feldspar has proved less useful as a guide to the nature of the source rock, though in theory some differences between feldspar of one provenance and that of another should exist (p. 126).

The heavy minerals have been found exceptionally useful as clues to the nature of the source rocks (Boswell, 1933, pp. 47–59). Some minerals are diagnostic of a particular type of source rock. Others, like quartz, are more nearly ubiquitous and occur in nearly all possible parent materials. In this case, as in the case of quartz, the varietal features, such as inclusions, serve as a guide to the rock type. Krynine's work on tourmaline, in which he was able to recognize thirteen subspecies of this mineral, illustrates the use of varietal properties (Krynine, 1946). Five main types of large-scale provenance were described by Krynine. These are (1) granitic tourmaline, (2) pegmatitic tourmaline, (3) tourmaline from pegmatized, injected metamorphic terranes, (4) sedimentary authigenic tourmaline, and (5) tourmaline reworked from older sediments. Each tourmaline type has distinctive optical and morphological properties which enable one to recognize and correctly interpret the provenance of the sediment.

The more common mineral suites indicative of provenance are given in Table 98.

HEAVY MINERAL ZONES

That beds of differing geologic ages, even in the same district, have differing assemblages of heavy minerals is a common observation. Are these differences random or systematic? What is their relation to the age of the beds? And what is the cause of such differences? These are questions which require consideration.

It now seems probable that the variations in mineral composition from bed to bed are not haphazard or random. Careful study of heavy mineral zones in Tertiary and Mesozoic sections, in which such zones appear to be the most clearly defined, shows two things. First, the number of mineral species appears to increase as one goes from older to younger beds; second, the order of appearance of the minerals, even in widely separated areas, is remarkably similar. If one neglects stray occurrences and counts only those minerals present in half or more of the samples studied, the trend appears quite clear. Stow (1938), for example, zoned the Cretaceous and Tertiary beds in the Bighorn Basin (Fig. 115). The zones defined by him contained, from older to younger, 3, 5, 6, and 7 species in the order listed. Cogen (1940) defined four heavy mineral zones in the Tertiary of the Gulf Coast region (Fig. 115). The number of mineral species (in half or more of the samples) were 5, 6, 8, and 8, in the four zones (from oldest to youngest). Anderson's (1948) work on the Coastal Plain sediments of Maryland (Fig. 116) discloses much the same increase in number of species as one approaches the present. The Triassic contained 5 species, the Lower Cretaceous has 6, the Upper Cretaceous 8 (Arundel) and 9 (Raritan), the Tertiary has 9 (Choptank and Pleistocene) or 10 (Yorktown).

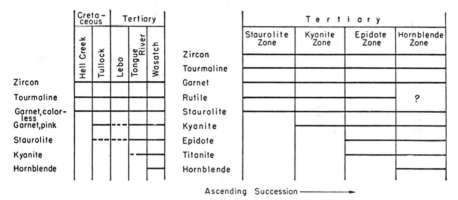

FIG. 115.   Heavy mineral zones. Solid line, present in more than half of samples; dashed line, present in less than half of the samples. Left, Big Horn Basin (data from Stow, 1938); right, Gulf Coast (data from Cogen, 1940).

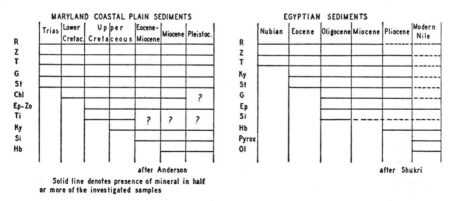

FIG. 116.   Heavy mineral zones. Same conventions as in Fig. 115. Left, Atlantic Coastal plain of Maryland (data from Anderson, 1948); right, Egyptian sediments (data from Shukri and others, 1954).

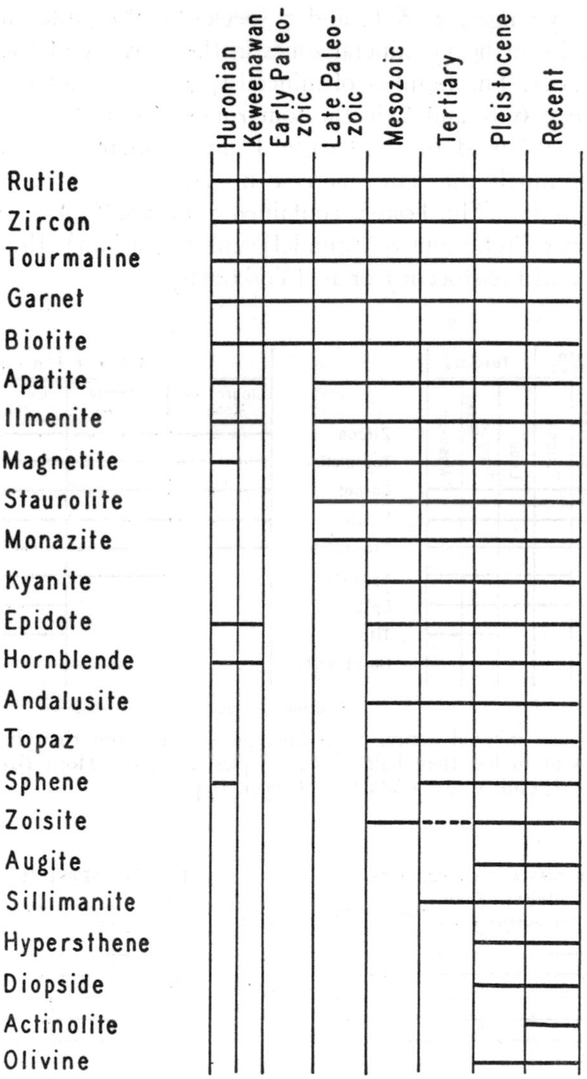

Column headers (left to right): Huronian · Keweenawan · Early Paleozoic · Late Paleozoic · Mesozoic · Tertiary · Pleistocene · Recent

Rutile
Zircon
Tourmaline
Garnet
Biotite
Apatite
Ilmenite
Magnetite
Staurolite
Monazite
Kyanite
Epidote
Hornblende
Andalusite
Topaz
Sphene
Zoisite
Augite
Sillimanite
Hypersthene
Diopside
Actinolite
Olivine

Fig. 117. Mineral persistence chart. Line indicates presence of mineral in *relative* frequency (Recent = 100) of 50 or greater (Pettijohn, 1941, p. 619).

Not only is this increase common in individual districts or stratigraphic sections but it seems to be true on a world-wide basis as noted by Boswell (1933) and Pettijohn (1941) (Fig. 117). Pettijohn, in particular, has made an analysis of the literature on the mineralogy of sands of all ages. If the species reported in more than half of the investigated formations of each

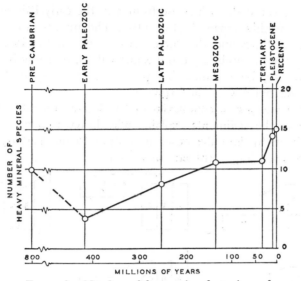

FIG. 118. Number of heavy-mineral species and age of deposit. The number of species in more than half of the reported formations is plotted against the age of the beds (Pettijohn, 1941).

TABLE 99. Order of Appearance of Index Species in Heavy Mineral Zones[a]

Stow (1938)	Cogen (1940)	Anderson (1948)	Evans, Hayman, and Majeed (1933)	Shukri (1954)
Cretaceous-Tertiary Wyoming	Tertiary Gulf Coast	Triassic-Cretaceous-Tertiary Atlantic Coastal Plain	Tertiary Burma	Cretaceous-Tertiary Egypt
		Rutile[b]	Rutile[b]	Rutile[b]
Zircon[b]	Zircon[b]	Zircon[b]	Zircon[b]	Zircon[b]
Tourmaline[b]	Tourmaline[b]	Tourmaline[b]		Tourmaline[b]
Garnet[b]	Garnet[b]	Garnet[b]	Garnet	
Staurolite	Staurolite[b]	Staurolite[b]	Staurolite	Staurolite
Kyanite	Kyanite			Kyanite
		Chloritoid	Chloritoid	
	Epidote	Epidote	Epidote	Epidote
	Sphene	Sphene		Garnet
		Kyanite		
Hornblende	Hornblende	Hornblende	Hornblende	Hornblende

[a] Only minerals common to 3 or more authors included in table.
[b] Present in lowest formation; order in table not significant.

time period are counted, an increase from 5 in the early Paleozoic to 17 in the Recent is readily apparent (Fig. 118). The increase in complexity is greatest in later times and the curve rises steeply in the Pleistocene and Recent. Only the Precambrian record is anomalous, probably because of the formation *in situ*, by metamorphic processes, of many mineral species, notably epidote, hornblende, and sphene.

The general increase in complexity of the heavy mineral suite with decreasing age of the sediments explains why heavy mineral zones are so difficult to define in the older rocks in contrast to the Tertiary. The older strata carry a much impoverished mineral suite.

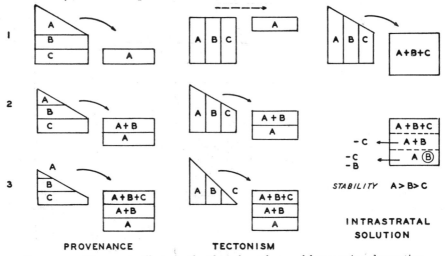

Fig. 119.   Diagram to illustrate the three hypotheses of heavy mineral zonation.

As noted above, the mineral zones of several unrelated and geographically separated areas are alike, not only in the increase in number of minerals species in each zone but also in the order of appearance of many of the dominant minerals (Figs. 115, 116, 117, and Table 99). It is certainly not accidental that hornblende is most typical of the highest zones and that the lowest zones are restricted to minerals like tourmaline, zircon, rutile, staurolite, and garnet. Kyanite, epidote, and titanite seem more characteristic of the intermediate zones. The minerals in the lower zones, as a rule, are also present in the higher zones, so that, as noted, the latter have an enlarged or enriched suite. These observations are not without exception. The order of appearance of the species is not always the same; there are cases where the minerals of the lower zones do not persist into the higher ones. And there are cases where a mineral seems to appear prematurely, then drop out and reappear again at a higher stratigraphic level.

How then are the apparent increase in complexity of the suite and the apparently standard order of appearance of the several species to be explained? Several hypotheses have been set forth (Fig. 119). One explains the heavy minerals zones as stability zones. This view supposes that all sediments deposited had about the same suite at the time of deposition, but that because of intrastratal solution, the deeper and older beds have lost all unstable species. The probability of survival is a function of depth of burial and of time. The deeper the burial and/or the older the rock the less probable the presence of a given species. Pettijohn (1941) has supported this hypothesis and pointed out that the order of appearance, from older to younger zones, of the several index minerals is the inverse of the stability order as determined by other studies unrelated to the mineral zoning problem. Moreover, there is considerable direct evidence of the efficacy of intrastratal solution such as Bramlette's observations on the contrasting heavy mineral content of calcareous sandstones and their matrix (Bramlette, 1941) as well as the visual evidence of corrosion and solution of many species in the deeper zones (Edelman and Doeglas, 1931).

This interpretation has been challenged by Krynine (1942) who attributed the zoning, as do nearly all the earlier students of the subject, to provenance. Krynine did not explain the order of appearance common to many otherwise unrelated sections. It is conceivable, however, that progressive denudation would lead to increasing complexity of the suite. As erosion proceeded, deeper levels in the crust would become contributors to the basin of sedimentation. Moreover, the minerals of the deeper zones are, on the average, the least stable, so that there might be both a normal order of succession and a succession that would correlate with the stability order.

A third alternative explanation might be a correlation between the mineral sequence and progressive uplift in the source area. Under this thesis, the terrane, of varied lithology, would lie near base level at the initial stages and would be progressively elevated. During the initial stages only the most stable species escape destruction in the soil profile; in the final stages even the least stable minerals would appear in the sediment.

Heavy mineral zones, then, of somewhat similar character and with a similar sequence of species might be produced in several unlike ways. It is important to discriminate between these alternatives. Obviously if the heavy minerals zones are stability zones only, they have little or no stratigraphic significance. If they result from progressive denudation or progressive tectonism, the heavy suite will change with time, and the mineral zones might be very useful as an aid to stratigraphic correlation. The zoning may result from simultaneous operation of several factors and be related both to stability and to provenance. If so, the unraveling of the problem of zones and sorting out of factors of no stratigraphic value from those of value is much more complex than heretofore supposed. Perhaps varietal characters of the same species would assist in this task. The appearance of new and different varieties of zircon would be in nowise related to intrastratal solution or differential loss by weathering in the distributive province. Only progressive denudation and unroofing of new source rocks would explain the changing character of the zircon. Careful work with the tourmaline might, like zircon, assist in the solution of the mineral zone problem.

Although any of the hypotheses might be adequate for a local sequence or a single tectonic cycle, none is proved for the geologic column as a whole. The increasing complexity with decreasing age *could* be a reflection of stability only and to the author this seems most probable. It has been claimed, however, that the orogenies are becoming more closely spaced and that the rate of sedimentation shows a progressive increase with the passage of time. If so, the mineral assemblage should increase in complexity with time. On the other hand, none of the older sediments, even those following notable orogenies, seem to be so rich as the Pleistocene and Recent sands, and it is hard to escape the conclusion that their impoverishment is somehow related to long-continued intrastratal solution.

PROVENANCE AND TEXTURE

The texture of a clastic sediment, especially the "washed residue" group of sediments, is the result of the action of the washing processes on the original weathered residuum. Many of the textural attributes of the sediment are inherited from the weathered residues; others are imposed by the washing processes.

The texture of the residuum itself varies with the nature of the parent rock, the dominant weathering process, and the maturity of the end product. Immature or incompletely decomposed rock materials are coarse. If the source rock is block yielding, an angular rubble is produced; if the source rock itself is coarse-grained and undergoes granular distintegration instead, the residue is a coarse ill-sorted sand. The sand grains will be largely monomineralic, though the larger particles may be polygranular (Table 14, p. 50). In some cases these materials are no less well sorted than the average river sand (Fig. 120, A). If chemical decay is more advanced, a larger proportion of the material is contained in the silt grades (Fig. 120, C). Many of the products of weathering, both chemical and mechanical, have a size distribution that is closely similar to that produced by crushing, as is given by the Rosin law distribution (Krumbein and Tisdel, 1940) (Fig. 21).

Dake (1921) has pointed out the fact that in sandstones the proportion of sand grains over 0.6 millimeter in diameter is quite insignificant. This applies only to true quartz grains—not to the polygranular rock fragments.

According to Dake, the observed limit on the maximum size is determined by the size distribution of the quartz grains in the ultimate source rock, probably a rock of granitic texture and composition. Dake's examination of a number of granites, excluding pegmatites, showed that the prevalence of grains 1 millimeter or less was overwhelming. Of 420 grains measured, only 161 were over 0.6 millimeter, and about half of these (79) were so badly fractured that they would not yield sand grains larger than 0.6 millimeter.

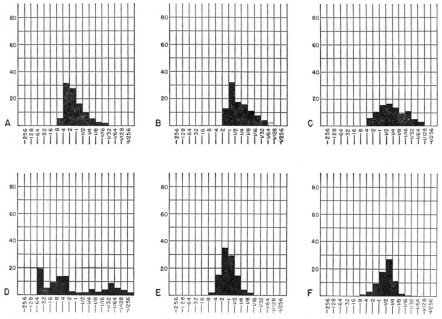

Fig. 120. Mechanical composition of residual materials and related deposits. **A:** Average of five samples of disintegrated granitic and gneissic boulders from glacial outwash (Krumbein and Tisdel, 1940). **B:** Detritus from weathered gneiss, District of Columbia (Wentworth, 1931). **C:** Average of two samples of residual soil over gneiss, North Carolina (Krumbein and Tisdel, 1940), (analyses incomplete, about 6 per cent under $\frac{1}{128}$ mm). **D:** Rain-washed slope detritus (Wentworth, 1931). **E:** Sand from dry wash, El Centro, Calif. (essentially a disintegrated granite). **F:** Dry wash, Superior, Ariz.

Thus only 20 per cent (82) were of such size and character as to yield sand exceeding 0.6 millimeter. Only 9 per cent were over 1 millimeter in size.

Ingerson and Ramisch (1942) have shown that broken and unworn grains of quartz from granites have an original elongation that is parallel to the crystallographic c axis and parallel also to the unit rhombohedral faces. Subsequent wearing off of the irregularities of such grains would produce elongate rounded grains of quartz, a large number of which are elongated parallel to the c axis as Wayland (1939) had noted earlier. The quartz grains of the schists are more elongated than those of the granites (Bokman, 1952). This initial difference in grain shape persists and assists in the determination of the provenance of a sand or sandstone.

The maturity of a sediment may be textural as well as compositional. The criteria for the recognition of the several stages of textural maturity have been stated by Folk (1951). The passage from an initial clayey, poorly sorted, angular sediment to a completely matured, rounded, and sorted sand is marked by three stages (Fig. 121). These are (1) removal of the clay, (2) attainment of good sorting of the nonclay fraction, and (3) rounding of the quartz grains. The first two steps are quickly achieved, even by the brief transport of ephemeral streams. The last stage is attained only after prolonged transport and characterizes only the mineralogically mature multi-cycle sands or the sands of certain beaches.

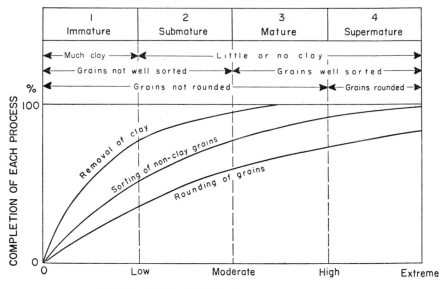

FIG. 121.   Stages of textural maturity (after Folk, 1951).

REFERENCES CITED AND BIBLIOGRAPHY

Allen, V. T. (1948), Weathering and heavy minerals, *J. Sediment. Petrol.*, vol. 18, pp. 38–42.

Anderson, J. L., and others (1948), Cretaceous and Tertiary subsurface geology, *Maryland Dept. Geol. Mines Water Resources, Bull.* 2, pp. 1–113.

Barrell, J. (1908), Relations between climate and terrestrial deposits, *J. Geol.*, vol. 16, p. 183.

Baturin, V. P. (1942), On stability and formation of minerals of abyssal geospheres in the stratisphere, *Compt. rend. acad. sci. URSS*, vol. 37, no. 1, pp. 32–34.

Bokman, John (1952), Clastic quartz particles as indices of provenance, *J. Sediment. Petrol.*, vol. 22, pp. 17–24.

Boswell, P. G. H. (1933), *On the mineralogy of sedimentary rocks*, London, Murby, pp. 37–46; 47–59.

Bramlette, M. N. (1941), The stability of minerals in sandstone, *J. Sediment. Petrol.*, vol. 11, pp. 32–36.

Cogen, W. M. (1940), Heavy mineral zones of Louisiana and Texas Gulf Coast sediments, *Bull. Am. Assoc. Petroleum Geol.*, vol. 24, pp. 2069 ff.

Dake, C. L. (1921), The problem of the St. Peter sandstone, *Missouri Univ. School Mines and Metal., Bull.*, tech. series, vol. 6, pp. 158 ff.

Dryden, Lincoln and Dryden, Clarissa (1946), Comparative rates of weathering of some common heavy minerals, *J. Sediment. Petrol.*, vol. 16, pp. 91–96.

Edelmann, C. H. (1931), Diagenetische Umwandlungserschienungen and detritischen Pyroxenen und Amphibolen, *Fortschr. Mineral Krist. Petrog.*, vol. 16, pp. 67–68.

Edelmann, C. H. and Docglas, D. J. (1931), Reliktstrukturen detritischen Pyroxene und Amphibole, *Mineral. u. Petrog. Mitt.*, vol. 42, pp. 482–490.

Evans, P., Hayman, R. J. and Majeed, M. A. (1933), The graphical representation of heavy mineral analyses, *Proc. World Petroleum Congr.*, 1933 (London), vol. 1, pp. 251–256.

Fairbairn, H. W. (1943), Packing in ionic minerals, *Bull. Geol. Soc. Amer.*, vol. 54, pp. 1305–1374.

Folk, R. L. (1951), Stages of textural maturity in sedimentary rocks, *J. Sediment. Petrol.*, vol. 21, pp. 127–130.

Goldich, S. S. (1938), A study in rock weathering, *J. Geol.*, vol. 46, pp. 17–58.

Goldstein, August, Jr. (1950), Mineralogy of some Cretaceous sandstones from the Colorado Front Range, *J. Sediment. Petrol.*, vol. 20, pp. 85–97.

Gruner, J. W. (1950), An attempt to arrange silicates in the order of reaction energies at relatively low temperatures, *Amer. Mineralogist*, vol. 35, pp. 137–148.

Hilgard, E. W. (1906), *Soils*, New York, Macmillan, pp. 377, 387.

Ingerson, Earl, and Ramisch, J. L. (1942), Origin of shapes of quartz sand grains, *Am. Mineralogist*, vol. 27, pp. 595–606.

Keller, W. D. (1954), The energy factor in sedimentation, *J. Sediment. Petrol.*, vol. 24, pp. 62–68.

Kennedy, W. Q. (1951), Sedimentary differentiation as a factor in Moine-Torridonian correlation, *Geol. Mag.*, vol. 88, pp. 257–266.

Krumbein, W. S. and Tisdel, F. W. (1940), Size distribution of source rocks of sediments, *Am. J. Sci.*, vol. 238, pp. 296–305.

Krynine, P. D. (1942), Provenance versus mineral stability as a controlling factor in the composition of sediments (abstract), *Bull. Geol. Soc. Amer.*, vol. 53, pp. 1850–1851.

Krynine, P. D. (1949), The origin of red beds, *Trans. N.Y. Acad. Sci.*, ser. 2, vol. 11, pp. 60–67.

Krynine, P. D. (1946), The tourmaline group in sediments, *J. Geol.*, vol. 54, pp. 65–87.

Leith, C. K. and Mead, W. J. (1915), *Metamorphic geology*, New York, Holt, pp. 16–17.

Mackie, Wm. (1925), The principles that regulate the distribution of particles of heavy minerals in sedimentary rocks, as illustrated by the sandstones of the northeast of Scotland, *Trans. Edinburgh Geol. Soc.*, vol. 11, pp. 138–164.

Milner, H. B. (1922), The nature and origin of the Pliocene deposits of the county of Cornwall, etc., *Quart. J. Geol. Soc. London*, vol. 78, p. 366.

Milner, H. B. (1940), *Sedimentary petrography*, 3d ed., London, Murby.

Payne, T. G. (1950), unpublished communication.

Pettijohn, F. J. (1941), Persistence of heavy minerals and geologic age, *J. Geol.*, vol. 49, pp. 610–625.

Polynov, B. B. (1937), *Cycle of weathering* (trans. by A. Muir), London, Murby.

Reiche, Parry (1943), Graphic representation of chemical weathering, *J. Sediment. Petrol.*, vol. 13, pp. 58–68.

Reiche, Parry (1950), A survey of weathering processes and products, *Univ. New Mexico Publ. Geol.*, no. 3.

Shukri, M. N. and El-Ayouty, M. K. (1954), The mineralogy of Eocene and later sediments in the Anqabia area—Cairo-Suez district, *Bull. Faculty Sci.*, Cairo Univ., no. 32, pp. 47–61.

Sindowski, F. K. H. (1949), Results and problems of heavy mineral analysis in Germany: a review of sedimentary-petrological papers, 1936–1948, *J. Sediment. Petrol.*, vol. 19, pp. 3–25.

Smithson, F. (1939), Statistical methods in sedimentary petrology, *Geol. Mag.*, vol. 76, pp. 417–427.

Smithson, F. (1941), The alteration of detrital minerals in the Mesozoic rocks of Yorkshire, *Geol. Mag.*, vol. 78, pp. 97–112.

Smithson, F. (1942), The Middle Jurassic rocks of Yorkshire: a petrological and palaeogeographical study, *Quart. J. Geol. Soc. London*, vol. 98, pp. 27–59.

Smithson, F. (1950), The mineralogy of arenaceous sediments, *Science Progress*, vol. 149, pp. 17–21.

Steidtmann, Edward (1908), A graphic comparison of the alteration of rocks by weathering with their alteration by hot solutions, *Econ Geol.*, vol. 3, pp. 381–409.

Stow, M. H. (1938), Dating Cretaceous-Eocene tectonic movements in Big Horn Basin by heavy minerals, *Bull. Geol. Soc. Amer.*, vol. 49, pp. 731–762.

Vogt, T. (1927), Geology and petrology of the Sulitelma district, *Norg. Geol. Undersökelse*, Nr. 121.

Wayland, R. G. (1939), Optical orientation in elongate clastic quartz, *Am. J. Sci.*, vol. 237, pp. 99–109.

12

Dispersal

INTRODUCTION

THE RESIDUES produced by the destruction of pre-existing rocks are subject, from the moment of their inception, to dispersal by various geologic agents —most especially by moving fluids—both air and water, and to a lesser extent by moving ice. The more common agents of dispersal sort the materials handled and modify them in various ways. Ultimately these materials come to rest somewhere as a sedimentary deposit—the sedimentary rock to be.

The geologist must, from his examination of the sedimentary rock, ascertain both the direction from which its components came and the distance which they traveled. The *direction* of travel may, in many cases, be determined by study of the vector properties (fabric, cross-bedding, and so forth) of the deposit (which register or record the direction of current movement). The *distance* of transport is less readily determined but must be in some way related to those scalar properties (mineral composition, roundness, and so forth) of the sediment which are modified by the sorting and abrasive action accompanying transportation. The problem is much complicated, however, by the fact that some of the effects of transport are cumulative and may be inherited from previous cycles of transport. The problem, though rendered complex, is not insoluble, and close observation of several unrelated properties may make possible reasonable estimates of the distance of travel (as well as the direction of movement).

Although the products of weathering may be widely dispersed, there is a tendency for those produced in any one area to move out in a systematic manner and to be spread out over a rather well-defined region or area. Such a region or area, whether large or small is a dispersal shadow deposited

PLATE 37

LIMESTONE FRAGMENTS AT VARIOUS STAGES OF ABRASION BY TUMBLING BARREL

Upper left: Original fragments; **upper right:** 0.5 mile; **left center:** 1.0 mile; **right center:** 5.0 miles; **lower left:** 9.0 miles; **lower right:** 20.0 miles. See Fig. 127 for data on size, shape, and roundness of these pebbles at various distances. (Krumbein, *J. Geol.*, vol. 49, 1941, p. 490.)

PLATE 38

EFFECT OF STREAM TRANSPORTATION ON GRANODIORITE PEBBLES, SAN GABRIEL CANYON, CALIF.

The upper sample was collected near the source of the gravel and has a roundness of 0.28; the lower sample was 5.5 miles downstream and shows a roundless of 0.44. (Krumbein, *Bull. Geol. Soc. Amer.*, vol. 51, 1940, pl. 1.)

downcurrent from the generating or source area. The dispersal shadow may be merely the peripheral area near an ore body contaminated by metallic ions migrating from said ore body, or a boulder train on the lee side of a resistant knob overridden by ice, or a great sedimentary sheet or apron peripheral to the source region and built out into the sea.

The problem of delimiting the area of dispersal or *petrographic province*, the problem of determining the direction of migration of material (ion, sand grain, or boulder) and the problem of estimating the distance which it has moved is common to each. In this chapter each of these problems will be outlined and the progress toward their solution summarized. We will first consider the *effects* of transportation on the scalar properties and the problem of estimating the distance of travel; second, the relations between vector properties and the current direction will be explored; finally, the mapping or delimitation of petrographic provinces and the closely related subject of facies will be outlined as will also the problem of provincial succession or modification through time.

The problems of provenance and dispersal are primarily the problems of the clastic sediments. The materials which go into solution and become a part of the oceans and reappear again as a chemical or biochemical precipitate carry no record of their provenance or distance and direction of transport. The chemical sediments, unlike the clastic sediments, are documents of milieu or the chemical environment in which they form. The clastic sediments, on the other hand, are documents of provenance and dispersal and are comparatively insensitive to the chemical environment in which they accumulate.[1]

SIZE AND DISPERSION

Introduction

The *effects* of transportation on the materials transported are only incompletely understood. The prevailing concepts are based mainly on deductive reasoning and supported by very little experimental or field data. Although most attention has been given to the effects of transport on the size of the materials moved, we cannot yet be certain as to the cause of the observed effects. In general the sands and gravels carried by streams appear to decrease in size downstream, and since the corners and surfaces of the larger materials are rounded and smoothed, it has been presumed that abrasion is an active process during transport and that the downcurrent decrease in size therefore is caused by such wear. In part this is probably true, but as pointed out be-

---

[1] Some sediments, notably the clays, though mechanically transported, are reactive, and therefore sensitive to the character of the medium in which they are deposited. They thus combine in some measure the qualities of both clastic and chemical sediments.

low, the size decline in some cases is probably not solely the result of abrasive action but instead of a progressive sorting action. What are the facts?

Size and Distance

Despite the general observation that the size of the clastic elements tends to decrease in the downcurrent direction, there are comparatively few actual field measurements of such changes. Sternberg (1874) was perhaps the first to record actual sizes of pebbles and study the relation of size to distance

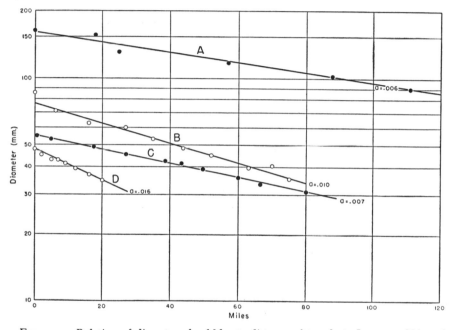

Fig. 122. Relation of diameter of pebbles to distance of travel. **A:** Largest cobbles of Rhine River (after Sternberg and Barrell, 1925). **B:** River Mur (after Grabau, 1913, from Hochenburger, 1886). **C:** Limestone test piece, T-33, in abrasion mill (after Wentworth, 1918). **D:** Limestone in abrasion mill (after Krumbein, 1941), a is coefficient of size reduction.

of transport. He measured the maximum and average size of the pebbles in the channel of the Rhine from Basel downstream a distance of about 160 miles (Fig. 122). Sternberg not only observed the decline in size in the downcurrent direction, but concluded that the decline was proportional to the weight of the pebble in water and to the distance traveled. This rule seems to be the best expression of our knowledge of the subject to date and is in agreement with some other field observations. As noted by Barrell

(1925), Sternberg's law may be expressed mathematically as a negative exponential, $W = W_o e^{-as}$, where W is the weight at any distance s, W_o is the initial weight of the pebble, and a is the coefficient of size reduction. This relation is also true if the size is expressed as the diameter rather than as the weight. Sternberg also noted that the gradient of a river follows a logarithmic curve; therefore the conclusion is that both gravel size and gradient of a single stream are related under the same general law.

This relationship has been emphasized by Shulits (1941). Shulits, however, assumed that the size decrease was due solely to abrasion and that the river profile therefore was in some way a function of the hardness of the

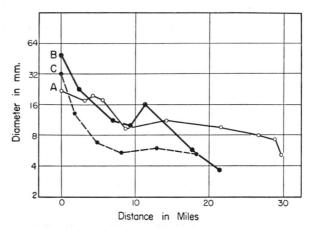

Fig. 123. Relation of mean size to distance of travel, Black Hills (S.D.) streams. **A:** Rapid Creek. **B:** Bear Butte Creek. **C:** Battle Creek (after Plumley, 1948).

materials carried. Shulits admits, however, that abrasion may not be involved and that the coefficient of weight decrease derived by study of the stream profile does not carry any implication as to the processes by which this decrease came about.

Actual field studies of other streams show that the gravel does in fact commonly decline exponentially. Such seems to be the case of the gravel in the river Mur (Hochenburger, in Grabau, 1913) and of the largest boulders in the Arroyo Seco (Krumbein, 1942). A similar exponential decline in size in the downcurrent direction has been noted on an alluvial fan (Chawner, in Krumbein, 1942). As Krumbein (1937) has shown that the surface of an alluvial fan declines exponentially and as Blissenbach (1952) has shown the maximum sizes of fragment and the slopes of several fans to be closely correlated, it seems probable that the size decline on these fans is also exponential.

Plumley (1948) measured the downstream decline in size of the gravels in three streams in the Black Hills of South Dakota. Both gradient and mean size of the gravels decreased in the downstream direction (Fig. 123). the relation between the two was expressed by Plumley as $M_\phi = a + bG$, where M_ϕ is the phi mean size, G is the gradient in feet per mile, and a and b are constants. The value of b is a measure of the slope of the curve. As the profile of the Black Hills streams was not an exponential, the size decline was not exponential.

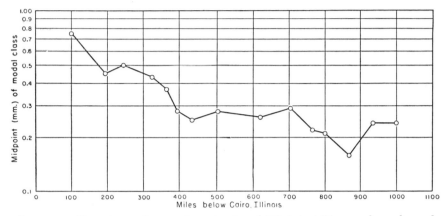

FIG. 124. Downstream decrease in grain size of Mississippi River sands as shown by mid-points of modal size class. Moving average of three values (data from Russell and Taylor, 1937).

The downcurrent size changes of the streams carrying primarily sands is less well known. The sands of the Mississippi decrease notably downstream (Fig. 124) as do the sands of the River Tessin (Burri, 1929). In both cases the downstream decrease fluctuates widely from station to station due to the accidents of sampling, and in the case of the Tessin, by marked size increases correlated with local oversteepened portions of the stream profile.

Systematic size decrease in the downcurrent direction of littoral drift is reported by MacCarthy (1931) and by Pettijohn and Lundahl (1943) (Figs. 125, 126). The latter authors report a 50 per cent decline in size in about 7 miles of shore drift, which is about the same magnitude of decrease reported by MacCarthy in about 130 miles of movement along an Atlantic coast beach, and about equal to the decline in the Mississippi in the last 1100 miles of its course. Krumbein and Griffith (1938) record a sharp decrease in size in limestone fragments in but a few hundred feet of movement away from the parent ledges in a pocket beach of Lake Michigan. An abnormal *increase* in the size of beach materials in the direction of their migration is reported from Cape Cod by Schalk (1938).

The effect of glacial transport on size is almost unknown, though Shaler (1893) reports a decrease in both the maximum and the average size of fragments within a boulder train in Rhode Island.

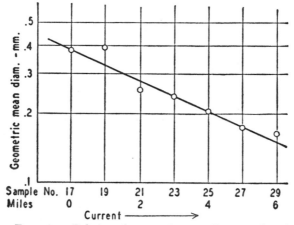

FIG. 125. Relation of geometric mean diameter of sand sample to position on beach, Cedar Point, Lake Erie (from Pettijohn and Lundahl, 1943).

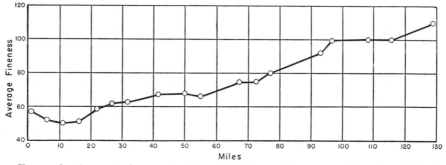

FIG. 126. Apparent decrease in size with distance of transport of sand on Atlantic coastal beach (from MacCarthy, 1931).

It is apparent from the above observations that in general the size of the clastic elements carried in a current progressively decreases in the direction of transport. It is apparent that the decrease in stream-carried materials is closely correlated with the gradient, the gradient or slope being a function of the third power of the bed-load diameters (Schoklitsch, 1933). If the gradient diminishes exponentially, so will the size. But as noted by Plumley, other factors, such as the mean discharge of the stream and the resistance of the materials, will also govern the decrease in size. Size decline during transport also characterizes shore-drift materials and probably ice-borne debris.

It is also clear that although the rate of size decline varies widely in different situations, theoretically the direction of current flow and perhaps the distance of transport of a clastic sediment could be estimated by mapping the maximum or mean size of the clastic elements and by drawing isopleths through equal size values and sketching normals thereto.

It remains to inquire into the causes of the size declines observed.

Size Reduction Processes

The downcurrent size decline of clastic sediments has generally been attributed to abrasion or other size reduction processes. It is by no means certain, however, that the observed diminution in size in any given case is due to abrasion. In some cases it cannot be so explained.

Abrasion

Abrasion is the general term meaning wearing away, or attrition. As such it is applied to almost any mechanical process of size reduction. Several workers, however, have recognized the operation of one or more size-reduction processes. Marshall (1927), for example, defines three processes of size reduction, namely, (1) abrasion (in a restricted sense), (2) impact, and (3) grinding. Marshall defines *abrasion* as the effect of rubbing one pebble against another. It is by far the slowest of the several processes of wear. *Impact* is the effect of definite blows of relatively large fragments on others which are relatively small. This action, of course, could occur only if there were an appreciable disparity in the sizes of the largest and smallest fragments. If such disparity does exist, and if the larger sizes greatly predominate, the smallest sizes undergo heavy losses in a short period of time. *Grinding* is the crushing of small grains by continued contact and pressure of pebbles of somewhat larger size. It was found to be more rapid in its action than impact. Sand, mixed with gravel, was reduced to silt and clay in but a few hours in an abrasion mill.

Wadell (1932a) has discussed the size-reduction processes and has recognized four; namely, solution, attrition, chipping, and splitting. The differences are primarily a matter of the ratio of the size of the particles removed to the size of the original fragment. The mode of action is not considered. If the particles removed are of molecular or smaller size, the term *solution* is applied. If the material removed is larger than a molecule but not visible with an ordinary microscope, the term *solution* perhaps should still be applied because a collodial suspension will be produced. If the particles are visible but in any case have a diameter less than $\frac{1}{150}$ that of the fragment subject to wear, the process is termed *attrition*. In case the material removed is still larger, such as would result from flaking off of the corners, the term *chipping* is appropriate. If the destruction process produces two or three subequal fragments, the term *splitting* may be employed. It seems likely that Marshall's impact and grinding result in chipping and splitting.

One type of abrasion, not often kept in mind and not yet properly evaluated, is *blasting*. This is the process of abrasion (or attrition) accomplished by the movement of fine particles past a larger stationary fragment. The familiar einkanter and dreikanter forms are the product of sandblast action by the sand. Less well known are the products of the wet-blasting action of streams (see page 66).

No complete or comprehensive study has been made of the effects of abrasion on sedimentary particles. Summaries of our knowledge of the subject have been presented by Russell (1939) and by Pettijohn (1942). The abrasive processes may be studied in the field and in the laboratory. In the field one may examine closely the sedimentary materials that have been transported; compare these with the untransported fragments and note the differences. Many, but not all, such differences are due to abrasive action. Some are the result of sorting action and it is difficult to know what should be assigned to such action and what is to be accredited to abrasion.

Controlled laboratory studies with abrasion mills or tumbling barrels offer another approach to the problem. Experimenters, beginning with Daubrée, have done important work on this problem. Experimental work, however, has several shortcomings. It is oversimplified; one cannot be certain that conditions in a mill even approximate those in a stream. Experimental work may be extrapolated beyond reasonable limits; since most abrasion mill

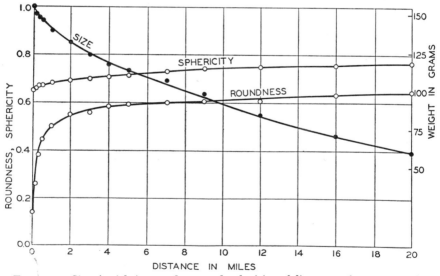

Fig. 127. Size (weight), roundness, and sphericity of limestone fragments as functions of distance during abrasion (after Krumbein, 1941). (See Plate 37).

studies dealt with large, pebble-sized fragments, conclusions drawn from such work have been erroneously applied to sand-sized materials.

The rate of abrasion is controlled by a number of factors of which one is the size of the materials. The rate of abrasion of gravels is markedly greater than that of sand. By means of abrasion mill tests, Wentworth (1919) found 700 miles of travel sufficient to reduce limestone pebbles from 180 to 10 grams. Ninety-five per cent of the original weight was lost by wear. Similarly Krumbein (1941) found the mean weight of a limestone sample to decrease 55 per cent in 20 miles of travel (Fig. 127). Marshall (1927), using more resistant graywacke, records a loss of 21 per cent in 360 hours (corresponding to about 360 miles of travel) in a laboratory mill.

TABLE 100.   Abrasion Mill Tests on Gravel and Sand (after Marshall)

Wt. of Sample (grams)	Number of Pebbles	Avg. Diam. (mm)	Wt. Loss in 24 hr (grams)	Loss per Particle (grams)	Loss per Particle (%)
5000	55	44.4	299.	5.5	6.0
5000	56,500	4.7	16.5	0.00029	0.33
5000	212,500	2.7	11.37	0.00005	0.22
5000	....	0.27	0.837	....	0.016

On the other hand, it has been repeatedly shown that, in the absence of coarse materials, the abrasion of sand is a much slower process. Daubrée (1879) noted this fact and concluded that a sand grain lost but 1/10,000 part of its weight in one kilometer of travel. Anderson (1926) subsequently confirmed the slowness of the abrasion of sand as did also Marshall (1929) (see Table 100). As is apparent from Marshall's data, material of pebble size appears to wear 300 to 400 times as rapidly as sand-size debris. If a pebble, therefore, becomes well worn in 50 miles, a sand grain might be expected to show the same wear at 15,000 to 20,000 miles. This expectation is in some measure confirmed by Thiel's (1940) experiments on the sand grades. The size reduction of coarse quartz sand was very small (Table 101).

TABLE 101.   Percentage by Weight Lost from Original Weights of Size Grades During 100 Days of Abrasion (after Thiel)

Diam. (mm)	Quartz (Hardness, 7)	Garnet (Hardness, 6)	Hornblende (Hardness, 5.5)	Apatite (Hardness, 5)
2 to 1	24.2	41.7	82.2	84.3
1 to ½	22.4	32.6	57.4	61.4

The 2- to 1-millimeter grade, for example, lost about 24 per cent of its weight during about 5000 miles of travel. This may seem to be a very significant loss and imply a substantial reduction in size. This is not the case. To reduce a grain with a diameter of 1 to ½ millimeter (assuming spherical shape) requires a ⅞ (or 87.5 per cent) loss of volume or weight. Even to reduce a cube that is 1 millimeter on a side, to a sphere having a diameter of 1 millimeter, means a removal of about 47.5 per cent of the original volume. It is apparent, therefore, that losses indicated by Thiel's experiments mean not only that no significant size reduction occurs in 100 days (5000 miles) of travel but that for quartz, at least, the loss is insufficient to produce significant modification of shape. Thiel's photographs confirm this conclusion and indicate that for quartz the loss is enough only to produce a minor rounding of the grains. That the rate of abrasion is a function of size was also shown by Thiel's experiments. Of the two grades studied, the larger showed the greater percentage lost for each of the mineral species used.

TABLE 102. Abrasion Mill Tests on Limestone Pebbles
(after Sarmiento)

Diameter (mm)	% Lost at End of Run (20 miles)	
	A	B
16	9	42
32	13	28
64	28	13

A. Each size taken alone.
B. All three sizes taken together.

The rate of abrasion is not only a function of size but is also influenced by the size of the associated materials. As noted above, Marshall showed that the finer sands were largely destroyed in a short time if gravel was also present in the abrasion mill. Sarmiento (1945) also showed that the rate of abrasion of fragments taken alone was quite different from that when taken together. An abrasion mill test with limestone pieces 16, 32, and 64 millimeters in diameter was continued until the abrasion was about equal to that involved in 20 miles of travel (Table 102). The relations shown in the table show that the larger sizes are more rapidly abraded than the smaller when each size is treated separately. In mixtures, however, the smaller sizes undergo the greatest loss, perhaps because of breakage and splitting of the smaller sizes under the conditions of the experiment. If the disparity between the sizes had been different, or the proportions changed, or the rigor (velocity) of action reduced, the results might have been different.

The rate of abrasion is obviously a function also of the abrasion resistance of the materials. Quartzites might be expected to behave differently from limestones. In the case of minerals the loss caused by abrasion is in considerable measure related to the hardness of the materials. In Thiel's experiment the coarse quartz sand lost about 24 per cent by weight whereas the apatite lost about 84 per cent. Minerals intermediate in hardness between quartz and apatite underwent abrasion losses intermediate between those of quartz and apatite (see Table 101). Cozzens (1931) has attempted to study quantitatively the rate of wear as a function of hardness. As anticipated, the durability index and the Mohs scale of hardness are closely correlated, at least for those minerals less than quartz in hardness. Cozzens' results have been discussed elsewhere (page 559).

The rate and manner of size reduction are also functions of the rigor of the action. Under some conditions, namely, those of very high velocities, some rock types appear to undergo considerable breakage. Bretz (1929), for example, has called attention to the numerous broken rounds in some of the gravels in the Washington scabland areas. According to Bretz, the percentage of pebbles and cobbles once rounded and now broken greatly exceeds that in the bars of the present-day Columbia River. He concluded, therefore, that the scabland gravels had been last moved by a flood of exceptional violence. Yet the gravels of modern streams subject to frequent floods have become rounded despite such episodes of violent action. Although normal abrasion seems to dominate over splitting, such breakage is by no means rare, since most gravels show some broken rounds. The latter do not generally exceed 15 per cent (Bretz, unpublished data). The proportion of broken rounds is probably dependent not only on violence of action (rigor) but also upon the ease with which the rock type splits and perhaps also upon some postdepositional fracturing processes.

There has been little experimental work on the relation between the rigor of action and the rate of size reduction. Only Schoklitsch (1933) seems to have attempted to evaluate this factor. As would be expected, the size reduction processes are accelerated as the velocity increases. Whether there are critical velocities for certain rocks or minerals above which chipping or splitting dominates over normal attrition is not known. As noted elsewhere (page 560). Krynine believed that certain minerals, such as kyanite, normally would be rounded (by abrasion) but above a critical velocity they would fracture and not round. Russell and Taylor (page 549) have even contended that large-scale splitting and fracturing of quartz grains occurs in the Mississippi River. The data that led to this conclusion, however, are capable of a somewhat different interpretation (see page 550). In conclusion it seems probable that in the absence of gravel the average current does not have a high enough velocity to reduce materially the grain size by such wholesale fracturing. Even in streams carrying gravel—such as those in the Black Hills —the sand appears to show progressive rounding as do the gravels, so that attrition must dominate over fracturing.

There have been a number of attempts to make quantitative studies of the several factors influencing the rate of abrasion. Most of these have shown that the size of a pebble or cobble in an abrasion mill decreases exponentially in accordance with what has been called Sternberg's law. The weight W, at any distance s is expressed as $W = W_oe^{-as}$, where W_o is the original weight and a is a coefficient of size reduction (Krumbein, 1941; Schoklitsch, 1933). The coefficient a is dependent on the nature of the rock (durability), the rigor of the abrasive action, the size of associated cobbles, and perhaps other factors. Schoklitsch has shown that:

1. The coefficient a is a constant for a particular kind of rock but it varies with the fourth root of the velocity of the abrasion mill.

2. The abrasion of a particle is controlled in part by the size distribution of the material with which it is associated. An increase in the mean size of the associated material causes a linear increase in a.

Wentworth (1931) also carried out additional experiments on abrasion. He attempted to measure (1) rate of wear (reduction index), (2) resistance to abrasion (durability index), (3) distance rigor, and (4) time rigor. Wentworth does not refer to Sternberg's law, but it is clear from his graphs that his data conform to it and that his reduction index is essentially the same as a, the coefficient of abrasion, and his durability index is essentially the ratio of the coefficients for quartz (taken as a standard) to that of the material in question.[2] The distance rigor and time rigor were defined as the "intensity of wear in daubrées per kilometer of distance" and "the intensity of wear in daubrées per day," respectively. A *daubrée* was defined by Wentworth as the removal of 0.1 gram from a 100-gram sphere of quartz. Wentworth was able to demonstrate that:

1. The rate of wear was independent of size over a considerable range of sizes, which is an indirect confirmation of Sternberg's law.

2. The rate of wear is a function of the size of the associated materials. The coarser the material, the greater the rate. The relationship, however, was not linear, as stated by Schoklitsch.

In conclusion, it is clear that size reduction by abrasion and related processes is a function of the size of the materials, their nature (durability), the nature and violence of action (rigor), the size and proportions of associated materials, and the duration or distance involved in the abrasive action.

In light of the field observations and experimental studies, what is the actual role played by abrasion in nature? The effectiveness of abrasion in nature is uncertain. That the larger fragments undergo considerable abrasion

---

[2] Wentworth's "reduction index" given in an earlier paper (1919) as $\dfrac{W_o - W}{W_oD}$ where W_o is the initial weight, W is the weight after the test, and D is the distance (in miles or kilometers). In the Jarvis Island paper (1931) the mean weight instead of the initial weight was used in the denominator.

is self-evident from their worn appearance and their rounded corners and subspherical form. But because the size of materials in a river declines exponentially in the downcurrent direction as does the size of materials abraded in a mill, it does not follow that the natural decrease in size is the result of abrasive action. As noted by Barrell, difficulties arise if this conclusion is drawn. Daubrée noted, for example, that granite fragments lose 0.001 to 0.004 of their weight per kilometer traveled in an abrasion mill. The highest rate attained by Daubrée is only 0.4 of the rate of wear implied by the data on the Rhine gravels, which presumably on the average are as resistant as granite. This is an unexpected result, because it might be supposed that the conditions of laboratory wear were more severe than in natural streams. Barrell therefore thought that some conditions must exist in river action which must lead to an excessive wear of gravel during its movement downstream. Such wearing action, according to Barrell, is that due to large amounts of sand which is swept over the gravel. Rubey (1933, p. 21) has attributed the rapid disappearance of quantities of pebbles and boulders being dumped into the Mississippi River by its tributaries and caving of banks of Pleistocene gravels to this wet-blasting action.

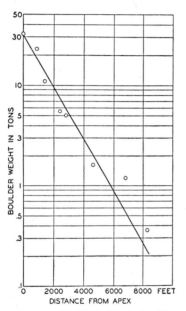

FIG. 128. Variation in boulder size on alluvial fan caused by La Crescenta floor (from Krumbein, 1942, based on data by Chawner).

If by abrasion sand grains lose but 0.0001 part of their weight per kilometer of travel, it seems unlikely that the 50 per cent size decline of Mississippi River sand observed between Cairo, Illinois, and the Gulf of Mexico, in a distance of about 1100 miles (1770 km) is attributable to abrasion. A size reduction of this magnitude implies an 87.5 per cent loss of original weight. As Theil has shown, 22–24 per cent was all that was lost in 5000 miles of abrasion of quartz sand in a mill. The ineffectiveness of abrasion is thus further substantiated.

Moreover, it does not seem likely that the pronounced size decrease observed in the materials of an alluvial fan from the apex outward can be in any way related to abrasion (Fig. 128). Is then the decrease in maximum boulder size, from 1.5 to 0.5 meters (66.7 per cent diminution in diameter, or 96 per cent decrease in volume) in less than 10 miles in the Arroyo Seco of California (Fig. 129) caused by wet blasting, breakage, or abrasion? The size decrease observed in the Black Hills streams was of like order of magnitude. In 30 miles of travel, for example, the mean diameter of the bed materials of Rapid Creek decreased from about 24 to about 5 millimeters, an 80 per cent decrease in diameter (Fig. 123). As noted by Plumley, the proportions of hard rocks (quartzite, quartz, etc.) to soft rocks (limestone, etc.) changed progressively downcurrent in the streams studied by him (Fig. 139).

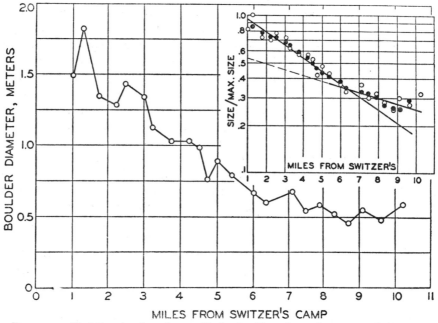

FIG. 129.   Variation in size of granodiorite boulders along the course of the Arroyo Seco, California (from Krumbein, 1942).

As this is most probably due to abrasion, the loss of a unit volume of material by such action was estimated in Rapid Creek to be about 50 per cent. A 50 per cent volume loss would correspond to about 20 per cent reduction in diameter of a unit sphere. One-fourth of the observed diameter decline of 80 per cent therefore is the result of abrasive action, and three-fourths must be explained in some other manner (Plumley, 1948, p. 570). Selective sorting has been postulated to account for the apparent size reduction.

Progressive Sorting

Most agents of transport tend to sort the particles carried according to their size, shape, and specific gravity. Our concern here is primarily the effect of the sorting process on the size of the constituent elements of the sediment. The action which is responsible for the size frequency distribution and its homogeneity at a given place has been called *local sorting* (Russell, 1939); that which involves assortment in the downcurrent direction was termed *progressive sorting*. The effects of progressive sorting are a systematic downcurrent decrease in the mean grain size of the sediment with a possible concomitant change in the standard deviation of the size distribution.

Two causes of such progressive sorting have been postulated. One supposes a progressive decrease in the competence of the transporting agent, whereas the other supposes a lagging behind of the larger particles because of fluctuations in competency.

A progressive decrease in competency may be produced in several ways. In streams, a decrease in gradient, if not compensated for by an increase in volume, would cause a decrease in velocity and hence in competency. Similarly a decrease in volume resulting from loss by seepage or by subdivision of the waters in a distributary system would result in decreased competency. A sedimentary deposit produced by an aggrading current would be expected to show a marked downcurrent sorting.

Perhaps, also, fluctuations in current flow might produce a progressive decline in mean grain size. At times of highest velocity, as during flood, all sizes of materials tend to move; at times of reduced flow only the smallest sizes are transported. Thus the larger particles moved only infrequently tend to lag behind, whereas the finer sizes tend to outrun the coarser in the downcurrent direction. It would seem probable, however, that in a stream this effect would be temporary, since the coarse material would eventually reach the mouth of the stream. As it does not, either this material is reduced by abrasion or the stream is aggrading.

How effective is the progressive sorting in nature and to what extent is it responsible for the commonly observed downcurrent decrease in size? As noted above, abrasion does not seem adequate to produce a size decrease of the magnitude commonly observed. Abrasion experiments with both gravel-sized and sand-sized debris failed to achieve a size reduction of the order of magnitude of that observed in natural streams for a given distance of travel. This was true in all natural situations but it is most apparent on alluvial fans and aprons. Very probably in most deposits which are products of an aggrading current, the change of grain size in the downcurrent direction is largely a sorting effect. Examples of facies changes thus produced are those measured in some alluvial fans (Fig. 128) (Chawner, in Krumbein, 1942), those reported in some high-level blanket gravels such as the Lafayette in western Kentucky and adjoining states (Potter, 1954) (Fig. 149), similar high-level gravels and related terraces of some Black Hills streams (Plumley, 1948), and the Brandywine gravels of Maryland (Schlee, 1956).

Where the downcurrent change in size is not accompanied by any changes in roundness one might conclude that the rounding had achieved its maximum value under the prevailing conditions of current flow (rigor). Where there is a concomitant downcurrent *decrease* in roundness and sphericity (see page 549) progressive sorting is most probably the process governing the size change. If so, the downcurrent size decrease on certain beaches (Mac-Carthy, 1931; Pettijohn and Lundahl, 1943) and in the Mississippi River (Russell and Taylor, 1938) are largely the result of a sorting action.

A progressive *increase* in mean size of beach sand in the direction of shore drift, such as that reported for Cape Cod (Schalk, 1938) almost certainly implies a sorting action. Such action abstracts or removes the fines to deeper water, leaving a residue on the beach with a higher average size than before. Under laboratory conditions, Krumbein (1944) obtained just the opposite results, namely, abstraction of the coarse materials and transfer of these to the underwater part of the beach, and hence formation of a water-level residue of finer grain. Both natural and experimental data, however, show that it is possible to derive a sediment with a larger mean grain size than that of the parent material from which it came.

Inasmuch as the abrasive and the sorting processes operate simultaneously in nature, the observed downcurrent size changes are in all probability a product of both actions. Only Plumley (1948) has attempted to evaluate the effects of each. As noted (page 540), three-quarters of the size change in the terraces of Rapid Creek in the Black Hills is the result of sorting and one-quarter is the result of abrasion. More quantitative field and experimental data are obviously needed to understand fully the relative roles of abrasion and sorting.

None of the studies known to the writer has demonstrated any progressive increase (or decrease) in the uniformity (coefficient of sorting) of the material in the downcurrent direction. It might be supposed that prolonged transport would improve the sorting of the individual deposits. Despite a large and impressive decrease in mean size of the terrace materials in each of three Black Hills streams, no progressive change in sorting was detectable (Plumley, 1948). On the other hand, a marked decrease in skewness was found in all cases.

REFERENCES CITED AND BIBLIOGRAPHY

Alling, H. L. (1944), Grain analyses of minerals of sand size in ball mills, *J. Sediment. Petrol.*, vol. 14, pp. 103–114.

Anderson, G. E. (1926), Experiments on the rate of wear of sand grains, *J. Geol.*, vol. 34, pp. 144–158.

Barrell, J. (1925), Marine and terrestrial conglomerates, *Bull. Geol. Soc. Amer.*, vol. 36, pp. 279–342.

Blissenbach, Erich (1952), Relation of surface angle distribution to particle size distribution on alluvial fans, *J. Sediment. Petrol.*, vol. 22, pp. 25–28.

Bretz, J H. (1929), Valley deposits immediately east of the channeled scabland of Washington, *J. Geol.*, vol. 37, p. 507.

Burri, Conrad (1929), Sedimentpetrographische Untersuchungen an alpinen Flüssanden, *Schweiz. mineralog. petrog. Mitt.*, vol. 9, pp. 205–240.

Cozzens, S. B. (1931), Rates of wear of common minerals, *Wash. Univ. Studies, Sci. and Technol.*, no. 5, new series, pp. 71–80.

Daubrée, A. (1879), *Etudes synthétiques de géologie experimentale*, Paris, Dunod.

Friese, F. W. (1931), Untersuchung von Mineralen auf Abnutzbarkeit bei Verfrachtung im Wasser, *Mineralog. petrog. Mitt.*, vol. 41, new ser., pp. 1–7.

Grabau, A. W. (1913), *Principles of stratigraphy*, New York, Seiler.

Krumbein, W. C. (1937), Sediments and exponential curves, *J. Geol.*, vol. 45, pp. 577–601.

Krumbein, W. C. (1941), The effects of abrasion on the size, shape, and roundness of rock fragments, *J. Geol.*, vol. 49, pp. 482–520.

Krumbein, W. C. (1942), Flood deposits of Arroyo Seco, Los Angeles County, California, *Bull. Geol. Soc. Amer.*, vol. 53, pp. 1355–1402.

Krumbein, W. C. (1944), Shore currents and sand movement on a model beach, *Beach Erosion Board, Tech. Memo. No. 7.*

Krumbein, W. C. and Griffith, J. S. (1938), Beach environment in Little Sister Bay, Wisconsin, *Bull. Geol. Soc. Amer.*, vol. 49, pp. 629–652.

MacCarthy, G. R. (1931), Coastal sands of the eastern United States, *Am. J. Sci.*, ser. 5, vol. 22, pp. 35–50.

Marshall, P. E. (1927), The wearing of beach gravels, *Trans. Proc. New Zealand Inst.*, vol. 58, pp. 507–532.

Marshall, P. E. (1928), Colloid substances formed by abrasion, *Trans. Proc. New Zealand Inst.*, vol. 59, pp. 609–613.

Marshall, P. E. (1929), Beach gravels and sands, *Trans. Proc. New Zealand Inst.*, vol. 60, pp. 324–365.

Pettijohn, F. J. (1942), Quantitative and analytical sedimentation, *Rept. Comm. Sedimentation, 1940–1941*, mimeographed, Nat. Research Council, pp. 43–61.

Pettijohn and Lundahl, A. C. (1943), Shape and roundness of Lake Erie beach sands, *J. Sediment. Petrol.*, vol. 13, pp. 69–78.

Plumley, W. J. (1948), Black Hills terrace gravels: A study in sediment transport, *J. Geol.*, vol. 56, pp. 526–577.

Potter, P. E. (1955), Petrology and origin of the Lafayette gravel, *J. Geol.*, vol. 63, pp. 1–38.

Rubey, W. W. (1933), The size-distribution of heavy minerals within a waterlaid sandstone, *J. Sediment. Petrol.* vol. 3, pp. 3–29.

Russell, R. D. (1939), Effects of transportation on sedimentary particles, *Recent Marine Sediments*, Tulsa, Amer. Assoc. Petroleum Geologists, pp. 32–47.

Russell, R. D. and Taylor, R. E. (1937), Roundness and shape of Mississippi River sands, *J. Geol.*, vol. 45, pp. 225–267.

Salminen, Antti (1935), On the weathering of rocks and the composition of clays, *Maatalouskoelaitoksen Maatutkimusosasto Agrogeologisia Julkaisuja*, no. 40 (reviewed in *J. Sediment. Petrol.*, vol. 6, 1936, p. 162).

Sarmiento, A. (1945), *Experimental study of pebble abrasion*, M.S. thesis, University of Chicago.

Schalk, Marshall (1938), A textural study of the outer beach of Cape Cod, Massachusetts, *J. Sediment. Petrol.*, vol. 8, pp. 41–54.

Schlee, J. S. (1956), *Sedimentological Analysis of the Upland Gravels of Southern Maryland*, Ph.D. thesis, The Johns Hopkins Univ.

Schoklitsch, A. (1933), Ueber die Verkleinerung der Geschiebe in Flussläufen, *Sitzber. Akad. Wiss. Wien, Math.-natur. Kl.*, sec. IIz, vol. 142, no. 8, pp. 343–366.

Schoklitsch, A. (1935), *Stauraumverlandung und Kolkabwehr*, Vienna, Springer, pp. 4–17.

Schoklitsch, A. (1936), *Geschiebebewegung im Flüssen und an Stauwerken*, Vienna, Springer, pp. 3–7.

Shaler, N. S. (1893), The conditions of erosion beneath deep glaciers, based upon a study of the boulder train from Iron Hill, Cumberland, R.I., *Harv. Mus. Comp. Zool., Bull.* 16, pp. 185–225.

Shulits, S. (1941), Rational equation of river-bed profile, *Trans. Am. Geophys. Union*, 22nd Ann. Meeting, pt. 2, pp. 622–630.

Sternberg, H. (1875), Untersuchungen über langen- und querprofil geschiebe-fuhrende Flusse, *Z. Bauwesen*, vol. 25, pp. 483–506.

Szádeczky-Kardoss, E. v. (1932), Flussschotteranalyse und der Abtragung-gebiet, *Mitt. berg u. huttenmänn. Abt. kgl. ungar. Hochschule Berg- und Forstw. Sopron*, vol. 4, pp. 1–38; vol. 5, 1933, pp. 1–23 (reviewed in *J. Sediment. Petrol.*, vol. 5, 1935, pp. 52–53).

Thiel, G. A. (1940), The relative resistance to abrasion of mineral grains of sand size, *J. Sediment. Petrol.*, vol. 10, pp. 102–124.

Wadell, Hakon (1932a), *Volume, shape and roundness of rock particles*, University of Chicago Ph.D. dissertation (unpublished).

Wadell, Hakon (1932b), Volume, shape and roundness of rock particles, *J. Geol.*, vol. 40, pp. 443–451.

Wadell, Hakon (1935), Volume, shape, and roundness of quartz particles, *J. Geol.*, vol. 43, pp. 250–280.

Wentworth, C. K. (1919), A laboratory and field study of cobble abrasion, *J. Geol.*, vol. 27, pp. 507–522.

Wentworth, C. K. (1922), A method of measuring and plotting the shapes of pebbles, *U.S. Geol. Survey Bull.* 730-C, pp. 91–102.

Wentworth, C. K. (1931), Pebble wear on the Jarvis Island beach, *Wash. Univ. Studies, Sci. and Technol.*, no. 5, new series, pp. 11–37.

ROUNDNESS, SPHERICITY, AND DISPERSION

Introduction

As in the case of fragment size, the disintegration of the parent material releases particles which, as they are moved, undergo a progressive modification of their roundness and shape. Normally as the size decreases the roundness and sphericity rise to a maximum. The factors affecting this change are many and the laws controlling them are poorly understood.

What are the initial characteristics of the fragments? Even if they are derived directly from an igneous rock, the initial values of sphericity and roundness are not zero. Freshly crushed quartz was found to have a projection sphericity of 0.70 to 0.72 (Thiel, 1940) which corresponds to a true sphericity of about 0.60 to 0.65. Limestone fragments, produced by crushing, have an initial sphericity of 0.65 and a roundness of 0.13 (Krumbein, 1941). Granodiorite fragments (16 to 32 mm in diameter) that were collected very near the ledges from which they came have a sphericity of 0.68 and a roundness of 0.16 (Krumbein, 1942). Theoretically, perhaps, the roundness should be initially zero; in fact, however, the edges are not infinitely sharp, but are a trifle blunted. A few minerals, such as mica, may have a very low initial sphericity; yet even crushed hornblende has a projection sphericity of 0.63 to 0.65 (Thiel, 1940).

Roundness and Distance

In all experimental studies of abrasion of sand and gravel, the roundness of the materials increased with the distance of travel of the materials. In all cases roundness increased most rapidly at first and then rose more slowly (Fig. 127). Though noted by Daubrée (1879), this observation was first given a clear quantitative demonstration by Wentworth, who first clearly defined and measured roundness (1919). It remained for Krumbein (1940) to attempt formulation of the relations in mathematical terms. Krumbein assumed that the rate of change of roundness was a function of the difference between the roundness at any point and a certain limiting roundness.[3] This relation may be expressed as $P = P_L(1 - e^{-kx})$, where P is the roundness at any point, P_L is the limiting roundness, x is the distance, and k is the coefficient of rounding. This equation seems to fit both experimental and field data (Krumbein, 1940; 1941). Later experimental work by Krumbein (1941, p. 482) showed that the relation of rounding to distance was more complex. Krumbein believed that the rate of rounding was first controlled, as above, by the difference between the roundness at any point and the limiting roundness, but as rounding proceeded the rate was governed by the sphericity, and the rate of sphericity increased. Plumley's work on the gravels of the Black Hills streams (Plumley, 1948, p. 566) cast doubt on the validity of Krumbein's equation, since the roundness was found to increase

---

[3] These assumptions are reasonable, since sharp edges and corners should be worn more easily than blunt edges or faces. This implies that rounding is more rapid when the fragment is angular and that it slows down as the piece becomes more rounded. Both experiment and field study seem to bear out this concept. There seems also to be a limiting roundness which, under the conditions of the experiment or those prevailing in the stream, the roundness approaches but never exceeds.

downstream but the sphericity showed no such systematic increase. Plumley concluded, instead, that the rate of change of roundness with distance is not only proportional to the difference between the roundness at any point and a limiting roundness, but proportional also to some power of the distance traveled. These conclusions were expressed mathematically as $P = P_L[1 - e^{-r(x)^n}]$, where P is the roundness at any point, P_L is the limiting roundness, x is the distance, and r and n are constants. Roundness measurements of the Minnekahta limestone pebbles in Rapid Creek and Battle Creek and those on limestone fragments rounded in an abrasion mill (Sarmiento, 1945) were found to fit the equation very well (Pl. 37).

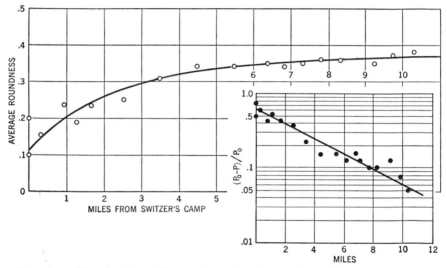

Fig. 130. Variation in pebble roundness along Arroyo Seco, California. Lowe grano-diorite, 16–32 mm class. Inset shows relation of ratio of the difference roundness at any point (P) and limiting roundness (P_0) to limiting roundness (after Krumbein, 1942).

As noted above, the rounding of gravels in streams closely resembles that observed in abrasion mills, and the laws governing one must also apply to the other. This observation, first made by Wentworth (1922), was substantiated by Krumbein (1940; 1941) (Fig. 130) and Plumley (1948) (Fig. 131). Studies of beach gravels made by Wentworth (1922b), Landon (1930), Krumbein and Griffith (1938), and Grogan (1945) (Fig. 132) have not yielded results wholly consistent either with each other or with the results obtained from studies of river gravels. Wentworth and Landon both report an inverse relation between flatness and roundness; i.e., the more rounded the fragment, the less flat it is (see Fig. 31). Grogan found the sphericity and roundness to be positively correlated, i.e., the better-rounded pebbles were also the more spherical. Although flatness and sphericity are not strictly the same, the greater the flatness, the less spherical the fragment. A similar but less clear correlation between roundness and sphericity is reported by Krumbein and Griffith. Grogan found a pronounced and

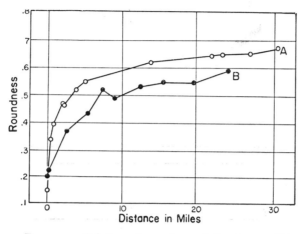

FIG. 131. Relation of roundness of limestone pebbles to distance of transport in Black Hills (S.D.) streams. **A:** Rapid Creek. **B:** Battle Creek (data from Plumley, 1948).

regular increase in roundness of the rhyolite pebbles of the Lake Superior beach as these were moved away from the parent ledges (Fig. 132). The roundness increased from about 0.26 to 0.61 in a migration of 2200 feet.

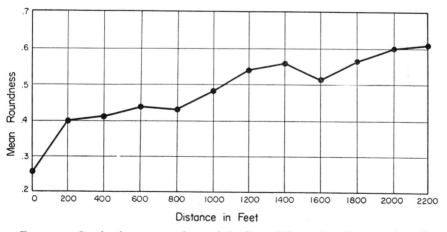

FIG. 132. Graph of mean roundness of rhyolite pebbles against distance of travel on Lake Superior beach. The dashed line represents a moving average of three successive measurements (from Grogan, 1945).

Although photographs of limestone fragments on a Lake Michigan beach published by Krumbein and Griffith show a marked rounding as they are carried away from the source ledges, the roundness measurement actually made did not support this observation. Landon's data were likewise contradictory. Although the size of materials studied by him on the west shore of Lake Michigan decreased in the direction of shore drift, the rounding did not show a systematic change. Landon believed these anomalies to be the result of a selective sorting action on the beach which removed the less flat (and better-rounded fragments) from the beach, whereas the flat (and less well-rounded) fragments tended to concentrate on the beach. Obviously our data are very meager and unsatisfactory.

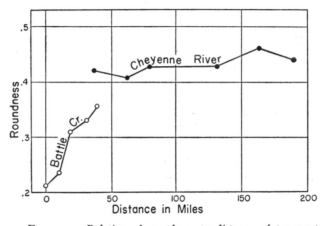

FIG. 133. Relation of roundness to distance of transport of quartz sand, 1–1.414 mm class, in South Dakota streams (after Plumley, 1948).

All field and laboratory data show that rounding of sand, unlike rounding of gravel, is a very slow process. As has been noted elsewhere, Daubrée (1879) found sand grains to lose but 0.0001 part of their weight per kilometer of travel. Thiel's (1940) abrasion experiments with quartz sand, 1 to 2 millimeters in diameter, showed but 22 per cent loss in 100 hours in an abrasion mill—equivalent to about 5000 miles of travel. This is an average loss of less than 0.0001 part per mile of travel. Marshall's data (Marshall, 1927) showed a loss of about 0.0005 part per mile of travel for grains between 2 and 3 millimeters in diameter. It is clear, therefore, that such small losses mean that several thousand miles of travel will do little more than dull the edges of the quartz grains. The only actual experimental data on roundness is that given by Marsland and Woodruff (1937), who found quartz to reach a roundness of 0.01 after 10 hours of wind-blast action at

35-mile velocities. The data of these experimenters suggest, however, that fracturing and breakages were common.

Field observations on rounding of sands are apparently ambiguous and contradictory. Russell and Taylor (1938) showed that the sand carried by the Mississippi River between Cairo, Illinois, and the Gulf of Mexico, de-

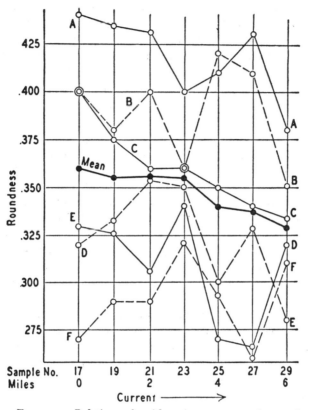

Fig. 134. Relation of arithmetic mean roundness of beach size grade and position, and unweighted arithmetic mean roundness of whole sample and position on beach, Cedar Point, Lake Erie, Ohio. A: 0.70–0.50 mm class. B: 0.50–0.35 mm class. C: 0.35–0.25 mm class. D: 0.25–0.177 mm class. E: 0.177–0.125 mm class. F: 0.125–0.088 mm class (from Pettijohn and Lundahl, 1943).

creased in roundness in the downcurrent direction. They concluded, therefore, that streams do not round sand and that the decrease in roundness was caused by progressive fracturing. The observed decline in roundness was from 0.239 to 0.179 or 23.5 per cent in 1100 miles. On the other hand, Plumley (1948) showed that the sands (1 to 1.414 mm grade) of Battle Creek, in the Black Hills of South Dakota, increased 71 per cent in roundness, from 0.21 to 0.36, in a distance of about 40 miles. The same sand grade of the Cheyenne River of South Dakota, however, was found by Plumley to show an increase in rounding of only 5 per cent, from 0.42 to 0.44, in about 150 miles of transport (Fig. 133). The observations of Pettijohn and Lundahl (1943) on the beach sands of Lake Erie showed an apparent decline in the roundness of the sand in the direction of travel. All size classes show a definite, though fluctuating decrease in average roundness, with the possible exception of the finest grade (Fig. 134). The unweighted mean shows an unvarying decline from 0.360 to 0.329, or about 8 per cent decrease in seven miles. The 0.35- to 0.25-millimeter class, on which sphericity measurements were made, declined 17.5 per cent. Pettijohn and Lundahl regarded the decrease in roundness as being only apparent and as being related to a sorting of the grains on the basis of sphericity. Since sphericity and roundness have been found to be positively correlated (p. 60), any downcurrent decline in sphericity would carry with it a somewhat larger decline in rounding. Since there appears to be a progressive downcurrent sorting on the basis of sphericity in some streams, the observed decrease in rounding is therefore a necessary concomitant change. Apparently in the larger slow-flowing streams, this sorting action takes place, so that any downstream increase in rounding is masked by the downcurrent sorting action. It is hardly conceivable that the steep-gradient, gravel-carrying streams of the Black Hills would round sand and that the Mississippi River would not (and would, as Russell and Taylor thought, actually decrease the rounding by progressive fracturing).

The role of wind action in sand rounding has been much debated. Very few data are actually available. Calver (1940) reports an increase in rounding in the direction of sand movement in the dunes of western Michigan. An appreciable though slight increase was noted in a few thousand feet of movement. In view of the slowness with which sand is rounded, there is some possibility that the changes in roundness observed by Calver might be the result of a concomitant sorting based on shape.

Shape (Sphericity) and Distance

The changes of shape with distance of travel (or time of action) have been given less study than has been accorded modification of roundness, perhaps because of the common failure to distinguish between these properties. Experimental work shows that gentle abrasion causes a progressive increase in sphericity with time. As with roundness, the sphericity changes most rapidly at first and more slowly later (Krumbein, 1941; Thiel, 1940) (Fig. 127). Also, as for roundness, the sphericity seems to approach a limit beyond which it does not go. This limit may be in part controlled by the structure of the material being abraded. Rocks with a pronounced fissility will remain disks and never become spherical no matter how prolonged their transport.

Reasoning concerning the abrasion process involved in shape modification would suggest that an exponential equation, similar to that governing rounding, should express the relations between sphericity and the duration of the abrasion process. Because the initial value of the sphericity cannot be zero, or even near it, the equation relating sphericity to abrasion must contain a term which makes allowance for this fact. The relation of sphericity to dis-

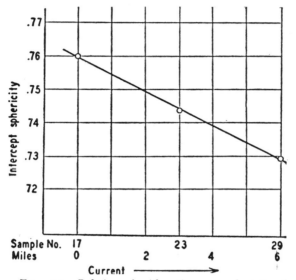

Fig. 135. Relation of arithmetic mean sphericity of 0.35–0.25 mm size grade and position on beach, Cedar Point, Lake Erie, Ohio (from Pettijohn and Lundahl, 1943).

tance has been given by Krumbein (1941) as $\phi = \phi_L(1 - e^{as}) + \phi_i e^{-as}$, where ϕ is the sphericity at any point, ϕ_L is the limiting sphericity, ϕ_i is the initial sphericity, s is the distance, and a is the coefficient of shape change. Although Krumbein's experimental data on gravel seem to fit this function fairly well, it is not clear whether such is the case in nature. Not only is the shape modified by abrasion under natural conditions, but during transport some sorting processes, in which sphericity is a factor, are also operative, so that the results observed are composite in origin.

Illustrative of the complexities of the problem are Krumbein's observations that there was no change in sphericity in the downstream direction of the flood gravels of the San Gabriel and Arroyo Seco, in spite of a well-marked increase in rounding. Likewise Plumley (1948) found little or no change in sphericity of the limestone fragments in the downstream direction in several Black Hills streams although the fragments of these streams exhibited a large downstream increase in roundness. Grogan (1945), on the other hand, reports a distinct though slight (from 0.55 to 0.64) increase in the sphericity of rhyolite fragments of a Lake Superior beach as these materials are moved away from the source ledges by the shore drift. Grogan's observations seem to support Wentworth's conclusion (Wentworth, 1922b)

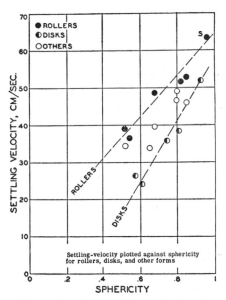

FIG. 136. Shape-settling velocity relations (from Krumbein, 1942).

that beach action does not produce flat pebbles but rather that the material becomes less flat, that is, more spherical the longer it is abraded.

Natural sands appear to decline in sphericity in the downcurrent direction. MacCarthy (1933) showed that the Atlantic coastal sands studied by him decrease in sphericity ("roundness" of MacCarthy) about 5.5 per cent in 128 miles of longshore movement. Pettijohn and Lundahl (1943) report a 4 per cent decrease in 7 miles of shore drift on a Lake Erie beach (Fig. 135). Similarly Russell and Taylor (1937) found a sphericity decline of 1.9 per cent in 1100 miles of travel down the Mississippi River. Plumley (1948) found no appreciable change in sphericity of the coarse sand carried in Battle Creek or the Cheyenne River of South Dakota in about 200 miles of transport. The apparent downcurrent decrease of sphericity was attributed by Russell and Taylor to progressive fracturing; by MacCarthy and Pettijohn and Lundahl to a selective sorting process. These latter authors presume that the sand is transported in suspension so that the less spherical grains settle more slowly than the more spherical and they are thus carried forward more rapidly than the other grains with which they were originally associated. This supposition seems to be borne out by experimental studies (Krumbein, 1942) (Fig. 136).

One may say, in conclusion, that the ultimate shape which a pebble or sand grain acquires is dependent not only on abrasion during transport, but also upon initial shape and upon the vectorial resistance to wear. In general, abrasive action during transport is not marked and the original shape seems not to be lost even by prolonged transport.

Conclusions

What is the geological significance of roundness and the usefulness of this property in ascertaining the distance, direction, and velocity of movement of the sedimentary materials?

As pointed out in the chapter on textures, roundness summarizes the abrasion history of a particle. As noted also the effects of abrasion are cumulative so that the roundness acquired in an early cycle of transport may be inherited and added to in a later epoch of transport. How far must a pebble be transported to become well-rounded $(P = 0.60)$? Can one, knowing the roundness of a fragment, calculate the distance of transport? Experimental work and field studies do not as yet permit a precise answer to these questions, but do suggest that distances of about the right order of magnitude can be estimated. Reduction of a cube to a sphere having a diameter equal to one edge of the cube involves removal of 47.5 per cent of the original volume or weight. It may be supposed, therefore, that weight loss of one-third to one-half would lead to a maximum roundness and that further reduction in size would not be accompanied by any increase in roundness. As can be seen from Krumbein's data (1941) a loss of weight of about one-third is associated with a roundness of about 0.60 (well-rounded). His data show also that further loss of weight did not result in much change in roundness. The limestone studied by him in an abrasion mill reached this roundness in 7 miles. Using Daubrée's figure of 0.001 to 0.004 loss in weight per kilometer travel of granite pebbles, to become well-rounded (that is, to lose one-third of the original weight) requires a transport of between 50 and 200 miles (84 to 333 km). The calculations are very crude but the results are probably of the correct order of magnitude.

Plumley (1948) found that limestone pebbles in two Black Hills streams became well-rounded (0.60 at about 11 and 23 miles, respectively) (Table 103). The quartzite pebbles in the Brandywine gravels of Maryland have a roundness of 0.59. The nearest ledges from which they could have come are about 45 miles distant.

TABLE 103.   Distance of Travel (miles) Needed to Produce a Well-Rounded
$(P > 0.6)$ Pebble

Rock Type	Locality	Distance (miles)	Reference
Limestone	Experimental	9.0	Sarmiento (1945)
Limestone	Experimental	7.0	Krumbein (1941)
Limestone	Rapid Creek	13.0±	Plumley (1948)
Limestone	Battle Creek	23.0±	Plumley (1948)

Knowing that most of the observed rounding is acquired in the first few miles of transport, it is evident that an angular or subangular gravel cannot have been moved more than a mile or two by a stream (see Pl. 38).

On the other hand, the slowness with which sand is abraded precludes the possibility of rounding sand in a single cycle of transport from the continental interior to the sea. Although quantitative data are as yet incomplete, it seems probable that surf action, however, could round sand in a single epoch of sedimentation. Highly rounded sand therefore does not always mean or require a multicycle origin. Although rounded sand does denote long continued abrasion, and therefore a long transport history, angular or subangular sand does *not* denote a brief transport. Both field and laboratory studies show that sand can travel many hundreds of miles without becoming rounded or well-rounded.

It should be further noted that both field and laboratory work suggest that in a given stream or experiment there is a limit to which the roundness approaches but cannot exceed. This limit is perhaps a function of the violence of motion or rigor. If this be so, even prolonged transport might not produce a well-rounded pebble. The distances given above therefore are minimal distances only.

Can one, knowing the roundness of a pebble, calculate the distance that it has come? Wentworth (1922a) attempted to do this for the quartz pebbles in the Pennsylvanian Lee conglomerate of Big Stone Gap, Virginia. He found these pebbles to have the same roundness as the quartzite fragments in the Russell Fork which had traveled 11.6 miles, but since they were four times as durable (as shown by mill tests), they had probably acquired their observed roundness in about 50 miles of transport. Such a calculation is obviously subject to many uncertainties and can only give results of about the right order of magnitude.

To some extent the ultimate rounding is a function of the character of the materials also. Some rocks, such as chert, are prone to fracture under given conditions, whereas other materials such as quartzite do not. For the same rigor and distance traveled the chert will be less well-rounded than the associated quartzites or vein quartz. This is essentially the same concept presented by Krynine (1942), who believes that certain minerals were indices of current velocities. Above certain velocities some minerals, kyanite for example, would fracture and remain angular; below this critical velocity the mineral would become rounded. This concept needs experimental verification.

Theoretically, the direction of transport could be determined by mapping the roundness values and drawing normals to the lines joining equal roundness values. The author knows of no case where this has been done.

Roundness is an index of maturity and as such should be closely correlated with the other indices of maturity. It is so correlated with sorting, though the correlation is very poor (Dapples, Krumbein, and Sloss, 1953). Sorting seems to be achieved very quickly, even by ephemeral streams, whereas rounding is acquired very slowly. Glacial outwash sands, for example, are moderately well sorted though they are quite angular. On the other hand most highly rounded sands, such as the St. Peter sandstone, are also very well sorted.

The roundness of a sand is probably correlated with its mineralogical maturity. The high-quartz sands are the best rounded; the arkoses and other immature sands are generally the most angular. No quantitative data have as yet been published, so the degree to which the roundness and the quartz content are correlated is unknown.

REFERENCES CITED AND BIBLIOGRAPHY

Calver, J. L. (1940), Roundness of grains in western Michigan dune sands, *Papers Mich. Acad. Sci.*, vol. 25, pp. 465–471.

Dapples, E. C., Krumbein, W. C., and Sloss, L. L. (1953), Petrographic and lithologic attributes of sandstones, *J. Geol.*, vol. 61, pp. 291–317.

Daubrée, A. (1879), *Etudes synthétiques de géologie experimentale*, 2 vols., Paris, Dunod.

Grogan, R. M. (1945), Shape variation of some Lake Superior beach pebbles, *J. Sediment. Petrol.*, vol. 15, pp. 3–10.

Krumbein, W. C. (1940), Flood gravel of San Gabriel Canyon, California, *Bull. Geol. Soc. Amer.*, vol. 51, pp. 639–676.

Krumbein, W. C. (1941), The effects of abrasion on the size, shape and roundness of rock fragments, *J. Geol.*, vol. 49, pp. 482–520.

Krumbein, W. C. (1942), Flood deposits of Arroyo Seco, Los Angeles County, California, *Bull. Geol. Soc. Amer.*, vol. 53, pp. 1355–1402.

Krumbein, W. C. (1942), Settling-velocity and flume-behavior of nonspherical particles, *Trans. Am. Geophys. Union*, 1942, pp. 621–633.

Krumbein, W. C. and Griffith, J. S. (1938), Beach environment in Little Sister Bay, Wisconsin, *Bull. Geol. Soc. Amer.*, vol. 49, pp. 629–652.

Krynine, P. D. (1942), Critical velocity as a controlling factor in sedimentation, *Bull. Geol. Soc. Amer.*, vol. 53, p. 1805 (abstract).

Landon, R. E. (1930), Analysis of beach pebble abrasion and transportation, *J. Geol.*, vol. 38, pp. 437–446.

MacCarthy, G. R. (1933), The rounding of beach sands, *Am. J. Sci.*, ser. 5, vol. 25, pp. 205–224.

MacCarthy, G. R. (1935), Eolian sands: a comparison, *Am. J. Sci.*, ser. 5, vol. 30, pp. 81–95.

Marshall, P. (1927), The wearing of beach gravels, *Trans. Proc. New Zealand Inst.*, vol. 58, pp. 507–532.

Marsland, P. S. and Woodruff, J. G. (1937), A study of the effects of wind transportation on grains of several minerals, *J. Sediment. Petrol.*, vol. 7, pp. 18–30.

Pettijohn, F. J. and Lundahl, A. C. (1943), Shape and roundness of Lake Erie beach sands, *J. Sediment. Petrol.*, vol. 13, pp. 69–78.

Plumley, W. J. (1948), Black Hills terrace gravels: a study in sediment transport, *J. Geol.*, vol. 56, pp. 526–577.

Russell, R. D., and Taylor, R. E. (1937), Roundness and shape of Mississippi River sands, *J. Geol.*, vol. 45, pp. 225–267.

Sarmiento, A. (1945), *Experimental study of pebble abrasion*, University of Chicago M.S. dissertation (unpublished).

Thiel, G. A. (1940), The relative resistance to abrasion of mineral grains of sand size, *J. Sediment Petrol.*, vol. 10, pp. 103–124.

Wentworth, C. K. (1919), A laboratory and field study of cobble abrasion, *J. Geol.*, vol. 27, pp. 507–521.

Wentworth, C. K. (1922a), A field study of the shapes of river pebbles, *U.S. Geol. Survey Bull.* 730-C, pp. 103–114.

Wentworth, C. K. (1922b), The shapes of beach pebbles, *U.S. Geol. Survey Prof. Paper* 131-C, pp. 75–83.

COMPOSITION AND DISPERSION

Introduction

It might be supposed that the residues produced by the disintegration and decomposition of the source rocks would undergo further alteration or change during their dispersal. Not only would the clay fraction be separated from the sand and gravel grades, but the latter two fractions themselves would undergo further modification and fractionation. It might be supposed, for example, that the processes operative during transport which are responsible for rounding of the debris transported would also modify the composition by selective abrasion and sorting.

Unfortunately, careful observations on what actually does happen during transit are exceedingly few. That some changes in composition do occur during transport seems highly probable. Mackie (1896), for example, reported a decline in feldspar content, from 42 per cent to 21 per cent in about 30 to 40 miles of transport in the River Findhorn. Plumley's (1948) more recent work on several streams draining the Black Hills discloses a similar enrichment of the stream sands in quartz and impoverishment in feldspar. On the other hand, Plumley found that in the sands of the Cheyenne River of the same area, the feldspar content was only slightly diminished in 150 miles of travel (Fig. 137). Russell (1937) likewise found only a slight decrease in feldspar content in 1100 miles of transport in the Mississippi River. Moreover, he found almost no change in the proportions of the heavy detrital minerals, and concluded therefore that progressive changes in composition during transport were negligible. Burri (1929), however, records a notable downstream change in heavy mineral composition along the course of the River Tessin.

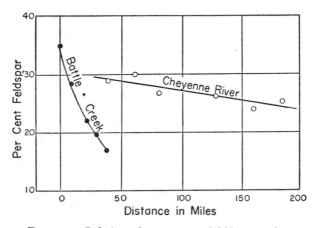

Fɪɢ. 137. Relation of percentage of feldspar to distance
of transport in 1–1.414 mm size class of Black Hills (S.D.)
streams (from Plumley, 1948).

Beach sands have also been found to show progressive, though somewhat
irregular changes in their mineral composition in the direction of shore
transport (Pettijohn and Ridge, 1933; Martens, 1935) (Fig. 138).

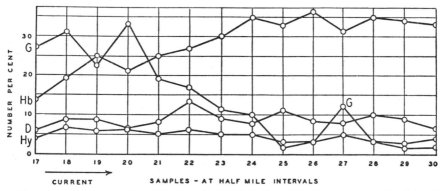

Fɪɢ. 138. Diagram of heavy mineral variations in 0.177–0.125 mm grade of beach
sand, Cedar Point, Lake Erie, Ohio. G, garnet; Hb, hornblende; D, diopside; Hy, hypersthene (from Pettijohn and Ridge, 1933).

Downstream changes in the composition of river gravels have long been
noted. Erdmann (Grabau, 1913) described the disappearance of certain rock
types in Swedish rivers and estimated the distance of travel required to
destroy various rock types completely. Plumley (1948) has recorded the
changing composition of the Black Hills stream gravels and has shown that
these materials undergo marked modifications in the downcurrent direction

(Fig. 139). Even glacial materials have been found to show progressive changes in composition in the direction of ice movement (Holmes, 1952).

In conclusion it can be said that downcurrent changes in composition of the medium and coarse-grained sediments do commonly occur and that such changes may be systematic and indicative of both *direction* of current flow and *distance* of transport (and perhaps even of current velocity). In some

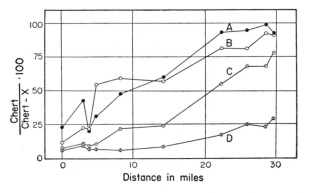

Fig. 139. Effect of transport on rock constituents of gravel in Rapid Creek, Black Hills, S.D. Ratio of chert to chert plus each component: **A:** Sandstone. **B:** Limestone. **C:** Precambrian metamorphics. **D:** Quartz plus quartzite (after Plumley, 1948).

cases, however, no such progressive changes seem to be evident, or such changes, if present, are feeble or erratic and nonsystematic. It seems desirable therefore to inquire into the causes of the changes, if any, in order to utilize these changes for determination of both distance and direction of transport.

Selective Abrasion

It has been commonly supposed that progressive compositional changes in both sands and gravels would occur because of the unequal resistance of the several components of these materials to abrasion. Such selective abrasion would result in progressive and systematic elimination of the softer and more cleavable materials and complementary enrichment of the harder and more durable components.

Accordingly some experiments have been conducted to determine the over-all resistance of mineral and rock fragments to the size-reduction processes. Wentworth (1922), for example, experimented with various rock types in a tumbling barrel or abrasion mill. Although he was primarily interested in the rounding of rock fragments, he did some work on the relative durability of several rock types (see also Szadecky-Kardoss, 1932, 1933).

Most experimental work on abrasion resistance, however, has been done on mineral rather than rock fragments. Friese (1931) determined the durability ("transportwiderstand") of a considerable number of minerals. Taking crystalline hematite as 100, he assigned a numerical value to the abrasion resistance of each mineral studied (Table 104). Cozzens (1931) likewise deter-

TABLE 104. Abrasion Resistance of Various Minerals
(after Friese, 1931)

Mineral	Transportwiderstand[a]
Monazite	105 to 130; avg, 117
Orthoclase	150
Diopside	160
Andalusite	220
Kyanite	260
Apatite	275
Common Olivine	290
Epidote	320
Ilmenite	325
Garnet	320 to 430; avg, 378
Magnetite	380
Topaz	390
Common Augite	420
Staurolite	420
Cordierite	480
Pyrite	500
Tourmaline	690 to 950; avg, 817

[a] As compared with crystalline hematite.

mined the rate of wear of common minerals. Cozzens worked on the rate of wear as a function of hardness. Apparently the durability index and Mohs scale of hardness are closely correlated, at least for minerals less than quartz in hardness. The exact function was not worked out fully, though it appears to be of the type $y = (x/a)^n$, where y is the durability index, x is the hardness (Mohs), a is the hardness of quartz (7), and n is an exponent (near 4). Erratic values were frequent and may be due to size-reduction processes other than abrasion, to the nonuniform nature of the hardness scale, and other properties of the minerals (such as elasticity).

Thiel (1940) experimentally determined the relative resistances of some of the common minerals. According to Thiel, the order of resistance is, beginning with the least resistant, (1) apatite, (2) hornblende, (3) microcline, (4) garnet, (5) tourmaline, and (6) quartz. In a later note Thiel (1945) added several other minerals to this list. The amended and expanded list of minerals, given in order from the least to the greatest resistance to abrasion, is: barite, siderite, fluorite, goethite, enstatite, kyanite, bronzite, hematite, augite, apatite, spodumene, hypersthene, diallage, rutile, hornblende, zircon, epidote, garnet, titanite, staurolite, microcline, tourmaline, and quartz. Though differing in some important particulars from Friese, the order is in the main consistent with the results of Friese.

Marsland and Woodruff (1937) also determined the mineral resistance to abrasion. Their work was based on air-blast action and showed the resistance to rounding to be, beginning with the least resistant, gypsum, calcite, apatite, magnetite, garnet, orthoclase, and quartz.

The abrasion-resistance orders of these various workers are observed orders determined experimentally. Abrasion resistance is in some way determined by the various mechanical properties of the grains. Thiel's order, for example, correlates roughly with the hardness. The average of the first five minerals is about 4.4, the next five average 5.6, the next averages 5.8, the next averages 6.8, and the last three are near 6.9. But cleavage as well as hardness plays a role in abrasion resistance, as does the "tenacity" of the mineral. Because hardness and other properties, in turn, are determined by the kind and arrangement of the atoms in the crystal lattice, some general character such as Fairbairn's packing and bonding indices (Fairbairn, 1943) might be expected to measure abrasion resistance. Such does not seem to be the case. The packing index shows a closer relation with resistance to decomposition than to wear.

Under given conditions of rigor, the several minerals may behave differently. Some, especially those with excellent cleavage, might be expected to fracture rather than undergo gentle attrition and rounding. Therefore certain species, notably kyanite, may serve as current velocity indices. Rounding of certain species would denote very gentle currents; absence of rounding of these minerals, but good rounding of other consanguinous species would indicate higher velocities (Krynine, 1942). These theoretical considerations have not yet been established by field or laboratory tests.

Do studies of sands and gravels in transit in nature show changes in composition consistent with the selective abrasion theory? On this point there is no agreement and much conflicting evidence. Russell (1937, 1939) takes the view that the sands of large streams show no or few mineral changes even during prolonged transport and that such feeble changes as do occur are not due to differential abrasion. His observations, on the mineralogy of the sands of the Mississippi between Cairo, Illinois, and the Gulf, 1100 miles distant, seem to support this conclusion. There appears to be only a small loss of feldspar relative to quartz and no appreciable loss of hornblende, pyroxene, and other relatively soft and cleavable minerals. Russell's conclusions seem to be confirmed by study of the sands of the Rhine (van Andel, 1950). The observation of Mackie and Plumley on the other hand seem to show that there is an appreciable loss of feldspar in comparatively short distances in high gradient streams. In the Black Hills streams the decline in feldspar content can hardly have been caused by anything except abrasion (Fig. 137). The similarity in density and sphericity of feldspar to quartz precludes a selective sorting process, and the size fraction studied by Plumley was so coarse (1–1.4 mm) that no progressive dilution of the feldspar content by contamination was likely.

The marked changes in mineral composition on the Cedar Point spit of Lake Erie, reported by Pettijohn and Ridge (1933) (Fig. 138), on the other hand, could not be attributed to selective abrasion, since the more durable minerals diminished and those less resistant increased in the direction of sand movement.

The downstream changes in composition of the gravels of the Black Hills streams (Fig. 139) and those earlier studied in Sweden seem to be related to selective abrasion. No experimental work was done, however, to see if the order of loss was actually that of the relative order of resistance to abrasion. The marked changes in lithologic composition of the glacial materials in central New York State, described by Holmes and attributed by him to selective abrasion by ice, are not certainly the result of such action. The decline in any given component may be only relative and the effect of dilution of this component by new materials added to the ice-load as the material was transported.

In conclusion, it can be said that the tendency to selective losses caused by abrasion exists and in some cases is operative but in other cases abrasion losses may be obscured by changes in composition from other causes. Progressive change in composition is certainly not sufficient proof of differential abrasion.

Selective Sorting

It is a common observation that somewhat homogeneous fractions can be extracted from complex mineral mixtures by various sorting processes. The prospector is able to recover heavy mineral fractions from natural sands by use of the miner's pan. Many of the ore-dressing procedures involve separation of one mineral from another by sorting processes dependent upon differences in density, size, or shape of the component grains. Nature also, therefore, might be expected to achieve crude separations by similar means.

Despite these observations, very little experimental work has been done on the sorting effects of water or air currents on mineral mixtures. Since sorting is dependent on size, shape, and specific gravity, the influence of each of these properties needs to be investigated. Although much experimental work has been done on settling velocity and the relation between this property and size, shape, and specific gravity, little of this knowledge has been carried over to the study of progressive changes in mineral composition in the downcurrent direction.

The relations between grain size and density have been most closely studied. Udden (1914) noted that in beach and stream sands, quartz is dis-

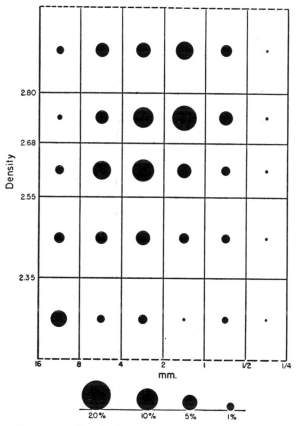

Fig. 140.   Size-density composition of beach materials, Christmas Island. The deposit is moderately well sorted, about eighty per cent in the 1–8 mm range. The several density fractions were obtained by use of heavy liquids. The percentage of the whole sample contained in each of the size-density classes is indicated by the black circles, the areas of which are proportional to the percentage. The distribution depicted indicates a general increase in density with a decrease in size (from Wentworth and Ladd, 1931).

tributed through more grades than the magnetite of the same sands, and also that the modal size of the quartz was one to three grades farther toward the larger sizes than the mode of the magnetite grains. The distance between the two modes in seven samples was about 1½ grades. In other words, the magnetite distribution is better sorted and finer grained than the associated quartz distribution. Apparently under the given conditions, magnetite is deposited with a grain of quartz of larger size. The differences in size are compensated for by differences in density, so that the grains of the two minerals are hydraulically equivalent. The size-density relationships in various sediments have been investigated (Wentworth and Ladd, 1931; Hawkes and Smythe, 1931) (Fig. 140).

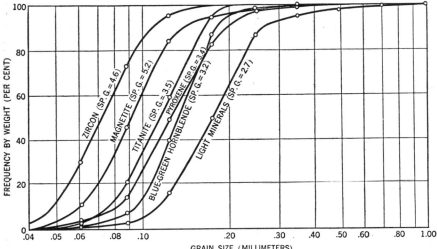

FIG. 141.   Size distribution by weight of light and selected heavy minerals in sample of sand from the Rio Grande, New Mexico (from Rittenhouse, 1943).

Rubey (1933) in particular has given a fairly complete theoretical analysis of the size relations in water-laid sands and the factors which control this distribution. Rubey's analysis, based on certain simplifying assumptions, gave the theoretical percentage frequency distribution curves of quartz, magnetite, and tourmaline in sands of fine, medium, and coarse grain. Lack of data made impossible a quantitative evaluation of all the factors governing the size distribution, so that the curves drawn by Rubey are subject to reservations. Nevertheless, the validity of the curves is supported in general by study of actual sands. Rubey showed that there would be important differences, not only in the percentage of the various heavy minerals in the different size grades of a particular sample, but also on the heavy-mineral composition of two sands of identical source that were deposited at the same time and distance from the source, but differing in average grain size or in sorting or in both these features.

The actual size distribution of the various minerals in modern sands has been worked out in some detail by Russell (1936), by Rittenhouse (1943), and others (Hawkes and Smythe, 1931; Van Andel, 1950). Rittenhouse showed that the size distribution of the heavy minerals is in general similar to that of the quartz, that the heavy minerals are finer in texture than the light minerals, that increasing specific gravity is accompanied by increasing fineness of the heavy minerals although there are some exceptions (zircon, sp gr 4.6, is much finer than magnetite, sp gr 5.2), and finally that the different species of heavy minerals in the same sands have different sorting (Fig. 141). On the basis of his analyses of actual sands, Rittenhouse determined the hydraulic equivalents of each of a number of common heavy minerals (Table 105). The hydraulic equivalent is the number of Udden

TABLE 105. Hydraulic Equivalents (after Rittenhouse, 1943)

Mineral	Sp Gr	Hydraulic Equivalent (Number of Udden size grades smaller than quartz)
Magnetite	5.2	1.0
Ilmenite	4.7	1.0
Zircon	4.6	0.9
Garnet	3.8 (variable)	0.6
Kyanite	3.6	0.3
Sphene	3.5	0.5
Pyroxene	3.4 (variable)	0.3
Hypersthene	3.4	0.4
Hornblende	3.2 (variable)	0.2
Apatite	3.2	0.4
Tourmaline	3.1	0.2

size grades between the size of a given mineral grain and the size of the quartz grain with which it was deposited or to which it is hydraulically equivalent. Rubey, for example, on the basis of Stoke's law,[4] concluded that a magnetite grain 0.63 millimeter in diameter would fall through water with the same velocity as a quartz grain 1.00 millimeter in diameter. In the finer-grained sands the size-ratio of $^{63}/_{100}$ of magnetite to quartz actually seems to be maintained, as shown by Rittenhouse's data. For coarser sands, where Stoke's law fails, the ratio is not the same.

[4] Stoke's law is the classic statement of the settling velocity of spherical particles. If standard conditions are assumed, namely, constant temperature, a given fluid, and a known specific gravity of the sphere, Stoke's law becomes $v = Cr^2$, where v is the velocity in centimeters per second, r is the radius of the sphere in centimeters, and C is a constant equal to $(2/9) (d_1 - d_2)g/\eta$, d_1 and d_2 are the densities of the sphere and the fluid, respectively, g is the acceleration due to gravity, and η is the viscosity of the fluid. Stoke's law has been shown to hold for small spheres—those under 0.08 mm in diameter. Large departures from theory are observed with grains over 0.2 mm in diameter (Krumbein and Pettijohn, 1938, p. 95).

Very little experimental work has been done on the sorting effects of water currents on mineral composition. Mackie (1923) states that the order of selectivity is (1) zircon, (2) iron ores, (3) garnet, (4) hornblende and other ferromagnesian minerals, and (5) quartz and feldspar. Smithson (1939) discussed the theory of selective transport of minerals and to a limited extent tested his conclusions by panning. He noted the general tendency of minerals to be sorted, the lighter from the heavier. Smithson also discussed the variations to be expected in certain ideal mixtures, assuming that some constituents are removed selectively by sorting. The problem is complex, however, because one characteristic of a mineral may work against another. The low sphericity of kyanite, despite its moderately high density, leads to a behavior more akin to a mineral of low density. Biotite is an even more striking example. The concentration of the micas in the silts rather than in the sands with which they were associated in the parent rock is thus explained. Present knowledge is incomplete and it is not possible to predict the behavior of any two minerals.

Actual examples of selective sorting in nature are few. The existence of placers, of course, implies some kind of sorting process (Trainer, 1930). The changing mineral composition of the sands transported along the Cedar Point spit of Lake Erie has been interpreted as a result of natural sorting (Pettijohn and Ridge, 1933). In the direction of transport garnet declines notably; hornblende shows a complementary increase (Fig. 138). Diopside and hypersthene, of intermediate specific gravity, show only a little change in frequency.

Progressive Dilution

Sediment from a given source area, as it moves out and away from such area, mingles with and becomes diluted by materials from other areas or places. The constituents of such a sediment, if they be distinctive or different from those with which they mingle, are progressively diluted as they move out from the source area. The progressive dilution of a given constituent results in a decrease in said constituent, which decrease might be mistaken as evidence for reduction by abrasion or the result of selective sorting.

Contamination might affect all size grades alike, though in the case of clastic sediments the grades are more commonly differentially contaminated. Locally derived materials tend to be coarse; far-traveled material is fine-grained. The coarser grades therefore are more heavily contaminated by locally derived debris, and the fine grades less so. Exceptionally the reverse is true. If the local material is a friable sand it may abnormally contaminate the sand fraction rather than the gravel portion (Krynine, 1937).

River channel sands and gravels might be expected to illustrate the principles outlined above. Materials from the headwaters would have diminished somewhat in size by the time they enter the middle reaches of the stream. Materials from the local bedrock in this section would be relatively coarse and would mingle with and dilute the materials from the headwater areas. Although all size grades would receive local contributions, the coarsest grades would receive a proportionally greater contribution. As pointed out by Cayeux (1929), the stream pebbles reflect in large measure the local bedrock whereas the sands are a clue to the character of the rocks in the

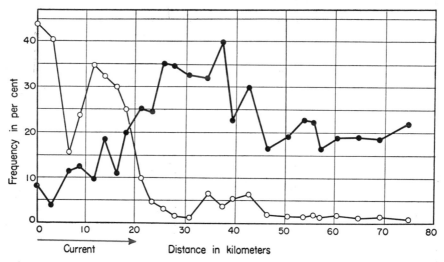

FIG. 142. Variations in heavy mineral composition of sands of River Tessin along the course of the stream (after Burri, 1929). Open circles, hornblende; black circles, staurolite.

headwaters area. One of the best illustrations of such progressive dilutions is Burri's study of the heavy minerals of the sands of the River Tessin (Burri, 1929). The decline in hornblende from 44 per cent to less than 1 per cent in about 80 kilometers of travel is almost certainly the result of progressive dilution of the bed load by nonhornblende-bearing sands (Fig. 142).

The contamination concept finds application in relation to unconformities. Locally derived, commonly angular, coarse debris is mingled with far-traveled and better-rounded debris. Full appreciation of the contamination principle will lead the investigator to recognition of multiple sources of the material of which any sediment is composed and to anticipate the basement rocks prior to their penetration with the drill.

The deposits of the continental ice sheets illustrate progressive dilution and show especially well the influence of the local bedrock on the character of the drift. The load carried by the ice is progressively modified by addition of new materials as the ice moves over varying types of bedrock. As a result the content of any specific component diminishes rapidly away from its source; a further result is the loading of the drift in any one place with locally derived materials. Careful analysis of the composition of the drift at several places therefore should enable one to deduce the direction of ice movement and to estimate the distance to the contributing ledges of any specific constituent.

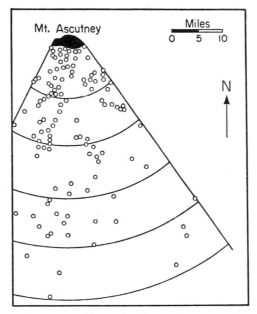

FIG. 143. Map of Mt. Ascutney boulder train, after Foster. Each circle represents a boulder; the arcs are spaced at ten-mile intervals (from Krumbein, 1937).

Boulder trains and the concentration in the drift of boulders derived from known sources illustrate the principles involved. Most boulder trains are derived from point sources, or at least from sources limited in extent. The boulders are dispersed in the lee of the source and are most thickly concentrated in the immediate vicinity of the source ledges (Figs. 143 and 144). As shown by Krumbein (1937), the boulder concentration per unit area diminishes exponentially with the distance from the source (Fig. 145). Maps published by Lundquist (1935) showing pebble counts (concentration in a small unit volume or sample) demonstrate rapid diminution away from the source; very probably also the decline is exponential (Fig. 144). The distribution and dispersion pattern of debris derived from a point source by the moving ice has been successfully used in prospecting for otherwise concealed ore bodies (Grip, 1953).

The best illustration of the problems involved is afforded by Holmes data from the glacial drift of west central New York (Holmes, 1952). The concentration of sandstone pebbles, here derived from a linear outcrop belt which lay athwart the direction of ice movement, shows a rapid decline in

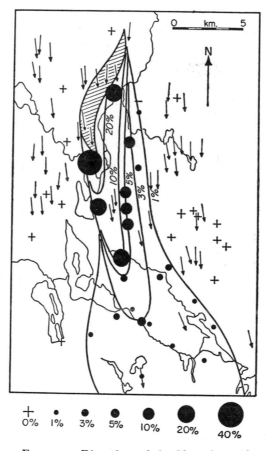

FIG. 144. Dispersion of boulders from the mica-slate district of Stallberg. Boulder counts by N. H. Magnusson; black circles moraine, dotted circles outwash. The transportation is in the direction of ice movement (shown by striations: arrows) (from Lundquist, 1935).

the downcurrent direction. The decline is exponential (Fig. 146). The concentration, high near the ledges, is halved in about 20 miles. Each successive 20 miles of transport results in successive halving of the sandstone percentage as determined by count in an index size class. Contouring of the sandstone percentages enables one to draw the normals to such lines of equal concentration and thus determine the direction and pattern of ice flow.[5]

It is obvious that air-borne materials from a given source would be deposited in the downcurrent or lee direction from such source. It has been shown that the thickness of such deposits diminishes exponentially away

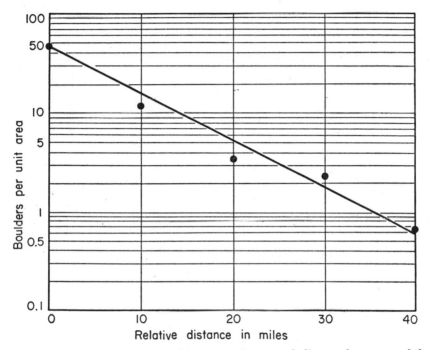

FIG. 145. Concentration of boulders per unit area and distance from source ledges, Mt. Ascutney boulder train (from Krumbein, 1937).

from the source. In Illinois, for example, the loess diminishes rapidly away from the river flats whence it came (Smith, 1942; Krumbein, 1937). Recent studies in Iowa show a similar rapid decrease, though the rate of decline may not be strictly exponential.

[5] Holmes ascribed the decrease of sandstone away from the source ledges to ice abrasion. Although some abrasion may indeed have taken place, the acquisition of new materials as the ice moved inevitably would depress the percentage of materials derived from bedrock upcurrent. It can readily be shown that if the ice acquires 50 per cent (or like proportion) of its load locally, the quantity of any given constituent will be exponentially decreased away from the source area (see Salisbury, 1900).

There appears also, in some cases at least (Shaler, 1895) a size decrease in the materials as they move away from their source. Such size decrease has been attributed to abrasion; it might also be due in part to the size of the sample. The smaller the sample the less likely is it to contain the larger sizes.

The thickness of volcanic ash also appears to diminish exponentially away from the crater from which it was expelled. Had such materials fallen into a basin in which sediments were accumulating at about a uniform rate, the resultant accumulation would show a diminished concentration of the contaminant away from the source of the extraneous material. That these theoretical considerations are correct seems to be borne out by some field

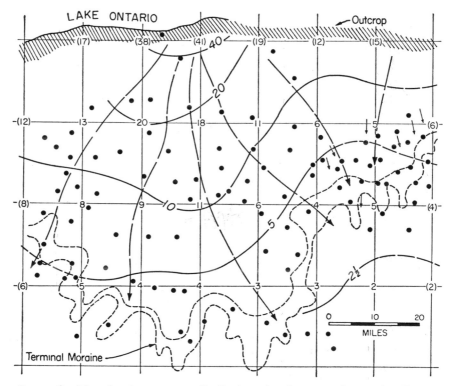

Fig. 146. Map showing per cent distribution of red-green sandstones in till, west-central New York. Generalized outcrop area of source beds, diagonal ruling; collecting localities, black dots; numerals at intersection of grid lines denote average for the four quadrangles centered on the respective values. Contours based on the averaged values; normals drawn to contours are the indicated directions of movement; arrows denote glacial striations and record actual movement (data from Holmes, 1952).

studies. The per cent of ash contained in marine sediments does diminish rapidly away from the volcano from which the ash came. The best data, however, are those on pollen concentrations (pollen grains per cubic centimeter) which show excellent agreement with theory (Hoffmeister, 1954). As is the case of pebble counts in glacial drift, the pollen concentration can be contoured, the direction of transport can be deduced, and the distance to the source can be estimated. In the case of pollen, the computed distance would be essentially the distance to the shore line. It is obvious, therefore, that the position and trend of the shore could thus be determined. It is also clear that it is immaterial whether the contaminant is wind-, water-, or ice-borne, and immaterial whether it is ash, pollen, or sandstone pebbles. The fall-out principle involved in all cases is essentially the same.

Although the concentration of one or more constituents may be depressed by dilution, ratios between two such depressed components should not be altered. As noted by Krynine (1937a, 1937b) these ratios may be more significant than actual percentages in recognizing reworking of older materials. If the critical ratios change in the downcurrent direction, selective sorting or selective abrasions or both may be involved. If the ratios remain unchanged, dilution alone is responsible for the depression of the absolute concentrations.

REFERENCES CITED AND BIBLIOGRAPHY

Burri, Conrad (1929), Sedimentpetrographische Untersuchungen an alpinen Flüssanden, Schweiz. mineralog. petrog. Mitt., vol. 9, pp. 205–240.

Cayeux, L. (1931), Introduction à l'étude pétrographique des roches sédimentaires, Paris, Impr. nationale.

Cozzens, A. B. (1931), Rates of wear of common minerals, Wash. Univ. Studies, Sci. Technol., n.s., no. 5, pp. 71–80.

Fairbairn, H. W. (1943), Packing in ionic minerals, Bull. Geol. Soc. Amer., vol. 54, pp. 1305–1374.

Friese, F. W. (1931), Untersuchungen von Mineralen auf Abnutzbarkeit bie Verfrachtung im Wasser, Mineralog. petrog. Mitt., vol. 41, n.s., pp. 1–7.

Grabau, A. W. (1913), Principles of stratigraphy, New York, Seiler.

Grip, Erland (1953), Tracing of glacial boulders as an aid to ore prospecting in Sweden, Econ. Geol., vol. 48, pp. 715–725.

Hawkes, L. and Smythe, J. A. (1931), Garnet-bearing sands of the Northumberland coast, Geol. Mag., vol. 68, pp. 345–361.

Hoffmeister, W. S. (1954), Microfossil prospecting for petroleum, U.S. Patent 2,686,108.

Holmes, C. D. (1952), Drift dispersion in west-central New York, Bull. Geol. Soc. Amer., vol. 63, pp. 993–1010.

Krumbein, W. C. (1937), Sediments and exponential curves, J. Geol., vol. 45, pp. 577–601.

Krumbein, W. C. and Pettijohn, F. J. (1938), Manual of sedimentary petrography, New York, Appleton-Century.

Krynine, P. D. (1937a), Glacial sedimentology of the Quinnipiac-Pequabuk lowland in southern Connecticut, Am. J. Sci., ser. 5, vol. 33, pp. 111–139.

Krynine, P. D. (1937b), Age of till on "Palouse Soil" from Washington, Am. J. Sci., ser. 5, vol. 33, pp. 205–216.

Krynine, P. D. (1942), Critical velocity as a controlling factor in sedimentation (abstract), *Bull. Geol. Soc. Amer.*, vol. 53, p. 1805.

Lundquist, G. (1935), Blockundersokningar, Historik och Metodik, *Sver. Geol. Undersökn.*, ser. 3, no. 390.

Mackie, Wm. (1896), The sands and sandstones of eastern Moray, *Trans. Edinburgh Geol. Soc.*, vol. 7, pp. 148–172.

Mackie, Wm. (1923), The principles that regulate the distribution of particles of heavy minerals in sedimentary rocks, as illustrated by the sandstones of the northeast of Scotland, *Trans. Edinburgh Geol. Soc.*, vol. 11, pp. 138–164.

Marsland, P. S. and Woodruff, J. G. (1937), A study of the effects of wind transportation on grains of several minerals, *J. Sediment. Petrol.*, vol. 7, pp. 18–30.

Martens, J. H. C. (1931), Persistence of feldspar in beach sand, *Am. Mineralogist*, vol. 16, pp. 526–531.

Martens, James H. C. (1935), Beach sands between Charleston, South Carolina, and Miami, Florida, *Bull. Geol. Soc. Amer.*, vol. 46, pp. 1563–1596.

Pettijohn, F. J. and Ridge, J. D. (1933), A mineral variation series of beach sands from Cedar Point, Ohio, *J. Sediment. Petrol.*, vol. 3, pp. 92–94.

Plumley, W. J. (1948), Black Hills terrace gravels: a study in sediment transport, *J. Geol.*, vol. 56, pp. 526–577.

Rittenhouse, Gordon (1943), The transportation and deposition of heavy minerals, *Bull. Geol. Soc. Amer.*, vol. 54, pp. 1725–1780.

Rubey, W. W. (1933), The size-distribution of heavy minerals within a water-laid sandstone, *J. Sediment. Petrol.*, vol. 3, pp. 3–29.

Russell, R. D. (1937), Mineral composition of Mississippi River sands, *Bull. Geol. Soc. Amer.*, vol. 48, pp. 1307–1348.

Russell, R. D. (1936), The size distribution of minerals in Mississippi River sands, *J. Sediment. Petrol.*, vol. 6, pp. 125–142.

Russell, R. D. (1939), Effects of transportation on sedimentary particles, in *Recent Marine Sediments*, Tulsa, Amer. Assoc. Petroleum Geologists, pp. 32–47.

Salisbury, R. D. (1900), The local origin of glacial drift, *J. Geol.*, vol. 8, pp. 426–432.

Shaler, N. S. (1893), The conditions of erosion beneath deep glaciers, based upon a study of the boulder train from Iron Hill, Cumberland, R.I., *Harvard Mus. Comp. Zool.*, Bull. 16 (g.s.2), pp. 185–225.

Smith, G. D. (1942), Illinois loess-variations in its properties and distribution, *Illinois Agric. Expt. Sta. Bull.* 490.

Szadecky-Kardoss, E. v. (1932), Flussschotteranalyse und Abtragunggebiet, *Mitt. berg- u. hüttenmänn. Abt. kgl. ung. Hochschule Berg- u. Forstw.* Sopron, vol. 4, pp. 1–38; vol. 5 (1933), pp. 1–23. Rev. in *J. Sediment. Petrol.*, vol. 5 (1935), pp. 52–53.

Thiel, G. A. (1940), The relative resistance to abrasion of mineral grains of sand size, *J. Sediment. Petrol.*, vol. 10, pp. 103–124.

Thiel, G. A. (1945), Mechanical effects of stream transportation on mineral grains of sand size (abstract), *Bull. Geol. Soc. Amer.*, vol. 56, p. 1207.

Trainer, D. W., Jr. (1930), Mineral concentrates of beach sand, *Am. Mineralogist*, vol. 15, pp. 194–197.

Udden, J. A. (1914), Mechanical composition of clastic sediments, *Bull. Geol. Soc. Amer.*, vol. 25, pp. 733–734.

Van Andel, Tj. H. (1950), *Provenance, transport and deposition of Rhine sediments*, Ph.D. dissertation, Univ. of Groningen.

Wentworth, C. K. (1922), A field study of the shapes of river pebbles, *U.S. Geol. Survey*, Bull. 730-C, pp. 103–114.

Wentworth, C. K. and Ladd, H. S. (1931), Pacific island sediments, *Univ. Iowa Studies Nat. Hist.*, vol. 13, no. 2, p. 31.

DISPERSAL SHADOWS: SEDIMENTARY PETROLOGIC PROVINCES AND SEDIMENTARY FACIES

Detrital materials released by weathering do not remain in the area in which they originate. They are dispersed. The dispersed materials come to rest in an area, the location, size, and shape of which are determined by the topography and the prevailing current system. The materials move downcurrent and if the current system is relatively stable, the materials will tend to lodge on the lee side of the generating source. Such a lee-side accumulation or shadow is a *sedimentary petrologic province*.

The concept of a sedimentary petrologic province has been attributed to Niggli (Baturin, 1937, p. 286). The exploration of the concept and the delineation of petrologic provinces in recent and ancient sediments has been largely the product of Edelman and his students (Edelman, 1933; Baak, 1936; Van Andel, 1950; Doeglas, 1940) and of Baturin (1931, 1937). Baturin (1937) defined a *terrigenous mineralogical province* as the area of sedimentation (both present and ancient sedimentation) characterized by one complex of light and heavy minerals which have the same source and are connected by one distributive province.[6] The term *sedimentary petrologic province* was suggested by Edelman for the same thing, that is, for the area underlain by sediments with a common provenance or origin. Normally this group of sediments is characterized by a distinctive mineral association.

The southern North Sea, for example, is floored with sand in part derived from the Fennoscandian highland, in part derived from Rhenish sources, and in part derived by erosion of the English coastal areas. The area delimited by the materials of Fennoscandian derivation is a sedimentary petrologic province; those areas defined by the materials of Rhenish or British derivation form additional provinces (Baak, 1936) (see Fig. 147). Provinces may overlap. Such overlap, if caused by oscillation of the boundary between two

[6] The term *distributive province*, first introduced by Brammall (Milner, 1922) implies the environment, embracing all rocks contributing to the formation of contemporaneously accumulated sediment.

provinces during time, leads to *provincial alternation*; if caused by mixing of sediments from two source areas at a given time the result is a *compound province* (composite terrigenous mineralogical province of Baturin). The study of sedimentary petrologic provinces is further complicated by the change in character of the distinguishing mineral association with time. Denudation of the source region may unroof new contributing sources and thus the defining assemblage is altered. Such changes result in *provincial succession* (Doeglas, 1940). The mapping of provinces is a difficult and time-consuming task, since their identification depends solely on a mineral association determined normally only by petrographic analysis.

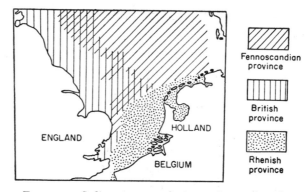

FIG. 147. Sedimentary petrologic provinces of southern North Sea (after Baak, *Recent Marine Sediments*, 1939, p. 345).

Exceptionally sedimentary provinces may be mapped by pebble counts. Such is the case with the glacial deposits. A boulder train is in fact a dispersal shadow formed downcurrent from the source ledges. A boulder train is therefore a small sedimentary petrologic province. Also the drift of one ice lobe differs in pebble content from that of another. The Saginaw lobe of Michigan, for example, contains boulders of a distinctive sort—especially the jasper conglomerates and tillites—not found in the drift of the contemporaneous Michigan lobe. The materials, though deposited at the same time, differ in their provenance; they belong therefore to differing petrologic provinces.

It seems probable that the red jasper pebble-bearing portion of the Lorrain quartzite (Precambrian) of the north shore of Lake Huron belongs to a different petrologic province than the rest of the Lorrain.

Sedimentary facies is the aspect or character of the sediment within beds of one and the same age. The sediments may have a common source and thus belong to the same province, but they may differ in their character from place to place. Sediments, for example, tend to diminish in grain size away from their source; sands, for example, shale out and pass into or intertongue with shales away from their source. Hence the field geologist may map the sand/shale ratio or depict the facies variation by plotting some other measurable property. A map of the sand/shale ratio expresses in a rough way the variation in mean grain size. In other cases facies maps reflect differing conditions of sedimentation. In an oxidizing environment the sands may be red; in a reducing environment they will be gray. Commonly these differ-

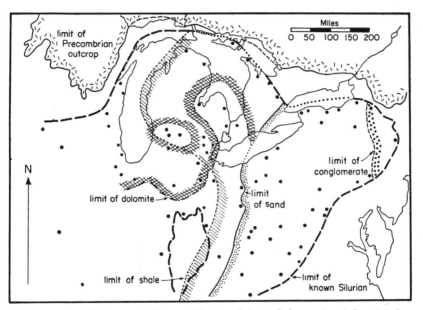

Fig. 148. Facies map of Lower Silurian of Great Lakes region (after Amsden, *Bull. Am. Assoc. Pet. Geol.*, vol. 39, 1955, p. 62). Limit of conglomerate 10 per cent; limit of sand about 12.5 per cent; limit of shale 25 per cent.

ences are areally distinct and mappable. Other facies, also chemically controlled, may be delineated. The distribution of limestone and dolomite within a formation or group of strata might be so mapped. Chemical facies and textural facies may be more or less independent and isofacial lines differently defined may even cross one another, as shown in a study of the facies of the Lower Silurian in the eastern United States (Amsden, 1955) (see Fig. 148).

Facies maps therefore delimit readily observable aspects or characters which are independent of the provenance of the sediment. A map of glacial sediments, discriminating between outwash and till, is a facies map; one discriminating between deposits characterized by differing pebble counts is a petrologic province map. Similarly a map depicting sand/shale ratios is a facies map; one depicting mineral assemblages in the sands is a province map. Both types are required to a full understanding of the sedimentary history of a given basin.

The construction of facies maps and their interpretation has been given a great deal of attention. The interested reader is referred to the pertinent literature on definitions and methods (Sloss, Krumbein, and Dapples, 1949; Moore, 1949; Krumbein, 1948, 1952, 1954) and to the many published examples.

Also essential to an understanding of the history of a sedimentary basin and related to both lithofacies and mineral provinces is the paleocurrent system reigning at the time of the sediment accumulation. Although the reconstruction of this system can be done by facies and provincial studies, it can more readily be done by systematic mapping of the vector properties of the sediment itself. The succeeding section of this chapter is devoted to paleocurrent reconstruction and interpretation.

REFERENCES CITED AND BIBLIOGRAPHY

Amsden, T. W. (1955), Lithofacies map of Lower Silurian deposits in central and eastern United States and Canada, Bull. Am. Assoc. Petroleum Geol., vol. 39, pp. 60–74.

Baak, J. A. (1936), Regional petrology of the southern North Sea, Ph.D. thesis, Wageningen, Netherlands.

Baturin, V. P. (1931), Petrography of the sands and sandstones of the productive series, Trans. Azerbaijan Petroleum Inst., Bull. 1, pp. 1–95.

Baturin, V. P. (1937), Paleogeography on the base of terrigenous components, Moscow, O.N.T.I., U.S.S.R.

Doeglas, D. J. (1940), The importance of heavy mineral analysis for regional sedimentary petrology, Nat. Research Council, Comm. Sedimentation Rept. 1939–1940, pp. 102–121.

Edelman, C. H. (1931), Mineralogische Untersuchungen von Sedimentgesteinen, Forschr. Mineral. Krist. Petrog., vol. 15, pp. 289–291.

Edelman, C. H. (1933), Petrologische provincies in het Nederlandsche Kwartair, Amsterdam,

Krumbein, W. C. (1948), Lithofacies maps and regional sedimentary-stratigraphic analysis, Bull. Am. Assoc. Petroleum Geol., vol. 32, pp. 1909–1923.

Krumbein, W. C. (1952), Principles of facies map interpretation, J. Sediment. Petrol., vol. 22, pp. 200–211.

Krumbein, W. C. (1954), The tetrahedron as a facies mapping device, J. Sediment. Petrol., vol. 24, pp. 3–19.

Milner, H. B. (1922), The nature and origin of the Pliocene deposits of the County of Cornwall, etc., Quart. J. Geol. Soc. London, vol. 78, p. 348.

Moore, R. C. (1949), Meaning of facies, Geol. Soc. Amer. Mem. 39, pp. 1–34.

Sloss, L. L., Krumbein, W. C., and Dapples, E. C. (1949), Integrated facies analysis, Geol. Soc. Amer. Mem. 39, pp. 91–123.

Van Andel, Tj. H. (1950), *Provenance, transport and deposition of Rhine sediments*, Ph.D. dissertation, Univ. of Groningen.

PALEOCURRENTS AND DISPERSION

Introduction

The vector properties of a clastic sedimentary deposit are those which are anisotropic—those which are related in some way to the current system prevailing at the time of deposition and are indeed a fossil record of such paleocurrents. Included here are cross-bedding and primary lineations and other markings (ripple marks, etc.) which are indicative of current flow (Table 106).

Systematic mapping of these primary structures enables one to study the current system of any period and to ascertain the areal extent of such systems and their stability in geologic time. The significance of such studies is obvious, for paleocurrents flowed down the regional slope within the area of sediment accumulation and the determination and mapping of regional slopes is of paramount importance in any paleogeographic reconstruction.

That the paleocurrent systems as determined from the vector properties of a sediment do define and delimit the regional slope is not wholly self-evident. Certainly the current flow of subaerial systems is downslope. The cross-bedding and other features of fluvial or alluvial sheets are a reliable indication of the downslope direction. Although local departures from the mean slope are to be expected, the mean direction of flow can hardly be other than downslope. In so far as the primary vector properties are due to subaqueous turbidity flows (striation casts and grooves, flow casts, etc.) the current direction indicated is clearly down the submarine slope. It is by no means clear, however, that the cross-bedding and other current features of shallow water marine sandstones are downslope. Conceivably such structures might register only a longshore current direction quite different from the regional slope and not in the source direction. Such a possibility was clearly stated by McKee (1940) who, however, later (1945) concluded that the cross-bedding shown in the marine Cambrian Tapeats sandstone of the Grand Canyon area was downslope and not a product of aberrant longshore currents. The evidence now at hand seems to indicate that this is generally true and that the current direction indicated is a reliable guide to both regional slope and source direction. The cross-beds of some sands show slump structures which indicate movement in the same direction as the current system—and since these are gravity initiated, they must be downslope. The current directions mapped in the shallow marine water sands are far too widespread and consistent to be a record of any local longshore current. And as noted by McKee, the current direction is consistent with and in the same direction as the facies changes induced by a shift from shallow water to deeper water environments.

In summary then, most of the current structures are certainly downslope and the remainder almost certainly so. Establishment of the regional slope is of considerable importance, since such slopes will be from the areas of the most recent orogenic maxima to the areas of subsidence or downwarp. The slope is therefore from older toward younger rocks; from source to sink. The slope direction is normal to the strand line, which in fact is but a special contour on the regional slope. It behooves the field geologist, therefore, to observe closely, to recognize the primary current structures, and to map these as systematically as the structural geologist maps those structures imposed on the rocks by tectonic forces.

The current origin of many primary structures of clastic sediments and the relation between fabric and current direction have long been known. Excepting only the early work of Ruedemann (1897), the systematic mapping of such features is a relatively recent development. The first such studies were generally related to a single feature. Hyde (1911), for example, mapped only the ripple marks in the Mississippian Berea sandstone of Ohio. Reiche (1938) mapped the cross-bedding of the Coconino sandstone of Arizona, and Shotton (1937) made a statistical and cartographic analysis of cross-bedding in the Lower Bunter sandstone of England. McKee (1940), like Reiche, measured and plotted the cross-bedding orientations of several Paleozoic sandstones of the Grand Canyon area. The results were shown both on polar coördinate diagrams and maps. Perhaps the first attempt to map all the primary structures and to make a comprehensive analysis of the paleogeography based on these observations was that done by Hans Cloos (1938) and his pupil van Bertsbergh (1940). Their work was done on the folded sediments of the Rhine geosyncline. Features mapped included strike of ripple marks, current direction inferred from asymmetrical ripples, strike and dip of cross-bedding, oriented fossils, and several linear structures. Several extended areal studies of cross-bedding have been made in more recent years (Schwarzacher, 1953; Potter, 1955; Potter and Olson, 1954; Brett, 1955; Bieber, 1953; Wilson, Watson, and Sutton, 1953; Illies, 1949; Lemcke, Engelhardt, and Füchtbauer, 1953) and several paleocurrent maps have been published based on both cross-bedding and other features (Stokes, 1953; Craig et al., 1951).

Geological field work involving the coarser clastic sediments can now be considered acceptable only if it includes mapping of the primary sedimentary structures of these rocks. Stratigraphic field studies omitting such features are as incomplete and unsatisfactory as geological maps of complex structures without observations of strike and dip of bedding, cleavage, lineation, and so forth.

Cross-Bedding and Paleogeography

The simplest and perhaps the most conspicuous structure of many arenaceous sediments is their cross-bedding. The abundance of such bedding and the ease with which it can be mapped, even in folded beds, and the great usefulness of the results are no doubt the reasons why cross-bedding has been studied and mapped more frequently than any other primary structure.

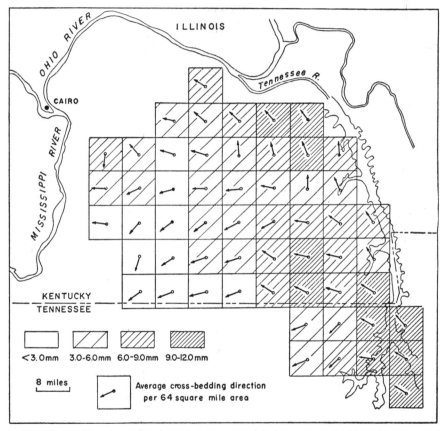

Fig. 149. Two-dimensional moving average of Lafayette cross-bedding direction and median size (after Potter, *J. Geol.*, vol. 63, 1955, p. 19).

Although Knight (1929) made a statistical analysis of both azimuthal and inclination frequencies of cross-bedding in several localities, Reiche's (1938) work on the Coconino sandstones of Arizona seems to be the first extended mapping of this feature in the United States. Shotton (1937) had earlier mapped the cross-bedding in the Lower Bunter sandstone in England. The sandstones studied by both Reiche and Shotton were thought to be of aeolian origin and the current flow pattern deduced from cross-bedding was therefore presumed to be the direction of the prevailing winds.

Subsequent studies have shown that the cross-bedding of water-laid sandstones commonly has a regionally consistent pattern. Potter (1955), for example, mapped the cross-bedding in the Lafayette gravels on the Smith-

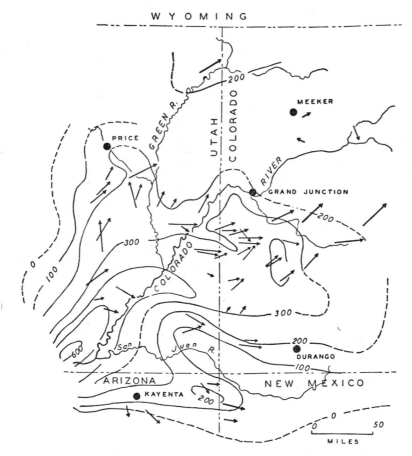

Fig. 150. Relations between cross-bedding directions (arrows) and isopach lines in Salt Wash member of the Morrison formation of southeastern Utah and adjacent states (data from Craig et al., 1955).

land surface in western Kentucky and was able to show that these deposits were essentially an ancient alluvial fan of the Tennessee (Fig. 149). Likewise the cross-bedding in the Saltwash member of the Morrison (Cretaceous) formation of Utah also showed a radial distribution pattern characteristic of an alluvial fan (Craig et al., 1951) (Fig. 150). Bieber (1953) and Potter and Olson (1954) mapped the regional pattern of the cross-bedding in basal Pennsylvanian sandstones of the Eastern Interior Basin and parts of the Appalachian Basin, and showed these sediments to have a regionally consistent current pattern indicating an eastern and northwestern source. Brett (1955) mapped the cross-bedding in the Precambrian Baraboo quartzite, which showed a clear north to south current flow pattern (Fig. 151). As the Baraboo is sharply folded, the original measurements of strike and dip of the cross laminations had to be rotated to ascertain their original attitude. Similar observations had been made earlier on the now-vertical Sturgeon

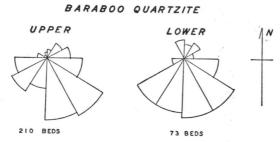

BARABOO QUARTZITE

FIG. 151. Comparison of cross-bedding azimuths in upper and lower halves of the Baraboo quartzite (Precambrian). (After Brett, *J. Geol.*, vol. 63, 1955, Fig. 2.)

quartzite (Precambrian) of the Menominee district in Michigan by Trow (1948). A similar study of the cross-bedding in the Moine series of Scotland showed this structure to have a regionally consistent pattern indicating a south to north current system (Wilson, Watson, and Sutton, 1953). Lemcke, Engelhardt and Füchtbauer (1953) mapped the cross-bedding of the sandstones and conglomerates of the Molasse in Augsburg region of Germany. The cross-bedding over an area roughly 100 kilometers in length and 40 kilometers width disclosed a consistent paleocurrent pattern.

It is now apparent that the cross-beddings of aeolian, fluviatile, and marine sandstones generally have regionally consistent patterns imposed by the ruling current system at the time of their deposition. In the stream-laid sandstones and conglomerates, the cross-bedding will dip down the regional slope. Although the significance of a regionally consistent azimuthal orientation of the cross laminations in marine sandstones is less clear, it seems likely that the pattern must in general signify downslope movement of the sand-depositing currents. A littoral current system would be a more local affair. Apparently, therefore, the cross-bedding of an ancient sandstone is indicative of the regional slope, movement away from source toward the basin, from older rocks to younger. It is obviously therefore of great paleogeographic significance.

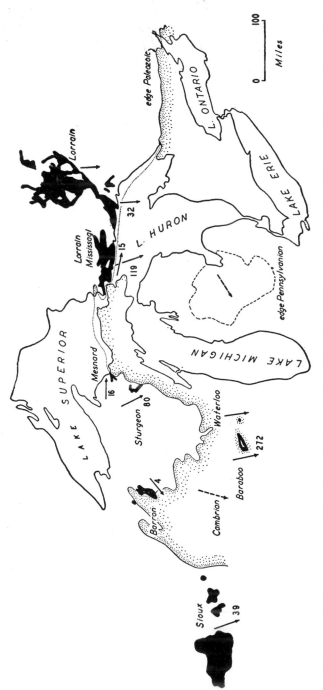

Fig. 152. Paleocurrent map of late Precambrian quartzites of the United States and Canada. Current directions primarily based on studies of cross-bedding. Numbers denote number of observations averaged. (After Pettijohn, Geol. Soc. Am., Bull., vol. 68, Fig. 1.)

In general the studies to date seem to bear out these conclusions. The Precambrian quartzites on which some cross-bedding data are available, all presumed to be late Precambrian, show movement south, southeast, and east from the presumed older Temiskaming (Archean) province (Fig. 152). The Pennsylvanian sandstones studied by Potter and Olson seem to show sediment movement southwest and west, presumably from the New England highlands uplifted during Taconic and Acadian orogenies.

The variability of the cross-bedding, i.e., its variance about the mean at any one place or through a region may be related to the tectonic stability (or lack of it). If the regional slope is maintained, the current flow pattern would be stable. If the slope is not so maintained by reason of lack of diastrophic movement, the surface of deposition approaches an equilibrium profile so that the currents become feeble and more random. Obviously more work is needed to relate cross-bedding to the geologic history of the region in which it occurs. Obviously, too, the spatial variations in thickness or scale of the cross-bedding and the coarseness of grain need to be made and correlated with the study of the cross-bedding direction.

Linear Structures and Paleocurrent Studies

With few exceptions the orientation of primary linear structures of sediments has not been recorded. And in most cases such records have been incomplete or, at best, made in conjunction with mapping of the cross-bedding. Most conspicuous exception is the work of Chenowith (1952) who recorded the orientation of markedly elongate fossils, especially high-spired gastropods and cephalopods, and the orientation of large parariples. These orientations proved to be consistent with one another and to show a regionally consistent pattern. Mention has been made elsewhere (page 181) of the mapping of primary lineation in sandstones (Cloos, 1938; Stokes, 1953) in conjunction with cross-bedding analysis.

The observations on the regional pattern of ripple mark orientation are somewhat conflicting. Van Bertsbergh (1940) apparently found both the oscillation and current ripples to be oriented normal to the current flow pattern deduced from cross-bedding. Hyde (1911) long ago noted a statewide preferential orientation of oscillation (symmetrical) ripples in the Berea sandstone of Mississippian age in Ohio. One hundred and forty-nine measurements over a distance of 115 miles show a remarkably consistent orientation. Hyde believed the ripples were parallel to a shoreline. Trow's observations on about 200 ripples, mainly of the symmetrical type, in the Precambrian Sturgeon quartzite of Michigan disclose a pattern less uniform than that of the Berea. The ripples, however, were generally parallel to and normal to the current system shown by cross-bedding analysis. Brett (1955) found the ripples in the Baraboo quartzite of Wisconsin, also Pre-

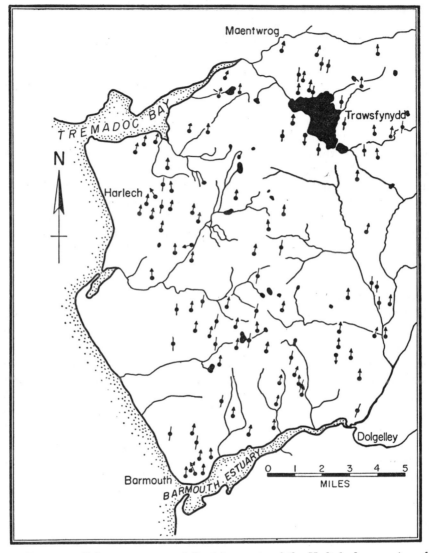

FIG. 153. Paleocurrent map of Cambrian strata of the Harlech dome region of Wales. Current directions based largely on flow casts and primary current lineations and sedimentary fabric (after Kopstein, 1954).

cambrian, to be essentially perpendicular to the current system shown by cross-bedding. His data were few (21 measurements only).

Theoretically the dimensional fabric of both sands and gravels should show a close correlation with the current system. Though some sporadic measurements have been made and show the theory to be essentially correct, few workers have systematically mapped the fabric of a sand or gravel.

Holmes (1941) did make a regional study of till fabric, as had Richter (1932; 1933), and in all cases, the fabric mapped was parallel with the ice current pattern determined from bedrock striations or from the trend of recessional moraines, eskers, and other depositional features.

The study of sand fabrics is incomplete and somewhat contradictory. Although several observers describe sand fabrics (Schwarzacher, 1951; Dapples and Rominger, 1945; Nanz, 1955), others have failed to find any. Griffiths and Rosenfeld (1951), for example, found no preferred orientation of the apparent long axes of sand grains in the plane of the bedding in specimens of the Third Bradford Sand (Devonian). On the other hand, Helmbold (1952) found and measured such orientation in the Tanner graywackes of Germany. Only Kopstein (1954), who reports such long-axis alignment in most specimens of the Cambrian from the Harlech dome area in Wales, systematically mapped these orientations (together with other current structures) for the purpose of determining direction of current flow. As fabric analyses are somewhat tedious to make, it is likely that they will be made only where the paleocurrent systems cannot be determined by other means.

The most conspicuous and most useful linear structures of current origin are the striation casts, groove casts, and flow casts found on the underside of many flagstone beds rhythmically graded and interbedded with shales. These features, briefly mentioned by Rich (1950) in the Portage group of western New York state, seem to be uniform in orientation over wide areas. The only systematic mapping, however, seems to be that of Kopstein (1954) in the Cambrian of Wales. The paleocurrent system depicted by plotting of these structures is exceedingly uniform over large areas and throughout very long periods of time [7] (Fig. 153). Unlike cross-bedding, the variability of direction is very low—a few degrees instead of a whole quadrant. Clearly the currents responsible for the deposition of the graded beds moved with glacier-like uniformity down a submarine slope which had a remarkable stability through a very long period of time.

Since current-bedding and graded-bedding are the earmarks of two very different facies of sand deposition, it is reasonable to expect the criteria of

TABLE 106.   Criteria of Current Direction and Sand Facies

Orthosandstones (current-bedded)	Parasandstones (graded-bedded)
CROSS-BEDDING	Cross-bedding
Primary current lineation	STRIATION CASTS AND GROOVES
Rib-and-furrow	FLOW CASTS
Fabric	Fabric

[7] The whole of the Cambrian in Kopstein's Harlech dome study.

current-flow direction and the stability and other characteristics of the current systems involved to be quite different in the two contrasting facies. The principal criteria and their relative importance are shown in Table 106.

REFERENCES CITED AND BIBLIOGRAPHY

Bieber, C. L. (1953), Current directions indicated by cross-bedding in deposits of early Mansfield age in southwestern Indiana, Proc. Indiana Acad. Sci., vol. 62, pp. 228–229.

Brett, Geo. W. (1955), Cross-bedding in the Baraboo Quartzite of Wisconsin, J. Geol., vol. 63, pp. 143–148.

Brinckman, Roland (1933), Über Kreuzschichtung im deutschen Buntsandsteinbecken, Nachr. Ges. Wiss. Göttingen, Math.-physik. Kl. 1933, p. 1–2.

Chenowith, P. A. (1952), Statistical methods applied to Trentonian stratigraphy in New York, Bull. Geol. Soc. Amer., vol. 63, pp. 521–560.

Cloos, Hans (1938), Primäre Richtungen in Sedimenten der rheinischen Geosynkline, Geol. Rundschau, vol. 29, pp. 357–367.

Craig, L. C. (1955), Stratigraphy of the Morrison and related formations, Colorado Plateau region: a preliminary report: U.S. Geol. Survey Bull. 1009E.

Dapples, E. C. and Rominger, J. F. (1945), Orientation analysis of fine-grained clastic sediments, J. Geol., vol. 53, pp. 246–261.

Griffiths, J. C. and Rosenfeld, M. A. (1951), Progress in measurement of grain orientation in Bradford Sand, Producers Monthly, vol. 15, pp. 24–36.

Helmbold, R. (1952), Beitrag zur Petrographie der Tanner Grauwacken, Heidelberger Beitr. Mineral. u. Petrog., vol. 3, pp. 253–288.

Holmes, C. D. (1941), Till fabric, Bull. Geol. Soc. Amer., vol. 52, pp. 1299–1354.

Holmes, C. D. (1952), Drift dispersion in west-central New York, Bull. Geol. Soc. Amer., vol. 63, pp. 993–1010.

Hyde, J. E. (1911), The ripples of the Bedford and Berea formations of central Ohio, with notes on the paleogeography of that epoch, J. Geol., vol. 19, pp. 257–269.

Illies, H. (1949), Die Schrägschichtung in fluviatilen und litoralen Sedimenten, ihre Ursachen, Messung, und Auswertung, Mitt. geol. Staatsinst. Hamburg, vol. 19, pp. 89–109.

Jüngst, H. (1931), Diagonal strukturen, ihre Auflösung und Darstellung, Z. deut. geol. Ges., vol. 83, p. 663.

Kiersch, G. A. (1950), Small-scale structures and other features of Navajo sandstone, northern part of San Rafael swell, Utah, Bull. Am. Assoc. Petroleum Geol., vol. 34, pp. 923–942.

Knight, S. H. (1929), The Fountain and Casper formations of the Laramie Basin, Univ. Wyoming Publ. Sci., Geol., vol. 1.

Kopstein, F. P. H. W. (1954), Graded bedding of the Harlech dome, Ph.D. thesis, Univ. of Groningen.

Kuenen, Ph. H. (1952), Paleogeographic significance of graded bedding and associated features, Koninkl. Ned. Akad. Wetenschap., Proc., ser. B, vol. 55, pp. 28–36.

Lemcke, K., von Engelhardt, W., and Füchtbauer, H. (1953), Geologische und sediment-petrographische Untersuchungen im Westteil der ungefalten Molasse des süddeutschen Alpenvorlandes, Beihefte, Geol. Jahrb., H. 11.

McKee, E. D. (1940), Three types of cross-laminations in Paleozoic rocks of northern Arizona, Am. J. Sci., vol. 238, p. 811–824.

McKee, F. D. and Resser, C. E. (1945), Cambrian history of the Grand Canyon region, Carnegie Inst. Wash., Publ. No. 563, pp. 125–128.

Nanz, R. H. (1955), Grain orientation in beach sands: a possible means for predicting reservoir trend, Program, 29th Ann. Meeting, S.E.P.M. New York.

Olson, J. S. and Potter, P. E. (1954), Variance components of cross-bedding direction in some basal Pennsylvanian sandstones of the Eastern Interior Basin: statistical methods, J. Geol., vol. 62, pp. 26–49.

Potter, P. E. (1955), Petrology and origin of the Lafayette gravel, Part I. Mineralogy and petrology, J. Geol., vol. 63, pp. 1–38.

Potter, P. E. and Olson, J. S. (1954), Variance components of cross-bedding direction in some basal Pennsylvanian sandstones of the Eastern Interior Basin: Geological applications, J. Geol., vol. 62, pp. 50–73.

Reiche, Parry (1938), An analysis of cross-lamination: the Coconino sandstone, J. Geol., vol. 46, pp. 905–932.

Rich, J. L. (1950), Flow markings, groovings, and intrastratal crumplings, etc., Bull. Am. Assoc. Petroleum Geol., vol. 34, pp. 717–741.

Richter, Konrad (1932), Die Bewegungsrichtung des Inlandeises rekonstruiert aus den Kritzen und Längsachsen der Geschiebe, Z. Geschiebeforsch., vol. 8, pp. 62–66.

Richter, Konrad (1933), Gefüge und Zusammensetzung des norddeutschen Jung-moranengebietes, Z. Geschiebeforsch. Beihefte, vol. 9, pp. 1–63.

Ruedemann, R. (1897), Evidence of current action in the Ordovician of New York, Am. Geologist, vol. 19, pp. 367–391.

Schlee, John (1955), Sedimentological analysis of the Upland Gravels of Maryland, Ph.D. thesis, The Johns Hopkins University.

Schwarzacher, W. (1951), Grain orientation in sands and sandstones, J. Sediment. Petrol., vol. 21, pp. 162–172.

Schwarzacher, W. (1953), Cross-bedding and grain size in the Lower Cretaceous sands of East Anglia, Geol. Mag., vol. 90, pp. 322–330.

Shotton, F. W. (1937), Lower Bunter sandstones of north Worcestershire and east Shropshire, Geol. Mag., vol. 74, pp. 534–553.

Stokes, W. L. (1953), Primary sedimentary trend indicators applied to ore-finding in the Carrizo Mountains, Arizona, and New Mexico, U.S. Atomic Energy Comm., RME-3043 (pt. 1).

Trow, J. W. (1948), The Sturgeon quartzite of the Menominee district, Michigan, Ph.D. dissertation, Univ. of Chicago.

von Bertsbergh, J. W. B. (1940), Richtungen der Sedimentation in der rheinischen Geosynkline, Geol. Rundschau, vol. 31, pp. 328–364.

Weir, G. W. (1951), Cross-lamination in the Salt Wash sandstone member of the Morrison formation (abstract), Bull. Geol. Soc. Amer., vol. 62, p. 1514.

Wilson, G., Watson, J., and Sutton, J. (1953), Current-bedding in the Moine series of northwestern Scotland, Geol. Mag., vol. 90, pp. 377–387.

13

Depositional Environments

INTRODUCTION

A SEDIMENTARY rock is not only a product of a specific provenance and transport history but it is also the product of its environment of deposition. Some sedimentary rocks, such as the chemical and biochemical precipitates, carry no record of their provenance or transport and reflect only their environment of origin; others, such as the clastic deposits, not only record the predepositional history, but in addition have imprinted on them some record of the depositional environment. Our task here is to analyze the problem of environmental reconstruction and to report on progress made to date in such reconstruction.

We must first consider what is meant by environment. To most geologists the term means a geographically restricted complex generally described in geomorphic terms. Thus a lagoon, a lake, a swamp, or a river flood plain constitutes environmental complexes referred to as lagoonal, lacustrine, paludal, or fluvial, respectively. The stratigrapher would like to assign a particular bed or facies to some such environmental complex.

Each such depositional environment is indeed a complex, characterized by a variable set of physical and chemical conditions. These may even vary from place to place within the confines of the geomorphic unit, so that the sediments likewise vary from place to place. Lake beach deposits more closely resemble sea beach materials than they do the deep-water lake sediments.

The character of a sediment, as noted elsewhere, is determined by both the intensity of the formative processes operating on it and by the time or duration through which such action is continued. The *intensity* is in large part controlled by the *local* environment. Sediments, for example, deposited in a turbulent environment, where the energy input is high will be coarse, well sorted, and if the energy input is maintained over a long period of time, they will be well rounded and otherwise texturally mature. Thus beach and dune deposits are much alike, and are in turn rather similar to some of the deposits of turbulent streams. The time or duration through which the action is extended, however, is a function primarily of the tectonic stability or instability of a region. Rapid uplift and equally rapid down-sinking lead to high relief, with the result that weathering is incomplete, transport is brief, and burial without reworking is rapid. The formative processes are cut short so that the resulting sediment is quite immature. The study of environments and the problem of environmental reconstruction is resolved into study of the local environment, its physical and chemical attributes, and a study of the tectonic realm or domain in which the local environment is set.

The local environment is characterized by both physical and chemical norms. The physical factors include current velocity, current stability (both as to velocity and direction), water depth, fluidity (viscosity and density) of the depositional medium, and so forth. The chemical factors are principally the oxidation-reduction potential (Eh), the acidity or alkalinity (pH), the concentration or salinity, and the temperature of the depositional medium. For the most part the criteria for determining the physical factors are textural and structural; for the most part the determination of the nature of the chemical milieu is dependent upon the mineral composition. There are, in addition, important, and in some cases conclusive, biological criteria for the recognition of both the physical and chemical environments. The characteristics of the local environment are, of course, in part determined by the size and shape of the basin of deposition and by the climate of the area in which it is located.

The tectonic environment is perhaps the most basic. Diastrophism is the fundamental geologic process and produces the inequalities in relief which set in motion the counteracting processes of erosion and sedimentation. In general it is the positive areas, which stand above the sea and constitute the lands, that are the sources of the sediments and the negative areas which are covered by the sea which are the basins in which the sediment is trapped. The strand or shoreline is the line of demarcation between source and sink. The geologist has long recognized the importance of the strand line and much effort has been expended in trying to locate this boundary in the times past. Not only does diastrophism determine which areas are sources of sediments and which are sinks, but it determines, through the rate of uplift and depression, the magnitude of the relief and therefore the time or duration of the formative processes and hence the maturity or immaturity of the sediment and the extent to which the processes of sedimentary differentiation may be carried.

In this chapter we will attempt, first, to discuss the parameters of the local environment and the criteria for their reconstruction, and second, attempt to formulate the principles relating tectonism to petrologic types and the criteria for the reconstruction of the tectonic framework of ancient times.

ENVIRONMENTAL PARAMETERS

Physical Parameters

The physical milieu is best described in terms of the dynamic and static properties of the depositional medium from which the sediment is laid down. The static properties include the density and viscosity of the medium (air versus water, for example) and the depth of the medium above the sediment-fluid interface; the dynamic factors include the turbulence of the medium (quiet versus rough water), the velocity of the depositing current, the direction of current flow, the stability of the flow pattern (in terms of both velocity and direction), and similar factors.

The Nature of the Depositing Medium

One of the factors in environmental analysis is the nature of the medium from which the clastic elements of the sedimentary rock were deposited. In other words, was the material deposited from air, water, or glacial ice? Clearly identification of the depositing medium would greatly advance our efforts at reconstruction of the environment.

As the transporting power of a current and the effectiveness of that current as a sorting agent depend on the viscosity or the density (or both) of the medium involved, there should be a correlation between the textures of the deposit formed and these properties of the moving medium. At the opposite poles are the air-laid materials, such as dune sand, and those which are ice-laid, namely, till. No more marked textural contrasts are known. The distinction between aeolian sands and some beach sands, however, is far less clear. The principal media and the materials deposited therefrom are schematically shown in Table 107.

In brief, as the density or viscosity increases, the lower is the velocity required to transport a given size; also as these properties increase, the less effective is the medium as a sorting agent. Dilute suspensions moved by air or water are effectively sorted; large sizes are transported only at high velocities. Concentrated suspensions or slurries carry larger fragments at the same velocities and deposit poorly sorted sediments. If the proportion of the solid to the fluid increases still more, the materials no longer flow as a Newtonian liquid but move only as a semisolid plastic body. Sorting is nil and the largest available blocks are moved and deposited concurrently with the finest particles. Mudflows and glacial ice belong to this latter category.

Table 107. Transporting Agents and Sedimentary Deposits

———————— Increasing Density and/or Viscosity ——————→			
Fluid		*Semisolid*	*Solid*
Air Water plus sediment		Sediment plus water	Ice plus sediment
Dilute suspension	Concentrated suspension		
Orthoarenites (orthoquartzite and calcarenite)	Para-arenites (graywackes)	Tilloids	Till and tillite
Current-bedded	Graded-bedded	Nonbedded	

The deposits of dilute suspensions are the orthoconglomerates and ortho-arenites—those with an intact framework of clastic elements; the deposits of the concentrated slurries and mudflows are the paraconglomerates and para-arenites or those with a disrupted framework and an argillaceous matrix. If the solid/fluid ratio is not too high the deposit is graded;[1] if the ratio exceeds some critical value Newtonian flow ceases and the deposit is not graded. Consequently the framework/matrix ratio, the presence or absence of grading and the type of grading are critical criteria in attempting to identify the agent of deposition.

Theoretically the differences in density and viscosity between air and water should lead to distinctive textural differences in the deposits of these two agents. Although various writers have attempted to formulate these differences, there seems to be no definitive textural criterion for distinguishing aeolian and aqueous sands. Udden (1914) devised an index of sorting which he thought made such a discrimination; he also thought that the difference in size between the chief mode and the secondary mode of bimodal sediments was different for aeolian and aqueous deposits. Later work does not seem to bear out Udden's conclusions. MacCarthy (1935) attempted to discriminate between aeolian and beach sands on the basis of their roundness. Although MacCarthy's "roundness" is in reality a shape modulus (Russell and Taylor, 1937, p. 73), there seems to be a real distinction between the beach and dune sands studied by MacCarthy. The dune sands are better rounded, although desert dunes were less well rounded than beach dunes. MacCarthy's results, though interesting, are based on much too small a sample to have general validity. A more extended study, based on 700 samples, seems to suggest that in dune sands the fine admixtures (p. 34) exceed the coarse by at least 2 or 3 to 1, whereas in the beach sands the ratio is near 1 to 1 or less (Keller, 1945). The use of the coarse

[1] The grading is of the symmict type, unlike that produced by a waning current, the fines are present throughout the bed (see p. 171. Fig. 59).

or fine admixtures is an uncertain procedure, since the proportions of the two are easily altered by shift of the class limits used in the analysis. Perhaps, as the data seem to imply, the grading curves are differently skewed for beach and dune sands.

It has long been believed that wind is able to round smaller grains of sand than is water (Ziegler, 1911). This concept has been challenged and has never been well established by quantitative studies.

More commonly sandstones have been ascribed to the action of wind or water on other characters than grain size or shape. Frosted quartz has been attributed to the action of wind although the proof of this statement is not yet certain.[2] Even if it is caused by aeolian action, the frosted character might be inherited from a previous cycle. Most weight, therefore, is usually given to the presumed differences in the bedding of dune and beach deposits. These have been well summarized by Thompson (1937). It has been said, for example, that dune sands will show a much greater spread in the direction of inclination of cross laminations than is shown by the cross laminations of aqueous origin (Twenhofel, 1932, p. 621). Data are at present inconclusive. Reiche's (1938) work on the Coconino, a presumed aeolian sand, showed a standard deviation ranging from 31 to 74 degrees for the various localities studied. Although comparable data do not exist for either known aqueous or aeolian sands, inspection of diagrams based on many measurements (Fig. 56) of cross-laminated sandstones of presumed aqueous origin does not show any markedly different spread or scatter between these and the Coconino.[3] More reliance has been placed on the *scale* of the cross-bedding than the consistency of its orientation. Large-scale tangential cross-bedding is ascribed to wind action. Subaerial cross beds are said to have a higher inclination than those deposited subaqueously.

Ripple marks produced by wind have a larger ripple index (p. 185) than do aqueous ripples. Moreover, the coarser grains of aeolian ripples are concentrated in the crests. Vertebrate tracks observed on the lee slopes of dunes appear always to go up the slope. Unfortunately, vertebrate tracks and aeolian ripples are exceedingly rare and seldom available when needed.

The deposits of glacial ice, the tills and tillites, have been described in detail elsewhere (p. 266) so that the criteria for recognizing an ancient tillite and the distinction between tilloids and tillites need not be reviewed here. Likewise the characteristics of the sands deposited by turbidity flows have been reviewed in the sections on graded bedding (p. 170) and graywackes (p. 301). The interested reader is referred to these portions of this book.

---

[2] Clearly rivers can remove frosting and induce a polish (Bond, 1954).

[3] Most of the diagrams are for areas rather than single localities and many are for a series of beds of considerable thickness. Restriction of time and space involved obviously would reduce the standard deviation.

Rough Water Versus Quiet Water

The bathymetric position of marine sediments is defined or described first of all with reference to wave base. Those sediments above wave base are deposited in a rough-water or turbulent environment and are constantly shifted about and reworked so that they tend to become texturally and mineralogically mature. Sediments deposited below wave base accumulate in a relatively quiet-water or still-water environment and are little disturbed by currents after deposition. Although environments may be classified as rough-water or quiet-water, some are alternately one and then the other. Thus three zones characterized by continuously turbulent, intermittently turbulent, and nonturbulent (laminar) flow can be defined. Baturin (1941) even recognized four such zones.

Wave base is not an absolute depth; it is a relative one. In small water bodies or semi-isolated bodies of small size, the waves generated are small and their effects extend only to a slight depth. On exposed coasts of the open seas the waves are larger and they may sweep the bottom many feet below the surface. Although the majority of currents and the scour which they produce are wave-generated, some currents, generally feeble, occur at great depths. Except for the turbidity currents these are able to move only the smallest-sized particles.

The rough-water environment is the zone characterized by sand and gravel deposits and by coquinas and the calcarenites. The sands are well sorted, well rounded, ripple marked, and presumably current bedded. Coarse clastics, however, are no certain criterion of shallow water (or even rough water) as they were once supposed to be. Sands are transported and deposited *below* wave base by turbidity underflows. These sands are marked by poor rounding, poor sorting, and graded structure and may be deposited upon fine-grained muds and silts without disturbing the delicate worm trails of the muddy bottoms. As noted by Bailey (1930, 1936) graded bedding and current bedding are indices of two contrasting environments of sand deposition, below and above wave base, respectively. Current-bedding, if produced in the deeper waters is on a very small scale.

Criteria indicative of quiet-water deposition include the delicate laminations which characterize some siltstones and shales. Some such paper-thin laminations may represent annual increments of sediment and thus become a measure of the rate of sedimentation. Only in the absence of any bottom turbulence could such laminations remain undisturbed.

Whereas the rough-water zone is characterized by scour-and-fill cross-bedding and the quiet-water zone is distinguished by the thin and even laminations, the intermittently quiet and rough-water environment is marked by alternately regular and irregular bedding. The larger (and coarser) beds are somewhat uneven in thickness and wavy in cross section. The finer laminations composing them are still more irregular and given to tapering out. Some of the siltstone or fine sandstone beds are broken up into a string of planoconvex segments as if their deposition had been succeeded by brief periods of erosion or ripple marking (Pl. 22, center).

The state of preservation of many fossils, their mode of attachment, and their orientation may be further clues to the turbulence of the surrounding medium. Delicate articulated forms suggest growth and burial in a current-free environment; disarticulated broken and sorted fossil debris suggest strong bottom currents.[4] The random orientation of concave-convex shells suggests an absence of appreciable currents and conversely a common orientation of these and other fossil structures is proof of stronger bottom currents. Preservation of delicate worm trails and like structures on mud surfaces (represented by casts on the underside of sandstone or siltstone beds) suggests very feeble bottom currents or none. The burrowing habit of forms living in a sandy environment may be a response to bottom scour.

Certain minerals are indicative of reducing conditions. Such conditions cannot be achieved in highly turbulent, aerated waters. Minerals formed in stagnate anaerobic waters include sedimentary pyrite and siderite. In certain lagoons and estuaries where wave and current action is negligible, these materials may form in the muds in comparatively shallow water.

Current Velocity, Direction, and Stability

Various attempts have been made to estimate the current velocity from the size of the clastic elements in a sediment. Such estimates are valid only

TABLE 108. Grain Size and Current Velocity

Grain Diameter (mm)	Observed Traction Velocity (cm/sec)	Calculated Suspension Velocity (cm/sec)
6.08	84.5[a]	45.3[c]
4.18	61.3[a]	36.3[c]
4.08	62.2[b]	35.9[d]
3.08	53.8[a]	29.7[c]
1.38	36.0[a]	18.0[c]
0.72	....	15.2[c]
0.59	31.6[b]	14.1[d]
0.35	....	13.7[c]
0.31	24.5[b]	13.2[d]
0.20	21.5[b]	10.7[d]

[a] Observed in flume experiments (Gilbert, 1914).
[b] Observed in flume experiments, U.S. Waterways Experiment Station, Vicksburg, Mississippi, 1935 (Nevin, 1946).
[c] Calculated (Rubey, 1938).
[d] Calculated (Nevin, 1946).

[4] Simple disarticulation alone may mean only a very slow rate of sedimentation.

Diagonal
cross-bedding

Convex
cross-bedding

Change-rolls

Diagonal
incline-bedding

Horizontal
stratum

Horizontal
strata

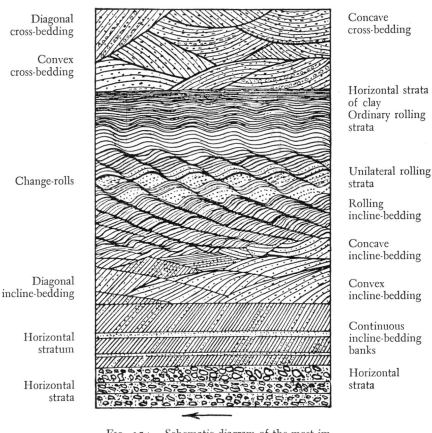

Concave
cross-bedding

Horizontal strata
of clay
Ordinary rolling
strata

Unilateral rolling
strata

Rolling
incline-bedding

Concave
incline-bedding

Convex
incline-bedding

Continuous
incline-bedding
banks

Horizontal
strata

FIG. 154. Schematic diagram of the most important forms of structures in stratified gravel, sands, and clay. The arrow indicates the direction of the current that laid down the deposits under the horizontal strata of clay; over the clay, the stream has run at right angles to the section shown (from Andersen, 1931, fig. 38).

for the orthosands and gravels, not for the paraconglomerates and sands of turbidity underflows. The values given in Table 108 are based on experiments in flumes by Gilbert (1914) and the U.S. Waterways Experiment Station at Vicksburg, Mississippi (Nevin, 1946). From the observed velocities of traction debris it is possible to calculate the velocity of the suspension load by use of Rubey's formula (1938). Anderson (1934) and others have noted that the bedding structures of a sediment are closely related to the velocity of the velocity of the currents involved. As shown in Fig. 154, the slow-moving currents deposit even-bedded silts and clays; faster movement initiates a rippling of the sand-water interface and produces small-scale ripple cross-bedding; at high velocities scour and fill lead to a strongly cross-bedded deposit. There is undoubtedly some relation between scale of the cross-bedding and current velocity, although the precise relations have not been quantitatively defined.

Other indices of current velocity are the percussion marks found on some pebbles transported by high velocity streams (p. 71), an abnormal percentage of broken rounds (p. 537), the rounding of kyanite and micas that is possible only if the current action is very gentle (p. 560).

Not only is the current strength an important attribute of the environment but so also is the persistence of the current in both direction and velocity. The persistence in direction is best determined by the variance of the cross-bedding or other vector of current origin; the persistence in velocity is expressed by the bed-to-bed variance in mean particle size.

Depth of Water

It is comparatively easy to distinguish between the turbulent and quiet water environments, i.e., between the sediments deposited above wave base and those deposited below. It is difficult, however, to estimate absolute depth of water.

The kind of fossils present may be a guide to water depth. Algal structures indicate deposition only in depths to which light has access. The depth of light penetration varies, of course, with the turbidity of the water but is never very great. In the more recent sediments, especially those of Tertiary age, the water depth can be estimated by paleoecologic data. The foraminiferal species are closely correlated with depth and by study of the habitats of present-day forms, the depth of water of older deposits containing these forms can be estimated (Phleger, 1955; Bandy, 1953). The interpretation of such faunal evidence is complicated, however, by the effects of temperature on the species range and by mechanical transport of shallow-water forms to deep water. In the older rocks the faunal content is a less sure guide to absolute depth.

Except that a quiet-water environment suggests greater depth and conversely a rough-water environment is more or less surely restricted to shallow depths, there is no certain criterion of absolute depth. Absence of carbonate sediments and a predominance of shales is probably an indication of comparatively deep waters. At the present time carbonate dissolves in depths exceeding 3000 fathoms. Before the Cretaceous, carbonate-secreting organisms were largely shallow-water benthonic forms; the absence of calcareous fossils therefore does not imply solution at abyssal depths.

If slump structures are prominent in the sediments, the probable depth of water can be estimated by assuming a bottom gradient sufficient to initiate

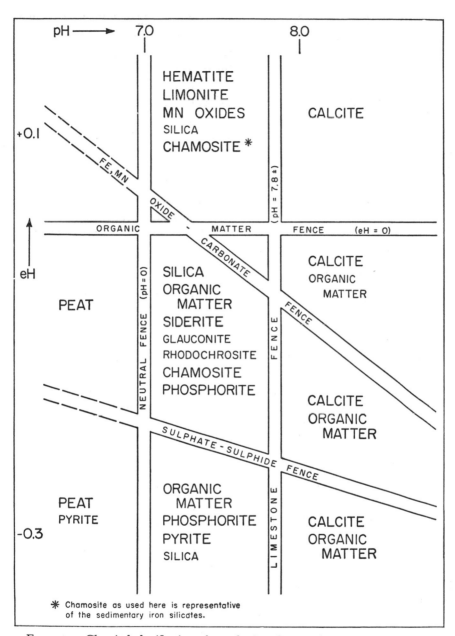

FIG. 155. Chemical classification of nonclastic sediments (evaporites excepted) based on pH and Eh (after Krumbein and Garrels, 1952).

slumping. A slope of 1.5 to 3 degrees may be considered likely (p. 189). The depth of the basin or trough can then be estimated if the deepest and most persistent part of the trough is well outlined by stratigraphic studies and if the location of the probable source area is known. By this method Briggs (1953, p. 436) estimated the waters in the Cretaceous San Joaquin valley trough to have been 3000 to 7000 feet deep.

It has been said that there are no deep-water sediments anywhere on the continent. The prevalence of structures characteristic of shallow turbulent waters throughout the geologic column gives considerable support to this idea. On the other hand, foraminiferal evidence shows that the Ventura Basin in parts of the Pliocene was of the order of 4000 to 5000 feet deep (Natland and Kuenen, 1951), a figure of the same order of magnitude as that calculated by Briggs for the San Joaquin Cretaceous. It seems probable that depths of this order were not uncommon in the more strongly negative areas at various times in the geologic past.

The Chemical Parameters

The chemical factors in the environment are primarily the salinity (concentration), the oxidation-reduction potential (Eh), and the acidity-alkalinity (pH). The minerals precipitated and the faunal elements present are closely related to these environmental factors. Another factor of interest to the geologist and of great importance in the distribution of the fauna is the temperature. A classification of chemical environments has been suggested by Teodorovich (Chilingar, 1955) and by Krumbein and Garrels (1952). Although a number of factors enter into and control the precipitation of minerals, the most important seem to be the Eh (oxidation-reduction potential) and the pH (acidity-alkalinity) (see Fig. 155).

Oxidation-Reduction Potential (Eh)

In a general way sediments are deposited under either oxidizing (aerobic) or reducing (anaerobic) conditions. The measure of the oxidizing capacity of the environment is the Eh, or the oxidation-reduction potential (Mason, 1949; Zobell, 1946). Whether or not an ancient sediment was deposited under oxidizing or reducing conditions is decided mainly on the basis of the mineralogy and what is known about the stability of the minerals under different oxidation potentials. The iron minerals in particular are most useful. Deposition of hematite indicates a fully aereated environment; iron sulfides (pyrite or marcasite) signify a reducing and wholly oxygen-deficient medium. Siderite is indicative of an intermediate oxidation potential (Krumbein and Garrels, 1952).

By the use of other minerals a further subdivision, based on Eh, of the chemical environment is possible. Teodorovich (Chilingar, 1955) recognized six such subdivisions. These are the strongly reducing or sulfide zone, the reducing (iron carbonate and iron sulfide) zone, weakly reducing (siderite and vivianite) zone, neutral (iron-rich chlorites with both ferric and ferrous iron) zone, weakly oxidizing (glau-conite) zone, and oxidizing (ferric oxide and hydroxide) zone.

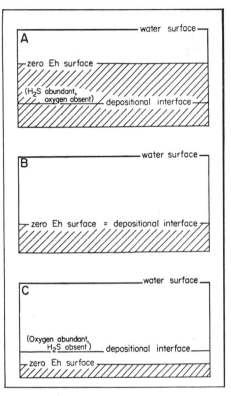

Other criteria of a low oxidation potential are the absence of a normal benthonic fauna and the presence of only such forms as can tolerate the toxic conditions produced by oxygen deficiency or those forms which are wholly free swimming or are attached to floating objects. In the former category are certain phosphatic brachiopods, especially *Lingula* and *Discina*, which are ubiquitous and hardy types capable of survival under adverse conditions. Conodonts, occasional fish remains, and spores and pollen complete the fauna or flora of those shales formed in a highly reducing environment. A further indication of oxygen deficiency is an abnormally high (over 2 or 3 per cent) content of organic matter or residues therefrom. Normal microbiological and scavenger action tends to destroy the organic residues which settle to the bottom.

FIG. 156. Relation of oxidation-reduction boundary and sediment-water interface (after Krumbein and Garrels, 1952).

Inhibition of such action, because of oxygen deficiency, leads to an increase in these materials and hence to black shales and the like.

As noted by Krumbein and Garrels and by Teodorovich, the oxidation-reduction surface, i.e., the plane separating the oxidizing from the reducing environment, may be above, coincide with, or be below the sediment-water interface (Fig. 156). In the more strongly reducing environments it is above the mud-water surface; in the oxidizing environment it is well below that interface. Inasmuch as the environment within a sediment is always reducing how does it happen that all sediments are not reduced? Whether a sediment is reduced or not depends on whether a reducing agent is present. Such an agent is organic matter, and as noted above, in an oxidizing environment the organic matter is mainly oxidized and destroyed by microbiological decay or by normal scavenging action. In the sediment deposited in this environment, therefore, little or none remains to effect reduction of the iron. As shown by studies of modern muds (Emery and Rittenberg, 1952) the diagenetic processes are reducing in character and such organic matter as is present does in part bring about reduction of the iron.

Alkalinity-acidity (pH)

The acidity or alkalinity of an environment is an important factor in determining whether or not certain minerals will precipitate. In a strongly acid environment, for example, the carbonates will not be deposited. The deposition of calcite is therefore evidence of a pH of at least 7.8 (see Fig. 155).

It may not be sufficient just to discriminate between an acid and an alkaline environment. Krumbein and Garrels (1952) would define three environments based on acidity, namely the most acid, pH less than 7.0; a more nearly neutral environment, pH 7.0 to 7.8; and an alkaline environment, pH over 7.8. Teodorovich (Chilingar, 1955) would define six environments based on pH: strongly alkaline (soda lakes) with pH over 9.0; alkaline, pH 8.0 to 9.0; weakly alkaline, pH 7.2 to 8.0; neutral, pH 6.6 to 7.2; slightly acid, pH 5.5 to 6.6; and acid (swamps) with pH 2.1 to 5.5.

The criteria for determination of the acidity or alkalinity of an ancient sediment are mainly mineralogical. As noted, the carbonates dissolve in an acid medium and precipitate in an alkaline environment. Krumbein and Garrels set a pH of 7.8 (about that of sea water) as a "limestone fence." Calcite is freely precipitated at this or higher pH values; it is a minor accessory only in slightly less alkaline environments, and its precipitation is completely inhibited as the pH drops below 7.0. Silica, on the other hand, tends to dissolve in the alkaline environment and to be precipitated in the acid environment. Extensive deposition of chert suggests a more acid environment than that responsible for calcite. The relations between the solubility of silica, calcium carbonate, and pH have been reviewed by Correns (1950).

As noted by Edwards and Baker (1951), the widespread occurrence of marcasite in association with coals is in striking contrast to the occurrence of pyrite in marine clays and shales. Presumably the difference is related to the pH. The coal swamp is strongly acid; the marine environment is neutral or mildly alkaline. The form of the iron sulfide therefore provides a further means for discriminating between acid and alkaline environments. Marcasite in a marine formation would be indicative of acidification subsequent to deposition.

In addition to the carbonates, silica, and the forms of iron sulfide which are pH-sensitive, it is believed that kaolin requires an acid environment for its formation, whereas an alkaline environment favors the formation of montmorillonite (Millot, 1949).

A more direct attempt to determine the pH of the environment of an ancient sediment is that of Shukri (1942) who believed that the pH of an aqueous extract of a shale would be essentially that of the water from which the mud was originally sedimented. Emery and Rittenberg (1952), however, noted a tendency for the interstitial waters of muds to have a slightly higher pH than the waters of the basin in which they accumulated.

Salinity

The salinity [5] of the waters in ancient basins varied from fresh to super-saline. As a guide to salinity most reliance is placed on the fauna. The fauna may be described as fresh-water, brackish, or normal saline. Ecologic studies of present faunas, especially the foraminiferal assemblages, have proved dependable guides to interpretation of the more recent past (Tertiary). The biological criteria for more ancient times are less certain.

In the case of more than normal salinity, the biota becomes sparse or disappears. The evidence of supersaline [6] conditions is recorded in the salt minerals formed. The sulfates, gypsum and anhydrite, are common; greater salinity leads to precipitation of halite. Only from the most concentrated brines are the potash salts precipitated.

Most difficulty arises from the waters that are not saline enough to precipitate the sulfates or chlorides but are appreciably more saline than normal sea water. These waters have been termed penesaline. Deposits formed under such conditions are generally nonfossiliferous. The evaporitic carbonates are said to indicate penesaline waters (Sloss, 1953). Such carbonates are chiefly the oolitic carbonates and the finely laminated dolomites interpreted as primary.

Salt crystal molds, in the absence of salt deposits proper, indicate at least a temporary salinity greater than normal. Salt crystals can form in shallow intermittently flooded areas even in regions of abundant rainfall, and do not therefore necessarily indicate prevalence of an arid condition.

Temperature

An important parameter of the environment of deposition is the temperature. Temperature affects the solubility of many minerals and gases and has

[5] Commonly defined as chlorinity, or parts per thousand of chlorine. Normal sea water has a chlorinity of about 19.4.

[6] There is some confusion in terminology. Saline may be used to designate salt water, such as sea water, or to signify a salinity appreciably greater than sea water. Supersaline may be used to designate the latter or to indicate a salinity of extraordinary kind from which even the potash salts are precipitated.

therefore an important effect on chemical precipitation. Certain salt minerals may be precipitated in the winter time but dissolved in the summer. At lower temperatures the solubility of CO_2 is greatly enhanced; hence the solution of calcium carbonate is promoted in cold waters, and conversely the precipitation of the same material is brought about by a rise in temperatures. The temperature also affects the composition of mixed crystals or solid solutions. Shell carbonate is richer in MgO at the lower temperature (Chave, 1954); the lower-temperature authigenic plagioclase is nearly pure albite, whereas that formed at higher temperatures contains more lime. The effect of temperature on the viscosity of water, though readily measurable, seems not to be geologically important. The temperature profoundly affects the behavior of water, however, if it passes below the freezing point of that liquid. Glaciers and glacial deposits form only at materially reduced temperatures.

Criteria formulated to determine past temperature (paleotemperatures) are geological, mineralogical, and ecological. Geological evidences of glacial temperatures are the tillites and pellodites. The criteria for the recognition of tillite has been reviewed elsewhere (p. 266); the recognition of pellodites—the glaciolacustrine varved clays—has also been summarized. The certain recognition of these deposits is not easy. The tillites are closely imitated by the tilloids; the only certain criterion of a glaciolacustrine deposit is the berg-rafted cobbles, and since other agents of rafting are known even this criterion is difficult to apply.

Mineralogical or chemical criteria of temperature are not clearly formulated and not wholly isolated from those related to other climatic factors. The red color of many soils (and hence perhaps the red pigmentation of many sediments) seems to be correlated with latitude (and hence temperature). The highly oxidized red pigmentation is a characteristic of the soils of low latitudes; the soils of the colder latitudes are not red. The color seems to be related to the rate of oxidation of the humus in the soil. Humus inhibits the oxidation of the iron; its destruction permits the oxidation.

Although the composition of certain solid solutions is a function of temperature such a geological thermometer has not been successfully used to discriminate between high and low temperature values in the limited range of temperatures which prevail at the surface of the earth. Presumably the stability of certain hydrides is temperature controlled. Anhydrite rather than gypsum is formed at relatively higher temperatures (p. 482).

Most recent effort to measure paleotemperatures is related to the temperature-controlled fractionation of the isotopes of oxygen, O^{16} and O^{18}. As the proportions of these isotopes can be shown experimentally and theoretically to be temperature dependent, the temperature of formation of a mineral can theoretically be determined if the ratio has not been affected by postdepositional exchanges or replacement. Some success has been achieved in determining the temperature of the shell formation of some belemnites and other fossil forms (Urey et al., 1951; Epstein, Buchsbaum, Lowenstam, and Urey, 1951) (Fig. 157).

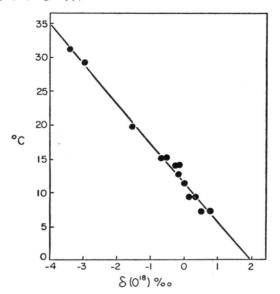

FIG. 157.   Plot of O^{18} concentrations versus temperature: calcium carbonate samples, heat-treated. Abscissa is ratio (after Epstein et al., 1951).

Both faunal and floral evidence has been cited respecting paleotemperature. It seems probable that in Tertiary beds at least valid distinctions between cold-water and warm-water faunas can be made. The Foraminifera, in particular, have been useful in establishment of paleotemperatures (Bandy, 1953). The determination of temperature by biological criteria is difficult in the older formations, and in all cases the biota is affected by other ecologic facts in addition to temperature. These complications render interpretations more difficult.

REFERENCES CITED AND BIBLIOGRAPHY

Andersen, S. A. (1931), Om Aase og Terrasser inden for Susaa's Vandomraade og deres Vidnesbyrd om Isafsmeltningens Forløb, Danmarks Geol. undersøgelse, II Raekke Nr. 54, 1931, pp. 21–31. See also J. Geol., vol. 42, 1934, p. 551.

Bandy, Orville L. (1953), Ecology and paleoecology of some California Foraminifera. Part I. The frequency distribution of Recent Foraminifera off California, J. Paleontology, vol. 27, pp. 161–182.

Bandy, Orville L. (1953), Ecology and paleoecology of some California Foraminifera. Part II. Foraminiferal evidence of subsidence rates in the Ventura Basin, *J. Paleontology*, vol. 27, pp. 200–203.

Bailey, E. B. (1930), New light on sedimentation and tectonics, *Geol. Mag.*, vol. 67, pp. 86–88.

Bailey, E. B. (1936), Sedimentation in relation to tectonics, *Bull. Geol. Soc. Amer.*, vol. 47, pp. 1716–1718.

Baturin, V. P. (1941), On stratification and a law of sedimentation of clastic deposits, *Compt. rend. acad. Sci. U.R.S.S.*, vol. 31, pp. 137–140.

Bond, Geoffrey (1954), Surface textures of sand grains from the Victoria Falls area, *J. Sediment. Petrol.*, vol. 24, pp. 191–195.

Briggs, L. I. Jr. (1953), Upper Cretaceous sandstones of Diablo Range, California, *Univ. Calif. Publ. Geol. Sci.*, vol. 29, pp. 417–452.

Chave, Keith (1954), Aspects of the biogeochemistry of magnesium. 2. Calcareous sediments and rocks, *J. Geol.*, vol. 62, pp. 587–599.

Chilingar, G. V. (1955), Review of Soviet literature on petroleum source-rocks, *Bull. Am. Assoc. Petroleum Geol.*, vol. 39, pp. 764–767.

Correns, Carl W. (1950), Zur Geochemie der Diagenese, *Geochim. et Cosmochim. Acta*, vol. 1, pp. 49–54.

Edwards, A. B., and Baker, G. (1951), Some occurrences of supergene iron sulphides in relation to their environments of deposition, *J. Sediment. Petrol.*, vol. 21, pp. 34–46.

Emery, K. O., and Rittenberg, S. C. (1952), Early diagenesis of California basin sediments in relation to origin of oil, *Bull. Am. Assoc. Petroleum Geol.*, vol. 36, pp. 735–806.

Epstein, Samuel, Buchsbaum, Ralph, Lowenstam, Heinz, and Urey, H. C. (1951), Carbonate-water isotopic temperature scale, *Bull. Geol. Soc. Amer.*, vol. 62, pp. 417–426.

Gilbert, G. K. (1914), The transportation of debris by running water, *U.S. Geol. Survey, Prof. Paper 86*.

Keller, W. D. (1945), Size distribution of sand in some dunes, beaches, and sandstones, *Bull. Am. Assoc. Petroleum Geol.*, vol. 29, pp. 215–221.

Krumbein, W. C. and Garrels, R. M. (1952), Origin and classification of chemical sediments in terms of pH and oxidation-reduction potentials, *J. Geol.*, vol. 60, pp. 1–33.

Lowenstam, H. A. and Epstein, S. (1954), Paleotemperatures of the post-Aptian Cretaceous as determined by oxygen isotope method, *J. Geol.*, vol. 62, pp. 207–248.

MacCarthy, G. R. (1935), Eolian sands: A comparison, *Am. J. Sci.*, 5th ser., vol. 30, pp. 81–95.

Mason, B. (1949), Oxidation and reduction in geochemistry, *J. Geol.*, vol. 57, pp. 62–72.

Millot, Georges (1949), Relations entre la constitution et la genèse des roches sédimentaires argileuses, *Géol. appl. et prospect. miniere*, vol. 2, nos. 2–4, p. 352.

Natland, M. L. and Kuenen, Ph. H. (1951), Sedimentary history of the Ventura

Basin, California and the action of turbidity currents, *Soc. Econ. Paleon. and Mineralogists, Special Publ. No. 2*, pp. 76–107.

Nevin, Charles (1946), Competency of moving water to transport debris, *Bull. Geol. Soc. Amer.*, vol. 57, pp. 651–674.

Phleger, F. B. (1955), Ecology of Foraminifera in southeastern Mississippi delta area, *Bull. Am. Assoc. Petroleum Geol.*, vol. 39, pp. 712–752, and other papers.

Reiche, Parry (1938), An analysis of cross-lamination: The Coconino sandstone, *J. Geol.*, vol. 46, pp. 905–932.

Rubey, W. W. (1938), The force required to move particles on a stream bed, *U.S. Geol. Survey Prof. Paper 189-E*, pp. 121–140.

Russell, R. D., and Taylor, R. E. (1937), Bibliography on roundness and shape of sedimentary particles, *Rept. Com. Sediment.*, 1936–37, Nat. Research Council, pp. 65–80.

Shukri, M. N. (1942), The use of pH values in determining the environment of deposition of some Liassic clays and shales, *Bull. Fac. Sci. Fouad I Univ.*, 24, pp. 61–65.

Sloss, L. L. (1953), The significance of evaporites, *J. Sediment. Petrol.*, vol. 23, pp. 143–161.

Teodorovich, G. I. (1946), (Sedimentary geochemical facies), *Biulleten Moskovskogo Obschestva Ispytalelei Prirody, Geol. Div.*, vol. 22, no. 1 (see review of this and related papers by C. V. Chilingar, *Bull. Am. Assoc. Petroleum Geol.*, vol. 39, 1955, pp. 764–768).

Thompson, W. O. (1937), Original structures of beaches, bars and dunes, *Bull. Geol. Soc. Amer.*, vol. 48, p. 747.

Twenhofel, W. H. *et al.* (1932), *Treatise on sedimentation*, 2nd ed., Baltimore, Williams and Wilkins, pp. 621–622.

Udden, J. A. (1914), Mechanical composition of clastic sediments, *Bull. Geol. Soc. Amer.*, vol. 25, pp. 655–744.

Urey, H. C. *et al.* (1951), Measurement of paleotemperatures and temperatures of the Upper Cretaceous of England, Denmark, and the southeastern United States, *Bull. Geol. Soc. Amer.*, vol. 62, pp. 399–416.

Ziegler, V. (1911), Factors influencing the rounding of sand grains, *J. Geol.*, vol. 19, pp. 157–191.

Zobell, C. E. (1946), Studies on redox potential of marine sediments, *Bull. Am. Assoc. Petroleum Geol.*, vol. 30, pp. 477–513.

SEDIMENTARY BASINS

Certainly an important part of any environmental analysis is determination of the size, shape, and bottom configuration of the basin in which the sediments in question accumulated. This problem involves some knowledge of modern sedimentary basins, the various classes and characteristics of such basins, and their general architecture. As most basins are tectonic this is essentially a study of the geotectonic elements of the earth and their behavior.

The geologist, however, must approach the problem from the record and determine from the sedimentary fill where the basin margin or shore line was, where the axis lay, and what the bottom configuration was like.

Finding Ancient Shore Lines

The shore line is a critical line. In general it is the dividing line between areas of erosion and sedimentation, although there are many exceptions to this rule. It is the dividing line between the continental and marine environments and the corresponding faunas and floras. Geologists have long recognized the significance and importance of the strand line and have expended much effort in attempting to locate the position and trend of ancient shore lines (Menard and others, 1955). Those of the recent past can be recognized by certain geomorphic features—beach ridges, sea cliffs, and so forth—and can readily be mapped. The shore lines of the earlier times, however, cannot be so recognized or mapped. The location of the shore line for a given time, within the Silurian, for example, is a very difficult task. Nonetheless many attempts to locate the strand and to construct paleogeographic maps have been made (Moore, 1941).

The shore lines of the more ancient periods can be located only from the record left in the sediments deposited in those times. What criteria are there for locating or finding ancient shore lines? The criteria fall into three classes. In the first class are those based on the recognition of certain structures or textures believed characteristic of the littoral zone. Included here is the presumed beach structure (Thompson, 1937), various beach markings (swash marks, beach cusps, etc.), tidal flat markings, and so forth. Many of the supposed littoral structures are very rare or, if found, may be indicative also of other situations. Mud cracks, for example, although plentiful on some tidal mud flats, are also found on river flats and are probably more diagnostic of continental rather than littoral environments (Barrell, 1906). At best the deposits of the strand line are thin, discontinuous, most readily prone to destruction, and altogether very rare in the geologic record. In the absence of any certainly recognizable strand line features or if the features are not definitive but are known to occur also in other environments, how can one locate an ancient shore line?

A second approach, one of the most fruitful, is the recognition of difference between fresh-water, brackish, and marine faunas. If a bed with a marine fauna passes (laterally) into one with a fresh-water fauna, clearly a strand zone separates the two. It can be argued that the distinction between marine and fresh-water biota becomes less clear the older the period involved. Nonetheless such distinctions can generally be made. It is difficult to utilize this information to delineate a shore line unless the organisms involved are closely associated with a mappable facies.

A third and relatively new approach involves the search for an areal pattern which is closely correlated with the position and trend of the shore line. The best example is that afforded by the concentration (number per gram) of land-derived spores and pollen. The concentration (in the shales) of these materials rises (exponentially) as one approaches the shore. Lines of equal concentration therefore are parallel to the shore; the line where the concentration rises most steeply is close to or at the shore (Hoffmeister, 1954). Theoretically the concentration of any land-derived materials could be similarly used; air-borne materials are perhaps the most satisfactory.

In a general way sediments coarsen toward their source. Presumably therefore the clastic marine sediments would be distributed in texturally defined belts parallel to the shore line. Since the sand/shale ratio is a measure of mean grain size, contours based on this ratio would be parallel to the shore. A very high sand/shale ratio would indicate proximity to the shore line.[7]

Another illustration of the pattern approach is that given by Krumbein and Nagel (1953), who plotted the number of sand beds in an intertonguing sand-shale sequence. Since the sands were of the littoral type and the shales were marine, the line showing the maximum number of sands is statistically the average position of the shore line during the time interval studied (Fig. 158).

Since the shore line is but a special contour on the regional slope, the direction of this as well as other contours may be inferred from a study of paleocurrent systems. In so far as the mean current direction is downslope, the normals to the current flow lines would be contour lines and parallel to the strand or basin margin. Although a paleocurrent study can no more than suggest the trend of the shore line, such a study in conjunction with other observations can further serve to delineate an ancient shore line.

In conclusion, it seems most likely that the mapping of ancient shore lines will be most successful if it is done in connection with mapping of faunal and litho-facies, paleocurrents, and spore or pollen concentrations. The delineation of the strand line by finding strand line sediments with distinctive textures or structures is difficult; it is virtually impossible if the data must be secured from drilling. Inasmuch as the strand is a constantly shifting line, any line mapped must be the average position of the shore—a statistical

---

[7] The concept of textural belts conformal with the strand line has been challenged by Shepard (1948, p. 150) and other students of recent sediments. Indeed bottom-sediment maps on the present-day shelves seem to support the contention of these critics. The present-day sediments of shallow waters show a patchwork distribution and are not the simple conformal graded textural belts usually postulated. Nevertheless the geologic record in many places shows that broad systematic variations in sediment character and texture do exist (see Krumbein and Nagel, 1953; Amsden, 1955). Apparently the shallow-water sediments of the present-day shelves are either not adjusted to the recent rise of sea level (Kuenen, 1950. p. 304) or they constitute an insignificant body of sediment seldom preserved in the older records.

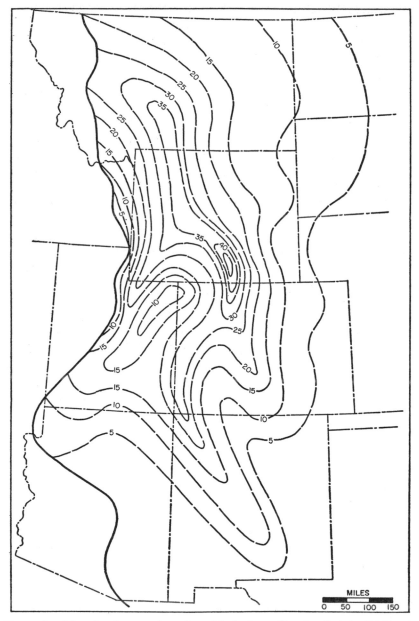

MILES
0   50   100   150

F<small>IG</small>. 158. Map showing number of sand beds (exceeding ten feet in thickness) in Upper Cretaceous of Great Plains and Rocky Mountain areas (after Krumbein and Nagel, *Bull. Am. Assoc. Pet. Geol.*, 1953, p. 593).

shore line rather than the actual shore line. The mean position of the shore is more readily found by the pattern approach rather than by the search for criteria definitive of strand line deposits.

Inasmuch as all marine strata must thin and pinch out at the shore line, it might be supposed that the zero isopach of any marine bed would be the position of the shore. This may be true but in many cases the zero isopach is only the position of the beveled edge of a bed. Distinction between the initial zero isopach and a zero isopach produced by erosion cannot be made unless other criteria are taken into account (see Krumbein and Sloss, 1951, p. 445).

Bottom Slope and Configuration of the Basin

The configuration of the basin of deposition is determined only by study of the sediments which accumulated in the basin. Inasmuch as these are in part eroded away and in part concealed beneath younger beds, the reconstruction of the outline and depth of the basin is difficult. Reconstruction is in part achieved if the ancient basin margins, especially the shore line of the basin if marine, can be mapped.

An isopach map will enable one to locate the greatest depth of subsidence but not necessarily the greatest depth of water in the original basin. The direction of slope of the bottom can be reconstructed from paleocurrent studies. The steepness of the slopes, however, is more difficult to determine. If much or most of the accumulated sediments collected above wave base, the basin was shallow and no great submarine slopes could have existed. If the sediments are deep water sediments, the slopes can be estimated if the distance to the shore line is known. On overly steep slopes slump structures produced by subaqueous slides will be conspicuous. The direction of slump can be determined from the folds preserved, and as pointed out in the section above, the depth of the basin can be calculated if the angle of slope needed to initiate slumping is known.

REFERENCES CITED AND BIBLIOGRAPHY

Amsden, T. W. (1955), Lithofacies map of Lower Silurian deposits in central and eastern United States and Canada, *Bull. Am. Assoc. Petroleum Geol.*, vol. 39, pp. 60–74.

Barrell, J. (1906), Relative geological importance of continental, littoral, and marine sedimentation, *J. Geol.*, vol. 14, pp. 524–568.

Hoffmeister, W. S. (1954), Microfossil prospecting for petroleum, *U.S. Patent No. 2,686,108.*

Krumbein, W. C. and Nagel, F. G. (1953), Stratigraphy of "Upper Cretaceous," Rocky Mountains, *Bull. Am. Assoc. Petroleum Geol.*, vol. 37, pp. 940–960.

TABLE 109. Consanguineous Associations (facies)

Consanguineous Association	Sedimentary Domain or Realm		Appalachian Examples
	A		
Graywacke suite (flysch)	Marine, geo-synclinal	Bathyl to abyssal	
Graywacke			
Slate-shale			Rennselaer
Siliceous shale			Martinsburg
Chert			(upper)
(Greenstone)			"Portage"
(Basic tuffs)			
	B		
Subgraywacke suite (molasse)			
B₁ Subgraywacke-protoquartzite	Paralic, reducing	Neritic to nonmarine (paludal-fluvial)	Pocono Tuscarora
Micaceous shales			
Coal			
B₂ Subarkose and red subgraywacke	Paralic, oxidizing	Nonmarine, fluvial	Juniata Catskill
Red mudstones and shales			
	C		
Orthoquartzite-carbonate suite			Oriskany
C₁ Orthoquartzite	Cratonic; marine to shelf marine	Neritic to intertidal	Onondaga Conococheague Beekmantown
Limestones, bio-chemical and mechanical			
Mottled dolomite			
Replacement dolomite			
C₂ Evaporite facies	Penesaline to saline; epi-continental	Neritic to bathyl	Beekmantown? Salina
Primary dolomite			
Anhydrite-gypsum			
Halite			
Potash salts			
C₃ Euxinic facies	Euxinic: epi-continental to geosyn-clinal	Neritic to bathyl	Romney Chattanooga
Black shale			
Sedimentary pyrite			
Bedded siderite			
Bedded phosphorites			
Black chert			
	D		
Arkosic suite	Terrestrial: graben or half graben	Nonmarine: fluvial, lacustrine, paludal	Triassic
Arkose			
Lithic arenites			
Conglomerates			
Black shale (rare)			
Freshwater limestone (rare)			
(Melaphyre and diabase)			

Krumbein, W. C. and Sloss, L. L. (1951), Stratigraphy and sedimentation, San Francisco, Freeman.

Kuenen, Ph. H. (1950), Marine geology, New York, Wiley.

Menard, H. W. Jr. ed. (1955), Finding ancient shorelines, Special Publ. No. 3, Soc. Econ. Paleon. and Mineralogists.

Moore, R. C. (1941), Stratigraphy, Geol. Soc. Amer., 50th Ann. Volume, pp. 177–220.

Shepard, F. J. (1948), Submarine geology, New York, Harper & Brothers.

Thompson, W. O. (1937), Original structures on beaches, bars, and dunes, Bull. Geol. Soc. Amer., vol. 48, pp. 723–752.

SEDIMENTATION AND TECTONICS

Introduction

A *consanguineous association* is a natural group of sedimentary rocks related to one another by origin. They may all be formed, for example, in a reducing environment as are the sedimentary sulfides, bedded siderites, and black shales. Or they may be the product of a saline environment as are the bedded sulfates, anhydrite and gypsum, and halite. Such an association is commonly called a facies, such as the *black shale facies* and the *evaporite facies*.[8]

Consanguineous associations are recurrent throughout geologic time. The graywacke-shale association is found in rocks ranging from Archean to Tertiary in age. Evaporites occur in nearly every geologic system from the Cambrian on. The fundamental problem is to recognize and define such natural associations, to determine or define the major domains or realms of sedimentation which produce such consanguineous assemblages, and finally to determine the ultimate geological factors which produce such realms. In short, the problem is to explain the distribution of sedimentary rocks in time and space.

The more commonly recognized ecologic groupings of sedimentary rocks are shown in Table 109, together with the presumed realms of sedimentation responsible for them.

Consanguineous Associations (facies)

Orthoquartzite-Carbonate Association

The suite characterized primarily by orthoquartzitic sandstones and carbonates—mostly limestones and dolomites—has been described as the

---

[8] The term *facies* has been used in two unlike ways. It has been defined as "areally segregated parts of differing nature belong to any genetically related body of sedimentary deposits" (Moore, 1949, p. 8). Facies has also been defined as a "term applicable to every distinguishable sedimentary record of a depositional environment" (Moore, 1949, p. 15). The term *lithofacies* has been proposed for the latter concept. Facies is here used in this sense.

shelly facies or *calcareous facies* in recognition of the importance of the carbonate rocks in this assemblage. It has also been designated the *Arbuckle facies* or the *Champlain facies*, terms appropriate for certain areas, or as the *platform facies* or *stable shelf* or *foreland facies* in recognition of the presumed structural stability of the site of deposition.

In general the total thickness of this facies is small, although there are notable exceptions. In the thinner sections the formations also are thinner; they show abrupt vertical variations, marked bedding planes, and many breaks in faunal and lithologic sequence. The number of formations is large and the individual units are thin (Table 110). The rocks are abundantly fossiliferous. This facies therefore is the stratigrapher's delight.

TABLE 110. Representative Orthoquartzite-Carbonate Sections

	A	B	C	D	E	F
Percentage Sandstone	25	48	15	29	32	29
Percentage Shale	7	22	5	42	17	21
Percentage Limestone	68	30	80	29	51	50
Total Thickness (ft)	7900	1950	2725	2450	2630	....
No. Formations	21	26	26	....	5	....
Average Thickness of Formation (ft)	376	75	105	....	524	....

A. Cambro-Ordovician of west-central Vermont.
B. Cambro-Ordovician of southwestern Wisconsin.
C. Cambro-Ordovician of southeastern Missouri.
D. "Lower Huronian" of Marquette district, Michigan.
E. Paleozoic, Bighorn Mountains, Wyoming.
F. Average of A to E, inclusive.

This association is, as the name implies, largely orthoquartzitic sandstones and limestones and dolomites. Shale is a subordinate component, even in the thicker sections. Carbonates are generally dominant, forming up to 80 per cent or more of the section. The sandstones, both calcareous and quartzitic, are clean-washed, pure quartz, well-rounded, and generally very mature. Cross-bedding and ripple marking are common. The limestones and dolomites are characterized by sandy interbeds or by numerous scattered quartz grains. The carbonates are varied in origin; some are abundantly stromatolitic and obviously algal; these form both biostromes, and together with other organisms, reefs. Many limestones are calcarenitic, are locally cross-bedded, and consist of oolites or sorted shell debris or nonskeletal granules (false oolites) or mixtures of all these. Flat-pebble conglomerates are common, as are mud-cracked calcilutites. Many alternations of calcarenite, calcilutite, algal beds, and flat-pebble conglomerates characterize these carbonates. Mottled dolomites, laminated primary dolomite, and saccharoidal replacement dolomites are common.

Shales are comparatively rare; the sandstones and carbonates follow one another or grade into one another without intervening shales. Such shales as are present are saprogenic and have a high alumina/soda ratio.

Commonly this facies rests unconformably on a stable crystalline basement with only a few inches or few feet of arkosic and conglomeratic material just above the unconformity. Feldspar is absent in the higher beds, or if present, is restricted to areas near buried granitic monadnocks or to a few scattered well-rounded grains. Most commonly the basal sandstone is followed by limestone or dolomite although in places the carbonate rocks themselves rest directly on the underlying basement. Shales, if they are present, follow the carbonate stage of deposition and seem to be the record of deepening waters.

The orthoquartzite-carbonate facies appears to be the product of sedimentation marginal to a very low-lying stable land surface. The evidence of stability is in the maturity of the sands produced and by the general paucity of clastic materials and the dominance of carbonates. The slight total thickness and the undeformed character of many sections further testify to the stability of the site of deposition.

Throughout the depositional history the water was exceedingly shallow and was many times withdrawn. The cross-bedding of both carbonates and orthoquartzites indicates local zones of turbulence; the innumerable algal biostromes and the mud-cracked calcilutites are indicative of extremely shallow waters and of temporary withdrawals. The flat-pebble conglomerates, if they be desiccation breccias, likewise suggest repeated withdrawals of the water. In many cases the deposition may have been in the intertidal zone and in no case was the water more than a few tens of feet deep.

Typical examples of this facies are the many lower Paleozoic sections in the upper Mississippi valley and the Great Lakes area. This region, one of extraordinary stability during most of the Paleozoic, is but a slightly buried extension of the Canadian shield. The deposits formed are largely carbonates, rarely more than a few thousand feet thick and notably sandy only near the higher portions of the shield—parts presumably emergent and providing the sand (Fig. 159).

In places near the bordering geosynclines the orthoquartzite-carbonate facies attains an astonishing thickness (Arbuckle limestone, for example). Such carbonate build-ups are similar in most respects to the thinner facies found on the interior platform although sands are perhaps fewer or at least relatively less important. Apparently a thick carbonate platform can be built out into or encroach on the bordering geosynclines if the continental interior is low or submerged and yields no important volume of clastic material. These thicker carbonate deposits were involved in the later orogenies affecting the geosynclinal accumulations. In part perhaps the unusual thickness

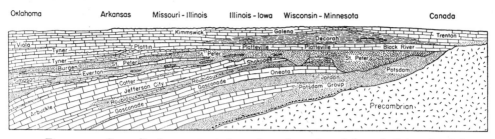

FIG. 159. Generalized, reconstructed, north-south section of the early Paleozoic of the Mississippi Valley. Typical orthoquartzite-carbonate association (modified from Dake by Thiel, 1935).

may be the result of sweeping of carbonate debris from the interior continental platform into the adjoining more negative geosynclinal tract. The area of lime production may be large and the belt of lime accumulation relatively small.

The carbonate front or embankment encroaching on the geosyncline may be comparatively steep and at times unstable so that large slumps occur, generating turbidity currents which transfer the shallow—nearly intertidal—carbonate muds and sands into the depths of the geosyncline. Such turbidity-transported carbonate may be graded and texturally similar to the graywackes (Carrozi, 1952). These may be the only carbonates in the geosynclinal tract proper. Some of the widespread intraformational limestone breccias may be thus formed.

The paucity of shale in the orthoquartzite-carbonate facies is not fully understood. If the carbonates are or were (prior to dolomitization) wholly calcarenites, then the calcarenites and the normal quartzose arenites were the product of deposition in a turbulent environment. In such a case the finer silts or clays from the land would be by-passed into deeper less turbulent waters. Inasmuch, however, as many of the carbonates are in fact calcilutites or lime muds, it is difficult to believe that argillaceous materials were by-passed. It has been suggested that the clays were winnowed out in an earlier cycle and that the sands associated with the carbonates are second-cycle and derived only from earlier sandstones. Perhaps, as has been suggested also, the land areas were deserts and the clay fraction was removed by the wind to leave only a sandy dune complex to be invaded and redistributed by the advancing sea.

In many cases deepening of the seas and rise of a borderland or island arc brought lime deposition to an end. Shale deposition succeeded carbonate deposition, and if the sea areas became silled, the shales were black shales. Such black shale, associated with cherts, phosphorites, or bedded siderites and pyrite, was most likely to have formed in the deeper more readily sealed parts of the basin—principally in the bordering geosyncline. If the climate became arid during the deposition of the orthoquartzite-carbonates, the evaporite facies may appear and be interbedded with the more normal strata of this facies.

The Graywacke Suite (flysch)

The graywacke suite, because it is typical of many geosynclines, has been called the *geosynclinal facies* or *orogenic facies*. It has also been called the *argillaceous facies* owing to the dominance of shales in this facies. Local names Magog, Ouachita, and Flysch have been used, and some—flysch, for example—have been extended to characterize sediments of any area or age similar in character to those of the type section. The choice of terms to be applied depends on whether one wishes to emphasize the composition, the Alpine counterpart, or the tectonic environment. The latter is perhaps somewhat misleading, since other types of sediments, as noted elsewhere, also collect in geosynclines.

The graywacke suite is marked by its great thickness and its predominantly argillaceous character. It is almost wholly clastic, although at some stages bedded cherts or radiolarites were deposited. The thickness is phenomenal and is measured in tens of thousands of feet. Deposition was continuous, or nearly so, and without interruption. The bedding is well marked, uniform, and rhythmic. The principal material is shale or silty shale regularly interbedded with beds of graywacke varying from an inch or two in thickness to several feet. These strata are characteristically described as *rhythmites* or, in the older literature, as *flagstone grits*. Graded bedding of the graywackes is the rule; cross-bedding and ripple marking are relatively uncommon. Cross-bedding, if present, is confined to the finer silty sands and is very small scale. Curly bedding or hassock structure, also known as slip bedding, is common.

The sandstones are microbreccias or grits, contain numerous shale fragments and, as pointed out elsewhere (p. 312), are not the products of normal bottom currents. They appear to record infrequent, somewhat catastrophic, incursions of slump-generated turbidity underflows. Such flows transfer sediments once deposited in comparatively shallow waters to a deep still-water environment. Closely associated with these rhythmites may be coarser breccias (tilloids) containing in some cases large erratic blocks.

The shales apparently accumulated relatively slowly; their accumulation being periodically interrupted by the almost instantaneous deposition of the sandy beds. The proportions of shale to sand varies but in general the section is largely shale (Table 111). The proportion of mud to sand is even higher if it be recalled that the graywackes contain an argillaceous detrital matrix and contain mudstone particles of sand dimensions. In general the mud/sand ratio is about that carried by the large rivers of the present time. The average Mississippi delta deposit is 29 per cent sand and 71 per cent mud (silt plus clay). As can be seen from Table 111 the average of several sections shows a sandstone to shale ratio of about 31 to 64.

Noteworthy is the absence of carbonates, except as concretions in the siltstone beds. Limestone, however, has been reported as graded beds in some sections—the presumed product of an intrusion of a carbonate-laden turbidity flow. In other sections radiolarites or other bedded cherts are present.

TABLE 111. Proportions of Rock Types in Flysch Facies

	A	B	C[a]	D	E	F
Per cent sandstone	42	17	32	27	39	31
Per cent shale	58[b]	66	61	73	59	64
Per cent limestone	tr	17	....	tr	1–2	4
Per cent conglomerate	1	....	....	....	tr	....

A. Upper Cretaceous (Chico), California (Trask and Hammer, 1934, p. 1366).
B. Carboniferous, Anadarko basin, Oklahoma (Bokman, 1954).
C. Carboniferous (Stanley), Arkansas-Oklahoma (Bokman, 1953, p. 155).
D. Tertiary, northern Sumatra.
E. Cretaceous, southern California (Briggs, 1953, p. 35).
F. Average, A to E, inclusive.
 [a] Includes 7 per cent siltstone.
 [b] Includes sandy shale.

Greenstones, commonly spilitic and pillowed, are associated closely with graywackes (Tyrrell, 1933). These basic flows appear to have been erupted on the sea floor concurrently with the sedimentation. Closely associated also are water-lain basic tuffs which grade into and resemble the coarser graywackes. The sections bearing basic volcanics have been described as eugeosynclinal by Stille and Kay (Kay, 1947); those devoid of volcanics are miogeosynclinal.

Slump bedding, convolute folding, and injection as dikes and sills seem to characterize many of the graywackes.

The typical graywacke assemblage commonly increases in coarseness upward. Conglomerates, if any, appear high in the section. The upward increase in coarseness is associated with an increase in the proportion and coarseness of the sands. The sands, moreover, become cleaner and are subgraywackes and even protoquartzites rather than graywackes. Variegated shales and coal beds make their appearance. The typical flysch facies has been displaced by the molasse facies—a product of paralic sedimentation.

The origin of the flysch facies with its rhythmic interbedding of shale and graded graywackes was long misunderstood. The coarseness of the grits and the general unfossiliferous nature of the beds, or the presence in some cases of plant debris, led some workers to believe the sediments were shallow water or even continental in origin. The evenness of the beds, absence of cross-bedding and the common occurrence of radiolarites led others to regard them as deep-water marine. The radiolarian cherts of some sections and the graptolites of others leave no doubt about the marine origin of the flysch facies. The general absence of a benthonic fauna, the dark carbonaceous shales, the thin-bedded and even-bedded sand layers, and the corresponding absence of large-scale cross-bedding or of wedging, lenticular bedding, and scour-and-fill channels are suggestive of deep water. The deep-water Foraminifera of the shales interbedded with the graywackes of the Pliocene of the Ventura basin in California (Natland and Kuenen, 1951; Bandy, 1953) strongly supports a deep-water origin for analogous sections of other ages and places. The turbidity-flow mechanism readily explains the grading characteristic of the coarser grits and the occurrence of such coarse clastics in a deep-water environment, and the presence of a shallow-water fauna in the graded beds.

Inasmuch as the graywacke rhythmites are characteristic only of the excessively thick and deformed sections, they are a product of geosynclinal sedimentation. They accumulated rapidly and without interruption in a comparatively deep-water (1000 to 5000 feet) marine environment. The sediments consist of waste products of a high land mass inasmuch as they are texturally and mineralogically very immature. They were derived both from low-rank metamorphic and crystalline terranes—in part from strata earlier deposited in the same geosyncline. They follow the euxinic or silled-basin stage and precede the paralic stage in the normal geosynclinal cycle. In the deeper, shorter-lived eugeosynclines they are associated with pillow lavas and tuffs.

Thick sections of this facies are very common. Most of the Archean sections in the Temiskaming province of the Canadian shield are graywackes, slates, ferruginous cherts, and greenstones (Pettijohn, 1943). The later Precambrian (Tyler, Michigamme) of northern Michigan consists of graywackes and slates plus basic volcanics. The Rensselaer graywacke (Ordovician?) of New York is a graywacke-slate complex with some volcanics (Balk, 1953). The Lower Paleozoic of the Caledonian geosyncline is thus characterized (Jones, 1938), as is the Carboniferous of the Armorican geosyncline of southern England and Wales and the Harz mountain district of Germany. This suite characterizes the Franciscan (Jurassic?) of California, the Eocene of the Olympic Mountains of Washington and much of the Alpine Tertiary (Bailey, 1936). Essentially the same assemblage, with fewer or no volcanics characterizes the Carboniferous of the Ouachita and Marathon mountains.

Nearly all the sections studied show the flysch assemblage of graded graywackes, gritty mudstones breccias, and shales to be followed by the molasse association consisting of cross-bedded subgraywackes and protoquartzites, micaceous shales, and coal beds. Clearly the marine deep-water geosynclinal conditions have been replaced by paralic conditions including fresh and brackish water environments. Subsidence became less general and short periods of stability permitted the formation of coal beds and cleaner sands.

Subgraywacke Association (molasse)

The molasse is a thick clastic association of Tertiary age found in the Swiss Plain and in the Alpine foreland of southern Germany. Rocks of similar character elsewhere have also been designated molasse (van Waterschoot van der Gracht, 1931, p. 998).

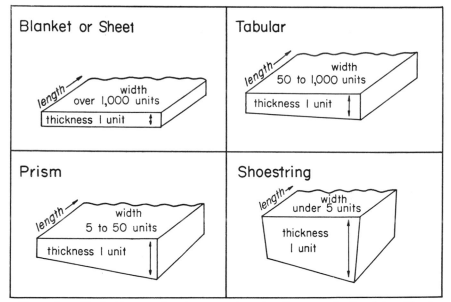

Fig. 160. Block diagrams showing geometry of sedimentary bodies (after Krynine, 1948, p. 148).

The molasse association consists mainly of sandstones and shales. In general it is coarser than the flysch and contains notable conglomerates. It may, like the flysch, be thousands of feet thick; it may in other cases be much thinner. The thicker molasse belongs to the orogenic belt and is itself deformed; the thinner molasse is a more distal portion of the same clastic wedge that lies beyond the orogenic belt proper.

The sands and shales of the molasse are immature products of denudation. The sands are mainly subgraywackes and protoquartzites rather than gray-wackes. They more commonly form shoestring bodies rather than sheets (Fig. 160). Typically they are calcareous or sideritic and are markedly cross-bedded. The proportion of sand to shale is higher in the molasse than in the

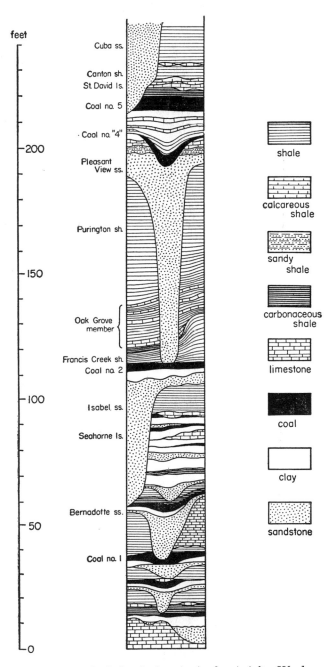

feet

Cuba ss.

Canton sh.
St. David ls.

Coal no. 5

· Coal no. "4"

—200

Pleasant
View ss.

Purington sh.

—150

Oak Grove
member

Francis Creek sh.
Coal no. 2

—100

Isabel. ss.

Seahorne ls.

Bernadotte ss.

—50

Coal no. 1

—0

shale

calcareous
shale

sandy
shale

carbonaceous
shale

limestone

coal

clay

sandstone

FIG. 161. Cyclothemic deposits (molasse) (after Wanless, 1931).

flysch. The shales are micaceous and vary from red to gray in color. Clay ironstone concretions, septaria, and plant fossils are common in the shales. Closely associated with these clastics are thin nodular fresh-water limestones and coal seams with their underclays. For the coal-bearing sequences, the term *coal measures* has long been used. The several members of this sequence are cyclically interbedded. To these cycles the term *cyclothem* has been applied (Weller, 1930; Wanless and Weller, 1932). Although the composition of the cyclothem varies from one region to another, in general, it is a sequence of thin beds recording subsidence alternating with periods of comparative stability. The latter are represented by the coal beds and their underclays. The intercalation of some beds bearing marine fossils and the presence of thin marine limestones as well as coal indicates sedimentation to be both marine and nonmarine (Fig. 161). The molasse of the older systems, before the advent of land plants, are not, of course, conspicuously coal-bearing.

In some molasse sequences red sandstones and red mudstones are conspicuous. The red color and the mudstone conglomerates—mud fragments in sand matrix—indicate oxidation and desiccation and hence deposition under subaerial conditions.

The molasse association is thus neither continental nor marine but both; it consists of an association of sediments formed in varying local environments including those of the beach and foreshore, the tidal lagoon, and both river channels with their point bars and the backwater swamps. In short, the area of molasse sedimentation is a deltaic coastal plain and its inland extensions.

The sediment supplied to this domain is partitioned among the various local environments and is differentiated texturally (and hence chemically and mineralogically) according to the energy input of the local situation. The deposits are primarily sands and shales. The sands are the product of the high energy turbulent environments—beaches and river channels. The shales are the products of the low-energy or still-water environments—the coastal lagoons and the alluvial swamps. The sands are therefore mainly shoestring sands deposited either parallel to the shore line (barrier beaches and offshore bars) or more or less normal thereto (fluvial channel sands) (Fig. 162). In general the beach sands were derived from the continental interior by river transport and should therefore be texturally and mineralogically more mature than the river sands proper. This seems to be borne out by actual observations in the present Gulf Coastal plain (Nanz, 1954). Only under rare or exceptional conditions is a sheet sand formed as a result of a uniform and uninterrupted transgression of the beach.

In general the shore is a prograding one, so that the molasse-type sediments encroach upon and replace the offshore marine sediments of the geosyncline. The latter sediments may be largely shale and sand also but the beds are wholly marine and the sands are of the thin graded type (flags) transported and deposited by turbidity currents. These are the typical sediments of the flysch phase of the tectonic cycle; the paralic sediments belong to the molasse phase.

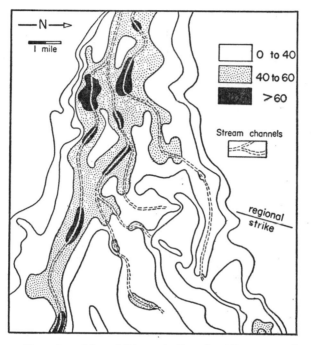

FIG. 162. Map of "shoestring" sands. Oligocene sand, distributary channels of shoal-water delta (after Nanz, *Bull. Am. Assoc. Pet. Geol.*, vol. 38, 1954, p. 110).

Sedimentation of the type described has been termed *paralique* by Tercier (1940). Paralic sedimentation is defined as sedimentation in areas peripheral to or within the continental framework characterized by intense terrigenous alluviation. Although the deposits are in part marine and in part brackish, more commonly they are continental. Geologic examples are many. The Juniata (Ordovician) red mudstones and sandstones and the superjacent protoquartzite and conglomerates (Tuscarora) and associated redbeds (Bloomsburg) of the Silurian, of the Appalachian region comprise a lower Paleozoic molasse. Likewise the red sands and shales of the Catskill (Devonian), the protoquartzites (Pocono) and red shales (Mauch Chunk) of the Mississippian and the coal measures of the Pennsylvanian constitute an upper Paleozoic molasse in the same region. The Atoka and overlying beds comprise a corresponding late Paleozoic molasse in the Ouachita area of Arkansas and Texas; the Haymond and Gaptank constitute a molasse in the Marathon basin area (van der Gracht, 1931). Much of the Carboniferous of Europe, the Neogene of Sumatra, Borneo, and Java, as well as the Molasse proper of the Alps constitute other examples.

Black Shale Facies (euxinic)

The black shale facies is most commonly just black shale. Such shale is thinly laminated, papery, and black. It has an abnormally high content of carbon (5 per cent or more), is rich in iron sulfide (pyrite), and is noted for its concentration of rare elements (V, U, Cu). Carbonates are rare except as cone-in-cone layers or as septarian nodules. The black shale fauna is restricted to a few inarticulate phosphatic brachiopods (*Discina*), conodonts, and resinous spores.

In some black shale sections chert is present, both as scattered nodules, or more typically in thin layers interbedded with the black shale. The proportion of bedded chert may increase and constitute an important stratigraphic unit. Less commonly pyritiferous limestones, bedded or sedimentary pyrite, bedded siderite, and bedded phosphates are associated with the black shale.

In general black shale sections are not very thick—several hundred feet is generally the greatest thickness. They may, however, be rather widespread. Their rate of accumulation is perhaps the slowest of all sediments, since many feet of clastics or carbonates at one place are the equivalent of a few feet of black shale in another locality.

Clearly the black shale association is one characterized by a highly reducing environment. It must be one with a very low oxidation-reduction potential.

The oxidation-reduction potential is largely a function of the availability of atmospheric oxygen. In a sealed environment, i.e., one cut off from the atmosphere, natural processes of slow oxidation (putrefaction and organic metabolism) slowly deplete the surrounding medium of its oxygen. A strongly reducing environment is thus created. Such an environment may be sealed off from the atmosphere by a density stratification of the waters resulting from marked differences in salinity. This is the so-called euxinic environment (Fig. 163). This environment is best illustrated by the Black Sea. This body of water is over 2000 meters deep in places. Only the upper 50 meters are well enough aerated to support life. All the waters below 100 to 200 meters are toxic by reason of the presence of H_2S. The bottom muds contain 23 to 35 per cent of organic matter, in contrast to the average recent sediment which contains only 2.5 per cent of organic matter (Trask, 1939, p. 441). Bottom life, except for anaerobic bacteria, is absent.

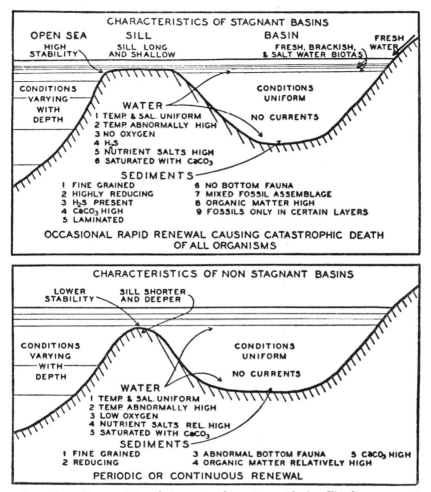

FIG. 163. Characteristics of stagnant and nonstagnant basins. Fine lines represent isopycnals (from Fleming and Revelle, *Recent Marine Sediments*, 1939, p. 96).

The hydrology of the Black Sea, which is the type euxinic basin, has long been known from the work of Androussow (1897) and others. This nearly land-locked body of water is connected with the Mediterranean by the narrow, river-like Straits of Thrace, the Sea of Marmora, and the Dardanelles. The Black Sea fills a deep, steep-sided basin covering 360,850 square kilometers and with a capacity of 280,000 cubic kilometers. The greatest depth is 1227 fathoms, and the floor lies mainly between 800 and 1200 fathoms. The basin is fringed by a narrow shelf sea.

The salt content of the Black Sea averages 1.8 per cent, is least in the northeast corner (1.4 per cent), and is greater in depth, reaching 2.1 per cent at 100 fathoms and 2.2 per cent at 1000 fathoms. The temperature varies abnormally with depth. It is 15°C to 24°C on the surface and falls to 7.26° to 6.96° at 30 to 45 fathoms and rises a little to 8.8°C at 100 fathoms, 9.0°C at 200 fathoms, and 9.3°C at 1200 fathoms.

The anomalous salinity and temperature variations with depth are explained by the inhibited vertical circulation. The lesser salinity of the surface waters and their lower density therefore are due to inflow of fresh water from rivers entering the Black Sea. The surplus flows out through the Straits of Thrace. But at the same time there is an inflow through the Straits of more saline, and therefore heavier, warmer water from the Mediterranean.

In the Straits, therefore, there are two currents: an upper and a lower. The uppermost removes 370,000 cubic feet per second, and the lower current brings in 200,000 cubic feet per second. At least 1700 years would be required for the lower waters of the Black Sea to be renewed, whereas the upper waters are renewed every year. The surface waters to a depth of 125 fathoms are therefore of normal character, well-aerated, and able to support abundant flora and fauna. Convection currents are confined to the upper 100 fathoms. Below this zone lies the heavy salt water so depleted of oxygen that at great depth H_2S appears in important amounts. The toxicity of the bottom waters prohibits normal life.

The uninterrupted rain of pelagic organisms from the surface waters to the deeper zone settles on the bottom and does not nourish a single benthonic organism, as is the rule in open seas and oceans. The organic matter is only partially decomposed by anaerobic bacteria. These bacteria also attack the sulfates, reducing them to sulfides and generating H_2S. The H_2S, in turn, reacts with iron salts and is precipitated as black amorphous mud. The suggested reactions are

$$RSO_4 + 2\,C \rightarrow 2\,CO_2 + RS, \quad RS + CO_2 + H_2O \rightarrow H_2S + RCO_3$$

Somewhat similar conditions prevail in other landlocked waters. Norwegian fjords (Ström, 1936, 1939) well illustrate sedimentation under anaerobic conditions. Conditions in these fjords are similar to those in the Black Sea, though on a smaller scale. The fjords, moreover, showed some variations among themselves, because of the varying degrees of isolation from the North Sea. The differences were related mainly to sill depth and therefore to rate of removal of bottom waters. Under certain exceptional circumstances complete renewal may take place with lifting of the foul bottom waters and catastrophic destruction of the fauna of the upper waters. The bottom deposits of the fjords are black, organic muds with highest determined content of organic carbon of 23.4 per cent.

The general characteristics of barred basins have been reviewed by Woolnough (1937) and by Fleming and Revelle (1939) (Fig. 163).

Considerable difference of opinion exists on the possibility of stagnation occurring in the open sea. Are the true black shales of the geologic record the products of sedimentation in a barred basin or were they deposited in the open sea? At the present time certain deep holes in the ocean are very low in dissolved oxygen and but little change would be required to produce stagnation of the type required for deposition of pyritic black shale. According to van der Gracht (1931), the existence of polar icecaps results in an active equatorward circulation of cold oxygen-bearing waters. Were the icecaps not present, the circulation would stop, and the bottom waters of large areas of the present ocean would become anaerobic.

The true euxinic sediments are exclusively marine. There is no bottom life (see discussion of black shales). Chlorophyl porphyrins are preserved but they are poor in N and Br. Vanadium and Cu (0.05 and 0.01 per cent, respectively) are present in more than normal concentration.

Closely associated with some black shales are other highly reduced sediments such as sedimentary iron sulfides and siderite. Also associated in some places are phosphorites and bedded cherts. Such abnormal concentrations of iron, phosphorus, silica, and organic matter are possible only in a *starved basin*, which has been defined (Adams, Frenzel, Rhodes, and Johnson, 1951) as a basin which received a minimum of clastic material by reason of the distance from the source or by intervening troughs or basins which trapped the incoming sediment or by reason of great depth and inability of waves or currents to carry their traction load beyond the basin margin. In view of the effectiveness of turbidity currents as distributors of muds and sand, the latter explanation of starvation seems least probable.

Geologic formations representing euxinic sedimentation are (1) the black pyritic and carbonaceous slates of the Precambrian of Iron County, Michigan, with their associated bedded cherts and siderites, (2) the dark graptolitic shales with associated radiolarian cherts of the Ordovician of New York state, (3) the black shales and limestones of the Upper Devonian and Lower Carboniferous (Culm) of the Variscan orogenic cycle of North America and Europe, (4) the Kupferschiefer of the western European Permian, (5) the black cherts, phosphorites, and black shales of the Phosphoria formation (Permian) of the north Rocky Mountain area of the United States, and (6) the several horizons of the Mesozoic and Tertiary of the outer zones of the Alpine chains throughout the world.

That the pyritic black shales were deposited under anaerobic conditions is unquestioned. Whether, however, the basin of accumulation was shallow or deep and whether it was landlocked or freely connected with the sea or even only a stagnant area in the open sea has been much debated.[9] It seems most probable that some impediment to convection currents is necessary and that

[9] The "shallow" versus "deep" water origin of the Chattanooga and correlative black shales is uncertain. For a review of this question see Rich (1951), Twenhofel (1939), Ruedemann (1934), Grabau and O'Connell (1917).

the best hindrance is a density stratification related to salinity differences. Such is readily obtained in a barred basin.

Anaerobic conditions can be generated in a sediment just below the mud-water interface. In this case the anaerobic environment is the result of microbiological oxidation in the mud coupled with a slow rate of downward diffusion of oxygen. Such oxygen depletion is characteristic of certain shallow lagoonal or estuarine muds. Black shales thus formed are not likely to be so extensive as those accumulated in a barred basin.

Euxinic sediments seem commonly to occur above the carbonate-orthoquartzite association and below the graywacke-shale assemblage. Their occurrence is perhaps a record of the transition between the open-sea deposition of carbonates and craton-derived sands and the influx of sediments from a rising island arc. The initial rise of the future arc results in shoals or barriers which lead to partial isolation of the locus of deposition and restricted or inhibited circulation—conditions conducive to stagnation of bottom waters and deposition of reduzates and related sediments (James, 1954).

Evaporite Facies

The evaporite assemblage is a sequence of bedded sulfates (gypsum or anhydrite) and halite beds closely associated with evaporitic and normal carbonates (Table 112). The sulfates are the most common; halite is less

TABLE 112.   Salinity Series

	Fresh	Brackish	Normal	Penesaline	Saline	Hypersaline
Mineralogy and Lithology	Freshwater limestone		Biochemical carbonates; biostromal or biohermal limestone; calcarenites	Evaporite carbonates; laminated primary dolomite; oolites; anhydrite	Halite	K-Mg salts
Biology	Freshwater fauna	Brackish water fauna	Normal benthos	Fauna extinguished; some transported plankton		

common, and most rare are the bedded potash salts (polyhalite, etc.). The salt beds vary from a few feet to many tens of feet thick. The total evaporite section, however, is not likely to exceed a thousand feet in thickness.[10]

The associated carbonates are thinly laminated primary dolomites and dolomites with many large included crystals of anhydrite. Oolitic limestones

[10] Excessive thicknesses of salt drilled in some places are the result of flow and intrusion of the salt into stocks or domes.

may be present; reef limestone is common and may separate the evaporite section from a normal marine facies (Sloss, 1953); (King, 1948).

According to Sloss many evaporite sections are cyclic. The lowermost bed is a normal limestone; which is followed by an anhydritic dolomite in turn overlain by the evaporites proper—anhydrite and salt. The sequence is then reversed so that the evaporites are overlain by anhydritic dolomite above which lies a normal limestone.

Clearly evaporites form by extraction of dissolved salts by an evaporation process.[11] This can be accomplished only by desiccation in an arid climate. Since normal sea water is greatly undersaturated in the salts involved, a large volume of such water would have to be evaporated to produce a brine from which salt can be deposited.

The most striking modern example which illustrates the precipitation of salt is the Gulf of Kara-Bugaz on the east side of the Caspian Sea. This gulf is separated from the Caspian by a bar 60 miles long and is connected to the sea by a shallow channel only a few hundred meters wide. The climate of the region is semiarid and no large streams, therefore, enter the Gulf to offset the evaporation from its surface. To replace the evaporation losses there is a constant flow over the bar from the Caspian. The sill prevents any backflow which, owing to salinity differences, would normally take place. As a result of continued evaporation, the salinity of the waters of the Gulf have risen to 16 to 28 per cent as compared with the 1.3 per cent of the adjoining Caspian. The inflow is estimated to carry in each day some 350,000 tons of salt. The waters of the Gulf thus are increasing in salinity. They no longer support animal life, and saline deposits are forming on the bottom (Grabau, 1920, p. 132).

The planktonic (free-floating) and nektonic (free-swimming) biota swept into the saline basin by the inflowing current are killed instantly by the salt brines. And because of both the strong salinity and anaerobic bottom conditions (a result of inhibition of convection by salinity stratification), organic debris is preserved and entombed in the accumulating sediments.

The deposits of such a barred basin should exhibit an order of precipitation of the salt minerals similar to that determined experimentally (Clarke, 1924, p. 219). The first precipitated materials are the iron and aluminum hydroxides, together with a small amount of calcium carbonate and silica. Though present in very small amounts in sea water, the constant replenishment by inflow leads to a rather considerable volume of such precipitates.

Ultimately, if the proper conditions are maintained, gypsum is precipitated. If the temperature of the waters is sufficiently high, anhydrite is deposited instead. Further concentration leads to the formation of beds of

[11] Except in rare cases by reaction between acid sulfate waters and limestone, forming replacement anhydrite or gypsum.

rock salt or rhythmically banded gypsum or anhydrite, probably governed by seasonal temperature changes. Only desiccation of the most extreme type leads to the formation of the hygroscopic salts of potash and magnesia.

This, the normal cycle of salt precipitation, may be interrupted and hence be incomplete, or it may reappear at several places in the stratigraphic section.

Evaporites occur in nearly every geologic system younger than the Cambrian (Krumbein, 1951; Sloss, 1953). They are found in the Ordovician of the Illinois Basin, the Silurian of New York, Ohio, Michigan, and Iowa, the Devonian of the Williston Basin, the Mississippian of Michigan, Illinois, the Williston Basin and West Virginia, the Pennsylvanian of the Paradox Basin of Utah, the Permian of the Gulf Coast, West Texas, and New Mexico, the Jurassic of the upper Gulf Coast, Wyoming, and Montana, Idaho, and Utah, and the Cretaceous of Florida and the Gulf Coast area.

Not only do evaporites signify aridity but they indicate a delicate adjustment to a sill—requiring a critical depth for a time long enough to precipitate a considerable thickness of salt. This adjustment is possible only in a comparatively stable area. The reef association suggests that the reef itself may constitute the sill or barrier isolating the evaporite basin.

Arkoses and Red-Bed Sedimentation

Many geologists would recognize or define "red bed facies" as a natural consanguineous association more or less as they recognize an evaporite or a carbonate facies. Indeed red beds are the oxidized facies at the opposite pole from the reduzate or black shale facies. In terms of the tectonic framework in which the sedimentation processes must operate, the red bed suite is in part oxidized molasse and thus a part of the orogenic belts proper and in part a product of sedimentation in rift valleys or grabens. The latter is represented best by the Newark series (Triassic) of the eastern United States.

According to Krynine (1941, 1950), the Newark series consists of a sedimentary wedge 125 miles long, bordered on the east by a normal fault with a displacement of 17,000 to 35,000 feet. The wedge is built of coalescing alluvial fans radiating westward from the fault and thinning from 16,000 to 1500 feet in 32 miles. The strata are coarse, gray and pink, fluvial arkoses, conglomerates, red feldspathic sandstones, and subordinate red siltstone and shales. Some variegated and dark siltstones of paludal and lacustrine origin are also present. The relative proportions of the various types of sediment are given in Table 113, col. A. Fifty-two per cent of the rocks are red in color.

The Triassic of the Deep River basin in North Carolina is similar in many respects to that of Connecticut (Reinemund, 1955). A higher proportion of

TABLE 113. Proportions of Sediments in Terrestrial Piedmont (Rift Valley) Facies

	A	B	C	D
Conglomerate	10	20	19	17
Sandstone (arkose)	64	70	55	63
Shale and Siltstone	25	10	22	20
Limestones	....	....	4	1

A. Newark series, Triassic, Connecticut (Krynine, 1950).
B. Keweenawan, Precambrian, Michigan, and Wisconsin.
C. Old Red Sandstone, Devonian, Scotland.
D. Average of A, B, and C.

the coarse clastics are schist arenites [12] rather than arkoses. The paludal deposits are relatively more important and include a number of workable coal beds. As in some of the other troughs of Triassic in the eastern United States, the sediment filling seems to have been supplied from *both* sides of the trough. The Keweenawan (late Precambrian) of the Lake Superior region also closely resembles the Newark series but perhaps is considerably thicker. Like the Newark series it is almost entirely clastic and is predominantly red. In addition to the thick conglomerates and red sandstones it, like the Newark series, contains lava flows—mostly amygdaloidal basalts with a few felsites—and is injected by numerous sills and dikes of diabase. The proportion of volcanic rocks in the Keweenawan is appreciably greater than in the Newark series proper. Although the bulk of the Keweenawan rocks are red, there are some dark siltstones and shales (Nonesuch) which are copper-bearing (White and Wright, 1954). Characteristic of this facies, therefore, is the coarseness of the clastics, the highly feldspathic character of these beds, their red color, and the absence of limestones. The coarseness of the clastics is reflected in the high percentage of sandstone in the section and by the great fanglomerates [13] that are most typical of this suite. Even many of the shales are in fact siltstones or fine sandstones. Noted exception to the red cover are the singular but subordinate black shales (and in some places, coals) that are found associated with the red beds. In some sections the black shales are copper-bearing shales of the Mansfield type.

Clearly this facies is nonmarine, was rapidly accumulated, and was deposited mainly under strongly oxidizing conditions. Although once interpreted as a product of an arid climate, Krynine believes the thick red clay, the huge swamps, and the flora suggest high precipitation (above 50 inches) and high temperatures (70°F to 80°F). Desiccation marks indicate alternating wet and dry seasons.

[12] A term proposed by Knopf for sandstones consisting mainly of rock particles, principally schists (Krynine, 1937).
[13] A term proposed by Lawson (1925).

This facies appears to consist of fanglomerates deposited near the boundary fault scarps and of channels, floodplains, and swamp deposits in the more remote areas. The channel fillings are commonly gray arkose, whereas the floodplain deposits are red arkose, siltstones, and shales. Krynine has attributed the channel fillings to erosion of fresh *gray* materials from the bottom of V-shaped canyons in the highland source area; and the finer-grained weathered *red* materials he has attributed to erosion of residual soils from interfluves between the canyons. The swamp deposits are black, as a result of reducing action of organic materials. These organic materials alone would preclude a hypothesis of desert origin, such as is commonly applied to the red-bed suite. The black carbon-bearing shales are likely to be the only fossil-bearing members of the whole assemblage.

The Newark-type association, as noted above, resembles in many ways the oxidized or red molasse. It has even been considered a molasse and designated *postorogenic* facies, i.e., considered to be the accumulated flood of coarse clastics shed by the newly uplifted mountain chain. The Newark series and the Keweenawan are not, however, a molasse in this sense. They appear to be related to a tectonic belt of different character, namely, a fault trough or graben. Such rift valleys appear to be unrelated to the erection of a folded mountain belt. Because of the high relief generated by faulting, the sediments are very coarse, and as the rifting seems to be intracontinental (rather than marginal to the continent), the sedimentation is terrestrial. The associated swamps or lakes seem to be a product of derangement of the rift-valley drainage by tectonic movements, lava accumulation, or more simply by piedmont alluvial fans which encroach on the valley flood and divide the trough into segments. Tilting, faulting, and contemporaneous eruption of melaphyres is the rule; true Alpine folding has not taken place.

The true molasse, on the other hand, is a paralic or coastal plain deposit and the thicker molasse is itself involved in the Alpine orogeny. Although similar in some respects to the rift-valley or graben deposits, it lacks the lavas, is more extensive, and much of it is deposited in a reducing environment—some of it is in fact marine. Unlike the graben facies which is derived from both sides of the structure, the molasse is derived primarily from just one side—the side of the mountain chain with which it is associated.

The term red-bed facies is thus rather loosely used. In most cases it consists of red clastics—red sands and red siltstones and shales. Generally it is a molasse deposited under oxidizing conditions; in some cases, however, it is a graben-deposited facies associated with normal faults and attendant basaltic upwellings.

Summary

In the foregoing section we have reviewed the principal consanguineous assemblages or *facies* commonly recognized by the field geologist. Such facies or assemblages are characterized by distinctive rock suites which have some characters or attributes in common, impressed on the assemblage by the realm or domain of sedimentation in which they formed. But are the facies defined and described above coequal and mutually exclusive? Are they not defined on overlapping (and hence not mutually exclusive) attributes?

Analysis of the foregoing facies shows that some are primarily nonclastic and are defined on a chemical attribute such as the state of oxidation (euxinic facies) or on the presence or absence of certain highly water-soluble salts (evaporite facies). Other facies are primarily clastic and are differentiated by the type of sandstone and the proportion of sand and shale or similar attributes. The flysch facies, for example is a graywacke-slate facies; the molasse facies is a subgraywacke-shale facies; the carbonate facies is nearly shale-free and closely associated with orthoquartzites. However, there is considerable overlap in the parameters used to define the several facies groups. The flysch facies is deposited under reducing conditions; the molasse facies is in part reducing and in part oxidizing. Perhaps as our knowledge becomes more complete both geochemical and ordinary petrologic factors will be used to define facies so that many subdivisions not now recognized will be made.

Despite the seeming inconsistencies in the facies categories commonly recognized, the groups as now defined seem to be geologically significant. The chemical facies express degrees of isolation of the basin of sedimentation from the open ocean or the degree of isolation of the environment of deposition from the atmosphere. In the first case the salinity of the water varies from fresh to supersaline, depending on the ratio of inflow into the basin to the outflow from the same. In the second case the oxygen potential varies from fully ventilated to wholly anaerobic. The clastic facies recognized are an expression of the tectonic stability or instability of the site of deposition, the correlated maturity or immaturity of the debris supplied to the basin of deposition, and the manner of sand transport and distribution. Rapid subsidence carries the site below the wave base. If ample clastic materials are available they will consist of muds, settled from above, and immature sands introduced by turbidity underflows. The result is a rhythmically interlayered and even-bedded accumulation of graywackes and shales. If the subsidence is less rapid or if the sedimentation exceeds subsidence, the sedimentation is paralic rather than flysch, and the clastic materials— sands and muds—are distributed according to different principles. The submature sands collect at the loci of maximum turbulence and the shales form in the backwater nonturbulent environment. As a result the sands are deposited in barrier beaches and river channels and the shales form in tidal lagoons and in backwater swamps. The deposit consists of shoestring sands of the subgraywacke type and much shale, some oxidized and some not. If subsidence is at a minimum the fractionation of sand and mud is complete, and the latter is winnowed out and removed to the deep sea. The sand, deposited and redeposited, becomes mature and remains to form a blanket sand of the orthoquartzitic type.

In a general way the supply of clastics is a function of the relief. So also the maturity of the debris supplied is related to relief inasmuch as under conditions of high relief the weathering process is interrupted midcycle and but partially weathered immature materials are contributed to the basin of deposition. Hence under conditions of maximum supply of clastic materials and maximum subsidence, the sediments are coarsest and least mature. Conversely under lowest relief, near peneplane, the volume of clastic materials is least and that supplied is most mature. In a general way, therefore, the chemical facies are dominant in regions of greatest tectonic stability and are associated with the most mature clastics, whereas the clastic facies predominate in regions of tectonic instability. Hence, although sedimentary facies are not all defined by the same parameters, the categories recognized are mutually complementary and not wholly so illogical as they might seem.

Classification of Sedimentary Domains

A number of attempts have been made to classify the domains [14] of sedimentation. More or less traditional is that of Barrell (1906) in which sediments are classed as continental, littoral, or marine. Each of these major realms is subdivided into lesser categories (Table 114). The problem, however, is to determine or define those realms of sedimentation which correspond to and explain the natural consanguineous associations of sediments recurrent throughout the geologic record. The geographic-geomorphic classification of Barrell and Twenhofel (1950) does not do this, nor is there any correlation between the observable petrologic types and this classification of environments. More recent efforts to classify sedimentary realms have attempted to group the environments according to different principles. Tercier (1940), for example, recognized the inadequacy of both the bathymetric classification of facies of E. Haug (1900) and the continental-marine grouping of environments. Instead, Tercier believed there were more natural groupings, some of which included both marine and nonmarine environments and also both deep and shallow water zones.

The five domains recognized by Tercier were:

1. Areas of paralic sedimentation. These are areas primarily within or

---

[14] The term *domain* rather than *basin* is preferred. The conditions within a basin may be radically altered so that one kind or class of sediments ceases to be deposited and a wholly unlike group of sediments is formed instead. The basin has been only slightly altered but the domain of sedimentation is greatly changed. An aerated lime-depositing basin, for example, may become silled and the bottom waters fouled so that a euxinic domain is created and black shales, siderites, etc., accumulate. A radical change in the sedimentation has taken place within one and the same basin.

peripheral to the continental platform characterized by intense terrigenous alluviation. Although the deposits are in part marine and in part brackish, more commonly they are continental. Clastic sedimentation is dominant and thickness may reach several thousands of meters. Geologic examples include the coal measures of the Carboniferous of North America and Europe, the Molasse of the Alps, and the Neogene of Sumatra, Burma, and Java.

TABLE 114. Geographic or Geomorphic Classification of Environment of Deposition (modified from Barrell, 1906)

I. Continental (above tidal reach)
  A. Terrestrial
    1. Glacial
    2. Aeolian
    3. Pluvial
    4. Fluvial
  B. Paludal (swamp)
  C. Lacustrine (lake)
    1. Freshwater
    2. Saline
II. Mixed continental and marine environments
  A. Littoral (between tides)
    1. Tidal lagoon
    2. Beach
  B. Delta
  C. Estuarine
III. Marine (below tidal limits)
  A. Offshore (neritic facies)
  B. Epicontinental sea
  C. Oceanic and mediterranean (bathyl and abyssal)

NOTE: Like many classifications, the above plan has internal inconsistencies and contradictions. In places the classification is based on the agent (ice, wind); in other places the basis is salinity (freshwater, saline); in still other places the geomorphic factor is the basis for classification (beach, delta, etc.). The several subdivisions are not therefore comparable. Some are complex and overlap others. The delta, for example, contains lakes and swamps and thus overlaps the lacustrine and paludal categories.

2. Areas of epicontinental sedimentation. These include the shallow ephemeral marine embayments in which sediments accumulate that are dominantly chemical or organic, and subordinately clastic (neritic facies). Only a slight total thickness is attained. They are marked by frequent but slight subsidence and elevation, with resultant cyclical transgression and regression of the sea. Geologic examples would include most of the early Paleozoic of the Upper Mississippi Valley.

3. Areas of geosynclinal sedimentation marked by heterogeneity and thickness of the deposits, now mainly exposed in the great mountain chains of the world. These deposits accumulated in narrow down-sinking tracts adjacent to complementary mountain ranges of high relief. Sediments are mainly

marine, in part neritic, and in part bathyl or even abyssal. Clastics, particularly shales, dominate but some organic sediments are also present. Tercier bases his description of the geosyncline on the Alpine type. He recognizes, therefore, several subfacies which are named from their Alpine counterparts,[15] namely, (a) the Flysch and Wildflysch and (b) the pre-Alpine or brianconnais facies. The Flysch and Wildflysch are typically thick clastic sediments characterized by exotic blocks, breccias, grits, and shale, with minor intercalated marls and radiolarites. The pre-Alpine facies is a more orderly deposit with important calcareous members. It resembles more closely the epicontinental platform sediments. The Flysch and pre-Alpine facies are complementary; generally the first overlies the second but it is possible for the two to coexist in the same geosyncline.

4. Areas of oceanographic sedimentation (deep sea). These are the abyssal depths remote from land in which sediments are exclusively marine, siliceous, and of chemical or organic origin. The radiolarian and diatomaceous oozes of the present deep sea are modern representatives of the group. According to Tercier some of the radiolarites are regarded as ancient equivalents.

5. Areas of the continent other than those included under 1 or 2. Here are deposited the wholly continental sediments. Lacustrine, fluvial, glacial, and aeolian deposits are examples.

Other efforts at classifications of sedimentary environments or realms of sedimentation likewise are attempts to find meaningful groupings, in general with an emphasis on the architecture of the basin of accumulation. Such a classification is that of Weeks (1952), who grouped depositional basins into those in mobile belts and those in stable regions. The primary differences are related to total subsidence and the rate of sedimentation. Generally, though not always, the deposits of the mobile belts are orogenically deformed. These mobile belts or *geosynclines* may be within the continents (intracontinental) or they may be marginal to the same. The latter may be open (as is the Gulf Coast geosyncline) or closed marginally by an island arc. Sedimentation in the stable regions may take place on a foreland shelf, in an interior basin, in a graben or half graben, or in a stable coastal area. Week's classification of sedimentary basins is a classification based primarily on the architecture of the basin; it is not strictly a classification of sedimentary domains, although a close correlation between the nature of the sedimentary deposits and the architecture of the basin is inevitable. As in the case of Tercier's classification, the domain or realm of sedimentation within

---

[15] The extension of the terms flysch and molasse to similar or analogous associations in other areas has been criticized (Eardley and White, 1947). Although the terms may have been misapplied, there is real need for these terms. Part of the difficulty stems from inadequate description of the original flysch and molasse. In part this lack has been remedied (Kuenen and Carozzi, 1953).

a given basin (a geosyncline for example) may change radically with time. It is this observation, perhaps, that led Kay (1951, p. 88) to deny any relationship between geosynclines and kind of sedimentation.

Krumbein, Sloss, and Dapples (1949, 1950) proposed but three realms of sedimentation, all structurally defined, namely (1) stable and unstable shelves, (2) intracratonic basins, and (3) geosynclines. They believed a distinctive stratigraphy and assemblage of rocks characterized each of these regions. The intracratonic basin was the most difficult to define and may have included several dissimilar types (Van Houten, 1950).

A more recent attempt to define realms (of marine sedimentation) is that of Rich (1951). His classification (undathem, clinothem, and fondothem) is related primarily to bathymetric position. It is basically a return to the Haug facies classification (neritic, bathyl, and abyssal). Although Rich has given a good description of several important sedimentary associations, his interpretation of those attributed to a *clino* environment and the distinction between this environment and that termed *fondo* is questionable. The only evidence of slope seems to be the turbidity current and slump-generated structures. Since these can be experimentally produced on nonsloping surfaces (Kuenen and Migliorini, 1950, p. 99) no appreciable bottom slope is implied. Moreover, sedimentation by turbidity currents seems to have produced nearly horizontal surfaces of deposition on the present sea floor

TABLE 115. Classification of Domains and Facies of Sedimentation

I. Basin of tectonic origin (major facies)
   A. Nonlinear, mildly negative (intracratonic and cratonic)
      1. Open (epicontinental and shelf seas) (orthoquartzite-carbonate facies)
      2. Restricted (silled basins)
         a. Humid climate (euxinic facies)
         b. Arid climate (evaporite facies)
      3. Isolated basins
         a. Humid climate (freshwater lacustrine facies)
         b. Arid climate (soda and salt facies)
   B. Linear, strongly negative
      1. Geosynclines
         a. Restricted and "starved" (euxinic facies) abyssal and bathyl
         b. Restricted marine (flysch facies)
         c. Nonrestricted, paralic (molasse facies)
            i. Oxidizing ("red beds")
            ii. Reducing ("coal measures")
      2. Rift valleys (grabens) ("red beds")
II. Nontectonic (minor facies)
   A. Gradational
      1. Spelian (caves)
      2. Paludal and limnal (glacial kettles, etc.)
   B. Volcanic (crater lakes, etc.)
III. "Permanent" or deep sea basins

(Heezen, Ewing, and Ericson, 1954). Foreset beds of large deltas are inclined less than one degree. That the deposits on such a surface are appreciably different than those on a surface with no slope seems improbable and has never been proved.

It is clear that neither the geographic-geomorphic classification of environments nor the facies classification based solely on bathymetric position explains the natural consanguineous groups of sediments observed in the geologic record. Inasmuch as the emphasis in this book is on the rocks and therefore upon these natural groupings or associations, the domains of sedimentation which best correlate with such groupings will be defined. The classification of such domains or realms is closely akin to that earlier proposed (first edition, 1949) (Table 115).

The Geosynclinal Cycle

The correlation between the character of the sedimentary assemblage and the mobility of the tract of accumulation is complicated not only by the variety and degrees of mobility but also by the change in character of any given tract with time. The initial sediments in a mobile tract, for example, may be quite different from those which followed. From observations in various areas has developed the concept of a geosynclinal cycle. Marcel Bertrand (1897) was one of the first to formulate the facies concept and to recognize that the several facies commonly followed one another in a systematic way. According to Bertrand the normal sequence in a geosynclinal belt is: (1) gneissic facies (basement of older rock), (2) shaly Flysch (a thick argillaceous facies deposited in the axial portion of the geosyncline which is debris derived from older rocks), (3) coarse Flysch (border deposit derived by reworking of the currently uplifted older strata of the geosyncline), and (4) gravels and coarse grits (red-grit facies) deposited at the foot of the mountains after elevation of the chain. This concept was apparently largely an outgrowth of the study of the history of the Alpine geosyncline. Bertrand, however, noted that this succession of facies was repeated in other geosynclinal tracts of other periods also.

Krynine (1941, 1942, 1945) attempted to generalize this concept of Bertrand and to apply it to the Appalachian geosyncline in particular. According to Krynine there are three tectonic stages, namely (1) peneplanation (or early geosynclinal) characterized by deposition of first-cycle orthoquartzites and carbonates on a fluctuating flat surface, (2) a geosynclinal stage proper marked by trough deposition interrupted by marginal upwarping and shift of earlier deposited sediments to the center of the trough after low-rank metamorphism—the graywacke suite—and (3) postgeosynclinal stage or uplift (commonly marked by faulting) after folding and magmatic intrusion of the geosyncline characterized by arkoses.

The validity of these generalizations has been questioned (Kay, 1949). It is clear, however, that there are certain recurrent natural consanguineous assemblages of sedimentary rocks and that in many cases these assemblages succeed one another in a regular or systematic manner. Such sequential orders repeated many times during the Precambrian and later eras gives considerable support to the concept of a normal geosynclinal cycle. This concept is briefly summarized in Fig. 164 and Table 116.

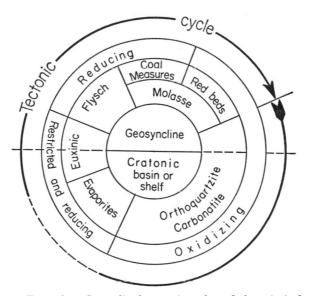

Fig. 164. Generalized tectonic cycle and the principal sedimentary facies. The evaporites are mainly a cratonic facies and generally have an orthoquartzite-carbonate association but their formation is not a normal event in the tectonic cycle.

TABLE 116. The Major Tectonic Cycle and Associated Sediments

Stage 1. Cratonic conditions and deposition of shield-derived orthoquartzites and of carbonates upon flooded craton or along cratonic border of geosyncline. More distal parts of geosyncline are starved and receive little or no sediment.

Stage 2. Mild upwarp in geosyncline and elevation of geanticlinal ridge; silled basin deposition of cherts, bedded siderites, pyrite, black shales, and phosphorites (euxinic facies).

Stage 3. Strong upwarp of geanticlinal ridges and island arcs with flood of clastic materials (flysch) increasing in coarseness upwards; submarine extrusives and tuffs.

Stage 4. Completion of trough filling; conversion to nonmarine stage. Paralic sedimentation (molasse), at first reducing (delta and swamp) and then oxidizing (fluvial).

Stage 5. Deformation and uplift.

Theoretical Considerations

It is difficult to make observations or to discuss them without reference to theory. The author has tried, however, to classify and describe the principal observable sedimentary facies and to call attention to the cyclical manner in which they commonly follow one another. Whether the observations made are correct and complete or not will be determined only by further observation and study.

Although some conjectures respecting the realms or domains of sedimentation represented by the principal facies were presented and an attempt to classify these domains was made, no unified coordinating theory of sedimentation has been formulated. This section will be devoted to this task and a discussion of some of the unresolved problems which remain.

The conclusion reached in recent years is that although sedimentation (and hence the kind of sedimentary rocks formed) is affected by many factors, the most fundamental is tectonic. The influence of tectonics on sedimentation has been pointed out by a number of geologists, but that it is the most fundamental factor has not been generally appreciated.[16]

Diastrophism is the major geologic process, the functioning of which produces surface irregularities and sets in motion the counteracting processes of gradation. Erosion and its complementary process, sedimentation, are parts of the major process of gradation, and together they tend toward the development of a plane surface. Were it not for diastrophism, the earth's surface would not be disturbed by rising and sinking movements, and sedimentation therefore would cease; thus diastrophism is the ultimate *cause* of sedimentation.

But most important, tectonics has a direct influence on the rates of erosion and sedimentation and thereby controls the *kind* of sedimentation and sedimentary products. The maturity of a clastic sediment is determined by the balance between the rate of erosion and the rate of weathering. Thus tectonics, because of its effect on relief and hence on the rate of erosion,

---

[16] The concept of tectonic control of sedimentation was clearly stated by Jones (1938). Basing his statement on the Lower Paleozoic of Great Britain, Jones recognized two facies, termed the *shelly facies* and the *graptolitic facies*. The former, an orthoquartzite-carbonate facies, is a product of sedimentation in shallow water on a stable surface; the latter is a thick argillaceous (flysch) accumulation in a strongly subsiding geosyncline. Bailey (1930, 1936) pointed out the tectonic control of the structure and composition of two contrasting sand facies—the current-bedded and the graded-bedded. Like Bailey, Tyrrell (1933) and Fischer (1933) believed graywackes to be the product of geosynclinal sedimentation. The extension of the terms *flysch* and *molasse*, which characterize the Alps, to similar facies elsewhere is tacit acceptance of the theory of tectonic control of facies. Such usage appears in the writings of many geologists, notably Bertrand (1897), Tercier (1940), and van der Gracht (1931). In America the influence of tectonics on sedimentation was most strongly emphasized by Krynine (1941, 1942, 1943, 1948), Pettijohn (1943), Dapples, Krumbein and Sloss (1948), and others (Cady, 1950).

exerts an important control over sediment maturity. The rate of sedimentation is a function of both rate of supply and rate of subsidence—both a function of tectonism. The balance between them determines whether the sediment is deposited below wave base or above. Hence the textures and structures of the sediment and the geometry of the sedimentation units are tectonically controlled. And finally, inasmuch as diastrophism is periodic, or episodic, the equilibria (between erosion and weathering or between supply and subsidence) established at any time or place are upset; it follows that the re-establishment of equilibrium proceeds in an orderly manner so that there is a continuous change in the character of the sediment with time—hence an orderly sequence of facies which have been called the geosynclinal or tectonic cycle. Each of these concepts needs to be explored further.

The influence of tectonics on maturity of the clastic sediments has been repeatedly stressed in this book (see Chapter 11). The feldspar content of the sandstones is the most useful index of maturity (see p. 509). As shown by Krynine (1935), relief rather than climate is generally the chief factor which determines the feldspar content of a sand. High relief results in removal or erosion of incompletely weathered materials and hence promotes the production of feldspathic and other immature sands. Low relief leads to complete destruction of the feldspar and the formation of residues capable of yielding orthoquartzitic sands. Presumably there are similar but less striking differences in the clays produced from regions of high and low relief.[17] Inasmuch as relief is a product of tectonism and requires energetic uplift for its maintenance, the maturity of the residues derived from a land surface are an index to tectonic activity. Furthermore, rapid uplift and rapid erosion commonly are associated with rapid sedimentation (and rapid subsidence). The sediments supplied to the rapidly subsiding basins are deposited without appreciable reworking. On the other hand, the mature sediments, especially the sands of a stable region, are subject to repeated shifting about, reworking, repeated washing, so that they tend to become texturally as well as compositionally mature.

The main influence of tectonism, however, is the effect on the total sediment supply and the rate of subsidence, the balance between which determines the relation of the surface of deposition and sea level. Strongly negative areas ("geosynclines") are inundated and covered with deep marine waters. The mud and sand, if in adequate supply, are distributed mainly by turbidity underflows and hence show the rhythmic bedding and grading

---

[17] In such circumstances where the sediments derived from a land area contain both mature and immature products of weathering, the mature products are fine-grained and accumulate mainly in the shales; the immature products are coarse-grained and appear in the sandstones. Shales generally are less differentiated chemically than are the sandstones (p. 102). The alumina/soda ratio, however, may be used as an index to maturity (p. 509).

characteristic of the flysch facies. If the depositional surface is raised to sea level or above it, either by accelerated sedimentation or by decreased subsidence, the sand and mud are distributed according to different principles. The former collects in the loci of maximum turbulence (bars and channels); the latter collects in the areas of minimum turbulence (backwater lagoons and swamps). Hence the sands form linear, texturally mature bodies (shoestring sands) intercalated in a thick accumulation of silt and clay. Thus the petrologic character of the sandstones, the geometry of these deposits of this facies (molasse) are radically unlike that of the flysch even though the bulk composition of the two is essentially the same.

If the subsidence is marked but the sediment supply restricted, the basin is starved and collects only a thin black shaly residuum or is the locus of chemical deposition characteristic of an euxinic environment the products of which are cherts, siliceous pelagic limestones, or phosphorites.

Only in the absence of tectonism can the textural and chemical fractionation processes be carried to completion. It is no accident that the evaporites, the high-purity quartz sands (orthoquartzites), most dolomites and carbonates are seldom, if ever, associated with the flysch or molasse facies. These deposits require a stable surface or, in the case of the evaporites, maintenance of a critical depth of water over a sill.

The sedimentary record is essentially a record of basin filling. The most impressive fills are the geosynclinal accumulations. Although *geosyncline* is difficult to define [18] and not all are alike, there is what may be called the normal geosynclinal cycle. The geosyncline is initiated, filled, and commonly, though not always, deformed. The sediments which accumulate during the different stages are more or less petrographically distinct (Fig. 165). The early stages of the geosynclinal cycle are commonly marked by a starved section—the euxinic facies, mainly black shales with, perhaps, very thin and even-bedded intercalated siltstones, siliceous limestone, or chert. This facies is succeeded by the normal flysch facies—the rhythmically bedded dark shales and graywackes. The flysch, in turn, gives way to the molasse facies in which the sandstones (subgraywackes and protoquartzites) become coarser, cleaner, and cross-bedded. They form shoestring bodies. Coals appear (Fig. 166). Reducing conditions may be replaced by an oxidizing environment and red mudstones and red sands become abundant.

[18] There is no general agreement on the definition of a *geosyncline*, and hence there are no wholly acceptable criteria for the recognition of either ancient or modern geosynclines. Kay has extended the term to include structures not considered geosynclines by others. Not all geosynclines are alike and some kind of a classification is needed. Stille has classified geosynclines (orthogeosynclines) as (1) eugeosynclines and (2) miogeosynclines. The former is marked by contemporaneous basic volcanics; the latter is amagmatic. The interested reader is referred to the writings of Stille (1941), Kay (1947, 1951), Weeks (1952), Glaessner and Teichert (1947), and others.

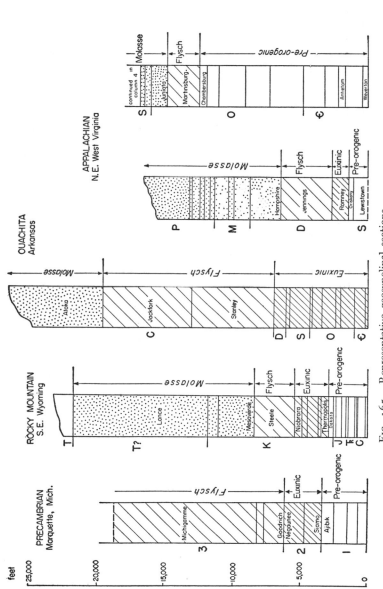

FIG. 165. Representative geosynclinal sections.

Stippling: molasse, open diagonal ruling; flysch, close diagonal ruling; euxinic, blank: orthoquartzite-carbonate (and evaporites).
€, Cambrian; O, Ordovician; S, Silurian; D, Devonian; M, Mississippian; P, Pennsylvanian; C, Carboniferous; Ŧ, Triassic; J, Jurassic;
K, Cretaceous; T, Tertiary. Precambrian cycle divided into three groups, 1, 2, and 3.
Sections from Wilmarth stratigraphic charts.

Illustrates the geosynclinal cycle. Note that the Appalachian section illustrates two such cycles; the first cycle is characterized by abnormal pre-orogenic carbonate "build-up" and a relatively thin orogenic section. The latter is a "distal" record of the Taconic orogeny of New England.

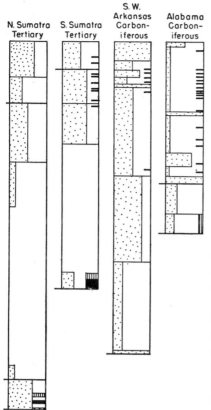

In some geosynclines, the pregeosynclinal or early geosynclinal stage is an orthoquartzite-carbonate facies. The sands, craton-derived, are interbedded with dolomites and limestones. These in turn may give way to the euxinic facies to be followed by the flysch and molasse. If conditions be proper the carbonate facies may be very thick.[19]

The change from the orthoquartzitic sands of this facies to the graywackes and related sandstones of the later stages is in part associated with a change in source of material as well as accelerated tectonism. The orthoquartzites are craton-derived; the graywackes may be derived mainly from the rising geanticlinal welts within the geosyncline.[20]

In general the tectonic cycle outlined is one of increasing coarseness from the base upward; of an increasing volume of clastic material; of eventual overtake of subsidence by sedimentation with resultant shoaling of the waters and passage from reducing marine to nonmarine, at first reducing or neutral, and then oxidizing [21] (see Fig. 165).

Fig. 166. Representative geological sections. Stipple, sand; blank, shale, ruled, limestone; black, coal (after Schuppli, *Bull. Am. Assoc. Petrol. Geol.*, vol. 30, 1946, p. 3).

The concept of a geosynclinal cycle,

[19] The differences between the carbonate-bearing and noncarbonate sections may be one of position. Nearest the craton, orthoquartzitic sands and carbonates may be deposited; more remote sections are starved and without either. In some geosynclines, however, carbonates seem wholly absent.

[20] The filling and deformation of a geosyncline may be complex. Some geosynclines undergo deformation at several stages, which in part are contemporaneous with the sedimentation as noted by Bertrand. Deposits first formed may be in some places elevated and eroded. The debris from these earlier deposits is redeposited within the main geosynclinal trough. The geosyncline is "cannibalistic" as Krynine has aptly expressed it, and tends to feed upon itself.

[21] The cycle outlined has commonly been called the *delta cycle* (Barrell, 1912). Perhaps many geosynclinal fills are essentially deltaic accumulations. The question is one more of semantics rather than geology. The Gulf Coast "geosyncline" is a major fill. Several deltaic accumulations are involved and the thick accumulation within this geosyncline, although contributed by the rivers involved, seems not to be localized in the deltaic areas (Lowman, 1949, p. 1991). This view, however, has not been universally held (Russell, 1940).

especially the correlation of specific sedimentary facies with the several stages of the cycle, has been criticized. Kay (1949, p. 136), for example, says that "orthoquartzites are characteristic of the geosynclines when the craton was the principal source, graywackes when the tectonic lands were the sources." In other words, provenance and not tectonism is believed to be the cause of the major sedimentary facies. Perhaps the orthoquartzites are cratonic in origin and the graywackes are derived from the tectonic lands, but the differences in compositional maturity of these sands express the differences in the relief and rates of erosion and uplift in the respective source areas. During the geosynclinical cycle the importance of the respective sources is materially altered, so that the major facies are correlated with stage irrespective of possible differences in source.[22]

In conclusion perhaps one can say that the lithology, relief, and climate of the source area will determine the composition of the sands, whereas the environment of deposition will control the textures, structures, and geometry of the sand bodies. Inasmuch as tectonism determines relief of the source area and negativity of the site of deposition, it exerts an over-all control of the stratigraphy and petrology of the major sedimentary facies.

Engel and Engel (1953, p. 1038) suggest that "the recently proposed tectonic frameworks of sedimentation are so severely tailored that only a few sedimentary series can wear them well." Certainly too few sections have been properly analyzed to permit safe generalization. Our concepts are highly colored by studies of the Alpine and Appalachian geosynclinal sections. The Gulf Coast geosyncline,[23] certainly the most thoroughly probed modern geosyncline, does not fit the pattern of the type geosyncline. Its fill is being derived from the distant continental interior—from neither a borderland (Appalachia type) nor a tectonic land (island arc).

Some geologic sections may not be a part of the tectonic cycle outlined above. The Newark series (Triassic) of the eastern United States and its Precambrian counterpart, the Keweenawan series of the Lake Superior region, do not appear to be a molasse; they are instead, local terrestrial rift-valley or graben facies. The relation of rift valleys to the normal orogenic belts is unknown. They may be related to the foundering of old shield areas and not orogenic in character.

---

[22] That provenance, rather than tectonism, is responsible for the several sand facies has also been expressed by others. Folk (1954), for example, attributes the arkoses to a granitic terrane and the graywackes to a metamorphic terrane. The author, however, attributes the differences between these rocks to the mechanics of transport and deposition, these being markedly different in two contrasting environments tectonically controlled. Arkose, to be sure, is of granitic derivation but some graywackes (feldspathic graywackes) are likewise derived mainly from acid plutonic source rocks.

[23] There are some who deny the Gulf Coast fill is geosynclinal; offshore drilling and geophysical data are making this view more and more difficult to defend (Storm, 1945).

Although the flysch facies is geosyncline-bound, the molasse sediments may overflow the geosyncline and spread into adjoining more stable areas. The coal-bearing molasse of the Appalachian cycle, for example, is thickest in the Appalachian areas but a thin distal wedge spread far into the continental interior.

REFERENCES CITED AND BIBLIOGRAPHY

Adams, J. E., Frenzel, H. N., Rhodes, M. L., and Johnson, D. P. (1951), Starved Pennsylvanian Midland Basin, *Bull. Am. Assoc. Petroleum Geol.*, vol. 35, pp. 2600–2606.

Bailey, E. B. (1930), New light on sedimentation and tectonics, *Geol. Mag.*, vol. 47, pp. 1716–1718.

Bailey, E. B. (1936), Sedimentation in relation to tectonics, *Bull. Geol. Soc. Amer.*, vol. 47, pp. 1716–1718.

Balk, Robert (1953), Structure of graywacke areas and Taconic Range, east of Troy, New York, *Bull. Geol. Soc. Amer.*, vol. 64, pp. 811–864.

Bandy, O. L. (1953), Ecology and paleoecology of some California Foraminifera. Part II, Foraminiferal evidence of subsidence rates in the Ventura Basin, *J. Paleon.*, vol. 27, pp. 200–203.

Barrell, J. (1906), Relative geological importance of continental, littoral, and marine sedimentation, *J. Geol.*, vol. 14, pp. 316–356.

Barrell, J. (1912), Criteria for the recognition of ancient delta deposits, *Bull. Geol. Soc. Amer.*, vol. 23, pp. 377–446.

Bertrand, Marcel (1897), Structure des alpes francaises et récurrence de certain faciès sédimentaires, *Compt. rend. congr. intern. géol.*, 6th sess. 1894, pp. 163–177.

Bokman, J. (1954), Relative abundance of common sediments in Anadarko Basin, Oklahoma, *Bull. Am. Assoc. Petroleum Geol.*, vol. 38, pp. 648–654.

Cady, Wallace M. (1950), Classification of geotectonic elements, *Trans. Am. Geophys. Union*, vol. 31, pp. 780–785.

Cady, W. M., McKelvey, V. E., and Wells, F. G. (1950), Geotectonic relationships of mineral deposits, *Bull. Geol. Soc. Amer.*, vol. 61, p. 1447.

Carozzi, A. (1952), Tectonique, courants de turbidité et sédimentation. Application au Jurassique supérieur des chaines subalpines de Haute-Savoie, *Rev. gen. sci.*, vol. 59, pp. 229–245.

Clarke, F. W. (1924), Data of geochemistry, *U.S. Geol. Survey Bull.* 770.

Dapples, E. C., Krumbein, W. C., and Sloss, L. L. (1948), Tectonic control of lithologic associations, *Bull. Am. Assoc. Petroleum Geol.*, vol. 32, pp. 1936–1937.

Eardley, A. J. and White, Max (1947), Flysch and molasse, *Bull. Geol. Soc. Amer.*, vol. 58, pp. 979–990.

Engel, A. E. J. and Engel, C. G. (1953), Grenville Series in the northwest Adirondack Mountains, New York, *Bull. Geol. Soc. Amer.*, vol. 64, pp. 1013–1097.

Fischer, G. (1933), Die Petrographie der Grauwacken, *Jahrb. preuss. geol. Landesanstalt*, vol. 54, pp. 320–343.

Fleming, R. H. and Revelle, Roger (1939), Physical processes in the ocean, *Recent Marine Sediments*, Amer. Assoc. Petroleum Geologists, pp. 95–102.

Fisk, H. N. (1955), Sand facies of recent Mississippi delta deposits, *World Petroleum Congr., Proc.*, Sec. I/C, Preprint 3.

Folk, R. L. (1954), The distinction between grain size and mineral composition in sedimentary-rock nomenclature, *J. Geol.*, vol. 62, pp. 344–359.

Glaessner, M. F., and Teichert, C. (1947), Geosynclines: A fundamental concept in geology, *Am. J. Sci.*, vol. 245, pp. 465–483, 571–591.

Grabau, A. W. (1920), *Principles of salt deposition*, New York, McGraw-Hill, p. 132.

Grabau, A. W. and O'Connell, M. (1917), Were the graptolitic shales, as a rule, deep- or shallow-water deposits? *Bull. Geol. Soc. Amer.*, vol. 28, pp. 2–5, 959.

Haug, E. (1900), Les géosynclinaux et les aires continentales. Contribution à l'étude des transgressions et des régressions marines, *Bull. soc. géol. France*, sér. 3, vol. 28, pp. 617–711.

Heezen, B. C., Ewing, M., and Ericson, D. B. (1954), Reconnaissance survey of the abyssal plain south of Newfoundland, *Bull. Geol. Soc. Amer.*, vol. 65, p. 1261.

James, H. L. (1954), Sedimentary facies of iron-formation, *Econ. Geol.*, vol. 49, pp. 235–293.

Jones, O. T. (1938), On the evolution of a geosyncline, *Proc. Geol. Soc. London*, vol. 94, pp. lx–cx.

Kay, Marshall (1944), Geosynclines in continental development, *Science*, vol. 99, pp. 461–462.

Kay, Marshall (1947), Geological nomenclature and the craton, *Bull. Am. Assoc. Petroleum Geol.*, vol. 31, pp. 1289–1293.

Kay, Marshall (1951), North American Geosynclines, *Geol. Soc. Amer.*, Mem. 48, p. 143.

King, P. B. (1948), Geology of the southern Guadalupe Mountains, Texas, *U.S. Geol. Survey Prof. Paper 215*.

Krumbein, W. C. (1951), Occurrence and lithologic associations of evaporites in the United States, *J. Sediment. Petrol.*, vol. 21, pp. 63–81.

Krumbein, W. C., Sloss, L. L., and Dapples, E. C. (1949), Sedimentary tectonics and sedimentary environments, *Bull. Am. Assoc. Petroleum Geol.*, vol. 33, pp. 1859–1891.

Krumbein, W. C., Sloss, L. L., and Dapples, E. C. (1950), Diastrophism and sedimentation—a reply, *Bull. Am. Assoc. Petroleum Geol.*, vol. 34, pp. 316–318.

Krynine, P. D. (1935), Arkose deposits in the humid tropics. A study of sedimentation in southern Mexico, *Am. J. Sci.*, ser. 5, vol. 29, pp. 353–363.

Krynine, P. D. (1941), Differentiation of sediments during the life history of a landmass, *Bull. Geol. Soc. Amer.*, vol. 52, p. 1915 (abstract).

Krynine, P. D. (1941), Paleogeographic and tectonic significance of arkoses, *Bull. Geol. Soc. Amer.*, vol. 52, pp. 1918–1919.

Krynine, P. D. (1942), Differential sedimentation and its products during one complete geosynclinal cycle, *Anales congr. panamer. ing. minas y geol.*, Santiago, Chile, pp. 536–561.

Krynine, P. D. (1943), *Diastrophism and the evolution of sedimentary rocks*, Am. Assoc. Petroleum Geol. (Distinguished Lecture Series) mimeographed.

Krynine, P. D. (1943), Diastrophism and the evolution of sedimentary rocks, *Penn. Min. Industries Tech. Paper*, 84A.

Krynine, P. D. (1945), Sediments and the search for oil, *Producers Monthly*, vol. 9, pp. 17–22.

Krynine, P. D. (1949), The origin of red beds, *Trans. N.Y. Acad. Sci.*, ser. 2, vol. 11, pp. 60–67.

Krynine, P. D. (1950), Petrology, stratigraphy, and origin of the Triassic sedimentary rocks of Connecticut, *Connecticut State Geol. Nat. Hist. Survey Bull.* 73.

Krynine, P. D. (1951), A critique of geotectonic elements, *Trans. Am. Geophys. Union*, vol. 32, pp. 743–748.

Kuenen, Ph. H. (1950), *Marine geology*, New York, Wiley, pp. 195–208.

Kuenen, Ph. H., and Carozzi, A. (1953), Turbidity currents and sliding in geosynclinal basins of the Alps, *J. Geol.* vol. 61, pp. 363–373.

Kuenen, Ph. H., and Migliorini, C. I. (1950), Turbidity currents as a cause of graded bedding, *J. Geol.*, vol. 58, pp. 91–127.

Lawson, A. C. (1925), The petrographic designation of alluvial fan formations, *Univ. Calif. Publ. Dept. Geol., Bull.*, vol. 7, pp. 325–334.

Lowman, S. W. (1949), Sedimentary facies in Gulf Coast, *Bull. Am. Assoc. Petroleum Geol.*, vol. 33, pp. 1939–1997.

Moore, R. C. (1949), Stratigraphy, *Geol. Soc. Amer., 50th ann. volume*, pp. 177–220.

Nanz, R. H. Jr. (1954), Genesis of Oligocene sandstone reservoir, Seeligson field, Jim Wells and Kleberg counties, Texas, *Bull. Am. Assoc. Petroleum Geol.*, vol. 38, pp. 96–117.

Natland, M. L., and Kuenen, Ph. H. (1951), Sedimentary history of the Ventura Basin, California, and the action of turbidity currents, *Soc. Econ. Paleon. Min., Special Publ.* no. 2, pp. 76–107.

Payne, T. G. (1942), Stratigraphic analysis and environmental reconstruction, *Bull. Am. Assoc. Petroleum Geol.*, vol. 26, pp. 1697–1770.

Pettijohn, F. J. (1943), Archean Sedimentation, *Bull. Geol. Soc. Amer.*, vol. 54, p. 947.

Reinemund, J. A. (1955), Geology of the Deep River coal field, North Carolina, *U.S. Geol. Survey, Prof. Paper* 246.

Rich, J. L. (1951), Three critical environments of deposition, and criteria for recognition of rocks deposited in each of them, *Bull. Geol. Soc. Amer.*, vol. 62, pp. 1–20.

Ruedemann, R. (1934), Paleozoic plankton of North America, *Geol. Soc. Amer., Mem.* 2, pp. 43–51.

Russell, R. J. (1940), Quaternary history of Louisiana, *Bull. Geol. Soc. Amer.*, vol. 51, pp. 1199–1234.

Sloss, L. L. (1953), The significance of evaporites, *J. Sediment. Petrol.*, vol. 23, pp. 143–161.

Storm, L. W. (1945), Resume of facts and opinions on sedimentation in Gulf Coast regions of Texas and Louisiana, *Bull. Am. Assoc. Petroleum Geol.*, vol. 29, pp. 1304–1335.

Ström, K. M. (1936), Land-locked waters: Hydrography and bottom deposits in badly ventilated Norwegian fjords with remarks upon sedimentation under anaerobic conditions, *Skrifter Norske Videnskaps- Akad. Oslo, Mat.-Natur. Kl.*, vol. 1, no. 7, pp. 1–85.

Ström, K. M. (1939), Land-locked waters and the deposition of black muds, in *Recent Marine Sediments*, Amer. Assoc. Petroleum Geologists, pp. 356–372.

Tercier, J. (1940), Dépôts marins actuels et séries géologique, *Eclogae Geol. Hclv*, vol. 32, pp. 47–100.

Trask, P. D. (1932), Organic content of recent marine sediments, in *Recent Marine Sediments*, Amer. Assoc. Petroleum Geologists, pp. 428–453.

Twenhofel, W. H. (1939), Environments of origin of black shales, *Bull. Am. Assoc. Petroleum Geol.*, vol. 23, pp. 1178–1198.

Twenhofel, W. H. (1950), *Principles of sedimentation* (2nd ed.), New York, McGraw-Hill.

Tyrrell, G. W. (1933), Greenstones and greywackes, *Compt. rend. reunion intern. etude Precambrien*, pp. 24–26.

Usiglio, J. (1849), cited by Clarke (1924), p. 219.

Van Houten, F. B. (1948), Origin of red-banded early Cenozoic deposits in Rocky Mountain region, *Bull. Am. Assoc. Petroleum Geol.*, vol. 32, pp. 2083–2126.

Van Houten, F. B. (1950), Diastrophism and sedimentation, *Bull. Am. Assoc. Petroleum Geol.*, vol. 34, pp. 314–316.

Van't Hoff, J. H. (1909), *Zur Bildung der ozeanischen Salzablagerungen,* Braunschweig, Vierweg.

van Waterschoot van der Gracht, W. A. J. M. (1931), Permocarboniferous orogeny in south-central United States, *Bull. Am. Assoc. Petroleum Geol.*, vol. 15, pp. 991–1057.

van Waterschoot van der Gracht, W. A. J. M. (1931), The Permo-carboniferous orogeny in the south-central United States, *Verhandel. Koninkl. Ned. Akad. Wetenschap.*, vol. 27, no. 3.

Wanless, H. R., and Weller, J. M. (1932), Correlation and extent of Pennsylvanian cyclothems, *Bull. Geol. Soc. Amer.*, vol. 43, pp. 1003–1016.

Weller, J. M. (1930), Cyclical sedimentation of the Pennsylvanian period and its significance, *J. Geol.*, vol. 38, pp. 97–135.

White, W. S. and Wright, J. C. (1954), The White Pine copper deposit, Ontonagon County, Michigan, *Econ. Geol.*, vol. 49, pp. 675–715.

Woolnough, W. G. (1937), Sedimentation in barred basins, and source rocks of petroleum, *Bull. Am. Assoc. Petroleum Geol.*, vol. 21, pp. 1101–1157.

14

Lithification and Diagenesis

INTRODUCTION

Lithification is that complex of processes that converts a newly deposited sediment into an indurated rock. Lithification may be partial or incomplete. It may occur shortly after deposition—may even be concurrent with it—or it may occur long after deposition.

Diagenesis refers primarily to the reactions which take place within a sediment between one mineral and another or between one or several minerals and the interstitial or supernatant fluids.

In mechanically accumulated sediments or in sediments consisting of a mechanical transported fraction and a chemically precipitated fraction, there is no a priori reason why such materials should be in chemical equilibrium with one another. Under proper conditions, such as a rise in temperature or in the presence of a suitable medium, reactions between the several phases present may take place. Such reactions are *diagenetic* at the lower temperatures and pressures and *metamorphic* at more elevated temperatures and pressures.

The term *diagenesis*, first used in 1888 by von Gümbel, has been variously defined. All writers would exclude metamorphic changes from the domain of diagenesis, but as pointed out by Deverin (1924), no distinction between diagenesis and metamorphism is possible. Diagenesis is, in fact, the beginning of metamorphism because it leads to modification of the textures, structures, and mineral composition of a sediment. Such modifications are the earmarks of metamorphism according to Grubenmann.

Efforts have been made to distinguish between the chemical rearrangements and replacements that take place on the sea floor from those that

648

occur after the sediment has been removed from direct contact with sea water. To the first group of changes the term *halmyrolosis* has been applied (Hummel, 1922). Many of the changes in regions of very slow sedimentation involve the decomposition of silicates, and these changes are analogous in cause and effect to weathering on the land, and hence, in fact, have been termed *submarine weathering*. A common result is an enrichment in iron in the gel-forming minerals. To those changes taking place after uplift or consolidation, the terms *epigenesis* or, less commonly, *metharmosis* (Kessler, 1922) have been applied. Diagenesis includes halmyrolosis and metharmosis and by degrees passes into metamorphism. The continuity of the processes of internal reorganization and replacement must be fully recognized.

The processes of weathering and those of diagenesis although seemingly quite different and unrelated, are at times rather difficult to separate from one another (Krumbein, 1947; Blackwelder, 1947). A sediment, for example, after consolidation and uplift may be subjected to further changes such as intrastratal solution. Is such solution, leading to the formation of stylolites for example, diagenetic or is it a result of weathering? Are retrograde changes to be designated retrograde diagenesis just as there are changes designated retrograde metamorphism or is retrograde diagenesis just weathering?

Some writers would include those physical changes which take place after deposition and before consolidation in their definition of diagenesis. Included are compaction and various types of soft-sediment deformation. These changes occur mainly while the sediment is still in the environment of deposition. Except for compaction and expulsion of pore fluids and their dissolved solids, the physical changes are not here included in the diagenetic realm.

Evidences of diagenetic reactions consist of evidences of postdepositional recrystallization, replacements, overgrowths, porphyroblastic growths *de novo*, segregations of mineral materials, and intrastratal solution (which see). No doubt the mineral assemblage produced by diagenesis is an equilibrium assemblage. To date little effort has been made to ascertain what mineral assemblages may be expected from given compositions. The application of the mineral facies principle to the low-grade assemblages and reactions should prove profitable.

Diagenetic changes are achieved by the ordinary processes of chemical reorganization such as solution, precipitation, crystallization, recrystallization, oxidation, reduction, and so forth. Diagenesis, however, is best understood if the processes operating are analyzed in terms of the geologic character of the process and its effects. From this point of view the principal diagenetic processes are cementation, diagenetic reorganization (authigenesis), diagenetic differentiation and segregation, diagenetic metasomatism, intrastratal solution, and compaction.

Cementation is the process of precipitation of mineral matter in the pores or voids of a clastic sediment, the end result of which is rock induration. It is the principal way in which sandstones and conglomerates become lithified. Diagenetic reorganization or authigenesis is the result of *reaction between* the several constituents of a sediment, both detrital and chemical in origin, and the formation of certain new minerals or the enlargement or outgrowth of others already present. The new minerals thus formed are the authigenic minerals. Diagenetic differentiation is the redistribution of materials *within* a sediment, leading to segregation of the minor constituents into nodules, concretions, and related bodies. Diagenetic metasomatism involves introduction of materials from *without*, leading to replacement without appreciable volume changes of the bed concerned as in the production of a replacement dolomite. Intrastratal solution is implied in all diagenetic change, but a separate discussion of this process seems warranted inasmuch as it leads to the formation of certain visible structures such as stylolites and microstylolites. Compaction is the reduction of pore space and expulsion of interstitial fluids resulting from grain rearrangements under load. Compaction is greatest and most important only in the finest-grained sediments.

REFERENCES CITED AND BIBLIOGRAPHY

Andrée, K. (1911), Die Diagenese der Sedimente, ihre Beziehungen zur Sedimentbuildung und Sedimentpetrographie, *Geol. Rundschau*, vol. 2, pp. 61–74, 115–130.

Blackwelder, Eliot (1947), Diagenesis and weathering, *Bull. Am. Assoc. Petroleum Geol.*, vol. 31, p. 500.

Correns, C. W. (1950), Zur Geochemie der Diagenese, *Geochim. et Cosmochim. Acta*, vol. 1, pp. 49–54.

Déverin, L. (1924), L'étude lithologique des roches sédimentaires, *Schweiz. mineralog. petrolog. Mitt.*, vol. 4, pp. 45–48.

Emery, K. O. and Rittenberg, S. C. (1952), Early diagenesis of California basin sediments in relation to origin of oil, *Bull. Am. Assoc. Petroleum Geol.*, vol. 36, pp. 735–806.

Hummel, K. (1922), Die Entstehung eisenreicher Gesteine durch Halmyrolse, *Geol. Rundschau*, vol. 13, pp. 40–81.

Kessler, P. (1922), Ueber Lochverwitterung und ihre Beziehungen zur Metharmose (Umbildung) der Gesteine, *Geol. Rundschau*, vol. 12, pp. 237–270.

Krumbein, W. C. (1942), Physical and chemical changes in sediments after deposition, *J. Sediment. Petrol.*, vol. 12, pp. 111–117.

Krumbein, W. C. (1947), Analysis of sedimentation and diagenesis, *Bull. Am. Assoc. Petroleum Geol.*, vol. 31, pp. 168–174.

Schuchert, Chas. (1920), Diagenesis in sedimentation, *Bull. Geol. Soc. Amer.*, vol. 31, pp. 425–432.

CEMENTATION AND DECEMENTATION

Introduction

The chemically precipitated material which forms the cement of many medium- and coarse-grained clastic sediments is an important constituent of such rocks. If the voids are completely filled, the cement constitutes from one-fourth to one-third of the whole rock. A cemented sandstone stratum 100 feet thick, for example, contains within it enough cementing material to form a layer 25 to 30 feet thick if these materials were segregated instead of dispersed throughout the bed. Cementation, moreover, is the last step in the formation of the sedimentary rock, and our knowledge is incomplete and unsatisfactory unless the origin and manner of emplacement of the cement is fully understood.

The introduction of a cement obviously affects both the porosity and the permeability of the rock, and is therefore of considerable interest to those persons concerned with either the movement of fluids through the rock or the total volume of such fluids. Cementation, if carried to completion, produces a tight sand capable of neither holding nor transmitting such fluids as ground water, petroleum, or natural gas. Conceivably the cementation process may result in displacement of the contained fluids or the building up of pressures in closed systems.

Kinds and Relative Abundance of Cementing Minerals

Many species of minerals are known to play the role of cement. Some, however, are relatively rare and therefore quantitatively unimportant. The most common cementing material is silica, generally quartz. The quartz cement is most commonly deposited as an overgrowth on the detrital quartz grains.

Under some rather uncommon conditions, the silica is deposited as opal or chalcedony instead of quartz (Pl. 17, E). Sandstones with opaline cement are chiefly of late geologic age. The factors leading to the formation of opal rather than quartz are not known. The opal-cemented Ogallala of Kansas (Frye and Swineford, 1946) has been interpreted as an opal replacement of a calcite-cemented sandstone. Ash beds associated with this formation are thought to be the source of the replacing silica. The close association of opal-cemented sands and ash beds seems rather common.

Various carbonate minerals, especially calcite, are common cementing agents. Dolomite is less common and siderite is comparatively rare. Siderite is not so rare, perhaps, as commonly believed, since it is almost never seen in outcrop owing to its instability in the presence of the atmosphere. Many of the ferruginous or iron oxide cemented sandstones may have been in fact sideritic sandstones. Examination of some of the spotted sandstones shows that each spot, which is a small area cemented by limonite, is derived by oxidation of siderite, some of which is preserved in the unaltered state in the center of the limonite-cemented areas (Pl. 17, C). Iron oxide, in part siderite derived, and more rarely, iron sulfide, also occur as cements. Barite and anhydrite are minor cementing agents and are only locally important, as are some zeolites (Gilbert and McAndrews, 1948).

Some sandstones contain clay. Some of this seems to be material entrapped at the time of deposition, and is therefore a detrital component. In other cases, however, the clay is coarsely crystalline and may possibly be introduced and precipitated from solution.

Tallman (1949) examined some 275 sandstones widely distributed in time and space, and attempted to ascertain the relative abundance of the several types of cement. He found that in sandstones of Mesozoic age or younger that carbonate and silica cements were about equally abundant. In the late Paleozoic, silica was found in three-quarters of the sandstones studied and carbonate in the remaining one-quarter. In the early Paleozoic and Precambrian, silica cemented four-fifths of all sandstones examined. The significance of Tallman's observations is not clear. Perhaps the carbonate cements were once as common in the earlier rocks as in the later ones and have been replaced by silica during the course of time. Perhaps also the carbonate of the earlier sandstones was removed by leaching so that the sands are now friable and contain only a small residue of silica, and therefore are classified as silica-cemented though carbonate once was the dominant cementing agent.

Textures of Cements

The relation of the cement to the detrital framework of a sand is of considerable interest and importance. If the mineral composition of the cement is the same as that of the detrital grains, the cement is deposited in crystallographic continuity on the detrital grains, the end result of which is an interlocking crystalline aggregate—a quartzite if the rock is largely quartz, and a nonmetamorphic marble (orthomarble of Brooks, 1954) if the rock be a calcite-cemented encrinite.[1]

If the cement is mineralogically unlike the detrital material it may show various textural relations. Calcite, for example, in partially cemented sandstones appears under the microscope as a fringe-like deposit on the borders of the sand grains. In most carbonate-cemented sands, however, the calcite cement forms a crystalline mosaic between the grains. Each pore is filled with a single crystal or at most with two or three such crystals (Fig. 167, A).

[1] Conceivably an arkose might be converted to a granite by secondary enlargement of both the quartz and the feldspar. Such a recomposed granite would be neither igneous nor metamorphic.

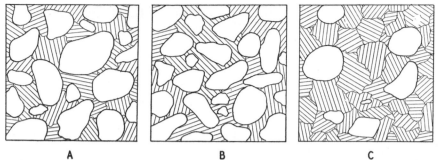

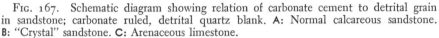

FIG. 167. Schematic diagram showing relation of carbonate cement to detrital grain in sandstone; carbonate ruled, detrital quartz blank. **A:** Normal calcareous sandstone. **B:** "Crystal" sandstone. **C:** Arenaceous limestone.

In a few sandstones, however, the crystals of calcite are large—1 centimeter or more in diameter (Fig. 167, B). Such sandstones are said to show *luster-mottling*. Incomplete cementation of such sandstones results in the formation of sand crystals, which are large calcite euhedra that are loaded with inclusions of detrital sand. Most noted examples of this phenomena are the sand crystals from the Miocene of Devil's Hill in the Badlands of South Dakota (Pl. 8, bottom and 17, B; see also p. 202) and the sandstone at Fontainbleau in the Paris basin. In other, rather uncommon cases, the quartz grains are widely separated or floating in a field of carbonate (Fig. 167, C).[2] Anderson interprets such rocks as an original mixture of clastic quartz and *clastic* carbonate. The clastic carbonate may have recrystallized, thereby losing all traces of its clastic origin. Such rocks grade into limestones with a few wind-blown quartz grains. Waldschmidt (1941), on the other hand, attributes the separation of the quartz grains of some sandstones to the growth of the cement and the forceful wedging apart of the grains. In other cases the corrosion of the quartz grains by the cement and the total replacement of the smaller grains leaves many widely separated quartz grains. The end result of this process of calcification would be a limestone. The writer knows of no example of such extensive replacement.

Paragenesis of Cementing Minerals

Some sandstones have more than one species of cementing mineral. If more than one such mineral is present, it is important to determine the paragenesis or relative age of the cementing minerals. Waldschmidt (1941) studied the sandstones of the Rocky Mountain area, ranging in age from Pennsylvanian to Cretaceous, and concluded that a definite order of precipitation could be established. According to him this order is quartz followed

[2] In many cases the isolated grains are not actually unsupported. Because of the random character of a thin-section cut, the plane of the section may not have passed through the point of contact between two adjacent grains so that they appear not to be in contact.

PLATE 39

DIAGENESIS I (SECONDARY ENLARGEMENT OF QUARTZ)

A: Cambrian sandstone, Iron Mountain, Mich. Crossed nicols, $\times$40.

Dusty borders mark outlines of original quartz grains. A quartzite formed by cementation with quartz in crystallographic continuity with detrital grains.

B: Bruce limestone, Lower Huronian, Bruce Mines, Ont., Canada. Crossed nicols, $\times$42.

A crystalline limestone, originally a calcareous silt containing some bits of angular detrital quartz and a few larger quartz sand grains. One of the latter, shown in the figure, shows secondary enlargement but without reconstruction of the quartz-crystal form. Note ringlike arrangement of carbonate inclusions along boundary of original quartz grain.

C: Arbuckle limestone, Cambrian, Carter County, Okla. Ordinary light, $\times$40.

Originally a calcareous oolite containing a few scattered well-rounded detrital quartz grains. The oolites (and matrix) have been dolomitized, so that most of their internal structure has been destroyed and the boundaries of many have become vague. The quartz grains have been enlarged by addition of quartz which has replaced both matrix and oolites. Note carbonate inclusions. See **D**.

D: Detail of **C**. Ordinary light, $\times$90.

Shows reconstructed quartz crystal with ringlike arrangement of inclusions along border of detrital nucleus. Carbonate was engulfed upon enlargement of quartz.

E: Hale formation, Morrow group, Pennsylvanian, Fayetteville, Ark. Ordinary light, $\times$40.

A calcareous oolite, cemented by clear calcite. Detrital quartz nuclei of oolites have been enlarged by outgrowth which has replaced oolite. Note minute carbonate inclusions of quartz in which faintly seen is structure of replaced oolite.

F: Siliceous oolites, Cambrian, State College, Penna. Crossed nicols, $\times$45.

Detail of a siliceous oolite with detrital quartz center. Core is outlined by dustlike ring of carbonate inclusions. Secondary quartz in crystallographic continuity with detrital nucleus is surrounded by microcrystalline chert. Space between oolites is filled by quartz crystals directed radially outward from oolites.

Ring of dusty carbonate inclusions is interpreted as engulfed carbonate matrix during outgrowth of quartz in original carbonate oolite prior to chertification.

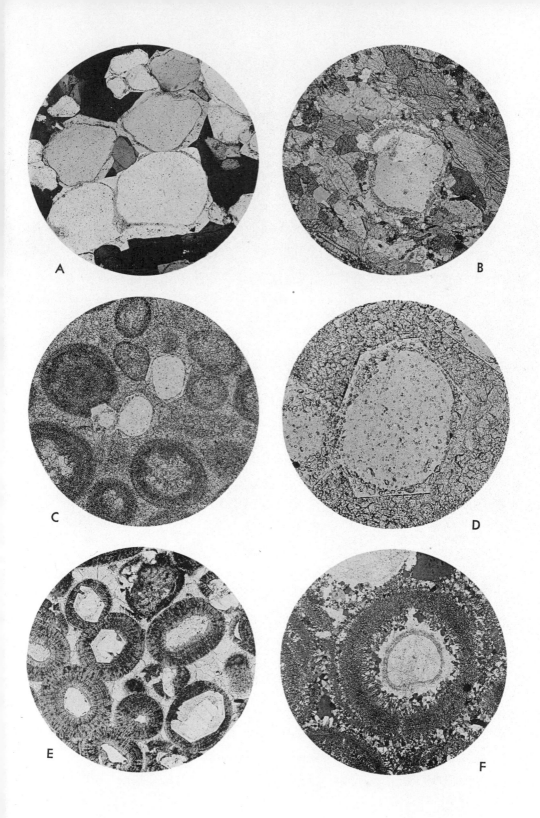

A

B

C

D

E

F

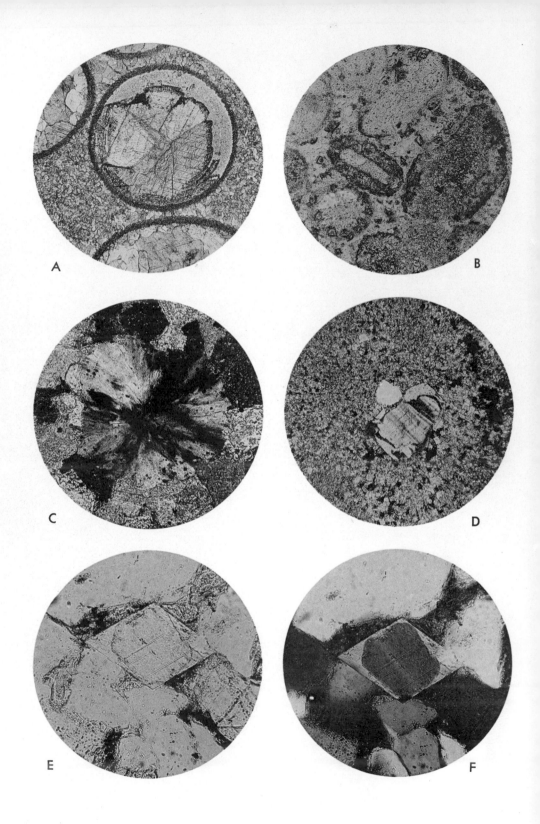

A

B

C

D

E

F

PLATE 40

DIAGENESIS II

A: Oolitic limestone, Cambrian, Tyrone, Penna. Crossed nicols, ×40.
Incompletely silicified oolite in dolomitic matrix. Original calcareous (probably aragonite) oolite was replaced by mosaic of coarsely crystalline calcite. Note cleavage cracks of latter which pass through concentrically arranged inclusions—vestigial remnants of the original concentric structure. Silica (chert) now eating into and replacing calcite mosaic. Matrix has been dolomitized. Illustrates a complex sequence of replacements.

B: Oolitic chert from Shakopee dolomite, Ordovician, Utica, Ill. Ordinary light, ×44.
Microcrystalline chalcedony in which outlines of original oolites are dimly visible. Note chert pseudomorphs of rhombic euhedra. The latter doubtless were dolomite. Hence the mineral sequence seems to have been: (1) aragonite (?) of original oolite, (2) partial replacement of both oolites and their matrix by dolomite, and (3) silicification of the whole rock and conversion to chert.

C: Spherulite of chalcedony in Niagaran dolomite, Silurian, Thornton, Ill. Crossed nicols, ×85.
Note irregular outline of spherulite, lack of concentric structure, and radial arrangement of fibers of chalcedony. The latter is shown to be the case by the pseudouniaxial cross which appears when the nicols are crossed.

D: Enlarged detrital feldspar in dolomitic Altyn limestone, Belt series (Precambrian), Glacier National Park, Montana. Crossed nicols, ×40. See also Fig. 93.
To somewhat corroded core of twinned feldspar has been added secondary deposit of that same mineral.

E: Enlarged feldspar in Croixan sandstone, Cambrian, Wis. Ordinary light, ×85.
Note simple rhombic outline of reconstructed feldspar, cleavage crossing both secondary outgrowth and nucleus, and faint outline of detrital core.

F: Same as **E**. Crossed nicols, ×85.
Note sharp differentiation between detrital core and secondary rim, because of difference in composition, which results in slightly different extinction positions for two parts of the reconstructed crystal.

by calcite, or if there are three cementing minerals, quartz followed by dolomite, in turn followed by calcite, or if there are four cementing minerals, the three last named would be followed by anhydrite. In some rocks with three minerals the order was quartz, dolomite, and anhydrite. Other studies have shown somewhat different sequences in time. Gilbert (1949), for example, from a study of some Tertiary sandstones in California, found the relative order of quartz and dolomite was reversed and that in some sandstones the calcite may be somewhat earlier than the quartz. Heald (1950), who examined some Paleozoic sandstones of West Virginia, concluded that the carbonates were younger than the quartz.

In general, the order of precipitation of the several cementing minerals is established on the principle that those minerals precipitated first will be better formed or more euhedral and will be attached to the walls of the interstices. The last-deposited minerals must occupy the remaining unfilled space and be molded about the early formed crystals. But can it be assumed that the minerals were formed in open spaces? Hadding (1929), Cayeux (1929), and others (Swineford, 1947) have described sandstones first cemented by calcite which was later partly or completely replaced by quartz. Evidence of such replacement lies in the scattered inclusions of calcite in the secondary quartz. Possibly, therefore, the euhedralism of some quartz and dolomite crystals means only that these are metacrysts formed during replacement, and are therefore the last- instead of the first-formed minerals.

Waldschmidt's tabulations (1941) show a dominance of quartz over carbonate in the cement of older sandstones and a dominance of dolomite over calcite in the older carbonate-cemented sandstones. The younger sandstones are calcite-cemented if they have a mineral cement at all. These relations are to be expected if the replacement is postdepositional. Longer time would permit greater substitution of quartz for carbonate and dolomite for calcite. Goldman (Mills and Wells, 1919, pp. 15–16) has noted that the approach to quartzite was in general greatest in the deepest beds although this relation was highly variable.

Origin of Cement

The problems of *how* and *when* sands become cemented and the *source* of the cementing material are still unresolved. There has been renewed interest in these problems in recent years.

It was long supposed that meteoric or artesian circulation carried the cementing materials into the sandstone and there deposited their silica or carbonate. It is known that ground waters do carry these materials in solution, that artesian flow does occur, and that materials may be precipitated from solution. Van Hise (1904) reviewed the problem at some length. He supposed that the silica (or other cementing material) was dissolved in the belt of weathering and redeposited in the belt of cementation. Downward moving waters would dissolve as they were warmed up, and upward moving waters would precipitate as they moved to cooler regions. Van Hise pointed out, however, that the silica content of ground water was very low. On the average there is only 1 part of silica to 50,000 of water. To cement a cubic mile of sand (with average porosity of 26 per cent) would require 130,000 cubic miles of average ground water. Owing to the fact that some sandstones, especially those in the deeper basins, are filled with salt waters, many have supposed that no meteoric waters have ever circulated through them, and therefore another source for their cement must be sought.

R. H. Johnson (1920) proposed, therefore, that the silica be derived from connate waters. Connate water is essentially trapped sea water and because sea water contains even less silica on the average than ground water, it is clear that the connate waters of the sandstone would provide only a negligible and wholly inadequate quantity of silica. Johnson, therefore, suggested that the connate waters of shales may be the source of the silica. Shales are originally more porous than the sands and undergo a much greater compaction. The entrapped fluids must escape and the interbedded sandstones may be indeed the channelways of escape. Under the elevated temperatures incident to burial, the shale waters may contain a higher than normal content of silica, which might be deposited in the sandstones. To date there has been no evidence that such solutions are adequate in silica content or volume to cement the sands. Some cemented sandstones occur without any associated shales. How did these sands become cemented?

The difficulties of ascribing the cements to either artesian or connate waters have led some workers to look within the formation for a source of silica. An intrastratal origin has been postulated by Waldschmidt (1941), Gilbert (1949), and others. Waldschmidt concluded that solution of silica at points of grain contact and precipitation of the same in the voids was responsible for the silica-cemented sandstones. This concept, as noted by Waldschmidt, is essentially Riecke's principle applied to nonmetamorphic rocks. As evidence that the process was operative Waldschmidt pointed to the interlocking boundaries of quartz grains. The concave-convex contact between quartz grains (analogous to the pitted pebbles of some conglomerates, Kuenen, 1942) and the sutured (microstylolitic) boundaries between others are apparent evidences in support of Waldschmidt's conclusion. Unfortunately clear examples of such contacts between the original detrital grains are rather rare; the suturing or interlocking is commonly between the quartz *overgrowths* rather than the detrital grains proper.[3] The mechanism

---

[3] An exception is the sandstone with an abundance of detrital chert particles described by Sloss and Feray (1948). In this sandstone microstylolitic boundaries are very common. The chert seems especially suspectible to solution.

therefore has been deemed inadequate by some students of the subject. Pye (1944) and later Goldstein (1948) concluded that some or most of the silica might have come from the solution of the fines which the sand may have once contained. It is a well-known principle that in a given solution the finer particles may dissolve at the same time the larger ones are growing. Conceivably, therefore, the larger grains in a sandstone might grow at the expense of the smaller ones. As the fines are destroyed in the process, there is little direct evidence of the correctness of this theory of cementation. More recently, Heald (1953, 1955) has suggested that the silica was derived by intrastratal solution along stylolitic seams, Heald points out that stylolites are more common in sandstones and quartzites than is generally realized, and that solution along such seams might produce some of the silica required for cementation.

Krynine (1941) who deemed both intrastratal solution and artesian flow inadequate mechanisms of cementation concluded, from a study of the Oriskany and other sandstones, that "probably close to 95 per cent of the 'secondary' silica in the Oriskany (and in many if not most other quartzites and cherts) is really of primary, penecontemporaneous sedimentary origin." Krynine says that the precipitation of the silica cement "takes place at the bottom of the sea immediately following the deposition of the sand grains." Krynine does not present the evidence to support this conclusion, and the low concentrations of silica in sea water and the absence of present-day cementation of marine sands contemporaneous with their formation make the hypothesis untenable.

Jane Taylor (1950) studied the grain contacts in sandstones from various depths in deep wells in Wyoming. She classified the contacts as *tangential, long, concavo-convex,* and *sutured.* Normal sands had 1.6 contacts per grain; [4] at 2885 feet they exhibited 2.5 contacts per grain and at 8343 feet the contacts per grain were 5.2. Obviously, therefore, sandstones do undergo a condensation process which tends to bring the grains in closer contact with one another. Taylor thought this was accomplished by intrastratal solution and precipitation and by solid flow of the quartz grains. In the latter case the pore volume would be reduced and the sand mechanically bonded. Little chemically precipitated silica would be needed. Taylor cited various evidences of pressure, such as bent micas and fractured quartz grains, but solid flow itself is difficult to prove, and the concave-convex contacts seen by Taylor may be, as Waldschmidt supposed, a solution effect. Taylor's work is important, however, in attempting to state in quantitative terms the extent to which a sandstone has been condensed.

Experiments by Fairbairn (1950) and Maxwell and Verrall (1954) suggest

[4] More recent experimental work on artificial sands by Gaither (1953) has shown that the freshly deposited sand would have 0.85 contact per grain.

that under considerable pressure and proper interstitial fluids solutions and reprecipitation of the quartz in sands does occur. Crushing, fracturing, and recrystallization of strained grains were also involved.

It is clear, therefore, that the time and manner of origin of the silica cement in sandstone are not yet clearly established. It is clear that sandstones may undergo a condensation or pore space reduction. This may be achieved by mechanical action in part and in part by intrastratal solution and reprecipitation, and by simple filling of voids by introduced materials.

Other cements, the carbonates, for example, pose problems similar to those of silica. These cements too may be in part introduced and in part intrastratal. The carbonate, for example, may be the product of solution and reprecipitation of calcareous shells. A sandstone with two or more cementing minerals is a further problem and none of the theories of sandstone cementation has adequately dealt with this problem. Most authors have been content to establish the relative age of the several cementing minerals without explaining why under their theory of cementation, there should be two cementing materials or why they are deposited in a particular order.

Decementation

If the void-filling fluids and the solid grains of a sandstone do not form a closed system, that is, if fluids move out as well as in or if ions can diffuse out and in, the materials precipitated in the voids might also be dissolved out of them. In other words, leaching of the cement, or *decementation* might take place. To date little evidence has been produced to show that decementation has occurred and none has been presented to show that it occurs on a large scale.

The partial replacement of the quartz and other detrital grains by the carbonate cement of some sandstones is evidence that some silica was removed. If the cement is quartz and there is evidence that it formed by replacement of a carbonate matrix, there is an implied removal of much carbonate. That carbonate removal has occurred in the Oriskany was a conclusion reached by Krynine (1941). Krynine observed small quantities of carbonate in the recesses of some pores and believed it to be residual carbonate left after leaching. If it were only a partial pore filling, it would show euhedral outlines on the free margins. Apparently these were lacking. Similarly Graf and Lamar (1950) interpreted the hour-glass-shaped brown carbonate in the Fredonia oolite of Illinois as vestigial carbonate left after wholesale removal by solution. One is inclined to suspect that many of the highly friable and loosely cemented sandstones, such as the St. Peter, were once carbonate cemented and have since been decemented. The frosted and etched surfaces of the quartz grains of this and other friable sandstones may be the record of the attack upon the quartz grains of the now vanished carbonate. The general paucity of carbonate cement in the older sandstones noted by Tallman (1949) may be in part due to removal of the carbonate.

In conclusion, there seems to be no reason why there should not be extensive carbonate removal from calcareous sandstones, since there is extensive internal solution in many limestones. There is, in fact, some evidence that such has indeed been the case. And as with the limestones, such solution can go on under phreatic conditions far below the water table, and as in the limestones also, the process may be reversed and the voids filled once more by precipitated materials.

REFERENCES CITED AND BIBLIOGRAPHY

Brooks, H. K. (1954), The rock and stone terms limestone and marble, Am. J. Sci., vol. 252, pp. 755–760.

Cayeux, L. (1929), Les roches sédimentaires de France. Roches siliceuses, Paris, Imprimerie nationale, p. 250.

Fairbairn, H. W. (1950), Synthetic quartzite, Am. Mineralogist, vol. 35, pp. 735–748.

Frye, J. C. and Swineford, Ada (1946), Silicified rock in the Ogallala formation, Kansas State Geol. Survey Bull. 64, pt. 2, pp. 33–76.

Gaither, A. (1953), A study of porosity and grain relationships in experimental sands, J. Sediment. Petrol., vol. 23, pp. 180–195.

Gilbert, C. M. (1949), Cementation of some California Tertiary reservoir sands, J. Geol., vol. 57, pp. 1–17.

Gilbert, C. M., and McAndrews, M. G. (1948), Authigenic heulandite in sandstone, Santa Cruz County, California, J. Sediment. Petrology, vol. 18, pp. 91–99.

Goldstein, August, Jr. (1948), Cementation of Dakota Sandstone of the Colorado Front Range, J. Sediment. Petrol., vol. 18, pp. 108–125.

Graf, D. L. and Lamar, J. E. (1950), Petrology of Fredonia oolite in southern Illinois, Bull. Am. Assoc. Petroleum Geol., vol. 34, pp. 2318–2336.

Hadding, Assar (1929), The pre-Quaternary sedimentary rocks of Sweden: Part III. The Paleozoic and Mesozoic sandstones of Sweden, Lunds Univ. Arsskr. NF Avd., vol. 25, nr. 3.

Heald, M. T. (1950), Authigenesis in West Virginia sandstones, J. Geol., vol. 58, pp. 624–633.

Heald, M. T. (1953), Significance of stylolites in sandstones (abstract), Bull. Geol. Soc. Amer., vol. 64, p. 1432.

Heald, M. T. (1955), Stylolites in sandstone, J. Geol., vol. 63, pp. 101–114.

Irving, R. D., and Van Hise, C. R. (1884), On secondary enlargements of mineral fragments in certain rocks, U.S. Geol. Survey, Bull. 8, pp. 1–56.

Johnson, R. H. (1920), The cementation process in sandstone, Bull. Am. Assoc. Petroleum Geol., vol. 4, pp. 33–35.

Krynine, P. D. (1941), Petrographic studies of variation in cementing material in the Oriskany sand, *Proc. 10th Penna. Mineral Ind. Conf., Penn. State Coll., Bull.* 33, pp. 108–116.

Kuenen, Ph. H. (1942), Pitted pebbles, *Leidische Geol. Mededeel.*, vol. 13, pp. 189–201.

Maxwell, J. C. and Verrall, Peter (1954), Low porosity may limit oil in deep sands, *World Oil*, April, May.

Mills, R. Van A., and Wells, R. C. (1919), The evaporation and concentration of waters associated with petroleum and natural gas, *U.S. Geol. Survey, Bull.* 693, pp. 15–16.

Pye, W. D. (1944), Petrology of Bethel sandstone of south-central Illinois, *Bull. Am. Assoc. Petroleum Geol.*, vol. 28, pp. 63–122.

Sloss, L. L., and Feray, D. E. (1948), Microstylolites in sandstone, *J. Sediment. Petrol.*, vol. 18, pp. 3–13.

Swineford, Ada (1947), Cemented sandstones of Dakota and Kiowa formations in Kansas, *Kansas Geol. Survey Bull.* 70, pt. 4, p. 86.

Tallman, S. L. (1949), Sandstone types: their abundance and cementing agents, *J. Geol.*, vol. 57, pp. 582–591.

Taylor, Jane M. (1950), Pore-space reduction in sandstones, *Bull. Am. Assoc. Petroleum Geol.*, vol. 34, pp. 701–716.

Van Hise, C. R. (1904), Treatise on metamorphism, *U.S. Geol. Survey, Mono.* 47, pp. 866–868.

Waldschmidt, W. A. 1941), Cementing materials in sandstones and their influence on the migration of oil, *Bull. Am. Assoc. Petroleum Geol.*, vol. 25, pp. 1839–1879.

AUTHIGENESIS

Introduction

As noted, the minerals of a sediment, in part detrital and in part chemical in origin, are not necessarily in chemical equilibrium with one another or with the interstitial fluid at the time of deposition. The authigenic processes are largely processes attempting to establish an equilibrium assemblage or facies by elimination of the unstable species, growth of stable species, and the production of new and stable species by appropriate chemical reactions.

The processes involved include reduction, especially of the iron. Many red muds, containing ferric oxide, are deposited in a reducing environment. If the rate of sedimentation is not too great or the supply of reducing materials (mainly organic matter) is not used up, the red mud is converted to a gray, green, or blue mud. Dehydration is another common process. Hydrated opaline silica tends to become dehydrated and crystallized. Gypsum may be dehydrated to form anhydrite. The converse is also common. Reaction between solid and liquid phases is an important diagenetic process. The clay materials react with the iron and magnesium present and form chlorites and other iron silicates. They also take up potash and form glauconite or a clay mica. Carbonate of calcium picks up magnesium and becomes dolomite. Although reactions between solids is perhaps characteristic of more truly metamorphic changes, the penetration and replacement of detrital quartz by chlorite and sericite of the matrix, so commonly seen in graywackes, seems to be such a reaction (p. 304). If a mineral is stable, i.e., in equilibrium with its environment, it may serve as a nucleus or seed crystal and grow in size. Feldspars, quartz, and some other minerals are commonly added to and display secondary enlargement.

Not all possible reactions between minerals take place. Many minerals therefore exist in an alien environment because the temperature rise needed to overcome barriers to reaction were never reached.

Any new or regenerated mineral is an *authigenic mineral*.

Authigenic Minerals

Tester and Atwater (1934) distinguish between *authigenic* and *secondary* minerals. An authigenic mineral is a new mineral generated or formed at the place of its occurrence. There may have been more than one period of authigenic growth, and there may or may not be a nucleus; if a nucleus to the first period of authigenic growth is present, it is of detrital origin. Secondary enlargement is growth around a nucleus of the same material and with optical continuity. Owing to slight composition differences, as in the case of the feldspars, the younger overlay does not always have the same extinction point as the nucleus. Tester and Atwater therefore call this outgrowth authigenic but not secondary. Few writers make this distinction. In this discussion, *authigenic* will be used to designate growth on the spot, and *secondary enlargement* is a particular manifestation of authigenesis, which is characterized by growth on a detrital grain of the same or closely related mineral (i.e., the minerals involved must be members of the same isomorphous series).

Baturin (1937) has used the term *authigenic* in a different sense from that customarily employed. Authigenic minerals, according to him, have formed in the sediment before burial and consolidation, whereas *epigenic* minerals are those formed in the sediment after burial. Baturin apparently attempts to discriminate between the products of early diagenesis (halmyrolisis) and later diagenesis (metaharmosis).[5]

[5] It is difficult to draw the line between the products of earliest diagenesis and those more properly formed by the sedimentation processes. Diagenesis normally is a *postdepositional* process. Although the term authigenic is used to describe a mineral formed or crystallized where it now is (in opposition to allogenic or detrital), the term as used refers primarily to minerals formed after deposition of the original sediment. It would not normally be applied, for example, to the aragonite of a coral skeleton, or other primary materials. Difficulty arises in trying to decide whether a mineral like glauconite is an original primary constituent of the sediment or a postdepositional or secondary (authigenic or diagenetic) component.

The number of minerals which have been shown to form in a sediment after its deposition is large. A few only, such as glauconite and certain zeolites, especially phillipsite, are known to have formed on the sea bottom. Many of the others may have so formed but much evidence points to their origin in a postconsolidation period. Common authigenic products include various forms of silica (quartz and chalcedony), the common carbonates (calcite, dolomite, and siderite), the feldspars (albite and orthoclase), many clay minerals (illite and sericite), and chlorites, titania (rutile, anatase, brookite), the common sulfates (gypsum, anhydrite, and barite), and the iron sulfides (marcasite and pyrite). Rarer authigenic minerals include tourmaline, zircon, and certain zeolites. A few other species, such as garnet, have been reported as authigenic, though proof of such origin is in doubt.

Authigenic Quartz and Chalcedony

Quartz occurs both as secondary rims on detrital grains and as small euhedra in limestones. The secondary outgrowths were described by Sorby in 1880. Shortly thereafter Irving and Van Hise (1884) recorded many examples of such enlargement of quartz from North American formations.

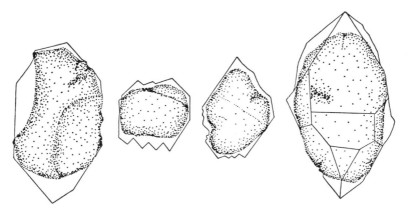

FIG. 168. Quartz crystal enlarged by secondary growth. The shaded outline represents the boundary of the sand grain; the solid lines, the reconstructed crystal after secondary growth (after Irving and Van Hise, 1884).

This phenomenon is widespread and may be universal in all sandstones in which crystalline quartz serves as a cement. In the least-cemented sandstones, the quartz grains may be broken apart readily and examined microscopically. The quartz outgrowths (Fig. 168; Pl. 1, C) restore the fundamental form and symmetry of the quartz crystal. If the detrital grain is stained with iron oxide, the nucleus and secondary rim are readily distinguished. In the better-welded quartzites, however, the distinction between the detrital and authigenic quartz is less clear and in some cases cannot be made (compare Pls. 39, A and 16, B).

The detrital quartz of certain arenaceous limestones has also been enlarged by secondary growth. Many of these enlarged grains are marked by entrapment of minute carbonate grains at the boundary between the detrital core and the new overlay of quartz (see Pl. 39, C and D). The crystal form of the quartz is restored in some cases and is more perfect than that in the sandstones inasmuch as the widely scattered quartz grains grew without interference by similar growth on neighboring grains. The overgrowth replaces the carbonate of the rock and takes place after consolidation as is shown by the transgression of quartz euhedra across the boundaries of calcareous oolites and other structures (Pl. 39, E) (Henbest, 1945).

Authigenic silica in limestones is more commonly chalcedonic rather than quartzose. Authigenic silica is most abundant as small spherulites of chalcedony, as minute disseminated patches (including the dolocastic chert seen in some insoluble residues) and as large nodular bodies (chert nodules) which may coalesce to form irregular layers. The chert problem has been reviewed elsewhere (p. 439).

Authigenic Feldspar

Authigenic and secondary feldspar occur in rocks of all ages, as inspection of a list of papers reporting its occurrence will demonstrate (see bibliography). It occurs in sandstones, shales, and limestones although its occurrence in shale has been demonstrated or reported only once. In sandstone it occurs more commonly as secondary rims or overgrowths on detrital feldspars. In limestone, the feldspar occurs as minute euhedra.

In sandstones, the differentiation between detrital nucleus and the secondary rim is readily made (Pl. 40, F). The nucleus usually is rounded, and commonly is altered sufficiently (kaolinized) or coated with a film of iron oxide, so that the contrast between the clouded core and limpid overgrowth is marked. In its growth the marginal material tends to develop crystal faces and assume a regular crystal form, usually of simple rhombic outline. As a rule the authigenic feldspar forms only a small fraction of the whole rock; exceptionally it may constitute a large and significant part—even one-half (Berg, 1952).

The nucleus of the great majority of grains seems to be the triclinic feldspar, microcline. The marginal growths appear to be an untwinned potash feldspar (orthoclase). In other cases other types of feldspar constitute the nucleus, even including labradorite. The secondary growth on such nuclei is the pure soda feldspar, albite. Where the rim is of different composition from the core, as is commonly the case, the whole grain does not show simultaneous extinction (Fig. 169). Further evidence of a difference in composition is afforded by differences in twinning and differences in refractive indices.

The secondary growth must have taken place after the deposition of the nucleus. The new feldspar is seen to be molded around adjacent interfering quartz grains. In some cases, however, evidence for several periods of secondary growth is present. The first-deposited rim itself may be worn prior to the last outgrowth of feldspar (Goldich, 1934; Stewart, 1937).

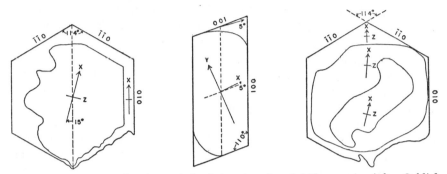

FIG. 169.   Diagram showing optical relations in enlarged feldspar grains (after Goldich, 1934). Left, (001) section; center, (010) section; right, (001) section of grain with two zones of secondary overgrowth.

The occurrence of minute feldspar euhedra in limestone has long been known. An excellent resumé of the literature on this topic is given by Boswell (1933). There are also a number of more recent papers on the authigenic feldspars of the carbonate rocks (Honess, A. P., and Jeffries, C. E., 1940; Stringham, 1940; Tester, A. C., and Atwater, G. E., 1934; van Straaten, 1948). Albite, microcline, and orthoclase are reported from limestones and dolomites of all ages. Though generally present as very minor accessories, feldspar is known in a few cases to form as much as 40 per cent of the rock (Daly, 1917). The feldspar crystals are very small—less than 1 millimeter and most commonly about 0.1 millimeter or less in size. They are disseminated through the enclosing rock, where they may replace oolites (Daly, 1917) (Fig. 93) or fossils (Stringham, 1940). They are limpid and usually unaltered by kaolinization. Carbonaceous inclusions zonally arranged are known; so also are included carbonates, which in some cases show a linear or patterned arrangement inherited from the structure of the replaced brachiopod shells (van Straaten, 1948). Glauconite also is included in some feldspars.

The feldspar crystals are well formed and of simple morphology. The unit prism (110) and the basal pinacoid (001) together produce a simple rhombohedral form. Some display the peculiar Roc Tourne twins. A similar crystal habit and twinning have never been seen in the feldspar of igneous and metamorphic rocks.

Authigenic feldspar rarely has been reported from shales. That it may be present in the high-potash shales and be more important than heretofore supposed is shown by the work of Gruner and Thiel (1937). A sample of the Glenwood shale (Ordovician) from Minneapolis, Minnesota, was shown by x-ray and chemical analysis to be about two-thirds potash feldspar. Similarly, certain size fractions of the Decorah and other Cambro-Ordovician shales were *chiefly* feldspar. All the shales were notably high in potash (6 to 10 per cent), and it is probable that other high-potash shales are also characterized by authigenic feldspar. Authigenic albite has been described from the Green River shales (Eocene) of Wyoming (Moore, 1950).

The circumstances leading to the formation of authigenic feldspar are not fully understood. Most workers today concede a contemporaneous origin for the mineral and reject a metamorphic or hydrothermal origin (Goldich, 1934). The authigenic feldspars in sediments are nearly always pure alkali feldspar.[6] It is known, both from petrological and experimental evidence, that the mixed feldspar, i.e., both soda-lime and potash-soda feldspars, are formed only at higher temperatures. The sedimentary feldspar is therefore a low-temperature product. The absence of any evidence of hydrothermal activity, coupled with the untwinned character of the feldspars and their unmixed character, rule out any possible hydrothermal origin.

Most investigators, especially the earlier writers, supposed that the feldspar was formed on the sea floor in the still unconsolidated mud, and regarded the sea water as the source of the potash or soda involved in the growth of the authigenic material. Grandjean (1910) noted the absence of feldspar in limestones of fresh-water origin. Recently the view that marine waters were necessary for the formation of authigenic feldspar has been readvanced, and the presence of such feldspar is taken as a criterion of marine origin (Crowley, 1939). Grandjean thought that the feldspar would cease to grow following burial. Reynolds (1929), van Straaten (1948), and others, however, consider it unlikely that the feldspar would form before burial and consolidation. As no growing feldspar crystals have been found in recent carbonate muds, and as van Straaten notes, fossils and oolites are replaced by authigenic feldspar, it seems likely that the feldspar is a postconsolidation product. The euhedral form of the crystals is no valid criterion of growth in an unconsolidated medium. Metamorphic rocks provide many examples of the growth of crystal euhedra in an essentially solid matrix. Tester and Atwater (1934) have shown that the feldspar of the Decorah and Galena dolomite was late,

[6] Berg (1952) estimates the authigenic feldspar in the Cambrian Franconia sandstone of Minnesota to be $Or_{98}Ab_2$. The albite of the Lowville limestone at Bellefonte, Pennsylvania, was found to be $Ab_{98.3}An_{1.7}$ (Honess and Jeffries, 1940).

perhaps following dolomitization. The presence of feldspar in sandstones containing connate waters would seem to show that circulating meteoric waters are not required for the growth of this mineral.

The conditions of formation and the source of the alkali ions needed for feldspar growth remain unknown. Van Straaten (1948) believes that a high concentration of alkali is necessary, as is perhaps the presence of CO_2. He suggests that the requisite materials may be supplied by the connate waters expelled from shales. Not all workers agree. Berg (1952), for example, attributes the potassium to sea water and the alumina and silica to clay materials in the sediment. It is not known, in any case, why the feldspar in some limestones is pure albite, whereas in others it is pure potash feldspar.

Authigenic Carbonates

Calcite appears to be an authigenic derivative of aragonite, which is the chief constituent of some invertebrate shells and skeletal structures. Since aragonite is metastable, it inverts to calcite in a relatively short time. Also, just as authigenic quartz appears as overgrowths on detrital quartz, so calcite may occur as an overgrowth on detrital calcite. The latter is mainly echinoderm debris, especially the ossicles and plates of crinoids, transported and deposited as detritus, which in time is bound together by a calcite cement deposited in optical and crystallographic continuity with the fragments (Pl. 28, A). Calcite may also occur as large sand-filled crystal euhedra (sand crystals) in some sandstones (p. 202).

Dolomite is mainly authigenic, principally in the carbonate rocks, as rhombic euhedra transecting and replacing earlier structures such as fossils and oolites (Pl. 29, B and C). In many cases the rhombs are zoned (Pl. 29, D); the zones being formed by alternations of calcite and dolomite or by inclusion-rich (hematitic) portions of the crystal. Dolomite rhombs appear in some cherts where it is not known whether they play the role of unreplaced residuals or as metacrysts. Dolomite may be distributed in scattered rhombs, or it may occur as an anastomosing network of irregular branching tubes and nodules (mottled dolomite), or it may form an interlocking mosaic completely replacing calcite. The origin and distribution of the dolomite— the dolomite problem—is discussed elsewhere (p. 421).

Siderite occurs as spherulites and as rhombic euhedra. The latter have been observed in some limestones and in chamosite and stilpnomelane mudstones, and are therefore presumed to be authigenic.

Authigenic Mica and Chlorite

As noted elsewhere (p. 349), the materials of clay size are reorganized most readily. Montmorillonite, and to a lesser extent kaolinite, are converted to the clay mica which is known as illite (or bravasite). The alteration is achieved by reaction of potassium-bearing waters (generally sea water) with the clay mineral. Potassium is preferentially fixed in the lattice of the hydromica. Unlike the sodium or calcium of montmorillonite, it is not replaceable. Such fixation of potassium apparently explains why this element, unlike sodium, does not accumulate in the ocean.

Chlorite, like the clay mica, apparently is authigenic. It appears to be formed from kaolinite and perhaps montmorillonite by the addition of magnesium (as brucite layers interleaved with the usual three-layer montmorillonite structure) (Grim, 1953).

Land-derived muds probably contain much degraded illite, chlorite, and kaolinite.[7] Upon contact with sea water, these materials pick up those ions needed to restore the crystal lattice. Reconstitution of these minerals is thus an important diagenetic change.

The factors affecting the diagenesis of the clay minerals are poorly understood. Apparently the pH of the environment is most important; to a lesser extent the oxidation-reduction potential and the concentration of such ions as potassium and magnesium also are involved. In the normal marine environment, the transformations are presumed to proceed readily; in freshwater lakes and other abnormal environments, the resulting clay mineralogy may be quite different from that of the open sea.

The transformations continue after burial so that in time montmorillonite and kaolinite tend to disappear and only the clay mica and chlorite are present.

Glauconite, Chamosite, and Related Minerals

Chamosite, an iron-rich member of the chlorite group, is thought by some writers to be an original precipitate (Hallimond, 1925); by others it is regarded as authigenic (Deverin, 1945). The oolitic chamosite is most probably an original or primary precipitate; that seen replacing crinoid debris or other fossil material is certainly authigenic. Stilpnomelane and minnesotaite, two closely associated iron-rich minerals, are considered by Gruner (1946) to be original precipitates. It seems more probable, however, that they are authigenic or low-rank metamorphic derivatives of some original iron-rich precipitate (James, 1955, p. 265).

Glauconite is a related mineral generally regarded as a product of authigenesis, although its formation appears to be contemporaneous with the accumulation of the sediment in which it occurs. Takahashi (1939) states that, "Glauconitization is one of the processes of submarine metamorphism that gives rise to the mineral glauconite" and that, "Glauconite seems to be formed under marine conditions by a process of hydration of silica and sub-

[7] Degraded clay minerals are those which have been partially leached of their alkalies and alkaline earths.

sequent absorption of bases and loss of alumina. Glauconite may originate from a number of mother materials . . . which . . . during glauconitization lose alumina, silica and alkalies except potash, and gain ferric iron and potash." Galliher (1935) considered glauconite a product of the submarine weathering of biotite. In the sediments of Monterey Bay, California, biotite was observed in all degrees of alteration from fresh biotite to glauconite. The characteristics of glauconite, its occurrence, and its origin have been summarized elsewhere (p. 467).

Authigenic Titania

The euhedral form and manner of occurrence of rutile, brookite, and anatase in the heavy residues of some sandstones leads to the conclusion that these minerals are commonly authigenic as well as detrital. Statistical data (p. 506) show that anatase and rutile are more common in the older sandstones than in those of younger age. This observation is in keeping with the authigenic concept. The antipathetic relations shown between these minerals and sphene, noted by Boswell (1924), further confirm this view and suggest, moreover, sphene as a source of the titania. These minerals also may form at the expense of leucoxene and ilmenite.

Many argillaceous rocks are crowded with fine needles of rutile which have probably been formed during diagenesis from the titanic acid set free by the decomposition of biotite. This is the probable manner of occurrence of TiO_2 in the shales.

Authigenic Sulfates

Both gypsum and anhydrite are known to be authigenic. Gypsum commonly occurs as large euhedra in a fine-grained anhydrite presumably formed from the anhydrite by hydration. It is also present in some shales as rather large crystals, several centimeters long, where it has grown at the expense of the shale as is shown by the large quantity of shaly matter included within the crystal. The gypsum euhedra of Ellsworth, Ohio, are well known. A spectacular example of authigenic gypsum are the crystal aggregates from the muds of Laguna Madra, Texas (Masson, 1955).

Anhydrite of authigenic origin is common as a minor cementing mineral of many sandstones. Celestite and barite play a similar role. Barite, in addition, forms symmetrical sand-filled crystal aggregates known as rosettes (see p. 202).

Authigenic sulfides

Authigenic pyrite and marcasite are common in many sediments (Newhouse, 1927). Black amorphous iron sulfide seems to be present in some modern muds. Apparently after burial this material is segregated and crystallized as scattered pyrite cubes, in part replacing the matrix material (Pl. 24, D), as crystal aggregates of marcasite or pyrite (Edwards and Baker, 1951), as small spherulites, and as replacements of fossil wood (Schwartz, 1927) and shells.

Inasmuch as sulfides may be carried by ground waters or by magmatic waters, the presence of sulfides is not sufficient proof of their authigenic nature. The close correlation between the sulfide content and the content of carbonaceous or organic matter in many sediments strongly suggests a diagenetic or sedimentary origin for the sulfides proper. A close correlation with veins and fractures, on the other hand, would suggest introduction from without.

Authigenic Tourmaline

Tourmaline is a common though minor constituent in most sandstones. Although it may form a considerable part of the heavy mineral residue, such residues generally are only 0.1 per cent or less of the whole rock. In a few cases the detrital tourmaline of these residues shows authigenic overgrowths. In the United States such outgrowths have been described from the Devonian of Michigan (Alty, 1933), the Oriskany (Devonian) of the Appalachian region (Stow, 1932), and the upper Cambrian Gatesburg of Pennsylvania (Krynine, 1946). Our knowledge of authigenic tourmaline in sedimentary rocks has been summarized by both Boswell (1933) and Deverin (1934). Additional occurrences have been reported by Rao (1952).

The authigenic outgrowth on tourmaline is nearly colorless and is generally deposited at the negative pole of the crystal. This appears to be a response to the hemimorphic habit of tourmaline. Although tourmaline is generally regarded as indicating pneumatolytic action at high temperature, its widespread occurrence in sediments remote from centers of igneous activity, leads to the conclusion that like the feldspars, it can form at low temperatures.

Authigenic Zircon

Although zircon, like tourmaline, is a common heavy mineral, it is a very minor constituent of most sandstones. Rare outgrowths show that it also can be authigenic (Butterfield, 1936). The outgrowths take the form of toothlike serrations attached to the prism faces. These, in fact, are small pyramids. The enlargement therefore is mainly at angles to the principal axis of the zircon grain.

REFERENCES CITED AND BIBLIOGRAPHY

Alty, S. W. (1933), Some properties of authigenic tourmaline from Lower Devonian sediments, Am. Mineralogist, vol. 18, pp. 351–355.

Baturin, V. P. (1937), *Paleogeography on the base of terrigenous components*, Moscow, O.N.T.I., U.S.S.R., p. 285 (in Russian with English summary).

Berg, R. R. (1952), Feldspathized sandstone, *J. Sediment. Petrol.*, vol. 22, pp. 221–223.

Boswell, P. G. H. (1924), Petrography of the sands of the Upper Lias and Lower Inferior Oolite in the west of England, *Geol. Mag.*, vol. 61, pp. 246–264.

Boswell, P. G. H. (1933), *On the mineralogy of the sedimentary rocks*, London, Murby, pp. 87–96, 100–101.

Butterfield, J. A. (1936), Outgrowths on zircon, *Geol. Mag.*, vol. 73, pp. 511–516.

Crowley, A. J. (1939), Possible criterion for distinguishing marine and non-marine sediments, *Bull. Am. Assoc. Petroleum Geol.*, vol. 23, pp. 1716–1720.

Daly, R. A. (1917), Low-temperature formation of alkaline feldspars in limestones, *Proc. Nat. Acad. Sci. U.S.*, vol. 3, pp. 659–665.

Déverin, L. (1934), Sur la tourmaline authigène dans les roches sédimentaires, *Schweiz. mineralog. petrog. Mitt.*, vol. 14, pp. 528–529.

Déverin, L. (1945), Etude pétrographique des minerais de fer oolithique du Dogger des Alpes suisses, *Beitr. Geol. Schweiz. Geotech. Ser. Lf 13, bd 2*.

Edwards, A. B. and Baker, G. (1951), Some occurrences of supergene iron sulphides in relation to their environments of deposition, *J. Sediment. Petrol.*, vol. 21, pp. 34–46.

Galliher, E. W. (1935), Glauconite genesis, *Bull. Geol. Soc. Amer.*, vol. 46, pp. 1351–1366.

Goldich, S. S. (1934), Authigenic feldspar in sandstone of southeastern Minnesota, *J. Sediment. Petrol.*, vol. 4, pp. 89–95.

Grandjean, F. (1910), Deuxième note sur le feldspath néogène des terrains sédimentaires nonmétamorphique, *Bull. soc. franc minéral*, vol. 33, pp. 92–97.

Grim, R. E. (1953), *Clay mineralogy*, New York: McGraw-Hill.

Gruner, J. W. (1946), *The mineralogy and geology of the taconites and iron ores of the Mesabi range, Minnesota*, St. Paul, Iron Range Resources and Rehabilitation Commission.

Gruner, J. W. and Thiel, G. A. (1937), The occurrence of fine-grained authigenic feldspar in shales and silts, *Am. Mineralogist*, vol. 22, pp. 842–846.

Hallimond, A. F. (1925), Iron Ores: Bedded ores of England and Wales, *Spec. Repts. Mineral Resources, Petrog. Chem. G. Brit.*, vol. 29, Geol. Survey Mem. 29.

Henbest, L. G. (1945), Unusual nuclei in oolites from the Morrow Group near Fayetteville, Arkansas, *J. Sediment. Petrol.*, vol. 15, pp. 20–24.

Honess, A. P., and Jeffries, C. D. (1940), Authigenic albite from the Lowville Limestone at Bellefonte, Pennsylvania, *J. Sediment. Petrol.*, vol. 10, pp. 12–18.

Irving, R. D. and Van Hise, C. R. (1894), On secondary enlargement of mineral fragments in certain rocks, *U.S. Geol. Survey Bull. 8.*

James, H. L. (1955), Sedimentary facies of iron-formation, *Econ. Geol.*, vol. 49, pp. 235–293.

Krynine, P. D. (1946), The tourmaline group in the Oriskany sandstone, *Am. Mineralogist*, vol. 17, pp. 150–152.

Masson, P. H. (1955), An occurrence of gypsum in southwest Texas, *J. Sediment. Petrol.*, vol. 25, pp. 72–77.

Moore, Fred E. (1950), Authigenic albite in the Green River oil shales, *J. Sediment. Petrol.*, vol. 20, 1950, p. 227.

Newhouse, W. H. (1927), Some forms of iron sulphide occurring in coal and other sedimentary rocks, *J. Geol.*, vol. 35, pp. 73–83.

Rao, C. Gundu (1952), Authigenic tourmaline from the Satyavedu Stage (Upper Gondwanas) near Madras, *Current Sci.*, vol. 21, pp. 336–337.

Reynolds, D. L. (1929), Some new occurrences of authigenic potash feldspar, *Geol. Mag.*, vol. 66, pp. 390–399.

Schwartz, G. M. (1927), Iron sulphide pseudomorphs of plant structures in coal, *J. Geol.*, vol. 35, pp. 375–377.

Singewald, J. T., Jr., and Milton, C. (1929), Authigenic feldspar in limestone at Glen Falls, New York, *Bull. Geol. Soc. Amer.*, vol. 40, pp. 463–468.

Sorby, H. C. (1880), On the structure and origin of non-calcareous stratified rocks, *Proc. Geol. Soc. London*, vol. 36, pp. 62–64.

Stewart, Duncan, Jr. (1937), An occurrence of detrital authigenic feldspar, *Am. Mineralogist*, vol. 22, pp. 1000–1003.

Stow, M. H. (1932), Authigenic tourmaline in the Oriskany sandstone, *Am. Mineralogist*, vol. 17, pp. 150–152.

Stringham, B. (1940), Occurrence of feldspar replacing fossils, *Am. Mineralogist*, vol. 25, pp. 139–144.

Takahashi, Jun-Ichi (1939), Synopsis of glauconitization, in *Recent Marine Sediments*, Tulsa, Amer. Assoc. Petroleum Geologists, pp. 503–512.

Tester, A. C. and Atwater, G. I. (1934), The occurrence of authigenic feldspars in sediments, *J. Sediment. Petrol.*, vol. 4, pp. 23–31.

van Straaten, L. M. J. U. (1948), Note on the occurrence of authigenic feldspars in nonmetamorphic sediments, *Am. J. Sci.*, vol. 246, pp. 569–572.

DIAGENETIC DIFFERENTIATION

Involved also in diagenesis are segregations of mineral matter. Materials scattered diffusely throughout the rock may dissolve and diffuse towards centers of reprecipitation. According to Ramberg the free energy of such materials is less if they are collected together in a few comparatively large segregations than if they be more uniformly diffused throughout the rock. The segregation process is a sort of diagenetic differentiation. It leads to the formation of concretions and related bodies.

These segregations take many forms. Some are large crystals or symmetrical crystal aggregates (sand crystals, spherulites, rosettes, etc.). Others are irregular microcrystalline bodies (chert nodules, etc.). Some of the segregated materials replace the matrix of the host rock (as do the chert nodules); in other cases the segregation thrusts aside the enclosing rock; in some cases the segregated matter is deposited in open spaces (pores, fractures, vugs).

The diverse forms and structures exhibited by these bodies, their varied composition, and the problems of origin have been considered in detail elsewhere (p. 196).

DIAGENETIC METASOMATISM

Evidence that many minerals are replacements of earlier constituents has been cited at many places in this text. It is appropriate at this point to analyze some general problems pertaining to such replacement.

To what extent has such replacement taken place on a large scale—on a scale too great to be attributed simply to internal reorganization? In other words, are the authigenic minerals merely minor constituents of the host rock or has the latter ever been completely replaced? Little doubt remains that large-scale replacements have occurred in some rocks, whereas in other rocks the authigenesis is partial or very minor. Dolomitization may go to completion, for example, and produce a rock composed solely of dolomite. Feldspathization, on the other hand, is generally a very minor phenomenon, and authigenic feldspar rarely is anything but a minor constituent.

If replacement is complete, how can one distinguish between such a metasomatite and an original chemical precipitate? In the absence of pseudomorphs proof of a replacement origin is difficult to affirm or deny. Many cherts, dolomites, siderites, and phosphate rocks are clearly replaced limestones, whereas the stratigraphic relations, textures, and composition of others make it almost certain that they are primary chemical precipitates. The criteria for discrimination between those of metasomatic origin and those produced by direct precipitation are not always clear and decisive. These criteria have been reviewed in the sections of this book dealing with these controversial rocks.

If the rock be a replacement product, whence came the materials needed for such replacement? Obviously no biochemical limestone contains enough magnesia to convert the rock to a dolomite. Nor does any limestone contain enough silica to convert it to a chert. Magnesium must be introduced in the one case and silica added to the other. Presumably these constituents were derived from the sea water with which the sediment was in contact or from connate waters contained in the bed or expelled from adjacent beds or from circulating artesian or juvenile waters. If the replacing materials were derived from sea water, presumably the replacement was early or nearly contemporaneous with the accumulation of the sediment; if connate or artesian or juvenile waters were responsible, the replacement may have taken place long after consolidation and uplift. The criteria for determining the time of replacement and the source of the introduced materials are also far from satisfactory or conclusive.

INTRASTRATAL SOLUTION

Introduction

Intrastratal solution is that solution which takes place within a sedimentary bed after deposition. Solution may take place early or late in the postdepositional history of the rock. It may or may not be accompanied by simultaneous precipitation of the material dissolved.

The effects of intrastratal solution (and concomitant precipitation if any) are many and varied. The loss of materials, without corresponding gain, leads to an increase in porosity—the so-called *secondary porosity*. If accompanied by precipitation of the same or unlike materials, there may be a net loss of porosity and resultant expulsion of intergranular fluids. Concurrent solution and reprecipitation of the substance dissolved may lead to thorough cementation of the rock—production of an orthoquartzite from a friable sand, for example. Differential solution of the minor accessories or heavy minerals may make obscure the interpretation of the heavy suite and thus render stratigraphic correlation and provenance studies difficult.

It is important therefore to examine the criteria for intrastratal solution, to estimate the magnitude or extent of such solution, and to discuss further the geological effects.

Criteria of Intrastratal Solution

Evidences that solution has taken place in a sedimentary stratum are many and varied. In some rocks, notably those which are chemically homogeneous, solution concentrated along planes normal to the rock pressure produces stylolitic surfaces the two sides of which mutually penetrate one another (see p. 213). In other rocks the solution is concentrated at the points of contact of the clastic elements of which the rock is composed. In such cases there may be mutual microstylolitic penetration of these elements (pebbles, sand grains, fossil debris). In other cases the less soluble element is impressed into the more soluble component; indented or pitted pebbles or sand grains are thus evidence of intrastratal solution (Kuenen, 1942).

In a random section of a normal sand, the grains show about 0.65 to 1.60 contacts per grain. The exact number of contacts is dependent on the shape, sorting, and packing of the component grains. Randomly packed, uniformly sized spheres show 0.64 contact per grain (Gaither, 1953). A large number of grains *appear* to be unsupported by their neighbors and are said to be floating. If the sand has undergone intrastratal solution at points of contact between the grains, the sand is condensed and the grains are brought closer together and into contact with additional grains. The average number of contacts per grains increases. Many orthoquartzites, for example, average 2.5 to 3.0 contacts per grain. Almost certainly a figure of 2.0 or more is therefore indicative of condensation—probably the result of intrastratal solution (see Fig. 170).

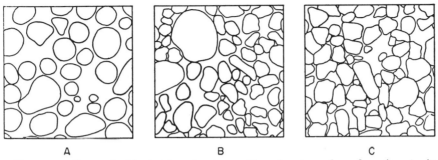

A   B   C

FIG. 170.   Camera lucida sketches showing packing of grains and condensation. A: Arbuckle calcareous oolite, fewer than 0.5 contact per grain. B: Lake Superior sandstone (Cambrian), 1.5 contacts per grain. C: Montebello sandstone (Devonian), 2.6 contacts per grain.

Molds, vugs, and other solution openings are known to every geologist. The molds of shells are common in many dolomites and in some sandstones. Less well known are the molds left by the removal of oolites without destruction of their matrix. Such pores have been termed *oolicasts* (Imbt and Ellison, 1946), though the term cast is inappropriate unless the openings are subsequently filled, as indeed they may be (Choquette, 1955).

Etched grains constitute good evidence of solution (Bramlette, 1929). It is not always clear, however, that the etching was achieved after rather than before deposition although the fragile spine-like projections or teeth on some of the heavy minerals, notably amphiboles and pyroxenes, could hardly have survived transport (Fig. 171) (Edelman, 1931; Edelman and Doeglas, 1931).

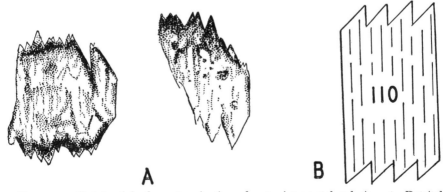

A   B

FIG. 171.   Sketch of hacksaw terminations due to intrastratal solution. A: Detrital augite. B: Schematic diagram of the hacksaw structure of a detrital augite parallel to (110) (after Edelman and Doeglas, 1931).

In some cases it can be proved that the hacksaw or cockscomb character was formed *in situ* after deposition (Ross, Miser, and Stephenson, 1929).

Very slight solvent action might produce only a frosted or mat surface as does hydrofluoric acid on glass. Possibly, therefore, the frosted quartz grains common in some limestones and dolomites and those of calcareous sandstones owe their frosted surfaces to intrastratal solution. The carbonate of these rocks appears to etch or corrode the embedded quartz (Pl. 17, B). Many of the older Paleozoic sandstones, now notably friable, such as the St. Peter (Ordovician), are characterized by frosted grains. Are these the product of solution and corrosion by a carbonate matrix which itself has since been removed by solution? In some such sandstones there remain hourglass and other residuals of the original carbonate cement (Graf and Lamar, 1950; Krynine, 1941).

Convincing proof of the efficacy of intrastratal solution is the contrast in character of the heavy mineral assemblage within a calcareous concretion and the matrix in which it occurs. Bramlette (1941) showed that the calcareous concretions of certain California sandstones contained about 40 per cent hornblende (in their heavy mineral fraction) whereas the matrix had but 5 per cent (Table 117). Obviously the hornblende in the adjoining sandstone matrix has been lost by leaching but is preserved within the concretion which constitutes a sealed environment. Students of heavy minerals long have noted an apparent increase in complexity of heavy-mineral suites with decreasing geologic age (Thoulet, 1913; Boswell, 1923; Pettijohn, 1941). Although there is considerable uncertainty as to why this should be true, it is possible, if not probable, that the older sediments have lost the less stable species by intrastratal solution (see p. 519).

TABLE 117.　Percentage of Heavy Mineral Grains in Calcareous Concretions and Their Matrix (after Bramlette, 1941)

	Zircon	Garnet	Titanite	Epidote-zoisite	Hornblende
Hambre Sandstone	12	3	10	37	5
Hambre Concretion	5	3	6	17	44
Modelo Sandstone	20	15	22	2	....
Modelo Concretion	12	5	10	53	R

Not only have the younger sediments a greater variety of heavy minerals, but the order of appearance of these minerals, as one proceeds from older to younger rocks, is essentially the reverse order of their stability determined by other independent observations. The suggestion has been made, therefore, that the heavy mineral zones are stability zones and owe their existence and character to selective removal of the less stable species in the deeper zones by intrastratal solution.

Magnitude and Mechanics of Intrastratal Solution

Although the evidence of intrastratal solution is abundant, evidence indicating the magnitude or importance of such solution is meager. Stockdale (1926) counted the number of stylolitic seams in limestones, and from this count and the amplitude of the seams estimated the total quantity of material removed by solution from such surfaces. Stockdale assumed that the height of the longest stylolitic column was a measure of the thickness lost by production of the seam in question. His assumption seems to be justified in

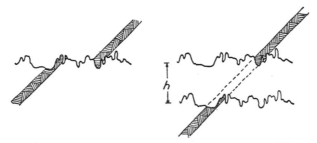

FIG. 172.   Sketch of apparent offset of vein by stylolite showing how thickness of layer dissolved during formation of stylolite can be estimated (after Conybeare, 1949).

that the thickness of the clay capping on the columns seems to be consistent with the quantity of insolubles known to occur in the rock presumed to have been dissolved. Stockdale estimated that from 5 to 40 per cent of the original volume of the formation was lost by stylolitic solution. The estimates could be checked further by the relation of stylolites to veins. Oblique veins, antedating stylolite formation, show an *apparent* offset by the stylolite. The offset is a consequence of removal of rock material and can be used as a measure of the same (Fig. 172).

The number of contacts per grain in the sands, oolites, and similar clastic or mechanical sediments is a measure of the magnitude of the intrastratal solution, although there is no way at present of translating such a number into percentage lost. One can only conclude that the condensed character of some sands implies a very considerable rearrangement of minerals—probably by intrastratal solution and precipitation.

If the friable sands with frosted quartz are the result of removal of a once all-pervading carbonate cement, then intrastratal solution and decementation is indeed a large-scale process.

Although it is clear that intrastratal solution would occur in the vadose zone, it is not so evident nor easy to prove that it occurs below the water table—in some cases far below. Bretz (1942) and others have presented cogent evidence of phreatic cave development in limestones far below the water table. The extraordinary oxidation and leaching of silica involved in the formation of the Lake Superior hematite deposits can hardly have occurred above the water table. That stylolitic development and other less spectacular effects of intrastratal solution originated below the water table or even in strata never subjected to artesian solution is highly probable. The formation of stylolites requires pressures—pressures which exceed some critical threshold value (Dunnington, 1954). They must be formed, therefore, by solution at depth. The orientation of the stylolitic surfaces parallel to the axial planes of folds or to pressure joints shows that they are not a product of surficial agents. The apparent increase in number of contacts per grain in some sandstones with increasing depth (Taylor, 1950) suggests further that intrastratal solution may be promoted by the higher pressures and temperatures of the relatively deeper zones.[8] One must not conclude that porosity thereby increases with depth as intrastratal solution at depth is only a part of an internal rearrangement process leading to solution on surfaces or points of stress and concomitant precipitation in adjacent porous areas.

There is, of course, both solution and removal of materials in the near-surface zone. It has been presumed that the porosity is notably high near unconformities for this reason. Near-surface solution is a part of the weathering process and not intrastratal in the usual meaning of that term.

REFERENCES CITED AND BIBLIOGRAPHY

Boswell, P. G. H. (1923), Some aspects of the petrology of sedimentary rocks, *Proc. Liverpool Geol. Soc.*, vol. 13, pp. 231–303.

Bramlette, M. N. (1929), Natural etching of detrital garnet, *Am. Mineralogist*, vol. 14, pp. 336–337.

Bramlette, M. N. (1941), The stability of heavy minerals in sandstone, *J. Sediment. Petrol.*, vol. 11, pp. 32–36.

Bretz, J H. (1942), Vadose and phreatic features of limestone caverns, *J. Geol.*, vol. 50, pp. 675–811.

Choquette, P. W. (1955), A petrographic study of the "State College" siliceous oolite, *J. Geol.*, vol. 63, pp. 337–347.

[8] Perhaps the critical pressure required for the solution of carbonate is less than that required for silica. At lower pressures, therefore, carbonate goes into solution, migrates to the pores of the rock, and etches or corrodes the quartz. At higher pressures the silica is dissolved at points of contact and is precipitated in the pores, replacing carbonate. In any case the secondary overgrowth on the quartz of many sandstones replaces the carbonate of the matrix although the detrital quartz grains show evidence of earlier corrosion by the cement. These observations may be, however, explained by variations in pH (Correns, 1950).

Correns, C. W. (1950), The geochemistry of diagenesis, *Geochim. et Cosmochim. Acta*, vol. 1, pp. 49–54.

Dunnington, H. V. (1954), Stylolite development post-dates rock induration, *J. Sediment. Petrol.*, vol. 24, pp. 27–49.

Edelman, C. H. (1931), Diagenetische Umwandlungserschienungen an detritischen Pyroxenen und Amphibolen, *Fortschr. Mineral. Krist. Petrog.*, vol. 16, pp. 67–68.

Edelman, C. H. and Doeglas, D. J. (1931), Reliktstrukturen detritischer Pyroxene und Amphibole, *Mineralog. petrog. Mitt.*, vol. 42, pp. 482–490.

Gaither, A. (1953), A study of porosity and grain relationships in experimental sands, *J. Sediment. Petrol.*, vol. 23, pp. 180–195.

Graf, D. L., and Lamar, J. E. (1950), Petrology of Fredonia oolite in southern Illinois, *Bull. Am. Assoc. Petroleum Geol.*, vol. 34, pp. 2318–2336.

Imbt, W. C., and Ellison, S. P. Jr. (1947), Porosity in limestone and dolomite petroleum reservoirs, *Drilling and Production Practice*, 1946, pp. 364–372.

Krynine, P. D. (1941), Petrographic studies of variations in cementing material in the Oriskany sand, *Penn. State Coll. Bull.* 33, pp. 108–116.

Krynine, P. D. (1942), Provenance versus mineral stability as a controlling factor in the composition of sediments (Abstract), *Bull. Geol. Soc. Amer.*, vol. 53, pp. 1850–1851.

Kuenen, Ph. H. (1942), Pitted pebbles, *Leidsche Geol. Mededeel.*, vol. 13, pp. 189–201.

Pettijohn, F. J. (1941), Persistence of minerals and geologic age, *J. Geol.*, vol. 49, pp. 610–625.

Ross, C. S., Miser, H. D. and Stephenson, L. W. (1929), Waterlaid volcanic rocks of early Upper Cretaceous age in southwestern Arkansas, southeastern Oklahoma, and northeastern Texas, *U.S. Geol. Survey Prof. Paper* 154–F, pp. 175–202.

Stockdale, P. B. (1926), The stratigraphic significance of solution in rocks, *J. Geol.*, vol. 34, pp. 399–414.

Taylor, Jane (1950), Pore-space reduction in sandstones, *Bull. Am. Assoc. Petroleum Geol.*, vol. 34, pp. 701–716.

Thoulet, J. (1913), Notes de lithologie sous-marine, *Ann. inst. oceanog.*, V, fasc. 9.

COMPACTION

Observations show that shales undergo a marked compaction. The open spaces are eliminated or greatly reduced by closer packing, crushing, and deformation of the grains, as well as by more or less recrystallization. The porosity therefore may be taken as a measure of the degree of compaction which the shale has undergone. In general in any given area, those rocks which are oldest and which have been covered by the greatest depth of overburden show the lowest porosities (Sorby, 1908; Hedberg, 1926, 1936).

Athy (1930) has shown the relation between the porosity of a shale and its depth of burial. This relation takes the form $P = p(e^{-bx})$, where P is porosity, p is the average porosity of surface clays, b is a coefficient, and x is the depth of burial. Athy finds the surface clays to have a porosity of 45 to 50 per cent, whereas shale at 6000 feet has only 5 per cent of pore space. Compaction equivalent to 20 per cent of the original bulk volume has occurred by the time a clay has been buried to 1000 feet, 35 per cent at 2000 feet, and 40 per cent at 3000 feet. As shown by Jones (1944), the rate of compaction is most rapid at the time of or shortly after deposition; it decreases greatly with the passage of time.

The relation between porosity and depth of burial has also been studied by Rubey (1930), but inasmuch as the shales investigated by Rubey had been deformed, the porosity observed was a function of both the depth of burial and the degree of tilt. In general the more steeply dipping rocks have a lower porosity (Table 68). The relationship can be expressed quantitatively (p. 354), so that correction for the tilt can be made. Such correction of the observed porosities by reduction of all readings to zero dip showed that the porosity values computed tend to increase with depth. This conclusion is a further confirmation of the observations of Sorby and Hedberg.

Rubey used the data thus obtained to estimate the thickness of rock once present but now eroded from above the highest formation exposed. Using a modified version of the Sorby depth-porosity equation, estimates of a thickness were obtained which were in fairly good agreement with estimates derived from wholly different data.

It is also possible to reduce all porosities in a given suite of samples to a common depth and zero dip. Such a calculation made by Rubey showed a considerable range in values which appeared to correlate with the grain size of the sediment. The fine-grained samples (those containing the smaller and flatter particles) showed a larger compaction (indicated by a smaller porosity) than the coarser-grained samples. This is in accord with both theory and experiment.

Several corollaries follow from the above observations. Noteworthy are the structural effects of compaction and decrease in porosity, namely, the thinning of fold limbs and the differential compaction that produces anticlines over buried noncompactible hills or analogous structures. It may be that in some areas the anticlines and basins observed are no more than a less accentuated reflection of the relief of the surface on which the beds were deposited. Such compaction anticlines have actually been shown to be localized over a buried granite ridge or over buried reefs.[9] Neither the granite nor the core rock of the reef are compactible. Also of geological importance is the rather

[9] The fine-grained carbonate muds appear to be subject to compaction in a degree and manner similar to that of ordinary shales or clays (Terzhagi, 1940).

large volume of fluid expelled from the compaction of shales which presumably escapes through the interbedded sandstones. These solutions may carry mineral matter capable of precipitation in the sandstones as a cement.

REFERENCES CITED AND BIBLIOGRAPHY

Athy, L. F. (1930), Density, porosity and compaction of sedimentary rocks, *Bull. Am. Assoc. Petroleum Geol.*, vol. 14, pp. 1–24.

Hedberg, H. D. (1926), The effect of gravitational compaction on the structure of the sedimentary rocks, *Bull. Am. Assoc. Petroleum Geol.*, vol. 10, pp. 1035–1072.

Hedberg, H. D. (1936), Gravitational compaction of clays and shales, *Am. J. Sci.*, ser. 5, vol. 31, pp. 241–297.

Jones, O. T. (1944), The compaction of muddy sediments, *Quart. J. Geol. Soc. London*, vol. 100, pp. 137–160; vol. 102 (1946), pp. 209–210.

Rubey, W. W. (1927), The effect of compaction on the structure of sedimentary rocks—a discussion, *Bull. Am. Assoc. Petroleum Geol.*, vol. 11, pp. 625–628.

Rubey, W. W. (1930), Lithologic studies of fine-grained Upper Cretaceous sedimentary rocks of the Black Hills region, *U.S. Geol. Survey Prof. Paper* 165A, pp. 34–38.

Sorby, H. C. (1908), On the application of quantitative methods to the study of the structures and history of rocks, *Quart. J. Geol. Soc. London*, vol. 64, pp. 227–231.

Terzaghi, R. D. (1940), Compaction of lime mud as a cause of secondary structure, *J. Sediment. Petrol.*, vol. 10, pp. 78–90.

15

Historical Geology of Sediments

INTRODUCTION

THE earth is believed to have undergone a long and complex geochemical evolution leading to the differentiation of the crust and to the formation of the hydrosphere and atmosphere. The presumed history of these fluid envelopes has been discussed by various writers (Daly, 1907; Rubey, 1951; Urey, 1952; and others). All writers agree that at some early time in the earth's history the conditions at the surface of the earth were radically different from those of the present time. The oceans were presumed to have a lesser volume than now; the salinity of the waters was perhaps much less; the atmosphere may have had a higher CO_2 content and even may have been reducing. If these views are correct, the sediments formed during the earliest times should be notably different from those of the later geologic eras and should record the geochemical evolution of the earth's crust and of the hydrosphere and atmosphere. Is there, in the sedimentary record, any evidence of a secular trend in composition or other characteristics to support this concept?

Geologists have found that the record of the past can be understood in terms of the present. This concept, variously termed the actualistic principle or the doctrine of uniformitarianism, has indeed been a fruitful one. There seems to be no rock or structure, even in the earliest Precambrian terranes, that cannot be found in the later periods. This observation gives strong support to the view that as far as the record goes, conditions during the earliest times were not materially different from those of the present and that secular changes of the first magnitude are nonexistent. This conclusion, however, has not been universally accepted. It has been pointed out that many sediments are the products of biochemical action, that many other sediments are modified or affected by the action of organisms, and that inasmuch as the biota has undergone a vast and complex evolution there should be some corresponding change in the kind and character of the sediments closely related to organic activity. The lime-secreting habit of the invertebrates was not acquired until Cambrian times and clearly, therefore, limestones produced by such activity could not have formed in the earlier times. Likewise the absence of land plants in the earlier times should have had a considerable influence on the rate of sedimentation. Some writers have argued that there is evidence in the geologic record of a reducing atmosphere in the earliest Precambrian and presumed that the oxidizing atmosphere of the present is a result of gradual release of oxygen by the photosynthetic action of green plants.

Despite the plausibility of these arguments, it is difficult to demonstrate any secular changes in the character of the sediments. The oldest strata, probably in excess of 3×10^9 years, consist of normal clastic rocks. The conglomerates contain well-worn cobbles and pebbles of many types of rocks (Pettijohn, 1943) showing that erosion and sedimentation went on then as now. These conglomerates, "so perfectly resemble recent accumulations of gravels alternating with sand beds that, at first glance, they might be taken for such if it were not for the tilting up of the strata" (Eskola, 1932). The presence of tillites of Precambrian age demonstrates the presence of glaciers then as now. There certainly cannot have been a progressive cooling of the earth's surface as was once commonly believed. Many of the Precambrian sediments are mature. Some of the quartzites are accumulations of quartz sand not exceeded in roundness and silica content by any later sandstones. Such high concentrations of quartz imply thorough and complete weathering of the quartz-bearing source rocks. Such mature weathering probably could not be accomplished in the absence of a plant cover on the lands. Despite the absence of fossils of land plants before the Devonian, it seems probable, therefore, that a plant cover existed even in the early Precambrian. The nature of the cover is not clear—perhaps a heavy cover of lichens and other primitive plants.

Although there is a general similarity of the earlier sediments to those of later times, some recent work seems to show small or second-order differences in the average composition of sediments of various ages. These apparent differences have been explained as related to differences in the biota of the earlier times or to small but real differences in the composition of the atmosphere and hydrosphere or to postdepositional alteration of the sediments, which is progressive and nonreversible. If the differences are related to metamorphism or diagenesis then no evolution of the environment is implied.

CHEMICAL EVOLUTION OF THE LUTITES

Best illustration of an apparent geochemical evolution is the study made of the shales and slates by Nanz (1953). Clarke's average Paleozoic shale seems to differ from the average shale of Mesozoic and Cenozoic times (Table 61, p. 344). An average for Precambrian slates shows a systematic difference from both that of Palezoic and later shales. The CaO and CO_2 content, for example, seem to show a progressive increase with decrease in age. This may be due to the rise in the lime-secreting habit of marine invertebrates, especially the planktonic Foraminifera during the Cretaceous. The accumulation of lime carbonate in deeper-water deposits, including many shales, is related to the rain of the tests of lime-secreting planktonic Foraminifera. In the earlier times the lime was fixed primarily by benthonic invertebrates and was presumably confined to the shallowest waters.

The progressive differences in the silica, alumina, and potash content of the shales (Fig. 173) are explained by Nanz as a record of a progressive change in texture. As shown by Grout (1925; see page 101), the percentage of these constituents is a function of

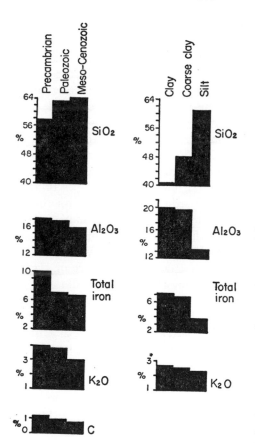

Fig. 173. Diagram showing differences in chemical composition of lutites of various ages (after Nanz, 1953).

grain size. There would seem, therefore, to be a secular change in grain size of the shales, which carries with it the concomitant change in chemical composition. The older shales on the average therefore are finer-grained than the younger shales.

A further notable trend in composition is the changing ratio of ferrous to ferric iron. In the older lutites ferrous iron exceeds ferric; in the younger shales the converse is true. The high content of ferrous iron in many Precambrian clastics and the transportation of iron and deposition of sedimentary siderite on a large scale have been cited by a number of workers as evidence of a reducing atmosphere (MacGregor, 1927; Rankama, 1954). That this conclusion need not follow has been pointed out by James (1954), Nanz (1953), and others. Clearly in some cases the sediments were precipitated in a strongly reducing environment. Inasmuch as such reducing environments exist at the present time, in the Black Sea for example (Androussow, 1897), despite our strongly oxidizing atmosphere, they could also have existed in Precambrian times and consequently do not imply a reducing atmosphere. Nevertheless a higher proportion of reduced iron in the older record requires an explanation. As noted by Nanz, the more reduced state of the iron in the slates may be a result of metamorphism. The average Paleozoic slate is almost identical in composition with the average Paleozoic shale except for the reduced state of the iron (Table 61, p. 344). The higher ferrous iron content of the Precambrian slates may therefore record only the difference in metamorphism between these rocks and those of the later times. Direct evidence of an oxidizing atmosphere has been pointed out (James, 1954). Hematitic oolites, associated with detrital quartz sand grains, denote deposition in turbulent aerated waters. As the ferric oolites occur in some Precambrian iron formations as well as in those of later times, an oxidizing environment is most certainly necessary. It is difficult to believe that such an environment could exist if the earth's atmosphere were reducing.[1] The Precambrian red beds of the Keweenawan, which resemble in all essential details those of the Newark series (Triassic) of the eastern United States, and the red quartzites of the Huronian would seem to require a strongly oxidizing environment for the formation of the red pigment.

The character of the clay minerals of the ancient shales is said to be different from that of the younger shales (Grim, 1953, p. 356). This difference is attributed, however, to postdepositional alterations of the clay minerals.

Data on the carbon content of shales are inadequate. In general there does not appear to be a significant difference related to age.[2]

EVOLUTION OF THE CARBONATES

Some years ago Daly (1907, 1909) pointed out that the earlier carbonate rocks appear to be richer in $MgCO_3$ than those of later times (Table 118).

[1] Unlike the converse, i.e., a reducing environment isolated from an oxidizing atmosphere, the turbulent environment implied by oolite formation and the clastic quartz association requires agitated shallow waters, an environment difficult to seal off from an atmosphere of unlike composition.

[2] Nanz's averages seem to show a *decline* with decreasing age of the lutite. The higher value for the Precambrian is somewhat misleading, since the inclusion of one or two exceptionally carbonaceous slates greatly affects the average value.

Daly supposed that the lime and magnesia entering the Precambrian (pre-Devonian) seas was quantitatively precipitated. The evidence for this was the similarity in ratio of $CaCO_3$ to $MgCO_3$ in these rocks to that of streams draining the Canadian Precambrian shield. No accumulation of magnesium salts in the sea was believed to have occurred in Precambrian times. Daly explained this apparent quantitative removal of calcium and magnesium by the ammonia generated by decomposing organic matter. Later evolution of a scavenging fauna removed the organic matter as rapidly as it formed. Lime-secreting forms removed the calcium from sea water; the magnesium, however, was left to accumulate. Daly's data may, however, be interpreted in another way. Circulating waters bearing magnesium are known to convert limestones to dolomite. The older a rock, the greater the probability that such a change would have taken place. If so, the older carbonates should show, as they do, a higher magnesium content.

TABLE 118.   Lime-Magnesia Ratio in Limestones of Various Ages
(after Daly, 1909)

	Ca-Mg Ratio	No. of Analyses
Pre-Devonian	3.35 to 1	392
Devonian	6.29 to 1	106
Carboniferous	12.45 to 1	238
Cretaceous	56.32 to 1	77
Tertiary	53.09 to 1	26
Quaternary and Recent	35 to 1	26
		865

Presumably the cement of the calcareous sandstones might be expected to show the same secular variation in the ratio of $CaCO_3$ to $MgCO_3$ as to the limestones if the difference in the ratio which correlates with age were due to postdepositional replacement. Data on the composition of carbonate cements have not been collected.

EVOLUTION OF THE SANDSTONES

Do the older sandstones differ from those of later times? The immature character of the graywackes, which are common in many Precambrian sections, has been attributed to the absence of a plant cover and their high ferrous iron content has been ascribed to a reducing atmosphere (MacGregor, 1927). Neither conclusion is justified. Tertiary graywackes are similar in all essential particulars to those of the older times (see column G, Table 51, p. 306).

The cement of the older sandstones seems to be more largely silica rather than carbonate. Tallman (1949) reports about a 50–50 ratio of calcareous to siliceous cements in post-Paleozoic sandstones but only a 20–80 ratio in the Paleozoic and older rocks. This observation has been attributed to substitution, by replacement, of quartz for calcite in the older rocks. Such diagenetic replacement, like the dolomitization of limestone, is nonreversible and its effects are cumulative.[3]

Most commonly cited difference between the younger and the older sandstones is the number and variety of the minor accessory minerals, i.e., the heavy minerals. As long ago noted by Boswell (1923) and others, the older sandstones have a very restricted heavy mineral suite. The number and variety of heavy minerals increase as the age of the sand decreases. Modern or Pleistocene sands have the richest heavy mineral assemblages (Pettijohn, 1941) (Fig. 118). These differences have been attributed either to increasing complexity of the terrane from which the sands were derived or to removal of the less stable species from the older sandstones (Boswell, 1923; Pettijohn, 1941). The older a sand, the greater is the probability that it has been leached and hence has lost the less stable heavy detritals. In a general way the order of persistence of minerals in time is closely correlated with their stability. Not only do the older sands contain a more restricted suite, but the minerals species present are the more stable ones.

But the mineral composition is not only a function of intrastratal solution. The mineral composition is also determined by the intensity and duration of the weathering affecting the source rocks. Under conditions of intense weathering and low relief, the sands produced will be mature and lacking in unstable heavy minerals. The progressive increase in complexity of the heavy mineral assemblage with decreasing age of the sands could reflect, therefore, a progressive increase in tectonism and resultant relief. That such may be the case is suggested by the data on the feldspar content of sandstones (Table 26, p. 123). Except for the Precambrian there seems to be a progressive increase in feldspar content with decreasing age. Inasmuch as feldspar apparently is stable within the sandstone—since it commonly shows authigenic overgrowths—it seems unlikely that the feldspar-poor older sands lost feldspar by intrastratal leaching. More probably they were impoverished in feldspar when they were deposited. As feldspar seems to be a good index of relief and a

---

[3] Inspection of Tallman's specimens showed that many of the carbonate-cemented sands contain a little silica cement also. Many of the older sandstones have only a very little silica cement and have voids which are mainly empty—so much so that some, like the St. Peter, are friable. This observation suggests that these sands were also once carbonate cemented, and even though somewhat friable, were placed by Tallman in the silica-cemented category because of the residual silica cement. Actual count shows that the ratio of silica-cemented to nearly noncemented sandstones is about the same as silica to carbonate-cemented sands in the later times.

result of rapid erosion, the changing feldspar content may record a progressive increase in relief, rate of erosion and corresponding rate of sedimentation.

RATE OF SEDIMENTATION

The rate of sedimentation shows extremely wide variations from place to place at the present time. It is virtually impossible to determine an average rate of sedimentation for the present; it is more difficult to do so for past times. Nevertheless data presented by Barrell (1917) suggest a secular change in the rate of sedimentation. Barrell noted that if the maximum known thickness of strata deposited in each geologic period was divided by the time during which these strata were deposited, there seemed to be a progressive increase in the rate of sedimentation with decreasing age of the beds. The time allocated to each period was that assigned to the periods in question based on a few relatively well-established dates determined by lead-uranium ratios. Barrell's observations have been substantiated by Schuchert (1931) and Holmes (1947) who, however, revised both the thickness maxima and the time allocations on the basis of new information (Table 119).

TABLE 119.   Thickness Maxima, Geologic Time, and Rates of Sedimentation (after Holmes, *Principles of Geology*, 1945, p. 105)

Maximum Known Thickness of Strata in Feet		Approximate Duration	Years per Foot
Cenozoic	76,000[a]	70,000,000	920
Mesozoic	109,000	120,000,000	1100
Late Paleozoic	90,000	130,000,000	1445
Early Paleozoic	95,000	180,000,000	1895

[a] Revised.

That the data justify the conclusion that the rate of sedimentation has in fact shown a secular change has been challenged by Gilluly (1949). Gilluly pointed out that the probability of finding the section showing the maximum thickness decreases with the age of the deposit because of concealment of the older strata beneath the younger. It is more probable, therefore, that the thickness maxima of the younger beds are about correct, whereas those of the older systems are too small. Moreover, as noted by Gilluly, the maximal thickness of the Paleozoic includes much limestone generally conceded to accumulate more slowly than clastic sediment, and hence the mean rate for the Paleozoic is too low.

But as noted elsewhere, there are other evidences of a changing rate of sedimentation. The chemical composition of the shales shows a secular trend presumed to reflect an increase in silt content with decreasing age—a change to be expected if the rate of sedimentation has progressively increased. The younger sandstones appear to be richer in feldspar and in the less stable heavy mineral species than the older sands—an observation best explained by derivation of these sands from more rugged areas, which implies also a more rapid rate of erosion and hence a more rapid rate of sedimentation.

CRITIQUE OF APPARENT SECULAR CHANGES

Evaluation of the data which constitute the evidence for presumed secular trends in the nature and character of the sedimentary rocks is difficult. In all cases the validity of the sample is clearly in doubt. Since five-sixths of the geologic record is without a valid chronology, the time span represented by the data is generally a very small part of the whole recorded history of the earth's crust. Until the geologic column for the Precambrian is well established, this defect in the sample will remain. Even for the later times the sample is very small and without good geographic spread. Most of the data are from the United States and northern Europe. In addition to these inadequacies of the sample, it may be that the sample is biased by the selective preservation of certain sedimentary facies and the loss of others. Further difficulties are due to metamorphism of the older rocks. How many of the observed or apparent differences are related to progressive, nonreversible metamorphic or diagenetic and metasomatic changes?

In conclusion, therefore, one can say that no major or significant secular trend has been established. Some apparent trends of second-order magnitude appear to exist, but whether they are due to systematic bias of the sample, to postdepositional alterations related to age, or to real differences in the environment of deposition is not certainly known.

REFERENCES CITED AND BIBLIOGRAPHY

Androussow (1897), La mer noire, *Guide des excursions du VII congres geol. intern.*, vol. 29.

Barrell, J. (1917), Rhythms and the measurement of geologic time, *Bull. Geol. Soc. Amer.*, vol. 28, pp. 745–904.

Boswell, P. G. H. (1924), Some further considerations of the petrology of sedimentary rocks, *Proc. Liverpool Geol. Soc.*, vol. 14, pp. 1–33.

Daly, R. A. (1909), First calcareous fossils and the evolution of the limestones, *Bull. Geol. Soc. Amer.*, vol. 20, pp. 153–170.

Daly, R. A. (1907), The limeless ocean of pre-Cambrian time, *Am. J. Sci.*, 4th ser., vol. 23, pp. 93–115.

Eskola, Pentti (1932), Conditions during the earliest geological times, *Ann. Acad. Sci. Fennicae*, ser. A, vol. 36, pp. 5–74.

Gilluly, James (1949), Distribution of mountain building in geologic time, *Bull. Geol. Soc. Amer.*, vol. 60, pp. 561–590.

Grim, R. E. (1953), *Clay mineralogy*, New York, McGraw-Hill, pp. 356–357.

Grout, F. F. (1925), Relation of texture and composition of clays, *Bull. Geol. Soc. Amer.*, vol. 36, pp. 393–416.

Holmes, Arthur (1947), The construction of a geological time scale, *Trans. Geol. Soc. Glasgow*, vol. 21, pp. 117–152.

James, H. L. (1954), Sedimentary facies of iron-formation, *Econ. Geol.*, vol. 49, pp. 236–293.

Kaiser, Erich (1931), Der Grundsatz des Aktualismus in der Geologie, *Z. deut. geol. Ges.*, vol. 83.

MacGregor, A. M. (1927), The problem of the Precambrian atmosphere, *S. African J. Sci.*, vol. 24, pp. 155–172.

Nanz, R. H., Jr. (1953), Chemical composition of pre-Cambrian slates with notes on the geochemical evolution of lutites, *J. Geol.*, vol. 61, pp. 51–64.

Pettijohn, F. J. (1941), Persistence of heavy minerals and geologic age, *J. Geol.*, vol. 49, pp. 610–625.

Pettijohn, F. J. (1943), Archean sedimentation, *Bull. Geol. Soc. Amer.*, vol. 54, pp. 925–972.

Rankama, Kalervo (1954), Geologic evidence of chemical composition of the Precambrian atmosphere (abstract), *Bull. Geol. Soc. Amer.*, vol. 65, p. 1297.

Rubey, W. W. (1951), Geologic history of sea water, *Bull. Geol. Soc. Amer.*, vol. 62, pp. 1111–1147.

Schuchert, Chas. (1931), Geochronology or the age of the earth on the basis of sediments and life, *Nat. Research Council, Bull.* 80, pp. 10–64.

Tallman, S. L. (1949), Sandstone types: Their abundance and cementing agents, *J. Geol.*, vol. 57, pp. 582–591.

Urey, H. C. (1952), On the early chemical history of the earth and the origin of life, *Proc. Nat. Acad. Sci. U.S.*, vol. 38, pp. 351–363.

Index of Names

Numbers in italics denote complete citation in the References Cited and Bibliographies.

Abelson, P. H., 154, *155*
Aberdeen, Esther, 42, 52
Ackerman, Ernst, 261, 266, 275
Adams, J. E., 442, 444, 625, *644*
Adams, S. F., 211, *211*
Agar, W. M., 440, *445*
Albee, A. L., 104, *107*
Aldrich, H. R., 442, 444, 464
Allen, V. T., 19, 51, 232, 240, 295, 300, 301, 314, 322, 330, 351, 356, 357, 365, 370, 372, 468, 469, 503, *522*
Alling, H. L., 27, 30, 51, 232, 240, 352, 371, 453, 457, 464, 481, 485, *542*
Allison, V. C., 410, *412*
Alty, S. W., 670, *670*
Amsden, T. W., 421, 425, 575, 576, 607, *609*
Andersen, S. A., 178, 595, *603*
Anderson, A. G., 47, *51*
Anderson, G. E., 120, 121, 535, *542*
Anderson, M. S., 356, *371*
Anderson, J. L., 515, 517, *522*
Andrée, K., 178, 393, *412*, 650
Androussow, N., 363, 371, 461, 465, 623, 685, *689*
Apfel, E. T., 159, *178*
Ashley, G. H., 457, 465, 467, 469
Athy, L. F., 354, 371, 680, 681
Atterberg, A., 29, *51*
Atwater, G. I., 622, 665, 666, 672
Austin, C. R., 362, *373*

Baak, J. A., 573, 574, *576*
Bagnold, R. A., 28, 39, 40, 46, 51, 168, *178*
Bailey, E. B., 164, 170, 173, 176, 178, 301, 304, 312, 314, 443, 444, 593, 604, 617, 638, 644
Baker, C. L., 265, 275

Baker, G., 201, 211, 323, 465, 600, 604, 670, 671
Baker, H. A., 25, *51*
Balk, Robert, 306, 308, 314, 480, 485, 617, *644*
Bandy, O. L., 596, 603, 603, 604, 617, *644*
Barbour, E. H., 97, 202, 211, 378, 379
Barghoorn, E. S., 488, 497
Barnes, V. E., 417, 421, 426
Barrell, J., 193, 195, 259, 511, 523, 529, 542, 606, 609, 632, 633, 642, 644, 688, 689
Barth, T. F. W., 105, 107, 237, 241, 323, 324, 328, 330, 381, 410, 425
Barton, D. C., 126, 127, 328, 330
Bartrum, J. A., 210, 211
Bassler, R. S., 205, 211
Bastin, E. S., 72, 72, 104, 105, 107, 111, 116, 214, 217, 439, 440, 444
Bates, R. L., 208, 211
Baturin, V. P., 508, 523, 573, 576, 593, 604, 662, 671
Bavendamm, W., 409, 412
Bayley, W. S., 418, 425
Beales, F. W., 419, 420, 425
Beavan, P. A., 454, 466
Becker, G. F., 78, 90
Becker, Hans, 225, 227
Beers, R. F., 155, *155*
Bell, H. S., 183, 194, 195
Berg, George, 465
Berg, R. R., 370, 371, 664, 666, 667, 671
Bergenback, R. E., 408, 412
Berkey, C. P., 428, *444*
Berman, H., 138, *140*
Bertrand, Marcel, 636, 638, *644*
Berz, K. C., 455, 465
Bieber, C. L., 178, 578, 580, 586
Birse, D. J., 425

691

Index of Subjects

Abrasion, analysis of, 533
    durability index, 538
    effect on mineral composition, 559; on
        roundness, 545; on shape, 551; on
        size, 534, 535; on sphericity, 551; on
        surface textures, 68
    experimental study of, 534
    factors governing, 535
    geologic significance of, 539
    of gravels, 535, pl. 38
    of limestone, 534, 536, pl. 37
    of sand, 535
    rate of, 535
    selective, 558
Abrasion and rigor of action, 537, 538
Abrasion mill, 534
    rounding of limestone in, 535, 536, pl. 37
    tests, 535; on gravel, 535; on sand, 535
Abrasion resistance, order of, 536
Acaustobiolith, 433
Accretion, 197
Actualistic principle, see Uniformitarianism
Admixtures, 34, 35
Agglomerate, 279, 331
Aggregates, naming of, 22
    sedimentary, 21
Algae, calcareous, 221
Algal balls, 222
Algal bedding, 221
Algal limestone, 391, pl. 26
Algal pebbles, see Algal pisolites
Algal pisolites, 222, pl. 26, 391
Algal structures, 221, 394, 399
Allogenic minerals, 108
Allophane, 135
Alluvial fan, boulders on, 539
        See also Fanglomerate
Alluvial gravels, 245
    size parameters of, 48
Analysis, chemical, 99
    mechanical, 30
Anatase, authigenic, 669

Anaerobic sedimentation, 622
Anauxite, 135
Anemoclasts, 233
Angular, defined, 58
Anhydrite, authigenic, 669
    bedded, 479
    properties of, 151
    rock, see Evaporites
Ankerite, 145
Anthracite, 490
Anthraxylon, 492
Apposition fabric, 73
Aquafacts, 66
Aragonite, 144
Arenites, defined, 16
    pyroclastic, see Tuffs
    schist, 629
        See also Sandstone
Arenyte, see Arenites
Argillites, defined, 340, 342
    composition of, 342
    examples of, pl. 23, pl. 24
    varved, pl. 23
Arkose, 291, 322, 323, 324, 335, pl. 20
    basal, 325
    chemical analyses of, 324
    geologic significance of, 328
    mineral analyses of, 323
    origin of, 328
    structures of, 324
    textures of, 324
Arkose suite, 236, 628
Ash, volcanic, 366, pl. 21
Associations, consanguineous, 610, 611,
        615, 618, 622
        See also Facies
Atmoclasts, 233
Atmoliths, 234
Attapulgite, 135
Atterberg scale, 18, 29
Attrition, 533
Attritus, 492